BETH HILLEL LIBRARY
WILMETTE, ILLINOIS

Nazi Germany's War Against the Jews

A Publication of
The American Jewish Conference
New York, N. Y.
1947

THE AMERICAN JEWISH CONFERENCE
521 FIFTH AVENUE
NEW YORK 17, N. Y.

Printed in the United States of America

Nazi Germany's War Against the Jews

PROPOSALS OF THE AMERICAN JEWISH CONFERENCE
FOR INCLUSION IN THE GERMAN PEACE TREATY

Foreword by
HENRY MONSKY
*Chairman of the Interim Committee
of the American Jewish Conference*

THE COMPLETE ACCOUNT OF GERMANY'S DESTRUCTION
OF EUROPEAN JEWRY AS REVEALED IN THE EVIDENCE
ASSEMBLED AT NURNBERG

PART ONE
THE TWENTY-FIVE YEAR CAMPAIGN
An Analysis of the Documentary Material and Testimony

PART TWO
THE TRIAL AND PUNISHMENT
Excerpts from the Official Proceedings at Nurnberg

PART THREE
THE DOCUMENTARY EVIDENCE
*Official German Reports, Statutes, Decrees and Orders, and
Other Documentary Material Collected by the American
and British Prosecuting Staffs at Nurnberg*

Prepared and Compiled by
SEYMOUR KRIEGER

TABLE OF CONTENTS

	Page
Foreword by Henry Monsky	I
Statement of the American Jewish Conference on the German Peace Treaty	V
Proposals for Inclusion in the Treaty	IX
Preface	XIX

PART ONE: THE TWENTY-FIVE YEAR CAMPAIGN

Introduction	I-i
Chapter I. Anti-Semitism Prior to 1933	I-1
Chapter II. Germany and Austria Under the Nazis	I-4
Boycott Action of April 1, 1933	I-5
"Jews Are Not Germans"	I-5
The Nurnberg Laws	I-6
Austria After March, 1938	I-8
Aktion November 9-10, 1938	I-8
Work Forbidden	I-13
Chapter III. Western Europe Under the Nazis	I-17
Nurnberg Moves to Holland	I-17
Vichy and the Gestapo Against French Jewry	I-19
Chapter IV. Einsatzstab Rosenberg	I-20
Plunder of Art Treasures	I-21
M-Action (Furniture Action)	I-23
The Hohe Schule	I-23
Chapter V. The East — Up to the "Final Solution"	I-25
Poland	I-25
Ghettos	I-25
Discriminatory Decrees	I-26
Forced Labor	I-26
Confiscation of Property	I-27
The Wehrmacht in the Soviet Union	I-27
Criminal Code for Poles and Jews	I-28
Evacuation from Galicia	I-28
Starvation	I-30
Bohemia and Moravia	I-30
Chapter VI. Genesis of Last Stage: A "Judenrein" Europe	I-31

Chapter VII. The Final "Solution": Genocide I-38
    Murder Camps I-39
    Gas Wagons I-41
    Screening Teams I-42
    Execution Squads I-42
    Einsatzgruppe A in the Baltic States I-43
    Einsatzgruppen in U.S.S.R. I-49
    Execution of Ukrainian Jews I-50
    Executions in Borisow, White Ruthenia, and Riga . . I-52
    Last Days of the Rowno and Dubno Ghettos I-52
    Aktion at Sluzk I-56
    "The Warsaw Ghetto Is No More" I-58
    The Fate of the Hungarian Jews I-63
    The Slaughter Stops I-68

Chapter VIII. The Propaganda Front I-70
    Early Efforts: 1933 . . . . I-70
    Jewish Question in German Foreign Policy I-71
    Hitler's Political Testament I-75

PART TWO: THE TRIAL AND PUNISHMENT

The Four-Power Agreement II-1
The Indictment II-12
Excerpts from Opening Addresses II-21
    Opening Address: Robert H. Jackson II-21
    Opening Address: Francois de Menthon II-31
    Opening Address: R. H. Rudenko II-40
Excerpts from Closing Addresses II-52
    Closing Address: Robert H. Jackson II-52
    Closing Address: Hartley Shawcross II-54
    Closing Address: R. H. Rudenko II-67
The Judgment II-73

PART THREE: THE DOCUMENTARY EVIDENCE

Explanatory Note . . . . III-i
List of Documents . . . . III-v
The Documentary Evidence III-1
Biographical Data III-593
Glossary III-608

FOREWORD

THE relentless war waged against the Jewish people by Nazi Germany and its allies brought ruin and death to millions of Jews and wrecked the whole structure of rights under which Jews lived since the period of emancipation.

The story of that war, as unfolded by the Nazis in their own words and writings, is told in this volume. Assembled here are all the major relevant documents gathered for the International Military Tribunal at Nurnberg. It is an authentic and accurate record of one of the most barbaric and degrading chapters in the history of mankind.

"Nazi Germany's War Against the Jews" is published by the American Jewish Conference as the democratic powers prepare the German Peace Treaty. If that treaty is to reflect the determination of the democratic world to right the wrongs committed by Nazi Germany, it must take into account the long, incessant and frightful German war against the Jewish people.

The American Jewish Conference, consisting of elected delegates of more than sixty Jewish organizations and every major Jewish community in the United States and representative of the great majority of the Jews of this country, was established in 1943 to plan common action to secure the rights and status of the Jewish people in the post-war world. Fundamental to that task is the presentation at the Peace Table of the case of the Jewish people against Germany. Life cannot be restored to the six million Jews butchered by the Nazis. But Jews who survived must be assured peace and dignity if the victorious powers are to succeed in building a better world for all peoples—be they large or small, powerful or weak.

To that end, the Interim Committee of the American Jewish Conference has formulated proposals which, it is urged, should be incorporated in the German Peace Treaty. These articles are respectfully submitted here for the consideration of the Council of Foreign Ministers.

Unrepresented as a people at the Peace Table and unable to act there as their own advocates, the Jewish people present these proposals to the peace-makers in the fervent hope that they will receive sympathetic consideration.

The right of all people to freedom, equality and justice must be guaranteed in the new world that will emerge when peace comes. Our plea is that, in common with all men, Jews may enjoy, in a world dedicated to the ways of peace, the rights for which the United Nations fought.

HENRY MONSKY, *Chairman*
Interim Committee

February 13, 1947

Proposals

of the

American Jewish Conference

For Inclusion in

The German Peace Treaty

Statement of the American Jewish Conference on the German Peace Treaty

★

GERMANY'S systematic war against the Jews was carried on with ever-increasing bestiality throughout the 12 years of the existence of the Nazi regime. It reduced flourishing Jewish communities to handfuls of homeless camp inmates. It despoiled prosperous Jewish settlements and robbed all Jews within Hitlerite Germany's grasp, the dead and surviving alike, of all their possessions. It cost the lives of more than half of Europe's pre-war Jewish population — six million men, women and children.

Germany's eternal guilt for this crime cannot be wiped out by the hands of men. Jews, who for more than 2,000 years have taught the world that man should not hate nor seek vengeance, do not ask for vengeance now. They ask for justice.

No obligations contained in a treaty can bring the dead back to life, or alleviate the past suffering of living victims of the aggressor. But they can and must secure some reparation of past wrongs and provide some safeguards for the future.

The incorporation of the following principles into the German Peace Treaty is designed to secure at least a minimum of justice for the first victims of Nazi Germany. Without it, no settlement with Germany can be just and no peace lasting.

1. Germany must acknowledge her guilt for her crime against the Jews. Without such acknowledgment, the German Peace Treaty would distort the records of history beyond recognition. It would, moreover, prevent that process of atonement which Germany must undergo before she can again be received into the family of civilized nations.

2. Germany must cleanse her public and private life from the insidious poison of anti-Semitism. She must show by her conduct that she is ready and willing to purge herself of diseased ideologies of race superiority. Equal rights for all and non-discrimination must be implanted and secured as the guiding principles of her laws and practices. The enjoyment of human rights and fundamental freedoms by all must

take the place of the omnipotence of the State as the foundation stone of her constitutional theory and practice.

3. Germany's readjustment to the principles of democracy will be a slow process. Her past conduct has shown that the treatment of Jews within her borders cannot be left to her discretion for many years to come. Their status and treatment must therefore be a matter of international concern and supervision.

4. To attest her atonement for her crimes against the Jews, Germany must effectively punish all those who had a hand in the persecution of Jews or benefited from it.

5. Jews who have been deprived of their nationality by discriminatory laws and practices must have the right to reacquire it but shall not be compelled to do so.

6. No Jew should be forced to remain on soil soaked with his brother's blood. Jews in Germany must have the unfettered right to emigrate from Germany and to take their belongings with them.

7. All Jewish displaced persons, who find themselves in Germany as the result of force or circumstance, must have the protection of Allied or other international authorities. They must never be allowed to fall under German jurisdiction, but Germany, responsible for the uprooting of these people from their former homes, must provide the means for their subsistence until these unfortunate people can go to the country of their choice.

8. Jews who will remain in Germany must be given freedom of association and the right to pursue their religious, communal and other activities with the same status and privileges they enjoyed before January 30, 1933, the date of Hitler's ascent to power.

9. The property of which individual Jews have been robbed must be returned to them or to their heirs. Heirless Jewish property must be transferred to and applied by a responsible Jewish body to be set up, for the purpose of relief and resettlement of Jewish victims of Nazi persecution. The beneficiaries of persecution must not be allowed to retain their ill-gotten gains and Germany must not become the heir of the Jews she has murdered. Such a provision responds to basic requirements of justice. Its omission would have a disastrous effect on the mentality of Europe, which would then conclude that robbery of the weak pays even if wars against the strong fail.

10. Germany must indemnify fully all Jews who have suffered in their person or property from measures and acts of Nazi persecution.

11. To further the process of German education in principles of justice, reparations should be paid by Germany for the damage and suffering she has caused by her persecution of the Jews. It can be no more than token because the damage and destruction she has wrought on the

Jews is immeasurable. Such reparation should include Jewish cultural property owned by non-Jewish German public institutions. This would be but a partial replacement of the vast Jewish cultural treasure wantonly destroyed by Germany.

12. Jews and their property must be exempted from any measures which are applied by the Allies to the property of enemy nationals, since it would be grossly unjust to treat them as enemy. Jews and their property must equally be protected against being used by Germany for payment of her war debts.

13. The enforcement of treaty provisions concerning Jews cannot be left to German authorities. These clauses must be supervised by international machinery to which Jewish individuals, their organizations and communities must have access. In addition, the principles contained in the treaty provisions must be enacted as part of German constitutional law and Germany must be obligated to implement them by appropriate legislation, to be approved by the Allied authorities.

The following proposals are of a minimal character, both in extent and effect. Little is being asked on behalf of those who have lost so much. But inclusion of these provisions in the German Peace Treaty is mandatory if that treaty is to be an instrument for the reconstitution of a moral society and the vindication of the principles for which the democratic world sacrificed blood and treasure.

Proposals for Inclusion In the Treaty

★

PART I. POLITICAL CLAUSES

Article I.

(1) Germany acknowledges her guilt for the heinous crime, unparalleled in its enormity and barbarity, which she has committed, under the Nazi regime, against the Jews; the persecution and infliction of inhuman cruelties and suffering on all Jews within her grasp; the wholesale extermination of entire Jewish communities in Europe; the destruction, pillage and plunder of Jewish cultural and other property; the infamous campaigns of lies, vilification and defamation of Jews, their religion, traditions and institutions; and the foul murder of six million Jews, executed with the utmost brutality.

(2) Germany, having by her conduct under the Nazi regime, shown that the treatment of Jews within her borders cannot be left to her exclusive domestic jurisdiction, acknowledges and agrees that the status and treatment of Jews in Germany is a matter of international concern.

Article II.

(1) Germany shall take all measures to secure to all persons under German jurisdiction, without distinction as to race, sex, language or religion, the enjoyment of human rights and of the fundamental freedoms, including full equality before the law, freedom of expression, of press and publication, of religious worship and practice, of political opinion, of association, and of public meeting, as well as freedom to pursue their economic activities and to preserve and develop their cultural entity.

(2) Germany further undertakes that, with the exception of such special regulations affecting foreigners as are by international custom normally applicable, the laws in force in Germany shall not, either in their content or in their application, discriminate or entail any discrimination between persons under German jurisdiction on the ground of their race, sex, language or religion, whether in reference to their persons, property, business, professional or financial interests, status, political or civil rights or any other matter.

Article III.

Germany undertakes to repeal, with retroactive effect, all discriminatory legislation, restrictions and administrative practices introduced under the Nazi regime, on account of racial origin, religion, or political belief; to keep in force the laws approved by Allied authorities in Germany concerning the abrogation of such legislation, restrictions and administrative practices, and not to enact, engage in, or permit any such discriminatory legislation, restrictions and administrative practices.

Article IV.

(1) Germany undertakes to dissolve all organizations favoring anti-Semitic or other Fascist theories of discrimination, and not to permit or assist the existence on German territory or abroad of organizations or activities which have as their aim denial to the people of their democratic rights.

(2) Germany undertakes to declare as a punishable offense against the democratic order the advocacy of, or incitement to racial, ethnic or religious hatred.

(3) Germany undertakes, in particular, to destroy and prohibit the publication of any literature, painting, record, film or other material whatsoever which furthers the advocacy of, or incitement to racial, ethnic or religious hatred.

Article V.

(1) Germany shall take all necessary steps to insure the apprehension and surrender for trial of

(a) Persons accused of having committed, ordered or abetted war crimes and crimes against peace or humanity;

(b) Nationals of any Allied or Associated Power accused of having violated their national law by treason or collaboration with the enemy during the war.

(2) Germany undertakes to bring to trial within two years from the coming into force of the present treaty and to impose adequate punishment on all persons who, since January 30, 1933, ordered, conspired to commit, committed, aided or abetted the murder, extermination, deportation, enslavement and disfranchisement of Jews, or any other act of persecution of Jews, affecting their person or property.

The provisions of any amnesties, statutes of limitation and of any laws, government orders, administrative or judicial decisions or practices, based on principles of discrimination practiced in Germany after January 30, 1933, or superior orders by any authority whatsoever, shall not be a defense.

Article VI.

Germany undertakes to restore their citizenship to former German nationals who, by discriminatory laws and practices in force in Germany at any time since January 30, 1933, were deprived of German citizenship, if within two years from the coming into force of the present treaty they formally express their desire to resume German citizenship.

Article VII.

(1) Jews in Germany shall have the right to emigrate and transfer their property and interests, free of taxes and other charges.

(2) Germany undertakes to make available, by suitable equitable arrangements, foreign exchange to facilitate such transfers, as well as the transfers of the proceeds of the sale of immovable property, of pensions, annuities and similar payments accruing now or in the future.

(3) Jews who escaped, who were deported, or who emigrated from Germany after January 30, 1933, and prior to the coming into force of the present treaty shall have the same right to transfer their property and the proceeds thereof.

Article VIII.

(1) Germany shall have no authority, right of control, or jurisdiction over Jewish displaced persons in Germany. Such persons shall be under the exclusive authority, control and jurisdiction of Allied or appropriate international authorities recognized by them.

(2) Germany undertakes to provide all facilities, goods, services and funds deemed proper and adequate by the Allied or other international authorities to maintain Jewish displaced persons so long as they remain in Germany.

Article IX.

Germany undertakes to restore and repair synagogues and Jewish cemeteries in Germany which have been pillaged or damaged under the Nazi regime, and to maintain in perpetuity the synagogues and cemeteries of destroyed or decimated Jewish communities, and pay the cost of exhumation and re-burial in Jewish cemeteries of Jews who died as a result of persecution during the Nazi regime.

Article X.

(1) Jews in Germany shall have the right to form and join associations and freely to pursue their religious, cultural, press, social, welfare and educational activities, including the establishment and maintenance of religious and secular schools of all grades.

(2) Jewish communities and institutions shall enjoy the same status, privileges, and immunities enjoyed by Jewish communities and institution before January 30, 1933; in particular, legal personality, the rights of self-taxation and tax-exemption.

(3) Jewish educational and religious institutions shall enjoy the privileges of state institutions of similar character. All Jewish institutions and their personnel shall be granted the same facilities and privileges, including budgetary support and civil service status, which are accorded to similiar state institutions and their personnel.

Article XI.

Relatives of Jews who perished as a result of persecution under the Nazi regime shall, irrespective of nationality or residence, be entitled to the same rights, privileges and allowances as are granted to the relatives of German war dead.

PART II. ECONOMIC CLAUSES

Article XII.

(1) Germany undertakes to pay an appropriate sum as a token for reparations owed by Germany for the damage and suffering caused by her persecution of the Jews under the Nazi regime. This sum is to be transferred to the body described in Article 15 (2).

(2) In order partially to repair the loss sustained by the Jewish people as the result of the destruction or dispersion of objects of religious, artistic, literary or historical value which constituted a part of their cultural heritage and which under the Nazi regime were taken from their lawful owners by force or duress, Germany shall transfer to the body described under Article 15 (2), upon its request, all similar objects owned by non-Jewish German public institutions.

Article XIII.

(1) Germany undertakes, within 18 months of the coming into force of the present treaty, to indemnify free of taxes or other charges, Jewish individuals and communities, corporations or associations which are owned or controlled by Jews, their heirs and successors, for all losses, damages and impositions, charges, fines and levies suffered since January 30, 1933, by reason of acts of discrimination, restriction, internment, forced labor, violence, or persecution.

(2) Germany undertakes to use property and funds, derived from the confiscation of property of the Nazi party, Nazi organizations and individuals, for the purpose of restitution, compensation and indemnification of persons who suffered personal or property injury or other damage through discriminatory measures on the ground of their race or religion.

Article XIV.

(1) Germany shall promptly restore in full, with their accessories, all the property, rights and interests which have been under her control and which, since January 30, 1933, have been subject to measures of sequestration, confiscation, or control or any other measures of dispossession based on discrimination against Jewish individuals and communities, corporations, or associations which are owned or controlled by Jews, or, if restoration is impossible, full compensation shall be made therefor.

(2) In the case of Jewish officials and employees of public or private enterprises, and Jews who occupied positions in the professions, who

lost or relinquished their positions, employment or professional practice after January 30, 1933, restoration shall include reinstatement with comparable status, salary, promotions, pension rights and other privileges to which they would have been entitled had they retained their positions, employment or professional practice uninterruptedly, from the date of dismissal to the date of reinstatement, and full compensation for the period of interruption. Where such reinstatement is impossible, full compensation shall be made.

Article XV.

(1) Germany shall nullify all measures including seizures, sequestration or control taken against Jewish property since January 30, 1933, and shall invalidate transfers effected since January 30, 1933, involving property, rights and interests of any description belonging to Jews, unless such transfers would have been effected irrespective of the existence of the Nazi regime. Prompt restitution of such property, rights and interests shall be effected. Where restitution in whole or in part is not possible, full compensation shall be made therefor.

(2) All property, rights and interests of Jewish individuals, Jewish communities, corporations or associations, owned or controlled by Jews, required to be restored or transferred or for which compensation or indemnification is to be made under any of the articles contained in Part II hereof, remaining heirless or unclaimed for six months after the coming into force of the present treaty shall be transferred by Germany or allied authorities to an appropriate Jewish body representative of Jews throughout the world, to act as trustee for Jewish interests, and the laws of escheat shall not apply. The property transferred shall be used by that body for purposes of relief, rehabilitation and resettlement of surviving Jewish victims of Nazi and Fascist persecution and discrimination. Such transfer shall be effected within twelve months of the coming into force of the present treaty.

(3) No restrictions or controls concerning the functions of the body described in (2), in particular as regards application and transfer in or from Germany of property, may be imposed by Germany, and no charges, taxes, or deductions of any kind may be levied by Germany on property transferred to or by that body.

(4) Property of Jews who perished since January 30, 1933, shall pass free of succession duties, taxes, fees, or other charges by any German authority, to the estate of such persons or to their heirs or successors, including the body described in (2).

Article XVI.

(1) The tribunals dealing with claims arising from any of the articles contained in Part II hereof, or from legislation pursuant thereto, shall consist of one judge of Allied nationality as president of the court, one member of the same group which was the object of persecution under

the Nazi regime to which the claimant belongs, and one German judge. The presidents of the tribunals shall lay down uniform rules of procedure and evidence for the tribunals. The tribunals shall be established within six months from the coming into force of the present treaty and shall discharge their functions expeditiously.

(2) All expenses in establishing claims under any of the articles contained in Part II hereof, or legislation pursuant thereto, including the assessment of losses or damage shall be borne by Germany.

(3) Claims arising under any of the articles contained in Part II hereof shall have priority over all other claims concerning the property, rights and interests affected.

Article XVII.

(1) Germany undertakes that all property, rights and interests passing under any of the articles contained in Part II hereof shall be restored or transferred free of all encumbrances and charges of any kind to which they may have become subject as a result of the war and without the imposition of any charges by the German government in connection with their return or transfer.

(2) Jewish individuals and communities, corporations or associations, which are owned or controlled by Jews, and their property, shall be exempted from any taxes, levies or imposts, imposed on their assets in Germany or elsewhere by Allied or German authorities for the purpose of meeting charges arising out of the war, or of meeting the costs of occupying forces, or of reparation payable to any of the United Nations. Any sums which have been so paid shall be refunded.

(3) Property of Jewish individuals and communities, corporations or associations which are owned or controlled by Jews, wherever situated, and irrespective of the nationality, domicile or residence of the owner, shall not be used for the payment of reparations or the satisfaction of other claims arising from the war, by the Allied and Associated Powers and their nationals against Germany and her nationals, notwithstanding the fact that such property has been subject to control by reason of the state of war existing between Germany and the Allied and Associated Powers.

(4) Nothing in any of the articles of this treaty, recognizing the title of any of the United Nations to German assets, shall be deemed to include any assets of Jewish individuals and communities, corporations or associations which are owned or controlled by Jews, irrespective of their nationality, residence or domicile.

PART III. ENFORCEMENT AND SUPERVISION

Article XVIII.

The provisions contained in Part I and Part II hereof, being matters of international concern, shall be subject to the supervision and enforcement by the appropriate organs of the United Nations. The Allied authorities and their organs and international agencies charged with the supervision of the execution of the terms of the present treaty shall have jurisdiction, at the instance of individuals and bodies concerned, in all disputes regarding the interpretation and execution of the terms of Part I and Part II hereof.

Article XIX.

(1) The provisions contained in Part I and Part II hereof shall have full force and effect as part of the law of Germany. They may be invoked by individuals and bodies concerned, before German courts and other authorities.

(2) Germany undertakes to enact the principles laid lown in the above articles as part of her constitutional law and to enact adequate legislation, where necessary, to carry out the terms of the present treaty. Such legislation shall be submitted for approval to the Allied authority set up to supervise the execution of the present treaty. No changes in the laws enacted in pursuance of the present treaty shall be permissible without the prior consent of the Allied authority. No other laws, administrative provisions, or judicial decisions shall be valid if they are in conflict with the terms of the present treaty or with legislation enacted in pursuance thereof.

The foregoing Statement and Proposals were approved by the Interim Committee of the American Jewish Conference on January 22, 1947.

HENRY MONSKY, *Chairman*,
Interim Committee

LOUIS LIPSKY, *Chairman*,
Executive Committee

Nazi Germany's War
Against the Jews

PREFACE

"NAZI Germany's War Against the Jews" is divided into three parts. Part One, "The Twenty-five Year Campaign," tells the story of Nazi aggression against the Jews from the beginnings of the Nazi Party in 1920 until Germany's downfall in the spring of 1945. It is based entirely on the documentary evidence assembled for the Nurnberg Trial.

Part Two, "The Trial and Punishment," records the Jewish case as it was presented before the International Military Tribunal. Included are the Four-Power Agreement, the Charter of the Tribunal, and those portions of the indictment, the addresses of the chief prosecutors, and the judgment, which dealt with Nazi crimes against the Jews.

Part Three, "The Documentary Evidence," includes all major documents concerning Jews which were assembled for the trial.

Seymour Krieger, member of the bar of the District of Columbia, wrote Part One and analyzed and arranged the documents for Parts Two and Three. Mr. Krieger was a member of the Office of the United States Counsel for the Prosecution of the Axis War Criminals, serving on Justice Robert H. Jackson's staff throughout the trial.

Part One

The Twenty-five Year Campaign

INTRODUCTION

THE Nazi Government's persecution, enslavement and slaughter of the Jews throughout Europe is the most systematically brutal record in history. The anti-Jewish policy of the Nazi Party, first formulated in the Party Program of February 24, 1920, proclaimed that no Jew could be a member of the German race. Between that time and January 30, 1933, when Hitler was appointed Chancellor of the Reich, the Jews of Germany were subjected to continuous attacks by leaders and members of the Nazi Party in speech, press and deed.

Immediately after the Party took possession of the German State, the entire executive and legislative machinery of the Reich was turned against the Jews. They were driven out of government service, they were denied the right to practice any profession, their German citizenship was revoked; they lost every conceivable right and privilege of membership in organized society.

On November 9-10, 1938, hundreds of synagogues in Germany were destroyed in a "spontaneous" uprising ordered by the German government. Thousands of Jews were thrown into concentration camps. Jews were murdered in their homes and in the streets of Germany. That terrible night was the beginning of the annihilation of German Jewry.

When the Wehrmacht overran Austria, Czechoslovakia, Poland, Denmark, Norway, Holland, Belgium, France, Greece, Yugoslavia, vast areas of the Soviet Union and Hungary, the entire weight of the Nazi government and its war machine was thrown against the Jews of those unhappy lands. The Nazi armies carried their racist pestilence with them into all occupied territories. The infamous Nurnberg Laws were incorporated into the national laws of all the occupied lands. The life and property of every Jew was threatened by the sinister arms of the all-grasping Hakenkreuz. The tempo of persecution heightened with the march of the Wehrmacht across Europe. Jewish property was confiscated, Jews were deprived of all means of livelihood, their food supply was cut off, they were confined in ghettos upon pain of death. They were ruthlessly deported by the hundreds of thousands to slave labor camps.

Finally, in the summer of 1941, Teutonic fury reached its zenith. The Nazis determined to annihilate all Jews throughout occupied Europe. Until autumn of 1944, the combined efforts of the German occupying authorities, the Gestapo, the Security Service and the Wehrmacht were bent on the accomplishment of this task.

Extermination camps were set up and put into operation. Transports brought hundreds of thousands of Jews from all corners of Europe to gas chambers and crematoria. Prisoners of war on the Eastern Front were screened and all Jews were executed. Thousands of Jews were murdered in gas wagons. Execution squads of the Security Service roamed the occupied areas of the East to shoot or bury alive hundreds of thousands of Jews. *In this last frenzy, four million Jews were massacred in gas chambers and an additional two million helpless men, women and children of Jewish faith were murdered by execution squads of the Security Service.*

These vast crimes were methodically committed—and methodically recorded. That record, punctiliously described in official German government reports, was unfolded in great detail before the International Military Tribunal, sitting at Nurnberg, from November 14, 1945 to October 1, 1946. The authenticity of those official German documents has not been and cannot be challenged. These documents and the testimony introduced before the Tribunal prove, by credible evidence, an almost incredible story.

CHAPTER 1

ANTI-SEMITISM PRIOR TO 1933

ANTI-SEMITISM has been called the emotional foundation of the National Socialist Movement (Document 2844-PS).[1] It was one of the basic tenets of the Party and the rallying cry of all fanatical Nazis.

The Nazi Party Program, proclaimed by Adolf Hitler on February 24, 1920 indicated the extent to which the Nazis sought to limit the rights and status of Jews from the outset (Document 1708-PS):[2]

"4. Only a member of the race can be a citizen. A member of the race can only be one who is of German blood, without consideration of creed. Consequently no Jew can be a member of the race.

"5. Whoever has no citizenship is to be able to live in Germany only as a guest, and must be under the authority of legislation for foreigners.

"6. The right to determine matters concerning administration and law belongs only to the citizen. Therefore we demand that every public office, of any sort whatsoever, whether in the Reich, the county or municipality, be filled only by citizens. We combat the corrupting parliamentary economy, office-holding only according to party inclinations without consideration of character or abilities.

"7. We demand that the state be charged first with providing the opportunity for a livelihood and way of life for the citizens. If it is impossible to sustain the total population of the State, then the members of foreign nations (non-citizens) are to be expelled from the Reich.

"8. Any further immigration of non-citizens is to be prevented. We demand that all non-Germans, who have immigrated to Germany since 2 August 1914, be forced immediately to leave the Reich."

From the adoption of the Party Program until January 30, 1933, when Hitler was appointed Reich Chancellor, the Nazis, in their campaign to seize control of the German state, relentlessly singled out the Jews for attack.

Alfred Rosenberg, fountain-head of Nazi teaching, and later the Fuehrer's Delegate for the Ideological Training of the NSDAP

---
[1] Part III—page 421
[2] Part III—page 266

(National Socialist German Workers Party) in his book, "Writings of the Years 1917-1921" (Document 2842-PS),[3] advocated the adoption of the following "national-political measures":

"3. Jews have no right to speak and write on or be active in German politics.

"4. Jews have no right to hold public offices, or to serve in the Army either as soldiers or as officers. However, their contribution of work may be considered.

"5. Jews have no right to be leaders of cultural institutions of the state and community (theaters, galleries, etc.) or to be professors and teachers in German schools and universities.

"6. Jews have no right to be active in state or municipal commissions for examinations, control, censorship, etc. Jews have no right to represent the German Reich in economic treaties; they have no right to be represented in the directorate of state banks or communal credit establishments.

"7. Foreign Jews have no right to settle in Germany permanently. Their admission into the German political community is to be forbidden under all circumstances. . . ."

This set the pattern for the future. In 1921 Rosenberg urged all Germans to gather into a "steel-hard racial united front" with the following battle-cry (Document 2432-PS):[4]

". . . This one challenge must go through the whole country: get the Jews out of all parties, institute measures for the repudiation of all citizenship rights of all Jews and half Jews, banish all eastern Jews, exercise strictest vigilance over the native ones, break up Zionism, which is involved in English-Jewish politics, confiscate its money, and banish its members to their English protector or to the Promised Land. Possible 'Jew Strikes' must be dealt with accordingly."

Adolf Hitler incited mob violence in a speech on July 28, 1922 (Document 2405-PS):[5]

"Is it not these criminals, this Jewry, who are the real foes of the Republic, these men who from the day of its birth burdened it with the lie that this people was guilty of the World War? And have they not undermined the Republic and thereby given to the foreign powers the spiritual arms with which these Powers for the last three years shower blows upon us and oppress us and say to us 'You deserve it, for you yourselves have confessed your guilt!' And have they not opposed the Republic, who have so reduced all power of resistance that today every Hottentot State is in a position to lord it over Germany? And do they not ceaselessly oppose Germany, who have brought

[3] Part III—page 419
[4] Part III—page 371
[5] Part III—page 368

us, once the people of honour, so low that we have a reputation for the meanest economic corruption and the most debased political outlook?"

And on April 27, 1923, Hitler cried:

"Clear away the Jews! Our people has genius enough—we need no Hebrews. If we were to put in their place intelligences drawn from the great body of our people, then we have found anew the bridge which leads to the community of the people."

Words became acts. In the very first days of their parliamentary activity in the Reichstag, the Nazis on May 27, 1924, introduced a motion to place all members of the Jewish race under special laws and, on August 25, 1924, to exclude members of the Jewish race from all public affairs. Wilhelm Frick, who was to become Hitler's Minister of the Interior, had this to say on July 17, 1925 (Document 2840-PS):[6]

"Never before have the rights of the civil service officials been violated more than in this republic. The best proof for this is the 'Reduction of Personnel Decree.' We, however, demand that a beginning be made particularly in the reduction of two civil service categories. The first we refer to are the so-called officials of the Revolution. The other category consists of the members of the Jewish Race. We deem it below our dignity to be governed by people of that race."

In MEIN KAMPF, the Nazi Bible, written in 1925, Hitler stated this as the most tremendous task of the National Socialist Movement (Document 2662-PS):[7]

"It must open the eyes of the people with regard to foreign nations and must remind them again and again of the true enemy [the Jew] of our present-day world. In the place of the hate against Aryans—from whom we may be separated by almost everything, to whom, however, we are tied by common blood or the great tie of a common culture—it must dedicate to the general anger the evil enemy of mankind, as the true cause of all suffering.

"It must see to it, however, that, at least in our country, he be recognized as the most mortal enemy and that the struggle against him may show, like a flaming beacon of a better era, to other nations too, the road to salvation for a struggling Aryan mankind."

This was the mission Hitler gave the German people.

---

[6] Part III—page 418
[7] Part III—page 400

CHAPTER 2

GERMANY AND AUSTRIA UNDER THE NAZIS

ON JANUARY 30, 1933, Hitler was appointed Reich Chancellor by President von Hindenburg. The NSDAP won 288 of the 647 seats in the Reichstag, in the elections on March 5. The Nazis captured the necessary majority by taking into "protective custody" a large number of Communist deputies and officials. They then assumed full legislative powers, including the power to amend the Weimar Constitution, by pushing through an "Enabling Act" on March 24, 1933. This placed the entire machinery of government in their hands.

The Nazi grip then closed on every phase of German life. Other political parties were persecuted, their property confiscated, their officers and members imprisoned. On July 14, 1933, a new law declared the NSDAP the only legal political party and made it a criminal offense to maintain or form any other political organization.

To consolidate their power by paralyzing all potential opposition, the NSDAP leaders began a ruthless campaign against the trade unions, the churches, and the Jews. On May 20, 1933, pursuant to an April 21 directive issued by Robert Ley, the NSDAP confiscated the properties of the free trade unions and placed their leaders in "protective custody." The Nazi government proceeded more cautiously to combat the influence of the Christian churches, whose doctrines were fundamentally at variance with National Socialist philosophy and practice. While the extreme step of banning the practice of the Christian religion was not taken, the NSDAP made strenuous efforts to limit the influence of Christianity on the German people.

Persecution of the Jews now became official state policy. The Nazis planned it deliberately. They executed their ghastly plans with the precision and thoroughness of mechanized savages.

The week of March 6-13, 1933, witnessed the first wave of anti-Jewish terror. The Nazi cry "Juda Verrecke" (Death to Jews) had accompanied the tramp of storm troop boots since 1925 and on the morning of March 6 the words came alive with death in their wake.

SA men roamed the streets, beating, looting, killing. (Documents 1759-PS[8] and L-198).[9]

Boycott Action of April 1, 1933

The first official act of the Nazi government against the Jews was the boycott of Jewish enterprises on April 1, 1933. The central committee for the boycott was headed by Julius Streicher, and included Robert Ley, Heinrich Himmler and Hans Frank (Document 2156-PS).[10] On March 31, 1933, Streicher issued a number of orders in connection with the boycott. The use of force was to be avoided; SA and SS members were forbidden to enter Jewish establishments; the only duty of the defensive guards was to inform the public that the proprietor of the establishment was a Jew (Document 2154-PS).[11] Streicher thus called upon the German people to support the boycott (Document 2410-PS):[12]

"But even this last hope of theirs shall be frustrated! Millions of Germans longed to see the day on which the German people would be shaken up in its entirety to recognize at last the world enemy in the Jew. World Jewry intended to do harm to the German people and has done good. At 10 A.M. Saturday 1 April, the defensive action of the German people against the Jewish world criminal will begin. A defensive fight begins, such as never has been dared before throughout the centuries. World Jewry asked for the fight, it is to have it! It is to have it until it shall have recognized that the Germany of the brown battalions is not a Germany of cowardice and of submission. World Jewry is to have the fight until victory shall be ours!

"National Socialists! Strike the world enemy! And if the world were full of devils, still we must succeed!"

The following brief description of the boycott appears in the book, "From the Imperial House to the Reich Chancellory," by Dr. Joseph Goebbels (Document 2409-PS):[13]

"1 April 1933.

"The boycott against the world atrocity propaganda has incited Berlin and the entire Reich to the fullest extent. For my own information I drive through the Tauentzien street. All Jewish stores are closed. At their entrances SA sentries are standing. The public has declared its solidarity everywhere. An exemplary discipline prevails. An imposing spectacle! Everything takes its course in the utmost tranquility, within the Reich too."

"Jews Are Not Germans"

Beginning April 7, 1933, a flood of restrictive legislation poured out, depriving Jews of every conceivable right that they might have had as German citizens or even as human beings. A law was enacted barring

---

[8] Part III—page 279
[9] Part III—page 78
[10] Part III—page 342
[11] Part III—page 341
[12] Part III—page 370
[13] Part III—page 368

non-Aryans from admission to the practice of law and providing for the cancellation of admission to the bar of non-Aryan lawyers (Document 1400-PS).[14] A law, reestablishing professional civil service, provided for the dismissal of officials of non-Aryan descent (Document 1397-PS).[15] Four days later a regulation defined non-Aryans and prohibited them from holding civil service positions (Document 2012-PS).[16] This was supplemented by the law of June 30, providing that a non-Aryan may not be appointed a Reich official (Document 1400-PS)[17] and this law, in turn, was implemented by the provision of October 14, 1936, that only an official of German blood may be promoted (Document 2326-PS).[18]

An April 22, 1933 statute removed non-Aryan patent agents from the roster (Document 2868-PS).[19] In the same month, a law directed against overcrowding of German schools and higher institutions reduced the number of non-Aryan students (Document 2022-PS).[20] This was followed by the general decree of September 10, 1935, establishing separate Jewish schools (Document 2894-PS);[21] and in November, 1938, Jews were barred from German universities (Document 2683-PS).[22] Jewish segregation from German life continued.

By statute enacted May 6, 1933, Jews were denied the right to practice the profession of tax adviser (Document 2869-PS).[23] On July 26, the German naturalization of Eastern Jews was revoked (Document 2870-PS).[24] On October 4, admission to the profession of editor was prohibited to non-Aryans (Document 2083-PS).[25] On May 21, 1935, after military service in Germany had been made compulsory, Aryan descent was made a prerequisite for active military service (Document 2984-PS).[26]

THE NURNBERG LAWS

All of these acts culminated in the promulgation on September 15, 1935 of the infamous Nurnberg Laws at the annual Nazi Party Rally in the medieval German town. Those laws consisted of the Reich Citizenship Law which provided that (Document 1416-PS):[27] "A citizen of the Reich is only that subject, who is of German or kindred blood and who, through his conduct, shows that he is both desirous and fit to serve faithfully the German people and the Reich," and the Law for the Protection of German Blood and German Honor (Document 3179-PS),[28] which prohibited marriages between Jews and Germans, denied

[14] Part III—page 249
[15] Part III—page 248
[16] Part III—page 331
[17] Part III—page 249
[18] Part III—page 362
[19] Part III—page 421
[20] Part III—page 332
[21] Part III—page 433
[22] Part III—page 404
[23] Part III—page 422
[24] Part III—page 423
[25] Part III—page 333
[26] Part III—page 441
[27] Part III—page 255
[28] Part III—page 473

I-6

The Twenty-five Year Campaign

Jews the privilege of employing German women in their households, and forbade Jews from hoisting the Reich national flag. On November 14, 1935, the First Regulation to the Reich Citizenship Law defined the term "Jew" and provided that a Jew may not be a citizen of the Reich (Document 1417-PS).[29] The effect of the Nurnberg Laws was to cut off the Jew from the German body politic, to give legislative sanction to the deprivations that the Jews had already suffered, and to pave the way for an even more intensive persecution.

In conversation with a representative of President Roosevelt on September 23, 1935, Hjalmar Schacht tried to soften the impression of the Nurnberg Laws (Document EC-450):[30] "I never was in favor of our treatment of the Jews, but the new laws announced at Nurnberg give protection to the Jews. They are now guaranteed the same rights as any other minority within Germany, such as Poland, for example."

The Nazis did not rest on their laws. The German mind was pounded with exhortations to carry out their intent. Typical was an article in the book, "The SA Man," entitled, "Finish Up With the Jews," published on July 27, 1935 (Document 3050AE-PS):[31]

"German women finally wake up and do not buy any more from Jews. And you, German girl, also finally wake up and do not go with Jews any longer.

"The Jew is also a person? Quite right! Nobody has ever argued that point. The only question is: What kind of a person is he? Oh, I know, German women, your groceryman is such an obliging and decent Jew, and your friend, German girl, is such a nice and polite person! Yes, I understand.

"To the devil finally with this nursery tale.
> Snake remains a snake, and
> Jew remains a Jew!***

"***German women, if you buy from Jews and German girl, if you carry on with Jews, then both of you betray your German Volk and your Fuehrer, Adolf Hitler, and commit a sin against your German Volk and its future! Finally, wake up German woman, aren't you ashamed to give your household money to Jews? Do you know what you are doing thereby? You give the deadly enemy of the German Volk as well as your own and your children's deadly enemy the weapons into his hands for the fight against Germany. Must that be? Can't you really go two or three houses further and obtain your needs from a German national?

"And you, German girl, you give your best, your honor and your blood to one of a strange race?

"Aren't you ashamed of yourself?"

The Nurnberg Laws were not the end. The Nazi legislative mill ground out new decrees. On January 8, 1937, financial assistance was

---
[29] Part III—page 256
[30] Part III—page 20
[31] Part III—page 456

I-7

refused to civil servants to pay for services rendered by Jewish doctors, dentists, lawyers, etc. (Document 3240-PS).[32] On April 26, 1938, registration of Jewish-owned property was required (Document 1406-PS).[33] On July 25, Jews were prohibited from practicing medicine (Document 2872-PS).[34] On August 17, a decree was enacted executing the law requiring Jews to use only such names as prescribed in the Minister of Interior's directives (Document 1674-PS).[35] On October 5, all German passports of Jews in the Reich were invalidated (Document 2120-PS).[36]

Austria After March, 1938

When German troops crossed the frontier on March 12, 1938 and Austria was united with the Reich, the entire body of German anti-Jewish legislation became Austrian law. Three days later, it was decreed that Jewish officials may not take the oath of office (Document 2311-PS).[37] Joseph Buerkel, the Fuehrer's Deputy for the Plebiscite in Austria, wrote to Goering on March 26 concerning an order for a boycott against Jewish stores and Aryanization of Jewish-owned businesses in Austria (Document 3577-PS).[38] On May 20, a specific decree introduced the Nurnberg Laws (Document 2124-PS).[39] On September 27, Jews were barred from practicing law (Document 2874-PS).[40]

Aktion November 9-10, 1938

The night of November 9-10, 1938 unleashed an orgy of arson, destruction and murder against Jews throughout Germany and Austria. It was called a "spontaneous" demonstration of German wrath evoked by the shooting of legation secretary vom Rath in Paris. Teletyped instructions were flashed to police officials and Gestapo agents to guide their actions during the "spontaneous" riots which were "going to take place." The *Voelkischer Beobachter* for November 11, 1938 reported the events under the head "Anti-Jewish Demonstrations Throughout the Reich" (Document 2712-PS):[41]

"Berlin, 10 November.

"On the announcement of the death of German diplomat vom Rath, who was killed at the hands of a cowardly Jewish assassin, spontaneous demonstrations have developed throughout the Reich."

Proof that the anti-Jewish violence was planned and organized by the Nazi Party and carried out with the advance approval and active participation of the German police is overwhelming.

---

[32] Part III—page 475
[33] Part III—page 250
[34] Part III—page 424
[35] Part III—page 264
[36] Part III—page 337
[37] Part III—page 361
[38] Part III—page 551
[39] Part III—page 338
[40] Part III—page 425
[41] Part III—page 409

The Twenty-five Year Campaign

Here are the facts: On the evening of November 9, 1938, Goebbels told Party leaders attending a social evening in the Munich old town hall that the Fuehrer, at his suggestion, had decided that demonstrations hostile to Jews, during which Jewish shops would be demolished and synagogues fired, were not to be prepared or organized by the Party, but so far as they originated "spontaneously," they were not to be discouraged. It was understood by all Party leaders, from Goebbels' oral instructions, that the Party should not appear to be the instigator of the demonstrations but that it should organize and execute them (Document 3063-PS).[42] Instructions to that effect were telephoned immediately to their district bureaus by a large number of Party members present.

At 1:20 a. m., November 10, the following teletype message was issued to state police and main offices of the Gestapo on the subject of "Measures Against Jews Tonight" (Document 3051-PS):[43]

"Because of the attempt on the life of the Secretary of the Legation vom Rath in Paris tonight, 9-10 November 1938, demonstrations against Jews are to be expected throughout the Reich. The following instructions are given on how to treat these events:

"1. The Chiefs of the State Police, or their deputies, must get in telephonic contact with the political leaders [Gauleitung oder Kreisleitung] who have jurisdiction over their districts and have to arrange a joint meeting with the appropriate inspector or commander of the regular Police [Ordnungspolizei] to discuss the organization of the demonstrations. At these discussions the political leaders have to be informed that the German Police has received from the Reichsfuehrer SS and Chief of the German Police the following instructions, in accordance with which the political leaders should adjust their own measures.

"*a.* Only such measures should be taken which do not involve danger to German life or property. (For instance synagogues are to be burned down only when there is no danger of fire to the surroundings.)

"*b.* Business and private apartments of Jews may be destroyed but not looted. The police is instructed to supervise the execution of this order and to arrest looters.

"*c.* On business streets, particular care is to be taken that non-Jewish business should be protected from damage.

"*d.* Foreigners, even Jews, are not to be molested.

"2. The demonstrations which are going to take place should not be hindered by the police provided that the instructions quoted above in section 1 are carried out. The police has only to supervise compliance with the instructions.

"3. Upon receipt of this telegram, in all synagogues and offices of the Jewish communities the available archives should be seized by the police, to forestall destruction during the demonstrations. This refers only to valuable

[42] Part III—page 464
[43] Part III—page 459

historical material, not to new lists of taxes, etc. The archives are to be turned over to the competent SD offices.

"4. The direction of the measures of the Security Police concerning the demonstrations against Jews is vested with the organs of the State Police, inasmuch as the inspectors of the Security Police are not issuing their own orders. In order to carry out the measures of the Security Police, officials of the Criminal Police as well as members of the SD of the 'Verfuegungstruppe' and the Allgemeinen SS may be used.

"5. Inasmuch as in the course of the events of this night the employment of officials used for this purpose would be possible, in all districts as many Jews, especially rich ones, are to be arrested as can be accommodated in the existing prisons [Haftraeumen]. For the time being only healthy men not too old are to be arrested. Upon their arrest, the appropriate concentration camps should be contacted immediately, in order to confine them in these camps as fast as possible. Special care should be taken that the Jews arrested in accordance with these instructions are not mistreated.

"6. The contents of this order are to be forwarded to the appropriate inspectors and commanders of the Ordnungspolizei and to the districts of the SD [SD-Oberabschnitte and SD-Unterabschnitte], adding that the Reichsfuehrer SS and Chief of the German Police ordered this police measure. The Chief of the Ordnungspolizei has given the necessary instructions to the Ordnungspolizei, including the fire brigade. In carrying out the ordered measures, the closest harmony should be assured between the Sicherheitspolizei and the Ordnungspolizei.

"The receipt of this telegram is to be confirmed by the Chiefs of the State Police or their deputies by telegram to the Gestapo, care of SS Standartenfuehrer Mueller.

/s/ Heydrich,
SS Gruppenfuehrer."

The teletyped instructions were carried out scrupulously throughout Germany and Austria. Heydrich detailed the following summary of the Aktion to Goering on the next day (Document 3058-PS):[44]

"The reports of the State Police offices which have so far been received up to 11.11.1938 [give] the following general impression:

"In numerous cities, looting of Jewish shops and business premises has occurred. In order to avoid further looting, strong action was taken in all cases. 174 persons were arrested for looting.

"The extent of the destruction of Jewish shops and houses can not yet be verified by figures. The figures given in the reports: 815 shops destroyed, 171 dwelling-houses set on fire or destroyed, only indicate a fraction of the actual damage caused, as far as arson is concerned. Due to the urgency of the reporting, the reports received to date are entirely limited to general statements such as 'numerous' or 'most shops destroyed.' Therefore the figures given must have been exceeded considerably.

"191 Synagogues were set on fire, and another 76 completely destroyed. In

---
[44] Part III—page 463

The Twenty-five Year Campaign

addition 11 parish halls [Gemeindehauser], cemetery chapels and similar buildings were set on fire and 3 more completely destroyed.

"20,000 Jews were arrested, also 7 Aryans and 3 foreigners. The latter were arrested for their own safety.

"36 deaths were reported and those seriously injured were also numbered at 36. Those killed and injured are Jews. One Jew is still missing. The Jews killed include one Polish national, and those injured include 2 Poles.

(Signed) Heydrich"

Sensitivity to adverse criticism abroad or perhaps a mechanical observance of the proprieties compelled the police and the state prosecutor to begin an investigation of the deaths and looting on the night of November 9-10. This embarrassed the Nazi Party and, to forestall punishment of its members, the Supreme Court of the Party took jurisdiction over these cases. The report of the judicial proceedings before the Supreme Court of the Party (Document 3063-PS)[45] is an extraordinary document.

Nazi Party men served as jurors at the trials. Cases against sixteen Party members were heard. In fourteen, the Party Court asked Hitler to quash the proceedings in the state criminal courts. Two of the accused Party members were handed over to the criminal court for prosecution. They were accused of the crime of rape against Jewesses, an offense particularly obnoxious to Nazis because it violated the Law for the Protection of German Blood and Honor. A third Party member, who was accused of moral crimes against a Jewess, was placed in protective custody. The three Party members involved in moral crimes were expelled from the NSDAP. Two of the Party members on whose behalf Hitler had been asked to intervene, were found guilty of killing Jews and were given disciplinary warnings and deprived of the right to hold public office for three years. Proceedings against the others charged with murder of Jews were either suspended or minor punishments were pronounced.

The Party Court's opinion excused the killings on the ground that they were motivated by justifiable hatred against the Jews or because the accused reasonably thought that the Nazi Party leaders had ordered reprisals for the death of vom Rath. The Court's opinion clarifies the whole sequence of the November 9-10 events (Document 3063-PS):[46]

"Therefore Party Member Dr. Goebbels' instruction that the Party was not to organize this demonstration was most likely interpreted by each Party leader present in the town hall to mean that the Party should not appear as the organizer. Party Member Dr. Goebbels probably meant it in that way for politically interested and active circles who might participate in such demonstrations as members of the Party and its branches. Naturally they could be

---
[45] [46] Part III—page 464

mobilized only through the offices of the Party and its branches. Thus a series of subordinate leaders understood some unfortunately phrased orders which reached them orally or by phone, to mean that Jewish blood would now have to flow for the blood of Party Member vom Rath; that at any rate the leadership did not attach importance to the life of a Jew. For example, not the Jew Gruenspan but all Jewry was guilty of the death of Party Member vom Rath. The German people were therefore taking revenge on all Jewry. The synagogues were burning in the entire Reich. Jewish residences and businesses were to be laid waste. Life and property of Aryans had to be protected. Foreign Jews were not to be molested. The drive was being carried out by order of the Fuehrer. The police were withdrawn. Pistols were to be brought. At the least resistance the weapon was to be used without consideration. As an SA man each one would certainly know what he had to do, etc. (Enclosure 10, pages 5 ff, enclosure 20 and enclosure 11 pages 5 ff.)

"It is a matter of course that, under the circumstances described, even an ambiguous order must direct the responsibility upwards. The same is true of a misunderstood order. (Enclosure 11 Heike case, and enclosure 12.)

"It is another question, whether an intentionally ambiguous order, given with the expectation that the receiver of the order would recognize the intention of the one who gave it and would act accordingly, is not an example of the discipline of the past. In times of struggle such an order may, in individual cases, be necessary, in order to achieve a political success without giving the government any possibility of discovering the origin of the Party. This viewpoint is now obsolete. The public, down to the last man, realizes that political drives like those of 9 November were organized and directed by the Party, whether this is admitted or not.

"When all the synagogues burn down in one night, it must have been organized in some way and can only have been organized by the Party. But the soldiers should never be put in a position of having any doubts in regard to the intention of the commander—whether the order really means what it says; for there is a possibility that such doubts may lead to the wrong results in important matters, or there might be doubts in a case when the commander wants to be certain that his order is understood and carried out literally. In any case, soldierly discipline and with it the National Socialist concept of discipline is undermined thereby."

There is perhaps no document which more clearly demonstrates the brazen perversion of justice under the Nazis than this exoneration of rape, theft and murder. The Nazi Party judges were "responsible only to their National Socialistic conscience, and subordinates of no political leader" except the Fuehrer (Document 2402-PS).[47]

There was a peculiar aftermath to Aktion November 9-10. Six million dollars' worth of plate glass windows had been broken in Jewish shops. The Nazis discovered, to their dismay, that most of the plate glass windows had been insured and that Aryan insurance companies would have to stand the loss. Moreover, replacements for the glass had

---

[47] Part III—page 367

to come from Belgium and the amount of damage represented about half the annual production of the Belgian glass industry.

The Nazis speedily found a solution. The Cabinet hastily convened on November 12 under the chairmanship of Goering, with Funk, Heydrich and Goebbels present (Document 1816-PS).[48] It was decided that the insurance money payable to the Jews would be confiscated by the state, that the Jews would be fined one billion marks, and that measures should be taken immediately to eliminate Jews from the German and Austrian economies and to Aryanize their property.

Work Forbidden

The Nazis had a chain of command, an order, a law, for each of their lawless acts. The fine of one billion reichsmarks upon the Jews of German nationality was imposed by a statute (Document 1412-PS)[49] which declared:

"The hostile attitude of Jewry towards the German people and Reich, which does not even shrink back from committing cowardly murder, makes a decisive defense and harsh punishment necessary."

Another statute (Document 1662-PS)[50] executed on the same date, November 12, eliminated Jews from German economic life; prohibited Jews from operating retail shops, mail order houses, and handicraft enterprises; made it unlawful for Jews to offer goods or services in any market or to advertise or accept orders; and provided that no Jew could manage a firm or be a member of a cooperative.

"Spontaneous" demonstrations also took place in Austria on the night of November 9-10 (Document 2237-PS).[51] They were followed by the same confiscatory economic measures. On November 18, the Austrian Governor in Vienna was authorized to confiscate property of persons or societies whose activities were "inimical" to the people of the State and confiscations previously made by the Gestapo were ratified (Document 3450-PS).[52] Goering had warned the Viennese shortly after the Anschluss (Document 3460-PS):[53]

"I must address myself with a serious word to the city of Vienna. The city of Vienna can no longer rightfully be called a German city. So many Jews live in this city. Where there are 300,000 Jews, you cannot speak of a German city.

"Vienna must once more become a German city, because it must perform important tasks for Germany in Germany's Ostmark. These tasks lie in the sphere of culture as well as in the sphere of economics. In neither of them can we, in the long run, put up with the Jew.

---

[48] Part III—page 292
[49] Part III—page 254
[50] Part III—page 261
[51] Part III—page 353
[52] Part III—page 540
[53] Part III—page 541

"This, however, should not be attempted by inappropriate interference and stupid measures but must be done systematically and carefully. As Delegate for the Four-Year Plan I commission the Reichsstatthalter in Austria jointly with the Plenipotentiary of the Reich, to consider and take any steps, necessary for the redirection of Jewish commerce, i.e., for the Aryanization of business and economic life, and to execute this process in accordance with our laws, legally but inexorably."

The billion mark fine and the confiscated Jewish property were fed into the gigantic maw of Nazi rearmament. On November 18, 1938, at a meeting of the Reich Defense Council, Goering thus linked German rearmament with the anti-Semitic persecution (Document 3575-PS):[54]

"3. Finances. Very critical situation of the Reich Exchequer. Relief initially through the billion imposed on Jewry, and through profits accruing to the Reich in the Aryanization of Jewish enterprises."

After the violence of November 9-10, 1938, legislative restrictions and confiscations fell upon the unfortunate Jews of Germany and Austria with unabated fury. On November 28, a police regulation was adopted imposing restrictions with respect to the time and place that Jews might appear in public (Document 1415-PS).[55]

Five days later, it was decreed that Jews could be ordered to sell or liquidate industrial enterprises, real estate, securities. They were prohibited from dealing in that type of property or converting it into jewels, gems, and objects of art which they could carry with them (Document 1409-PS).[56]

One week later, Goering issued an order to the Reich leaders of the NSDAP eliminating Jews from German economic life and taking over Jewish business and funds (Document 1208-PS).[57] No rights, however petty, escaped the dragnet of the all-inclusive restrictions. Drivers' licenses and registration papers were revoked (Document 2682-PS).[58] Hitler prohibited the use of sleeping and dining cars by Jews and banned them from certain hotels, restaurants, swimming pools, mineral baths, and similar public places (Document 069-PS).[59] A Jewish tenant could not invoke the protection of the tenancy laws against an Aryan landlord, and an Aryan could dissolve a lease with a Jew at any time simply by giving notice (Document 1419-PS).[60] On July 4, 1939, a decree was adopted authorizing the Reichsminister of the Interior to abolish or take over all Jewish organizations and foundations (Document 2876-PS).[61]

With the outbreak of World War II on September 1, 1939, Nazi

---

[54] Part III—page 550
[55] Part III—page 254
[56] Part III—page 251
[57] Part III—page 244
[58] Part III—page 402
[59] Part III—page 111
[60] Part III—page 258
[61] Part III—page 427

The Twenty-five Year Campaign

persecution of the Jews was intensified and extended throughout occupied Europe.

German Jews who had escaped from Germany were pursued by the on-rushing Wehrmacht. After France fell, the German ambassador to the Petain Government cabled to Berlin on October 1, 1940 on the subject of the citizenship status of German Jews living in occupied France, taking the "first step for the solution of the whole problem" (Document EC-265).[62] On September 18, 1941, in the occupied Dutch territories, a decree blocked the property of Jews who emigrated from the German Reich (Document 3326-PS).[63]

Meanwhile in Germany, on September 1, 1941, the Reichsminister of the Interior decreed that Jews could appear in public only if they wore a yellow Jewish star on the left side of the outer garment (Document 2673-PS).[64] It had already been made clear that Germans and Jews were not to mix socially. But with unfailing precision, the Gestapo office for the Nurnberg-Furth Area commanded on November 3, 1941 that Aryans must not maintain friendly relations with Jews or show themselves with Jews conspicuously in public, on pain of being sent to a concentration camp (Document L-152).[65]

On March 24, 1942, the Reichsminister of the Interior severely limited the use of public transportation facilities by Jews (Document L-167).[66] On September 18, 1942, the Reichsminister for Nutrition and Agriculture ordered that Jews could not buy meat, meat products, eggs, wheat products, or milk after October 14, 1942, sharply reduced their right to purchase other rationed foods and limited the hours of the day during which Jews could shop (Document 1347-PS).[67]

By 1943, the Jews of Germany were virtually prisoners. They had few rights left and these were soon to go. On April 1, 1943, the Reichsminister of Justice ordered the public prosecutors to send Jews released from penal institutions to the death camps of Auschwitz or Lublin (Document 701-PS).[67a]

And finally, the Thirteenth Regulation under the Reich Citizenship Law, dated July 1, 1943, placed Jews beyond the pale of the law and turned them over to the Gestapo. That regulation provided that criminal actions committed by Jews should be subject to direct police action and also that the property of Jews should escheat to the State after their death (Document 1422-PS).[68] Two days later Himmler commanded the Gestapo to execute the Thirteenth Regulation and ordered that any Jew

---

[62] Part III—page 16
[63] Part III—page 513
[64] Part III—page 401
[65] Part III—page 46
[66] Part III—page 51
[67] Part III—page 246
[67a] Part III—page 163
[68] Part III—page 259

I-15

suspected of trying to escape should be arrested immediately (Document 3085-PS).[69]

The Jews of Germany and Austria thus shared the terrible fate which befell Jews throughout German occupied Europe. They were deported into slavery by the thousands (Document 3803-PS)[70] and they were sent to extermination camps for mass slaughter (Documents 3868-PS[71] and 1472-PS).[72]

---

[69] Part III—page 473
[70] Part III—page 565
[71] Part III—page 569
[72] Part III—page 260

CHAPTER 3

WESTERN EUROPE UNDER THE NAZIS

BETWEEN September 1, 1939 and June 22, 1941, the German Armed Forces occupied substantially the entire European continent except for the U.S.S.R. Austria and Czechoslovakia had fallen before the war. Poland was occupied in about three weeks. On April 9, 1940 the invasion of Denmark and Norway began; on May 10 the German forces invaded the Netherlands, Belgium, Luxemburg and France; and on April 6, 1941 the German aggression against Yugoslavia and Greece commenced. All these military campaigns were rapidly concluded and the German occupying authorities settled down to impose Nazi ideology upon the conquered.

NURNBERG MOVES TO HOLLAND

The German occupying authorities, without loss of time or momentum, now undertook their relentless persecution of the Jews in their power. On October 22, 1940 a decree ordered registration of all Jewish enterprises in the occupied Dutch territories (Document 3333-PS).[73] The decree defined the term "Jew" and specified the degree of Jewish interest or participation to warrant registration. Registration was the first step toward confiscation.

A German report from the Hague describes the Aryanization of Dutch banks as of November 30, 1940 (Document EC-465):[74]

"The Jewish element is very little represented within the 25 leading banks. There are only a large number of Jews in brokerage and agent circles on the Amsterdam Bourse. For a long time already I have worked through open conversation with the participating banks so that the Jewish partners and employees are separated. Apart from the brokerage and agent firms mentioned above, the de-Jewing had been completely carried out as early as the end of the month of this report. Negotiations on taking over the firms Warburg & Co., Lippmann Rosenthal & Co. and Hugo Kaufmanns Bank have begun and are in part ready for conclusion."

---

[73] Part III—page 518
[74] Part III—page 23

I-17

Attacks on persons went side by side with attacks on property. Employment of German nationals of German or related blood was forbidden in Jewish households (Document 3334-PS).[75]

On January 10, 1941 persons entirely or partly of Jewish race who were living in occupied Holland were required to register (Document 3323-PS).[76] As in the case of property, registration of Jews was preliminary to the imposition of far more drastic measures. For example, on February 11, 1941 enrollment at Dutch universities and colleges of persons entirely or partly of Jewish blood was restricted (Document 3325-PS).[77]

Jewish-owned real estate had to be registered and the Netherlands Real Estate Administration was authorized on August 11, 1941 to take it over for administration (Document 2112-PS).[78] The exercise by Jews of professional, industrial or other pursuits aimed at profits was made subject to administrative license (Document 3328-PS).[79] On November 22, 1941, Jews in occupied Holland were banned from architecture, handicraft, music, literature, theatre, films and journalism (Document 3329-PS).[80] Finally, on May 21, 1942, all Jewish property claims in occupied Dutch territories had to be registered (Document 3336-PS).[81]

As their property was Aryanized, Holland's Jews were moved to the East. According to a report of the United Nations Information Organization, at the end of 1943, 120,000 Jews had been deported from Holland, tens of thousands being employed in labor camps of the East (Document L-26).[82]

Arthur Seyss-Inquart was Reich Commissioner for the occupied Netherlands from May 18, 1940 until the end of the war. In his book "Four Years in Holland, 1944" he presents the guiding concept of his administration (Document 3430-PS):[83]

"The Jews are the enemy of National Socialism and the national socialistic Reich. From the moment of their emancipation, their methods were directed to the annihilation of the common and moral worth of the German people and to replace national and responsible ideology with international Nihilism. The fatal meaning of Judaism became completely clear to the German people during the years of the World War. It was really they who stuck the knife in the back of the German army which broke the resistance of the Germans, and, in the year 1918, it was they who wanted to dissolve and decompose all national tradition and also moral and religious beliefs of the German people. The Jews for us are not Dutchmen. *They are those enemies, with whom we can neither come to an armistice nor to peace.* This applies here, if you wish, for the duration of the occupation. Do not expect an order from

---

[75] Part III—page 520
[76] Part III—page 511
[77] Part III—page 512
[78] Part III—page 334
[79] Part III—page 514
[80] Part III—page 516
[81] Part III—page 521
[82] Part III—page 39
[83] Part III—page 539

me which stipulates this, except regulations concerning police matters. *We will beat the Jews wherever we meet them* and those who join them must bear the consequences. *The Fuehrer declared that the Jews have played their final act in Europe,* and therefore they played their final act."

VICHY AND THE GESTAPO AGAINST FRENCH JEWRY

Hitler signed the Armistice with Petain in the railroad car at Compiegne on June 22, 1940. Freight cars were soon prepared to transport the Jews and Poles who had found refuge in France to concentration camps in the East.

By November, 6504 Jews from Baden and the Pfalz had been deported to unoccupied France and an additional 47,187 Jews were deported from Lorraine to Lyons (Document 2916-PS).[84]

Later Drancy, a suburb of Paris, became the main embarkation center for deportation of Jews in France to Auschwitz. French men and women risked their lives to save Jews but, despite resistance by the general population, the Vichy government and the Gestapo succeeded in deporting an estimated 120,000.

Economic measures against the Jews followed the predetermined pattern. On May 31, 1941, the Military Commander in Belgium and Northern France ordered Jews to shut down their businesses or sell their assets (Document 3611-PS):[85]

"The Military Commander can forbid the continuation of business to Jews and firms obligated to register. He can furthermore order Jews from firms obligated to register to shut down or sell their business as well as to sell shares or other assets. If these orders are not complied with within a period to be determined, the Military Commander can appoint a commissionary administrator for the execution of the decreed measures."

An example of the treatment of the Jews in the occupied West is contained in the teletype dated February 3, 1942 from Supreme Headquarters in Berlin to the Military Commander of France (Document 1012-PS).[86] That telegram dealt with a conference between Keitel and the Fuehrer on measures to be taken in cases of assault and acts of violence. The telegram stated:

". . . . . Sharp and deterring punishment must be instituted by shooting a large number of arrested Communists and/or Jews and persons who have previously committed assault and by arresting at least one thousand Communists, and/or Jews for shipment. Field Marshal Keitel awaits corresponding instructions for submission to the Fuehrer."

---

[84] Part III—page 437
[85] Part III—page 554
[86] Part III—page 165

CHAPTER 4

EINSATZSTAB ROSENBERG

EINSATZSTAB Rosenberg was Rosenberg's special staff for seizure of Jewish property, libraries, and art treasures throughout German occupied Europe. Its looting activities were so widespread, its plans so well worked out, its operations so efficient, and the scope and magnitude of its haul so large that the imagination is staggered. Almost immediately after the campaign in the West, Hitler ordered the Gestapo and the military commanders throughout occupied Holland, Belgium, Luxemburg, and France to cooperate with Rosenberg in confiscating documents "valuable for Germany" found in state libraries, archives, chanceries of the high church authorities and lodges whose political activities were directed against the Germans. Hitler's command was referred to in a secret order signed by Keitel on July 5, 1940 (Document 137-PS).[87] On September 17, 1940, the Fuehrer ordered Rosenberg to begin seizure of art possessions belonging to Jews who had fled the approach of the Wehrmacht (Document 015-PS).[88]

On the same day, Keitel notified the Chief of the High Command for the Military Administration in Occupied France that Rosenberg had been clearly authorized by the Fuehrer personally to search lodges, libraries, and archives in occupied territories of the West for material valuable to Germany and to transport these to Germany (Document 138-PS).[89] On October 10, 1940, Reinecke, the Chief of the General Department, Supreme Headquarters, Berlin, suggested that a similar order be addressed to the German military administration in Belgium to cooperate with the Einsatzstab Rosenberg (Document 139-PS).[90] On May 1, 1941, Goering directed all Party, State, and Wehrmacht services to support the Einsatzstab Rosenberg in its battle against Jews and Freemasons throughout all German occupied territories (Document 1117-PS),[91] and on August 20, 1941, Rosenberg, as Reichsminister for the Occupied Eastern Territories, notified his subordinates that an Einsatzstab was being set up in the East for the seizure of Jewish property, libraries, and art treasures (Document 145-PS).[92]

---

[87] Part III—page 121
[88] Part III—page 104
[89] Part III—page 122
[90] Part III—page 123
[91] Part III—page 237
[92] Part III—page 126

Hitler formalized Einsatzstab Rosenberg on March 1, 1942 by disseminating the following decree to all offices of the Armed Forces, the Nazi Party, and the German State (Document 149-PS):[93]

"Jews, freemasons, and the ideological enemies of National Socialism who are allied with them are the originators of the present war against the Reich. Spiritual struggle according to plan against these powers is a measure necessitated by war.

"I have therefore ordered Reichsleiter Alfred Rosenberg to accomplish this task in cooperation with the Chief of the High Command of the Armed Forces. To accomplish this task, his Einsatzstab for the occupied territories has the right to explore libraries, archives, lodges, and other ideological and cultural establishments of all kinds for suitable material and to confiscate such material for the ideological tasks of the NSDAP and for scientific research work by the university [Hohe Schule]. The same rule applies to cultural goods which are in the possession of or are the property of Jews, which are abandoned or whose origin cannot be clearly established. The regulations for the execution of this task with the cooperation will be issued by the Chief of the High Command of the Armed Forces in agreement with Reichsleiter Rosenberg.

"Necessary measures for the eastern territories under German administration will be taken by Reichsleiter Rosenberg in his capacity as Reich Minister for Occupied Eastern Territories.

(Signed) A. HITLER."

The entire machinery of the Wehrmacht, the Nazi Party, and the State participated in the work of Einsatzstab Rosenberg. On June 1, 1944, Utikal, Einsatzstab Chief of Staff, reported to Berlin that Einsatzstab had sent a special unit to Hungary and requested complete support from all offices of the State and Armed Forces (Document 158-PS).[94] Five days later, Utikal sent a similar message to Berlin concerning the dispatch of a special Einsatzstab unit to Denmark and Norway (Document 159-PS).[95]

The work of Einsatzstab Rosenberg fell into three principal categories: plunder of art treasures, M-Action (furniture action), and the Hohe Schule.

Plunder of Art Treasures

Seizure of Jewish art possessions in the occupied western territories was begun by Einsatzstab Rosenberg immediately after the Fuehrer's order of September 10, 1940 (Document 015-PS).[96] Jewish art collections left behind in Paris were seized first. Every city and village of occupied France was then combed for Jewish art collections. Einsatzstab Rosenberg worked in close collaboration with the Security Police and

---

[93] Part III—page 127
[94,95] Part III—page 135
[96] Part III—page 104

the squad for the protection of the foreign currency market, and succeeded in capturing the bulk of Jewish art collections in France and bringing it safely to Germany. The most important part of the loot consisted of seventy-nine collections of Jewish art connoisseurs in France, including those of the Rothschild family, which had been distributed in Paris, in Bordeaux, and in the Loire district. In addition all vacant Jewish apartments in France were searched for art objects which might have been left behind. Systematically, the art treasures were collected in central points in Paris, inventoried, photographed, and packed by the art specialists of Einsatzstab Rosenberg.

From September 17, 1940, to April 7, 1943, ten transports of ninety-two cars, or a total of 2,775 crates, including paintings, antique furniture, and objects of art, were sent to Germany (Document 015-PS).[97] Rosenberg kept the Fuehrer well advised of progress and on March 20, 1941, reported the inventory of objects of the highest artistic value then included more than 4,000 individual items (Document 014-PS).[98] After July 1944, Robert Scholz, Chief of Rosenberg's Special Staff for Pictorial Art, submitted a comprehensive report covering the work to July, 1944 (Document 1015B-PS).[99] The report described techniques of seizure and stated that 21,903 art objects of all types had been seized and inventoried. The inventory included the following categories:

"5,281 paintings, pastels, water-colors, drawings.
   684 miniatures, glass and enamel paintings, books and manuscripts.
   583 plastics, terra-cottas, medallions and plaques.
2,477 articles of furniture of value to art history.
   583 textiles (Gobelins, rugs, embroideries, Coptic materials).
5,825 hand-made art works (porcelains, bronzes, faiences, majolica, ceramics, jewelry, coins, art objects made with precious stones).
1,286 East Asiatic art works (bronzes, plastics, porcelains, paintings, folding screens, weapons).
   259 art works of antiquity (sculptures, bronzes, vases, jewelry, bowls, cut stones, terra-cottas).

"These figures will be increased, since seizures in the West are not yet completed, and it has not been possible to make a scientific inventory of part of the seized objects because of the lack of experts.

"The extraordinary artistic and material value of the seized art works cannot be expressed in figures. The paintings, period furniture of the 17th and 18th centuries, the Gobelins, the antiques and renaissance jewelry of the Rothschilds are objects of such a unique character that their evaluation is impossible, since no comparable values have so far appeared on the art market.

"A short report, moreover, can only hint at the artistic worth of the collection. Among the seized paintings, pastels and drawings there are several

---
[97] Part III—page 104
[98] Part III—page 102
[99] Part III—page 166

The Twenty-five Year Campaign

hundred works of the first quality, masterpieces of European art, which could take first place in any museum. Included therein are absolutely authenticated signed works of Rembrandt van Rijn, Rubens, Frans Hals, Vermeer van Delft, Velasquez, Murilio, Goya, Sebastiano del Piombo, Palma Vecchio, etc."

Scholz reported that from March, 1941 to July, 1944, the Special Staff for Pictorial Art brought twenty-nine large shipments, including 137 freight cars, with 4,174 cases of art works into Germany. He also stated that twenty-five portfolios of the most valuable art works seized in the West were presented to the Fuehrer on April 20, 1943, together with three large volumes of a provisional catalogue of the paintings, and an interim progress report. Additional portfolios of pictures were in preparation.

After the war in Germany ended, thirty-nine such portfolios were captured by American forces and presented in evidence before the International Military Tribunal at Nurnberg. These beautifully bound volumes containing hundreds of fine photographs of paintings, antique furniture, textiles, and hand-made works of art confiscated by Einsatzstab, give some indication of the vast scope of the looting.

M-Action (Furniture Action)

M-Action originated December 18, 1941, with a memorandum from Rosenberg to the Fuehrer (Document 001-PS).[100] Rosenberg reported that in carrying out Hitler's order for the seizure of Jewish cultural possessions in France, many of the home furnishings had disappeared from unguarded Jewish homes. He asked permission to seize the home furnishings of Jews living in all parts of the occupied West, to relieve the shortage of furnishings in the East. Hitler assented and the seizure was undertaken by Rosenberg on a vast scale. Rosenberg later reported that up to October 11, 1942 about 40,000 tons of household goods had been seized in France, Belgium, and the Netherlands, and transported to Germany and the East (Document 041-PS).[101] On August 8, 1944, Rosenberg's office reported that 69,619 Jewish homes had been confiscated in the West, yielding 69,512 sets of furnishings, and that 26,984 railroad cars, the equivalent of 674 trains, were required to transport those furnishings to Germany and the East (Document L-188).[102]

The Hohe Schule

The Hohe Schule was to be the Nazi ideological and research center under the direction of Rosenberg. On January 29, 1940, Hitler ordered Rosenberg to continue his preparations, already under way, toward setting up that institution, which was to be established after the

---
[100] Part III—page 98
[101] Part III—page 108
[102] Part III—page 75

I-23

war. All sections of the Party and State were to cooperate (Document 136-PS).[103] Einsatzstab units ransacked libraries, lodges, and cultural institutions of all kinds throughout occupied Europe to collect material for the Hohe Schule at Frankfurt-on-the-Main. A report from Paris disclosed the seizure in the West of the largest Jewish library in the world, consisting of 350,000 volumes, to be placed in the Hohe Schule (Document 090-PS).[104] An additional 200,000 volumes were to be added from Holland.

The names of valuable Jewish libraries in Amsterdam, confiscated to provide material for the Hohe Schule, were listed in an Einsatzstab report from the Netherlands (Document 176-PS).[105] A 1943 report revealed the gigantic looting of libraries. Names of Jewish libraries and book collections in Paris, Amsterdam, Riga, Minsk, Kiev, and other cities in the East were listed. It was even reported that books were taken from Jewish communities in Greece. Approximately 550,000 volumes had already been collected in Berlin, of which 220,000 volumes had been prepared for shipment to Frankfurt-on-the-Main, and an additional 300,000 volumes had already been received at the district office in Frankfurt-on-the-Main (Document 171-PS).[106] The last paragraph is particularly significant:

"Apart from the actual importance of the Jewish question, the library for the research of the Jewish question assumes a high position in the realm of German libraries with its present collection of about 550,000 volumes because this Frankfurt library could be brought to such a degree of completeness as regards the literature on the Jewish question as never before in Europe or elsewhere. In the New Order of Europe Organization *the* library for the Jewish question not only for Europe but for the world will arise in Frankfurt-on-the-Main."

---

[103] Part III—page 121
[104] Part III—page 117
[105] Part III—page 139
[106] Part III—page 136

CHAPTER 5

THE EAST — UP TO THE "FINAL SOLUTION"

EVEN before German troops occupied Bohemia and Moravia on March 15, 1939, the Nazis were planning eastward extension of their anti-Jewish program. In a conference with the Slovak Deputy Prime Minister Dr. Durkansky, on plans for the establishment of an "independent" Slovakia, Goering made the ominous prophecy that the Jewish problem in Slovakia would be solved as in Germany (Document 2801-PS).[107] That prophecy was fulfilled not only in Slovakia but in all the Eastern areas occupied by the Wehrmacht.

POLAND

The full impact of persecution fell upon the Jews of Poland twenty days after the Wehrmacht rolled across the Polish frontier. On September 21, 1939 Heydrich, Chief of the Security Police, sent a special delivery letter to all his subordinates on the Jewish problem in the occupied zone (Document 3363-PS).[108] He referred to a Berlin conference held on that day, and stated that the ultimate solution of the Jewish problem was to be kept strictly secret. The letter stated that the first prerequisite for the ultimate goal was the concentration of Jews in the ghettos in the larger cities, where Jews were to be confined. Heydrich referred specifically to the occupied area in the East, including Poland, and stated that the Aryanization of Jewish property and the emigration of the Jews should be planned immediately. He ordered his subordinates to report to him continuously on the census of Jews in their areas, the names of the cities designated for the ghettos, the time set for the concentration of Jews in the cities, and to survey all Jewish industries in the area to ascertain whether these could continue in operation after the Jews had been removed.

GHETTOS

The ghetto idea was carried out with German thoroughness. German authorities attempted to drive all the Jews of Warsaw into the ghetto a

---
[107] Part III—page 417
[108] Part III—page 532

I-25

few weeks after the occupation, but the Jews secured a temporary stay by paying a heavy fine. The Warsaw ghetto was established in October-November, 1940. Jews were forbidden to take anything with them except hand luggage. German police confiscated food carried into the ghetto by Poles and shot at sight anyone who tried to bring in food. Ghettos were also established in Lodz and Cracow. Food rations were extremely low, and the terribly over-crowded housing conditions and bad sanitary conditions in the ghettos resulted in a high death rate (Document 2613-PS).[109] The starving Jewish population had to purchase black market food which was smuggled over the ghetto walls at the risk of life (Document L-165).[110]

Hans Frank, Governor General of Poland, told his staff on December 16, 1941 (2233Q-PS):[111]

"Severe measures must and will be adopted against Jews leaving the ghettos. Death sentences pending against Jews for this reason must be executed as quickly as possible. This order according to which every Jew found outside the ghetto is to be executed, must be carried out without fail * * *."

DISCRIMINATORY DECREES

On October 26, 1939, the General Government of Poland prohibited Jewish ritual slaughter of animals (Document 2704-PS).[112] On the same day the Governor General decreed forced labor for all Jews and ordered that Jews be impressed into forced labor troops under the jurisdiction of the Senior SS and Police Leader (Document 3468-PS).[113] On November 23, all Jews residing in Poland were required to wear the Jewish star on their right sleeves, and simultaneously Jewish businesses were required to be marked with the Jewish star (Document 3468-PS).[114]

FORCED LABOR

Hans Frank, in his diary, stressed the importance of forced labor for the Jews (Document 2233G-PS):[115]

"* * * By spring 1,000,000 Poles and Jews from East and West Posen, Danzig, Poland and Upper Silesia must be received by the general government. The resettlement of the ethnic Germans and the taking on of Poles and Jews (10,000 daily) must be accomplished according to plan. Especially urgent is the institution of *forced labor for the Jews*. The Jewish population if possible must be extracted from the Jewish cities and be put to *work on roads*. The critical questions of housing and feeding are still to be cleared up * * *"

[109] Part III—page 392
[110] Part III—page 48
[111] Part III—page 352
[112] Part III—page 406
[113] [114] Part III—page 541
[115] Part III—page 351

Nazi Germany's War Against the Jews

The diary records that the question was discussed at a conference of department chiefs of the General Government in December (Document 2233A-PS):[116]

"The question of forced labor for the Jews could not be solved satisfactorily from one day to the other. Prerequisite for this would be the card indexing of the male Jews from 14 to 50 years of age. In this it had to be ascertained which trade the Jews had so far carried on, because just in those territories the Jews had had various skilled trades, and it would be a loss if this manpower would not be usefully exploited. To do this, sweeping planning is necessary. For the time being the Jews had to be gathered in columns and had to be employed wherever there was a pressing need. It is the task of the chief of the district to determine these needs."

Confiscation of Property

The German authorities did not lose time in confiscating Jewish property in Poland. On January 24, 1940 a decree detailed the manner in which abandoned property and Jewish credits were to be sequestered (Document 2540-PS).[117] A September 17 decree provided for the outright confiscation of Jewish property (Document 1665-PS).[118]

On March 4, 1941 German citizenship legislation was introduced into the Western Polish provinces annexed to the Reich (Document 2917-PS).[119] This statute incorporated the discriminatory features of the Nurnberg Laws.

The Wehrmacht in the Soviet Union

With the attack upon the Soviet Union, June 22, 1941, German aggression against the Jews everywhere reached its peak. A single document summarized the entire program within its four corners. It was the most comprehensive statement of German objectives. That document was a secret memorandum dated August 13, 1941, from the Reich Commissioner for the Ostland (the Baltic countries and White Russia) to Rosenberg, Reich Minister for Occupied Eastern Territories, on the subject of provisional directives on the treatment of Jews in the Ostland (Document 1138-PS).[120] The memorandum indicated that these directives were simply preliminary and the minimum measures to be taken where, and just so long as, further measures were not possible toward the final solution of the Jewish question. The term "Jew" was defined. Jews were ordered to register. They were to be marked with the Jewish star. They were prohibited from changing their residence, using sidewalks, public means of transportation, or any type of public facilities. They were denied the right to attend theaters, libraries, museums

---

[116] Part III—page 345
[117] Part III—page 373
[118] Part III—page 262
[119] Part III—page 438
[120] Part III—page 238

The Twenty-five Year Campaign

or schools. They were not allowed to own automobiles or radio sets. Kosher slaughtering was prohibited. Jewish doctors and dentists could treat only Jewish patients, and Jewish veterinarians were denied the right to practice their profession. They were forbidden to practice law, to act as notary public, legal adviser or agent, to operate banks or pawn shops and to trade in real estate or engage in migratory trade. All Jews were required to report all their property. All property of the Jewish population, except a bare minimum required for subsistence, was to be confiscated and secured. The directive further stated that Jews were to be cleaned out from the countryside, and removed from all commerce, particularly from the trade in agricultural products and foodstuffs. Jews were to be concentrated and confined in the ghettos. And finally, Jews capable of working were to be drafted for forced labor and were to be paid, not on the basis of work done, but just enough to remain alive.

CRIMINAL CODE FOR POLES AND JEWS

On December 4, 1941, a decree was adopted changing the criminal procedure against Poles and Jews in the Western Polish provinces annexed to Germany (Document 2746-PS).[121] The purpose was to impose heavier sentences upon Poles and Jews. The decree speeded procedure and provided for the immediate execution of sentences. It also deprived Poles and Jews of the right to prosecute cases in their own names, to join the public prosecutor in an action, or to appeal (Document R-96).[122] And on September 18, 1942, Himmler, the Reichsfuehrer SS and Chief of German Police, entered into an agreement with Thierack, the Minister of Justice, to the effect that after that date, Jews, Poles, Gypsies, Russians and Ukrainians in the East were no longer to be judged by the courts but were to be dealt with directly by the Reichsfuehrer SS (Document 654-PS).[123]

EVACUATION FROM GALICIA

The ruthlessness with which the deportations in Poland were carried out is eloquently revealed in the report of Katzmann, SS Gruppenfuehrer and Lieutenant General of the Police, entitled, "Solution of the Jewish Problem in the District of Galicia." This report, dated June 30, 1943, describes in great detail how 434,329 Jews were evacuated from Galicia. It lists Jewish property confiscated in the evacuation (Document L-18):[124]

"On the occasion of these actions, many more difficulties occurred owing to the fact that the Jews tried every means in order to dodge evacuation [Aus-

---

[121] Part III—page 412
[122] Part III—page 573
[123] Part III—page 162
[124] Part III—page 23

siedelung]. Not only did they try to flee, but they concealed themselves in every imaginable corner, in pipes, chimneys, even in sewers, etc. They built barricades in passages of catacombs, in cellars enlarged to dugouts, in underground holes, in cunningly contrived hiding-places in attics and sheds, within furniture, etc.

* * * * *

"Underground bunkers were found with entrances concealed in a masterly manner opening sometimes into flats, sometimes into the open. In most cases the entrances had only so much width that just one person could crawl through it. The access was concealed in such a manner that it could not be found by persons not acquainted with the locality. Here nothing succeeded but the assistance of some Jews to whom anything whatever was promised in exchange.

* * * * *

"Thirty-three Jewish bandits were shot. Some sawed-off carbines and quick-firing rifles and pistols of Russian make were confiscated. Polish game-keeper taking part in the combing-out action was shot dead by the bandits. During the arrests in Lwow, one SS-man was wounded by a shot in the left shank. The two German drivers were paid as recompense for their exemplary conduct 2,000 Zl. each.

* * * * *

"In the same way we succeeded on May 21, 1943, in destroying a Jewish gang who again were armed with 0.8 cal. pistols of Italian origin. (In the meantime all Italian soldiers left the district of Galicia.)

"Only some days later, the 31 May, we succeeded again, during a new comb-out, in destroying six dug-outs of major size containing 139 Jewish bandits.

"On June 2, 1943, again some Jews who attempted to escape to Hungary by means of a military car owned by the Hungarian Army, were arrested and, since they resisted, shot. Here again considerable valuables were confiscated. The Hungarian soldiers participating in the action were adequately rewarded.

"The evacuation having been completed, nevertheless, still minor actions are necessary in order to track Jews in hiding and concealment. This is proved by the fact that every day some persons are caught in possession of forged identity cards and passes. . .

"Since we received more and more alarming reports on the Jews becoming armed in an ever increasing manner, we started during the last fortnight in June 1943 an action throughout the whole district of Galicia with the intent to use strongest measures to destroy the Jewish gangsterdom. Special measures were found necessary during the action to dissolve the Ghetto in Lwow where the dug-outs mentioned above had been established. Here we had to act brutally from the beginning, in order to avoid losses on our side; we had to blow up or to burn down several houses. On this occasion the surprising fact arose that we were able to catch about 20,000 Jews instead of 12,000 Jews who had registered. We had to pull at least 3,000 Jewish corpses out of every kind of hiding places; they had committed suicide by taking poison.

"Only thanks to the sense of duty of every single leader and man have we succeeded to get rid of this PLAGUE in so short a time."

STARVATION

The sentence of death by starvation was imposed on 1,200,000 Polish Jews by Hans Frank at a cabinet meeting in Cracow, on August 24, 1942 (Document 2233E-PS):[125]

"The feeding of a Jewish population, estimated heretofore at 1.5 million, drops off to an estimated total of 300,000 Jews, who still work for German interests as craftsmen or otherwise. For these the Jewish rations, including certain special allotments which have proved necessary for the maintenance of working capacity, will be retained. The other Jews, a total of 1.2 million, will no longer be provided with foodstuffs."

BOHEMIA AND MORAVIA

Anti-Jewish persecution followed the German Panzer units as they sped through the Czech provinces. By decree, on September 1, 1941, Jews in Bohemia and Moravia were not allowed to travel without permission nor to appear in public without wearing a Jewish star (Document 2877-PS).[126] A special order issued by the Ministry of Agriculture of the Protectorate on December 2, 1942 sharply curtailed their rights to buy food, thus exposing the remnants of the Jewish community to death by starvation. Jews were permitted to shop for food only one hour a day after the Germans and Czechs had nearly exhausted the meager food stocks. Deportation of Jews from Bohemia and Moravia to Poland began on a large scale in June, 1942, and by the end of the year no Jewish life in Bohemia and Moravia was left. More than 72,000 out of the 90,000 Czech Jews had been deported (Document 1689-PS).[127]

---

[125] Part III—page 348
[126] Part III—page 429
[127] Part III—page 265

CHAPTER 6

GENESIS OF LAST STAGE: A "JUDENREIN" EUROPE

AS anti-Jewish persecution passed through the successive stages of legislative discrimination, economic pauperization, ghettoization and slavery in labor camps, it became apparent that the Nazis would be satisfied only with the biological extermination of all the Jews of Europe. While the Nazis threatened to destroy Jewry almost continuously from 1925, the actual decision to annihilate the Jews was made just prior to the campaign against the U.S.S.R. The development of Nazi thought and speech on this subject shows that the ultimate solution was the logical culmination of the entire Nazi anti-Jewish campaign and also shows that the ultimate decision was made at the highest level of the Nazi Party and State and implicated the entire nation.

In 1925 one of the battle cries of the Nazi Party had been "Juda Verrecke" [Death to Jews] (Document 1759-PS).[128] A 1933 article in the National Socialist Monthly edited by Hitler stated that the discriminatory laws against the Jews were mainly educational and gave direction to the final solution of the Jewish question (Document 2904-PS).[129] The article contained the following prophetic language: "Plans and programs must contain an aim pointing to the future and not merely consisting of the regulation of a momentarily uncomfortable situation." The same idea was expressed in "The Care for Race and Heredity in the Legislation of the Reich," published in Leipzig in 1943, just 10 years later, which declared that the aim of racial legislation might be regarded as already achieved and that many regulations would lose their practical importance as Germany approached achievement of the final goal in the Jewish problem (Document 2841-PS).[130]

The following prediction was made in "The Archive" in January 1935 (Document 3418-PS):[131]

---

[128] Part III—page 279
[129] Part III—page 434
[130] Part III—page 419
[131] Part III—page 536

"If international finance Jewry inside and outside Europe, should succeed in throwing the nations into another *World War* the result will not be the bolshevization of the earth and thus the victory of Jewry, but the *destruction of the Jewish race in Europe!*"

On January 15, 1939 Rosenberg asserted in an address at Detmold (Document 2843-PS):[132] "For Germany the Jewish problem is solved only when the last Jew has left Germany." And in a speech to the Reichstag on January 30, 1939, Hitler said (Document 2663-PS):[133]

"Once more I will assume the part of a prophet: If the international Jewish financiers within and without Europe succeed in plunging the nations once more into a world war, then the result will be not the bolshevization of the world and thereby the victory of Jewry—but the annihilation of the Jewish race in Europe."

Streicher repeated this theme on October 31, 1939 (Document 2583-PS):[134]

"This is our mission at home, to approach these future decisions without hesitation, to do our duty and to remain strong. We know the enemy, we have called him by name for the last 20 years: He is the World Jew. And we know, that the Jew must die."

In his testimony before the International Military Tribunal on November 30, 1945 (Pages 615-618 of Official Transcript) Lahousen described a conference he had attended with his chief, Admiral Canaris, on September 12, 1939 on the Fuehrer's train during the Polish campaign. At that conference General Keitel had said that the Fuehrer had decided upon the extermination through shooting of the Polish intelligentsia, nobility, clergy and, of course, the Jews.

On August 8, 1940 the SS periodical, "The Black Corps" carried the following statement on the Jewish question (Document 2668-PS):[135]

"Just as the Jewish question will be solved for Germany only when the last Jew has been deported, the rest of Europe should also realize that the German peace which awaits it must be a peace without Jews."

In late autumn of 1940 Hans Frank wrote in his diary (Document 2233C-PS):[136]

". . . . Well now, there are not so many lice and Jews any more, and conditions here in the Government General have changed and improved somewhat already. Of course, I could not eliminate all lice and Jews in only one year's time. But in the course of time, and above all, if you help me, this end will be attained."

Rosenberg, in a speech at Frankfurt-on-the-Main on March 28, 1941, said (Document 2889-PS):[137]

---

[132] Part III—page 420
[133] Part III—page 400
[134] Part III—page 376
[135] Part III—page 401
[136] Part III—page 346
[137] Part III—page 430

The Twenty-five Year Campaign

"Since Germany with its blood and its nationalism has now broken for always this Jewish dictatorship for all Europe, and has seen to it that Europe as a whole will become free from the Jewish parasitism once more, we may, I believe, also say for all Europeans: For Europe the Jewish question is only then solved when the last Jew has left the European continent."

As has been pointed out above, prior to the attack on the U.S.S.R. there had been many dire prophecies and veiled threats; but the actual decision to annihilate the Jews had not yet been reached. As a matter of fact, in a speech at Posen on October 4, 1943, Himmler complained that there had been too much talk and not enough action. He declared that all the Party members were saying, "The Jewish race is being exterminated, that is quite clear, it's in our program—elimination of the Jews, and we're doing it, exterminating them." But, he continued, talk was easy and no one had actually tackled the job of exterminating the Jews until the SS came along and took on the tough assignment of stacking corpse upon corpse in piles of 500 to 1000 (Document 1919-PS).[138]

The decision to annihilate the Jews was reached by Hitler in June of 1941. Otto Ohlendorf, an official of the Security Service, was designated by Himmler to lead a special task force (Einsatzgruppe D) which would accompany the Wehrmacht in the East to exterminate Jewish men, women, and children (Document 2620-PS).[139] Ohlendorf testified before the International Military Tribunal on January 3, 1946, that before the beginning of the campaign against the Soviet Union, Hitler had, in conversation with the High Command, announced his decision to annihilate the Jews and political commissars of the Red Army and had ordered the High Command to act accordingly. Ohlendorf also testified that, in the course of 1941, his unit had liquidated approximately 90,000 men, women, and children—most of them Jews (Pages 2007-2009 of Official Transcript; Document 2620-PS).[140]

Hoess, commandant of the Auschwitz extermination camp from May 1940 until December 1, 1943, testified before the International Military Tribunal on April 15, 1946 (Page 7787 of Official Transcript):

"In the summer of 1941, I had the order to see the Reichsfuehrer SS Himmler in Berlin personally. He told me in its approximate sense—I can't repeat it verbatim—'The Fuehrer has ordered the final solution of the Jewish question. We, the SS, must carry out that order. If, now, at this moment this is not being carried out, then the Jewish people will later on destroy the German people. Auschwitz,' he said, 'had been chosen because from the point of view of railway connections, it was most favorably situated and also because the extensive site was most suited for the purpose of guarding.'"

---
[138] Part III—page 324
[139] [140] Part III—page 397

Hoess then went on to testify that during the time he was in charge at Auschwitz two and a half million people were murdered there and an additional 500,000 died of disease and starvation (Page 7811 of Official Transcript; Document 3868-PS).[141]

There are official German documents supporting the testimony of Ohlendorf and Hoess that the decision to exterminate the Jews had actually been reached in June, 1941. Heydrich issued a series of directives to the Chiefs of Security Police and Secret Service teams assigned to prisoner-of-war camps, on June 28, 1941. He ordered them to screen out certain groups among the prisoners of war on the eastern front, including professional revolutionists, leading Communists, and all Jews and to execute them (Document 078-PS).[142] Another version of that directive was issued on July 17 (Document 502-PS).[143] A fortnight later Goering wrote to Heydrich, Chief of the Security Police and Security Service (Document 710-PS):[144]

"Complementing the task that was assigned to you on 24 January 1939, which dealt with the carrying out of emigration and evacuation, a solution of the Jewish problem, as advantageous as possible, I hereby charge you with making all necessary preparations in regard to organizational and financial matters for bringing about a complete solution of the Jewish question in the German sphere of influence in Europe."

It is apparent that Heydrich understood that his assignment was the total elimination of the Jews; for even a month earlier in commenting upon the proposed draft of the decree (Document 2746-PS)[145] of December 4, 1941, regarding criminal justice against Poles and Jews in annexed eastern territories, Heydrich had written (Document R-96):[146]

"Although it may safely be assumed that in the future there will be no more Jews in the annexed eastern territories, I am of the opinion that under present circumstances it is very urgent to provide martial law not only for Poles but for Jews as well."

In Cracow on December 16, Hans Frank said that the Jews must be done away with in one way or another and that the war would be only a partial success for Germany if Jewry survived it. He said that the Jews must be annihilated wherever they were found and wherever it was possible. He realized that the annihilation of over two and a half million people was a difficult assignment and he was aware that efficient measures would have to be devised to accomplish that goal. On this point, he said (Document 2233D-PS):[147]

"The Jews represent for us also extraordinarily malignant gluttons. We have now approximately 2,500,000 of them in the General Government,

---

[141] Part III—page 569
[142] Part III—page 113
[143] Part III—page 155
[144] Part III—page 165
[145] Part III—page 412
[146] Part III—page 573
[147] Part III—page 347

[Poland, excluding provinces then annexed to Germany] perhaps with the Jewish mixtures and everything that goes with it, 3,500,000 Jews. We cannot shoot or poison those 3,500,000 Jews, but we shall nevertheless be able to take measures, which will lead, somehow, to their annihilation, and this in connection with the gigantic measures to be determined in discussions from the Reich. The General Government must become free of Jews, the same as the Reich. Where and how this is to be achieved is a matter for the offices which we must appoint and create here. Their activities will be brought to your attention in due course."

Inter-office correspondence within Rosenberg's ministry proves conclusively that by December, 1941, the annihilation of the Jews in the East had become a matter of official state policy. On October 31, Dr. Liebbrandt, who was in charge of the Main Political Division of the Ministry for the Occupied Eastern Territories, wrote to Rosenberg's subordinate, the Reich Commissioner for the Ostland at Riga, demanding an explanation of his order forbidding the execution of Jews in Libau (Document 3663-PS).[148]

On November 15, the Reich Commissioner replied that he had forbidden the executions because of the manner in which they were carried out. He asked for instructions on the liquidation of Jews and whether the inquiry of October 31 was to be regarded as a directive to liquidate all Jews in the East and whether, in the course of this liquidation, any attention should be paid to age or sex of the Jews or the economic interests of the Wehrmacht. He also pointed out that he had been unable to find any directive to liquidate the Jews in any of the regulations or decrees which he thought might be applicable (Document 3663-PS).[149] The response, dated December 18, from the Ministry for the Occupied Eastern Territories, signed by Braeutigam, Liebbrandt's assistant, left no doubt that it was official policy to liquidate Jews in the East (Document 3666-PS):[150]

"Clarification of the Jewish question has most likely been achieved by now through verbal discussions. Economic considerations should fundamentally remain unconsidered in the settlement of the problem. Moreover, it is requested that questions arising be settled directly with the senior SS and Police leaders."

The following excerpt from Hans Frank's diary for August 24, 1942, furnishes proof that the identical policy in effect in the occupied territories of the U.S.S.R. was also applicable to the General Government of Poland (Document 2233E-PS):[151]

"Not unimportant manpower has been taken from us in the form of our old proven Jewish communities. It is clear that the working program is made

---

[148] [149] Part III—page 554
[150] Part III—page 556
[151] Part III—page 348

difficult when in the middle of this program, during the war, the order for complete annihilation of the Jews is given. The responsibility for this cannot be placed upon government of the General Government. The directive for the annihilation of the Jews comes from higher quarters."

The intentions of the Nazis were more clearly expressed with each passing day—at meetings of high officials, through the printed word, in the death camps themselves. On September 18, 1942, Thierack, Reich Minister of Justice, conferred with Himmler. Thierack's notes on that conference indicated that the following agreement had been reached (Document 654-PS):[152]

"The delivery of anti-social elements from the execution of their sentence to the Reich Fuehrer of SS to be worked to death. Persons under protective arrest, Jews, Gypsies, Russians and Ukrainians, Poles with more than 3-year sentences, Czechs and Germans with more than 8-year sentences, according to the decision of the Reich Minister for Justice. First of all the worst anti-social elements amongst those just mentioned are to be handed over. I shall inform the Fuehrer of this through Reichsleiter Bormann."

On October 9, an article in the official German Publication "Decrees, Regulations, Announcements" referred to preparatory measures for the solution of the Jewish problem in Europe and rumors of what was happening to Jews in the East (Document 3244-PS).[153] Official cognizance was here taken of the well-founded rumors and an attempt was made both to counteract and rationalize them:

"In the course of the work on the final solution of the Jewish problem discussions about 'very strict measures' against the Jews, especially in the Eastern territories, have lately been taking place within the population of the various areas of the Reich. Investigations showed that such discussions —mostly in a distorted and exaggerated form—were passed on by soldiers on leave from various units committed in the East, who had the opportunity to eye-witness these measures.

"It is conceivable that not all 'Blood Germans' are capable of demonstrating sufficient understanding for the necessity of such measures, especially not those parts of the population which do not have the opportunity of visualizing bolshevist atrocities on the basis of their own observations.

"In order to be able to counteract any formation of rumors in this connection, which frequently are of an intentional, prejudiced character, the following statements are issued for information about the present state of affairs:

"For about 2000 years, a so-far unsuccessful battle has been waged against Judaism. Only since 1933 have we started to find ways and means in order to enable a complete separation of Judaism from the German masses. . . .

"Since even our next generation will not be so close to this problem and will no longer see it clearly enough on the basis of past experiences and since

---
[152] Part III—page 162
[153] Part III—page 475

The Twenty-five Year Campaign

this matter which has now started rolling demands clearing up, the whole problem must still be solved by the present generation.

"A complete removal or withdrawal of the millions of Jews residing in the European economic space [Wirtschaftsraum] is therefore an urgent need in the fight for the security of existence of the German people. . . .

"It lies in the very nature of the matter that these problems which in part are very difficult, can be solved only with ruthless severity in the interest of the final security of our people."

That Jews were sent to Auschwitz for extermination was indicated in the official secret telegram dated December 16, 1942, sent by SS Gruppenfuehrer Mueller, head of the Gestapo (Document 1472-PS).[151] The telegram stated that physically handicapped and old Jews and children were included among 45,000 Jews to be transported and that when the Jews arrived at Auschwitz, the following month, at least 10,000 to 15,000 laborers would be available. The inference was clear that the remaining Jews, who were unfit for labor, were to be slaughtered in the gas chambers of Auschwitz.

---
[151] Part III—page 260

CHAPTER 7

THE FINAL "SOLUTION": GENOCIDE

ONCE they had decided to annihilate all the Jews of Europe, the Nazis, with Teutonic deliberateness and thoroughness, proceeded to carry out that policy as quickly and efficiently as possible. All sections and offices of the German State, the Nazi Party, and the German Armed Forces throughout the entire area under Nazi domination collaborated. A special office was set up within the Gestapo, Section IV B of the Reich Security Main Office, which worked exclusively on Jewish matters (Documents L-185[155] and L-219).[156] It was headed by Adolf Eichmann, who traveled all over occupied Europe rounding up Jews and transporting them to extermination camps where they were slaughtered by the hundreds of thousands.

The plan of operation was almost identical in all countries under the German yoke. Jews were first marked, then divested of all their property, and, finally, deported for extermination in the gas chambers of the large camps especially created for this purpose. One of Eichmann's assistants, Wisliczeny, testified before the International Military Tribunal on January 3, 1946, on his participation in the evacuation to Auschwitz for mass slaughter of 35,000 Jews from Slovakia in May, 1942, and 54,000 Jews from Greece in May, 1943 (Pages 2058-2069 of Official Transcript). Other officers of Section IV B covered specified areas of occupied Europe to direct the herding and deportation of Jews to the gas chambers (Document 2605-PS).[157]

Many methods were used to exterminate the Jews. They were transported in gas wagons, closed vans in which they were suffocated by carbon monoxide. Special teams of the Security Police (Einsatz Kommandos) were turned loose in the prisoner-of-war camps on the Eastern Front to screen the prisoners-of-war and execute political commissars of the Red Army, Jews, and other groups. Execution squads (Einsatzgruppen) of the Security Police roamed far and wide over the East

---
[155] Part III—page 74
[156] Part III—page 96
[157] Part III—page 378

The Twenty-five Year Campaign

slaughtering helpless men, women, and children by the hundreds of thousands. And finally, there were the mass extermination camps.

Murder Camps

To accomplish their end in the quickest possible way, the Nazis set up large extermination camps which were operated for murder on a mass basis. The most notorious and largest of these centers was at Auschwitz. Hoess, commandant of that camp from May 1, 1940, to December 1, 1943, testified at Nurnberg that he installed the extermination facilities there at the express order of Himmler, who had told him that Hitler had ordered the final solution of the Jewish question (Page 7787 of Official Transcript). Here is the description of the creation and operation of Auschwitz in his own affidavit (Document 3868-PS):[158]

"2. I have been constantly associated with the administration of concentration camps since 1934, serving at Dachau until 1938; then as Adjutant in Sachsenhausen from 1938 to May 1, 1940, when I was appointed Commandant of Auschwitz. I commanded Auschwitz until 1 December 1943, and estimate that at least 2,500,000 victims were executed and exterminated there by gassing and burning, and at least another half million succumbed to starvation and disease making a total dead of about 3,000,000. This figure represents about 70% or 80% of all persons sent to Auschwitz as prisoners, the remainder having been selected and used for slave labor in the concentration camp industries. Included among the executed and burnt were approximately 20,000 Russian prisoners of war (previously screened out of prisoner-of-war cages by the Gestapo) who were delivered at Auschwitz in Wehrmacht transports operated by regular Wehrmacht officers and men. The remainder of the total number of victims included about 100,000 German Jews, and great numbers of citizens, mostly Jewish from Holland, France, Belgium, Poland, Hungary, Czechoslovakia, Greece, or other countries. We executed about 400,000 Hungarian Jews alone at Auschwitz in the summer of 1944."

* * * * * *

"4. Mass executions by gassing commenced during the summer 1941 and continued until fall 1944. I personally supervised executions at Auschwitz until the first of December 1943 and know by reason of my continued duties in the Inspectorate of Concentration Camps WVHA (SS Main Economic and Administration Office) that these mass executions continued as stated above. All mass executions by gassing took place under the direct orders, supervision, and responsibility of RSHA (Reich Security Main Office). I received all orders for carrying out these mass executions directly from RSHA."

* * * * * *

---
[158] Part III—page 569

"6. The 'final solution' of the Jewish question meant the complete extermination of all Jews in Europe. I was ordered to establish extermination facilities at Auschwitz in June 1941. At that time, there were already in the general government three other extermination camps; Belzek, Treblinka, and Wolzek. These camps were under the Einsatz Kommando of the Security Police and SD. I visited Treblinka to find out how they carried out their extermination. The Camp Commandant at Treblinka told me that he had liquidated 80,000 in the course of one-half year. He was principally concerned with liquidating all the Jews from the Warsaw Ghetto. He used monoxide gas and I did not think that his methods were very efficient. So when I set up the extermination building at Auschwitz, I used Cyclon B, which was a crystallized prussic acid which we dropped into the death chamber from a small opening. It took from 3 to 15 minutes to kill the people in the death chamber depending upon climatic conditions. We knew when the people were dead because their screaming stopped. We usually waited about one-half hour before we opened the doors and removed the bodies. After the bodies were removed our special commandos took off the rings and extracted the gold from the teeth of the corpses.

"7. Another improvement we made over Treblinka was that we built our gas chambers to accommodate 2,000 people at one time, whereas at Treblinka their 10 gas chambers only accommodated 200 people each. The way we selected our victims was as follows: we had two SS doctors on duty at Auschwitz to examine the incoming transports of prisoners. The prisoners would be marched by one of the doctors who would make spot decisions as they passed. Those who were fit for work were sent into the camp. Others were sent immediately to the extermination plants. Children of tender years were invariably exterminated since by reason of their youth they were unable to work. Still another improvement we made over Treblinka was that at Treblinka the victims almost always knew that they were to be exterminated and at Auschwitz we endeavored to fool the victims into thinking that they were to go through a delousing process. Of course, frequently they realized our true intentions and we sometimes had riots and difficulties due to that fact. Very frequently women would hide their children under the clothes but of course when we found them we would send the children in to be exterminated. We were required to carry out these exterminations in secrecy but of course the foul and nauseating stench from the continuous burning of bodies permeated the entire area and all of the people living in the surrounding communities knew that exterminations were going on at Auschwitz."

Hoess' testimony is corroborated by the affidavit of Wilhelm Hoettl, a member of the Security Service, to the effect that Adolf Eichmann had told him that a total of six million Jews had been killed by the Germans, including four million in the mass extermination centers and two million in the East by the execution squads of the Security Service (Document 2738-PS).[159]

---

[159] Part III—page 410

GAS WAGONS

Another Nazi death weapon was the so-called gas wagon. This was a truck with a closed body in which the Jews were placed, ostensibly for transport. Actually they were transported and gassed at the same time. A report, dated May 16, 1942, signed by SS Untersturmfuehrer Becker, describes the operation of these gas vans in detail (Document 501-PS):[160]

"The overhauling of vans by groups D and C is finished. While the vans of the first series can also be put into action if the weather is not too bad, the vans of the second series *(Saurer) stop completely in rainy weather.* If it has rained for instance for only one half hour, the van cannot be used because it simply skids away. It can only be used in absolutely dry weather. It is only a question now whether the van can only be used standing at the place of execution. First the van has to be brought to that place, which is possible only in good weather. The place of execution is usually 10-15 km away from the highways and is difficult to access because of its location; in damp or wet weather it is not accessible at all. If the persons to be executed are driven or led to that place, then they realize immediately what is going on and get restless, which is to be avoided as far as possible. There is only one way left; to load them at the collecting point and to drive them to the spot.

"I ordered the vans of group D to be camouflaged as house-trailers by putting one set of window shutters on each side of the small van and two on each side of the larger vans, such as one often sees on farm-houses in the country. The vans became so well-known, that not only the authorities, but also the civilian population called the van 'death van,' as soon as one of these vehicles appeared. It is my opinion, the van cannot be kept secret for any length of time, not even camouflaged. . . .

"Because of the rough terrain and the indescribable road and highway conditions the caulkings and rivets loosen in the course of time. I was asked if in such cases the vans should be brought to Berlin for repair. Transportation to Berlin would be much too expensive and would demand too much fuel. In order to save those expenses I ordered them to have smaller leaks soldered and if that should no longer be possible, to notify Berlin immediately by radio, that Pol. Nr. . . . . is out of order. Besides that I ordered that during application of gas all the men were to be kept as far away from the vans as possible, so they should not suffer damage to their health by the gas which eventually would escape. I should like to take this opportunity to bring the following to your attention: several commands have had the unloading after the application of gas done by their own men. I brought to the attention of the commanders of those S.K. concerned the immense psychological injuries and damages to their health which that work can have for those men, even if not immediately, at least later on. The men complained to me about head-aches which appeared after each unloading. Nevertheless they don't want to change the orders, because they are afraid prisoners

---

[160] Part III—page 150

called for that work, could use an opportune moment to flee. To protect the men from these damages, I request orders be issued accordingly.

"The application of gas usually is not undertaken correctly. In order to come to an end as fast as possible, the driver presses the accelerator to the fullest extent. By doing that the persons to be executed suffer death from suffocation and not death by dozing off as was planned. My directions now have proved that by correct adjustment of the levers death comes faster and the prisoners fall asleep peacefully. Distorted faces and excretions, such as could be seen before, are no longer noticed.

"Today I shall continue my journey to group B, where I can be reached with further news."

Screening Teams

About a month before the attack against the Soviet Union, Heydrich, Head of the Security Police, and General Wagner, General Quartermaster of the Army, agreed on plans for the rear guard operations of the Einsatzkommandos of the SD on the Eastern Front. Schellenberg, an SS Brigade Fuehrer, testified at Nurnberg on January 4, 1946, on the Heydrich-Wagner conference (Pages 2080-2084 of Official Transcript).

Heydrich's "Directives for the Chiefs of Security Police and Secret Service Teams Assigned to PW Camps", dated June 28, 1941, referred to his agreement with the Supreme Command of the Army (Document 078-PS).[161] Heydrich instructed screening teams to seek out and execute the following categories in the prisoner-of-war camps.

"1. all outstanding functionaries of the State and of the Party, especially

"2. professional revolutionists.

"3. the functionaries of the Comintern,

"4. all leading Party functionaries of the Russian Secret Police [KPDSU] and their associated organizations in the Central, district, and county Committees,

"5. all the Peoples' Commissars and their Assistants,

"6. all the former Polit-Commissars in the Red Army,

"7. all leading personalities of the Central and Middle Offices among the State authorities,

"8. the leading economic personalities,

"9. the Soviet Russian Intelligence agents,

"10. all Jews,

"11. all persons who are established as being instigators or fanatical communists."

A later version of these directives issued on July 17, 1941 enumerated the same eleven categories. There was no doubt as to the fate of the prisoners selected (Document 502-PS):[162]

---
[161] Part III—page 113
[162] Part III—page 155

The Twenty-five Year Campaign

"Executions are not to be held in the camp or in the immediate vicinity of the camp. If the camps in the General-Government are in the immediate vicinity of the border, then the prisoners are to be taken for special treatment, if possible, into the former Soviet-Russian territory."

These screening teams operated throughout the entire Soviet campaign (Documents 2622-PS[163] and 2542-PS).[164]

Execution Squads

Four Einsatzgruppen were created within the Security Service on the eve of the Soviet campaign to accompany the German armies into the USSR. Their assignment was the extermination of Communist functionaries and Jewish men, women, and children. Einsatzgruppe A was directed by Stahlecker; Einsatzgruppe B was headed by Nebe; Rasche, and later Thomas, was in charge of Einsatzgruppe C; and Ohlendorf was in charge of Einsatzgruppe D (Document 2620-PS).[165] These execution squads followed the Wehrmacht and methodically carried out their brutal work of rounding up Jews and slaughtering them in their homes, on the streets, and in the public squares. They murdered two million helpless Jews. Numerous official German reports, written by the chiefs of the execution squads themselves, described their gruesome work proudly and in great detail.

Einsatzgruppe A in the Baltic States

SS Brigade Commander Stahlecker, who headed the Einsatzgruppe A, reported to Himmler on his group's activities from June 23, 1941, to October 15, in Latvia and Lithouania. He was a prolific writer (Document L-180):[166]

"Action-Group A, after preparing their vehicles for action proceeded to their area of concentration as ordered on 23 June 1941, the second day of the campaign in the East. Army Group North consisting of the 16th and 18th Armies and Panzer-Group 4 had left the day before. Our task was to hurriedly establish personal contact with the commanders of the Armies and with the commander of the army of the rear area. It must be stressed from the beginning that cooperation with the Armed Forces was generally good, in some cases, for instance with Panzer-Group 4 under Col. Gen. Hoeppner, it was very close, almost cordial. Misunderstandings which cropped up with some authorities in the first days, were cleared up mainly through personal discussions.

* * * * * *

"Similarly, native anti-Semitic forces were induced to start pogroms against Jews during the first hours after capture, though this inducement proved to be very difficult. Following out orders, the Security Police was determined

---
[163] Part III—page 399
[164] Part III—page 374
[165] Part III—page 397
[166] Part III—page 56

to solve the Jewish question with all possible means and most decisively. But it was desirable that the Security Police should not put in an immediate appearance, at least in the beginning, since the extraordinarily harsh measures were apt to stir even German circles. It had to be shown to the world that the native population itself took the first action by way of natural reaction against the suppression by Jews during several decades and against the terror exercised by the Communists during the preceding period. . . .

* * * * * *

"A. *The Baltic Area.* I. *Organization Measures.* 1. *Formation of auxiliary police and of police.* In view of the extension of the area of operations and the great number of duties which had to be performed by the Security Police, it was intended from the very beginning to obtain the cooperation of the reliable population for the fight against vermin—that is mainly the Jews and Communists. Beyond our directing of the first spontaneous actions of self-cleansing, which will be reported elsewhere, care had to be taken that reliable people should be put to the cleansing job and that they were appointed auxiliary members of the Security Police. The difference of the situation in each part of the area of operations also had to be taken into account. In Lithouania, activist and nationalist people formed themselves into so-called partisan-units at the beginning of the Eastern Campaign, in order to take active part in the fight against Bolshevism. According to their own report they suffered 4,000 casualties.

* * * * *

"II. *Cleansing and Securing the Area of Operations.* 1. *Instigation of self-cleansing actions.* Considering that the population of the Baltic countries had suffered very heavily under the government of Bolshevism and Jewry while they were incorporated in the U. S. S. R., it was to be expected that after the liberation from that foreign government, they (i. e., the population themselves) would render harmless most of the enemies left behind after the retreat of the Red Army. It was the duty of the Security Police to set in motion these self-cleansing movements and to direct them into the correct channels in order to accomplish the purpose of the cleansing operations as quickly as possible. It was no less important in view of the future to establish the unshakable and provable fact that the liberated population themselves took the most severe measures against the Bolshevist and Jewish enemy quite on their own, so that the direction by German authorities could not be found out.

"In Lithouania this was achieved for the first time by partisan activities in Kowno. To our surprise it was not easy at first to set in motion an extensive pogrom against Jews. Klimatis, the leader of the partisan unit, mentioned above, who was used for this purpose primarily, succeeded in starting a pogrom on the basis of advice given to him by a small advanced detachment acting in Kowno, and in such a way that no German order or German instigation was noticed from the outside. During the first pogrom in the night from 25. to 26.6 the Lithouanian partisans did away with more than 1,500 Jews, set fire to several synagogues or destroyed them by other means and burned down a Jewish dwelling district consisting of about 60 houses. During the following nights about 2,300 Jews were made harmless in a similar way.

The Twenty-five Year Campaign

In other parts of Lithouania similar actions followed the example of Kowno, though smaller and extending to the Communists who had been left behind.

"These self-cleansing actions went smoothly because the Army authorities who had been informed showed understanding for this procedure. From the beginning it was obvious that only the first days after the occupation would offer the opportunity for carrying out pogroms. After the disarmament of the partisans the self-cleansing actions ceased necessarily.

"It proved much more difficult to set in motion similar cleansing actions in *Latvia*. Essentially the reason was that the whole of the national stratum of leaders had been assassinated or destroyed by the Soviets, especially in Riga. It was possible though through similar influences on the Latvian auxiliary to set in motion a pogrom against Jews also in Riga. During this pogrom all synagogues were destroyed and about 400 Jews were killed. As the population of Riga quieted down quickly, further pogroms were not convenient.

"So far as possible, both in Kowno and in Riga evidence by film and photo was established that the first spontaneous executions of Jews and Communists were carried out by Lithouanians and Latvians.

"In *Esthonia* by reason of the relatively small number of Jews no opportunity presented itself to instigate pogroms. The Esthonian self-protection units made harmless only some individual Communists whom they hated especially, but generally they limited themselves to carrying out arrests.

"2. *Combating Communism*. Everywhere in the area of operation counter-actions against communism and Jewry took first place in the work of the Security Police.

* * * * * *

"3. *Action against Jewry*. From the beginning it was to be expected that the Jewish problem in the East could not be solved by pogroms alone. In accordance with the basic orders received, however, the cleansing activities of the Security Police had to aim at a complete annihilation of the Jews. Special detachments reinforced by selected units—in Lithouania partisan detachments, in Latvia units of the Latvian auxiliary police—therefore performed extensive executions both in the towns and in rural areas. The actions of the execution detachments were performed smoothly. When attaching Lithouanian and Latvian detachments to the execution squads, men were chosen whose relatives had been murdered or removed by the Russians.

"Especially severe and extensive measures became necessary in *Lithouania*. In some places—especially in Kowno—the Jews had armed themselves and participated actively in *franc tireur* war and committed arson. Besides these activities the Jews in Lithouania had collaborated most actively hand in glove with the Soviets.

"The sum total of the Jews liquidated in Lithouania amounts to 71,105.

"During the pogroms in Kowno 3,800 Jews were eliminated, in the smaller towns about 1,200 Jews.

"In *Latvia* as well the Jews participated in acts of sabotage and arson after the invasion of the German Armed Forces. In Duenaburg so many fires were lighted by the Jews that a large part of the town was lost. The electric power station burnt down to a mere shell. The streets which were mainly inhabited by Jews remained unscathed.

"In Latvia up to now 30,000 Jews were executed in all. Five hundred were made harmless by pogroms in Riga.

"Most of the 4,500 Jews living in Esthonia at the beginning of the Eastern Campaign fled with the retreating Red Army. About 200 stayed behind. In Reval alone there lived about 1,000 Jews.

"The arrest of all male Jews of over 16 years of age has been nearly finished. With the exception of the doctors and the Elders of the Jews who were appointed by the Special Commandos, they were executed by the Self-Protection Units under the control of the Special Detachment 1a. Jewesses in Pernau and Reval of the age groups from 16 to 60 who are fit for work were arrested and put to peat-cutting or other labor.

"At present a camp is being constructed in Harku, in which all Esthonian Jews are to be assembled, so that Esthonia will be free of Jews within a short while.

"After the carrying out of the first larger executions in Lithouania and Latvia it became soon apparent that an annihilation of the Jews without leaving any traces could not be carried out, at least not at the present moment. Since a large part of the trades in Lithouania and Latvia are in Jewish hands and others carried on nearly exclusively by Jews (especially those of glaziers, plumbers, stovebuilders, cobblers) many Jewish partisans are indispensable at present for repairing installations of vital importance for the reconstruction of towns destroyed and for work of military importance. Although the employers aim at replacing Jewish labor with Lithouanian or Latvian labor, it is not yet possible to displace all employed Jews especially not in the larger towns. In cooperation with the labor exchange offices, however, all Jews who are no longer fit for work are being arrested and shall be executed in small batches.

"In this connection it may be mentioned that some authorities of the Civil Administration offered resistance, at times even a strong one, against the carrying out of larger executions. This resistance was answered by calling attention to the fact that it was a matter of carrying out basic orders.

"Apart from organizing and carrying out measures of execution, the creation of ghettos was begun in the larger towns at once during the first days of operations. This was especially urgent in Kowno because there were 30,000 Jews in a total population of 152,400. Therefore, at the end of the first pogrom a Jewish Committee was summoned who were informed that the German authorities so far had not seen any reason to interfere in the quarrels between Lithouanians and Jews. The sole basis for creating a normal situation would be to construct a Jewish ghetto. Against remonstrations made by the Jewish Committee, it was declared that there was no other possibility to prevent further pogroms. On this the Jews at once declared themselves ready to do everything in their power to transfer their co-racials to the town district of Viriampol which was intended as a Jewish ghetto and with the greatest possible speed. This district lies in the triangle between the Memel river and a tributary; it is connected with Kowno by one bridge only and can, therefore, easily be locked off.

The Twenty-five Year Campaign

"In Riga the so-called 'Moskau suburb' was designated as a ghetto. This is the worst dwelling district in Riga, already now mostly inhabited by Jews. The transfer of the Jews into the ghetto-district proved rather difficult because the Latvians dwelling in that district had to be evacuated and residential space in Riga is very crowded. Twenty-four thousand of the 28,000 Jews living in Riga have been transferred into the ghetto so far. In creating the ghetto, the Security Police restricted themselves to mere policing duties, while the establishment and administration of the ghetto as well as the regulation of the food supply for the inmates of the ghetto were left to Civil Administration; the Labor Offices were left in charge of Jewish labor. . . .

"The number of Jews executed up to the present may be seen in the schedule on encl. 8."

* * * * * *

"Action-Group B liquidated so far 7,620 Jews in Borissow."

* * * * * *

"The active anti-Semitism which flared up quickly after the German occupation did not falter. Lithuanians are voluntarily and untiringly at our disposal for all measures against Jews, sometimes they even execute such measures on their own."

* * * * * *

Enclosure 8. Survey of the number of executed persons.

Area	Jews	Communists	Total
Lithouania			
Kowno town and surroundings (land)	31,914	80	31,994
Schaulen	41,382	763	42,145
Wilna	7,015	17	7,032
	80,311	860	81,171
Latvia			
Riga town and surroundings (land)			6,378
Mitau			3,576
Libau			11,860
Wolmar			209
Duenaburg	9,256	589	9,845
	30,025	1,843	31,868
Esthonia	474	684	1,158
White-Ruthenia	7,620		7,620
Total:			
Lithouania	80,311	860	81,171
Latvia	30,025	1,845	31,868
Esthonia	474	684	1,158
White-Ruthenia	7,620		7,620
	118,430	3,387	121,817

To be added to these figures:
In Lithouania and Latvia Jews annihilated by pogroms.................. 5,500
Jews, Communists and partisans executed in old-Russian area.............. 2,000
Lunatics executed 748

                                                                                                                                    122,455
Communists and Jews liquidated by State Pol. and Security
    Service Tilsit during search actions 5,502

                                                                                                                                    135,567

Map showing 'Number of persons liquidated in the Baltic countries as per 25.10.1941.'
The following figures have been entered into the map:
District of Libau in area of Courland 11,860
District of Mitau in area of Semgslen 3,576
District of Riga town in area of [sic] 6,378
District of Riga town in area of Livland 209
District of Fellin 1,158
District of Duenaberg in area of Lettgslen 9,845
in area of Schaulen 42,145
District of Kowno 31,994
in area of Wilna-land 7,032

Additionally pogrom [sic]
    in Lithouania and Latvia about 5,500
    border area Lithouania 5,502

Einsatzgruppe A later reported "the execution up to the present time of 229,052 Jews" in the Baltic provinces (Document 2273-PS):[107]

"The total number of Jews in Latvia amounted in June 1935 to 93,479 or 4.79% of the total population ...

"When the German troops marched in there were still 70,000 Jews in Latvia. The remainder had fled with the Bolsheviks. The Jews left behind were actively engaged in sabotage and setting fire to places. In Dueanaburg so many fires of this kind were started by the Jews that a large part of the town was destroyed.

"After the terror of the Jewish-Bolshevik rule—altogether 33,038 Letts were transported, imprisoned or murdered—an extensive pogrom carried out by the population might have been expected. In fact, however, only a few thousand Jews were eliminated by local forces on their own initiative. In Latvia it was necessary to carry out extensive mopping-up operations by means of Sonderkommandos with the help of forces picked from the Latvian Auxiliary Police (mostly relations of the Letts who had been carried off or murdered).

"Up to October 1941 approximately 30,000 Jews had been executed by these Sonderkommandos. The remaining Jews who were still indispensable from the economic point of view were collected in Ghettos, which were established in Riga, Duenaburg and Libau.

"As a result of punishments instituted for not wearing the Jewish star, black market, thieving, fraud, but also to prevent the danger of epidemics in

[107] Part III—page 355

the ghettos, further executions were subsequently carried out. In this way 11,034 Jews were executed in Duenaburg on 9.11.41, and, as a result of an action ordered and carried out by high authorities and police chiefs, 27,800 were executed in Riga at the beginning of December 1941, and, in the middle of December 1941, 2,350 were executed in Libau. At the moment there are in the ghettos (other than Jews from the Reich) Latvian Jews in

Riga approximately 2,500
Duenaburg approximately 950.
Libau approximately 300.

"These are indispensable at the moment as they are specialized workers necessary for maintaining the country's economy."

Einsatzgruppen in U.S.S.R.

Activity and Situation Report No. 6 of the Task Forces (Einsatzgruppen) of the Security Police and Security Service in the U.S.S.R. covering the month of October, 1941 precisely describes the methodical execution of Jews in the Ostland, White Ruthenia, and the Ukraine (Document R-102)[168]

[*White Ruthenia*]
"c) *Jews.*

"Now as ever it is to be noted that the population on their own part refrains from any action against Jews. It is true that the population reports collectively of the terror of the Jews to which they were exposed during the time of the Soviet regime, or they complain about new encroachments of the Jews, but nevertheless, they are not prepared to take part in any pogroms.

"All the more vigorous are the actions of the task forces of the Security Police and the SD against the Jews who make it necessary that steps be taken against them in different spheres.

"In Gorodnia 165 Jewish terrorists and in Tschenrigow 19 Jewish Communists were liquidated. 8 more Jewish communists were shot at Beresna.

"It was experienced repeatedly that the *Jewish women showed an especially obstinate behaviour.* For this reason 28 Jewesses had to be shot in Krugoje and 337 at Mogilew.

"In Borissow 321 Jewish saboteurs and 118 Jewish looters were executed.

"In Bobruisk 380 Jews were shot who had engaged to the last in *inciting and horror* propaganda (Hetz-und-Greuelpropaganda) against the German army of occupation.

"In Tatarsk the Jews had left the ghetto of their own accord and returned to their old home quarters, attempting to expel the Russians who had been quartered there in the meantime. All male Jews as well as 3 Jewesses were shot.

"In Sadrudubs the Jews *offered some resistance* against the establishment of a ghetto so that 272 Jews and Jewesses had to be shot. Among them was a political commissar.

"In Mogilew too, the Jews attempted to sabotage their removal to the ghetto. 113 Jews were liquidated.

---
[168] Part III—page 579

"Moreover four Jews were shot on account of *refusal to work* and 2 Jews were shot because they had ill-treated wounded German soldiers and because they did not wear the prescribed markings.

"In Talka 222 Jews were shot for anti-German propaganda and in Marina Gorka 996 Jews were shot because they had sabotaged orders issued by the German occupation authorities.

"At Schklow 627 more Jews were shot, because they had participated in acts of sabotage.

"*Witebsk*. On account of the extreme danger of an epidemic, a beginning was made to liquidate the Jews in the ghetto at Witebsk. This involved approximately 3000 Jews."

* * * * * *

[*Ukraine*]
"c) *Jews*.

"The embitterment of the Ukrainian population against the Jews is extremely great because they are thought responsible for the explosions in Kiev. They are also regarded as informers and agents of the NKVD, who started the terror against the Ukrainian people. As a measure of retaliation for the arson at Kiev, all Jews were arrested and altogether 33,771 Jews were executed on the 29th and the 30th September. Money, valuables and clothing were secured and put at the disposal of the National-Socialist League for Public Welfare (NSV) for the equipment of the National Germans (Volksdeutschen) and partly put at the disposal of the provisional city administration for distribution to the needy population.

"In Shitomir 3145 Jews had to be shot, because from experience they have to be regarded as bearers of Bolshevik propaganda and saboteurs.

"In Cherson 410 Jews were executed as a measure of retaliation for acts of sabotage. Especially in the area east of the Dnjepr the solution of the Jewish question has been taken up energetically by the task forces of the Security Police and the SD. The areas newly occupied by the Commandos were purged of Jews. In the course of this action 4891 Jews were liquidated. At other places the Jews were marked and registered. This rendered it possible to put at the disposal of the Wehrmacht for urgent labor, Jewish worker groups up to 1000 persons."

Execution of Ukrainian Jews

The execution of 150,000 to 200,000 Jews in the Ukraine was described on December 2, 1941, in a report to General Thomas, Chief of the Industrial Armament Department of the High Command. The author, one of Thomas' inspectors, was not in complete sympathy with the "horrible" action. It was one of the few documents in which a German official expressed doubts and reservations (Document 3257-PS):[109]

"Jewish problem.

"Regulation of the Jewish question in the Ukraine was a difficult problem because the Jews constituted a large part of the urban population. We therefore have to deal—just as in the General Government [GG.]—with a mass

---
[109] Part III—page 477

The Twenty-five Year Campaign

problem of policy concerning the population. Many cities had a percentage of Jews exceeding 50%. Only the rich Jews had fled from the German troops. The majority of Jews remained under German administration. The latter found the problem more complicated through the fact that *these Jews represented almost the entire trade* and even *a part of the manpower in small and medium industries* besides the business which had in part become superfluous, as a direct or indirect result of the war. *The elimination therefore necessarily had far reaching economic consequences and even direct consequences for the armament industry.*

"The attitude of the Jewish population was anxious—obliging from the beginning. They tried to avoid everything that might displease the German administration. That they hated the German administration and army inwardly goes without saying and cannot be surprising. However, there is no proof that Jewry as a whole or even to a greater part was implicated in acts of sabotage. Surely, there were some terrorists or saboteurs among them [who] just as much represented a danger to the German armed forces. The output produced by Jews who, of course, were prompted by nothing but the feeling of fear, was satisfactory to the troops and the German administration.

"The Jewish population remained temporarily unmolested shortly after the fighting. Only weeks, sometimes months later, specially detached formations of the police [Ordnungspolizei] executed a planned shooting of Jews. This action as a rule proceeded from east to west. It was done entirely in public with the use of the Ukrainian militia and unfortunately in many instances also with members of the armed forces taking part voluntarily. The way these actions which included men and old men, women and children of all ages were carried out was horrible. The great masses executed make this action more gigantic than any similar measure taken so far in the Soviet Union. So far about 150,000 to 200,000 Jews may have been executed in the part of the Ukraine belonging to the Reichskommissariat [RK]; no consideration was given to the interests of economy.

"Summarizing it can be said that the kind of solution of the Jewish problem applied in the Ukraine which obviously was based on the ideological theories as a matter of principle had the following results:

"a. Elimination of a part of partly superfluous eaters in the cities.

"b. Elimination of a part of the population which hated us undoubtedly.

"c. Elimination of badly needed tradesmen who were in many instances indispensable even in the interests of the armed forces.

"d. Consequences as to foreign policy—propaganda which are obvious.

"e. Bad effects on the troops which in any case get indirect contact with the executions.

"f. Brutalizing effect on the formations which carry out the executions—regular police—(Ordnungspolizei)."

Ohlendorf, head of Einsatzgruppe D, operating in the southern sector of the Soviet front, stated that in the course of 1941 his task force "liquidated approximately 90,000 men, women and children. The majority ... were Jews" (Document 2620-PS).[170]

---
[170] Part III—page 397

Executions in Borisow, White Ruthenia and Riga

The reports of executions of Jews continued with monotonous similarity up to October, 1944. An official report, dated October 24, 1941, received by the intelligence officer Lahousen, minutely detailed the slaughter of 6,500 Jews in Borisow (Document 3047-PS).[171] On July 31, 1942, Kube, Commissar General for White Ruthenia, reported to the Reich Commissar for the Ostland the liquidation of 55,000 Jews in White Ruthenia, as well as plans to execute 9,000 Jews in Baranowitschi the following month and to eliminate Jewry once and for all in White Ruthenia (Document 3428-PS).[172]

Like an accountant's inventory, a report from Riga, on November 6, 1942, listed the spoils. One truck, eighty peasant carts, forty-two bicycles, sixty-two horses, and five cows had been captured and 8,350 Jews had been executed (Document 1113-PS).[173]

Last Days of the Rowno and Dubno Ghettos

Most of the Nazi reports on executions were impersonal documents, coldly recording places, times, and statistical data. An eye-witness account of the murder of the Jews in the Rowno and Dubno ghettos in the Ukraine in 1942 is of a different character. Its author was a construction engineer who tried to save some of his Jewish workers. His story, conveying some of the horror of the events he witnessed, was one of the more effective statements used at Nurnberg (Document 2992-PS):[174]

"I, Hermann Friedrich Graebe, declare under oath:

"From September 1941 until January 1944 I was manager and engineer-in-charge of a branch office in Sdolbunow, Ukraine, of the Solingen building firm of Josef Jung. In this capacity it was my job to visit the building sites of the firm. Under contract to an Army Construction Office, the firm had orders to erect grain storage buildings on the former airport of Dubno, Ukraine.

"On 5 October 1942, when I visited the building office at Dubno, my foreman Hubert Moennikes of 21 Aussenmuehlenweg, Hamburg-Haarburg, told me that in the vicinity of the site, Jews from Dubno had been shot in three large pits, each about 30 meters long and 3 meters deep. About 1500 persons had been killed daily. All of the 500 Jews who had still been living in Dubno before the pogrom were to be liquidated. As the shootings had taken place in his presence he was still much upset.

"Thereupon I drove to the site, accompanied by Moennikes and saw near it great mounds of earth, about 30 meters long and 2 meters high. Several trucks stood in front of the mounds. Armed Ukrainian militia drove the people off the trucks under the supervision of an SS man. The militia men

---
[171] Part III—page 450
[172] Part III—page 537
[173] Part III—page 236
[174] Part III—page 442

I-52

acted as guards on the trucks and drove them to and from the pit. All these people had the regulation yellow patches on the front and back of their clothes, and thus could be recognized as Jews.

"Moennikes and I went directly to the pits. Nobody bothered us. Now I heard rifle shots in quick succession, from behind one of the earth mounds. The people who had got off the trucks—men, women, and children of all ages—had to undress upon the order of an SS man, who carried a riding or dog whip. They had to put down their clothes in fixed places, sorted according to shoes, top clothing and underclothing. I saw a heap of shoes of about 800 to 1000 pairs, great piles of under-linen and clothing. Without screaming or weeping these people undressed, stood around in family groups, kissed each other, said farewells and waited for a sign from another SS man, who stood near the pit, also with a whip in his hand.

"During the 15 minutes that I stood near the pit I heard no complaint or plea for mercy. I watched a family of about 8 persons, a man and woman, both about 50 with their children of about 1, 8 and 10, and two grown-up daughters of about 20 to 24. An old woman with snow-white hair was holding the one-year old child in her arms and singing to it, and tickling it. The child was cooing with delight. The couple were looking on with tears in their eyes. The father was holding the hand of a boy of about 10 years old and speaking to him softly; the boy was fighting his tears. The father pointed toward the sky, stroked his head, and seemed to explain something to him. At that moment the SS man at the pit shouted something to his comrade. The latter counted off about 20 persons and instructed them to go behind the earth mound. Among them was the family, which I have mentioned.

"I well remember a girl, slim and with black hair, who, as she passed close to me, pointed to herself and said, '23.' I walked around the mound, and found myself confronted by a tremendous grave. People were closely wedged together and lying on top of each other so that only their heads were visible. Nearly all had blood running over their shoulders from their heads. Some of the people shot were still moving. Some were lifting their arms and turning their heads to show that they were still alive. The pit was already 2/3 full. I estimated that it already contained about 1000 people.

"I looked for the man who did the shooting. He was an SS man, who sat at the edge of the narrow end of the pit, his feet dangling into the pit. He had a tommy gun on his knees and was smoking a cigarette. The people, completely naked, went down some steps which were cut in the clay wall of the pit and clambered over the heads of the people lying there, to the place to which the SS man directed them. They lay down in front of the dead or injured people; some caressed those who were still alive and spoke to them in a low voice. Then I heard a series of shots.

"I looked into the pit and saw that the bodies were twitching or the heads lying already motionless on top of the bodies that lay before them. Blood was running from their necks. I was surprised that I was not ordered away, but I saw that there were two or three postmen in uniform nearby. The next batch was approaching already. They went down into the pit, lined themselves up against the previous victims and were shot.

"When I walked back, round the mound I noticed another truckload of people which had just arrived. This time it included sick and infirm people. An old, very thin woman with terribly thin legs was undressed by others who were already naked, while two people held her up. The woman appeared to be paralyzed. The naked people carried the woman around the mound. I left with Moennikes and drove in my car back to Dubno.

"On the morning of the next day, when I again visited the site, I saw about 30 naked people lying near the pit—about 30 to 50 meters away from it. Some of them were still alive; they looked straight in front of them with a fixed stare and seemed to notice neither the chilliness of the morning nor the workers of my firm who stood around. A girl of about 20 spoke to me and asked me to give her clothes, and help her escape. At that moment we heard a fast car approach and I noticed that it was an SS detail. I moved away to my site. Ten minutes later we heard shots from the vicinity of the pit. The Jews still alive had been ordered to throw the corpses into the pit—then they had themselves to lie down in this to be shot in the neck.

* * * * *

"During the night of 13th July 1942 all inhabitants of the Rowno Ghetto, where there were still about 5000 Jews, were liquidated . . .

"I employed for the firm, in Rowno, in addition to Poles, Germans, and Ukrainians about 100 Jews from Sdolbunow, Ostrog, and Mysotch. The men were quartered in a building—5 Bahnhofstrasse, inside the ghetto, and the women in a house at the corner of Deutsche Strasse—98.

"On Saturday, 11 July 1942, my foreman, Fritz Einsporn, told me of a rumor that on Monday all Jews in Rowno were to be liquidated. Although the vast majority of the Jews employed by my firm in Rowno were not natives of this town, I still feared that they might be included in this pogrom which had been reported. I therefore ordered Einsporn at noon of the same day to march all the Jews employed by us—men as well as women—in the direction of Sdolbunow, about 12 km from Rowno. This was done.

"The Senior Jew [Judenrat] had learned of the departure of the Jewish workers of my firm. He went to see the Commanding Officer of the Rowno SIPO and SD, SS Major [SS Sturmbannfuehrer] Dr. Puetz, as early as the Saturday afternoon to find out whether the rumor of a forthcoming Jewish pogrom—which had gained further credence by reason of the departure of Jews of my firm—was true. Dr. Puetz dismissed the rumor as a clumsy lie, and for the rest had the Polish personnel of my firm in Rowno arrested. Einsporn avoided arrest by escaping from Sdolbunow. When I learned of this incident I gave orders that all Jews who had left Rowno were to report back to work in Rowno on Monday, 13 July 1942. On Monday morning I myself went to see the Commanding Officer, Dr. Puetz, in order to learn, for one thing, the truth about the rumored Jewish pogrom and secondly to obtain information on the arrest of the Polish office personnel. SS Major Puetz stated to me that no pogrom whatever was planned. Moreover such a pogrom would be stupid because the firms and the Reichsbahn would lose valuable workers.

"An hour later I received a summons to appear before the Area Commissioner of Rowno. His deputy, Stableiter and Cadet Officer [Ordensjunker] Beck, subjected me to the same questioning as I had undergone at the SD.

My explanation that I had sent the Jews home for urgent delousing appeared plausible to him. He then told me—making me promise to keep it a secret—that a pogrom would in fact take place on the evening of Monday, 13 July 1942. After lengthy negotiation I managed to persuade him to give me permission to take my Jewish workers to Sdolbunow—but only after the pogrom had been carried out. During the night it would be up to me to protect the house in the ghetto against the entry of Ukrainian militia and SS. As confirmation of the discussion he gave me a document, which stated that the Jewish employees of Messrs. Jung were not affected by the pogrom.

"On the evening of this day I drove to Rowno and posted myself with Fritz Einsporn in front of the house in the Bahnhofstrasse in which the Jewish workers of my firm slept. Shortly after 22:00 the ghetto was encircled by a large SS detachment and about three times as many members of the Ukrainian militia. Then the electric arclights which had been erected in and around the ghetto were switched on. SS and militia squads of 4 to 6 men entered or at least tried to enter the houses. Where the doors and windows were closed and the inhabitant did not open at the knocking, the SS men and militia broke the windows, forced the doors with beams and crowbars and entered the houses. The people living there were driven on to the street just as they were, regardless of whether they were dressed or in bed. Since the Jews in most cases refused to leave their houses and resisted, the SS and militia applied force.

"They finally succeeded, with strokes of the whip, kicks and blows with rifle butts in clearing the houses. The people were driven out of their houses in such haste that small children in bed had been left behind in several instances. In the street women cried out for their children and children for their parents. That did not prevent the SS from driving the people along the road, at running pace, and hitting them, until they reached a waiting freight train. Car after car was filled, and the screaming of women and children, and the cracking of whips and rifle shots resounded unceasingly.

"Since several families or groups had barricaded themselves in especially strong buildings, and the doors could not be forced with crowbars or beams, these houses were now blown open with hand grenades. Since the ghetto was near the railroad tracks in Rowno, the younger people tried to get across the tracks and over a small river to get away from the ghetto area. As this stretch of country was beyond the range of the electric lights, it was illuminated by signal rockets.

"All through the night these beaten, hounded and wounded people moved along the lighted streets. Women carried their dead children in their arms, children pulled and dragged their dead parents by their arms and legs down the road toward the train. Again and again the cries, 'Open the door!' 'Open the door!' echoed through the ghetto.

"About 6 o'clock in the morning I went away for a moment, leaving behind Einsporn and several other German workers who had returned in the meantime. I thought the greatest danger was past and that I could risk it. Shortly after I left, Ukrainian militia men forced their way into 5 Bahnhofstrasse and brought 7 Jews out and took them to a collecting point inside the ghetto. On my return I was able to prevent further Jews from being taken out. I went to the collecting point to save these 7 men.

"I saw dozens of corpses of all ages and both sexes in the streets I had to walk along. The doors of the houses stood open, windows were smashed. Pieces of clothing, shoes, stockings, jackets, caps, hats, coats, etc., were lying in the street. At the corner of a house lay a baby, less than a year old with his skull crushed. Blood and brains were spattered over the house wall and covered the area immediately around the child. The child was dressed only in a little shirt.

"The commander, SS Major Puetz, was walking up and down a row of about 80-100 male Jews who were crouching on the ground. He had a heavy dog whip in his hand. I walked up to him, showed him the written permit of Stabsleiter Beck and demanded the seven men whom I recognized among those who were crouching on the ground. Dr. Puetz was very furious about Beck's concession and nothing could persuade him to release the seven men. He made a motion with his hand encircling the square and said that anyone who was once here would not get away. Although he was very angry with Beck, he ordered me to take the people from 5 Bahnhofstrasse out of Rowno by 8 o'clock at the latest.

"When I left Dr. Puetz, I noticed a Ukrainian farm cart, with two horses. Dead people with stiff limbs were lying on the cart. Legs and arms projected over the side boards. The cart was making for the freight train. I took the remaining 74 Jews who had been locked in the house to Sdolbunow.

"Several days after the 13th of July 1942 the Area Commissioner of Sdolbunow, Georg Marschall, called a meeting of all firm managers, railroad superintendents, and leaders of the Organization Todt and informed them that the firms, etc., should prepare themselves for the 'resettlement' of the Jews which was to take place almost immediately. He referred to the pogrom in Rowno where all the Jews had been liquidated, i.e. had been shot near Kostolpol."

AKTION AT SLUZK

Numerous official German reports authenticate the foregoing eyewitness account. And occasionally, the brutality of Himmler's agents proved too much for German commissioners in the occupied territory who were moved, in isolated instances, to protest. The following excerpt from a report to the commissioner general at Minsk, dated October 30, 1941, on the Aktion against the Jews of Sluzk, was penned by the commissioner of that territory (Document 1104-PS):[175]

"For the rest, as regards the execution of the action, I must point out to my deepest regret that the latter bordered already on sadism. The town itself offered a picture of horror during the action. With indescribable brutality on the part of both the German police officers and particularly the Lithuanian partisans, the Jewish people, but also among them White Ruthenians, were taken out of their dwellings and herded together.

---
[175] Part III—page 229

The Twenty-five Year Campaign

"Everywhere in the town shots were to be heard and in different streets the corpses of shot Jews accumulated. The White Ruthenians were in greatest distress to free themselves from the encirclement. Regardless of the fact that the Jewish people, among whom were also tradesmen, were mistreated in a terribly barbarous way in the face of the White Ruthenian people, the White Ruthenians themselves were also worked over with rubber clubs and rifle butts. There was no question of an action against the Jews any more. It rather looked like a revolution.

"I myself with all my officials have been in it without interruption all day long in order to save what could yet be saved. In several instances I literally had to expel with drawn pistol the German police officials as well as the Lithouanian partisans from the shops. My own police was employed for the same mission but had often to leave the streets on account of the wild shooting in order to avoid being shot themselves.

"The whole picture was generally more than ghastly. In the afternoon a great number of abandoned Panje carriages with horses were standing in the streets so that I had to instruct the municipal administration to take care of the vehicles immediately. Afterwards it was ascertained that they were Jewish vehicles ordered by the armed forces to move ammunition. The drivers had simply been taken off the carriages and led away, and nobody had worried in the least about the vehicles.

"I was not present at the shooting before the town. Therefore I cannot make a statement on its brutality. But it should suffice, if I point out that persons shot have worked themselves out of their graves some time after they had been covered.

"Regarding the economic damage I want to state that the tannery has been affected worst of all. Twenty-six experts worked there. Of them, fifteen of the best specialists alone have been shot. Four more jumped from the truck during the transport and escaped, while seven others were not apprehended after they fled. The plant barely continues to operate today. Five wheelwrights worked in the wheelwright shop. Four of them have been shot and the shop has to keep going now with one wheelwright. Additional tradesmen such as carpenters, blacksmiths, etc., are still missing.

"Up till now it was impossible for me to obtain an exact survey. I have mentioned already in the beginning, that the families of tradesmen should be spared too. But now it seems that almost in all families some persons are missing. Reports come in from all over, making it clear that in one family the tradesman himself, in another family the wife and in the next one again the children are missing. In that way, almost all families have been broken up. It seems to be very doubtful whether under these circumstances the remaining tradesmen will show any interest in their work and produce accordingly, particularly as even today they are running around with bloody and bruised faces due to the brutality.

"The White Ruthenian people who had full confidence in us, are dumbfounded. Though they are intimidated and don't dare to utter their free opinion, one has already heard that they take the viewpoint that this day does not add to the glory of Germany and that it will not be forgotten. I am of the opinion that much has been destroyed through this action which we have achieved during the last months and that it will take a long time until we shall regain the confidence of the population which we have lost."

In transmitting this report to the Reich Commissioner for the Ostland, Kube, the Commissioner General for White Ruthenia made even more violent protest (Document 1104-PS):[176]

"I am submitting this report in duplicate so that one copy may be forwarded to the Reich Minister [Rosenberg]. Peace and order cannot be maintained in White Ruthenia with methods of that sort. To bury seriously wounded people alive who worked their way out of their graves again, is such a base and filthy act that this incident as such should be reported to the Fuehrer and Reich Marshal. The civil administration of White Ruthenia makes very strenuous efforts to win the population over to Germany in accordance with the instructions of the Fuehrer. These efforts cannot be brought in harmony with the methods described herein."

The protest reached Rosenberg, he admitted under cross-examination at Nurnberg. But the policies remained unchanged.

"THE WARSAW GHETTO IS NO MORE"

In April and May of 1943, the Warsaw Ghetto was destroyed and all of its Jews were murdered there or sent to Treblinka for extermination (Documents 1061-PS,[177] 3868-PS,[178] 3841-PS,[179] and 3840-PS).[180] The gutting of the Ghetto began as a move to evacuate the Jews to Treblinka, but the Jews resisted and there ensued a military action of extraordinary brutality. The report entitled "The Warsaw Ghetto is no more," written by Stroop, SS and Police Fuehrer in the Warsaw District, who was later captured, describes the action completely and gives a day-to-day meticulous account. It was a finely-bound, leather-covered volume, typed on heavy white paper with beautifully deckled edges, and contained a number of photographs. The report was signed by Stroop in a bold hand and bespoke his pride in the achievement (Document 1061-PS).[177]

"The creation of special areas to be inhabited by Jews, and the restriction of the Jews with regard to residence and trading is nothing new in the history of the East. Such measures were first taken far back in the Middle Ages; they could be observed as recently as during the last few centuries. These restrictions were imposed with the intention of protecting the Aryan population against the Jews.

"Identical considerations led us as early as February, 1940 to conceive the project of creating a Jewish residential district in Warsaw. The initial intention was to establish as the Ghetto that part of the City of Warsaw which has the Vistula as its Eastern frontier. The particular situation pre-

---

[176] Part III—page 229
[177] Part III—page 173
[178] Part III—page 569
[179] Part III—page 568
[180] Part III—page 567

The Twenty-five Year Campaign

vailing in Warsaw seemed at first to frustrate this plan. It was moreover opposed by several authorities particularly by the City Administration. They pointed in particular that disturbances in industry and trade would ensue if a Ghetto were founded in Warsaw, and that it would be impossible to provide the Jews with food if they were assembled in a closed area.

* * * * * *

"The necessity of erecting a Ghetto in the City of Warsaw as well became more and more urgent in the summer of 1940, since more and more troops were being assembled in the district of Warsaw after termination of the French campaign. At that time the Department for Hygiene urged the speedy erection of a Ghetto in the interest of preserving the health of the German Forces and of the native population as well. * * * In October 1940, the Governor ordered the Commissioner of the District, President for the City of Warsaw, to complete the resettlement necessary for establishing the Ghetto within the City of Warsaw by 15 November 1940.

"The Ghetto thus established in Warsaw was inhabited by about 400,000 Jews. It contained 27,000 apartments with an average of 2½ rooms each. It was separated from the rest of the city by partition and other walls and by walling-up of thoroughfares, windows, doors, open spaces, etc.

"It was administered by the Jewish Board of Elders, who received their instructions from the Commissioner for the Ghetto, who was immediately subordinated to the Governor. The Jews were granted self-administration in which the German supervising authorities intervened only where German interests were touched. In order to enable the Jewish Board of Elders to execute its orders, a Jewish Police force was set up, identified by special armbands and a special beret and armed with rubber truncheons. This Jewish Police force was charged with maintaining order and security within the Ghetto and was subordinated to the German and Polish Police.

"It soon became clear, however, that not all dangers had been removed by this confining the Jews to one place. Security considerations required removing the Jews from the city of Warsaw altogether. The first large resettlement action took place in the period from 22 July to 3 October 1942. In this action 310,322 Jews were removed. In January 1943 a second resettlement action was carried out by which altogether 6,500 Jews were affected.

"When the Reichsfuehrer SS visited Warsaw in January 1943 he ordered the SS and Police Leader for the District of Warsaw to *transfer to Lublin the armament factories and other enterprises of military importance which were installed within the Ghetto including their personnel and machines.* The execution of this transfer order proved to be very difficult, since the managers as well as the Jews resisted in every possible way. The SS and Police Leader thereupon decided to enforce the transfer of the enterprises in a large-scale action which he intended to carry out in three days. The necessary preparations had been taken by my predecessor, who also had given the order to start the large-scale action. I myself arrived in Warsaw on 17 April 1943 and took over the command of the action on 19 April 1943, 0800 hours, the action itself having started the same day at 0600 hours.

"Before the large-scale action began, the limits of the former Ghetto had been blocked by an external barricade in order to prevent the Jews from breaking out. This barricade was maintained from the start to the end of the action and was especially reinforced at night.

"When we invaded the Ghetto for the first time, the Jews and the Polish bandits succeeded in repelling the participating units, including tanks and armored cars, by a well-prepared concentration of fire. When I ordered a second attack, about 0800 hours, I distributed the units, separated from each other by indicated lines, and charged them with combing out the whole of the Ghetto, each unit for a certain part. Although firing commenced again, we now succeeded in combing out the blocks according to plan. The enemy was forced to retire from the roofs and elevated bases to the basements, dug-outs, and sewers. In order to prevent their escaping into the sewers, the sewerage system was dammed up below the Ghetto and filled with water, but the Jews frustrated this plan to a great extent by blowing up the turning off valves. Late the first day we encountered rather heavy resistance, but it was quickly broken by a special raiding party. In the course of further operations we succeeded in expelling the Jews from their prepared resistance bases, sniper holes, and the like, and in occupying during the 20 and 21 April the greater part of the so-called remainder of the Ghetto to such a degree that the resistance continued within these blocks could no longer be called considerable.

* * * * *

"When only a few days had passed, it became apparent that the Jews no longer had any intention to resettle voluntarily, but were determined to resist evacuation with all their force and by using all the weapons at their disposal. So-called battle groups had been formed, led by Polish-Bolshevists; they were armed and paid any price asked for available arms.

* * * * *

"The resistance put up by the Jews and bandits could be broken only by relentlessly using all our force and energy by day and night. *On 23 April 1943 the Reichsfuehrer SS issued through the higher SS and Police Fuehrer East at Cracow his order to complete the combing out of the Warsaw Ghetto with the greatest severity and relentless tenacity.* I therefore decided to destroy the entire Jewish residential area by setting every block on fire, including the blocks of residential buildings near the armament works. One concern after the other was systematically evacuated and subsequently destroyed by fire. The Jews then emerged from their hiding places and dug-outs in almost every case. Not infrequently, the Jews stayed in the burning buildings until, because of the heat and the fear of being burned alive they preferred to jump down from the upper stories after having thrown mattresses and other upholstered articles into the street from the burning buildings. With their bones broken, they still tried to crawl across the street into blocks of buildings which had not yet been set on fire or were only partly in flames. Often Jews changed their hiding places during the night, by moving into the ruins of burnt-out buildings, taking refuge there until they were found by our patrols.

"Their stay in the sewers also ceased to be pleasant after the first week. Frequently from the street, we could hear loud voices coming through the sewer shafts. Then the men of the Waffen SS, the Police or the Wehrmacht Engineers courageously climbed down the shafts to bring out the Jews and not infrequently they then stumbled over Jews already dead, or were shot at. It was always necessary to use smoke candles to drive out the Jews. Thus one day we opened 183 sewer entrance holes and at a fixed time lowered smoke candles into them, with the result that the bandits fled from what they believed to be gas to the center of the former Ghetto, where they could then be pulled out of the sewer holes there. A great number of Jews, who could not be counted, were exterminated by blowing up sewers and dug-outs.

* * * * * *

"Only through the continuous and untiring work of all involved did we succeed in catching a total of 56,065 Jews whose extermination can be proved. To this should be added the number of Jews who lost their lives in explosions or fires but whose numbers could not be ascertained.

* * * * * *

"The large-scale action was terminated on 16 May 1943 with the blowing up of the Warsaw synagogue at 2015 hours.

"Now, there are no more factories in the former Ghetto. All the goods, raw materials, and machines there have been moved and stored somewhere else. All buildings etc., have been destroyed. The only exception is the so-called Dzielna Prison of the Security Police, which was exempted from destruction.

* * * * * *

"Of the total of 56,065 Jews caught, about 7,000 were exterminated within the former Ghetto in the course of the large-scale action, and 6,929 by transporting them to T.II, which means 14,000 Jews were exterminated altogether. Beyond the number of 56,065 Jews an estimated number of 5,000 to 6,000 were killed by explosions or in fires."

Stroop dispatched daily teletype messages to Krueger, the higher SS Reich Police Fuehrer East at Cracow, recording the progress of the Ghetto operation. Some excerpts:

[April 22, 1943.]

"Our setting the block on fire achieved the result in the course of the night that those Jews whom we had not been able to find despite all our search operations left their hideouts under the roofs, in the cellars, and elsewhere, and appeared at the outside of the buildings, trying to escape the flames. Masses of them—entire families—were already aflame and jumped from the windows or endeavored to let themselves down by means of sheets tied together or the like. Steps had been taken so that these Jews as well as the remaining ones were liquidated at once. During the whole night there were shots from buildings which were supposed to be evacuated. We had no losses in our cordoning forces. 5,300 Jews were caught for the evacuation and removed."

* * * * * *

"Progress of the Ghetto Operation on 22 April 1943 up to 1200 hrs.

"One raiding party was dispatched to invade once more the block of buildings which for the greater part had burned out or was still aflame, in order to catch those Jews who were still inside. When shooting again started from one block against the men of the Waffen SS, this block also was set on fire, with the result that a considerable number of bandits were scared from their hide-outs and shot while trying to escape. Apart from those, we caught about 180 Jews in the yards of the buildings. The main body of our units continued the cleansing action from the line where we terminated this action yesterday. This operation is still in progress. As on the preceding days local resistance was broken and the dug-outs we discovered were blown up. Unfortunately there is no way of preventing part of the Jews and bandits from taking refuge in the sewers below the Ghetto, where we can hardly catch them since they have stopped the flooding. The city administration is not in a position to frustrate this nuisance. Neither did the use of smoke candles or the introduction of creosote into the water have the desired result. Cooperation with the Wehrmacht splendid."

* * * * *

[April 24, 1943.]
"* * * At 1815 hours a search party entered the premises, the building having been cordoned off, and found that a great number of Jews were within the building. Since some of these Jews resisted, I ordered the building to be set on fire. Not until all the buildings along the street and the back premises on either side were well aflame did the Jews, some of them on fire, emerge from these blocks, some of them endeavored to save their life by jumping into the street from windows and balconies, after having thrown down beds, blankets, and the like. Over and over again we observed that Jews and bandits, despite the danger of being burned alive, preferred to return into the flames rather than risk being caught by us. Over and over again the Jews kept up their firing almost to the end of the action; thus the engineers had to be protected by a machine gun when toward nightfall they had to enter forcibly a concrete building which had been very strongly fortified. Termination of today's operation; on 25 April 1943 at 0145 hours, 1,660 Jews were caught for evacuation, 1,814 pulled out of dug-outs, about 330 shot. Innumerable Jews were destroyed by the flames or perished when the dug-outs were blown up. 26 dug-outs were blown up and an amount of paper money, especially dollars was captured; this money has not yet been counted."

* * * * *

[April 25, 1943.]
"Today's operations of the search parties ended almost everywhere in the starting of enormous conflagrations. In this manner the Jews were forced to leave their hideouts and refuges. A total of 1,960 Jews were caught alive. The Jews informed us that among them were certain parachutists who were dropped here and bandits who had been equipped with arms from some unknown source. 274 Jews were killed. As in the preceding days, uncounted Jews were buried in blown up dug-outs and, as can be observed time and again, burned with this bag of Jews today. We have, in my opinion, caught a very considerable part of the bandits and lowest elements of the Ghetto. Intervening darkness prevented immediate liquidation. I am going to try to obtain a train for TII tomorrow. Otherwise liquidation will be carried out tomorrow. Today also, some armed resistance was encountered; in a dug-out three pistols and some explosives were captured. Furthermore, considerable

The Twenty-five Year Campaign

amounts of paper money, foreign currency, gold coins, and jewelry were seized today."

* * * * * *

[May 4, 1943.]

"The main forces were detailed about 1100 hours to comb out, mop up, and destroy two large blocks of buildings, containing the former firms Toebbens, Schulz and Co., and others. After these blocks had been completely cordoned off, we requested the Jews who were still within the buildings to come forward voluntarily. By this measure, we caught 456 Jews for evacuation. Not until the blocks of buildings were well aflame and were about to collapse did a further considerable number of Jews emerge, forced to do so by the flames and the smoke. Time and again the Jews try to escape even through burning buildings. Innumerable Jews whom we saw on the roofs during the conflagration perished in the flames. Others emerged from the upper stories in the last possible moment and were only able to escape death in the flames by jumping down. Today we caught a total of 2,283 Jews, of whom 204 were shot and innumerable Jews were destroyed in dug-outs and in the flames. The sum total of Jews caught rises to 44,089."

* * * * * *

[May 7, 1943.]

"The location of the dug-out used by the so-called select 'Party Directorate' is now known. It is to be forced open tomorrow. The Jews testify that they emerge at night to get fresh air, since it is unbearable to stay permanently within the dug-outs owing to the long duration of the operation. On the average the raiding parties shoot 30 to 50 Jews each night. From these statements it was to be inferred that a considerable number of Jews are still underground in the Ghetto. Today we blew up a concrete building which we had not been able to destroy by fire. In this operation we learned that the blowing up of a building is a very lengthy process and takes an enormous amount of explosives. The best and only method for destroying the Jews therefore still remains the setting of fires."

THE FATE OF THE HUNGARIAN JEWS

The Germans occupied Hungary on March 19, 1944, and the Hungarian Jews were the last group of European Jews to fall into Nazi hands. By this time, the Nazis had mastered the art of deportation and extermination. Within four months more than 400,000 Hungarian Jews were dead. The story of what happened to Hungary's Jews was contained in an affidavit by Rudolph Kastner, a Hungarian Zionist leader. It is one of the most comprehensive documents in the Nurnberg file and is remarkable for the author's description of the details of the Nazi plans and methods, which were not revealed to the world until after the capture of the Nazi archives (Document 2605-PS):[181]

---

[181] Part III—page 378

"*After the German occupation.*

"*19 March 1944:* Together with the German military occupation arrived in Budapest 'Special Section Commando' of the German Secret Police with the sole object of liquidating the Hungarian Jews. It was headed by Adolf Eichmann, SS Obersturmbannfuehrer, Chief of Section IV.B of the Reich Security Head Office. His immediate collaborators were: SS Obersturmbannfuehrer Hermann Krumey, Hauptsturmfuehrer Wisliczeny, Hunsche, Novak, Dr. Seidl, later Danegger, Wrtok. They arrested, and later deported to Mauthausen, all the leaders of Jewish political and business life and journalists, together with the Hungarian democratic and anti-Fascist politicians; taking advantage of the 'interregnum' following upon the German occupation lasting 4 days they have placed their Quislings into the Ministry of the Interior. These were Ladislas Endre and Ladislas Baky. Utilizing the Hungarian administrative organs they have:

"a. Arrested all Jews arriving or leaving Budapest (about 2,500 persons, who were interned at Kistarcsa).

"b. Excluded the Jews from using postal and telephone facilities.

"c. Took over for SS and German military purposes all Jewish public buildings, schools, and hospitals.

"*On 23 March 1944* the Quisling Cabinet was formed, the purpose of which was—according to the statement made by Wisliczeny (to us in June 1944 in Budapest)—solely the solution of the Jewish problem. During the deliberations preceding the formation of the Cabinet, Prime Minister Sztojay undertook in the presence of SS Obergruppenfuehrer Winckelmann, Hungary's SS Commander, SS Standartenfuehrer Wesenmayer, new German Minister, and Eichmann, that the Hungarian Government will do everything possible to help in the liquidation of Hungarian Jewry. One anti-Jewish decree followed another after the Sztojay Cabinet took over. At the same time Krumey and Wisliczeny appeared in the building of the Budapest Jewish Committee and informed Samuel Stern, President, that the matters concerning the Hungarian Jewish problem would be henceforth 'dealt with' within the competence of the SS. They warned the Jews against creating panic and obliged the Jewish leaders to form a 'Jewish Council.' A gigantic levy was imposed (money and goods worth about 11,000,000 pengoes had to be handed over). When President Stern made an inquiry at the Hungarian Ministry of the Interior he was told: 'You must fulfill the German demands . . .'

"*On 26 March 1944* the whole of Ruthenia, Upper Hungary and Northern Transylvania were declared operational territory at the request of the German General Staff. During the next days that followed Eichmann, Wisliczeny, and Hunsche had daily conferences with Ladislas Endre who received full authority from the Cabinet in matters concerning the Jews.

"*On 9 April 1944* the military authorities, with headquarters at Munkacs began the rounding-up of 320,000 Jews into Ghettos within the operational area. In order to prevent any armed resistance by the Jews, they were concentrated in brick factories (as at Kassa, Ungvar, Kolozsvar) or under the open sky (as at Nagybanyam, Marosvasarhely, Des), in a few cases they were allowed to retire into some sections of the cities (as in Nagyvarad, Mara-

The Twenty-five Year Campaign

morossiziget). Food allocations: daily 1/5 of a pound of bread and two cups of soup. From the Jews sent into the ghettos even matches were taken away.

"While an agreement was arrived at between Wesenmayer, German Minister and a representative of Sauckel on the one hand, and Prime Minister Sztojay, on the other, that Hungary would place 300,000 Jewish workers at the disposal of the Reich (who were to be selected by a mixed Hungarian-German committee), total deportation of all Jews was decided by Endre, Baky and Eichmann at a meeting in the Ministry of the Interior on the 14 April 1944.

"Novak and Lullay left on the next day for Vienna to discuss the question of transport facilities with the management of the German railways.

"A levy of 2,000,000 pengoes each was imposed by the Gestapo on the Jews of Novisad and Ungvar. Jewish shops were looted by Germans. Despite a German protest, the Hungarian Government ordered the closing down of all Jewish shops. The Jews resisted in the Ghetto of Munkacs. The Gestapo shot 27 of them, including the entire executive of the Jewish Community.

"*On 28 April 1944* the first deportation took place; 1,500 persons suitable as laborers were taken from the Kistarcsa internment camp to Auschwitz. There, they were compelled to write encouraging notes to their relatives with datelines from 'Waldsee.' The notes were brought by an SS Courier to Budapest and were distributed by the Jewish Council.

"In the meantime the Budapest Relief Committee received two messages from the Bratislava Committee. One message said that there was feverish work going on in Auschwitz to restore the gas chambers and crematoriums there, which were not working for months and a remark made by a SS NCO that 'soon we will get fine Hungarian sausages' was reported. The other message was to the effect that an agreement was reached, between the Hungarian, Slovakian, and German railway managements that, for the time being, 120 trains would be directed, via Presov, towards Auschwitz. This information was passed on to the Bratislava Relief Committee by an anti-Nazi Slovakian railway official. It was obvious that it concerned deportation trains.

"The delegate of the International Red Cross, to whom I have appealed for intervention, stated that in view of the Geneva Convention this was impossible for him. The Swedish and Swiss Legation promised that they would report to their governments and ask for instructions. After repeated appeals the Primate of the Catholic Church promised an intervention on behalf of the converted Jews. But Sztojay refused to listen.

"After consulting with all Jewish leaders we turned to the Germans. At first Krumey, Wisliczeny, and Hunsche negotiated with us: later Eichmann took over the negotiations. Eichmann arrived at Budapest on the first day of the German occupation, 19 March, 1944. Wisliczeny arrived there on March 22. The first time we negotiated was 3 April. At first the Germans demanded a compensation of 2,000,000 dollars and promised that in return for this sum they would not deport anyone. Later Eichmann declared: 'I can only sell the Hungarian Jews as from Germany. Brand should leave at once for Istanbul and inform the Jews there and the Allies that I am prepared to sell 1,000,000 Hungarian Jews, for goods, primarily vehicles. I would transport them to Auschwitz and "put them on ice." If my generous offer is accepted I will release all of them. If not, they will all be gassed.'

"In the meantime the organization of the ghettos had been directed by Wisliczeny, who had been traveling from town to town. The Hungarian police and gendarmerie was at his disposal everywhere. Officially he only acted as an 'Adviser' to the Hungarian authorities; in reality everything took place on German orders.

"*15 May 1944* general and total deportation began. One day before the evacuation all hospital cases, newly born babies, blind and deaf, all mental cases and prison inmates of Jewish origin were transferred to the ghettos. About 80-100 Jews were placed in each cattle-car with one bucket of water; the car was then sealed down. At Kassa the deportation trains were taken over from the escorting Hungarian gendarmerie by the SS. While searching for 'hidden valuables' the gendarmerie squads tortured the inmates with electric current and beat them mercilessly. Hundreds committed suicide. Those who protested or resisted were shot at once (as for instance Dr. Rosenfeld, solicitor of Marosvasarhely).

"The Hungarian press and radio kept quiet about the deportations. The Hungarian government denied in the foreign press that Jews were tortured.

"*Between 5 June and 8 June 1944* Eichmann told me: 'We accepted the obligation toward the Hungarians that not a single deported Jew will return alive!'

"*Up to 27 June 1944*, 475,000 Jews were deported.

"The Pope and the King of Sweden intervened with Horthy. Then followed the ultimatum-like appeal of President Roosevelt to stop the brutal anti-Jewish persecutions. Thereupon Horthy has forbidden the deportation of the Jews from the capital which was already fixed to take place on July 5.

"Endre, Baky, and the Germans protested against this decision and a further 30,000 Jews were deported from Transdanubia; the outer suburbs of Budapest were also emptied. Horthy dismissed Endre. But Eichmann, Endre, and Baky continued to try to liquidate the Jews of the capital with the collaboration of the gendarmerie. Liberators bombed Budapest and the railway junctions which were to be used by the deportation trains. Horthy has ordered the mobilization of the Army against an attempted coup d'etat (8 July). The gendarmerie thereupon went over to Horthy's side. But Eichmann emptied the camp of Kistarcsa by secretly collaborating with the Camp Commander and another 1,700 Jews were transported off in the direction of Auschwitz. On Horthy's orders the train was stopped at the frontier and the people were brought back. But Eichmann repeated his coup after three days and prevented any information reaching Horthy in time.

"*On 15 July 1944* an ultimatum was handed over by Wesenmayer, German Minister to the Hungarian Minister of Foreign Affairs, demanding the deportation of the Budapest Jews. The Hungarian Government replied in a note to the effect that it was prepared to transfer the Budapest Jews to satisfy demands of military security, but only within the borders of the country (27 July).

"Allied successes have strengthened the position of the Hungarian Government against the Germans. Lakatos, new Hungarian Prime Minister sent a note to the German Government demanding the recall of Eichmann and his staff from Hungary, the transfer of the German-controlled internment camps

The Twenty-five Year Campaign

to Hungarian authorities and the handing over of Hungarian politicians and high-ranking officers in German captivity to the Hungarians.

"On 25 August 1944 following instructions received from Himmler, Wesenmayer informed the Hungarian Government that its demands would be fulfilled by the Germans.

"But on 15 October 1944 a German coup ended the Horthy regime and Szalasy took over power. On 17 October Eichmann returned to Budapest by air. On his order the Arrow-Cross Party and the police began the deportation of all Jews locked into the houses marked by yellow stars; 25,000 Jewish people, mostly women were made to walk over 100 miles in rain and snow without food to the Austrian border; hundreds died on the way, more died in Austria through exhaustion and dysentery. On the border the transports were taken over by Wisliczeny; 20,000 Labor Service men shared the same fate.

"The German authorities were the same as before; the most active Hungarian collaborators were: Minister Emil Kovarcz, Solymosi, Under-Secretary of State, and Ladislas Ferenczi, Lt. Col. of the gendarmerie.

"On 8 December the deportations from Budapest stopped. According to Wisliczeny, Eichmann refused to carry out Himmler's order to stop deportations until he received written instructions from Himmler himself. Until 11 February 1945 the Arrow-Cross Party men did not stop to hunt down Jews in hiding, living on false papers; 10-15,000 Jews were shot on the shores of the Danube or in the streets during these 2 months. Thousands have died in the Ghettos, as well as in the 'protected houses' of the Swedish and Swiss Legations, as a result of enemy action, sickness or starvation.

The Losses of Hungarian Jewry

"The 1940-41 census found 762,000 persons of Jewish persuasion within what was then Hungarian territory. But the persecution was extended to the converted Jews, as well as to mixed marriages, of whom there were no official figures. Their numbers were estimated generally at 60,000.

"According to figures estimated in August 1945:

There are at present in Budapest	150,000 Jews
In the provinces	40,000 Jews
In Transylvania (returned to Rumania), in Ruthenia (attached to Russia), in Upper Hungary (attached to Slovakia), and in the Backa (returned to Yugoslavia), there are estimated to be	50,000 Jews
Total	240,000 Jews
In territory occupied by the Allies and in Russia, Sweden and Switzerland approximately	50,000 Jews
Total	290,000 Jews

"Of the 10,000 or so Slovakian, Polish, Yugoslav, and German Jews who were in Hungary at the time of the German occupation only about 750 are still alive, according to a reliable estimate.

I-67

"Therefore, a total of 540,000 Hungarians and 10,000 refugee Jews perished, of them—
      The Germans were responsible for the death of...450,000
      The Hungarians were responsible for the death of............................. 80,000
      Suicides, sickness, enemy (allied) action.. 20,000
                                                                                                                    ———
                                                                                                                    550,000

"The figures concerning the deported Jews originate from Wisliceny, who directed the deportations and was fully competent to give these figures."

Kastner's affidavit is corroborated by a vast number of official German documents. His statement that the Germans were responsible for the slaughter of 450,000 Hungarian Jews is supported by the statement of Hoess, commandant at Auschwitz, to the effect that in the summer of 1944, 400,000 Hungarian Jews were executed there. A British War Office report on the Auschwitz Camp (Document L-161)[182] stated that Hungarian Jews were liquidated at Auschwitz at the rate of 10,000 per day in July, 1944.

THE SLAUGHTER STOPS

As Allied victory and fear of retribution began to overtake the Nazi leadership, orders were given to stop the slaughter of Jews.

Kurt Becher, former SS colonel, revealed that Himmler ordered the end of further liquidation of the Jews between the middle of September and October, 1944 (Document 3762-PS).[183] According to Becher, Himmler's order was directed to the SS Generals Kaltenbrunner, Head of the Reich Security Main Office, and Pohl, Chief of Administration and Economic Main Office of the SS in Charge of Concentration Camps.

It read as follows:

"Effective immediately I forbid any liquidation of Jews and order that on the contrary, hospital care should be given to weak and sick persons. I hold you personally responsible even if this order should not be strictly adhered to by lower echelons."

There are other affidavits that the liquidation as a matter of official Nazi policy terminated prior to the end of 1944. In his affidavit (Document 2605-PS),[184] Kastner stated that deportations from Budapest stopped on December 8, 1944. At Nurnberg, Wisliceny, Eichmann's assistant for deportations from Slovakia and Greece, testified that Himmler gave the order to stop the destruction of Jews in October, 1944. (Page 2057 of Official Transcript.)

---

[182] Part III—page 48
[183] Part III—page 564
[184] Part III—page 378

I-68

The Twenty-five Year Campaign

The Nazis had by that time realized that they had lost the war. Toward the end, Himmler bargained with neutral intermediaries for the lives of the few Jews who remained. He ordered his SS minions to stop the slaughter in a futile attempt to ward off the retribution of which they had long been warned by Allied leaders and which now appeared inevitable.

CHAPTER 8

THE PROPAGANDA FRONT

THROUGHOUT the entire 25-year campaign, as persecution developed from legislative discrimination to massacre and spread from Germany throughout occupied Europe, the Nazis carried on a continuous and relentless propaganda war against the Jews, which reached into every country of the world.

It was a major weapon in the Nazi arsenal. The goal was a bloodless conquest of the world for Nazi ideology to be followed by domination by the Wehrmacht legions. Anti-Jewish propaganda had two immediate aims: the first, to justify to the world the persecution of the Jews; the second, to attempt to persuade other nations to adopt similar measures against the Jews, and thus to divide peoples within the democratic countries and subvert democratic principles and ideals.

Early Efforts: 1933

Fearing that their treatment of German Jews would be placed on the League of Nations agenda, Reich ministers met on September 12, 1933 to plan their strategy. They anticipated that the political commission at Geneva would discuss the plight of the Jewish minority in Germany and consider steps for its protection. Their formula was that any excesses against Jews in Germany were Germany's own business. To prepare the most effective counter-propaganda, Hitler was requested to appoint Goebbels, Reichsminister of Propaganda and Public Enlightenment, to the German delegation. It was decided that if "the League of Nations should come to decisions which were unbearable to the German way of life," then the Reich government would reserve the right to withraw Germany's delegation (Document 2907-PS).[185] Germany did withdraw from the International Disarmament Conference and the League of Nations in October, 1933.

Earlier that year, on March 27, Vice-Chancellor von Papen found it necessary to send a long radiogram to the Board of Trade for German-

---
[185] Part III—page 435

American Commerce in New York denying alleged interferences with American business interests and other excesses. Von Papen insisted that Jews were unmolested (Document D-635):[186]

"Hundreds of thousands of Jews irrespective of nationality, who have not taken part in political activities, are living here entirely unmolested. Operations of large Jewish enterprises and big Jewish publishing houses, such as Mosse, Ullstein and Frankfurter Zeitung, are absolutely normal. Synagogues and Jewish cemeteries are undisturbed."

The radiogram published in the New York Times on March 28, 1933 attributed stories of alleged excesses to "sources strongly interested in poisoning the friendly relations between Germany and America and systematically discrediting" the German government with the American people.

Jewish Question in German Foreign Policy

One of the most revealing of all documents on the propaganda picture is the German Foreign Office circular dated January 25, 1939, on the subject of the Jewish Question as a Factor in German Foreign Policy in the Year 1938 (Document 3358-PS).[187] The memorandum was sent to all German diplomatic and consular representatives abroad and it began with the following significant paragraph:

"It is certainly no coincidence that the fateful year 1938 has brought nearer the solution of the Jewish question simultaneously with the realization of the 'idea of Greater Germany', since the Jewish policy was both the basis and consequence of the events of the year 1938. The advance made by Jewish influence and the destructive Jewish spirit in politics, economy and culture paralyzed the power and will of the German people to rise again more perhaps even than the power-policy opposition of the former enemy allied powers of the World War. The healing of this sickness among the people was therefore certainly one of the most important requirements for exerting the force which in the year 1938 resulted in the joining together of Greater Germany, in defiance of the world."

The final goal of German anti-Jewish policy was to compel the emigration of the Jews from Germany. The various ways and means of encouraging and forcing that emigration were discussed. It was noted that liquidation of the Jewish wholesale trade, manufacturing trade, houses and real estate would gradually reach such a point that there would soon no longer be any Jewish property in Germany to speak of.

The circular stated that the forced emigration of Jews without means to all parts of the world provoked the opposition of native populations and in that way constituted the best propaganda for the German anti-

---

[186] Part III—page 9
[187] Part III—page 524

Jewish policy. With satisfaction it was noted that anti-Semitism was rising in the United States, in South America, France, Holland, Scandinavia, and Greece. There were reports from every German mission. German diplomatic and consular representatives abroad were instructed to further the anti-Semitic wave as part of German foreign policy. The circular ended as follows:

"These examples from reports from authorities abroad, can, if desired, be amplified. They confirm the correctness of the expectation that criticism of the measures for excluding Jews from German Lebensraum, which were misunderstood in many countries for lack of evidence, would only be temporary and would swing in the other direction the moment the population saw with its own eyes and thus learned, what the Jewish danger was to them. The poorer and therefore the more burdensome the immigrant Jew is to the country absorbing him, the stronger this country will react and the more desirable is the effect in the interests of German propaganda. The object of this German action is to be the future international solution of the Jewish question, dictated not by false compassion for the 'United Religious Jewish minority' but by the full consciousness of all peoples of the danger which it represents to the racial composition of the nations."

The propagation of anti-Semitism was an advance guard for the Wehrmacht. Thus, even before Czechoslovakia was occupied, Goering told Dr. Durkansky, Deputy Prime Minister of Slovakia, that the Jewish problem in Slovakia should be "solved" as in Germany (Document 2801-PS).[188] On June 29, 1939, Heydrich recommended to Ribbentrop that 41,000 marks be contributed to the "Woldemaras Supporters" in Lithouania, explaining—(Document 2953-PS):[189]

". . . . In order to make full use of anti-Semitic feeling in Lithouania it is intended to stage pogroms against the Jews. The sum of 100,000 Lit (about 41,000 Mark) is required for this illegal work. Besides that a leading 'Woldemaras Supporter' is enquiring whether the Reich would send weapons as well. The reply was given to the effect that money would possibly be provided but weapons, however, would definitely not be delivered.

"The fight against the Jews would result in a further increase in the escape of Jewish capital, causing Lithouania to be more dependent than ever on the German market."

As the war spread, the Nazi propaganda was accelerated. On September 24, 1942, Foreign Minister Ribbentrop telephoned a subordinate, Luther, to speed the "evacuation" of Jews from various countries in Europe. It was argued that Jews agitated against Germany and must be made responsible for acts of sabotage and attacks. After describing current evacuations in Slovakia, Croatia, Rumania, and the occupied ter-

---

[188] Part III—page 417
[189] Part III—page 439

The Twenty-five Year Campaign

ritories, Ribbentrop ordered Luther to approach the Bulgarian, Hungarian, and Danish governments to initiate the "evacuations" in those countries. Ribbentrop said that the Jewish question in Italy would be discussed either at a conference between Hitler and the Duce or between Ribbentrop and Count Ciano (Document 3688-PS).[190] The Royal Rumanian Grand General Staff and the German High Command, between August and October, 1941, agreed upon the evacuation of 110,000 Jews, for the purpose of liquidation, from Bukovina and Bessarabia into two forests in the Bug River area (Document 3319-PS).[191]

On February 25, 1943, Ribbentrop told the Duce that all Jews had been transported from Germany and occupied territories to the East. He justified this drastic measure on the ground that the Jews were the propagators of Anglo-American news and other rumors, and spread defeatism. He complained that the Jewish problem was not as efficiently approached in Italian military circles and the Duce agreed with him (Document D-734).[192]

Hitler, Ribbentrop and the Hungarian Regent, Horthy, met on April 17, 1943. Horthy was urged to adopt vigorous measures against the Jews. Horthy asked what more should be done since he had already deprived the Jews of almost all possibilities of livelihood. He stated that he could not kill them off. Ribbentrop retorted "that the Jews must either be exterminated or taken to concentration camps." Hitler argued that Jews were "pure parasites" and in Poland, for example, if Jews did not want to work they were shot (Document D-736).[193] After the German Armed Forces occupied Hungary the following March, the Nazis no longer had to rely on persuasion.

There has been captured a comprehensive German Foreign Office file which gives many details concerning the propaganda activity of the German Foreign Office (Document 3319-PS).[194] The Foreign Office approached this task with characteristic method and deliberateness. All German missions abroad were instructed to send to Berlin headquarters all available material about Jewish or anti-Jewish occurrences and to utilize information disseminated from Berlin in the most efficient manner, in the press, over the radio, and in public and private discussions. The file revealed the type of archives maintained on the Jewish question and methods for its use.

Every German mission had a special consultant on Jewish questions and on April 3-4, 1944, these met in Krummhuebel for a "work session" to compare notes and exchange ideas on the use of every propaganda medium in the fostering of anti-Semitism. A fortnight later,

---
[190] Part III—page 556
[191] Part III—page 485
[192] Part III—page 10
[193] Part III—page 12
[194] Part III—page 485

elaborate minutes were sent to the German missions at Ankara, Italy, Madrid, Paris, Lisbon, Bratislava, Sofia, Stockholm, Zagreb, Berne, Bucharest, and Copenhagen. This report went into great detail. It was pointed out that the physical elimination of Eastern Jewry would deprive Jewry of its "biological reserves." Representatives from Italy, Spain, Portugal, France, Sweden, Switzerland, Denmark, Rumania, Turkey, and Slovakia were present at that working conference, and each of them gave the conference the benefit of his views on the subject. The following excerpts are typical:

"*Dr. Klassen (France)* next presents a lengthy historical resume of the development of the Jewish problem and of anti-Semitism in France, and points out differences in the treatment of Jews in the Northern and Southern zones. In the Northern zone steps had been taken toward the Aryanization of Jewish concerns, and Jewish publications had been suppressed. According to French legislation for Jews, Jewish writers and actors were not forbidden to work but they could not own or manage a newspaper or a theater. Jews had vanished from government positions. An Institute for Jewish Questions was founded in France in 1940. An anti-Jewish exhibition met with great success. Apart from a few anti-Semitic clericals, the Catholic Church gave far-reaching support to Jewry in the sense of the democratic ideology. A few anti-Semitic films had a discouraging effect. The film medium should therefore be more widely used. The information activity must stem from the French tradition and be represented as the affair of the French.

* * * * *

"*Vice Consul Dr. Janke (Switzerland)* points out that while the majority of all Swiss are anti-Semitic by healthy instinct, there is lacking a realization of the actuality of the Jewish question. The influence of Jews is much less than in the other countries under democratic-plutocratic regimes. An anti-Jewish information activity would have to be handled with great care and without revealing its German origin, in order not to challenge the severe statutory restrictions and evoke mistrust of Germany. The sharp censorship, also, must be taken into account. For this reason the work must be camouflaged. Possibilities to be considered are anti-Jewish tracts, which should be constantly altered in format; also the exploitation of Jewish scandals, compilation of a list of all Jewish persons playing a leading role in the enemy countries, and the spreading of jokes about Jews. The inviting of Swiss personalities to attend the anti-Jewish congress would meet with difficulties."

The work session was a gathering of Nazi experts. It was more important to drill Nazi ideas in other minds. To that end, in the summer of 1944, Hitler ordered Rosenberg to stage an anti-Jewish international congress. It was late in the war and the Nazis were experiencing sharp reverses on both Eastern and Western fronts. In spite of that, and perhaps because of it, a new effort was to be made to sharpen an old weapon. Anti-Semitic propaganda was to be intensified on every front.

But this was not to be a Nazi congress. The memorandum describing the preparations (Document 1752-PS),[195] dated June 15, 1944, discloses that "it must be borne in mind that not a German authority but an international assembly is responsible for the Congress and issues invitations to it," and that "the preparations for the Congress have so far progressed with the greatest possibilities of disguise."

The Congress was scheduled to be held at Cracow on July 11, 1944, under the supervision of Rosenberg. A very full agenda was prepared. Participation on the honorary committee was promised by leading personalities from Italy, France, Hungary, and Holland. The Grand Mufti of Jerusalem had accepted on behalf of Arabia and was to be a lecturer, "Prime Minister" Gailani was representing Iraq and a special emissary of Rosenberg had travelled to Norway to extend a personal invitation to Prime Minister Quisling. Delegates from Sweden, Rumania, and Slovakia and illegal delegates from Switzerland, Spain, and Portugal had promised to attend

The purpose of the Congress was to combat the impression created by Allied propaganda that "National Socialism is retreating on all fronts." It was important to show the world that the invasion army on the Normandy beachhead was in reality fighting, not against "the barbarian Germany of annihilation of Jews but for World Jewry."

But the invading army on the Normandy beachhead rolled faster than the Nazis expected—so fast that the plans for the great international congress had to be scrapped. National Socialism was in fact retreating on all fronts. And no congress and no propaganda, however skillful, could refute the plain fact that Hitlerite Germany was now doomed to total military defeat.

Hitler's Political Testament

But even to the end, the Nazis were not willing to surrender their political creed. On April 29, 1945, one day before he is believed to have committed suicide, Hitler executed his political testament at Berlin. That document probably represents Hitler's last official act as head of the Nazi Party and German State. In it he set up the new government to succeed him, headed by Grand Admiral Doenitz. In it he charged his heirs. In it, he said, at the end (Document 3569-PS):[196]

"Above all I charge the leaders of the nation and those under them to scrupulous observance of the laws of race and to merciless opposition to the universal poisoner of all peoples, international Jewry."

Whether history will witness the rise of self-appointed executors, ready and willing to carry out Hitler's last will and testament depends on the ability of the democratic world to build a lasting and just peace.

---

[195] Part III—page 270
[196] Part III—page 545

Part Two

The Trial and Punishment

THE FOUR-POWER AGREEMENT

Agreement by the Government of the United States of America, the Provisional Government of the French Republic, the Government of the United Kingdom of Great Britain and Northern Ireland and the Government of the Union of Soviet Socialist Republics for prosecution and punishment of major Axis war criminals—8 August 1945.

* * *

WHEREAS the United Nations have from time to time made declarations of their intention that War Criminals shall be brought to justice;

AND WHEREAS the Moscow Declaration of the 30th October 1943 on German atrocities in Occupied Europe stated that those German Officers and men and members of the Nazi Party who have been responsible for or have taken a consenting part in atrocities and crimes will be sent back to the countries in which their abominable deeds were done in order that they may be judged and punished according to the laws of these liberated countries and of the free Governments that will be created therein;

AND WHEREAS this Declaration was stated to be without prejudice to the case of major criminals whose offenses have no particular geographical location and who will be punished by the joint decision of the Governments of the Allies;

NOW THEREFORE the Government of the United States of America, the Provisional Government of the French Republic, the Government of the United Kingdom of Great Britain and Northern Ireland and the Government of the Union of Soviet Socialist Republics (hereinafter called "the Signatories") acting in the interests of all the United Nations and by their representatives duly authorized thereto have concluded this Agreement.

Article 1.

There shall be established after consultation with the Control Council for Germany an International Military Tribunal for the trial of war criminals whose offenses have no particular geographical location whether they be accused individually or in their capacity as members of organizations or groups or in both capacities.

Article 2.

The constitution, jurisdiction and functions of the International Military Tribunal shall be those set out in the Charter annexed to this Agreement, which Charter shall form an integral part of this Agreement.

Article 3.

Each of the Signatories shall take the necessary steps to make available for the investigation of the charges and trial the major war criminals detained by them who are to be tried by the International Military Tribunal. The Signatories shall also use their best endeavors to make available for investigation of the charges against and the trial before the International Military Tribunal such of the major war criminals as are not in the territories of any of the Signatories.

Article 4.

Nothing in this Agreement shall prejudice the provisions established by the Moscow Declaration concerning the return of war criminals to the countries where they committed their crimes.

Article 5.

Any Government of the United Nations may adhere to this Agreement by notice given through the diplomatic channel to the Government of the United Kingdom, who shall inform the other signatory and adhering Governments of each such adherence.

Article 6.

Nothing in this Agreement shall prejudice the jurisdiction or the powers of any national or occupation court established or to be established in any allied territory or in Germany for the trial of war criminals.

Article 7.

This Agreement shall come into force on the day of signature and shall remain in force for the period of one year and shall continue thereafter, subject to the right of any Signatory to give, through the diplomatic channel, one month's notice of intention to terminate it. Such termination shall not prejudice any proceedings already taken or any findings already made in pursuance of this Agreement.

IN WITNESS WHEREOF the Undersigned have signed the present Agreement.

DONE in quadruplicate in London this 8th day of August 1945 each in English, French and Russian, and each text to have equal authenticity.

The Trial and Punishment

For the Government of the United States of America

Robert H. Jackson
....

For the Provisional Government of the French Republic

Robert Falco
....

For the Government of the United Kingdom of Great Britain and Northern Ireland

Jowitt C.
....

For the Government of the Union of Soviet Socialist Republics

I. T. Nikitchenko
....

A. N. Traenin
....

CHARTER OF THE INTERNATIONAL MILITARY TRIBUNAL
I. CONSTITUTION OF THE INTERNATIONAL MILITARY TRIBUNAL

Article 1.

In pursuance of the Agreement signed on the 8th day of August 1945 by the Government of the United States of America, the Provisional Government of the French Republic, the Government of the United Kingdom of Great Britain and Northern Ireland and the Government of the Union of Soviet Socialist Republics, there shall be established an International Military Tribunal (hereinafter called "the Tribunal") for the just and prompt trial and punishment of the major war criminals of the European Axis.

Article 2.

The Tribunal shall consist of four members, each with an alternate. One member and one alternate shall be appointed by each of the Signatories. The alternates shall, so far as they are able, be present at all sessions of the Tribunal. In case of illness of any member of the Tribunal or his incapacity for some other reason to fulfill his functions, his alternate shall take his place.

Article 3.

Neither the Tribunal, its members nor their alternates can be challenged by the Prosecution, or by the Defendants or their

Counsel. Each Signatory may replace its member of the Tribunal or his alternate for reasons of health or for other good reasons, except that no replacement may take place during a Trial, other than by an alternate.

Article 4.
- (a) The presence of all four members of the Tribunal or the alternate for any absent member shall be necessary to constitute the quorum.
- (b) The members of the Tribunal shall, before any trial begins, agree among themselves upon the selection from their number of a President, and the President shall hold office during that trial, or as may otherwise be agreed by a vote of not less than three members. The principle of rotation of presidency for successive trials is agreed. If, however, a session of the Tribunal takes place on the territory of one of the four Signatories, the representative of that Signatory on the Tribunal shall preside.
- (c) Save as aforesaid the Tribunal shall take decisions by a majority vote and in case the votes are evenly divided, the vote of the President shall be decisive; provided always that convictions and sentences shall only be imposed by affirmative votes of at least three members of the Tribunal.

Article 5.
In case of need and depending on the number of the matters to be tried, other Tribunals may be set up; and the establishment, functions, and procedure of each Tribunal shall be identical, and shall be governed by this Charter.

II. JURISDICTION AND GENERAL PRINCIPLES

Article 6.
The Tribunal established by the Agreement referred to in Article 1 hereof for the trial and punishment of the major war criminals of the European Axis countries shall have the power to try and punish persons who, acting in the interests of the European Axis countries, whether as individuals or as members of organizations, committed any of the following crimes.

The following acts, or any of them, are crimes coming within the jurisdiction of the Tribunal for which there shall be individual responsibility:
- (a) CRIMES AGAINST PEACE: namely, planning, preparation, initiation or waging of a war of aggression, or a war in violation of international treaties, agreements or

assurances, or participation in a common plan or conspiracy for the accomplishment of any of the foregoing;
(b) WAR CRIMES: namely, violations of the laws or customs of war. Such violations shall include, but not be limited to, murder, ill-treatment or deportation to slave labor or for any other purpose of civilian population of or in occupied territory, murder or ill-treatment of prisoners of war or persons on the seas, killing of hostages, plunder of public or private property, wanton destruction of cities, towns or villages, or devastation not justified by military necessity;
(c) CRIMES AGAINST HUMANITY: namely, murder, extermination, enslavement, deportation, and other inhumane acts committed against any civilian population, before or during the war, or persecutions on political, racial or religious grounds in execution of or in connection with any crime within the jurisdiction of the Tribunal, whether or not in violation of the domestic law of the country where perpetrated.

Leaders, organizers, instigators and accomplices participating in the formulation or execution of a common plan or conspiracy to commit any of the foregoing crimes are responsible for all acts performed by any persons in execution of such plan.

Article 7.

The official position of defendants, whether as Heads of State or responsible officials in Government Departments, shall not be considered as freeing them from responsibility or mitigating punishment.

Article 8.

The fact that the Defendant acted pursuant to order of his Government or of a superior shall not free him from responsibility, but may be considered in mitigation of punishment if the Tribunal determines that justice so requires.

Article 9.

At the trial of any individual member of any group or organization the Tribunal may declare (in connection with any act of which the individual may be convicted) that the group or organization of which the individual was a member was a criminal organization.

After receipt of the Indictment the Tribunal shall give such notice as it thinks fit that the prosecution intends to ask the Tribunal to make such declaration and any member of the organization will be entitled to apply to the Tribunal for leave to be heard by the Tribunal upon the question of the criminal character of the organization. The Tribunal shall have power to allow or reject the application. If the application is allowed, the Tribunal may direct in what manner the applicants shall be represented and heard.

Article 10.

In cases where a group or organization is declared criminal by the Tribunal, the competent national authority of any Signatory shall have the right to bring individuals to trial for membership therein before national, military or occupation courts. In any such case the criminal nature of the group or organization is considered proved and shall not be questioned.

Article 11.

Any person convicted by the Tribunal may be charged before a national, military or occupation court, referred to in Article 10 of this Charter, with a crime other than of membership in a criminal group or organization and such court may, after convicting him, impose upon him punishment independent of and additional to the punishment imposed by the Tribunal for participation in the criminal activities of such group or organization.

Article 12.

The Tribunal shall have the right to take proceedings against a person charged with crimes set out in Article 6 of this Charter in his absence, if he has not been found or if the Tribunal, for any reason, finds it necessary, in the interests of justice, to conduct the hearing in his absence.

Article 13.

The Tribunal shall draw up rules for its procedure. These rules shall not be inconsistent with the provisions of this Charter.

III. COMMITTEE FOR THE INVESTIGATION AND PROSECUTION OF MAJOR WAR CRIMINALS

Article 14.

Each Signatory shall appoint a Chief Prosecutor for the investigation of the charges against and the prosecution of major war criminals.

The Chief Prosecutors shall act as a committee for the following purposes:

(a) to agree upon a plan of the individual work of each of the Chief Prosecutors and his staff,

The Trial and Punishment

- (b) to settle the final designation of major war criminals to be tried by the Tribunal,
- (c) to approve the Indictment and the documents to be submitted therewith,
- (d) to lodge the Indictment and the accompanying documents with the Tribunal,
- (e) to draw up and recommend to the Tribunal for its approval draft rules of procedure, contemplated by Article 13 of this Charter. The Tribunal shall have power to accept, with or without amendments, or to reject, the rules so recommended.

The Committee shall act in all the above matters by a majority vote and shall appoint a Chairman as may be convenient and in accordance with the principle of rotation: provided that if there is an equal division of vote concerning the designation of a Defendant to be tried by the Tribunal, or the crimes with which he shall be charged, that proposal will be adopted which was made by the party which proposed that the particular Defendant be tried, or the particular charges be preferred against him.

Article 15.

The Chief Prosecutors shall individually, and acting in collaboration with one another, also undertake the following duties:

- (a) investigation, collection and production before or at the Trial of all necessary evidence,
- (b) the preparation of the Indictment for approval by the Committee in accordance with paragraph (c) of Article 14 hereof,
- (c) the preliminary examination of all necessary witnesses and of the Defendants,
- (d) to act as prosecutor at the Trial,
- (e) to appoint representatives to carry out such duties as may be assigned to them,
- (f) to undertake such other matters as may appear necessary to them for the purposes of the preparation for and conduct of the Trial.

It is understood that no witness or Defendant detained by any Signatory shall be taken out of the possession of that Signatory without its assent.

IV. FAIR TRIAL FOR DEFENDANTS

Article 16.

In order to ensure fair trial for the Defendants, the following procedure shall be followed:

(a) The Indictment shall include full particulars specifying in detail the charges against the Defendants. A copy of the Indictment and of all the documents lodged with the Indictment, translated into a language which he understands, shall be furnished to the Defendant at a reasonable time before the Trial.
(b) During any preliminary examination or trial of a Defendant he shall have the right to give any explanation relevant to the charges made against him.
(c) A preliminary examination of a Defendant and his Trial shall be conducted in, or translated into, a language which the Defendant understands.
(d) A defendant shall have the right to conduct his own defense before the Tribunal or to have the assistance of Counsel.
(e) A defendant shall have the right through himself or through his Counsel to present evidence at the Trial in support of his defense, and to cross-examine any witness called by the Prosecution.

V. POWERS OF THE TRIBUNAL AND CONDUCT OF THE TRIAL

Article 17.
The Tribunal shall have the power
(a) to summon witnesses to the Trial and to require their attendance and testimony and to put questions to them,
(b) to interrogate any Defendant,
(c) to require the production of documents and other evidentiary material,
(d) to administer oaths to witnesses,
(e) to appoint officers for the carrying out of any task designated by the Tribunal including the power to have evidence taken on commission.

Article 18.
The Tribunal shall
(a) confine the Trial strictly to an expeditious hearing of the issues raised by the charges,
(b) take strict measures to prevent any action which will cause unreasonable delay, and rule out irrelevant issues and statements of any kind whatsoever,
(c) deal summarily with any contumacy, imposing appropriate punishment, including exclusion of any Defendant or his Counsel from some or all further proceedings, but without prejudice to the determination of the charges.

The Trial and Punishment

Article 19.

The Tribunal shall not be bound by technical rules of evidence. It shall adopt and apply to the greatest possible extent expeditious and non-technical procedure, and shall admit any evidence which it deems to have probative value.

Article 20.

The Tribunal may require to be informed of the nature of any evidence before it is offered so that it may rule upon the relevance thereof.

Article 21.

The Tribunal shall not require proof of facts of common knowledge but shall take judicial notice thereof. It shall also take judicial notice of official governmental documents and reports of the United Nations, including the acts and documents of the committees set up in the various allied countries for the investigation of war crimes, and the records and findings of military or other Tribunals of any of the United Nations.

Article 22.

The permanent seat of the Tribunal shall be in Berlin. The first meetings of the members of the Tribunal and of the Chief Prosecutors shall be held at Berlin in a place to be designated by the Control Council for Germany. The first trial shall be held at Nuremberg, and any subsequent trials shall be held at such places as the Tribunal may decide.

Article 23.

One or more of the Chief Prosecutors may take part in the prosecution at each Trial. The function of any Chief Prosecutor may be discharged by him personally, or by any person or persons authorized by him.

The function of counsel for a Defendant may be discharged at the Defendant's request by any Counsel professionally qualified to conduct cases before the Courts of his own country, or by any other person who may be specially authorized thereto by the Tribunal.

Article 24.

The proceedings at the Trial shall take the following course:
(a) The indictment shall be read in court.
(b) The Tribunal shall ask each Defendant whether he pleads "guilty" or "not guilty."
(c) The prosecution shall make an opening statement.
(d) The Tribunal shall ask the prosecution and the defense what evidence (if any) they wish to submit to the Tribunal, and the Tribunal shall rule upon the admissibility of any such evidence.

(e) The witnesses for the Prosecution shall be examined and after that the witnesses for the Defense. Thereafter such rebutting evidence as may be held by the Tribunal to be admissible shall be called by either the Prosecution or the Defense.
(f) The Tribunal may put any question to any witness and to any Defendant, at any time.
(g) The Prosecution and the Defense shall interrogate and may cross-examine any witnesses and any Defendant who gives testimony.
(h) The Defense shall address the court.
(i) The Prosecution shall address the court.
(j) Each Defendant may make a statement to the Tribunal.
(k) The Tribunal shall deliver judgment and pronounce sentence.

Article 25.

All official documents shall be produced, and all court proceedings conducted, in English, French and Russian, and in the language of the Defendant. So much of the record and of the proceedings may also be translated into the language of any country in which the Tribunal is sitting, as the Tribunal considers desirable in the interests of justice and public opinion.

VI. JUDGMENT AND SENTENCE

Article 26.

The judgment of the Tribunal as to the guilt or the innocence of any Defendant shall give the reasons on which it is based, and shall be final and not subject to review.

Article 27.

The Tribunal shall have the right to impose upon a Defendant on conviction, death or such other punishment as shall be determined by it to be just.

Article 28.

In addition to any punishment imposed by it, the Tribunal shall have the right to deprive the convicted person of any stolen property and order its delivery to the Control Council for Germany.

Article 29.

In case of guilt, sentences shall be carried out in accordance with the orders of the Control Council for Germany, which may at any time reduce or otherwise alter the sentences, but may not increase the severity thereof. If the Control Council for Germany, after any Defendant has been convicted and sen-

The Trial and Punishment

tenced, discovers fresh evidence which, in its opinion, would found a fresh charge against him, the Council shall report accordingly to the Committee established under Article 14 hereof, for such action as they may consider proper, having regard to the interests of justice.

VII. EXPENSES

Article 30.

The expenses of the Tribunal and of the Trials, shall be charged by the Signatories against the funds allotted for maintenance of the Control Council for Germany.

THE INDICTMENT

Excerpts from indictment before International Military Tribunal, filed 18 October 1945.

* * *

I. The United States of America, the French Republic, the United Kingdom of Great Britain and Northern Ireland and the Union of Soviet Socialist Republics by the undersigned, Robert H. Jackson, Francois de Menthon, Hartley Shawcross and R. A. Rudenko, duly appointed to represent their respective Governments in the investigation of the charges against and the prosecution of the major war criminals, pursuant to the Agreement of London dated 8th August, 1945, and the Charter of this Tribunal annexed thereto, hereby accuse as guilty, in the respects hereinafter set forth, of Crimes against Peace, War Crimes, and Crimes against Humanity, and of a Common Plan or Conspiracy to commit those Crimes, all as defined in the Charter of the Tribunal, and accordingly name as defendants in this cause and as indicted on the counts hereinafter set out: HERMANN WILHELM GOERING, RUDOLF HESS, JOACHIM von RIBBENTROP, ROBERT LEY, WILHELM KEITEL, ERNST KALTENBRUNNER, ALFRED ROSENBERG, HANS FRANK, WILHELM FRICK, JULIUS STREICHER, WALTER FUNK, HJALMAR SCHACHT, GUSTAV KRUPP von BOHLEN und HALBACH, KARL DOENITZ, ERICH RAEDER, BALDUR von SCHIRACH, FRITZ SAUCKEL, ALFRED JODL, MARTIN BORMANN, FRANZ von PAPEN, ARTUR SEYSS-INQUART, ALBERT SPEER, CONSTANTIN von NEURATH and HANS FRITZSCHE, individually and as members of any of the Groups or Organizations next hereinafter named.

II. The following are named as Groups or Organizations (since dissolved) which should be declared criminal by reason of their aims and the means used for the accomplishment thereof and in connection with the conviction of such of the named defendants as were members thereof: DIE REICHSREGIERUNG (REICH CABINET); DAS KORPS DER POLITISCHEN LEITER DER NATIONALSOZIALISTISCHEN DEUTSCHEN ARBEITERPARTEI (LEADERSHIP CORPS OF THE NAZI PARTY); DIE SCHUTZSTAFFELN DER NATIONALSOZIALISTISCHEN DEUTSCHEN ARBEITERPARTEI (commonly known as the "SS") and including DIE SICHERHEITSDIENST (commonly known as the "SD"); DIE GEHEIME

The Trial and Punishment

STAATSPOLIZEI (SECRET STATE POLICE, commonly known as the "GESTAPO"); DIE STURMABTEILUNGEN DER N.S.D.A.P. (commonly known as the "SA"); and the GENERAL STAFF and HIGH COMMAND of the GERMAN ARMED FORCES. The identity and membership of the Groups or Organizations referred to in the foregoing titles are hereinafter in Appendix B more particularly defined.

COUNT ONE—THE COMMON PLAN OR CONSPIRACY
(Charter, Article 6, especially 6 (a))

III. Statement of the Offense

All the defendants, with divers other persons, during a period of years preceding 8th May, 1945, participated as leaders, organizers, instigators or accomplices in the formulation or execution of a common plan or conspiracy to commit, or which involved the commission of, Crimes against Peace, War Crimes, and Crimes against Humanity, as defined in the Charter of this Tribunal, and, in accordance with the provisions of the Charter, are individually responsible for their own acts and for all acts committed by any persons in the execution of such plan or conspiracy. The common plan or conspiracy embraced the commission of Crimes against Peace, in that the defendants planned, prepared, initiated and waged wars of aggression, which were also wars in violation of international treaties, agreements or assurances. . . . The common plan or conspiracy contemplated and came to embrace as typical and systematic means, and the defendants determined upon and committed, Crimes against Humanity, both within Germany and within occupied territories, including murder, extermination, enslavement, deportation, and other inhumane acts committed against civilian populations before and during the war, and persecutions on political, racial or religious grounds, in execution of the plan for preparing and prosecuting aggressive or illegal wars, many of such acts and persecutions being violations of the domestic laws of the countries where perpetrated.

* * * * * * *

IV (D) 3 (d). Implementing their "master race" policy, the conspirators joined in a program of relentless persecution of the Jews, designed to exterminate them. Annihilation of the Jews became an official State policy, carried out both by official action and by incitements to mob and individual violence. The conspirators openly avowed their purpose. For example, the defendant ROSENBERG stated: "Anti-Semitism is the unifying element of the reconstruction of Germany." On another occasion he also stated: "Germany will regard the Jewish question as solved only after the very last Jew has left the greater German living space . . . Europe will have its Jewish question solved only after the very last Jew has left the Continent." The defendant LEY declared: "We swear we are not going to abandon the struggle until the last Jew in Europe has been exterminated and is actually dead. It is not enough to isolate the Jewish enemy of mankind—the Jew has got to be exterminated." On another occasion he also declared: "The second German secret weapon is anti-Semitism because if it is consistently pursued by Germany, it will become a universal problem which all nations will be forced to consider." The defendant STREICHER declared: "The sun will not shine on the nations of the earth until the last Jew is dead." These avowals and incitements were typical of the declarations of the Nazi conspirators throughout the course of their conspiracy. The program of action against the Jews included disfranchisement, stigmatization, denial of civil rights, subjecting their persons and property to violence, deportation, enslavement, enforced labor, starvation, murder and mass extermination. The extent to which the conspirators succeeded in their purpose can only be estimated, but the annihilation was substantially complete in many localities of Europe. Of the 9,600,000 Jews who lived in the parts of Europe under Nazi domination, it is conservatively estimated that 5,700,000 have disappeared, most of them deliberately put to death by the Nazi conspirators. Only remnants of the Jewish population of Europe remain.

*　　*　　*　　*　　*　　*　　*

IV (F) 6. *The German invasion on June 22nd, 1941, on the U.S.S.R. territory in violation of non-aggression Pact of 23rd August, 1939.*

On June 22nd, 1941, the Nazi conspirators deceitfully denounced the non-aggression Pact between Germany and the U.S.S.R. without any declaration of war, invaded the Soviet territory thereby beginning a war of aggression against the U.S.S.R.

From the very first day of launching their attack on Soviet territory the Nazi conspirators in accordance with their detailed plans began to carry out the destruction of cities, towns and villages, the demolition of factories and plants, collective farms, electric stations and railroads, the robbery and barbaric devastation of the national cultural institutions of the peoples of the U.S.S.R., the devastation of museums, schools, hospitals, churches, historical monuments, the mass deportation of the

Soviet citizens for slave labour to Germany, as well as the annihilation of adults, old people, women and children especially Russians, Byelorussians, Ukrainians, the extermination of Jews, committed throughout the territory of the Soviet Union.

The above mentioned criminal offences were perpetrated by the German troops in accordance with the orders of the Nazi Government and the General Staff and High Command of the German Armed Forces.

* * * * * * *

COUNT TWO—CRIMES AGAINST PEACE
(Charter, Article 6 (*a*))
V. Statement of the Offense

All the defendants with divers other persons, during a period of years preceding 8th May, 1945, participated in the planning, preparation, initiation and waging of wars of aggression, which were also wars in violation of international treaties, agreements and assurances.

* * * * * * *

COUNT THREE—WAR CRIMES
(Charter, Article 6, especially 6 (*b*))
VIII. Statement of the Offense

All the defendants committed War Crimes between 1st September, 1939, and 8th May, 1945, in Germany and in all those countries and territories occupied by the German armed forces since 1st September, 1939, and in Austria, Czechoslovakia, and Italy, and on the High Seas.

All the defendants, acting in concert with others, formulated and executed a common plan or conspiracy to commit War Crimes, as defined in Article 6 (*b*) of the Charter. This plan involved, among other things, the practice of "total war" including methods of combat and of military occupation in direct conflict with the laws and customs of war, and the commission of crimes perpetrated on the field of battle during encounters with enemy armies, and against prisoners of war, and in occupied territories against the civilian population of such territories.

* * * * * * *

VIII (A) MURDER AND ILL-TREATMENT OF CIVILIAN POPULATIONS OF OR IN OCCUPIED TERRITORY AND ON THE HIGH SEAS

Throughout the period of their occupation of territories overrun by their armed forces the defendants, for the purpose of systematically terrorizing the inhabitants, murdered and tortured civilians, and ill-treated them, and imprisoned them without legal process.

Nazi Germany's War Against the Jews

The murders and ill-treatment were carried out by divers means, including shooting, hanging, gassing, starvation, gross over-crowding, systematic under-nutrition, systematic imposition of labour tasks beyond the strength of those ordered to carry them out, inadequate provision of surgical and medical services, kickings, beatings, brutality and torture of all kinds, including the use of hot irons and pulling out of finger nails and the performance of experiments by means of operations and otherwise on living human subjects. In some occupied territories the defendants interfered with religious services, persecuted members of the clergy and monastic orders, and expropriated church property. They conducted deliberate and systematic genocide, viz., the extermination of racial and national groups, against the civilian populations of certain occupied territories in order to destroy particular races and classes of people and national, racial or religious groups, particularly Jews, Poles and Gypsies and others.

* * * * * * *

VIII (A) 1. *In France, Belgium, Denmark, Holland, Norway, Luxemburg, Italy and the Channel Islands (hereinafter called the "Western Countries") and in that part of Germany which lies west of a line drawn due North and South through the centre of Berlin (hereinafter called "Western Germany") . . .*

Crimes committed in France or against French citizens took the following forms:—

Arbitrary arrests were carried out under political or racial pretexts; they were both individual and collective; notably in Paris (round-up of the 18th Arrondissement by the Field Gendarmerie, round-up of the Jewish population of the 11th Arrondissement in August, 1941, round-up of Jewish intellectuals in December, 1941, round-up in July, 1942; . . .

* * * * * * *

VIII (A) 2. *In the U.S.S.R., i.e., in the Byelorussian, Ukrainian, Esthonian, Latvian, Lithuanian, Karelo-Finnish, and Moldavian Soviet Socialist Republics, in 19 regions of the Russian Soviet Federated Socialist Republic, and in Poland, Czechoslovakia, Yugoslavia, Greece, and the Balkans (hereinafter called "the Eastern Countries") and in that part of Germany which lies*

The Trial and Punishment

East of a line drawn North and South through the centre of Berlin (hereinafter called "Eastern Germany").

From the 1st September, 1939, when the German armed forces invaded Poland, and from the 22nd June, 1941, when they invaded the U.S.S.R., the German Government and the German High Command adopted a systematic policy of murder and ill-treatment of the civilian populations of and in the Eastern Countries as they were successively occupied by the German armed forces. These murders and ill-treatments were carried on continuously until the German Armed Forces were driven out of the said countries.

Such murders and ill-treatments included:—

(*a*) Murders and ill-treatments at concentration camps and similar establishments set up by the Germans in the Eastern Countries and in Eastern Germany including those set up at Maidanek and Auschwitz.

The said murders and ill-treatments were carried out by divers means including all those set out above, as follows:

About 1,500,000 persons were exterminated in Maidanek and about 4,000,000 persons were exterminated in Auschwitz, among whom were citizens of Poland, the U.S.S.R., the United States of America, Great Britain, Czechoslovakia, France and other countries.

In the Lwow region and in the city of Lwow the Germans exterminated about 700,000 Soviet people, including 70 persons in the field of the arts, science and technology, and also citizens of the U.S.A., Great Britain, Czechoslovakia, Yugoslavia and Holland, brought to this region from other concentration camps.

In the Jewish ghetto from 7th September, 1941, to 6th July, 1943, over 133,000 persons were tortured and shot.

Mass shooting of the population occurred in the suburbs of the city and in the Livenitz forest.

In the Ganov camp 200,000 peaceful citizens were exterminated. The most refined methods of cruelty were employed in this extermination, such as disembowelling and the freezing of human beings in tubs of water. Mass shootings took place to the accompaniment of the music of an orchestra recruited from the persons interned.

* * * * * * *

VIII (A) 2. (*b*) Murders and ill-treatments at places in the Eastern Countries and in the Soviet Union, other than in the camps referred to in (*a*) above, included, on various dates during the occupation by the German Armed Forces:

The destruction in the Smolensk region of over 135,000 Soviet citizens. . . .

In Kamenetz-Podolsk Region 31,000 Jews were shot and exterminated, including 13,000 persons brought there from Hungary.

In the Odessa Region at least 200,000 Soviet citizens were killed.

In Kharkov about 195,000 persons were either tortured to death, shot or gassed in gas vans.

In Gomel the Germans rounded up the population in prison, and tortured and tormented them, and then took them to the centre of the city and shot them in public.

In the city of Lyda in the Grodnen region on 8th May, 1942, 5,670 persons were completely undressed, driven into pens in groups of 100 and then shot by machine guns. Many were thrown in the graves while they were still alive.

* * * * * * *

VIII (F) THE EXACTION OF COLLECTIVE PENALTIES.

The Germans pursued a systematic policy of inflicting, in all the occupied countries, collective penalties, pecuniary and otherwise, upon the population for acts of individuals for which it could not be regarded as collectively responsible; this was done at many places, including Oslo, Stavanger, Trondheim and Rogaland.

Similar instances occurred in France, among others in Dijon, Nantes and as regards the Jewish population in the occupied territories. The total amount of fines imposed on French communities add up to 1,157,179,484 francs made up as follows—

A fine on the Jewish population 1,000,000,000
Various fines 157,179,484

* * * * * * *

COUNT FOUR—CRIMES AGAINST HUMANITY.
(Charter, Article 6, especially 6 (*a*))
X. Statement of the Offense.

All the defendants committed Crimes against Humanity during a period of years preceding 8th May, 1945 in Germany and in all those countries and territories occupied by the German armed forces since 1st September, 1939 and in Austria and Czechoslovakia and in Italy and on the High Seas.

All the defendants, acting in concert with others, formulated and executed a common plan or conspiracy to commit Crimes against Humanity as defined in Article 6(*c*) of the Charter. This plan involved, among other things, the murder and persecution of all who were or who were suspected of being hostile

The Trial and Punishment

to the Nazi Party and all who were or who were suspected of being opposed to the common plan alleged in Count One.

* * * * * * *

X. (A.) MURDER, EXTERMINATION, ENSLAVEMENT, DEPORTATION AND OTHER INHUMANE ACTS COMMITTED AGAINST CIVILIAN POPULATIONS BEFORE AND DURING THE WAR.

For the purposes set out above, the defendants adopted a policy of persecution, repression, and extermination of all civilians in Germany who were, or who were believed to, or who were believed likely to become, hostile to the Nazi Government and the common plan or conspiracy described in Count One. They imprisoned such persons without judicial process, holding them in "protective custody" and concentration camps, and subjected them to persecution, degradation, despoilment, enslavement, torture and murder.

Special courts were established to carry out the will of the conspirators; favoured branches or agencies of the State and Party were permitted to operate outside the range even of nazified law and to crush all tendencies and elements which were considered "undesirable." The various concentration camps included Buchenwald, which was established in 1933 and Dachau, which was established in 1934. At these and other camps the civilians were put to slave labour, and murdered and ill-treated by divers means, including those set out in Count Three above, and these acts and policies were continued and extended to the occupied countries after the 1st September, 1939, and until 8th May, 1945.

X. (B.) PERSECUTION ON POLITICAL, RACIAL AND RELIGIOUS GROUNDS IN EXECUTION OF AND IN CONNECTION WITH THE COMMON PLAN MENTIONED IN COUNT ONE.

As above stated, in execution of and in connection with the common plan mentioned in Count One, opponents of the German Government were exterminated and persecuted. These persecutions were directed against Jews. They were also directed against persons whose political belief or spiritual aspirations were deemed to be in conflict with the aims of the Nazis.

Jews were systematically persecuted since 1933; they were deprived of their liberty, thrown into concentration camps where they were murdered and ill-treated. Their property was confiscated. Hundreds of thousands of Jews were so treated before the 1st September, 1939.

Since the 1st September, 1939, the persecution of the Jews was redoubled: millions of Jews from Germany and from the occupied Western Countries were sent to the Eastern Countries for extermination. . . .

In November, 1938 by orders of the Chief of the Gestapo, anti-Jewish demonstrations all over Germany took place. Jewish property was destroyed, 30,000 Jews were arrested and sent to concentration camps and their property confiscated.

Under paragraph VIII (A), above, millions of the persons there mentioned as having been murdered and ill-treated were Jews.

Among other mass murders of Jews were the following:

At Kislovdosk all Jews were made to give up their property: 2,000 were shot in an anti-tank ditch at Mineraliye Vodi: 4,300 other Jews were shot in the same ditch.

60,000 Jews were shot on an island on the Dvina near Riga.
20,000 Jews were shot at Lutsk.
32,000 Jews were shot at Sarny.
60,000 Jews were shot at Kiev and Dniepropetrovsk.

Thousands of Jews were gassed weekly by means of gas-wagons which broke down from overwork.

As the Germans retreated before the Soviet Army they exterminated Jews rather than allow them to be liberated. Many concentration camps and ghettos were set up on which Jews were incarcerated and tortured, starved, subjected to merciless atrocities and finally exterminated.

About 70,000 Jews were exterminated in Yugoslavia.

* * * * * * *

Wherefore, this Indictment is lodged with the Tribunal in English, French and Russian, each text having equal authenticity, and the charges herein made against the above named defendants are hereby presented to the Tribunal.

ROBERT H. JACKSON.
Acting on Behalf of the United States of America.
FRANCOIS DE MENTHON.
Acting on Behalf of the French Republic.
HARTLEY SHAWCROSS.
Acting on Behalf of the United Kingdom of Great Britain and Northern Ireland.
R. RUDENKO.
Acting on Behalf of the Union of Soviet Socialist Republics.

Berlin, *18th October*, 1945.

OPENING ADDRESS: ROBERT H. JACKSON

Excerpts from opening address of Justice Robert H. Jackson, Chief Prosecutor for the United States, before the International Military Tribunal, Nurnberg, Germany, on 21 November 1945.

* * *

[Page 108 of Official Transcript]

The Nazi Party declaration also committed its members to an anti-Semitic program. It declared that no Jew or any person of non-German blood could be a member of the nation. Such persons were to be disfranchised, disqualified for office, subject to the alien laws, and entitled to nourishment only after the German population had first been provided for. All who had entered Germany after August 2, 1914, were to be required forthwith to depart, and all non-German immigration was to be prohibited.

* * * * *

[Pages 111-123 of Official Transcript]

I was about to take up CRIMES COMMITTED AGAINST THE JEWS.

The most savage and numerous crimes planned and committed by the Nazis were those against the Jews. Those in Germany, in 1933, numbered about 500,000. In the aggregate, they had made for themselves positions which excited envy, and had accumulated properties which excited the avarice of the Nazis. They were few enough to be helpless and numerous enough to be held up as a menace.

Let there be no misunderstanding about the charge of persecuting Jews. What we charge against these defendants is not those arrogances and pretensions which frequently accompany the intermingling of different races and peoples and which are likely, despite the honest efforts of Government, to produce regrettable crimes and convulsions. It is our purpose to show plans and designs to which all Nazis were fanatically committed, to annihilate all Jewish people. These crimes were organized and promoted by the Party Leadership, executed and protected by the Nazi officials, as we shall convince you by written orders of the Secret State Police itself.

The persecution of the Jews was a continuous and deliberate policy. It was a policy directed against other nations as well as against the Jews themselves. Anti-Semitism was promoted to divide and embitter the democratic peoples and to soften their resistance to the Nazi aggression. As Robert Ley himself declared, "the second German secret weapon is Anti-Semitism because if it is constantly pursued by Germany, it will become a universal problem which all nations will be forced to consider."

Anti-Semitism also has been aptly credited with being a "spearhead of terror." The ghetto was the laboratory for testing repressive measures. Jewish property was the first to be expropriated, but the custom grew and included similar measures against anti-Nazi Germans, Poles, Czechs, Frenchmen, and Belgians. Extermination of the Jews enabled the Nazis to bring a practiced hand to similar measures against Poles, Serbs, and Greeks. The plight of the Jew was a constant threat to opposition and discontent among other elements of Europe's population—pacifists, conservatives, communists, Catholics, Protestants, socialists. It was, in fact, a threat to every dissenting opinion and to every non-Nazi's life.

The persecution policy against the Jews commenced with non-violent measures, such as disfranchisement and discriminations against their religion, and the placing of impediments in the way of success in economic life. It moved rapidly to organized mass violence against them, physical isolation in ghettos, deportation, forced labor, mass starvation, and extermination. The Government, the Party formations indicted before you as criminal organizations, the Secret State Police, the Army, private and semi-public associations, and "spontaneous" mobs that were carefully inspired from official sources, were all agencies that were concerned in this persecution. Nor was it directed against individual Jews for personal bad citizenship or unpopularity. The avowed purpose was the destruction of the Jewish people as a whole, an end in itself; a measure of preparation for war, and a discipline for conquered peoples.

The conspiracy, or common plan to exterminate the Jew was so methodically and thoroughly pursued that despite German defeat and Nazi prostration, this Nazi aim largely has succeeded. Only remnants of the European Jewish population remain in Germany, in the countries which Germany occupied, and in those which were her satellites or collaborators. Of the 9,600,000 Jews who lived in Nazi dominated Europe, 60 percent are authoritatively estimated to have perished. 5,700,000 Jews are missing from the countries in which they formerly lived, and over 4,500,000 cannot be accounted for by the normal death rate nor by immigration; nor are they included among displaced persons. History does not record a crime perpetrated

The Trial and Punishment

against so many victims or ever carried out with such calculated cruelty.

You will have difficulty, as I have, to look into the faces of these defendants and believe that in this Twentieth Century human beings could inflict such sufferings as will be proved here on their own countrymen as well as upon their so-called "inferior" enemies. Particular crimes, and the responsibility of defendants for them, are to be dealt with by the Soviet Government's Counsel, when committed in the East, and by Counsel for the Republic of France when committed in the West. I advert to them now only to show their magnitude as evidence of a purpose and a knowledge common to all defendants, of an official plan rather than of a capricious policy of some individual commander, and to show a continuity of Jewish persecution from the rise of the Nazi conspiracy to its collapse which forbids us to believe that any person could be identified with any part of Nazi action without approving this most conspicuous item in their program.

The Indictment itself recites many evidences of the anti-Semitic persecutions. The defendant Streicher led the Nazis in anti-Semitic bitterness and extremism. In March of 1942 he complained that Christian teachings have stood in the way of "radical solution of the Jewish question in Europe," and quoted enthusiastically as the Twentieth Century solution the Fuehrer's proclamation of February 24, 1942 that "the Jew will be exterminated." And on November 4, 1943, Streicher declared that the Jews, and I quote his words, "have disappeared from Europe and that the Jewish 'Reservoir of the East' from which the Jewish plague has for centuries beset the people of Europe, has ceased to exist." [Document No. 1965-PS, 4 November 1943]. Streicher now has the effrontery to tell us he is "only a Zionist" and he only wants to return the Jews to Palestine. But on May 7, 1942 he wrote:

"It is also not only a European problem! *The Jewish question is a world question!* Not only is Germany not safe in the face of the Jews as long as one Jew lives in Europe, but also the Jewish question is hardly solved in Europe so long as the Jews live in the rest of the world."

And the defendant Hans Frank, a lawyer by profession, I blush to say, summarized in his Diary in 1944 the Nazi policy thus: "The Jews are a race which has to be eliminated; whenever we catch one, it is his end." And earlier, speaking of his function as Governor General of Poland, Hans Frank confided to his diary this sentiment: "Of course I cannot eliminate all lice and Jews in only a year's time." [Document No. 2233C-PS, Vol. IV, 1940, p. 1158.] I could multiply endlessly this kind of Nazi ranting, but I will leave it to the evidence and turn to the fruit of this perverted thinking.

The most serious of the actions against Jews were outside of any law, but the law itself was employed to some extent. There were the infamous Nurnberg decrees of September 15, 1935. The Jews were segregated into ghettos and put into forced labor; they were expelled from their professions; their property was expropriated; all cultural life, the press, the theatre, and schools were prohibited them; and the SD [Security Service] was made responsible for them. [Documents Nos. 212-PS, 069-PS.] This was an ominous guardianship.

It was ordered that "An eventual act by the civilian population against the Jews is not to be prevented as long as this is compatible with the maintenance of order and security in the rear of fighting troops." And again, "The first main goal of the German measures must be the strict segregation of Jewry from the rest of the population. In the execution of this, first of all, is the seizing of the Jewish populace by the introduction of a registration order and similar appropriate measures. Then immediately, the wearing of the recognition sign, consisting of a yellow Jewish star, is to be brought about and all rights of freedom for Jews are to be withdrawn. They are to be placed in ghettos, and, at the same time, are to be separated according to sexes. The entire Jewish property is to be seized and confiscated, with the exception of that which is necessary for a bare existence."

The anti-Jewish campaign became furious in Germany following the assassination in Paris of the German Legation Councillor vom Rath. Heydrich, Gestapo head, sent a teletype to all Gestapo and SD offices with directions for handling "spontaneous" uprisings anticipated for the nights of November 9 and 10, 1938, and directed them to aid in the destruction of Jewish-owned property and protect only that of Germans. [Document No. 3051-PS.] No more cynical document ever came into evidence.

Then there is a report by an SS Brigade Leader, Dr. Stahlecker, to Himmler, dated in 1941 [Document No. L-180]—and it will be put in evidence—which recites the measures taken against Jews, as they proceeded in occupied countries, and I quote:

"Similarly, anti-Semitic forces were induced to start po-

The Trial and Punishment

groms against the Jews during the first hours of capture, though this inducement proved to be very difficult.

"Following our orders, the Security Police was determined to solve the Jewish question with all possible means and most decisively. But it was desirable that the Security Police should not put in an immediate appearance, at least in the beginning, since the extraordinarily harsh measures were apt to stir even German circles. It had to be shown to the world that the native population itself took the first actions by way of natural reaction . . ."

Of course, it is self-evident that these "uprisings" were managed by the Government and the Nazi Party. If we were in doubt, we could resort to Streicher's memorandum of April 14, 1939, which says, "The anti-Jewish action of November, 1938 did not arise spontaneously from the people. . . . Part of the party formation have been charged with the execution of the anti-Jewish action." [Document No. 406-PS.] Jews as a whole were fined a billion Reichsmarks. They were excluded from all businesses and claims against insurance companies for their burned properties were confiscated, all by decree of the defendant Goering.

Synagogues were the objects of a special vengeance. On November 10, 1938, the following order was given: "By order of the Group Commander, all Jewish Synagogues in the area of Brigade 50 have to be blown up or set afire. . . . The operation will be carried out in civilian clothing. . . . Execution of the order will be reported . . ." [Document No. 1721-PS.] Some 40 teletype messages to various police headquarters, which will be introduced to you, will tell the fury with which all Jews were pursued in Germany on that awful November night. The SS troops were turned loose and the Gestapo supervised. Jewish-owned property was destroyed. The Gestapo ordered twenty to thirty thousand "well-to-do Jews" to be arrested. Concentration camps were to receive them and the order provided healthy Jews, fit for labor, were to be taken. [Document No. 3051-PS.]

As the German frontiers were expanded by war, so the campaign against the Jews expanded. The Nazi plan never was limited to extermination in Germany; always it contemplated extinguishing the Jew in Europe and often in the world. In the West, the Jews were killed and their property taken over in occupied countries. But the campaign achieved its zenith of savagery in the East. The Eastern Jew has suffered as no people ever suffered. Their sufferings were carefully reported to the

Nazi authorities to show faithful adherence to the Nazi design. I shall refer only to enough of the evidence of these to show the extent of the Nazi design and common plan for killing Jews.

If I should recite these horrors in words of my own, you would think me intemperate and unreliable. Fortunately, we need not take the word of any witness but the Germans themselves. I invite you now to look at a few of the vast number of captured German orders and reports that will be offered in evidence, to see what a Nazi invasion meant. We will present such evidence as the report of Action Group A of October 15, 1941, which boasts that in overrunning the Baltic States, "Native anti-Semitic forces were induced to start pogroms against the Jews during the first hours after occupation . . ." [Document No. L-180.] The report continues:

"From the beginning it was to be expected that the Jewish problem in the East could not be solved by pogroms alone. In accordance with the basic orders received, however, the cleansing activities of the Security Police had to aim at a complete annihilation of the Jews. Special detachments reinforced by selected units—in Lithouania partisan detachments, in Latvia units of the Latvian auxiliary police — therefore performed extensive executions both in the town and in rural areas. The actions of the execution detachments were performed smoothly. . . .

"The sum total of the Jews liquidated in Lithuania amounts to 71,105. During the pogroms in Kowno 3,800 Jews were eliminated, in the smaller town about 1,200 Jews. . . .

"In Latvia, up to now a total of 30,000 Jews were executed. 500 were eliminated by pogroms in Riga."

Then there is a captured report from the Commissioner of Sluzk on October 20, 1941, which describes these executions in more detail. Let me quote from it:

". . . The first lieutenant explained that the police battalion had received the assignment to effect the liquidation of all Jews here in the town of Sluzk, within two days . . . Then I requested him to postpone the action one day. However, he rejected this with the remark that he had to carry out this action everywhere and in all towns and that only two days were allotted for Sluzk. Within these two days, the town of Sluzk had to be cleared of Jews by all means . . . All Jews without exception were taken out of the factories and shops and deported in spite of our agreement. It is true that part of the Jews was moved by way of the ghetto

The Trial and Punishment

where many of them were processed and still segregated by me, but a large part was loaded directly on trucks and liquidated without further delay outside of the town . . . For the rest, as regards the execution of the action, I must point out to my deepest regret that the latter bordered already on sadism. The town itself offered a picture of horror during the action. With indescribable brutality on the part of both the German police officers and particularly the Lithouanian partisans, the Jewish people, but also among them White Ruthenians, were taken out of their dwellings and herded together. Everywhere in the town shots were to be heard and in different streets the corpses of shot Jews accumulated. The White Ruthenians were in greatest distress to free themselves from the encirclement. Regardless of the fact that the Jewish people, among whom were also tradesmen, were mistreated in a terribly barbarous way in the face of the White Ruthenian people, the White Ruthenians themselves were also worked over with rubber clubs and rifle butts. There was no question of an action against the Jews any more. It rather looked like a revolution . . ." [Document No. 1104-PS.]

There are reports which merely tabulate the numbers slaughtered. [Document No. R-102.]

In Estonia, all Jews were arrested immediately upon the arrival of the Wehrmacht.

I call your attention to the fact that this is the report of the Wehrmacht, the Army, which became implicated in this business along with the SS. Jewish men and women above the age of 16 and capable of work were drafted for forced labor. (P.8) Jews were subjected to all sorts of restrictions and all Jewish property was confiscated. (P.8)

All Jewish males above the age of 16 were executed, with the exception of doctors and elders. Only 500 of an original 4,500 Jews remained. (P.8)

37,180 persons have been liquidated by the Sipo and SD in White Ruthenia during October.

In one town, 337 Jewish women were executed for demonstrating a 'provocative attitude.' (P.13) In another, 380 Jews were shot for spreading vicious propaganda. (P.13)

And so the report continues, listing town after town, where hundreds upon hundreds of Jews were murdered.

In one town 3,000; in another, 33,771; in another 3,145; in another 410; all listed in detail.

Other accounts tell not of the slaughter so much as of the

depths of degradation to which the tormenters stooped. For example, we will show the report made to defendant Rosenberg about the army and the SS in the area under Rosenberg's jurisdiction, which recited the following, [Document No. R-135] and I quote:

"In the presence of SS men, a Jewish dentist has to break all gold teeth and fillings out of mouth of German and Russian Jews *before* they are executed." (Document B.)

It also says:

Men, women and children are locked into barns and burned alive. (Document A.)

Peasants, women and children are shot on pretext that they are suspected of belonging to bands. (Document C.)

We of the Western World heard of Gas Wagons in which Jews and political opponents were asphyxiated. We could not believe it. But here we will produce for you the report of May 16, 1942 from the German SS officer, Becker, to his supervisor in Berlin, and this is the story that it tells: [Document No. 501-PS.]

Gas vans in C. group can be driven to execution spot, which is generally stationed 10 to 15 kms. from main road only in dry weather. Since those to be executed become frantic if conducted to this place, such vans become immobilized in wet weather. (Letter, p.1.)

Gas vans in D group camouflaged as cabin trailers, but vehicles well known to authorities and civilian population which calls them 'Death Vans'. (Letter, p.2.)

The writer of the letter ordered all men to keep as far away as possible during gassing. Unloading van after the gassing has 'atrocious spiritual and physical effect' on the men who have to unload them and they should be ordered not to participate in such work. (Letter, p.2.)

I shall not dwell on this subject longer than to quote one more sickening document which evidences the planned and systematic character of these Jewish persecutions. I hold an original report written with Teutonic thoroughness as to detail, illustrated with photographs to authenticate its almost incredible text, and beautifully bound in leather with the loving care bestowed to a proud work. It is the original report of the SS Brigade General Stroop in charge of the destruction of the Warsaw Ghetto, and Hans Frank was Governor General of Poland. Its title page carries the inscription, "The Jewish Ghetto in Warsaw no longer exists."

I shall ask your Honors to examine with care the photographs

The Trial and Punishment

(showing to Tribunal) with which this document abounds, showing the destruction of this Ghetto, showing the people driven before the flames, with the title "Jews and Bandits"; women and children and old men, not a man of fighting age in the picture except the German soldiers; the masses lined up against the wall for execution; the picture to illustrate the text showing that they jumped from the windows to escape the flames.

Now, let's read what General Stroop says in here:

"The resistance put up by the Jews and bandits could only be suppressed by energetic actions of our troops day and night. The Reichsfuehrer SS ordered, therefore on 23 April 1943 the cleaning out of the Ghetto with utter ruthlessness and merciless tenacity. I, therefore, decided to destroy and burn down the entire Ghetto without regard to the armament factories. These factories were systematically dismantled and then burned. Jews usually left their hideouts, but frequently remained in the burning buildings and jumped out of the windows only when the heat became unbearable. They then tried to crawl with broken bones across the street into buildings which were not afire. Sometimes they changed their hideouts during the night into the ruins of burned buildings. Life in the sewers was not pleasant after the first week. Many times we could hear loud voices in the sewers. SS men or policemen climbed bravely through the manholes to capture these Jews. Sometimes they stumbled over Jewish corpses; sometimes they were shot at. Tear gas bombs were thrown into the manholes and the Jews driven out of the sewers and captured. Countless numbers of Jews were liquidated in sewers and bunkers through blasting. The longer the resistance continued the tougher became the members of the Waffen SS Police and Wehrmacht who always discharged their duties in an exemplary manner. Frequently Jews who tried to replenish their food supplies during the night or to communicate with neighboring groups were exterminated."

This action eliminated, says the SS commander, "a proved total of 56,065 Jews. To that, he says, we have to add the number of those killed through blasting, fire, etc., which cannot be counted."

We charge that all of the atrocities against Jews were the manifestation and culmination of the Nazi plan to which every defendant in this box was a party. I know very well that some of these men did take steps to spare some particular Jew for some personal reason from the horrors that awaited the unrescued Jew. Some protested that particular atrocities were excessive, and discredited the general policy. While a few defendants may show some efforts to make specific exceptions to the policy of Jewish extermination, I have found no instance in which any defendant opposed the policy itself or sought to revoke or even modify it.

Determination to destroy the Jews was a binding force which at all times cemented the elements of this conspiracy. On many internal policies there were differences among the defendants. But there is not one of them who has not echoed the rallying cry of Nazism—GERMANY AWAKE, JEWRY PERISH!

OPENING ADDRESS: FRANCOIS DE MENTHON

Excerpts from opening address of Francois de Menthon, Prosecutor for the French Republic, before the International Military Tribunal, Nurnberg, Germany, on 17 January 1946.

* * *

[Pages 2908-2911 of Official Transcipt]

The crime which will undoubtedy remain the most tragically memorable among those committed by the Germans against the civilian populations of the occupied countries was that of deportation and internment in the concentration camps of Germany.

These deportations had a double aim: to assure supplementary work for the benefits of the German war machine, to eliminate from the occupied countries and progressively exterminate the elements most opposed to Germanism. They served likewise to empty prisons overcrowded with patriots and to remove the latter for good.

The deportations and the methods employed in the concentration camps were a stupefying revelation for the civilized world. Nevertheless they also are only a natural consequence of the National Socialist doctrine, for which man has no value in himself when he is not in the service of the German race.

It is not possible yet to give exact figures. It is probable that one would remain under the truth in speaking of 250,000 for France, 6,000 for Luxemburg, 5,200 for Denmark, 5,400 for Norway, 120,000 for Holland, 37,000 for Belgium.

The arrests are founded now in a pretext of a political nature; now on a pretext of a racial order. In the beginning they were individual; subsequently they took on a collective character, particularly in France from the beginning of 1941 on. Sometimes the deportation did not come until after long months of prison, but more often the arrest was made directly with a view to deportation under the regime of "protective custody." Everywhere imprisonment in the country of origin was accompanied by brutality, often by torture. Before being sent to Germany, the deportees were in general concentrated at an assembly camp. The formation of a convoy was often the first stage of extermination. The deportees traveled in cattle cars, 80 to 120 per car, no matter what the season. There were few convoys where no deaths occurred. In certain transports the proportion of deaths was more than 25 per cent.

The deportees were sent to Germany, almost always to concentration camps but sometimes also to prisons.

The prisons took in those deportees who had been condemned or were awaiting trial. The prisoners there were crowded together under inhumane conditions. Nevertheless the way the prisons were run was generally less severe than was the case with the camps. The work there was less out of proportion to the strength of the prisoners and the prison wardens were less hard than the SS in the concentration camps.

It appears to have been the plan followed by the Nazis in the concentration camps gradually to do away with the prisoners, but only after their working strength had been used to the advantage of the German war effort.

The Court has been told of the almost inconceivable treatment inflicted by the SS on the prisoners. We shall take the liberty of going into still further detail during the course of the statement of the French Public Prosecution for it should be fully known to what extent the Germans inspired by National-Socialist doctrine could stoop to dishonour.

The most terrible aspect is perhaps the desire to create moral degradation and debasement in the prisoner until he lost, if possible, all semblance of a human individual.

The usual living conditions imposed on the deportees in the camps were sufficient to ensure slow extermination through inadequate feeding, bad sanitation, the cruelty of the guards, the severity of the discipline, the strain of work out of proportion to the strength of the prisoner, and the haphazard medical service. Moreover you already know that many did not die a natural death, but were put to death by injections, the gas chambers, or from being inoculated with fatal diseases.

But more speedy extermination was often the case, it was often brought about by ill treatment: communal ice-cold showers in winter in the open air, prisoners left naked in the snow, cudgelling, dog bites, hanging by the wrist. Some figures will illustrate the result of these various methods of extermination. At Buchenwald, during the first period of 1945 there were 13,000 deaths out of 40,000 internees. At Dachau 13,000 to 15,000 died in the 3 months preceding the liberation. At Auschwitz, a camp of systematic extermination, the number of murdered persons came to several million.

As to the total number of those deported from France, the official figure is as follows:

Of 250,000 deported only 35,000 returned.

The deportees served as guinea pigs for numerous medical,

surgical or other experiments which generally led to their death. At Auschwitz, at Stuthoff in the prison at Cologne, at Ravensbruck, at Neurngeamme, numerous men, women and children were sterilized. At Auschwitz the most beautiful women were set apart, artificially fertilized and then gassed. At Stuthoff a special barrack, isolated from the others, by barbed wire, was used to inoculate men in groups of 40 with fatal illnesses. In the same camp women were gassed whilst German doctors observed their reactions through a peephole arranged for this purpose.

Extermination was often directly effected by means of individual or collective executions. These were carried out by shooting, by hanging, by injections, by gas lorry or gas chamber.

I should not wish to further stress the facts, already so numerous, submitted to your High Tribunal during the preceding days by the American Prosecution; but the representative of France, so many of whose citizens have died in these camps after horrible sufferings, could not pass in silence this tragic example of complete inhumanity. This would have been inconceivable in the 20th century if a doctrine of return to barbarism had not been established in the very heart of Europe.

* * * * * * *

[Pages 2916-2921 of Official Transcript]

As a consequence of such a doctrine [substituting an animalistic conception for a human one], the upsetting of the human condition does not only appear to be a means to which one has recourse in the presence of contrary opportunities such as those arising from war, but also it appears as an aim both necessary and desirable. The Nazis propose to classify mankind into 3 main categories. That of their adversaries or persons whom they consider inadaptable to their strange constructions: this category can be bullied in all sorts of ways and even destroyed. That of higher mankind which they claim is distinguishable by its blood or by some arbitrary means. That of inferior mankind, which does not deserve destruction and whose vital power should be used in a regime of slavery for the well-being of the "overlords," the masters. The Nazi leaders proposed to apply this conception everywhere where they could do so to territories more and more expansive; to populations becoming ever greater; and in addition they demonstrated the frightful ambition of succeeding in imposing it on intelligent people, of convincing their victims and of demanding from them, in addition to so many sacrifices, an act of faith. The Nazi war is a war of fanatical religion in which one can exterminate infidels and equally well force them to conversion. It should further be noted that the Nazis aggravated the excesses of those horrible times, for in a religious war converted adversaries were received like brothers, whereas the Nazis never gave their pitiable victims the chance of saving themselves even by the most complete recanting.

It is by virtue of these conceptions that the Germans undertook the Germanization of occupied territories, and had without doubt the intention of undertaking to Germanize the whole world. This Germanization can be distinguished from the ancient theories of pan-Germanism in as far as it is both a Nazification and an actual return to barbarism.

Racialism classifies occupied nations into two main categories; Germanization means for some a national socialist assimilation and for the others disappearance or slavery. For human beings classified as of higher races the most favoured condition assigned to them comprises the falling-in with the new concepts of the Germanic community. For human beings of the so-called "inferior race" it was proposed either to abolish all rights whilst awaiting and preparing their physical classification, or to assign them to servitude.

For both, racialism means acceptance of the Nazi myths.

This twofold program of absolute Germanization was not carried out in totality nor in all the occupied countries. The Germans had conceived it as a lengthy piece of labor, which they intended to carry out gradually, by a series of successive measures. This progressive approach is always characteristic of the Nazi method. It fits in, apparently, both with the variety of obstacles encountered, the hypocritical desire of sparing public opinion, and with a horrid lust for experimenting and scientific ostentation.

When the countries were liberated, the state of the Germanization varied a great deal according to the different countries, and in each country according to such and such a category of the population. At times the method was forced on to its extreme consequences; elsewhere one only discovers the appearance of preparatory arrangements.

But it is easy to note everywhere the trend of the same evil, interrupted at different moments in its development, but everywhere directed by the same inexorable movement.

As regards national status, the Germans proceeded on a pure and simple annexation basis in Luxemburg, in the Belgian cantons of Eupen and of Malmedy, and in the French depart-

The Trial and Punishment

ments of Alsace and of Lorraine. Here the criminal undertaking consisted in both the abolition of the sovereignty of the State, natural protector of its nationals, and the abolition for those nationals of the status they had as citizens of this State, a status recognized by domestic and international law.

The inhabitants of these territories thereby lost their original nationality, ceasing to be Luxemburgers, Belgians, or French. They did not acquire, however, full German nationality; they were admitted only gradually to this singular favor, on the further condition that they furnish certain justifications therefor.

The Germans sought to efface in them even the memory of their former country. In Alsace and in Moselle the French language was banned, names of places and of people were Germanized.

New citizens or mere subjects were equally subjected to the obligations relating to the Nazi regime; to forced labor naturally, and soon to military conscription. In case of resistance to these orders—unjust and abominable though they were, since it was a matter of arming the French against their allies and in reality against their own country—sanctions were brought to bear, not only against the parties concerned, but even against the members of their families, following the thesis of Nazi law, which brushes aside the fundamental principles of the law against repression.

Persons who appeared recalcitrant to Nazification, or even those who seemed of little use to Nazi enterprises, became the victims of large-scale expulsions, driven from their homes in a few short hours with their most scanty baggage, and despoiled of their property.

Yes this inhuman carrying away of entire populations, which will remain one of the horrors of our century, appears as favorable treatment when compared to the deportations which were to fill the concentration camps, in particular the Stuthof camp in Alsace.

At the same time that they oppressed the population by force and in contravention of all law, the Nazis undertook, according to their method, to convince the people of the excellence of their regime. The young people especially were to be educated in the spirit of National Socialism.

The Germans did not proceed to the annexation, properly speaking, of other areas than those we have named; it is beyond doubt, however, and confirmed by numerous indications, that they proposed to annex territories much more important by applying to them the same regime if the war had ended in victory.

But everywhere they prepared the abolition or the weakening of the national position by debarring or damaging the sovereignty of the state involved, and by forcing the destruction of patriotic feeling.

In all the occupied countries, whether or not there existed an apparent governmental authority, the Germans systematically disregarded the laws of occupation. They legislated, regulated, administered. Besides the territories actually annexed, the other occupied territories also found themselves in a state that might be defined as a state of pre-annexation.

This leads to a second aspect which is the attack on spiritual security. Everywhere, although with variation in time and space, the Germans applied themselves to abolishing the public freedoms, notably the freedom of association, the freedom of the press; and they endeavored to trammel the essential freedoms of the spirit.

The German authorities subordinated to the strictest censorship, even in matters devoid of military character, a press, many of whose representatives, moreover, were inspired by them. Manifold restrictions were imposed on the moving picture industry and commerce. Numerous works altogether without political character were banned, even textbooks. Religious authorities themselves saw their clerical province invaded and words of truth could not be heard.

After having curtailed freedom of expression even beyond the degree that a state of war and of occupation could have justified, the Germans developed their National Socialist propaganda systematically through the press, radio, film, meeting, book, poster.

All these efforts achieved so little result that one might attempt today to minimize their importance. Nevertheless, the propaganda conducted by means most contrary to the respect due human intelligence, and on behalf of a criminal doctrine, must go down in history as one of the shames of the National Socialist regime.

No less did the Germanization program compromise human rights in the other broad areas that we have defined: right of the family, right of professional and economic activity, juridical guarantees. These rights were attacked, these guarantees were curtailed.

The forced labor and the deportations infringed the rights of the family, as well as the rights of labor. The arbitrary ar-

The Trial and Punishment

rests suppressed the most elementary legal guarantees. In addition, the Germans tried to impose their own methods on the administrative authorities of the occupied countries and sometimes unfortunately succeeded in their attempts.

It is also known that racial discriminations were provoked against citizens of the occupied countries who were catalogued as Jews, measures particularly hateful, damaging to their personal rights, and to their human dignity.

All these criminal acts were committed counter to the rules of international law, and of the Hague Convention in particular, which limits the rights of armies occupying a territory.

The battle the Nazis waged against humanity completes the tragic and monstrous picture of the war criminality of Nazi Germany, which advanced under the banner of the abasement of man—a deliberate requirement of the National Socialist doctrine. This gives it its true character of a systematic attempt to return to barbarism.

Such are the crimes which National Socialist Germany committed while waging the war of aggression that she launched. The martyred peoples appeal to the justice of civilized nations and request your high Tribunal to condemn the National Socialist Reich in the person of its surviving chiefs.

Let the accused not be astonished at the charges brought against them and let them not dispute at all this principle of retroactivity, the permanence of which was guaranteed, against their wishes, by democratic legislation. War crimes are defined by international law and by the national law of all modern civilizations. The accused knew that acts of violence against the persons and property and human rights of enemy nationals were crimes for which they would have to answer before international justice.

The governments of the United Nations have addressed many a warning to them since the beginning of the hostilities.

* * * * * * *

[Page 2922 of Official Transcript]

The leaders of National Socialist Germany received other warnings. I refer to the speech of General de Gaulle of 13 January 1942; that of Churchill on 8 September 1942, the note of Mr. Molotov, Commissar of the People for Foreign Affairs of the Soviet Union, of 14 October 1942 and the second inter-allied declaration of 17 December 1942. The latter was made simultaneously at London, Moscow and Washington after receipt of information according to which the German authorities were engaged in exterminating the Jewish minorities in Europe. In this declaration, the Governments of Belgium, Czechoslovakia, Greece, Luxemburg, the Netherlands, Norway, Poland, the United States of America, the United Kingdom, the Soviet Union, Yugoslavia, and the French National Committee which represented the permanence of France, solemnly reaffirmed their will to punish the war criminals who are responsible for this extermination.

* * * * * * *

[Pages 2933-2934 of Official Transcript]

But perhaps it will seem to you that to doom to punishment hundreds of thousands of men who belonged to the SS, to SD, to the Gestapo, to the SA, awakens some objection. I should like to try to do away with that objection by showing you the dreadful responsibilities of these men.

Without the existence of these organizations, without the spirit which animated them, one would not succeed in understanding how so many atrocities could have been perpetrated. The systematic war of criminality could not have been carried out by Nazi Germany without these organizations, without the men who composed them. It is they who for Germany not only executed but willed this body of crime.

It may have seemed impossible to you that the monstrous barbarity of the National Socialist doctrine could have been imposed upon the German people, the heir, as are we, of the highest values of civilization. The education of the Nazi Party of the young men who formed the SS, the SD, and the Gestapo, expands the empire of Nazism over all Germany, the incarnated National Socialism, and permitted it to accomplish, thanks to the guilty passiveness of the whole German population, a part of its purpose. This youth, those who carried out the tenets of the regime were formed in a veritable doctrine of immoralism, which results from a notion of the world which served as inspiration for the regime. The myth of race . . . removed from criminal war its criminal character.

If it proved that a superior race is to annihilate races and peoples that are considered inferior and decadent, incapable of living a life as it should be lived, before what means of extermination will they recoil? The ethics of immorality, the result of the most authentic Nietzscheism, which considers the destruction of all conventional ethics is the supreme attitude of man. The crime against race is punished without pity. The crime on behalf of race is exalted without limit. The regime truly creates a logic of crime which obeys its own laws, which has

The Trial and Punishment

no connection whatsoever with what we consider ethical. With such a point of view, all horrors could have been justified and authorized. So many acts which appear incomprehensible to us, so greatly do they clash with our customary notions, were explained, were formulated in advance in the name of the racial community.

* * * * * * *

[Pages 2936-2937 of Official Transcript]

The truly diabolical enterprise of Hitler, and of his companions, was to assemble in a body of dogmas formed around the concept of race, all the instincts of barbarism, repressed by centuries of civilization, but always present within the depths of men, all the negations of the traditional values of humanity, without which nations, as well as individuals, question their conscience in the troubled hours of their evolution and of their life; to construct and to propagate a doctrine which organizes, regulates, and aspires to command crime.

The diabolical enterprise of Hitler, and of his companions, was also to appeal to the forces of evil in order to establish his domination over the German people, and subsequently the domination of Germany over Europe, and perhaps over the world. They planned to incorporate organized criminality into a system of war conduct, by unleashing within the whole nation the most savage passions.

Nationalism, and the service of their people and of their country, will perhaps be their explanation; far from constituting an excuse, if any excuse were possible in view of the enormity of their crime, these determining causes would make it still greater. They have profaned the sacred concept of country, linking it to a willed return to barbarism.

OPENING ADDRESS: R. H. RUDENKO

Excerpts from opening address of General R. H. Rudenko, Chief Prosecutor for the U.S.S.R., before the International Military Tribunal, Nurnberg, Germany, on 8 February 1946.

* * *

[Pages 4140-4150 of Official Transcript]

Having prepared and carried out the perfidious assault against the freedom-loving nations, Nazi Germany turned the war into a system of militarized banditry.

Mass murder of war prisoners, extermination of civilian populations, plunder of occupied territories and other war crimes, were committed as a part of a totalitarian lightning war, Blitzkrieg, projected by the Nazis. In particular, the terrorism practised by Nazis on the temporarily-occupied Soviet territories, reached fabulous proportions and was carried out with a fiendish cruelty.

"We must," said Hitler to Rauschnigg, "pursue a policy of systematic depopulation. If you ask me what I mean by the term 'depopulation,' I would tell you that I understand it as the complete removal of whole racial groups. And that is what I am going to do; such, roughly speaking, is my purpose. Nature is cruel, and so we have to be cruel too. If I can send the cream of the German nation into the hell of war . . . without any regret for the shedding of precious German blood, I have surely the right to remove millions of an inferior race, who multiply like flies!"

The Soviet Prosecution has at its disposal numerous documents, collected by the Extraordinary State Commission for the prosecution and investigation of crimes committed by the German Nazi aggressors and their accomplices, which constitute irrefutable evidence of countless crimes perpetrated by German authorities.

We have at our disposal a document, known as the "Appendix #2 to the Operational Order #8 of the Chief of the SIPO and SD, dated "Berlin, 17 June 1941", and signed by Heydrich who, at that time, held the office of Himmler's deputy. [Probably an earlier version of Documents 078-PS and 502-PS.] This document was worked out in collaboration with the High Command of the German Armed Forces. The ap-

The Trial and Punishment

pendices to Order #8, as well as Orders #9 and 14 and the appendices thereto, make it evident that the systematic extermination of Soviet people in Nazi concentration camps in the territories of U.S.S.R. and other countries occupied by the Nazi aggressors, was carried out under the form of "filtration, cleaning measures, purge, extraordinary measures, special treatment, liquidation, execution," and so on.

The perpetration of these crimes was entrusted to the "Sonderkommandos" especially formed for this purpose, by agreement between the Chief of Police and the SD and the High Command of the German Armed Forces.

The Appendix #1 to Order #14 shows that these "Sonderkommandos" acted independently on the basis of their special powers and in accordance with general directives given to them within the scope of camp regulations, maintaining close contact with the camp C.O.s and the officers of the counter intelligence.

It is to be noted that, during the German offensive aimed at Moscow, the Nazis created a special "Sonderkommando Moscow" which was supposed to carry out the mass killings of the inhabitants of Moscow.

Hitler's Government and the German Military Command were afraid that these monstrous Orders #8 and #14 might fall into the hands of the Red Army and the Soviet Government, and they took all possible measures to keep these Orders completely secret. In Order #14, Heydrich declared: "I especially emphasize that the Operational Orders #8 and #14, as well as the regulations pertaining thereto, must be immediately destroyed in case of imminent danger. Their destruction is to be reported to me."

Besides the above-mentioned orders, containing the program and plan for the Nazi annihilation of the Soviet population, numerous orders and regulations were issued to the civil "administration," as well as to the German military authorities, prescribing mass extermination, and mass execution of Soviet people. Keitel's order of 12 December 1941, reads as follows:

"In the Fuehrer's opinion the punishment by imprisonment or even life sentence would be considered as a symptom of weakness. Effective intimidation can be realized only by executions or measures which would leave the population in complete ignorance about the criminal's fate. This latter aim is reached through the deportation of criminals into Germany. The attached instructions for the prosecution of criminals is in accordance with the Fuehrer's opinion. It is approved by him. Keitel."

Nazi Germany's War Against the Jews

Among the diverse means employed by the Hitlerites for the extermination of Soviet citizens were also intentional infection with spotted fever and murder by poison gas in murder vans. Upon investigations by the Extraordinary State Commission of the Soviet Union it was found that at the front near their main line of defense, the Hitlerites had systematically constructed special concentration camps where they kept tens of thouands of children, women, not fit for work, and aged men. The approaches to these camps were mined. No barracks or shelters of any kind were built within the areas of the camps, and the internees had to camp on the bare ground. For the slightest infractions of established ruthless camp regulations, the internees were shot. Many thousands of typhus patients were found in these camps who, through contact with the population brought there by force from the surrounding villages, systematically infected them with the disease.

The document which will be presented by the Soviet Prosecution describes in detail these heinous crimes perpetrated by the German Fascist occupants.

The Prosecution possesses a document signed by the Untersturmfuehrer Becker May 16, 1942. This document [No. 501-PS] is a report to his superiors concerning the use of murder vans. This is what one reads in this monstrous document:

[General Rudenko then quoted excerpts from this document which will be found in Part I, Chapter 7, Page 41.]

The names have already been mentioned here of the camps of Maidanek and Auschwitz with their gas-chambers, in which over 5½ million people, citizens of Poland, Czechoslovakia, U.S.S.R., U.S.A., Great Britain, France and other democratic countries, people who were not guilty of a single offense, were killed. I must name the concentration camps of Smolensk, Stavropol, Kharkov, Kiev, Lwow, Poltava, Novgorod, Orel, Rowno, Dnepropetrovsk, Odessa, Kamenetz-Podolsk, Gomel, Kerch, of the Stalingrad region, of Kaunas, Riga, Mariampol, of the Lithouanian S.S.R., of Kloga, of the Esthonian S.S.R. and many others in which hundreds of thousands of Soviet citizens belonging to the civilian population, and also soldiers and officers of the Red Army, were tortured to death by the Hitlerites.

The Germans also carried out mass shootings of Soviet citizens in the Lisenitz forest, which is on the outskirts of Lwow in the direction of Tarnopol. It was to this forest that the Germans daily drove or brought in motor vehicles large parties of Soviet prisoners of war from the camp "Citadel," internees from the Yanov camp and from the Lwow prison as well as

The Trial and Punishment

peaceful Soviet citizens who had been seized on the squares and streets of Lwow in the course of numerous round-ups.

Investigation made by the Extraordinary State Commission established the fact that the Germans shot over 200 thousand people in the Lisenitz forest.

These mass murders, this arbitrary regime of terror, was fully approved by the defendant Rosenberg, in his speech at the meeting of the German Labor Front in November 1942:

"Apparently," declared Rosenberg, "if we are to subjugate all these peoples, (i.e. peoples inhabiting the territory of the U.S.S.R.), the arbitrary rule and tyranny will be an extremely suitable form of Government."

Later, when the Red Army started to clear of the German Fascist hordes the Soviet Union territory temporarily occupied by them, and when the organs of Soviet authorities began discovering abominable crimes perpetrated by Fascist monsters and finding numerous graves of Soviet citizens, soldiers and officers, tortured to death by the Fascists—the German command took urgent measures to conceal and destroy all traces of their crimes. For this purpose, the German command organized everywhere exhumations of corpses from the graves and their cremation. Special order of the Obersturmfuehrer, dated Rowno, 3 August 1943-IVAI-#35/43c, and addressed to the Regional Leader of Gendarmerie in Kamen-Kashirsk, prescribed "to supply immediately information concerning location and number of graves (common) of persons to whom special repressive measures were applied in the district."

Among the documents discovered in the Gestapo building of the Rowno district, has been found a report concerning the execution of the above-mentioned order with the enumeration of about 200 localities, where such graves were found. One can see by these lists, that the German Fascist henchmen chose as burial-grounds for the interment of their victims primarily secluded and isolated points.

At the end of the list, we read: "the list includes all the tombs, including those of the commandos which worked here previously."

I will now quote an extract of the appeal to the public opinion of the world of the representatives of several thousand former internees at Auschwitz:

"The gassing of countless numbers of people took place upon the arrival of 'transports' from various countries, including: France, Belgium, Holland, Greece, Italy, Hungary, Czechoslovakia, Germany, Poland, the U.S.S.R., Norway and others. The new arrivals had to pass before an SS doctor or else before the SS Commandant of the camp. The latter pointed his finger to the right or left. The left meant death by gas. Out of a transport of 1,500, an average of 1,200 to 1,300 were immediately sent to be gassed. Now and then, the quota of people who were sent to the camps was a little higher. It often occurred that the SS doctors Mengele and Thilo performed this selection whilst whistling a jolly ditty. The people, destined to be gassed, were obliged to undress in front of the gas-chambers, after which they were whipped into the gas-chamber. Then, the door of the underground gas-chamber was shut and the people were gassed.... Death came approximately four minutes later. After eight minutes the gas-chamber was opened, and workmen belonging to a special outfit, the so-called 'Sonderkommando,' transported the bodies to the cremation ovens which burned day and night.

"There was a shortage of ovens at the time of the arrival of transports from Hungary, consequently enormous ditches were dug for the purpose of burning the bodies. Fires made of wood soaked in gasoline were laid in these ditches and bodies were thrown therein. However, the SS men frequently hurled alive children and adults into those ditches, where the most unfortunate perished a terrible death. To effect a saving in gasoline, fats and oils necessary for cremations were often derived from the bodies of gassed peoples. Fats and oils for technical purposes and for the manufacture of soap were also obtained from bodies."

The petition ends with the following words: "Together with 10,000 saved inmates of all nationalities we demand that the crimes and the inconceivable atrocities of the Hitlerites should not remain unpunished."

This just demand is supported by the entire civilized world and by all freedom-loving peoples.

The organized mass annihilation of prisoners of war constitutes one of the vilest crimes of the Hitlerite conspirators.

Numerous facts of assassinations, tortures and maltreatment to which prisoners of war were subjected have been definitely established. They were tortured with red-hot irons, their eyes were gouged, their extremities were severed, etc.

The systematic atrocities and short shrift justice against captured officers and men of the Red Army were not chance episodes or the results of the criminal activities of individual officers of the German Army and German officials.

The Trial and Punishment

The Hitlerite Government and the High Command of the German Army ruthlessly exterminated prisoners of war. Numerous documents, orders and decrees of the Nazi Government and orders of the German Supreme Command testify to this.

As early as March 1941—as the German Lieutenant-General Osterreich testified during his interrogation—a secret conference took place at the headquarters of the High Command in Berlin, when measures were planned for the organization of camps for Russian prisoners of war, and "rules" laid down for their treatment. These "rules" and "measures" were essentially a plan for the extermination of Soviet prisoners of war, as is made clear in Osterreich's evidence.

Many Soviet prisoners of war were shot or hanged whilst others perished from hunger and infectious diseases, from cold and tortures, systematically employed by the Germans according to a plan which was developed beforehand and had as its object the mass extermination of Soviet persons.

In appendix 3 to order No. 8 of the Chief of the Security Police and SD, dated the 17th of July 1941, a list is given of Prisoner of War camps set up in the area of the 1st Military district and of the so-called Government-General. In the 1st Military district, camps were set up, in particular in Prokuls, Heidekrug, Schierwinds, Schutzenrode (Ebenrode) in Prostken, Suwalki, Fischbor-Tursen and Ostwlyenka. In the so-called Government-General, camps were set up at Ostrov-Mesovetzky, Sedlitz, Byelopedlasko, Kholm, Jaroslavl, etc. In the appendix to operational order No. 9, issued in development of order No. 8 of the 17th July 1942, lists are given of the camps for Soviet prisoners of war situated in the territory of military districts 2, 4, 6, 8, 10, 11 and 13, at Hammerstein, Schneidemuehl and many other places.

In these prisoner of war camps, as well as in camps for the civilian population, extermination and tortures were practiced, referred to by the Germans as "filtering, execution, special regime." The "Gross-Lazarett" set up by the Germans in the town of Slavuta has left grim memories. The whole world is familiar with the atrocities perpetrated by the Germans against Soviet prisoners of war and those of other democratic states at Auschwitz, Maidanek and many other camps.

The directives of the German Security Police and of the SD —worked out in collaboration with the Staff of the Supreme Command of the Armed Forces, whose chief was the defendant Keitel—were applied here. Operational order No. 8 stated:

"Executions must not take place in the camp or in the

immediate vicinity of the camp. If the camps in the Government-General are situated in the immediate vicinity of the frontier, the prisoners intended for special treatment should, if possible, be transported to former Soviet districts. Should executions be necessary owing to violations of camp discipline, the chief of the operational detachment should in this case approach the camp commandant.

"The activities of the 'Sonderkommandos' sanctioned by the Army commanders of the Rear Areas (district commandants dealing with affairs connected with prisoners of war) must be conducted in such a way as to carry out 'filtering' with as little notice as possible, while the liquidation must be carried out without delay and at such a distance from the transit camps themselves, and from populated places, as to remain unknown to the rest of the prisoners of war and to the population."

The following "form" for the carrying out of executions is recommended in Appendix 1 to Operational Order No. 14 of the Chief of the Security Police and SD, dated "Berlin, the 29th October 1941, No. 21 B/41 G R S—IV A.I.Z.: Chiefs of operational groups decide questions about execution on their own responsibility, and give appropriate instructions to the Sonderkommandos. In order to carry out the measures laid down in the directives issued, the Kommandos are to demand from the commandants of the camps the handing over to them of the prisoners. The High Command of the Army has issued instructions to the commandants for meeting such demands.

"Executions must take place unnoticed, in convenient places, and, in any event, not in the camp itself, nor in its immediate vicinity. It is necessary to take care that the bodies are buried immediately and properly."

The report of the Operational Kommando (Obersturmbannfuehrer Lipper to Brigadefuehrer, Dr. Thomas) in Vinnitza, dated December 1941, speaks of the way in which all the above-mentioned instructions were carried out. It is pointed out in this report that, after the so-called "filtering" of the camp, only 25 persons who could be classed as "suspects" remained in the camp at Vinnitza.

"This limited number," the report states, "is explained by the fact that the local organizations, in conjunction with the commandants or with the appropriate counter intelligence officers, daily undertook the necessary measures, in accordance with the rules of the Security Police, against the undesirable elements in the permanent Prisoner of War camps." Thus, apart from

The Trial and Punishment

the mass executions conducted by "Sonderkommandos," specially created for this purpose, the systematic extermination of Soviet persons was widely practiced by commandants and their subordinates in camps for Soviet prisoners of war.

Among the documents of the Extraordinary State Commission for the investigation of crimes committed by the Germans in the temporarily seized territories of the U.S.S.R., there are several notes of the People's Commissar for Foreign Affairs, V. M. Molotov, on the subject of the extermination of prisoners of war and of their cruel treatment, and in these notes numerous instances of these monstrous crimes of the Hitlerite Government and of the German Supreme Command are quoted.

The note of V. M. Molotov, the People's Commissar for Foreign Affairs, dated the 25th of November 1941, on the subject of the revolting bestialities of the German authorities against Soviet prisoners of war, addressed to all ambassadors and ministers plenipotentiary of the countries with which the U.S.S.R. had diplomatic relations, pointed out that Red Army soldiers were subjected by the German High Command and by the German military units to brutal tortures and killings. The wild Fascist fanatics stabbed and shot on the spot defenseless sick and wounded Red Army soldiers who were in the camps; they raped hospital nurses and workers, and brutally murdered representatives of the medical personnel.

A special count of the victims of executions was conducted, on the instructions of the German Government and the Supreme Command. Thus, the directive given in Appendix 2 to Heydrich's Order No. 8, points out the necessity for keeping an account of the executions performed, i.e., of the extermination of prisoners of war, in the following form: 1. Serial number; 2. Surname and first name; 3. Date and place of birth; 4. Profession; 5. Last place of domicile; 6. Grounds for the execution; 7. Date and place of the execution.

A further specification of the tasks to be carried out by the Sonderkommandos for the extermination of Soviet prisoners of war was given in operational order No. 14, of the Chief of the Security Police and SD dated the 29th of October 1941.

* * * * * * * *

[Page 4154 of Official Transcript]

Yet another secret document concerning the utilization of women workers from the Eastern territories for domestic labor in Germany has been presented to the Tribunal by the prosecution. This document is composed of excerpts from the report on a meeting held by Sauckel on the 3rd September 1942. I quote some of these excerpts:

1. "The Fuehrer has ordered that between 400,000 and 500,000 Ukrainian women aged between 15 and 35 be brought immediately for domestic labor."

2. "The Fuehrer has expressed categorically his desire that a large number of these girls should be Germanized."

3. "It is the Fuehrer's will that, in 100 years' time, 250 million German-speaking people should live in Europe."

4. "Consider these women workers from the Ukraine as workers from the East, and put the sign 'Ost' (East) on them."

5. "Gauleiter Sauckel declared that, apart from the introduction of women workers for domestic labor, it was intended to utilize an additional million workers from the East."

6. "References to the difficulty of bringing stocks of grain to Germany from other countries did not worry him, Sauckel, at all. He would find ways and means to utilize Ukrainian grain and cattle, by mobilizing all the Jews in Europe and making of them a living chain of conveyors to get all the necessary equipment to the Ukraine."

[Page 4162 of Official Transcript]

Side by side with the barbarous destruction and looting of villages, towns, and national cultural monuments, the Hitlerites also mocked at the religious feelings of the believers among the Soviet population.

They burnt, looted, destroyed, and desecrated on Soviet territory 1,670 Greek-Orthodox churches, 237 Roman Catholic churches, sixty-nine chapels, 532 synagogues, and 258 other buildings belonging to religious institutions.

[Pages 4166-4169 of Official Transcript]

At the disposal of the Soviet Prosecution are the notes of Martin Bormann, found in the archives of the German Foreign Office, and captured by the Soviet troops in Berlin, on the conference held by Hitler on 2 October, 1940. This document refers to occupied Poland. It will be submitted to the Tribunal. At the moment I shall only quote from it a few points of the Hitlerite leadership program. The conference started with the statement by Frank that his activities as Governor General could be considered very successful: the Jews in Warsaw and other cities were locked up in ghettos.

"Very soon Cracow will be entirely cleared of Jews. There

The Trial and Punishment

must be no Polish landlords," the document went on to state. "Wherever they may be, they must be exterminated, no matter how brutal this may sound.

"All representatives of the Polish intelligentsia must be exterminated. This sounds brutal, but such is the law of life. Priests will be paid by us and, as a result, they will preach what we want. If we find a priest acting otherwise, we will make short work of him. The task of the priest consists in keeping the Poles quiet, stupid and dull-witted. This is entirely in our interests. The lowest German workman and the lowest German peasant must always stand above any Pole economically."

A special place among the unheard-of crimes of the Hitlerites is occupied by the bloody butchery of the Slavonic and Jewish peoples. Hitler said to Rauschnigg:

"After all these centuries of whining about the protection of the poor and lowly, it is about time we decided to protect the strong against the inferior. It will be one of the chief tasks of German statesmanship for all times to prevent by every means in our power the further increase of the Slav races. Natural instincts bid all living beings not merely to conquer their enemies but destroy them. In former days it was the victor's prerogative to destroy entire tribes, entire peoples."

If your Honors please, you have already heard the testimony of the witness Erich von den Bach-Zelewsky about Himmler's aims, as given by him in his speech at the beginning of 1941.

In answer to a question by a representative of the Soviet Prosecution, the witness declared, "In Himmler's speech it was mentioned that it was necessary to cut down the number of Slavs by 30 million."

You see by this what monstrous proportions the criminal ideas of the Hitlerite fanatics attained.

The Hitlerites vented their ferocity particularly on the Soviet intelligentsia.

Even before the attack on the U.S.S.R., directives were prepared regarding the merciless annihilation of Soviet people for political and racial reasons.

In Appendix 2 to Operational Order No. 8 of the Chief of the Security Police and SD, dated the 17th of June, 1941, it was stated, "It is above all essential to ascertain the identity of all prominent government and party officials, particularly professional activists and revolutionaries, persons working for the Comintern, all influential members of the Communist Party of the U.S.S.R. and the affiliated organizations in the Central Committee and the district and regional committees, all people's commissars and their deputies, all former political commissars in the Red Army, leading personalities of the state institutions of the central and middle administrative levels, leading personalities in economic life, the Soviet Russian intelligentsia and all Jews."

In a directive of the 17th of June, 1941, for Security Police and SD detachments, it is pointed out that it is necessary to take such measures, not only against the Russian people, but also against the Ukrainians, Byelorussians, Azerbaidzhanians, Armenians, Georgians, Turks and other nationalities.

The Soviet Prosecution will present to the Tribunal actual documents and facts in this connection. The Fascist conspirators planned the extermination to the last man of the Jewish population of the world, and carried out this extermination throughout the whole of their conspiratorial activity from 1933 onwards.

My American colleague has already quoted Hitler's statement of the 24th of February, 1942, that "the Jews will be annihilated." In a speech by the Defendant Frank, published in the "Cracow Gazette" on the 18th of August, 1942, it is stated:

"Anyone who passes through Cracow, Lwow, Warsaw, Radom, or Lublin today must in all fairness admit that the efforts of the German administration have been crowned with real success, as one now hardly sees any Jews."

The bestial annihilation of the Jewish population took place in the Ukraine, in Byelorussia, and in the Baltic States. In the town of Riga some 80,000 Jews lived before the German occupation. At the moment of the liberation of Riga by the Red Army there were 140 Jews left there.

It is impossible to enumerate in an opening statement the crimes committed by the defendants against humanity. The Soviet Prosecution has at its disposal considerable documentary material which will be presented to the Tribunal.

If your Honors please, I am appearing here as the representative of the Union of Soviet Socialist Republics, which bore the main weight of the attack of the Fascist invaders and which contributed on an enormous scale to the smashing of Hitlerite Germany and its satellites.

On behalf of the Soviet Union, I charge the defendants on all the counts enumerated in Article VI of the Charter of the International Military Tribunal.

Together with the Chief Prosecutors of the United States of America, Great Britain and France, I charge the defendants

The Trial and Punishment

with having prepared and carried out a perfidious attack on the peoples of my country and on all freedom-loving nations.

I accuse them of the fact that, having initiated a world war, they, in violation of the fundamental rules of international law and of the treaties to which they were signatories, turned war into an instrument of extermination of peaceful citizens, an instrument of plunder, violence and pillage.

I accuse the defendants of the fact that, having proclaimed themselves to be the representatives of the "Master Race," a thing which they have invented, they set, wherever their domination spread, an arbitrary regime of tyranny; a regime founded on the disregard for the elementary principles of humanity.

Now, when as a result of the heroic struggle of the Red Army and of the Allied Forces, Hitlerite Germany is broken and overwhelmed, we have no right to forget the victims who have suffered. We have no right to leave unpunished those who organized and were guilty of monstrous crimes.

In the name of the sacred memory of millions of innocent victims of the Fascist terror, for the sake of the consolidation of peace throughout the world, for the sake of the future security of nations, we are presenting the defendants a just and complete bill which must be paid. This is a bill on behalf of all mankind, a bill backed by the will and the conscience of all freedom-loving nations.

May justice be done.

CLOSING ADDRESS: ROBERT H. JACKSON

Excerpts from closing address of Justice Robert H. Jackson, Chief Prosecutor for the United States, before the International Military Tribunal, Nurnberg, Germany, on 26 July 1946.

* * *

[Page 14341 of Official Transcript]

The Nazi movement will be of evil memory in history because of its persecution of the Jews, the most far-flung and terrible racial persecution of all time. Although the Nazi party neither invented nor monopolized anti-Semitism, its leaders from the very beginning embraced it, incited it, and exploited it. They used it as "the psychological spark that ignites the mob." After seizure of power, it became an official state policy. The persecution began in a series of discriminatory laws eliminating the Jews from the civil service, the professions, and economic life. As it became more intense, it included segregation of Jews in ghettos, and exile. Riots were organized by party leaders to loot Jewish business places and to burn synagogues. Jewish property was confiscated and a collective fine of a billion marks was imposed upon German Jewry. The program progressed in fury and irresponsibility to the "final solution." This consisted of sending all Jews who were fit to work to concentration camps as slave laborers, and all who were not fit, which included children under 12 and people over 50, as well as any others judged unfit by an SS doctor, to concentration camps for extermination. [Document No. 2605-PS.]

Adolf Eichmann, the sinister figure who had charge of the extermination program, has estimated that the anti-Jewish activities resulted in the killing of six million Jews. Of these, four million were killed in extermination institutions, and two million were killed by Einsatzgruppen, mobile units of the Security Police and SD which pursued Jews in the ghettos and in their homes and slaughtered them by gas wagons, by mass shooting in anti-tank ditches and by every device which Nazi ingenuity could conceive. [Document No. 2738-PS.] So thorough and uncompromising was this program that the Jews of Europe as a race no longer exist, thus fulfilling the diabolic "prophecy" of Adolf Hitler at the beginning of the war.

* * * * * * *

The Trial and Punishment

[Page 14354 of Official Transcript]

The same war purpose was dominant in the persecution of the Jews. In the beginning, fanaticism and political opportunism played a principal part, for anti-Semitism and its allied scapegoat, mythology, was a vehicle on which the Nazis rode to power. It was for this reason that the filthy Streicher and the blasphemous Rosenberg were welcomed at Party rallies and made leaders and officials of the State or Party. But the Nazis soon regarded the Jews as foremost amongst the opposition to the police state with which they planned to put forward their plans of military aggression. Fear of their pacifism and their opposition to strident nationalism was given as the reason that the Jews had to be driven from the political and economic life of Germany. Accordingly, they were transported like cattle to the concentration camps, where they were utilized as a source of forced labor for war purposes.

At a meeting held on 12 November 1938, two days after the violent anti-Jewish pogroms instigated by Goebbels and carried out by the Party Leadership Corps and the SA, the program for the elimination of Jews from the German economy was mapped out by Goering, Funk, Heydrich, Goebbels, and the other top Nazis. The measures adopted included confinement of the Jews in ghettos, cutting off their food supply, "Aryanizing" their shops, and restricting their freedom of movement. [Document No. 1816-PS.] Here another purpose behind the Jewish persecutions crept in, for it was the wholesale confiscation of their property which helped finance German rearmament. Although Schacht's plan to have foreign money ransom the entire race within Germany was not adopted, the Jews were stripped to the point where Goering was able to advise the Reich Defense Council that the critical situation of the Reich exchequer, due to rearmament, had been relieved "through the billion Reichsmark fine imposed on Jewry, and through profits accrued to the Reich in the Aryanization of Jewish enterprises." [Document No. 3575-PS.]

CLOSING ADDRESS: HARTLEY SHAWCROSS

Excerpts from closing address of Sir Hartley Shawcross, Chief Prosecutor for the United Kingdom of Great Britain and Northern Ireland, before the International Military Tribunal, Nurnberg, Germany, on 27 July 1946.

* * *

[Pages 14491-14493 of Official Transcript]

You will remember too the plan for Poland discussed in Hitler's train on 12th September 1939 by Ribbentrop, Keitel and Jodl as described in the evidence of the witness Lahausen and the discussion between Hitler, Schirach and Frank three weeks later after dinner in the Fuehrer's apartment.

"There should be one master only for the Poles—the German: two masters side by side cannot and must not exist and therefore all representatives of Polish intelligentsia are to be exterminated. This sounds cruel but such is the law of life."

Such were the plans for the Soviet Union, for Poland and for Czechoslovakia. Genocide was not restricted to extermination of the Jewish people or of the gypsies. It was applied in different forms to Yugoslavia, to the non-German inhabitants of Alsace-Lorraine, to the people of the Low Countries and of Norway. The technique varied from nation to nation, from people to people. The long term aim was the same in all cases.

The methods followed a similar pattern: first a deliberate programme of murder, of outright annihilation. This was the method applied to the Polish intelligentsia, to gypsies and to Jews. The killing of millions, even by the gas chambers and mass shootings employed, was no easy matter. The defendants and their confederates also used methods of protracted annihilation, the favourite being to work their victims to death, hence Himmler's bond with the Minister of Justice in September 1942 under which anti-social elements were handed over to the SS "to be worked to death." On the 14th of the same month Goebbels was recommending this method in terms:

"With regard to the destruction of social life Dr. Goebbels has the opinion that the following groups should be exterminated: Jews and gypsies unconditionally, Poles who have to serve 3-4 years of penal servitude, and Czechs and Germans who are sentenced to death or penal servitude for life or to security custody for life. The idea of exterminating them by labour is the best."

Another favourite technique of extermination was by starvation. Rosenberg, the great architect of this policy of national murder, told his collaborators in June 1941:—

"The object of feeding the German people stands this year without a doubt at the top of the list of Germany's claims on the East, and there the southern territories and the Northern Caucasus will have to serve as a balance for the feeding of the German people. We see absolutely no reason for any obligation on our part to feed also the Russian people with the products of that surplus territory. We know that this is a harsh necessity bare of any feelings. A very extensive evacuation will be necessary without any doubt and it is sure that the future will hold very hard years in store for the Russians."

The method applied in Alsace was deportation. A captured report reads:

"The first expulsion action was carried out in Alsace in the period from July to December, 1940: in the course of it, 105,000 persons were either expelled or prevented from returning. They were in the main Jews, gypsies and other foreign racial elements, criminals, anti-social and incurably insane persons, and in addition Frenchmen, and Francophiles. The Patois-speaking population was combed out by these series of deportations in the same way as the other Alsatians."

The report goes on to state that new deportations are being prepared and after reciting the categories affected, sums up the measures being taken:

"The problem of race will be given first consideration and this in such a manner that persons of racial value will be deported to Germany proper and racially inferior persons to France."

The Nazis also used various biological devices, as they have been called, to achieve genocide. They deliberately decreased the birthrate in the occupied countries by sterilization, castration and abortion, by separating husband from wife and men from women and obstructing marriage.

* * * * * * *

[Page 14496 of Official Transcript]

The immediate needs of the war machine no doubt saved the Western Territories from similiar destruction but the Tribunal have ample evidence of the plunder of France, the Low Countries and the other territories which these men exploited to the utmost possible extent. In view of the nature of their murderous policy, it is not surprising that the men charged by the defendants to carry it out were brutes. In Rosenberg's domain, for instance, there was Koch, who was recommended by Rosenberg for the post of Commissar in Moscow because of the very fact of his "absolute ruthlessness." It was Koch who caused the slaughter of several hundred innocent human beings in the Zuman wood area so that he could have a private hunting reserve. Another of Rosenberg's agents was Kube, who wrote:

> "We have liquidated in the last ten weeks about 55,000 Jews in White Ruthenia. In the territory Minskland, Jewry has been eliminated without endangering the manpower demands: in the pre-eminently Polish territory Lida 16,000 Jews, in Zlonin 8,000 Jews and so forth have been liquidated."

* * * * * * *

[Pages 14498-14507 of Official Transcript]

There is one group to which the method of annihilation was applied on a scale so immense that it is my duty to refer separately to the evidence. I mean the extermination of the Jews. If there were no other crime against these men, this one alone, in which all of them were implicated, would suffice. History holds no parallel to these horrors.

As soon as the prospect of a Second World War became a certainty, Streicher, who had preached this infamous doctrine as far back as 1925, began in earnest to advocate annihilation. As he, on his own admission, had been instrumental in effecting the Nurnberg Decrees by years of propaganda in favour of racial laws, so now, in January 1939, anticipating the war which was to come, he began, in articles published in the Stuermer with "the full support of the highest Reich authority," to demand with all vehemence the physical extinction of the Jewish race. Unless words have completely lost their meaning, what do these mean but murder:

"They must be exterminated root and branch"
"Then will the criminal race be forever eradicated"
"Then will they slay the Jews in masses"
"Prepare a grave from which there can be no resurrection"

Almost immediately after the war had started the organized extermination of the Jewish race began. Hoess has told you:

> "The final solution of the Jewish question means the complete extermination of all Jews in Europe. I was ordered to establish extermination facilities in Auschwitz in June

The Trial and Punishment

1941. At that time there were already in the Government General 3 other extermination camps, Belzek, Treblinka and Wolzek."

Already the Jews in Germany and Poland had been concentrated in the ghettos of the Government General. Over dinner in the Fuehrer's apartment in October 1940, Frank had explained and I quote:

"The activities in the Government General could be termed very successful. The Jews in Warsaw and other cities were now locked up in ghettos, Krakow would very shortly be cleared of them. Reichsleiter von Schirach remarked that he still had more than 50,000 Jews in Vienna when Dr. Frank would have to take over from him."

When the order actually came, therefore, the preparatory measures, so far as they affected Poland and Germany, had already been taken. Of the destruction of the ghettos and the slaughter of their populations General Stroop's report on the Warsaw action is eloquent evidence. But the fate of the Jews in Warsaw was only typical of the fate of the Jews in every other ghetto in Poland.

When they were not slaughtered in the ghettos themselves, they were transported to the gas chambers. Hoess, Commandant of Auschwitz, described the procedure:

"I visited Treblinka to find out how they carried out their exterminations. The Camp Commandant at Treblinka told me that he had liquidated 80,000 in the course of one half-year. He was principally concerned with the liquidation of the Jews from the Warsaw ghetto."

Hoess describes the improvements that he made at Auschwitz. He introduced the new gas, Cyclon B, which

"took from 3-15 minutes to kill the people in the death chamber, dependent upon climatic conditions. We knew when the people were dead because their screaming stopped.... Another improvement we made over Treblinka was that we built our gas chambers to accommodate 2,000 people at a time, whereas at Treblinka their 10 gas chambers only accommodated 200 people each."

And he describes the selection of the victims from the daily transports that arrived:

"Those who were fit for work were sent into the camp. Others were sent immediately to the extermination plant. Children of tender years were invariably exterminated since, by reason of their youth, they were unable to work. Still another improvement we made over Treblinka was that at Treblinka the victims almost always knew they were to be exterminated and at Auschwitz we endeavoured to fool the victims into thinking that they were going through delousing process. Of course, frequently they realized our true intentions. Very frequently the women would hide their children under their clothes but of course when we found them we would send the children in to be exterminated. We were required to carry out these exterminations in great secrecy, but of course the foul and nauseating stench from the continuous burning of bodies permeated the entire area and all the people living in the surrounding communities knew that exterminations were going on at Auschwitz."

So also must they have known in the districts surrounding Belzek, Treblinka, Wolzek, Mauthausen, Sachsenhausen, Flossenburg, Neuengamme, Gusen, Natzweiler, Lublin, Buchenwald and Dachau.

I do not repeat these things in order to make the blood run cold. It is right that a few of these typical matters should be extracted from the great mass of the evidence which is accumulated here so that one may see this thing in its true perspective and appreciate the cumulative effect of what has been proved.

Whilst the German Armies surged into Russia and the Baltic States, the Einsatz Commandos followed in their wake. Their dreadful work had been planned and prepared in advance. In the file describing the operations of the Task Force A there is a map of the Baltic countries showing the number of Jews that were living in each State who were to be hounded out and killed. Another map shows the results achieved after those two or three months' work—a total of 135,567 Jews destroyed. In another report on their operations during October 1941, it is proudly stated that they continued "on the march with the advancing troops into the sectors which have been assigned to them."

These actions were not only the work of the SS and Himmler. They were carried out in co-operation with the Army Commanders with the full knowledge of Keitel and Jodl and, indeed, because every soldier fighting in the East must have known about them, with the knowledge also of every member of the Government and of the commanders of its Armed Forces.

"Our task," so states the report of the Task Force A, "was hurriedly to establish personal contact with the commanders of the armies and with the commander of the rear army. It must

The Trial and Punishment

be stressed from the beginning that co-operation with the armed forces was generally good. In some cases, for instance, with Panzer Group 4 under Col. Gen. Hoeppner, it was very close, almost cordial."

The German Generals were "almost cordial" as they weltered in the blood of hundreds of thousands of helpless, innocent men, women and children. Perhaps they enjoyed this work—in the same way as the members of the Einsatz Commandos themselves apparently enjoyed it.

"It should be mentioned," states the report, "that the leaders of the armed SS and of the uniformed police, who are reserves, have declared their wish to stay on with the Security Police and the SD."

*   *   *   *   *   *   *

Nor was it only cordiality and understanding that the army authorities showed. In some cases they themselves took the initiative. After describing the murder of inmates of lunatic asylums that had fallen into their hands, the Einsatz Commando report continues:

"Sometimes authorities of the Armed Forces asked us to clear out in a similar way other institutions which were wanted as billets. However, as the interests of the Security Police did not require any intervention, it was left to the authorities of the Armed Forces to take the necessary action with their own forces."

*   *   *   *   *   *   *

How can operations of this kind, extending for months and years over vast territories, carried out with the co-operation of the Armed Forces as they advanced and in the rear areas that they administered have remained unknown to the leaders in Germany? Even their own Commissioners in the occupied territories protested. In October 1941 the Commissioner for White Ruthenia was forwarding to the Reich Commissioner for Eastern Territories at Riga a report on the operations in his district. Some idea of the horror of those operations can be seen from the report:

"Regardless of the fact that the Jewish people, among whom were also tradesmen, were mistreated in a terribly barbarous way in the face of the White Ruthenian people, the White Ruthenians themselves were also worked over with rubber clubs and rifle butts ... the whole picture was generally more than ghastly ... I was not present at the shooting before the town. Therefore I cannot make a statement on its brutality. But it should suffice if I point out that persons shot have worked themselves out of their graves some time after they had been covered."

But protests of this kind were of no avail; the slaughter continued with unabated ghastliness.

In February 1942, in Heydrich's activity and situation report on the Einsatz Commandos in the U.S.S.R. of which a copy was addressed to Kaltenbrunner personally, it was stated:

"We are aiming at cleansing the Eastern countries completely of Jews . . . Estonia has already been cleared of Jews. In Latvia the number of Jews in Riga, of which there were 29,500 has now been reduced to 2,500."

By June 1943, the Commissioner for White Ruthenia was again protesting. After referring to 4,500 enemy dead, he says:

"The political effect of this large scale operation upon the peaceful population is simply dreadful in view of the many shootings of women and children."

The Reich Commissar for Eastern Territories, forwarding that protest to Rosenberg, the Reich Minister for Occupied Eastern Territories in Berlin, added:

"The fact that Jews receive special treatment requires no further discussions. However, it appears hardly believable that this is done in the way described in the report of the General Commissar. What is Katyn against that? Imagine only that these occurrences would become known to the other side and exploited by them. Most likely such propaganda would have no effect if only because people who read and heard about it simply would not be ready to believe it."

How true that comment is. Are we ready even now to believe it? Describing the difficulty of distinguishing between friend and foe, he says:

"Nevertheless it should be possible to avoid atrocities and to bury those who have been liquidated. To lock men, women and children into barns and set fire to them does not appear to be a suitable method of combating bands, even if it is desired to exterminate the population. This method is not worthy of the German cause and hurts our reputation severely."

Of these Jews murdered in White Ruthenia, over 11,000 were slaughtered in the district of Libau, and 7,000 of them had been killed in the naval port itself.

How can any of these defendants plead ignorance of these things? When Himmler was speaking of these actions openly

The Trial and Punishment

amongst his SS Generals and all the officers of his SS Divisions in April 1943, he told them:

"Anti-Semitism is exactly the same as delousing. Getting rid of lice is not a question of ideology. It is a matter of cleanliness. In just the same way, anti-Semitism for us has not been a question of ideology but a matter of cleanliness which now will soon have been dealt with. We shall soon be deloused. We have only 20,000 lice left, and then the matter is finished off within the whole of Germany."

And again in October of that year:

"Most of you must know what it means when 100 corpses are lying side by side, or 500, or 1,000."

Meanwhile, the mass murder of the Jews at Auschwitz and the other extermination centres was becoming a State industry with many by-products. Bales of hair, some of it, as you will remember, still plaited as it had been shorn off the girls' heads, tons of clothing, toys, spectacles and other articles went back to the Reich to stuff the chairs and clothe the people of the Nazi State. The gold from their victims' teeth, 72 transports full, went to fill the coffers of Funk's Reichsbank. On occasion, even the bodies of their victims were used to make good the wartime shortage of soap.

The victims came from all over Europe. Jews from Austria, Czechoslovakia, Hungary, Rumania, Holland, Soviet Russia, France, Belgium, Poland and Greece were being herded together to be deported to the extermination centers or to be slaughtered on the spot.

In April 1943, Hitler and Ribbentrop were pressing the Regent Horthy to take action against the Jews in Hungary. Horthy asked:

"What should he do with the Jews now that he had deprived them of almost all possibilities of livelihood; he could not kill them off. The Reich Foreign Minister declared that the Jews must be either exterminated or taken to concentration camps. There was no other possibility."

Hitler explained:

"In Poland the state of affairs had been fundamentally cleared up. If the Jews there did not want to work they were shot. If they could not work they had to succumb. They had to be treated like tuberculosis bacilli. This was not cruel if one remembered that even innocent creatures of nature, such as hares and deer, have to be killed so that no harm is caused by them."

In September 1942, Ribbentrop's State Secretary, Luther was writing:

"The Reich Foreign Minister has instructed me today by telephone to hasten as much as possible the evacuation of the Jews from different countries.... After a short lecture on the evacuation now in progress in Slovenia, Croatia, Rumania and the Occupied Territories, the Reich Foreign Minister had ordered that we are to approach the Bulgarian, Hungarian and Danish Governments with the goal of getting evacuation started in those countries."

By the end of 1944, 400,000 Jews from Hungary alone had been executed in Auschwitz. In the German Embassy in Bucharest, the files contained a memorandum:

"110,000 Jews are being evacuated from Bukovina and Bessarabia into two forests in the area of the river Bug.... The purpose of the action is the liquidation of these Jews."

Day by day, over years, women were holding their children in their arms and pointing to the sky while they waited to take their place in blood-soaked, communal graves. 12,000,000 men, women and children have died thus, murdered in cold blood; millions upon millions more today mourn their fathers and mothers, their husbands, their wives and their children. What rights has any man to mercy who has played a part—however indirectly—in such a crime?

Let Graebe speak again of Dubno:

[Sir Hartley then quoted at length from the vivid eye-witness description by Graebe of the murder of Jews at Dubno in the Ukraine in 1942. (Document 2992-PS) which will be found in Part I, Chapter 7, Page 52.]

*   *   *   *   *   *   *

[Pages 14517-14519 of Official Transcript]

It was not Himmler, but the Reich Foreign Minister who proudly reported to the Duce in February, 1943, that,

"All Jews had been transported from Germany and from the territories occupied by her to reserves in the East."

His bald recommendations to Horthy two months later and the record of the conference called by Steengracht, his permanent Under Secretary of State, betray the meaning of these ghastly euphemisms.

No one was more insistent on merciless action in the occupied territories than Ribbentrop. You will remember his advice to the Italians on how to deal with strikes:

"In such a case only merciless action is any good. In the

The Trial and Punishment

occupied territories we would not get anywhere with soft measures in the endeavour to reach an agreement."

Advice which he proceeded to reinforce by referring with pride to the successes of "brutal measures" in Norway, "brutal action" in Greece, and in France and Poland the success of "Draconian" measures.

Were Keitel and Jodl less involved in murder than their confederates? They cannot deny knowledge or responsibility for the operations of the Einsatz Commandos with whom their own Commanders were working in close and cordial cooperation. The attitude of the High Command to the whole question is typified by Jodl's remark about the evacuation of Danish Jews:

"I know nothing of this. If a political measure is to be carried out by the Commander, Denmark, the OKW must be notified by the Foreign Office."

You cannot disguise murder by calling it a political measure.

Kaltenbrunner, as chief of the RSHA, must be guilty. The Reports of the Einsatz Commandos were sent to him monthly. You will remember the words of Gisevius, a witness for the defense:

"We asked ourselves whether it was possible that an even worse man could possibly be found after such a monster as Heydrich . . . Kaltenbrunner came . . . and things got worse every day . . . We had the experience that perhaps the impulsive actions of a murderer like Heydrich were not as bad as the cold legal logic of a lawyer who was handling such a dangerous instrument as the Gestapo."

You will remember his description of those horrible luncheon parties at which Kaltenbrunner discussed every detail of the gas chambers and of the technique of mass murder.

Rosenberg's guilt as the philosopher and theorist who made the ground fertile for the seeds of Nazi policy is not in doubt, and it is beyond belief that he, as Reich Minister for Eastern Occupied Territories, did not know of and support the destruction of the ghettos and the operations of the Einsatz Commandos. In October, 1941, when the operations of those Commandos were at their height, one of Rosenberg's ministerial departmental chiefs was writing to the Reich Commissioner for the East in Riga informing him that the Reich Security Main Office had complained that he had forbidden the executions of the Jews in Libau and asking for a report upon the matter. On 15th November, the report comes back addressed to the Reich Minister for Occupied Eastern Territories:

"I have forbidden the wild execution of Jews in Liepaja because they were not justifiable in the manner in which they were carried out. I should like to be informed whether your enquiry of 31st October is to be regarded as a directive to liquidate all Jews in the East? Shall this take place without regard to age and sex and economic interests? ... Of course, the cleansing of the East of Jews is a necessary task; its solution, however, must be harmonized with the necessities of war production."

Frank—if it is not sufficient to convict him that he was responsible for the administration of the Government General and for one of the bloodiest and most brutal chapters in Nazi history—has himself stated:

"One cannot kill all lice and all Jews in one year."

It is no coincidence that that was exactly Hitler's language. And again:

"As far as the Jews are concerned, I want to tell you quite frankly that they must be done away with in one way or another ... Gentlemen, I must ask you to rid yourselves of all feeling of pity. We must annihilate the Jews wherever we find them and whenever it is possible in order to maintain the structure of the Reich as a whole ... We cannot shoot or poison 3,500,000 Jews, but we shall nevertheless be able to take measures which will lead to their annihilation."

Can Frick, as Minister of the Interior, have been unaware of the policy to exterminate the Jews? In 1941 one of his subordinates, Heydrich, was writing to another—the Minister of Justice:

"It may safely be assumed that in the future there will be no more Jews in the annexed Eastern territories."

Can he, as Reich Protector for Bohemia and Moravia deny responsibility for the deportations of thousands of Jews from his territory to the gas chambers of Auschwitz, only a few miles across the frontier?

Of Streicher one need say nothing. Here is a man more responsible, perhaps, than any, for the most frightful crime the world has ever known. For 25 years the extermination of the Jews had been his terrible ambition. For 25 years he had educated the German people in the philosophy of hate, of brutality, of murder. He had incited and prepared them to support the Nazi policy, to accept and participate in the brutal persecution and slaughter of millions of his fellow men. Without him these

The Trial and Punishment

things could not have been. It is long since he forfeited all right to live.

* * * * * * *

[Excerpts from Pages 14523-14529]

Can Raeder have been ignorant of the murder of thousands of Jews at Libau in the Baltic? You will remember the evidence that many were killed in the naval port and the facts reported by his naval officers at the Local Headquarters to Kiel. We now know from the report of the Commando which dealt with the Jews of Libau that at the end of January 1942 they had accounted for 11,860 in that district alone. Raeder who, on Heroes Day, 1939, spoke of the clear and inspiring summons to fight international Jewry. Do you really believe, when he was always helping individual Jews, he had never heard of the horrors of concentration camps or the murder of millions? Yet he still went on.

* * * * * * *

Von Schirach. What need one say of him? That it were better that a millstone had been placed around his neck. . . . ? It was this wretched man who perverted millions of innocent German children so that they might grow up and become what they did become—the blind instrument of that policy of murder and domination which these men carried out.

The infamous "Heu Aktion" by which between forty and fifty thousand Soviet children were kidnapped into slavery was a product of his work. You will remember the weekly SS reports on the extermination of the Jews found in his office.

* * * * * * *

As to Seyss-Inquart, you will remember Goering's instructions to him on the 26th March, 1938, to institute anti-Semitic measures in Austria, followed by the Progress Report on 12th November by one of his officials. As far as concerns the Jews in the Netherlands, he admits that he knew they were being deported but says he was powerless to stop it as it was ordered from Berlin. He has further said that he knew they went to Auschwitz but he says he was sent there to enquire about them, was told they were well off and arranged for them to send mail from Auschwitz to Holland. It is likely that Seyss-Inquart who admits knowledge of large-scale crimes against the Jews in the Netherlands, for example: "a drive to force the Jews to be sterilized," who admits that many and grave excesses occurred in the Netherlands concentration camps and indeed that in wartime he "considered that almost inevitable," who pleads that in comparison with camps elsewhere "it was perhaps not quite so bad in the Netherlands"—is it possible that he was really deceived as he says into thinking the people in Auschwitz were "comparatively well off?"

* * * * * * *

Neurath who has told the Tribunal that he joined Hitler's Government to keep it peace-loving and respectable, knew within a few weeks that the Jews were being persecuted, that reputable foreign papers and reputable German papers too for that matter were quoting official figures of ten to twenty thousand internees.

* * * * * * *

That reassurance [to Czechoslovakia at the time of the Anschluss] ought never be forgotten—there can be few things more grimly cynical than von Neurath who had listened to the Hosbach speech solemnly telling M. Mastny that Hitler would stand by the Arbitration Treaty with Czechoslokavia. As soon as Hitler had marched into Prague, he it was who became protector of Bohemia and Moravia. You have heard his admission that he applied all decrees for the treatment of the Jews which had appeared in Germany between 1933 and 1939.

* * * * * * *

On the 18th December 1941 he [Fritzsche] referred to the fate of European Jews in the following words:

"The fate of Jewry in Europe has turned out to be as unpleasant as the Fuehrer predicted it would be in the event of a European war. After the extension of the war instigated by the Jews, this unpleasant fate may also spread to the New World, for you can hardly assume that the nations of the New World will pardon the Jews for the misery of which the nations of the Old World did not absolve them."

There were few more dreadful or hate-provoking accusations among the whole miasma of Nazi lies against the Jews, than that of instigating the war which brought such misery to humanity, yet this educated and thoughtful defendant deliberately made it.

CLOSING ADDRESS: R. H. RUDENKO

Excerpts from Closing Address of General R. H. Rudenko, Chief Prosecutor for the U.S.S.R., before the International Military Tribunal, Nurnberg, Germany, on 29 July 1946.

* * *

[Page 14605 of Official Transcript]

The initiation of the systematic persecution and extermination of the Jewish population, is connected with the name of Goering.

It was he who signed the misanthropic Nurnberg decrees, the decrees for the expropriation of Jewish property, for the imposing on the Jews of the penalty of 1 billion marks and other decrees; such activity was in full keeping with . . . Goering's cannibalistic conception of the world.

At the trial Goering denied that he was an adherent of the racial theory whilst in 1935, he made a speech before the Reichstag in the defense of the Nurnberg racial provocators. On that occasion, he loudly declared:

". . . God has created races, He did not will equality and for this reason we reject energetically every attempt to pervert the idea of the purity of race. . . ."

* * * * * * *

[Page 14609 of Official Transcript]

The misanthropic Nurnberg laws, [Document No. 3179-PS] for the publishing of which the defendant [Hess] is also responsible, contain a special provision authorizing Frick and Hess to issue the necessary decrees to carry these laws into effect. Hess signed the law on the "protection of race and honour," the decree of 14 September 1935 depriving the Jews of their right to be employed at public offices, and also the decree of 20 May 1938 extending the Nurnberg laws to Austria. The question of the part played by Hess in organizing a network for spies and terroristic groups abroad, in creating SD (Security Service) and recruitment of SS units has been sufficiently elucidated at this trial.

* * * * * * *

[Page 14610 of Official Transcript]

The name of Martin Bormann is closely connected with the setting up of Hitler's regime. He was one of those who committed the most outrageous crimes, aiming at the annihilation of hundreds of thousands of people.

Nazi Germany's War Against the Jews

Together with the defendant Rosenberg, Bormann carried on a propaganda of racial theories and persecutions of Jews with cruel perseverance.

Numerous instructions were issued by him aiming at the discrimination of Jews in Hitlerite Germany, which afterward had such a fatal effect and resulted in the annihilation of Jews. By this activity of his, he won the confidence of Hitler, he was "authorized to represent the party in the field of government activity" (regulations and orders of the party chancellory v. II p. 228) and he did represent it.

Thus, as chief of the party chancellory, he directly participated in the annihilation of Jews, Gypsies, Russians, Ukrainians, Poles and Czechoslovaks.

* * * * * * *

[Page 14617 of Official Transcript]

Ribbentrop himself admitted at the Trial that he had negotiated with the Governments of European countries about the banishment of the Jews.

According to the record of Ribbentrop's conversation with Horthy, "The Minister of Foreign Affairs declared to Horthy that the Jews should be either exterminated or sent to concentration camps. There could be no other decision."

* * * * * * *

[Pages 14628-14630 of Official Transcript]

There is only one point of the accusation against Kaltenbrunner, on which I deem it necessary to dwell. Together with other RSHA organizations, Kaltenbrunner took over from Heydrich five "Einsatzgruppen." The citizens of the Soviet Union remember well these criminal organizations of German Fascism, headed by Kaltenbrunner.

The "Einsatzgruppe A" reached the approaches to Leningrad. It created the "Fort of Death #9" near Kaunas, the secret points for mass extermination of human beings in Panarai; it carried out the executions by shooting in the woods of Salaspinsk and Bikerneksk near Riga; it erected gallows in the parks of one of Leningrad's suburbs—the Pushkino.

The "Einsatzgruppe B" settled down in the vicinity of Smolensk. It burnt alive the peasants of Byelorussia; it shot down the victims of the awful Pinsk "action"; it drowned thousands of Byelorussian women and children in the Masyr marshes; it operated with murder vans in Minsk; it liquidated the ghetto in the Upper Gardens district of Smolensk.

The "Einsatzgruppe C" was quartered in Kiev. This group carried on the mass "action" in Babiyar near Kiev, an execu-

The Trial and Punishment

tion unmatched for its cruelty, when 100,000 Soviet citizens perished on a single day.

The "Einsatzgruppe D" operated in the southern regions of the temporarily occupied territories of the Soviet Union. This group was the first to experiment with the murder vans on the Soviet citizens in the district of Stavropol and in Krasnodar.

And when Kaltenbrunner's fate will be decided, all these human beings, asphyxiated in the "murder vans" near Stavropol, buried alive in the graves near Kiev and Riga, burnt alive in the Byelorussian villages, can not be forgotten.

All these innocent victims are on his dirty conscience.

* * * * * * *

[Pages 14631 of Official Transcript]

The important fact is that Rosenberg, having assembled all these excrements of science, raised the racial theories to a degree of racial fanaticism, and educated in this spirit the members of the Nazi party and the German youth. And when the representatives of the "master race" elaborated and committed acts of aggression, when the German oppressors enslaved and exterminated nations and peoples, when the factories of death were created at Maidanek and Auschwitz, Rosenberg's share in all these crimes was great.

All this was the outcome of the Fascist racial ideology, the essence of which consists in the idea that the "Aryan, north-Germanic" race is a "master race," and that all other races and nations belong to "lower strata."

* * * * * * *

[Page 14636 of Official Transcript]

And finally, I shall speak about the ridiculous theory of Rosenberg's so-called "noble anti-Semitism." It is absurd to argue with Rosenberg's counsel, who affirms that there exists such a thing as a "noble anti-Semitism," and all the more absurd it is to argue with Rosenberg. In my statement to the Tribunal, I threw light upon the Fascist propaganda contained in the defense speeches. Now, I would like to recall to the Tribunal the text of two of Rosenberg's documents:

In his directive of 29 April 1941, he wrote:

"The general solution of the Jewish problem must at the present moment be carried out by methods of a temporary character. Slave labor for Jews, the creation of Ghettos, etc., must be the solution of this problem." [Document No. 1024-PS]

[Page 14637 of Official Transcript]

Even more cynical and frank is the statement made by Rosenberg in November 1942, when he, in his capacity of Minister for the Occupied Eastern Territories, addressed a conference of the German labor front:

"We must not be satisfied," said Rosenberg, "with the deportation of Jews to another country and with the creation here or there of a large Jewish ghetto; no, our object must always remain the same. The Jewish problem in Europe and in Germany will be solved only when there are no more Jews left on the European continent."

And the operations "Kotbus", the extermination of Jews in the Baltic towns, in the Ukraine and Byelorussia [Document No. R-135]—all these were carried out in conformity with Rosenberg's theories and with his agreement.

* * * * * *

[Page 14641 of Official Transcript]

It was not Frank's fault, that as early as in 1944, dreaming to make "minced meat" of the Poles and Ukrainians he was compelled to add: "If we win the war." At this time he could not be as emphatic in his utterings as on 2 August 1943, when at the reception of the Party speakers in the Royal Palace in Cracow he spoke about the exterminated Polish Jews:

"Here we started out with 3,500,000 Jews; now but a few workers remain from this number. All the others, we shall some day say, emigrated."

* * * * * *

[Pages 14643-14644 of Official Transcript]

His counsel even tried to represent Frank as "a singularly peaceful anti-Semite," who, entertaining a negative attitude towards the Jewish people, never initiated massacres of the Jews or even instigated them. It is incomprehensible in this case how the following words of Frank would be interpreted by the counsel:

"The Jews are a race that should be exterminated. Wherever we catch even one he shall be done away with."

Or his declaration at the government meeting of 12 August 1942, when he said:

"That 1.2 million Jews have been condemned by us to starvation is quite comprehensible. It stands to reason that if these Jews do not die of starvation, this will lead to precipitated active measures directed against the Jews."

The Trial and Punishment

[Pages 14648-14649 of Official Transcript]

Notwithstanding the fact that during the war years, the defendant Julius Streicher did not formally hold functions directly connected with the perpetration of murders and mass executions, it is hard to overestimate the crimes committed by this man.

Together with Himmler, Kaltenbrunner, Pohl and those who conceived, constructed and switched into action the gas chambers and gas wagons; together with those who personally committed mass actions, Streicher must bear responsibility for the most cruel crimes of German Fascism.

The inflaming of national and racial dissension, the cultivation of depraved cruelty and the calling to murder—all this was not only the Party function of this man, but also the source of his income.

And it is not by accident, that in his greeting to Streicher dated April 1937, which is already known to the Tribunal, Himmler expressed his high esteem for the merits of "Der Stuermer" and of its publisher.

One can consider Streicher as the actual spiritual father of those who quartered the children of Treblinka. Had it not been for the "Stuermer" and its publisher, German Fascism would not have been able to educate at such short notice those mass cadres of murderers who personally put into effect the criminal plans of Hitler and his gang, by murdering over 6 million European Jews.

Over a period of many years, Streicher spiritually corrupted the children and youth of Germany. The so-called "children's editions" of the "Stuermer" have been submitted to the Tribunal.

And therefore, together with Baldur von Schirach, Streicher must bear responsibility for the selection of Jewish children from the Lwow ghetto, for target practice by the morally depraved "Hitler Jugend." It is not by accident, that von Schirach held in so high an esteem Streicher's "historical merits."

The fanatical "Nurnberg Laws" were only the "beginning of the struggle" for this "Number One Judeophobe" as he called himself, who was also the organizer of the first Jewish pogroms. As the Tribunal can recall, after these laws were issued, Streicher called for the physical extermination of the Jews in Europe and he wrote: "This problem will only be solved when world Jewry is exterminated."

I will not dwell again, either, on the shameless and mendacious "ritual numbers" of the Stuermer, which were to incite the SS men towards the killing of millions of guiltless persons and to justify any atrocity directed against the Jews. These proofs of Streicher's guilt which, among others, were submitted to the Tribunal, are of common knowledge and not subject to any doubt.

In 1939 he anticipated Maidanek and Treblinka and wrote that "perhaps graves alone" will testify to the previous existence of Jews in Europe.

In 1943, when the gas chambers of Treblinka and Auschwitz were already engulfing millions of victims, the "Stuermer" published articles inciting to the liquidation of the ghetto, articles which were full of lies and maliciousness and finally the "Stuermer" could state with sadistic satisfaction that:

"The Jews of Europe have disappeared."

Streicher lied all his life. He attempted to lie, here in Court. I do not know whether he believed he would be able to deceive anybody by these lies, or whether he lied from habit or out of fear.

But it seems to me that it must be apparent, even to the defendant himself, that his last lie will not deceive anybody and will not bring about his salvation.

* * * * * * *

[Page 14659 of Official Transcript]

In his capacity of Reich Deputy and Gauleiter of Vienna, Schirach directed personally the eviction of 60,000 Jews from Vienna, who afterwards were exterminated in the concentration camps of Poland. The documents presented by the Prosecution—weekly reports addressed to Schirach—prove the fact that he was informed of all the numerous crimes perpetrated by the German armed forces and the occupation authorities in the East, and, in particular, about the tragic fate of the tens of thousands of Jews deported from Vienna.

THE JUDGMENT

Excerpts from Judgment of International Military Tribunal, delivered at Nurnberg, Germany, 30 September 1946.

* * *

THE UNITED STATES OF AMERICA, THE FRENCH REPUBLIC, THE UNITED KINGDOM OF GREAT BRITAIN AND NORTHERN IRELAND, AND THE UNION OF SOVIET SOCIALIST REPUBLICS
—against—
HERMANN WILHELM GOERING, RUDOLF HESS, JOACHIM VON RIBBENTROP, ROBERT LEY, WILHELM KEITEL, ERNST KALTENBRUNNER, ALFRED ROSENBERG, HANS FRANK, WILHELM FRICK, JULIUS STREICHER, WALTER FUNK, HJALMAR SCHACHT, GUSTAV KRUPP VON BOHLEN UND HALBACH, KARL DOENITZ, ERICK RAEDER, BALDUR VON SCHIRACH, FRITZ SAUCKEL, ALFRED JODL, MARTIN BORMANN, FRANZ VON PAPEN, ARTUR SEYSS-INQUART, ALBERT SPEER, CONSTANTIN VON NEURATH, and HANS FRITZSCHE, individually and as Members of any of the Following Groups or Organizations to which They Respectively Belonged, **Namely:** DIE REICHSREGIERUNG (REICH CABINET); DAS KORPS DER POLITISCHEN LEITER DER NATIONAL-SOZIALISTISCHEN DEUTSCHEN ARBEITERPARTEI (LEADERSHIP CORPS OF THE NAZI PARTY); DIE SCHUTZSTAFFELN DER NATIONAL-SOZIALISTISCHEN DEUTSCHEN ARBEITERPARTEI (commonly known as the "SS") and including DIE SICHERHEITSDIENST (commonly known as the "SD"); DIE GEHEIME STAATS-POLIZEI (SECRET STATE POLICE, commonly known as the "GESTAPO"); DIE STURMABTEILUNGEN DER NSDAP (commonly known as the "SA") and the GENERAL STAFF and HIGH COMMAND of the GERMAN ARMED FORCES all as defined in Appendix B to the Indictment.

The International Military Tribunal in Session at Nurnberg, Germany

THE RT. HON. LORD JUSTICE LAWRENCE (member for the United Kingdom of Great Britain and Northern Ireland) President

THE HON. MR. JUSTICE BIRKETT (alternate member for the United Kingdom of Great Britain and Northern Ireland)

THE HON. FRANCIS BIDDLE (member for the United States of America)
THE HON. JOHN J. PARKER (alternate member for the United States of America)
M. LE PROFESSEUR DONNEDIEU DE VABRES (member for the French Republic)
M. LE CONSEILLER FALCO (alternate member for the French Republic)
MAJOR-GENERAL JURISPRUDENCE I. T. NIKITCHENKO (member for the Union of Soviet Socialist Republics)
LT.-COLONEL A. F. VOLCHKOV (alternate member for the Union of Soviet Socialist Republics)

Prosecutors

Mr. Justice Robert H. Jackson:
 Chief Prosecutor for the United States of America.
M. Champetier de Ribes:
 Chief Prosecutor for the French Republic.
Rt. Hon. Sir. Hartley Shawcross, KC, MP.:
 Chief Prosecutor for the United Kingdom of Great Britain and Northern Ireland.
State Counsellor of the 2nd Class, R. H. Rudenko:
 Chief Prosecutor for the Union of Soviet Socialist Republics.

JUDGMENT

The Court:

On the 8th August 1945, the Government of the United Kingdom of Great Britain and Northern Ireland, the Government of the United States of America, the Provisional Government of the French Republic, and the Government of the Union of Soviet Socialist Republics entered into an agreement establishing this Tribunal for the trial of War Criminals whose offences have no particular geographical location. In accordance with Article 5, the following Governments of the United Nations have expressed their adherence to the Agreement:

Greece, Denmark, Yugoslavia, the Netherlands,
Czechoslovakia, Poland, Belgium, Ethiopia, Australia,
Honduras, Norway, Panama, Luxemburg, Haiti, New Zealand,
India, Venezuela, Uruguay, and Paraguay.

By the Charter annexed to the Agreement, the constitution, jurisdiction and functions of the Tribunal were defined.

The Tribunal was invested with power to try and punish

The Trial and Punishment

persons who had committed crimes against peace, war crimes and crimes against humanity as defined in the Charter.

The Charter also provided that at the trial of any individual member of any group or organization the Tribunal may declare (in connection with any act of which the individual may be convicted) that the group or organization of which the individual was a member was a criminal organization.

In Berlin, on the 18th October 1945, in accordance with Article 14 of the Charter, an indictment was lodged against the defendants named in the caption above, who had been designated by the Committee of the Chief Prosecutors of the signatory Powers as major war criminals.

A copy of the indictment in the German language was served upon each defendant in custody at least thirty days before the Trial opened.

This indictment charges the defendants with crimes against peace by the planning, preparation, initiation and waging of wars of aggression, which were also wars in violation of international treaties, agreements and assurances: with war crimes: and with crimes against humanity. The defendants are also charged with participating in the formulation or execution of a common plan or conspiracy to commit all these crimes. The Tribunal was further asked by the Prosecution to declare all the named groups or organizations to be criminal within the meaning of the Charter.

The defendant Robert Ley committed suicide in prison on the 25th October 1945. On the 5th November 1945 the Tribunal decided that the defendant Gustav Krupp von Bohlen und Halbach could not then be tried because of his physical and mental condition, but that the charges against him in the indictment should be retained for trial thereafter, if the physical and mental condition of the defendant should permit. On the 17th November 1945 the Tribunal decided to try the defendant Bormann in his absence under the provisions of Article 12 of the Charter. After argument, and consideration of full medical reports, and a statement from the defendant himself, the Tribunal decided on the 1st December 1945 that no grounds existed for a postponement of the trial against the defendant Hess because of his mental condition. A similar decision was made in the case of the defendant Streicher.

In accordance with Articles 16 and 23 of the Charter, Counsel were either chosen by the defendants in custody themselves, or at their request were appointed by the Tribunal. In his absence the Tribunal appointed Counsel for the defendant Bormann, and also assigned Counsel to represent the named groups or organizations.

The Trial which was conducted in four languages—English, Russian, French and German—began on the 20th November 1945, and pleas of "Not Guilty" were made by all the defendants except Bormann.

The hearing of evidence and the speeches of Counsel concluded on 31st August 1946.

403 open sessions of the Tribunal have been held. 33 witnesses gave evidence orally for the Prosecution against the individual defendants, and 61 witnesses, in addition to 19 of the defendants, gave evidence for the Defense.

A further 143 witnesses gave evidence for the Defense by means of written answers to interrogatories.

The Tribunal appointed Commissioners to hear evidence relating to the organizations, and 101 witnesses were heard for the Defense before the Commissioners, and 1,809 affidavits from other witnesses were submitted. Six reports were also submitted, summarizing the contents of a great number of further affidavits.

38,000 affidavits signed by 155,000 people were submitted on behalf of the Political Leaders, 136,213 on behalf of the SS, 10,000 on behalf of the SA, 7,000 on behalf of the SD, 3,000 on behalf of the General Staff and OKW, and 2,000 on behalf of the Gestapo.

The Tribunal itself heard 22 witnesses for the organizations. The documents tendered in evidence for the prosecution of the individual defendants and the organizations numbered several thousands. A complete stenographic record of everything said in court has been made, as well as an electrical recording of all the proceedings.

Copies of all the documents put in evidence by the Prosecution have been supplied to the Defense in the German language. The applications made by the defendants for the production of witnesses and documents raised serious problems in some instances, on acount of the unsettled state of the country. It was also necessary to limit the number of witnesses to be called, in order to have an expeditious hearing, in accordance with Article 18 (c) of the Charter. The Tribunal after examination, granted all those applications which in their opinion were relevant to the defense of any defendant or named group or organization, and were not cumulative. Facilities were provided for obtaining those witnesses and documents granted

The Trial and Punishment

through the office of the General Secretary established by the Tribunal.

Much of the evidence presented to the Tribunal on behalf of the Prosecution was documentary evidence, captured by the Allied armies in German army headquarters, Government buildings, and elsewhere. Some of the documents were found in salt mines, buried in the ground, hidden behind false walls and in other places thought to be secure from discovery. The case, therefore against the defendants rests in a large measure on documents of their own making, the authenticity of which has not been challenged except in one or two cases.

The Charter Provisions

The individual defendants are indicted under Article 6 of the Charter, which is as follows:

"Article 6. The Tribunal established by the Agreement referred to in Article 1 hereof for the trial and punishment of the major war criminals of the European Axis countries shall have the power to try and punish persons who, acting in the interests of the European Axis countries, whether as individuals or as members of organizations, committed any of the following crimes.

"The following acts, or any of them, are crimes coming within the jurisdiction of the Tribunal for which there shall be individual responsibility:

"(a) Crimes Against Peace: namely, planning, preparation, initiation or waging of a war of aggression, or a war in violation of international treaties, agreements or assurances, or participation in a common plan or conspiracy for the accomplishment of any of the foregoing:

"(b) War Crimes: namely, violations of the laws or customs of war. Such violations shall include, but not be limited to, murder, ill-treatment or deportation to slave labor or for any other purpose of civilian population of or in occupied territory, murder or ill-treatment of prisoners of war or persons on the seas, killing of hostages, plunder of public or private property, wanton destruction of cities, towns or villages, or devastation not justified by military necessity:

"(c) Crimes Against Humanity: namely, murder, extermination, enslavement, deportation, and other inhumane acts committed against any civilian population, before or during the war, or persecutions on political, racial or religious grounds in execution of or in connection with any crime within the jurisdiction of the Tribunal, whether or not in violation of the domestic law of the country where perpetrated.

"Leaders, organizers, instigators and accomplices participating in the formulation or execution of a common plan or conspiracy to commit any of the foregoing crimes are responsible for all acts performed by any persons in execution of such plan."

These provisions are binding upon the Tribunal as the law to be applied to the case. The Tribunal will later discuss them in more detail; but, before doing so, it is necessary to review the facts. For the purpose of showing the background of the aggressive war and war crimes charged in the indictment, the Tribunal will begin by reviewing some of the events that followed the first World War, and in particular, by tracing the growth of the Nazi Party under Hitler's leadership to a position of supreme power from which it controlled the destiny of the whole German people, and paved the way for the alleged commission of all the crimes charged against the defendants.

THE ORIGIN AND AIMS OF THE NAZI PARTY

On 5th January 1919, not two months after the conclusion of the Armistice which ended the first World War, and six months before the signing of the Peace Treaties at Versailles, there came into being in Germany a small political party called the German Labour Party. On the 12th September 1919 Adolf Hitler became a member of this party, and at the first public meeting held in Munich, on 24th February 1920, he announced the party's programme. That programme, which remained unaltered until the party was dissolved in 1945, consisted of twenty-five points, of which the following five are of particular interest on account of the light they throw on matters with which the Tribunal is concerned:

"Point 1. We demand the unification of all Germans in the Greater Germany, on the basis of the right of self-determination of peoples.

"Point 2. We demand equality of rights for the German people in respect to the other nations; abrogation of the peace treaties of Versailles and Saint Germain.

"Point 3. We demand land and territory for the sustenance of our people and the colonisation of our surplus population.

"Point 4. Only a member of the race can be a citizen. A member of the race can only be one who is of German blood, without consideration of creed. Consequently no Jew can be a member of the race . . .

"Point 22. We demand abolition of the mercenary troops and formation of a national army."

Of these aims, the one which seems to have been regarded

The Trial and Punishment

as the most important, and which figured in almost every public speech, was the removal of the "disgrace" of the Armistice, and the restrictions of the peace treaties of Versailles and Saint-Germain. In a typical speech at Munich on the 13th April 1923, for example, Hitler said with regard to the Treaty of Versailles:

> "The treaty was made in order to bring twenty million Germans to their deaths, and to ruin the German nation ...
> At its foundation our movement formulated three demands:
> 1. Setting aside of the Peace Treaty.
> 2. Unification of all Germans.
> 3. Land and soil to feed our nation."

The demand for the unification of all Germans in the Greater Germany was to play a large part in the events preceding the seizure of Austria and Czechoslovakia; the abrogation of the Treaty of Versailles was to become a decisive motive in attempting to justify the policy of the German Government; the demand for land was to be the justification for the acquisition of "living space" at the expense of other nations; the expulsion of the Jews from membership of the race of German blood was to lead to the atrocities against the Jewish people; and the demand for a national army was to result in measures of re-armament on the largest possible scale, and ultimately to War.

On the 29th July 1921, the Party which had changed its name to National Sozialistische Deutsche Arbeiter Partei (NSDAP) was re-organized, Hitler becoming the first "Chairman."

* * * * * * *

In order to place the complete control of the machinery of Government in the hands of the Nazi leaders, a series of laws and decrees were passed which reduced the powers of regional and local governments throughout Germany, transforming them into subordinate divisions of the government of the Reich. Representative assesmblies in the Laender were abolished, and with them all local elections. The Government then proceeded to secure control of the Civil Service. This was achieved by a process of centralization, and by a careful sifting of the whole Civil Service administration. By a law of the 7th April it was provided that officials "who were of non-Aryan descent" should be retired; and it was also decreed that "officials who because of their previous political activity do not offer security that they will exert themselves for the national state without reservation shall be discharged."

* * * * * * *

In their determination to remove all sources of opposition,

the NSDAP leaders turned their attention to the trade unions, the churches and the Jews.

* * * * * * *

From the earliest days of the NSDAP, anti-Semitism has occupied a prominent place in National Socialist thought and propaganda. The Jews, who were considered to have no right to German citizenship, were held to have been largely responsible for the troubles with which the nation was afflicted following on the war of 1914-1918. Furthermore, the antipathy to the Jews was intensified by the insistence which was laid upon the superiority of the Germanic race and blood. The second chapter of Book 1 of "Mein Kampf" is dedicated to what may be called the "Master Race" theory, the doctrine of Aryan superiority over all other races, and the right of Germans in virtue of this superiority to dominate and use other peoples for their own ends. With the coming of the Nazis into power in 1933, persecution of the Jews became official state policy. On the 1st April 1933, a boycott of Jewish enterprises was approved by the Nazi Reich Cabinet, and during the following years a series of anti-Semitic laws were passed, restricting the activities of Jews in the Civil Service, in the legal profession, in journalism and in the armed forces. In September 1935, the so-called Nuremberg Laws were passed, the most important effect of which was to deprive Jews of German citizenship. In this way the influence of Jewish elements on the affairs of Germany was extinguished, and one more potential source of opposition to Nazi policy was rendered powerless.

* * * * * * *

Persecution of the Jews

The persecution of the Jews at the hands of the Nazi Government has been proved in the greatest detail before the Tribunal. It is a record of consistent and systematic inhumanity on the greatest scale. Ohlendorf, Chief of Amt III in the RSHA from 1939 to 1943, and who was in command of one of the Einsatz groups in the campaign against the Soviet Union testified as to the methods employed in the extermination of the Jews. He said that he employed firing squads to shoot the victims in order to lessen the sense of individual guilt on the part of his men; and the 90,000 men, women and children who were murdered in one year by his particular group were mostly Jews.

When the witness Bach Zelewski was asked how Ohlendorf could admit the murder of 90,000 people, he replied:

"I am of the opinion that when, for years, for decades, the doctrine is preached that the Slav race is an inferior race, and Jews not even human, then such an outcome is inevitable."

But the defendant Frank spoke the final words of this chapter of Nazi history when he testified in this court:

"We have fought against Jewry: we have fought against it for years: and we have allowed ourselves to make utterances and my own diary has become a witness against me in this connection—utterances which are terrible. . . . A thousand years will pass and this guilt of Germany still will not be erased."

The anti-Jewish policy was formulated in Point 4 of the Party Program which declared "Only a member of the race can be a citizen. A member of the race can only be one who is of German blood, without consideration of creed. Consequently, no Jew can be a member of the race." Other points of the program declared that Jews should be treated as foreigners, that they should not be permitted to hold public office, that they should be expelled from the Reich if it were impossible to nourish the entire population of the State, that they should be denied any further immigration into Germany, and that they should be prohibited from publishing German newspapers. The Nazi Party preached these doctrines throughout its history. "Der Stuermer" and other publications were allowed to disseminate hatred of the Jews, and in the speeches and public declarations of the Nazi leaders, the Jews were held up to public ridicule and contempt.

With the seizure of power, the persecution of the Jews was intensified. A series of discriminatory laws were passed, which limited the offices and professions permitted to Jews; and restrictions were placed on their family life and their rights of citizenship. By the autumn of 1938, the Nazi policy towards the Jews had reached the stage where it was directed towards the complete exclusion of Jews from German life. Pogroms were organized, which included the burning and demolishing of synagogues, the looting of Jewish businesses, and the arrest of prominent Jewish business men. A collective fine of one billion marks was imposed on the Jews, the seizure of Jewish assets was authorized, and the movement of Jews was restricted by regulations to certain specified districts and hours. The creation of ghettos was carried out on an extensive scale, and by an order of the Security Police Jews were compelled to wear a yellow star to be worn on the breast and back.

It was contended for the Prosecution that certain aspects of this anti-Semitic policy were connected with the plans for aggressive war. The violent measures taken against the Jews in November 1938 were nominally in retaliation for the killing of an official of the German Embassy in Paris. But the decision to seize Austria and Czechoslovakia had been made a year before. The imposition of a fine of one billion marks was made, and the confiscation of the financial holdings of the Jews was decreed, at a time when German armament expenditure had put the German treasury in difficulties, and when the reduction of expenditure on armaments was being considered. These steps were taken, moreover, with the approval of the defendant Goering, who had been given responsibility for economic matters of this kind, and who was the strongest advocate of an extensive rearmament program notwithstanding the financial difficulties.

It was further said that the connection of the anti-Semitic policy with aggressive war was not limited to economic matters. The German Foreign Office circular in an article of January 25th 1939, entitled "Jewish question as a factor in German Foreign Policy in the year 1938", described the new phase in the Nazi anti-Semitic policy in these words:

"It is certainly no coincidence that the fateful year 1938 has brought nearer the solution of the Jewish question simultaneously with the realization of the idea of Greater Germany, since the Jewish policy was both the basis and consequence of the events of the year 1938. The advance made by Jewish influence and the destructive Jewish spirit in politics, economy, and culture, paralyzed the power and the will of the German people to rise again, more perhaps even than the power policy opposition of the former enemy Allied powers of the World War. The healing of this sickness among the people was therefore certainly one of the most important requirements for exerting the force which, in the year 1938, resulted in the joining together of Greater Germany in defiance of the world."

The Nazi persecution of Jews in Germany before the war, severe and repressive as it was, cannot compare, however, with the policy pursued during the war in the occupied territories. Originally the policy was similar to that which had been in force inside Germany. Jews were required to register, were forced to live in ghettos, to wear the yellow star, and were used as slave laborers. In the summer of 1941, however, plans were made for the "final solution" of the Jewish question in Europe. This "final solution" meant the extermination of the Jews, which early in 1939 Hitler had threatened would be one of the

The Trial and Punishment

consequences of an outbreak of war, and a special section in the Gestapo under Adolf Eichmann, as head of Section B 4 of the Gestapo, was formed to carry out the policy.

The plan for exterminating the Jews was developed shortly after the attack on the Soviet Union. Einsatzgruppen of the Security Police and SD, formed for the purpose of breaking the resistance of the population of the areas lying behind the German armies in the East, were given the duty of exterminating the Jews in those areas. The effectiveness of the work of the Einsatzgruppen is shown by the fact that in February 1942 Heydrich was able to report that Esthonia had already been cleared of Jews and that in Riga the number of Jews had been reduced from 29,500 to 2,500. Altogether the Einsatzgruppen operating in the occupied Baltic States killed over 135,000 Jews in three months.

Nor did these special units operate completely independently of the German Armed Forces. There is clear evidence that leaders of the Einsatzgruppen obtained the co-operation of Army Commanders. In one case the relations between an Einsatzgruppen and the Military authorities was described at the time as being "very close, almost cordial"; and in another case the smoothness of an Einsatzcommando's operation was attributed to the "understanding for this procedure" shown by the army authorities.

Units of the Security Police and SD in the occupied territories of the East, which were under civil administration, were given a similar task. The planned and systematic character of the Jewish persecutions is best illustrated by the original report of the SS Brigadier-General Stroop, who was in charge of the destruction of the Ghetto in Warsaw, which took place in 1943. The Tribunal received in evidence that report, illustrated with photographs, bearing on its title page: "The Jewish Ghetto in Warsaw no longer exists." The volume records a series of reports sent by Stroop to the Higher SS and Police Fuehrer East. In April and May of 1943, in one report, Stroop wrote:

"The resistance put up by the Jews and bandits could only be suppressed by energetic actions of our troops day and night. The Reichsfuehrer SS ordered therefore on the 23rd April 1943 the cleaning out of the Ghetto with utter ruthlessness and merciless tenacity. I therefore decided to destroy and burn down the entire Ghetto, without regard to the armament factories. These factories were systematically dismantled and then burnt. Jews usually left their hideouts, but frequently remained in the burning buildings, and jumped

Nazi Germany's War Against the Jews

out of the windows only when the heat became unbearable. They then tried to crawl with broken bones across the street into buildings which were not afire. . . . Life in the sewers was not pleasant after the first week. Many times we could hear loud voices in the sewers. . . . Tear gas bombs were thrown into the manholes, and the Jews driven out of the sewers and captured. Countless numbers of Jews were liquidated in sewers and bunkers through blasting. The longer the resistance continued, the tougher became the members of the Waffen SS, Police, and Wehrmacht, who always discharged their duties in an exemplary manner."

Stroop recorded that his action at Warsaw eliminated "a proved total of 56,065 people. To that we have to add the number of those killed through blasting, fire, etc., which cannot be counted." Grim evidence of mass murders of Jews was also presented to the Tribunal in cinematograph films depicting the communal graves of hundreds of victims which were subsequently discovered by the Allies.

These atrocities were all part and parcel of the policy inaugurated in 1941, and it is not surprising that there should be evidence that one or two German officials entered vain protests against the brutal manner in which the killings were carried out. But the methods employed never conformed to a single pattern. The massacres of Rowno and Dubno, of which the German engineer, Graebe, spoke, were examples of one method, the systematic extermination of Jews in concentration camps, was another. Part of the "final solution" was the gathering of Jews from all German occupied Europe in concentration camps. Their physical condition was the test of life or death. All who were fit to work were used as slave laborers in the concentration camps; all who were not fit to work were destroyed in gas chambers and their bodies burnt. Certain concentration camps such as Treblinka and Auschwitz were set aside for this main purpose. With regard to Auschwitz, the Tribunal heard the evidence of Hoess, the Commandant of the camp from May 1st 1940 to December 1st 1943. He estimated that in the camp of Auschwitz alone in that time, 2,500,000 persons were exterminated, and that a further 500,000 died from disease and starvation. Hoess described the screening for extermination by stating in evidence:

"We had two SS doctors on duty at Auschwitz to examine the incoming transports of prisoners. The prisoners would be marched by one of the doctors who would make spot decisions as they walked by. Those who were fit for work were

The Trial and Punishment

sent into the camp. Others were sent immediately to the extermination plants. Children of tender years were invariably exterminated since by reason of their youth they were unable to work. Still another improvement we made over Treblinka was that at Treblinka the victims almost always knew that they were to be exterminated and at Auschwitz we endeavored to fool the victims into thinking that they were to go through a delousing process. Of course, frequently they realized our true intentions and we sometimes had riots and difficulties due to that fact. Very frequently women would hide their children under their clothes, but of course when we found them we would send the children in to be exterminated."

He described the actual killing by stating:

"It took from three to fifteen minutes to kill the people in the death chamber, depending upon climatic conditions. We knew when the people were dead because their screaming stopped. We usually waited about one-half hour before we opened the doors and removed the bodies. After the bodies were removed our special commandos took off the rings and extracted the gold from the teeth of the corpses."

Beating, starvation, torture, and killing, were general. The inmates were subjected to cruel experiments at Dachau in August 1942, victims were immersed in cold water until their body temperature was reduced to 28° Centigrade, when they died immediately. Other experiments included high altitude experiments in pressure chambers, experiments to determine how long human beings could survive in freezing water, experiments with poison bullets, experiments with contagious diseases and experiments dealing with sterilization of men and women by X-rays and other methods.

Evidence was given of the treatment of the inmates before and after their extermination. There was testimony that the hair of women victims was cut off before they were killed, and shipped to Germany, there to be used in the manufacture of mattresses. The clothes, money and valuables of the inmates were also salvaged and sent to the appropriate agencies for disposition. After the extermination the gold teeth and fillings were taken from the heads of the corpses and sent to the Reichsbank.

After cremation the ashes were used for fertilizer, and in some instances attempts were made to utilize the fat from the bodies of the victims in the commercial manufacture of soap. Special groups traveled through Europe to find Jews and subject them to the "final solution." German missions were sent to such satellite countries as Hungary and Bulgaria, to arrange for the shipment of Jews to extermination camps and it is known that by the end of 1944, 400,000 Jews from Hungary had been murdered at Auschwitz. Evidence has also been given of the evacuation of 110,000 Jews from part of Rumania for "liquidation." Adolf Eichmann, who had been put in charge of this program by Hitler, has estimated that the policy pursued resulted in the killing of 6,000,000 Jews, of which 4,000,000 were killed in the extermination institutions.

THE LAW RELATING TO WAR CRIMES AND CRIMES AGAINST HUMANITY

Article 6 of the Charter provides:

"(b) War Crimes: namely, violations of the laws or customs of war. Such violations shall include, but not be limited to, murder, ill-treatment or deportation to slave labor or for any other purpose of civilian population of or in occupied territory, murder or ill-treatment of prisoners of war or persons on the seas, killing of hostages, plunder of public or private property, wanton destruction of cities, towns or villages, or devastation not justified by military necessity;

"(c) Crimes against Humanity: namely, murder, extermination, enslavement, deportation, and other inhumane acts committed against any civilian population, before or during the war; or persecutions on political, racial or religious grounds in execution of or in connection with any crime within the jurisdiction of the tribunal, whether or not in violation of the domestic law of the country where perpetrated"

As heretofore stated, the Charter does not define as a separate crime any conspiracy except that one set out in Article 6(a), dealing with crimes against peace.

The Tribunal is of course bound by the Charter, in the definition which it gives both of war crimes and crimes against humanity. With respect to war crimes, however, as has already been pointed out, the crimes defined by Article 6, section (b), of the Charter were already recognized as war crimes under international law. They were covered by Articles 46, 50, 52, and 56 of the Hague Convention of 1907, and Articles 2, 3, 4, 46, and 51 of the Geneva Convention of 1929. That violations of these provisions constituted crimes for which the guilty individuals were punishable is too well settled to admit of argument.

The Trial and Punishment

But it is argued that the Hague Convention does not apply in this case, because of the "general participation" clause in Article 2 of the Hague Convention of 1907. That clause provided:

"The provisions contained in the regulations (Rules of Land Warfare) referred to in Article I as well as in the present convention do not apply except between contracting powers, and then only if all the belligerents are parties to the convention."

Several of the belligerents in the recent war were not parties to this convention.

In the opinion of the Tribunal it is not necessary to decide this question. The rules of land warfare expressed in the convention undoubtedly represented an advance over existing international law at the time of their adoption. But the convention expressly stated that it was an attempt "to revise the general laws and customs of war", which it thus recognized to be then existing but by 1939 these rules laid down in the convention were recognized by all civilized nations, and were regarded as being declaratory of the laws and customs of war which are referred to in Article 6(b) of the Charter.

A further submission was made that Germany was no longer bound by the rules of land warfare in many of the territories occupied during the war, because Germany had completely subjugated those countries and incorporated them into the German Reich, a fact which gave Germany authority to deal with the occupied countries as though they were part of Germany. In the view of the Tribunal it is unnecessary in this case to decide whether this doctrine of subjugation, dependent as it is upon military conquest, has any application where the subjugation is the result of the crime of aggressive war. The doctrine was never considered to be applicable so long as there was an army in the field attempting to restore the occupied countries to their true owners, and in this case, therefore, the doctrine could not apply to any territories occupied after 1st September 1939. As to the war crimes committed in Bohemia and Moravia, it is a sufficient answer that these territories were never added to the Reich, but a mere protectorate was established over them.

With regard to crimes against humanity, there is no doubt whatever that political opponents were murdered in Germany before the war, and that many of them were kept in concentration camps in circumstances of great horror and cruelty. The policy of terror was certainly carried out on a vast scale, and in many cases was organized and systematic. The policy of persecution, repression and murder of civilians in Germany before before the war of 1939, who were likely to be hostile to the Government, was most ruthlessly carried out. The persecution of Jews during the same period is established beyond all doubt. To constitute crimes against humanity, the acts relied on before the outbreak of war must have been in execution of, or in connection with, any crime within the jurisdiction of the Tribunal. The Tribunal is of the opinion that revolting and horrible as many of these crimes were, it has not been satisfactorily proved that they were done in execution of, or in connection with, any such crime. The Tribunal therefore cannot make a general declaration that the acts before 1939 were crimes against humanity within the meaning of the Charter, but from the beginning of the war in 1939 war crimes were committed on a vast scale, which were also crimes against humanity; and insofar as the inhumane acts charged in the Indictment, and committed after the beginning of the war, did not constitute war crimes, they were all committed in execution of, or in connection with, the aggressive war, and therefore constituted crimes against humanity.

* * * * * * *

PREFACE TO INDIVIDUALS' JUDGMENT

Article 26 of the Charter provides that the Judgment of the Tribunal as to the guilt or innocence of any defendant shall give the reasons on which it is based.

The Tribunal will now state those reasons in declaring its Judgment on such guilt or innocence.

* * * * * * *

GOERING

* * * * * * *

Goering persecuted the Jews, particularly after the November 1938 riots, and not only in Germany where he raised the billion mark fine as stated elsewhere, but in the conquered territories as well. His own utterances then and in his testimony show this interest was primarily economic—how to get their property and how to force them out of the economic life of Europe. As these countries fell before the German Army, he extended the Reich's anti-Jewish laws to them; the Reichsgesetzblatt for 1939, 1940, and 1941 contains several anti-Jewish decrees signed by Goering. Although their extermination was in Himmler's hands, Goering was far from disinterested or inactive despite his protestations in the witness box. By decree of 31 July 1941 he directed Himmler and Heydrich to bring "about a complete solution of the Jewish question in the German sphere of influence in Europe."

There is nothing to be said in mitigation. For Goering was often, indeed almost always, the moving force, second only to his leader. He was the leading war aggressor, both as political and as military leader; he was the director of the slave labor program and the creator of the oppressive programme against the Jews and other races, at home and abroad. All of these crimes he has frankly admitted. On some specific cases there may be conflict of testimony but in terms of the broad outline, his own admissions are more than sufficiently wide to be conclusive of his guilt. His guilt is unique in its enormity. The record discloses no excuses for this man.

Conclusion

The Tribunal finds the defendant Goering guilty on all four counts of the Indictment.

* * * * * * *

RIBBENTROP

* * * * * * *

He played an important part in Hitler's "final solution" of the Jewish question. In September 1942 he ordered the German diplomatic representatives accredited to various Axis satellites to hasten the deportation of Jews to the East. In June 1942 the German Ambassador to Vichy requested Laval to turn over 50,000 Jews for deportation to the East. On February 25, 1943, Ribbentrop protested to Mussolini against Italian slowness in deporting Jews from the Italian occupation zone of France. On April 17, 1943, he took part in a conference between Hitler and Horthy on the deportation of Jews from Hungary and informed Horthy that the "Jews must either be exterminated or taken to concentration camps." At the same conference Hitler had likened the Jews to "tuberculosis bacilli" and said if they did not work they were to be shot.

* * * * * * *

In the administration of territories over which Germany acquired control by illegal invasion Ribbentrop also assisted in carrying out criminal policies particularly those involving the extermination of the Jews. There is abundant evidence, moreover, that Ribbentrop was in complete sympathy with all the main tenets of the National Socialist creed, and that his collaboration with Hitler and with other defendants in the commission of crimes against peace, war crimes and crimes against humanity was whole-hearted. It was because Hitler's policy and plans coincided with his own ideas that Ribbentrop served him so willingly to the end.

Nazi Germany's War Against the Jews

Conclusion

The Tribunal finds that Ribbentrop is guilty on all four Counts.

* * * * * * *

KEITEL

* * * * * * *

Lahousen testified that Keitel told him on 12 September 1939, while aboard Hitler's headquarters train, that the Polish intelligentsia, nobility and Jews were to be liquidated. On 20 October, Hitler told Keitel the intelligentsia would be prevented from forming a ruling class, the standard of living would remain low, and Poland would be used only for labor forces. Keitel does not remember the Lahousen conversation, but admits there was such a policy and that he had protested without effect to Hitler about it.

* * * * * * *

Conclusion

The Tribunal finds Keitel guilty on all four counts.

* * * * * * *

KALTENBRUNNER

* * * * * * *

During the period in which Kaltenbrunner was Head of the RSHA, it was engaged in a widespread program of War Crimes and Crimes against Humanity. Those crimes included the mistreatment and murder of prisoners of war. Einsatz Kommandos operating under the control of the Gestapo were engaged in the screening of Soviet prisoners of war. Jews, commissars and others who were thought to be ideologically hostile to the Nazi system were reported to the RSHA, which had been transferred to a concentration camp and murdered.

The RSHA played a leading part in the "final solution" of the Jewish question by the extermination of the Jews. A special section under the AMT IV of the RSHA was established to supervise this program. Under its direction approximately six million Jews were murdered, of which two million were killed by Einsatzgruppen and other units of the Security Police. Kaltenbrunner had been informed of the activities of these Einsatzgruppen when he was a Higher SS and Police Leader, and they continued to function after he had become Chief of the RSHA.

The murder of approximately four million Jews in concentration camps has heretofore been described. This part of the program was also under the supervision of the RSHA when Kaltenbrunner was head of that organization, and special missions of the RSHA scoured the occupied territories and the various Axis satellites arranging for the deportation of Jews to these extermination institutions. Kaltenbrunner was informed of these activities. A letter which he wrote on June 30, 1944, described the shipment to Vienna of 12,000 Jews for that purpose, and directed that all who could not work would have to be kept in readiness for "special action," which meant murder. Kaltenbrunner denied his signature to this letter, as he did on a very large number of orders on which his name was stamped or typed, and, in a few instances, written. It is inconceivable that in matters of such importance his signature could have appeared so many times without his authority.

Conclusion

The Tribunal finds that Kaltenbrunner is not guilty on Count One. He is guilty under Counts Three and Four.

* * * * * * *

ROSENBERG

* * * * * * *

Rosenberg is responsible for a system of organized plunder of both public and private property throughout the invaded countries of Europe. Acting under Hitler's orders of January 1940, to set up the "Hohe Schule," he organized and directed the "Einsatzstab Rosenberg," which plundered museums and libraries, confiscated art treasures and collections, and pillaged private houses. His own reports show the extent of the confiscations. In "Action-M" (Moebel), instituted in December 1941 at Rosenberg's suggestion, 69,619 Jewish homes were plundered in the West, 38,000 of them in Paris alone, and it took 26,984 railroad cars to transport the confiscated furnishings to Germany. As of July 14, 1944, more than 21,903 art objects, including famous paintings and museum pieces, had been seized by the Einsatzstab in the West.

With his appointment as Reich Minister for Occupied Eastern Territories on July 17, 1941, Rosenberg became the supreme authority for those areas. He helped to formulate the policies of Germanization, exploitation, forced labour, extermination of Jews and opponents of Nazi rule, and he set up the administration which carried them out. He took part in the conference of July 16, 1941, in which Hitler stated that they were faced with the task of "cutting up the giant cake according to our needs, in order to be able: first, to dominate it, second, to administer it, and third, to exploit it," and indicated that ruthless action was contemplated. Rosenberg accepted his appointment on the following day.

Rosenberg had knowledge of the brutal treatment and terror to which the Eastern people were subjected. He directed that the Hague Rules of Land Warfare were not applicable in the Occupied Eastern Territories. He had knowledge of and took an active part in stripping the Eastern Territories of raw materials and foodstuffs, which were sent to Germany. He stated that feeding the German people was first on the list of claims on the East, and that the Soviet people would suffer thereby. His directives provided for the segregation of Jews, ultimately in ghettos. His subordinates engaged in mass killings of Jews, and his civil administrators in the East considered that cleansing the Eastern Occupied Territories of Jews was necessary. In December 1941, he made the suggestion to Hitler that in a case of shooting 100 hostages, Jews only be used.

* * * * * * *

Conclusion

The Tribunal finds that Rosenberg is guilty on all four counts.

* * * * * * *

FRANK

* * * * * * *

Frank was appointed Chief Civil Administration Officer for occupied Polish territory and, on October 12, 1939, was made Governor General of the occupied Polish territory.

* * * * * * *

The persecution of the Jews was immediately begun in the General Government. The area originally contained from 2,500,000 to 3,500,000 Jews. They were forced into ghettos, subjected to discriminatory laws, deprived of the food necessary to avoid starvation, and fined systematically and brutally exterminated. On December 16, 1941, Frank told the Cabinet of the Governor General: "We must annihilate the Jews, wherever we find them and wherever it is possible, in order to maintain there the structure of Reich as a whole." By January 25, 1944, Frank estimated that there were only 100,000 Jews left.

At the beginning of his testimony, Frank stated that he had a feeling of "terrible guilt" for the atrocities committed in the occupied territories. But his defense was largely devoted to an attempt to prove that he was not in fact responsible; that he ordered only the necessary pacification measures; that the excesses were due to the activities of the police which were not under his control; and that he never even knew of the activities of the concentration camps. It has also been argued that the starvation was due to the aftermath of the war and policies

The Trial and Punishment

carried out under the Four Year Plan; that the forced labour programme was under the direction of Sauckel; and that the extermination of the Jews was by the police and SS under direct orders from Himmler.

It is undoubtedly true that most of the criminal programme charged against Frank was put into effect through the police, that Frank had jurisdictional difficulties with Himmler over the control of the police, and that Hitler resolved many of these disputes in favour of Himmler. It therefore may well be true that some of the crimes committed in the General Government were committed without the knowledge of Frank, and even occasionally despite his opposition. It may also be true that some of the criminal policies put into effect in the General Government did not originate with Frank but were carried out pursuant to orders from Germany. But it is also true that Frank was a willing and knowing participant in the use of terrorism in Poland; in the economic exploitation of Poland in a way which led to the death by starvation of a large number of people; in the deportation to Germany as slave labourers of over a million Poles; and in a programme involving the murder of at least three million Jews.

Conclusion

The Tribunal finds that Frank is not guilty on Count One but guilty under Counts Three and Four.

* * * * * * *

FRICK

* * * * * * *

An avid Nazi, Frick was largely responsible for bringing the German Nation under the complete control of the NSDAP. After Hitler became Reich Chancellor, the new Minister of the Interior immediately began to incorporate local governments under the sovereignty of the Reich. The numerous laws he drafted, signed, and administered, abolished all opposition parties and prepared the way for the Gestapo and their concentration camps to extinguish all individual opposition. He was largely responsible for the legislation which suppressed the Trade Unions, the Church, the Jews. He performed this task with ruthless efficiency.

* * * * * * *

Frick signed the law of March 13, 1938, which united Austria with the Reich, and he was made responsible for its accomplishment. In setting up German administration in Austria, he issued decrees which introduced German law, the Nurnberg

Decrees, the Military Service Law, and he provided for police security by Himmler.

* * * * * *

Always rabidly anti-Semitic, Frick drafted, signed, and administered many laws designed to eliminate Jews from German life and economy. His work formed the basis of the Nurnberg Decrees, and he was active in enforcing them. Responsible for prohibiting Jews from following various professions, and for confiscating their property, he signed a final decree in 1943, after the mass destruction of Jews in the East, which placed them "outside the law" and handed them over to the Gestapo. These laws paved the way for the "final solution," and extended by Frick to the Incorporated Territories and to certain of the Occupied Territories. While he was Reich Protector of Bohemia and Moravia, thousands of Jews were transferred from the Terezin Ghetto in Czechoslovakia to Auschwitz, where they were killed. He issued a decree providing for special penal laws against Jews and Poles in the Government General.

As the Supreme Reich Authority in Bohemia and Moravia, Frick bears general responsibility for the acts of oppression in that territory after 20 August 1943, such as terrorism of the population, slave labor, and the deportation of Jews to the concentration camps for extermination. It is true that Frick's duties as Reich Protector were considerably more limited than those of his predecessor, and that he had no legislative and limited personal executive authority in the Protectorate. Nevertheless, Frick knew full well what the Nazi policies of occupation were in Europe, particularly with respect to Jews, at that time, and by accepting the office of Reich Protector he assumed responsibility for carrying out those policies in Bohemia and Moravia.

* * * * * *

Conclusion

The Tribunal finds that Frick is not guilty on Count One. He is guilty on Counts Two, Three and Four.

* * * * * *

STREICHER

* * * * * *

Streicher is indicted on Counts One and Four. One of the earliest members of the Nazi Party, joining in 1921, he took part in the Munich Putsch. From 1925 to 1940 he was Gauleiter of Franconia. Elected to the Reichstag in 1933, he was an honorary general in the SA. His persecution of the Jews was notorious. He was the publisher of "Der Stuermer," an anti-Semitic

The Trial and Punishment

weekly newspaper, from 1923 to 1945 and was its editor until 1933.

*   *   *   *   *   *   *

For his twenty-five years of speaking, writing and preaching hatred of the Jews, Streicher was widely known as "Jew-Baiter Number One". In his speeches and articles week after week, month after month, he infected the German mind with the virus of anti-Semitism, and incited the German people to active persecution. Each issue of "Der Stuermer", which reached a circulation of 600,000 in 1935, was filled with such articles, often lewd and disgusting.

Streicher had charge of the Jewish boycott of April 1, 1933. He advocated the Nurnberg Decrees of 1935. He was responsible for the demolition on August 10, 1938, of the Synagogue in Nurnberg. And on November 10, 1938, he spoke publicly in support of the Jewish pogrom which was taking place at that time.

But it was not only in Germany that this defendant advocated his doctrines. As early as 1938 he began to call for the annihilation of the Jewish race. Twenty-three different articles of "Der Stuermer" between 1938 and 1941 were produced in evidence, in which extermination "root and branch" was preached. Typical of his teachings was a leading article in September 1938 which termed the Jew a germ and a pest, not a human being, but "a parasite, an enemy, an evil-doer, a disseminator of diseases who must be destroyed in the interest of mankind." Other articles urged that only when world Jewry had been annihilated would the Jewish problem have been solved, and predicted that fifty years hence the Jewish graves "will proclaim that this people of murderers and criminals has after all met its deserved fate." Streicher, in February 1940, published a letter from one of "Der Stuermer's" readers which compared Jews with swarms of locusts which must be exterminated completely. Such was the poison Streicher injected into the minds of thousands of Germans which caused them to follow the National Socialist policy of Jewish persecution and extermination. A leading article of "Der Stuermer" in May 1939, shows clearly his aim:

> "A punitive expedition must come against the Jews in Russia. A punitive expedition which will provide the same fate for them that every murderer and criminal must expect. Death sentence and execution. The Jews in Russia must be killed. They must be exterminated root and branch."

As the war in the early stages proved successful in acquiring more and more territory for the Reich, Streicher even intensified his efforts to incite the Germans against the Jews. In the record are twenty-six articles from "Der Stuermer," published between August 1941 and September 1944, twelve by Streicher's own hand, which demanded annihilation and extermination in unequivocal terms. He wrote and published on December 25, 1941:

"If the danger of the reproduction of that curse of God in the Jewish blood is to finally come to an end, then there is only one way—the extermination of that people whose father is the devil."

And in February 1944 his own article stated:

"Whoever does what a Jew does is a scoundrel, a criminal. And he who repeats and wishes to copy him deserves the same fate, annihilation, death."

With knowledge of the extermination of the Jews in the Occupied Eastern Territory, this defendant continued to write and publish his propaganda of death. Testifying in this trial, he vehemently denied any knowledge of mass executions of Jews. But the evidence makes its clear that he continually received current information on the progress of the "final solution." His press photographer was sent to visit the ghettos of the East in the spring of 1943, the time of the destruction of the Warsaw Ghetto. The Jewish newspaper, "Israelitisches Wochenblatt," which Streicher received and read, carried in each issue accounts of Jewish atrocities in the East, and gave figures on the number of Jews who had been deported and killed. For example, issues appearing in the summer and fall of 1942 reported the death of 72,729 Jews in Warsaw, 17,542 in Lodz, 18,000 in Croatia, 125,000 in Rumania, 14,000 in Latvia, 85,000 in Yugoslavia, 700,000 in all of Poland. In November 1943 Streicher quoted verbatim an article from the "Israelitisches Wochenblatt" which stated that the Jews had virtually disappeared from Europe, and commented, "This is not a Jewish lie." In December 1942, referring to an article in the "London Times" about the atrocities, aiming at extermination, Streicher said that Hitler had given warning that the second World War would lead to the destruction of Jewry. In January 1943 he wrote and published an article which said that Hitler's prophecy was being fulfilled, that world Jewry was being extirpated, and that it was wonderful to know that Hitler was freeing the world of its Jewish tormentors.

In the face of the evidence before the Tribunal it is idle for

Streicher to suggest that the solution of the Jewish problem which he favored was strictly limited to the classification of Jews as aliens, and the passing of discriminatory legislation such as the Nurnberg Laws, supplemented if possible by international agreement on the creation of a Jewish State somewhere in the world, to which all Jews should emigrate.

Streicher's incitement to murder and extermination at the time when Jews in the East were being killed under the most horrible conditions clearly constitutes persecution on political and racial grounds in connection with war crimes, as defined by the Charter, and constitutes a crime against humanity.

Conclusion

The Tribunal finds that Streicher is not guilty on Count One, but that he is guilty on Count Four.

* * * * * * *

FUNK

* * * * * * *

In his capacity as Under Secretary in the Ministry of Propaganda and Vice-Chairman of the Reichs-Chamber of Culture, Funk had participated in the early Nazi program of economic discrimination against the Jews. On November 12, 1938, after the pogroms of November, he attended a meeting held under the chairmanship of Goering to discuss the solution of the Jewish problem and proposed a decree providing for the banning of Jews from all business activities, which Goering issued the same day under the authority of the Four Year Plan. Funk has testified that he was shocked at the outbreaks of November 10, but on November 15 he made a speech describing these outbreaks as a "violent explosion of the disgust of the German people, because of a criminal Jewish attack against the German people," and saying that the elimination of the Jews from economic life followed logically their elimination from political life.

In 1942 Funk entered into an agreement with Himmler under which the Reichsbank was to receive certain gold and jewels and currency from the SS and instructed his subordinates, who were to work out the details, not to ask too many questions. As a result of this agreement the SS sent to the Reichsbank the personal belongings taken from the victims who had been exterminated in the concentration camps. The Reichsbank kept the coins and bank notes and sent the jewels, watches, and personal belongings to Berlin Municipal Pawn Shops. The gold from the eyeglasses, and gold teeth and fillings was stored in the Reichsbank vaults. Funk has protested that he did not know that the Reichsbank was receiving articles of this kind. The Tribunal is of the opinion that he either knew what was being received or was deliberately closing his eyes to what was being done.

* * * * * *

Conclusion

The Tribunal finds that Funk is not guilty on Count One but is guilty under Counts Two, Three, and Four.

* * * * * *

VON SCHIRACH

* * * * * *

When von Schirach became Gauleiter of Vienna the deportation of the Jews had already been begun, and only 60,000 out of Vienna's original 190,000 Jews remained. On October 2, 1940, he attended a conference at Hitler's office and told Frank that he had 50,000 Jews in Vienna which the General Government would have to take over from him. On December 3, 1940, von Schirach received a letter from Lammers stating that after the receipt of the reports made by von Schirach, Hitler had decided to deport the 60,000 Jews still remaining in Vienna to the General Government because of the housing shortage in Vienna. The deportation of the Jews from Vienna was then begun and continued until the early fall of 1942. On September 15, 1942, von Schirach made a speech in which he defended his action in having driven "tens of thousands upon tens of thousands of Jews into the Ghetto of the East" as "contributing to European culture."

While the Jews were being deported from Vienna, reports, addressed to him in his official capacity, were received in von Schirach's office from the office of the Chief of the Security Police and SD which contained a description of the activities of Einsatzgruppen in exterminating Jews. Many of these reports were initialed by one of von Schirach's principal deputies. On June 30, 1944, von Schirach's office also received a letter from Kaltenbrunner informing him that a shipment of 12,000 Jews was on its way to Vienna for essential war work and that all those who were incapable of work would have to be kept in readiness for "special action."

The Tribunal finds that von Schirach, while he did not originate the policy of deporting Jews from Vienna, participated in this deportation after he had become Gauleiter of Vienna. He knew that the best the Jews could hope for was a miserable existence in the ghettos of the East. Bulletins describing the Jewish extermination were in his office.

* * * * * * *

Conclusion

The Tribunal finds that von Schirach is not guilty on Count One. He is guilty under Count Four.

* * * * * * *

BORMANN

* * * * * * *

Bormann was extremely active in the persecution of the Jews not only in Germany but also in the absorbed or conquered countries. He took part in the discussions which led to the removal of 60,000 Jews from Vienna to Poland in cooperation with the SS and the Gestapo. He signed the decree of 31 May 1941 extending the Nurnberg Laws to the annexed Eastern Territories. In an order of 9 October 1942 he declared that the permanent elimination of Jews in Greater German territory could no longer be solved by emigration, but only by applying "ruthless force" in the special camps in the East. On 1 July 1943 he signed an ordinance withdrawing Jews from the protection of the law courts and placing them under the exclusive jurisdiction of Himmler's Gestapo.

* * * * * * *

Conclusion

The Tribunal finds that Bormann is not guilty on Count One, but is guilty on Counts Three and Four.

* * * * * * *

SEYSS-INQUART

* * * * * * *

As Reichs Governor of Austria, Seyss-Inquart instituted a program of confiscating Jewish property. Under his regime Jews were forced to emigrate, were sent to concentration camps and were subject to pogroms. At the end of his regime he cooperated with the Security Police and SD in the deportation of Jews from Austria to the East. While he was Governor of Austria, political opponents of the Nazis were sent to concentration camps by the Gestapo, mistreated and often killed.

* * * * * * *

As Deputy Governor General of the General Government of Poland, Seyss-Inquart was a supporter of the harsh occupation policies which were put in effect. In November 1939, while on an inspection tour through the General Government, Seyss-

Inquart stated that Poland was to be so administered as to exploit its economic resources for the benefit of Germany. Seyss-Inquart also advocated the persecution of Jews and was informed of the beginning of the AB action which involved the murder of many Polish intellectuals.

* * * * * * *

One of Seyss-Inquart's first steps as Reich Commissioner of the Netherlands was to put into effect a series of laws imposing economic discriminations against the Jews. This was followed by decrees requiring their registration, decrees compelling them to reside in ghettos and to wear the star of David, sporadic arrests and detention in concentration camps, and finally, at the suggestion of Heydrich, the mass deportation of almost 120,000 of Holland's 140,000 Jews to Auschwitz and the "final solution." Seyss-Inquart admits knowing that they were going to Auschwitz but claims that he heard from people who had been to Auschwitz that the Jews were comparatively well off there, and that he thought that they were being held there for resettlement after the war. In light of the evidence and on account of his official position it is impossible to believe this claim.

* * * * * * *

Conclusion

The Tribunal finds that Seyss-Inquart is guilty under Counts Two, Three and Four. Seyss-Inquart is not guilty on Count One.

* * * * * * *

VON NEURATH

* * * * * * *

As Reichs Protector, von Neurath instituted an administration in Bohemia and Moravia similar to that in effect in Germany. The free press, political parties and trade unions were abolished. All groups which might serve as opposition were outlawed. Czechoslovakian industry was worked into the structure of German war production, and exploited for the German war effort. Nazi anti-Semitic policies and laws were also introduced. Jews were barred from leading positions in Government and business.

* * * * * * *

Von Neurath has argued that the actual enforcement of the repressive measures was carried out by the Security Police and SD who were under the control of his State Secretary, Carl Herman Frank, who was appointed at the suggestion of Himmler and who, as a Higher SS and Police Leader, reported directly

The Trial and Punishment

to Himmler. Von Neurath further argues that anti-Semitic measures and those resulting in economic exploitation were put into effect in the Protectorate as the result of policies decided upon in the Reich. However this may be, he served as the chief German official in the Protectorate when the administration of this territory played an important role in the wars of aggression which Germany was waging in the East, knowing that War Crimes and Crimes against Humanity were being committed under his authority.

* * * * * * *

Conclusion

The Tribunal finds that von Neurath is guilty under all four counts.

* * * * * * *

Part Three

The Documentary Evidence

EXPLANATORY NOTE

THE documents in Part Three are arranged according to the series of number and letter designations that were given to them as they were discovered and classified, and, consequently, are not arranged in topical or chronological order.

Although some pieces of evidence were secured in Washington and London, by far the greater part was obtained in Germany. As the American armies swept into Germany, military investigating teams uncovered a wealth of documentary material which was sent for processing and safekeeping to document centers set up for this purpose.

This material was freely made available by the American Army to field investigators of the Office of the United States Chief Counsel (OCC). That office was created by Executive Order of President Truman, dated 2 May 1945, appointing Justice Robert H. Jackson as Representative of the United States and as its Chief Counsel in the preparation and prosecution of the case against the major Axis war criminals.

Special assistance was given by the Document Section, G-2 Division, SHAEF, and by the Document Sections of the Army Groups and armies operating in the European Theater. A number of useful collections of documents were discovered by the intelligence units of the armies and by the field teams of the OCC.

Documents were screened thoroughly, in accordance with the procedure described in the affidavit of Major William H. Coogan (Document 001A-PS). During this process more than 100,000 documents were individually examined in order to select those of importance. Of these, approximately 40,000 were found to be of value.

This group was further reduced through exacting standards of elimination to a total of some 2,000 documents, which it was proposed to offer in evidence before the International Military Tribunal sitting at Nurnberg. These documents are in process of publication by the United States Printing Office under the auspices of the Office of U. S. Chief of Counsel, and the War and State Departments. That publication, entitled "Nazi Conspiracy and Aggression", consists of eight volumes, of which six have already appeared.

The documentary material set forth in Part Three includes the documents relevant to the subject of "Nazi Germany's War

Against the Jews." They consist, in the main, of official papers found in archives of the German government and the Nazi Party, diaries and letters of prominent Germans, and captured reports and orders. There are included, in addition, excerpts from governmental and Party decrees, from official newspapers, and from authoritative German publications.

These documents are absolutely authentic. They have withstood the crucible of the entire trial before the International Military Tribunal from November 14, 1945 until October 1, 1946. The twenty-two Nazi leaders who were defendants in that trial were given every opportunity in the course of their defense to attack, among other things, the validity of the documentary evidence introduced against them. There were extraordinarily few attempts to show that any of the several thousand documents introduced were not authentic and even those few attempts failed.

The judgment of the Tribunal imposing death upon twelve defendants, prison terms upon seven, and acquitting only three demonstrated conclusively the weight of the documentary evidence. In the course of its judgment, the Tribunal noted that the case against the defendants rested in large measure on documents of their own making.

It should be borne in mind that these documents in the main are translations from the original German. The magnitude of the task confronting the American and British prosecuting staffs, coupled with a need for speed, naturally resulted in many imperfections.

The format of the original documents has been preserved in the printed translations, as far as possible. Italics represent underlinings in the original documents and editorial additions have been inserted in brackets. Certain passages of some documents may appear confused or incomplete, and occasionally this may be the result of hasty translation. More frequently, however, the jumble of language accurately reflects the chaos of the original German; for the language of the National Socialists was often merely a turgid and mystical aggregation of words signifying nothing.

CLASSIFICATION SYMBOLS. The documents processed by the American prosecution staff are classified under the cryptic categories of "EC," "L," "PS," and "R." The letters "EC" stand for "Economic Case," and designate those documents which were obtained and processed by the Economic Section of OCC working at Frankfurt. The "L" symbol was used as an abbreviation for "London" and designates those documents processed in the London office of the OCC. The letters "PS" are an abbreviation of "Paris-Storey" and denote those documents which, although obtained in Germany, were processed by the OCC office in Paris, as well as those documents later processed by the OCC staff in Nurnberg. The letter "R" stands for "Rothschild" and indicates the documents obtained through the screening and translation activities of Lt. Walter Rothschild, of the London Branch of the OSS.

The documents designated by the letters "D" and "M" are documents originally processed by the British prosecuting staff, known as the British War Crimes Executive. The letter "D" is merely a filing reference, and the letter "M" stands for the first name of the British Assistant Prosecutor.

Each document is headed by a bold type caption giving the title of the document and a brief summary of its contents. For easy reference, there is provided a complete list of the documents, with their captions. Both the documents and the list are arranged in alphabetical order by series designations (D, EC, L, M, PS and R). References will be found in the captions of the documents to "USA" and "GB" numbers. They represent the exhibit numbers given to the documents by the clerk of the International Military Tribunal as they were introduced in evidence: the "USA" numbers having been placed upon documents introduced by the United States Prosecutor, and the "GB" numbers assigned when the documents were introduced by the Prosecutor for the United Kingdom of Great Britain and Northern Ireland.

LIST OF DOCUMENTS

No.	Description	Page
D-183	Order of Gestapo Office, Darmstadt, 7 December 1938, on treatment of articles secured during protest action against Jews	1
D-229	Excerpts from a pamphlet, *"Judges Letters"*, concerning punishment for concealing Jewish identification, 24 April 1942; and crime against currency laws by a Jew, 26 May 1942	3
D-355	Affidavit of Walter Thoene, 8 October 1945, on mistreatment of Hungarian Jewesses working at heavy labor	5
D-411 (USA 556)	Army Order, dated 10 October 1941, covering letter on Conduct of Troops in Eastern Territories, to effect that soldiers must have full understanding for necessity of a severe but just revenge on subhuman Jewry	6
D-635 (GB 242)	Translation of Radiogram from Vice-Chancellor von Papen to Board of Trade for German-American Commerce, 27 March 1933, to effect that news circulating in United States about German excesses against the Jews emanates from sources interested in poisoning relations between Germany and America. Published in New York *Times*, Tuesday, 28 March 1933	9
D-734	Note of a conversation between Reich Foreign Minister and the Duce, 25 February 1943, in which Foreign Minister stated Italian military circles did not sufficiently appreciate the Jewish problem	10
D-736 (GB 283)	Notes on discussion between Fuehrer, Ribbentrop and Hungarian Regent Horthy, 17 April 1943, in which Ribbentrop said that Jews must be either exterminated or taken to concentration camps	12

III - v

No.	Description	Page
D-964	Affidavit dated 9 August 1946 of Szloma Gol, a Jewish resident of Vilna, Lithouania, concerning the exhuming in December 1943 of 68,000 graves and burning the bodies, including those in the batch of 10,000 Jews from Vilna ghetto who were shot in September 1941	13
EC-265	Telegram dated 1 October 1940 from Abetz, German Ambassador to the Petain Government, on citizenship status of Reich German Jews living in Occupied France	16
EC-305 (USA 303)	Excerpts from Minutes of meeting on 12 February 1940 under chairmanship of Goering on questions concerning the East, including the evacuation and forced labor of Jews	17
EC-433 (USA 832)	Excerpt from Koenigsberg Speech of Schacht at the German Eastern Fair (probably 1935) concerning the Jewish problem	19
EC-450 (USA 629)	Excerpt of Affidavit of S. R. Fuller, 18 October 1945, giving account of a conversation with Schacht, 23 September 1935, concerning Jewish question	20
EC-465	Excerpt from letter, 9 December 1940, from Commissar at the Netherlands Bank on status of Aryanization of the banks as of November 1940	23
L-18 (USA 277)	Report from Katzmann to General of Police Krueger, concerning "Solution of Jewish Question in Galicia", 30 June 1943, describing ruthless evacuation of 434,329 Jews	23
L-22 (USA 294)	Excerpt from report of War Refugee Board, Washington, D. C., estimating that 1,765,000 Jews were gassed in Birkenau (part of Auschwitz) between April 1942 and April 1944	39
L-26	Excerpts from United Nations Information Organization Report No. 8, 14 June 1944, *Conditions in Occupied Territories*, pp. 14, 16, commenting upon deportation of Jews from Greece and the Netherlands	39

No.	Description	Page
L-31	Excerpt from Communique of the Polish-Soviet Extraordinary Commission for Investigating the Crimes Committed by the Germans in the Mardanek Extermination Camp in Lublin, pp. 21, 26, in which reference was made to the wholesale murder of a vast number of Jews	41
L-53 (USA 291)	Order from Commandant of the SIPO and SD (Security Police and Security Service) for the Rodom District, 24 July 1944, on clearance of prisons, in which it was ordered that Jews were not to be liberated by the enemy or fall into their hands alive	42
L-61 (USA 177)	Express letter from Sauckel to Presidents of Landes Employment Offices, 26 November 1942, concerning employment of Jews and exchange of Jews in essential employment by Polish labor	44
L-152	Order, 3 November 1941, of Gestapo Office for Nurnberg-Fuerth area prohibiting friendly relations between Aryans and Jews	46
L-156	Circular letter from Office of Commissioner for Four-Year Plan, 26 March 1943, concerning removal of Jews for forced labor	47
L-161 (USA 292)	Excerpt from British War Office Report, Auschwitz Concentration Camp, 31 May 1945, concerning liquidation of 12,000 Hungarian Jews daily during July 1944	48
L-165 (USA 287)	Excerpt from *The Jewish Food Situation*, published in Polish Fortnightly Review of the Polish Ministry of Information, 15 December 1942, p. 7, describing food situation in the Warsaw Ghetto	48
L-167	Order of Minister of Interior, 24 March 1942, restricting use of public transportation facilities by Jews, and covering letters	51
L-179	Letter from RSHA (Reich Security Main Office) to police officials, 5 November 1942, concerning criminal procedure by the police against Poles,	

No.	Description	Page
	Jews and members of the Eastern peoples	54
L-180 (USA 276)	Excerpts from Report by SS Brigade Commander Stahlecker to Himmler, 15 October 1941, on activities of Action Group A in exterminating thousands of Jews in Latvia and Lithouania	56
L-185 (USA 484)	Excerpt from *Organization Plan of the RSHA* (Reich Security Main Office) showing function of SS Major Eichmann as concerned with Matters concerning Jews and Evacuations ...	74
L-188 (USA 386)	Report of 8 August 1944 on confiscation of Jewish homes, furniture, and possessions in France, Belgium and Holland up to 31 July 1944	75
L-198	State Department Dispatch by Consul General Messersmith, 14 March 1933, concerning physical attacks against American citizens in Berlin because they were Jews	78
L-199	Excerpts from newspaper *Berliner Tageblatt*, 29 March 1933, concerning the Anti-Jewish Boycott	87
L-201	Excerpts from newspaper *Berliner Boersen Zeitung*, 12 April 1933, on the murder of a Jewish lawyer	87
L-202	State Department Dispatch from D. H. Buffum, American Consul General at Leipzig, 21 November 1938, on anti-Semitic Onslaught in Germany as seen from Leipzig	88
L-205 (GB 157)	Telegram from Ambassador Kennedy at London to Department of State, Washington, 8 December 1938, reporting extremely violent statements against Jews by Ribbentrop, German Ambassador in London	93
L-217	Order, 20 November 1936, from Gestapo Office at Duesseldorf to effect that steps be taken to prevent the camouflage of Jewish businesses	94
L-219 (USA 479)	Excerpt from *Organization Plan of RSHA* (Reich Security Main Office) as of 1 October 1943, showing function of SS-Major Eichmann in charge of Jewish affairs and matters of evacuation	96

No.	Description	Page
M-1 (GB 178)	Excerpt from newspaper *Fraenkische Tageszeitung*, 24 June 1935, on Streicher's speech to the Hitler Youth on 22 June 1935 attacking the Jewish people	97
001-PS (USA 282)	Memorandum for the Fuehrer signed Rosenberg, 18 December 1941, concerning Jewish possessions in France and suggesting that 100 French Jews be executed	98
001A-PS (USA 1)	Affidavit of Major William H. Coogan, Chief of Documentation Division of the Office of U.S. Chief of Consul, 19 November 1945, describing manner in which captured German documents were collected, analyzed, numbered and translated	99
014-PS (USA 784)	Report of Rosenberg to the Fuehrer, 20 March 1941, concerning shipment of Jewish property	102
015-PS (USA 387)	Letter and Report of Rosenberg to Hitler, 16 April 1943, concerning seizure of ownerless Jewish art possessions	104
041-PS	Memorandum, Rosenberg to Hitler, 3 October 1942, concerning seizure of 40,000 tons of Jewish household goods in the West	108
053-PS	Excerpt from Report by Hans Koch, deputy of Reichsminister for Occupied Eastern Territories, 5 October 1941, concerning political situation in Ukraine, describing execution of 3500 Jews in Kiev	110
069-PS (USA 589)	Letter from Bormann to Rosenberg, 17 January 1939, enclosing order of 28 December 1938, concerning decisions on Jewish question	111
078-PS	Regulations issued by Heydrich, 28 June 1941, for treatment of political prisoners of war, providing for the execution of Jews	113
090-PS (USA 372)	Letter from Rosenberg to Schwarz, 28 January 1941, concerning registration and collection of Jewish libraries and art treasures, and synopsis of correspondence on subject	117

III - ix

No.	Description	Page
136-PS (USA 367)	Hitler order, 29 January 1940, concerning establishment of "Hohe Schule", the center for Nazi ideological research	121
137-PS (USA 379)	Order from Keitel to Commanding General of Armed Forces in the Netherlands, 5 July 1940, to cooperate with the Einsatzstab Rosenberg (Rosenberg's staff for seizing Jewish property, libraries and art treasures)	121
138-PS	Order from Keitel to Commanding General in Occupied France, 17 September 1940, to cooperate with the Einsatzstab Rosenberg	122
139-PS	Order of Reinecke, Chief of the General Department of OKW, 10 October 1940, concerning instructions to be given to Military Administration in Belgium to cooperate with Einsatzstab Rosenberg	123
140-PS	Order of Reinecke, Chief of the General Department of OKW, 30 October 1940, supplementing order of 5 July 1940, on seizure of Jewish possessions by Einsatzstab Rosenberg	124
141-PS (USA 368)	Goering order, 5 November 1940, concerning seizure of Jewish art treasures	125
145-PS (USA 373)	Rosenberg order 20 August 1941, concerning safeguarding the cultural goods in the Occupied Eastern Territories	126
149-PS (USA 369)	Hitler order, 1 March 1942, establishing authority of Einsatzstab Rosenberg to explore libraries and archives and confiscate material for the "Hohe Schule", Nazi center for ideological research	127
151-PS	Order from Reichsminister for Occupied Eastern Territories, 7 April 1942, concerning safeguarding of cultural goods, research material and Scientific Institutions in the East	128
154-PS (USA 370)	Letter from Lammers to high State and Party authorities, 5 July 1942, confirming Rosenberg's authority to seize material in connection with spiritual battle against Jews and Freemasons	130
155-PS	Instructions to Army Commands throughout occupied Europe, 30 Sep-	

No.	Description	Page
	tember 1942, to cooperate with units of the Einsatzstab Rosenberg	131
158-PS (USA 382)	Message, 1 June 1944, initialed Utikal, Chief of Einsatzstab (Rosenberg's staff for seizing Jewish property, libraries and art treasures), concerning a special unit dispatch to Hungary	135
159-PS (USA 380)	Message, 6 June 1944, initialed Utikal, Chief of Einsatzstab, concerning special units dispatched to Denmark and Norway	135
171-PS (USA 383)	Undated report on "Library for Exploration of the Jewish Question" by the Hohe Schule District Office	136
176-PS (USA 707)	Report on Einsatzstab Rosenberg Working Group Netherlands, signed Schimmer, listing lodges and Jewish libraries confiscated	139
212-PS (USA 272)	Memorandum from Rosenberg file concerning instructions for treatment of Jews in the East	144
342-PS	Decree, 13 October 1941, directing the confiscation of Jewish property in the Reich Commissariat Ostland	147
404-PS (USA 256)	Excerpts from Hitler, *Mein Kampf*, pp. 456, 457, 675, on racial superiority and attacking international world finance Jewry	149
501-PS (USA 288)	Collection of four documents on execution of Jews by gas wagons, June 1942, one signed by Dr. Becker, SS Untersturmfuehrer at Kiev, 16 May 1942 ..	150
502-PS (USA 486)	Regulations dated 17 July 1941 on discovering all professional revolutionaries, functionaries of the Komintern, Jews, etc. from among Soviet Prisoners of War in camps and executing them	155
579-PS	Three letters, District Commissioner, Employment Director at Riga, and Economic Directorate in Latvia, 21 July 1941, 10 February 1942, and 6 July 1942, concerning forced Jewish labor in Riga and Latvia	159
654-PS (USA 218)	Excerpts from notes of Thierack, Reich Minister of Justice, 18 September 1942, on discussion with Himmler concern-	

III - XI

No.	Description	Page
	ing delivery of Jews to Himmler for extermination through work	162
682-PS	Notes of Thierack, Reich Minister of Justice, on discussion with Goebbels, 14 September 1942, in Berlin, concerning groups to be exterminated, including Jews	163
701-PS (USA 497)	Letter from Minister of Justice to public prosecutors, 1 April 1943, to effect that Jews who are released from a penal institution are to be sent to the concentration camps Auschwitz or Lublin for the rest of their lives	163
710-PS (USA 509)	Letter from Goering to Heydrich, 31 July 1941, concerning solution of Jewish question	165
1012-PS	Teletype from OKW to Military Commander of France, 3 February 1942, concerning consultation of Hitler and Keitel about shooting of Jews and Communists	165
1015B-PS (USA 385)	Report on activities of special staff (Einsatzstab) for Pictorial Art, October 1940 to July 1944, to effect that 21,903 art objects, seized from Jews, were inventoried	166
1015I-PS (USA 385)	Letter from Goering to Rosenberg, 30 May 1942, on activities of Einsatzstab	171
1024-PS (USA 278)	Excerpts from Memorandum from Rosenberg file, 29 April 1941, concerning organization for handling problems in the Eastern Territories, suggesting that ghettos and forced labor will be lot of Jews	172
1028-PS (USA 273)	Memorandum from Rosenberg file, 7 May 1941, on decisive solution of Jewish problem through institution of ghettos or labor battalions	172
1061-PS (USA 275)	Official report of Stroop, SS and Police Leader of Warsaw, entitled "The Warsaw Ghetto is No More", describing destruction of Warsaw Ghetto in April/May 1943	173
1104-PS (USA 483)	Memorandum, 21 November 1943, enclosing copies of report concerning execution of Jews in Minsk	229

III - XII

No.	Description	Page
1113-PS	Excerpt from report of 6 November 1942 from Riga concerning action "Marsh-fever" noting that 8350 Jews were executed	236
1117-PS (USA 384)	Goering order, 1 May 1941, directing all party, state and Wehrmacht services to support Einsatzstab Rosenberg in battle against Jews and Freemasons throughout all occupied territories	237
1138-PS (USA 284)	Enclosure in letter from Reich Commissioner for Baltic States to Rosenberg, 13 August 1941, concerning provisional directives on treatment of Jews in area of Reichskommissariat Ostland (Baltic States and White Russia)	238
1189-PS	Excerpt from Special Instructions No. 44, 4 November 1941, on Feeding of Civilian Population in the Occupied Eastern Territories, in which it is provided that Jews are to receive one half the ration allowed "for population which does no work worth mentioning"	243
1208-PS (USA 590)	Goering order, 10 December 1938, concerning elimination of Jews from German economic life and confiscation of Jewish businesses and fortunes	244
1347-PS (USA 285)	Excerpt from decree, 18 September 1942, Reich Minister for Nutrition and Agriculture, concerning food supply for Jews	246
1397-PS	Excerpts from law for the reestablishment of the Professional Civil Service, 7 April 1933, providing for the dismissal of Officials of non-Aryan descent. 1933 *Reichsgesetzblatt*, Part I, p. 175	248
1400-PS	Excerpts from Law changing the regulations in regard to public officers, 30 June 1933, providing that non-Aryans may not be appointed a Reich official. 1933 *Reichsgesetzblatt*, Part I, p. 433	249
1406-PS	Excerpts from Decree for reporting of Jewish-owned property, 26 April 1938. 1938 *Reichsgesetzblatt*, Part I, p. 414	250

No.	Description	Page
1409-PS	Excerpts from order concerning utilization of Jewish property, 3 December 1938. 1938 *Reichsgesetzblatt*, Part I, p. 1709	251
1412-PS	Decree imposing one billion Reichsmark fine upon Jews of German nationality, 12 November 1938. 1938 *Reichsgesetzblatt*, Part I, p. 1579	254
1415-PS	Police regulation authorizing imposition upon Jews of restrictions on their appearance in public, 28 November 1938. 1938 *Reichsgesetzblatt*, Part I, p. 1676	254
1416-PS	Reich Citizenship Law of 15 September 1935. 1935 *Reichsgesetzblatt*, Part I, p. 1146	255
1417-PS (GB 258)	First Regulation to the Reichs Citizenship Law, 14 November 1935, defining term "Jew" and providing that a Jew cannot be a citizen of the Reich. 1935 *Reichsgesetzblatt*, Part I, p. 1333	256
1419-PS	Excerpts from law concerning Jewish Tenants, 30 April 1939, providing that a Jew cannot invoke protection of tenancy laws, that a lease may be dissolved, where only one party to it is a Jew, by the other party. 1939 *Reichsgesetzblatt*, Part I, p. 864	258
1422-PS	Thirteenth regulation under Reich Citizenship Law, 1 July 1943, depriving Jews of all protection of the law by providing that criminal actions committed by Jews shall be punished by the police	259
1472-PS (USA 279)	Cable dated 16 December 1942, signed by SS Gruppenfuehrer Mueller, concerning transportation during January 1943 of 45,000 Jews from Bialystock-District, Theresienstadt Ghetto, the occupied areas in the Netherlands and Berlin to Auschwitz for forced labor	260
1662-PS	Order eliminating Jews from German economic life, 12 November 1938	261
1665-PS	Excerpts from order concerning treatment of property of Nationals of the former Polish State, providing for the confiscation of property of Jews, 17 September 1940	262

III - xiv

No.	Description	Page
1674-PS	Excerpts from second decree for the execution of the law regarding the change of surnames and forenames, 17 August 1938, requiring that Jews may be given only such given-names as provided in Ministry of Interior directives	264
1689-PS (USA 286)	Excerpt from *"Czechoslovakia Fights Back,"* a document of the Czechoslovak Ministry of Foreign Affairs, 1943, describing elimination of Jewish life in Bohemia and Moravia	265
1708-PS (USA 255, USA 324)	The program of the NSDAP. *National Socialistic Yearbook*, 1941, p. 153	266
1724-PS (USA 266)	Announcement in Press Conferences, 4 August 1938, of breaking up of synagogue	270
1752-PS (GB 159)	Memorandum, dated 15 June 1944, concerning preparations for International Anti-Jewish Congress	270
1757-PS (GB 175)	Excerpts from report of Goering's Commissioners for investigation of Aryanisations carried out in Franconia between 9/11/38 and 9/2/39 and the irregularities connected therewith	273
1759-PS (USA 420)	Portion of affidavit of Raymond H. Geist, formerly American Consul and First Secretary of Embassy in Berlin, Germany, 1929-1939, dated 28 August 1945, describing Nazi Germany's anti-Jewish activities 1933-1938	279
1778-PS (USA 257)	Book *"The Poisonous Mushroom"* published in Nurnberg, 1938, concerning Jews	290
1816-PS (USA 261)	Stenographic report of the meeting on the Jewish question, under the Chairmanship of Fieldmarshal Goering, 12 November 1938	292
1919-PS (USA 170)	Excerpts from Himmler's speech to SS Gruppenfuehrers, 4 October 1943	324
1948-PS (USA 680)	Letter from Governor in Vienna, 7 November 1940, evidencing RSHA (Reich Main Security Office) instructions to recruit Jews for forced labor	326
1949-PS	Report of Statistical Office for Reich Gau Ostmark, 15 December 1939, on reduction in number of Jews especially in Vienna districts	327

No.	Description	Page
1950-PS (USA 681)	Secret letter from Lammers to von Schirach, 3 December 1940, reporting Hitler's decision to deport 60,000 Jews from Vienna	330
1965-PS (GB 176)	Article by Streicher, 4 November 1943, published in newspaper *Der Stuermer*, on disappearance of Jews from Europe	330
2012-PS	First regulation for administration of the law for the restriction of professional Civil Service, 11 April 1933, defining non-Aryans and prohibiting them from holding civil service positions	331
2022-PS	Law against overcrowding of German schools and higher institutions, 25 April 1933, reducing number of non-Aryans	332
2083-PS	Editorial Control Law, 4 October 1933, prohibiting non-Aryans from admission to the profession of editor	333
2112-PS	Excerpts from order of the Reich Commissioner for Occupied Netherlands Territories concerning Jewish Real Estate—providing for its registration and confiscation, 11 August 1941	334
2120-PS	Law invalidating all German passports of Jews residing in the Reich area, 5 October 1938	337
2124-PS (GB 259)	Decree introducing the Nurnberg Racial Laws into Austria, 20 May 1938	338
2154-PS (GB 167)	Additional orders of the Central Committee for defense against Jewish horror and boycott agitation, 31 March 1933, signed by Streicher.	341
2156-PS (USA 263)	Announcement of Central Committee for defense against Jewish horror and boycott agitation, 29 March 1933, published in National Socialist Party Correspondence No. 357	342
2171-PS	Excerpt from U. S. Government report B-2833 on *Numerical Expansion of Buchenwald Concentration Camp*, during years 1937-1945, with reference to substantial increase in November 1938	343
2233A-PS (USA 173)	Diary of Hans Frank, Governor General of Poland, Meetings of Depart-	

III - xvi

No.	Description	Page
	ment Chiefs in 1939/40, in which reference is made to shootings of Jews and forced labor for Jews	345
2233C-PS (USA 271)	Diary of Hans Frank, Governor General of Poland. *Tagebuch*, 1940, Part IV. October - December, containing statement that Jews in Poland will be eliminated	346
2233D-PS (USA 281)	Diary of Hans Frank, Governor General of Poland, 1941 October-December. Speech of the Governor General 16 December 1941 to effect that Jews, of whom there are over 2,500,000 in General Government, must be annihilated	347
2233E-PS (USA 283)	Diary of Hans Frank, Governor General of Poland. *Conference Volume*, Cabinet session in Cracow, 24 August 1942, on necessity of sending food to Germany from Poland even at expense of starving 1.2 million Jews	348
2233F-PS (USA 295)	Diary of Hans Frank, Governor General of Poland, Speech by Frank in Berlin 25 January 1944 in which he made statement that perhaps 100,000 Jews were left in the General Government	351
2233G-PS (USA 302)	Diary of Hans Frank, Governor General of Poland, 25 October to 15 December 1939 referring to resettlement of 1,000,000 Jews and institution of forced labor for the Jews	351
2233Q-PS	Diary of Hans Frank, Governor General of Poland, *Government Meetings*, October-December 1941. Meeting of 16 December 1941 in which Frank stated that death sentences must be imposed upon Jews leaving the ghettos	352
2237-PS	Letter from Reich Commissioner for the Reunion of Austria with the German Reich to Goering, 18 November 1938, concerning actions against the Jews in Vienna on 9/10 November 1938	353
2273-PS (USA 487)	Excerpt from a top secret report of Einsatz Group A on the execution of 229,052 Jews in Baltic Provinces	355

III - xvii

No.	Description	Page
2311-PS	Decree of Hitler on Administration of the Oath to the Officials of the Province of Austria, 15 March 1938, with provision that Jewish officials shall not be sworn in	361
2326-PS	Reich Principles Regarding Recruiting, Appointment and Promotion of Reich and Provincial Officials, 14 October 1936, providing that only an official of German blood may be promoted	362
2340-PS	Excerpts from German Public Officials law of 27 January 1937 providing, among other things, that only a person of German blood may become an official	363
2375-PS	Affidavit of Rudolf Mildner, Commander of the SIPO and SD (Security Police and Security Service) in Denmark, dated 16 November 1945, concerning anti-Jewish actions in Denmark	364
2376-PS	Affidavit of Rudolf Mildner, Commander of the SIPO and SD (Security Police and Security Service) in Denmark, dated 16 November 1945, concerning the official channels through which passed the orders for the deportation for forced labor and extermination of Jews throughout German occupied Europe	365
2402-PS	*Guide for the Party Courts,* 17 February 1934	367
2405-PS	Excerpts from German publications: Speeches by Hitler, 1922-1923, on Jewish question	368
2409-PS (USA 262)	Excerpts from the book *"From the Imperial House to the Reich Chancellory"* by Joseph Goebbels, concerning the anti-Jewish boycott of 1933	368
2410-PS	Articles by Julius Streicher on the "coming popular action" (anti-Jewish boycott), under banner headline "Beat the World Enemy" from the South German edition of the newspaper *Voelkischer Beobachter,* 31 March 1933	370
2432-PS	Excerpts from Rosenberg's *"Writings from the Years 1921-1923"* urging adoption of measures against the Jews	371

No.	Description	Page
2536-PS	Speech by Hans Frank, President of Academy of German Law and later Governor General of Poland, 3 October 1936, on the elimination of Jews from German jurisprudence	372
2540-PS	Excerpts from decree concerning sequestration of private property in the General Government of Poland, 24 January 1940	373
2542-PS (USA 489)	Affidavit of SS-Sturmbannfuehrer Kurt Lindow, 30 September 1945, in which statement is made concerning execution of Jewish soldiers on the eastern front by screening teams of the Gestapo	374
2583-PS	Quotation from speech made by Streicher on 31 October 1939 concerning the Jew as the world enemy	376
2602-PS	Excerpt from telegram, Wilson, U. S. Ambassador, to Secretary of State, Washington, 10 November 1938, reporting breaking of Jewish-owned shop windows and burning of synagogues	376
2603-PS	Report from Kemp, U. S. Consul General in Bremen, Germany, to Secretary of State, Washington, 10 November 1938, concerning anti-Jewish demonstrations in Bremen	377
2604-PS	Report of Honaker, American Consul General to U. S. Ambassador Wilson in Berlin, 12 November 1938, on anti-Semitic persecution in the Stuttgart Consular District	377
2605-PS (USA 242)	Affidavit, 13 September 1945, of Dr. Rudolf Kastner, former President of the Hungarian Zionist Organization, describing German persecution of Hungarian Jews	378
2613-PS	Excerpts from *"The Black Book of Poland"* describing ghettos in Poland and forced labor for Jews	392
2620-PS (USA 919)	Affidavit of Otto Ohlendorf, Chief of the Security Service (intelligence and counter-intelligence agency of the SS), 5 November 1945, concerning his participation in liquidation in the East of	

No.	Description	Page
	90,000 men, women and children, of whom the majority were Jews	397
2622-PS	Affidavit of Otto Ohlendorf, Chief of the Security Service (intelligence and counter-intelligence agency of the SS) concerning execution of Jewish prisoners of war on eastern front	399
2662-PS (USA 256)	Excerpt from *Mein Kampf*, 39th Edition, 1939, pp. 724-725 on the subject of the Jew as the evil enemy of mankind	400
2663-PS (USA 268)	Hitler's speech to the Reichstag, 30 January 1939, prophesying the annihilation of the Jewish race in Europe	400
2665-PS (USA 270)	The Jewish Question Past and Present, from *"World Battle"*, April-September 1941, p. 71	401
2668-PS (USA 269)	"And Don't Forget the Jews", from the *Black Corps*, 8 August 1940, No. 32, p. 2	401
2673-PS	Extract from *"The Archive"*, No. 90, 30 October 1941, p. 495, concerning police decree requiring Jews to wear Jewish star in public	401
2682-PS	Excerpts from newspaper *Voelkischer Beobachter*, 5 December 1938, No. 339, p. 5, concerning repeal of drivers' licenses and registration papers of Jews and restrictions against Jews prohibiting them from appearing in public in certain places in Berlin	402
2683-PS	Newspaper report in *Voelkischer Beobachter*, 15/16 November 1938, of decree barring Jews from German universities	404
2697-PS (USA 259)	Article: "The Chosen People of the Criminals" from newspaper *Der Stuermer*, No. 2, January 1935	404
2698-PS (USA 260)	Article: "Two Little Talmud Jews" from newspaper *Der Stuermer*, No. 50, December 1938	405
2699-PS (USA 258)	Article: "Ritual Murder" from newspaper *Der Stuermer*, No. 14, April 1937	405
2700-PS	Article: "The Ritual Murder" from newspaper *Der Stuermer*, No. 28, July 1938	406

No.	Description	Page
2704-PS	Decree concerning Prohibition of Jewish Religious Slaughter of animals, 26 October 1939, *Verordnungsblatt of the Governor General for Occupied Polish Territory*, 1939, p. 7	406
2705-PS	Decree of Reich Commissioner for Occupied Netherland Territories for the avoidance of cruelty to animals in slaughtering, *Official Gazette for Occupied Netherland Territories*, 3 August 1940	407
2709-PS (USA 265)	Report of Ralph C. Busser, American Consul-General in Leipzig, 5 April 1933, concerning anti-Jewish movement in central Germany	408
2711-PS (USA 267)	Article: "Symbolic Action" published in newspaper *Fraenkische Tageszeitung*—Nurnberg, 11 August 1938, concerning destruction of the Synagogue in Nurnberg	409
2712-PS	Account of spontaneous anti-Jewish demonstrations throughout Germany, from newspaper *Voelkischer Beobachter*, 11 November 1938	409
2738-PS (USA 296)	Affidavit of Wilhelm Hoettl, a member of the Security Service (intelligence and counter-intelligence agency of the SS), 26 November 1945, in which proof is given that 6 million Jews were killed by the Germans	410
2746-PS	Decree concerning organization of Criminal Jurisdiction against Poles and Jews in the Incorporated Eastern Territories, 4 December 1941	412
2752-PS	Affidavit of Willy Litzenberg, a member of the Gestapo, 8 November 1945, concerning activities of Einsatz groups in executing Jews in the East	416
2801-PS (USA 109)	Minutes of discussion between Goering and Slovak Minister Durkansky (undated, but probably late fall or early winter 1938-39) in which statement appears that Jewish problem will be solved in Slovakia as in Germany	417
2840-PS	Excerpt from *"Dr. Wilhelm Frick and His Ministry"*, 1937, pp. 180-181, on subject of early attempts (1924-25) by	

No.	Description	Page
	Nazi Party to eliminate the Jew from the German national body	418
2841-PS	Excerpt from *"Care for Race and Heredity in the Legislation of the Reich"*, Leipzig, 1943, p. 14, to effect that racial legislation prepared way for final solution of Jewish problem	419
2842-PS	Excerpt from *"Writings of the Years 1917-1921"*, by Alfred Rosenberg, Munich 1943, pp. 320-321, advocating national-political measures against the Jews	419
2843-PS	Excerpt from *Documents of German Politics*, Vol. VII, pp. 728-729, on Race Politics, commenting on Rosenberg's speeches, January and February 1939, advocating the elimination of Jews from Europe	420
2844-PS	Excerpt from *"The Program of the Nazi Party"* by Gottfried Feder, August 1927, Munich, p. 17, commenting on anti-Semitism	421
2868-PS	Excerpt from law relating to admission to profession of patent-agent and lawyer, 22 April 1933, providing that non-Aryan patent-agents may be taken off roster	421
2869-PS	Excerpt from law relating to the admission of tax advisors, 6 May 1933, providing that non-Aryans should not be admitted and that admissions already granted to such persons are to be withdrawn	422
2870-PS	Excerpts from executory decree for the law about the Repeal of Naturalization, 26 July 1933, providing for the repeal of the naturalization of Eastern Jews .	423
2872-PS	Fourth Decree relative to the Reich Citizenship Law, 25 July 1938, prohibiting Jews from practicing medicine .	424
2874-PS	Fifth Decree to the law relating to the Reich Citizenship Law, 27 September 1938, eliminating Jews from the bar in Germany and Austria	425

III - XXII

No.	Description	Page
2875-PS	Decree relating to the Exclusion of Jews from the German Economic Life, 12 November 1938	426
2876-PS	Tenth Decree relating to the Reich Citizenship Law, 4 July 1939, authorizing Reich Minister of Interior to abolish or take over all Jewish organizations and foundations	427
2877-PS	Police Decree concerning the "marking" of Jews, 1 September 1941, providing that Jews in Bohemia and Moravia may not travel without permission and may not appear in public without a Jewish star	429
2889-PS (USA 595)	Speech by Alfred Rosenberg on "The Jew Question as World Problem", 28 March 1941, published in newspaper *Voelkischer Beobachter*, Munich edition, 29 March 1941, advocating elimination of Jews from Germany and Europe	430
2894-PS	General Decree of 10 September 1935 issued by Rust, Reichsminister of Education, on establishment of separate Jewish schools, *Documents of German Politics*, 1937, p. 152	433
2904-PS	"*The Racial Problem and the New Reich*", published in The National Socialist Monthly, No. 38, May 1933, pp. 196-197, indicating that legislation is mainly educational and gives direction to the solution of the Jewish question	434
2907-PS	Notes of conference of Reich Ministers on 12 September 1933 concerning forthcoming session of the League of Nations Conference in Geneva where attacks against the Reich Government are to be reckoned with on account of the Jewish Question in Germany	435
2916-PS	Excerpt from survey of deportations of Jews and Poles up to 15 November 1940, from collection of restricted intra-office documents on Commitment of Manpower, Doctrines—Orders—Directives, edited December 1940 by Reich Commissioner for the Strengthening of	

III - XXIII

No.	Description	Page
	the National Character of the German People	437
2917-PS	Excerpts from decree concerning German people's list and German nationality in the Incorporated Eastern Territories, 4 March 1941, introducing Citizenship Legislation	438
2953-PS (GB 136)	Letter, 29 June 1939, from Heydrich to Ribbentrop, with enclosure concerning instigation of pogroms against Jews in Lithuania	439
2960-PS (USA 406)	Excerpt from *"The Reich Ministry of Interior"*, Berlin, 1940, p. 62, discussing the three "Nurnberg Laws"	440
2984-PS	Excerpt from law concerning Armed Forces, 21 May 1935, providing that Aryan descent is a prerequisite for active military service	441
2992-PS (USA 494)	Three affidavits on Hermann Friedrich Graebe, 10 and 13 November 1945, giving eye-witness accounts of slaughter of all Jews in Dubno, Ukraine, in October 1942 and slaughter of 5000 Jews in the Rowno Ghetto, Ukraine, on 13 July 1942, and order of Area Commissioner of Rowno, 13 July 1942, exempting Jewish workers of Jung firm from the pogrom	442
3047-PS (USA 80)	Excerpt from notes made by Lahousen (Assistant to Admiral Canaris, Head of Intelligence Section OKW) for the diary of Admiral Canaris, 19 September 1939, and complete report, dated 24 October 1941, on the execution of 6500 Jews in Borisow received by Lahousen in his official capacity as a German intelligence officer	450
3048-PS (USA 274)	Excerpt from speech by von Schirach before European Youth Congress in Vienna, on deportation to the Ghetto of the East tens of thousands of Jews from Vienna, published in newspaper *Voelkischer Beobachter*, 15 September 1942	455
3050AE-PS	Excerpts from series of articles designed to create and foster an anti-Jewish attitude, published in *"The SA Man"*	456

No.	Description	Page
3051-PS (USA 240)	Three teletype orders from Heydrich to all stations of the State Police, 10 November 1938, on measures against the Jews, and one order terminating the action	459
3058-PS (USA 508)	Letter from Heydrich to Goering, 11 November 1938, reporting results of the action against the Jews	463
3063-PS (USA 332)	Letter of transmittal, 13 February 1939, and report about the events and the judicial proceedings by the Supreme Nazi Party Court against persons who killed Jews during the course of the anti-Jewish demonstrations of 9 November 1938	464
3085-PS	Himmler's ordinance of 3 July 1943 charging Gestapo with execution of Thirteenth Ordinance under Reich Citizenship Law	473
3179-PS	Law for the Protection of German Blood and Honor, 15 September 1935	473
3240-PS	Excerpt from order signed by M. Bormann, 8 January 1937, refusing financial assistance to civil service employees to pay for services by Jewish doctors, dentists, lawyers, etc., published in *Decrees of the Deputy of the Fuehrer*, No. 5/37, pp. 383-385	475
3244-PS (GB 267)	Preparatory Measures for the Solution of the Jewish Problem in Europe—Rumors about the Position of the Jews in the East, 9 October 1942, published in *Decrees, Regulations, Announcements*, Vol. 2, pp. 131-132	475
3257-PS (USA 290)	Letter from Armament Inspector in the Ukraine to General Thomas, Chief of the Industrial Armament Department, OKW, 2 December 1941, enclosing report by Prof. Seraphim on the execution of 150,000 to 200,000 Jews in the Ukraine	477
3311-PS (USA 293)	Charge No. 6 against Hans Frank, submitted by Polish Government to International Military Tribunal, dated 5 December 1945, describing operation of extermination camp "Treblinka B"	

No.	Description	Page
	where several hundred thousands of Jews were slaughtered	480
3319-PS (GB 287)	Foreign Office Correspondence, August 1941 to April 1944, giving reports and notes on conferences on anti-Jewish action in foreign countries	485
3323-PS	Excerpts from decree concerning the obligations of Jews in the Netherlands to register, 10 January 1941	511
3325-PS	Decree of the Reich Commissioner for the Occupied Dutch Territories restricting the enrollment of Jews at Dutch Universities, 11 February 1941	512
3326-PS	Decree of the Reich Commissioner for the Occupied Dutch Territories blocking the property of Jews who emigrated to the Netherlands, 18 September 1941	513
3328-PS	Excerpts from decree of the Reich Commissioner for the Occupied Dutch Territories regulating all professional, industrial or other pursuits aimed at profits of Jews, 22 October 1941	514
3329-PS	Excerpts from decree of the Reich Commissioner for the Occupied Dutch Territories prohibiting Jews from working in the fields of architecture, handicraft, music, literature, theatre, films and journalism, 22 November 1941	516
3333-PS	Excerpts from decree of the Reich Commissioner for the Occupied Dutch Territories providing for the registration of all Jewish enterprises, 22 October 1940	518
3334-PS	Excerpts from decree of the Reich Commissioner for the Occupied Dutch Territories prohibiting the employment of German nationals of German or related blood in Jewish households, 19 December 1940	520
3336-PS	Excerpts from order of the Reich Commissioner for the Occupied Dutch Territories providing for the registra-	

III - XXVI

No.	Description	Page
	tion of all claims belonging to Jews, 21 May 1942	521
3358-PS (GB 158)	German Foreign Office Circular, 31 January 1939, on "The Jewish Question as a factor in German Foreign Policy in the Year 1938"	524
3363-PS	Special Delivery Letter, 21 September 1939, from Chief of the Security Police to Chiefs of all detail groups of the Security Police concerning the Jewish problem in occupied zone	532
3418-PS	Prophecy of Destruction of Jewish Race in Europe in the event of another World War, from *The Archive*, January 1935, p. 1605	536
3428-PS (USA 827)	Letter from Kube, Commissioner General For White Ruthenia, 31 July 1942, on Combating of Partisans and Action Against Jews in the District General of White Ruthenia, describing liquidation of 55,000 Jews	537
3430-PS	Excerpt from *"Four Years in Holland"*, 1944, by Reichsminister Seyss-Inquart, expressing implacable hatred toward Jews	539
3450-PS (USA 888)	Excerpts from Law of 18 November 1938 concerning the confiscation of property of enemies of the people and the State of Austria	540
3460-PS (USA 437)	Excerpt from speech of Hermann Goering urging inexorable elimination of Jews from economic life of Vienna	541
3468-PS (USA 705)	Excerpts from decrees of General Government of Poland, October-November 1939, concerning forced labor for Jews, requiring Jews to wear Star of David, and requiring Jewish enterprises to be marked by Jewish Star	541
3544-PS (USA 660)	Excerpts from interrogation of Walter Funk, 22 October 1945, concerning anti-Jewish economic measures	543
3545-PS (USA 659)	Excerpt from speech by Walter Funk, 15 November 1938, on elimination of Jews from the German economy, published in newspaper *Frankfurter Zeitung*, 17 November 1938	545

No.	Description	Page
3569-PS	Political Testament of Adolf Hitler, 29 April 1945, urging upon German nation merciless opposition to Jews	545
3575-PS (USA 781)	Excerpt from Top Secret Memorandum concerning the meeting of the Reich Defense Council, 18 November 1938, in which it was reported that fine imposed on Jewry and Aryanization of Jewish enterprises relieved very critical situation of the Reich Exchequer	550
3577-PS	Letter from Josef Buerkel, Deputy of the Fuehrer for the Plebiscite in Austria, to Goering, 26 March 1938, concerning Aryanization of Jewish-held business in Austria and disposition of resulting funds	551
3589-PS (USA 720)	Supplement No. 6 to Official Czechoslovak Report *"German Crimes Against Czechoslovakia"*, 7 January 1946, reporting that many thousands of Czechoslovak Jews were killed in gas chambers at Auschwitz	553
3611-PS	Excerpt from decree, 31 May 1941, authorizing Military Commander in Belgium and Northern France to order Jews to shut down their businesses or sell their assets	554
3663-PS (USA 825)	Letter from Liebbrandt (in charge of Main Division 2 of the Ministry for the Occupied Eastern Territories concerned with political affairs), 5 November 1941, to Reich Commissioner for the Ostland (Baltic Countries and White Russia), on subject of execution of Jews, and reply, 15 November 1941	554
3666-PS (USA 826)	Letter from Braeutigam (first assistant to Liebbrandt who was in charge of Main Division 2 of the Ministry for the Occupied Eastern Territories concerned with political affairs), 18 December 1941, on clarification of the Jewish question in the East	556
3688-PS	Notice from the German Foreign Office, 24 September 1942, concerning evacuation of Jews from occupied territories (Slovakia, Croatia, Rumania, Bulgaria,	

No.	Description	Page
	Hungary and Denmark), and regulation of the Jewish question in Italy...	556
3710-PS (USA 557)	Affidavit of Walter Schellenberg, 26 November 1945, on activities of Combat Groups (Einsatzgruppen) of the SIPO and SD (Security Police and Security Service) in executing Jewish prisoners of war on Eastern front and in carrying out mass executions of Jews in the East (Documents L-180, 078-PS, 502-PS and R-102)	557
3720-PS (USA 220)	Excerpts from interrogation of Albert Speer, 18 October 1945, on subject of forced labor of Hungarian Jews	561
3762-PS (USA 798)	Affidavit of Kurt Becher, formerly a Colonel in the SS, 8 March 1946, to effect that Himmler ordered end of further liquidation of Jews between the middle of September and October 1944	564
3803-PS (USA 802)	Covering letter enclosing a letter from Kaltenbrunner, 30 June 1944, concerning forced labor of Jews in Vienna ..	565
3840-PS (USA 803)	Affidavit of Karl Kaleske, adjutant to SS and Police Leader Stroop, 24 February 1946, concerning action against the Warsaw Ghetto, April 1943	567
3841-PS (USA 804)	Affidavit of Juergen Stroop, SS and Police Leader of Warsaw District, 24 February 1946, to effect that he conducted action against the Warsaw Ghetto in April 1943 pursuant to order of Himmler	568
3868-PS (USA 819)	Affidavit, dated 5 April 1946, of Rudolf Franz Ferdinand Hoess, Commandant of Auschwitz Extermination Camp from 1 May 1940 to 1 December 1943, concerning execution of 2,500,000 persons and death from starvation and disease of another 500,000, most of whom were Jews	569
R-96 (GB 268)	Correspondence from files of Minister of Justice, April-August 1941, in preparation of discriminatory decree of 4 December 1941 (2746-PS) regarding criminal justice against Poles and Jews in annexed Eastern territories	573

No.	Description	Page
R-102 (USA 470)	Excerpts from Activity and Situation Report No. 6 of the Task Forces (Einsatzgruppen) of the Security Police and the Security Service in the U.S.S.R., 1-31 October 1941, listing measures taken against Jews and the executions of Jews in various locations in the East	579
R-124 (USA 179)	Minutes of discussions between Speer and Hitler, 6 and 7 April 1944, concerning the importation of 100,000 Jews from Hungary for forced labor	587
R-135 (USA 289)	Correspondence May and June 1943 from the General Commissar in White Ruthenia and the Reich Commissar in the Ostland (Baltic Countries and White Russia) to the Reich Minister for the Occupied Eastern Territories concerning the executions of Jews	588

Biographical Data 593

Glossary of common German and Nazi Titles, Designations, and Terms, with their official abbreviations 608

THE DOCUMENTARY EVIDENCE

Translation of Document D-183. Order of Gestapo Office, Darmstadt, 7 December 1938, on treatment of articles secured during protest action against Jews.

* * *

Copy of a Copy.

Secret state police
State police station
Darmstadt
File No. II B 4 8521/38

Darmstadt, 7. Dec. 1938
Wilhelm - Glaessing - Str. 21

To the
SS - Section
Kassel.

Subject: Treatment of Articles Secured during Protest Action against Jews.
Ref: nil.
Enclosures: nil.

By order of the Prime Minister General Field Marshal Goering, the Secret State Police Department, Berlin, has issued the following orders regarding articles which were confiscated and secured:

1. The following applies to such articles, where the owner can still be established:

    a. Bonds [Wertpapiere], cash, jewelry, and articles for common use of high value, are to be listed, stating the owner, the value or estimated value, and reported to the competent State Police Department. Bonds, cash and jewelry, the value of which is less than 1.000. - RM are to be returned to their owner against receipt. This also applies to articles of common use, and objects of higher estimated value if proof exists that the owner will emigrate in the near future. Contact must first be made, however, with the appropriate agency of the President of the Finance Department. My decision must be obtained if particularly high values are involved.

III - 1

    b. Food and perishable articles of common use to the value of not more than 1.000. - RM, are to be handed, against receipt, to the competent local agencies of the Retail Trade concerned, for further sales. Only such food and articles of common use are excepted, where it can be proved that they belong to an Aryan business owner. These articles will be returned directly to the owners against receipt.

    c. Stocks of clothing are to be returned to the owners after consultation with local agencies of the retail trade concerned.

2. For articles the owners of which can no longer be ascertained, the following applies:

    a. Bonds, cash and articles of common use of high value (motor cars, furs and gowns) etc., will be delivered to the competent local agencies of the Finance President, against receipt. Lists will be submitted in duplicate.

    b. Food and perishable articles of common use will be transferred to the competent local National Socialist Welfare (NSV) agencies against receipt, for the purpose of distribution under their own authority.

    c. Where articles have already been handed to the National Socialist Welfare (NSV) under para 2(a), receipt on this transaction will also be submitted.

    I draw your attention to the fact that delivery of the articles must be carried out in co-operation with the competent State Police Departments. For the district of the 83rd SS troop this will be the State Police Department Giessen. Duplicate receipts will be submitted to the competent State Police Department, regarding any valuables which have been delivered directly to any of the Service Departments mentioned above.

    According to reports available here, it is likely that the appropriate notification has already been circulated by the office of the Reich Leader SS.

                                                 [Signature illegible]

Certified copy.
[Signature illegible]
SS - Sergeant.

The Documentary Evidence   D-229

Translation of Document D-229. Excerpts from a pamphlet, "Judges' Letters", concerning punishment for concealing Jewish identification, 24 April 1942; and crime against currency laws by a Jew, 26 May 1942.

* * *

[PAMPHLET "JUDGES' LETTERS"]
Information Pamphlet on the Reichs Ministry of Justice.

Confidential

5. *Concealment of Jewish Identification.*
Judgment of a Lower Court of 24th April 1942.

The Jewish proprietress of a boarding house failed to apply for the name SARA to be added to her own name in the official Telephone Directory. The Lower Court condemned her to a fine of RM30 or ten days' imprisonment. Reason given is: According to the decision of the District Court, Jews are obliged to have their names supplemented with the name SARA in the telephone book. The Jewess was therefore to be punished. The leniency of the punishment was explained by the fact that individual judges had sometimes not given their decisions along the lines laid down by the District Court.

Confidential.

No. 1, 1 Oct. 42.

GERMAN JUDGES.

According to the ancient Teutonic conception of justice, the leader of the Nation was also its supreme judge. If, therefore, the Fuehrer invests the authority of a judge on a third person, it not only implies that this person receives his judge's power from the Fuehrer and is responsible to him, but it also proves the close relationship between leadership and the duties of a judge.

* * * * * * *

I, therefore, decided to issue "Judges' Letters" which will be sent to all German judges and Attorney Generals. In particular these "Judges' Letters" will contain such findings, which, in my opinion, deserve to be specially discussed in view of their results or grounds for judgment. I propose to show by means of these findings how a better decision could, and should have been made. On the other hand, it is proposed to point out correct decisions of sufficient importance to the community.

The contents of the letters are confidential. They will be handed to all Judges and Attorney Generals by the departmental chiefs, against receipt.

III - 3

I am convinced that the "Judges' Letters" will contribute considerably towards the creation of a German corps of judges, homogeneous in spirit.

Berlin, 1 Oct 42.
(Sgd)   Dr. Thierach.
Reichs Minister of Justice.

No. 4
CRIME AGAINST FOREIGN CURRENCY LAWS BY A JEW.

Judgment by a County Court of 26 May 42.

The accused, a 36 year old Jew, took over the textile business of his deceased father in 1936 and emigrated to Holland in 1938. In 1941 he was arrested at Amsterdam.

*   *   *   *   *   *   *

The County Court decided that "for the reasons stated by the accused" a particularly serious case under para. 42 of the Foreign Currency Law of 4 Feb. 44 and para. 69 of the Foreign Currency Law of 12 Dec. 38, did not exist. It sentenced the accused to a total imprisonment of two years, and fined him 9,000 RM. The time spent in prison on remand will be deducted from the sentence.

The judgment, in considering the reasons for the sentence, is weighing up the mitigating circumstances and states that the accused was, in principle, without previous conviction; that he had been under a certain amount of stress owing to the action of his father and the stubbornness of his sister. One crime had inevitably been followed by another. Furthermore, by making a confession he had greatly assisted in clarifying the whole evidence. The lengthy period of criminal conduct is then quoted as an aggravating factor, as well as the fraudulent conduct towards German authorities. Certain demands made of former employees are also stressed.

COMMENTS BY THE REICHS MINISTER OF JUSTICE

In deciding the sentence, the Court is using the same considerations which would be applied if the accused had been a German national. This is not admissible. A Jew is an enemy of the German people who has plotted, stirred up and prolonged this war. Thus he has brought endless misery upon our German nation. He is not only of a different, but also of an inferior racial type. Justice demands that equal measures must not be applied to the unequal and that this racial point of view must not be overlooked in deciding the sentence. In passing a sentence on the accused, who was—as is typical for a Jew—a profiteer to the detriment of German interests, it ought to have been considered first and foremost that he had extracted considerable values from the German people over a period of years. Like all of his race, he deliberately and selfishly damaged vital German interests by ruthlessly profiteering and fraud. He has abused German hospitality which had enabled him and his father to accumulate a considerable fortune, and finally did not hesitate to entice Germans who were economically dependent on him, to commit grave breaches of the Foreign Currency Laws, which endangered their entire existence. The question of whether or not this was a particularly serious case, should have been examined with a view to the general aspect of the German people. It did not suffice in this connection to refer to the unconvincing statements of the accused himself who was certainly not under compulsion during all those four years, but who was acting in his own interest and on his own initiative. The typically Jewish conduct which is damaging National interests, calls for the sternest judgment and the most severe punishment. In view of those reasons considerations of the psychology of the Jew and his family should have been a matter of utter insignificance.

Translation of Document D-355. Affidavit of Walter Thoene, 8 October 1945, on mistreatment of Hungarian Jewesses working at heavy labor.

* * *

. Essen 8. 10. 45.

SWORN STATEMENT

I, the undersigned
Walter Thoene, born 30.10.1890 and living at Wolfsburg Ganghofer Str 13 make the following statement voluntarily.

I admit that I punched and beat Hungarian Jewesses which I had to supervise in No. 3 Steel Moulding Shop. I did not do this of my own free will but was ordered to do so by my works manager Reif, who was a Party Member like I was. Almost every day this unscrupulous man held me to it in no mistakable manner to driving on these Jewesses and getting better performances from them. He also always emphasized that I should not be trivial in the choice of means and, if necessary, hit them like hitting a piece of cold iron. As soon as I saw that these women were standing near the ovens, I had to drive them back to their work. And this whilst the poor women were so badly protected against the cold, as they only had thin rags on their bodies. Most of these people had no stockings on in severe frosty weather. In winter their legs were frozen blue and had scabby chilblains as big as a half-crown. The women received no food all day. They were fed in the camp. I could not bear to see the sufferings of the women, later on, and was glad when I was transferred from the Steel Forming Shop to the Railway during the last days of February.

I ought to mention the work in which the Jewesses were engaged was much too heavy for women. For instance they had to knock down the remains of walls with sledge hammers which weighed 8 to 10 pounds, or they had to carry or clean stones the whole day. They also had to unload sheet metal from Railway Wagons and carry it about 100 meters. Reif always inspected this work and made sure I kept an eye on the speed. If Reif hadn't always been standing behind me, I should definitely have treated the Jewesses better.

I ought to mention one case specially which happened in February 1945. I hit a woman with my clenched fist on the shoulder and she fell down. Reif who was standing about 6 meters away forced me to do it.

Signed: Walter THOENE

J.W.L. Rathborne Major.
President.
[Mil Gov Stamp]

Translation of Document D-411 (USA 556). Army Order, dated 10 October 1941, covering letter on Conduct of Troops in Eastern Territories, to effect that soldiers must have full understanding for necessity of a severe but just revenge on subhuman Jewry.

* * *

Appendix to 12 Inf. Div. I.c/Adj.
No. 607/41 Secret date 17.11 1941.

Copy of a Copy

High Command of the Army
Gen. Staff of the Army/Quarter
Master General Branch Admin.

H.Qu. High Command of the Army
28.10.41.

III - 6

SECRET!

(Qu.4/B)
II. 7498/41 g.
Subject: Conduct of Troops in the Eastern Territories

By order of the C.inC. Army, an enclosed copy of an order by G.O.C. 6th Army on the conduct of the Troops in eastern territories which has been described by the Fuehrer as excellent, is being forwarded with the request to issue corresponding instructions on the same lines if this has not already been done.

By order.

[signed] Wagner

Army H.Q., 10.10.41

Army Command 6.
Sec. Ia—AZ.7

SECRET!

Subject: Conduct of Troops in Eastern Territories.

Regarding the conduct of troops towards the bolshevistic system, vague ideas are still prevalent in many cases. The most essential aim of war against the Jewish-bolshevistic system is a complete destruction of their means of power and the elimination of asiatic influence from the European culture. In this connection the troops are facing tasks which exceed the one-sided routine of soldiering. The soldier in the eastern territories is not merely a fighter according to the rules of the art of war but also a bearer of ruthless national ideology and the avenger of bestialities which have been inflicted upon German and racially related nations.

Therefore the soldier must have full understanding for the necessity of a severe but just revenge on subhuman Jewry. The Army has to aim at another purpose, i.e. the annihilation of revolts in hinterland which, as experience proves, have always been caused by Jews.

The combatting of the enemy behind the front line is still not being taken seriously enough. Treacherous, cruel partisans and unnatural women are still being made prisoners of war and guerilla fighters dressed partly in uniforms or plain clothes and vagabonds are still being treated as proper soldiers, and sent to prisoner of war camps. In fact, captured Russian officers talk even mockingly about Soviet agents moving openly about the roads and very often eating at German field kitchens. Such an attitude of the troops can only be explained by complete thoughtlessness, so it is now high time for the commanders to clarify the meaning of the present struggle.

The feeding of the natives and of prisoners of war who are not working for the Armed Forces from Army Kitchens is an equally misunderstood humanitarian act as is the giving of cigarettes and bread. Things which the people at home can spare under great sacrifices and things which are being brought by the Command to the front under great difficulties, should not be given to the enemy by the soldier not even if they originate from booty. It is an important part of our supply.

When retreating the Soviets have often set buildings on fire. The troops should be interested in extinguishing of fires only as far as it is necessary to secure sufficient numbers of billets. Otherwise the disappearance of symbols of the former bolshevistic rule even in the form of buildings is part of the struggle of destruction. Neither historic nor artistic considerations are of any importance in the eastern territories. The command issues the necessary directives for the securing of raw materials and plants, essential for war economy. The complete disarming of the civil population in the rear of the fighting troops is imperative considering the long and vulnerable lines of communications. Where possible, captured weapons and ammunition should be stored and guarded. Should this be impossible because of the situation of the battle so the weapons and ammunition will be rendered useless. If isolated partisans are found using firearms in the rear of the army drastic measures are to be taken. These measures will be extended to that part of the male population who were in a position to hinder or report the attacks. The indifference of numerous apparently anti-soviet elements which originates from a "wait and see" attitude, must give way to a clear decision for active collaboration. If not, no one can complain about being judged and treated a member of the Soviet System.

The fear of the German counter-measures must be stronger than the threats of the wandering bolshevistic remnants. Being far from all political considerations of the future the soldier has to fulfill two tasks:

1. *Complete annihilation of the false bolshevistic doctrine of the Soviet State and its armed forces.*

2. *The pitiless extermination of foreign treachery and cruelty and thus the protection of the lives of military personnel in Russia.*

This is the only way to fulfill our historic task to liberate the German people once for ever from the Asiatic-Jewish danger.

        Commander in Chief
        [signed] von Reichenau
           Field Marshal.

Certified Copy:
signed [illegible]
 Captain.

Copy of Document D-635 (GB 242). *Translation of Radiogram from Vice-Chancellor von Papen to Board of Trade for German-American Commerce, 27 March 1933, to effect that news circulating in United States about German excesses against the Jews emanates from sources interested in poisoning relations between Germany and America. Published in New York Times, Tuesday, 28 March 1933.*

       * * *

Von Papen's message was as follows:

News which has reached you of alleged encroachments against American business interest and of other excesses is entirely without foundation. Business life, travel, and commercial intercourse have been proceeding absolutely normally since the national government has taken office. No complaints about interference with American interests have been reported by the American Chamber of Commerce in Berlin which on 10 March gave Ambassador Sackett a great farewell banquet.

      "State of Seige" Denied

Reports that a state of siege and news censorship exist are free interventions. The emergency decree under which mail and telegraphic communications can be supervised is directed against persons suspected of communistic plots. The national revolution, the goal of which is to free Germany from serious communistic danger and remove from the administration all inferior elements, has been accomplished with remarkable order.

The American Embassy has reported to the Reich Government less than a dozen cases of excesses against Americans, all of which are of a light nature and which by no means have been established as having been committed by National Socialists. Reports circulated in America and received here with indignation about alleged tortures of political prisoners and mistreatment of Jews deserve strongest repudiation.

Hundreds of thousands of Jews irrespective of nationality, who have not taken part in political activities, are living here entirely unmolested. Operations of large Jewish enterprises and big Jewish publishing houses, such as Mosse, Ullstein, and Frankfurter Zeitung, are absolutely normal. Synagogues and Jewish cemeteries are undisturbed.

Undoubtedly there have been a few regrettable excesses. However, since the declaration of the Chancellor on March 12 that illegal acts by individuals have to stop and will be most severely dealt with, nothing more has happened. News to the contrary which is circulated in America including a story of an alleged St. Bartholomew night, said to have been planned for the night of 4 March, clearly emanates from sources strongly interested in poisoning the friendly relations between Germany and America and systematically discrediting with the American people the national government, although it is based on a majority of the German people.

The radiogram, sent from the Foreign Office in Berlin to the trade board here at 230 Fifth Avenue was made public by Albert Degener, secretary-treasurer of the board.

Translation of Document D-734. Note of a conversation between Reich Foreign Minister and the Duce, 25 February 1943, in which Foreign Minister stated Italian military circles did not sufficiently appreciate the Jewish problem.

* * *

Note of a conversation between the Reich Foreign Minister and the Duce in the presence of von Mackensen, Alfieri and Bastianini on the 25th Feb 1943.

During the further course of the conversation, the Reich Foreign Minister came to speak about the possibilities of a landing by the British and Americans. It was in itself difficult to say where a landing would take place. But information was collecting according to which England intended to proceed against Corsica and Sardinia. In this connection the question of fortifying these islands became one of decisive importance. The Army engineers staffs, placed at the disposal of Italy are of the opinion that the fortification of Sardinia is totally inadequate and that, in case of a serious British landing, Sardinia would be occupied. The Fuehrer believed that the enemies were aware of the fact that the transport problem was becoming more and more difficult for them and they would therefore undertake landing operations as soon as possible.

Further, the Reich Foreign Minister dealt with the Jewish question. The Duce was aware that Germany took up a radical position on the question of the treatment of the Jews. As a result of the development of the war in Russia it had gained even greater clarity. All Jews had been transported from Germany and from the territories occupied by her to reserves in the East. He (the Reich Foreign Minister) knew that this measure was described as cruel, particularly by the enemies. But it was necessary, in order to be able to carry the war through to a successful conclusion. It could still be called relatively mild, considering its enormous importance. Experience had taught that wherever there were Jews, no pacification took place. The Jews were the propagators of the Anglo-American news and of other rumors, and spread all around them such defeatism that one was forced to apply special measures against them, not only for general ideological considerations, but also for purely practical ones.

France also had taken measures against the Jews, which were extremely useful. They were only temporary, because here too the final solution would be in the deportation of the Jews to the East.

He (the Reich Foreign Minister) knew that in Italian military circles—just occasionally amongst German military people too—the Jewish problem was not sufficiently appreciated. Only this could he understand as an order of the Commands Supreme which cancelled measures in the Italian occupation Zone of France that had been taken against the Jews by the French authorities acting under German influence.

The Duce contested the accuracy of this report and traced it back to the French tactics of causing dissension between Germany and Italy. The Jews had in fact been concentrated by the Italians in various camps. Nevertheless he admitted that the Reich Foreign Minister was right with regard to the remark that the military people had not got the right sentiment where the Jewish problem was concerned. He traced this back to their dissimilar mental preparation, amongst other things.

Referring to his discussions with Alfieri, the Reich Foreign Minister stressed the fact that the Jew was Germany's and Italy's greatest enemy. The British were perhaps sometimes somehow still decent people.

But the Jews hated National Socialist Germany and the Fas-

cist-Italy fanatically. If one was to allow 100,000 Jews to remain in Germany or Italy or one of the territories occupied by them, then—with the Jews' skill—this would be roughly equivalent to letting 100,000 Secret Service agents into one's country, giving them German nationality as camouflage and top of that equipping them with inexhaustible financial means.
Rome, the 27th Feb. 1943.

Translation of Document D-736 (GB 283). *Notes on discussion between Fuehrer, Ribbentrop and Hungarian Regent Horthy, 17 April 1943, in which Ribbentrop said that Jews must be either exterminated or taken to concentration camps.*

* * *

Note Fueh. 25/43.   Secret State Matter.
Notes   Secret Reich Matter.

On the discussion between the Fuehrer and the Hungarian Regent Horthy in Klessheim Castle on the morning of the 17th April 1943.

* * * * * * *

The Fuehrer then described to Horthy the German rationing measures which were carried out with perfect orderliness. There was no black market in Germany, and the peasants willingly delivered the quotas fixed for them. For produce which they placed at the Government's disposal over and above these quotas they were paid considerably higher prices by government offices in some cases even double the price, so that the peasants also had the possibility of getting hold of some money in this way. Horthy remarked to this that these problems were very difficult for Hungary. He had so far been unable to master the black market. The Fuehrer replied that it was the fault of the Jews who considered hoarding and profiteering as their main sphere of activity even during a world war, in exactly the same way as in England sentences for rationing offenses and the like now chiefly concerned Jews. To Horthy's counter-question as to what he should do with the Jews now that he had deprived them of almost all possibilities of livelihood, he could not kill them off—the Reich Foreign Minister declared that the Jews must either be exterminated or taken to concentration camps. There was no other possibility. To Horthy's remark that it was easier for Germany in this respect, because she did not possess so many Jews, the Fuehrer quoted figures which showed the extraordinarily great predominance of Jews in certain professions. Horthy replied that he had not known this at all. In this connection the Fuehrer came to speak of the town of Nurnberg, which had not tolerated any Jews within its walls for 400 years, while Furth admitted Jews. The result was that Nurnberg flourished greatly and Furth degenerated completely. The Jews did not even possess organizational value. In spite of the fears which he (the Fuehrer) had heard repeatedly in Germany also every thing continued to go its normal way without the Jews too. Where the Jews were left to themselves, as for instance in Poland, the most terrible misery and decay prevailed. They are just pure parasites. In Poland this state of affairs had been fundamentally cleared up. If the Jews there did not want to work, they were shot. If they could not work, they had to succumb. They had to be treated like tuberculosis bacilli, with which a healthy body may become infected. This was not cruel, if one remembered that even innocent creatures of nature, such as hares and deer, have to be killed, so that no harm is caused by them. Why should the beasts who wanted to bring us Bolshevism be spared more? Nations which did not rid themselves of Jews, perished. One of the most famous examples of this was the downfall of a people who were once so proud—the Persians, who now lead a pitiful existence as Armenians.

* * *   Salzburg, the 18th April 1943.

(SCHMIDT)

Translation of Document D-964. Affidavit dated 9 August 1946 of Szloma Gol, a Jewish resident of Vilna, Lithuania, concerning the exhuming in December 1943 of 68,000 graves and burning the bodies, including those in the batch of 10,000 Jews from Vilna ghetto who were shot in September 1941.

* * *

AFFIDAVIT OF
SZLOMA GOL.

I, Szloma Gol declare as follows:

1. I am a Jew and lived in Vilna, Lithuania. During the German occupation I was in Vilna ghetto.

2. The administration of Vilna ghetto was managed by the SA. The Town Commissioner of Vilna (Stadtkommissar) was an SA officer called Hinkst. The Landkommissar for Vilna was

an SA officer called Wolff. The Advisor on Jewish questions was an SA officer called Muerer.

3. In December 1943 80 Jews from the ghetto including 4 women and myself and my friend Josef Belic were ordered by an SA Sturmfuehrer, whose name I forget, to live in a large pit some distance from the town. This pit had originally been dug for an underground petrol tank. It was circular, 60 metres in diameter and 4 metres deep. When we lived in it the top was partially covered with boarding, and there were two wooden rooms partitioned off, also a kitchen and lavatory. We lived there 6 months altogether before we escaped. The pit was guarded by SA guards about whom I give details below.

4. One morning the Sturmfuehrer standing on the edge of the pit accompanied by 14 or 15 SA men said to us "Your brothers and sisters and friends are all near here. Treat them properly and if you complete your work we will send you to Germany, where each man can practice his own vocation." We did not know what this meant.

5. Thereupon the SA men threw chains into the pit, and the Sturmfuehrer ordered the Jewish foreman (for we were a working party) to fasten the chains on us. The chains were fastened round both ankles and round the waist. They weighed 2 kilos each, and we could only take small steps when wearing them. We wore them permanently for 6 months. The SA said that if any man removed the chains he would be hanged. The 4 women (who worked in the kitchen) were not chained.

6. After that we were taken out to work. We walked in chains 5 to 6 metres.

7. Our work consisted in digging up mass graves and piling the bodies on to funeral pyres and burning them. I was engaged in digging up the bodies. My friend Belic was engaged in sawing up and arranging the wood.

8. We dug up altogether 68,000 graves. I know this because two of the Jews in the pit with us were ordered by the Germans to keep count of the bodies: that was their sole job. The bodies were mixed, Jews, Polish priests, Russian Prisoners of War. Amongst those that I dug up I found my own brother. I found his identification papers on him. He had been dead two years when I dug him up: because I know that he was in a batch of 10,000 Jews from Vilna ghetto who were shot in September, 1941.

9. The procedure for burning the bodies was absolutely methodical. Parallel ditches 7 metres long were dug. Over these a square platform of boards was laid. A layer of bodies was put

on top, the bodies had oil poured on them and then branches were put on top and over the branches logs of wood. Altogether 14 such layers of bodies and fuel were put on each pyre. Each pyre was shaped like a pyramid with a wooden funnel sticking up through the top. Petrol and oil were poured down the funnel, and incendiary bombs put round the edge of the pyre. All this work was done by us Jews. When the pyre was ready the Sturmfuehrer himself or his assistant Legel (also in the SA) personally lit the pyre with a burning rag on the end of a pole.

10. The work of digging up the graves and building the pyres was supervised and guarded by about 80 guards. Of these over 50 were SA men, in brown uniform, armed with pistols and daggers and automatic guns (the guns being always cocked and pointed at us). The other 30 guards consisted partly of Lithuanians and partly of SD and SS. In the course of the work the Lithuanian guards themselves were shot presumably so that they should not say what had been done. The Commander of the whole place was the SA officer Muerer (the expert on Jewish questions) but he only inspected the work from time to time. The SA officer Legel actually commanded on the spot. At night our pit was guarded by 10 or 12 of these guards.

11. The guards (principally the SA guards) hit us and stabbed us. I still have scars on both legs and on my neck. I was once knocked senseless on to the pile of bodies, and could not get up, but my companions took me off the pile. Then I went sick. We were allowed to go sick for 2 days: the third day we were taken out of the pit "to hospital"—this meant to be shot.

12. Of 76 men in the pit 11 were shot at work. 43 of us eventually dug a tunnel from the pit with our bare hands, and broke our chains and escaped into the woods. We had been warned by a Czech SS man who said "they are going to shoot you soon, and they are going to shoot me too, and put us all on the pile. Get out if you can, but not while I am on guard".
I declare the above to be correct.

Signed
Szloma Gol

Sworn to at Nurnberg
9 August 1946.

EC-265　　　　　　　　　　Nazi Germany's War Against the Jews

Translation of Document EC-265. *Telegram dated 1 October 1940 from Abetz, German Ambassador to the Petain Government, on citizenship status of Reich German Jews living in Occupied France.*

* * *

Telegram (Open Text)
Paris, 1 October 1940   21.45 hrs.
Received: 1 October 1940   22.00 hrs.
No. 740, 1 Oct. 1940

The solution of the Jewish problem in the occupied territory of France requires, besides various measures, a regulation as soon as possible of the citizenship status of Reich German Jews who were living here at the beginning of the war regardless of the fact that they might have been interned or not. Heretofore the individual procedure of expatriation was based on Paragraph 2 of the Law from 14 July 1933 and refers only to actual violations of the duty of loyalty without considering racial membership. Suggest for the future a collective expatriation procedure for the occupied territory of France based on lists made here in agreement with Hoheitstrager (High Party Leaders) in which should be listed primarily the members of the following groups:

1. Jews, so-called ex-Austrians, that is, those who according to Circular [Runderlass] from 20 August 1938—R 17 178 did not change their Austrian passports for German passports before 31 December 1938.

2. Those Reich German Jews who by neglecting their duty of registration [Meldepflicht] violated Paragraph 5 of the Law for Registration Abroad (Auslandsmeldegesetz) from 3 February 1938. Measures requested above are to be considered only as a first step for the solution of the whole problem. I reserve for myself further proposals. Request telegraphic acknowledgment.

　　　　　　　　　　　　　　　　　　　　　　　　Abetz.

Prepared in 19 Copies.
From these have been sent:
No.　1 to R (Arb. St.)
No.　2 to RAM (Reich Foreign Minister)
No.　3 to S.S. (State Secretary)
No.　4 to Chef AO (Chief of Foreign Branch NSDAP)
No.　5 to BRAM (Plenipotentiary of Foreign Minister)
No.　6 to U.St.S. Pol. (Under State Secretary Political Div.)
No.　7 to U.St.S. Recht (Under State Secretary Legal Div.)

III - 16

No. 8 to Dir. Pers. (Director Personnel)
No. 9 to Dg.Pol. (Dirigent Political Div.)
No. 10 to D.W. (Director Economic Div.)
No. 11 to Dg.W. (Dirigent Economic Div.)
No. 12 to Dg. Recht (Dirigent Legal Div.)
No. 13 to Dir.Kult. (Director Cultural Div.)
No. 14 to Dr.Kult. (Dirigent Cultural Div.)
No. 15 to Dir.Presse (Director Press Div.)
No. 16 to Dir.Deutschld. (Director Germany Div.)
No. 17 to Dir.Prot. (Director Protocol)
No. 18 to Pers. Stab Hewel (Personal Staff (Hewel))
No. 19 to Landerref.pol. (Referent for France in Pol. Div.)

Translation of Document EC-305 (USA 303). *Excerpts from Minutes of meeting on 12 February 1940 under chairmanship of Goering on questions concerning the East, including the evacuation and forced labor of Jews.*

* * *

[in pencil]: Wi Rue Dept 383/40 Most Secret
Berlin 12 February 1940
V.P.2999 Top Secret
20 copies
8th copy
Most Secret
Meeting under the chairmanship of Minister President General Fieldmarshal Goering on questions concerning the East.

The following, among others, were present:
Reich Minister Graf Schwerin von Krosigk,
General Governor Reich Minister Frank,
Reichstatthalters Forster and Greiser,
Lord Lieutenants Koch and Wagner,
Reichsfuehrer—SS Himmler,
State Secretaries Koerner, Neumann, Landfried, Backe,
Dr. Syrup, Kleinmann, Alpers,
The Head of the Main Trust office East, Dr.h.c. Winkler.

By way of introduction the General Fieldmarshal explained that the strengthening of the war potential of the Reich must be the chief aim of all measures to be taken in the East. . . .

4. Special questions concerning the Government General:
* * * The General Government will have to receive the

Jews who are ordered to emigrate from Germany and the new Eastern Gaus. However, it must not occur again that transport trains are sent into the General Government without notification of the General Governor in the regular way and at the right time.

II.

The following reported on the situation in the Eastern Territories:

1. Lord Lieutenant Gauleiter:
* * *   There have been no evacuations. The Jews are employed on road construction and are needed for this purpose for a time. The Poles are employed in agriculture and in factories. Should the prisoners of war, employed in agriculture in East Prussia, be removed, as intended, into the interior of the Reich, East Prussia will need 115-120,000 Polish farm workers.

2. Reichsstatthalter Gauleiter Forster:
The population of the Danzig/West Prussia Gau (newly acquired territories) is 1.5 million, of whom 240,000 are Germans, 850,000 well-established Poles and 300,000 immigrant Poles, Jews and asocials (1,800 Jews). *87,000 persons have been evacuated, 40,000 of these from Gotenhafen.* From there, also the numerous shirkers, who are now looked after by welfare, will have to be deported to the General Government. Therefore, an evacuation of 20,000 further persons can be counted on for the current year.   * * *

3. Reichsstatthalter Gauleiter Greiser:
The Gau has approx. 4½ million inhabitants, of whom 400,000 are Germans and 400,000 Jews. *So far, 87,000 persons have been evacuated.* Among these are no workers, except those who were politically tainted; agricultural workers have not been deported.

*   *   *   *   *   *   *

4. Lord Lieutenant Gauleiter Wagner:
Agriculture is in good shape. Industry could increase its output by 30 to 50% if it were possible to eliminate the transportation difficulties. No evacuations have taken place so far. However, for the future the deportation of 100-120,000 Jews and 100,000 unreliable Polish immigrants is being considered.

*   *   *   *   *   *   *

The Reich Commissar for the consolidation of the German race, Reichsfuehrer-SS Himmler, reports that 40,000 Reich Germans had to be accommodated in Gotenhafen, and that room had to be made for 70,000 Baltic Germans and 130,000 Wolhynien Germans. Probably not more than 300,000 persons have been evacuated so far (the Polish population being 8 Mill.)

On the other hand it will probably be necessary to transfer into the Eastern Gaus 30,000 Germans from the Lublin area East of the Weichsel *which is to be reserved for Jews.*

Translation of Document EC-433 (USA 832). *Excerpt from Koenigsberg Speech of Schacht at the German Eastern Fair (probably 1935) concerning the Jewish problem.*

* * *

The obligation and will to serve in the armed forces compares to the obligation and will to serve the national economy.

Unfortunately, not all of our compatriots are conscious of this. First, there are the 10 percent who cannot be taught, who are known opponents and saboteurs, and to whom the Fuehrer recently directed very plain words. Then there are those of our contemporaries, about whom it is best to pray: "Lord, save me from my friends". Those are the people who heroically smear window panes in the middle of the night, who brand every German who trades in a Jewish store as a traitor, who condemn every former free-mason as a bum, and who, in the just fight against priests and ministers who talk politics from the pulpit, cannot themselves distinguish between religion and misuse of the pulpit. The goal at which these people aim is generally correct and good. There is no place in the Third "Reich" for secret societies, regardless of how harmless they are. The priest and preachers should take care of the souls, and not meddle in politics. The Jew must realize that their influence is gone for all times. We desire to keep our people and our culture pure and distinctive, just as the Jews have always demanded this of themselves since the time of the prophet Ezra. But the solution of these problems must be brought about under state leadership, and cannot be left to unregulated individual actions, which mean a disturbing influence on the national economy, and which have therefore been forbidden repeatedly by governmental agencies as well as party agencies. As always, according to the stage of legislation as well as several declarations of the Fuehrer's deputy, the Minister of the Interior and the Minister for Public Enlightenment and Propaganda (not to mention the Minister of Economics), Jewish enterprises are permitted to carry on their business activities. It is for the national government to decide whether and when these should be limited. However, all those who will not subordinate themselves to this decision of the government, act without discipline, and I shall hold them responsible, if their actions make impossible, the carrying out of the economic and financial policies, which were entrusted to us by the Fuehrer.

Economy is a very sensitive organism. Every disturbance, from whatever direction it may come, acts as sand in the machine. Since our economy is closely allied with that of foreign countries, not one of us, especially myself, as the minister responsible for the maintenance of the German economic machinery, can be indifferent to what consequences these disturbances can have at home and abroad. It is absolutely necessary for the leadership of our economic policies that confidence in Germany as a constitutional state remain unshaken. No one in Germany is deprived of his rights.

According to point 4 of the National-Socialist party program, the Jew can neither become a citizen or a fellow German. But point 5 provides legislation for him, that means, he must not be under arbitrary action, but under the law. *This legislation is being prepared and must be awaited*. Until such time, the existing laws must be observed. I also mention this here in connection with the whole of the church problem, which has for Germany a far greater importance than the Jewish problem.

Copy of Document EC-450 (USA 629). Excerpt of Affidavit of S. R. Fuller, 18 October 1945, giving account of a conversation with Schacht, 23 September 1935, concerning Jewish question.

* * *

STATE OF NEW YORK, }
} SS.:
COUNTY OF NEW YORK, }

S. R. Fuller, Jr., being first duly sworn according to law, deposes and says:

1. This affidavit has been prepared and executed at the written request of Lt. Col. John W. Griggs, officer in charge, Office of U.S. Chief Counsel for Prosecution of Axis Criminality, Room 4E869, The Pentagon, Washington, D.C. The letter of request from Lt. Col. Griggs, dated October 8, 1945, reads as follows:

"In accordance with the conversation of 6 October 1945 between you and Captain Conkling of this office, there is inclosed a photostatic copy of 'Enclosure B' of your memorandum to President Roosevelt, dated 11 October 1935.

"It is requested that you attach a signed affidavit to the inclosed photostat to the effect that it is a true account of your conversation with Dr. Hjalmar Schacht on 23 September 1935 and return the affidavit and photostat to this office."

2. The attached photostat, marked "Enclosure B", referred to in Lt. Col. Griggs' letter of October 8, 1945, above quoted, is a true copy, except for marginal numerals and the word "Hitler" on page 6 margin, of a memorandum of conversation between Dr. Hjalmar Schacht and me, which took place 23 September 1935 in Berlin.

3. The original memorandum was sent as "Enclosure B" with a confidential report from me to President Roosevelt, dated 11 October 1935. As I advised the President in this report, the transcription of the conversation recorded in "Enclosure B" is not word for word accurate; but it was made from longhand notes written by me immediately after the conversation, and is substantially word for word accurate, and is exactly accurate as to meaning.

[signed] S. R. Fuller, Jr.

Subscribed and sworn to before me this 18th day of October, 1945.

Alfred M. Reed,
Notary Public.
Alfred M. Reed,
Notary Public, Westchester County
Certificate filed in N.Y. Co., CLK's No.830, Reg.No.S39-R-6
Commission Expires March 30, 1946

Enclosure B

Memorandum of conversation between Dr. Hjalmar Schacht, Minister of Economics and President of the Reichsbank of Germany, and S. R. Fuller, Jr., 23 September, 1935, 2:30 p.m. to 3:30 p.m. at the American Embassy, Berlin.

The conversation took place in a library of the U.S. Embassy after a luncheon given for us by Ambassador Dodd at which were present, among others the Danish Minister; a representative of the German Foreign Office; First Secretary of the U. S. Embassy and Mrs. Flack; Ambassador and Mrs. Dodd; Mr.

Geist, acting U. S. Consul General in Berlin; Mrs. Fuller; Dr. and Mrs. Schacht. . . .

S. "Because of the international character of Jews and Roman Catholics, the Jews and Roman Catholics have been a domestic problem throughout history in many states, as you of course know. This is sometimes not appreciated or is forgotten by countries where these problems are not for the moment immediate. In Germany they have been very great."

F. "But Germany's treatment of the Jews is resented greatly by many countries; especially is there resentment in the United States. How many have you in Germany, 500,000?"

S. "Yes."

F. "Have you not, therefore, by your treatment of them made 500,000 martyrs?"

S. "I never was in favor of our treatment of the Jews, but the new laws announced at Nurnberg give protection to the Jews. They are now guaranteed the same rights as any other minority within Germany, such as Poland, for example."

F. "But they are denied the rights of citizenship."

S. "Yes."

F. "And their positions by these laws is an inferior one to the Germans?"

S. "Yes, that must always be. I called Mr. Warburg in to see me the other day and explained to him the protection Germany now guarantees to Jews; they can engage in their businesses from now on, and they can go about their business and will have proper governmental protection. I told Mr. Warburg to have his people stop making a noise and accept this protection."

F. "But if he can't stop them from making a noise and the Jewish people do not accept the inferior position given them in Germany with equanimity, what then?"

S. (Dr. Schacht made a wry face and shrugged his shoulders) "I don't know what may happen then."

F. "These restrictive laws refusing citizenship apply to the 100 percent Jews. What about the 50 percent and 25 percent Jews?"

S. "They will be gradually eliminated because of the law against intermarriage with gentiles or extra marital relations with gentiles."

Translation of Document EC-465. *Excerpt from letter, 9 December 1940, from Commissar at the Netherlands Bank on status of aryanization of the banks as of November 1940.*

* * *

The Commissar at the
Netherlands Bank
Amsterdam   The Hague, 9 Decemer 1940
                    SECRET
   Netherlands Bank, Money and Credit
Subject: Material for the November Report to the Fuehrer.
  (Follows my October Report of 9 November 1940)

* * * * * * *

K. Status of aryanization of the banks.

The Jewish element is very little represented within the 25 leading banks. There are only a large number of Jews in brokerage and agent circles on the Amsterdam Bourse. For a long time already I have worked through open conversation with the participating banks so that the Jewish partners and employees are separated. Apart from the brokerage and agent firms mentioned above, the de-Jewing had been completely carried out as early as the end of the month of this report. Negotiations on taking over the firms Warburg & Co., Lippmann Rosenthal & Co. and Hugo Kaufmanns Bank have begun and are in part ready for conclusion.

                              Signed: Wohlthat.

Translation of Document L-18 (USA 277). *Report from Katzmann to General of Police Krueger, concerning "Solution of Jewish Question in Galicia," 30 June 1943, describing ruthless evacuation of 434,329 Jews.*

* * *

State Secret
The SS & Police Leader
   in the District of Galicia
                                              June 30th 1943
Ref. 42/43 g.R.-Ch/Fr
                                                    2 Copies
                                                    1st copy
Re: Solution of Jewish Question in Galicia
Concerning: Enclose Report

Enclosure: 1 Report (executed in triplicate)
1 bound Copy

To:
The Superior SS and Police Leader East SS Obergruppenfuehrer and General of Police Krueger or deputy
Cracow

Enclosed I am submitting the 1st copy of the Final Report on the Solution of the Jewish Question in the District of Galicia for your information.

[Signed] KATZMANN
SS Gruppenfuehrer and Lt. Gen. of Police

SOLUTION OF THE JEWISH PROBLEM IN THE DISTRICT OF GALICIA

Owing to the term "Galician Jew," Galicia probably was the spot on earth which was best known and most frequently mentioned in connection with Jewry. Here they lived in immense multitudes, forming a world of their own, out of which the rising generations of world-Jewry were supplied. In all parts of Galicia one found Jews in their hundreds of thousands.

According to obsolete statistics of 1931 the number of Jews then was about 502,000. This number should not have decreased from 1931 up to the summer of 1941. Precise statements on the number of Jews present at the time when the German troops invaded Galicia are not available. By the Committees of Jews the number was stated to have been 350,000 at the end of 1941. That this statement was incorrect will be seen from the statement at the end of this report with regard to the evacuation of Jews. The town of Lemberg alone had about 160,000 Jewish inhabitants in July-August 1941.

The influence of this Galician Jewry, being considerable already under Austrian and Polish rule, increased to an almost incredible extent when the Soviets occupied this district in 1939.

Every important appointment within the country was filled by them. This explains the fact that in July 1941, after the occupation by German troops, Jews were found everywhere. Hence it was considered to be also our most urgent task to find a solution for this problem as soon as possible.

Our first measure consisted of marking every Jew by a white armlet bearing the Star of David in blue. By virtue of a decree of the Governor General the Department of the Interior was responsible for the marking and registration of Jews as well as for the formation of Committees of Jews. Our task, that of the Police, was first of all to counter effectively the immense black market carried on by Jews throughout the entire district and especially to take measures against loafing idlers and vagabonds.

The best remedy consisted of the formation, by the SS and Police Leader of Forced Labor Camps. The best opportunities for labor were offered by the necessity to complete the "Dg.4" road which was extremely important and necessary for the whole of the southern part of the front, and which was in a catastrophically bad condition. On October 15, 1941, the establishment of camps along the road was commenced, and despite considerable difficulties there existed, after a few weeks, only seven camps containing 4,000 Jews.

Soon more camps followed these first ones, so that after a very short time the completion of 15 camps of this kind could be reported to the Superior Leader of SS and Police. In the course of time about 20,000 Jewish labourers passed through these camps. Despite the hardly imaginable difficulties occurring at this work I can report today that about 160 km of the road are completed. [Photographs omitted.]

* * * * * * *

At the same time all other Jews fit for work were registered and distributed for useful work by the labor agencies. When the Jews were marked by the Star of David as well as when they were registered by the labor agencies, the first symptoms appeared of their attempts to dodge the orders of the authorities. The measures which were introduced thereupon, led to thousands of arrests. It became more and more apparent that the Civil Administration was not in a position to solve the Jewish problem in an approximately satisfactory manner. When, for instance, the Municipal Administration in Lwow had no success in their attempts to house the Jews within a close district which would be inhabited only by Jews, this question too was solved quickly by the SS and Police Leader through his subordinate officials. This measure became the more urgent as in winter 1941 big centres of spotted fever were noted in many parts of the town whereby not only the native population was endangered but also, and to a greater extent, the troops themselves, those stationed there as well as those passing through. During this removal of the Jews into a certain quarter of the town several sluices were erected at which all the work-shy and a social Jewish rabble were caught, during the screening and treated in a special way.

Owing to the peculiar fact that almost 90% of all artisans working in Galicia were Jews, the task to be solved could be fulfilled only step by step, since an immediate evacuation would not have served the interest of war economy. With regard to those Jews, however, who had a place in the labor process, no real effect could be found of their work. They used their job mostly only as a means to an end, namely in order first to dodge the intensified measures against Jewry and secondly to be able to carry on their black market activities without interference. Only by continuous police interference was it possible to prevent these activities. After it had been found in more and more cases that Jews had succeeded in making themselves indispensable to their employers by providing them with goods in scarce supply etc., it was considered necessary to introduce really draconic measures. Unfortunately it had to be stated that the Germans employed in the district, especially so-called "Operational Firms" or the "ill-famed Trustees" carried on the most extravagant black market activities with Jews. Cases were discovered where Jews, in order to acquire any certificate of labor, not only renounced all wages, but even paid money themselves. Moreover, the "organizing" of Jews for the benefit of their "employers" grew to so catastrophical extents that it was deemed necessary to interfere in the most energetic manner for the benefit of the German name.

Since the Administration was not in a position and showed itself too weak to master this chaos, the SS and Police Leader simply took over the entire disposition of labor for the Jews. The Jewish Labor Agencies which were manned by hundreds of Jews, were dissolved. All certificates of labor given by firms or administrative offices were declared invalid, and the cards given to the Jews by the Labor Agencies were revalidated by the Police Offices by stamping them.

In the course of this action again thousands of Jews were caught who were in possession of forged certificates or who had obtained surreptitiously certificates of labor by all kinds of pretexts. These Jews also were exposed to special treatment.

Army administration offices in particular had countenanced Jewish parasitism by giving special certificates to an uncontrollable extent.

Of the great number of certificates caught, only three will be enclosed; you will be able to conclude what methods were used with the intention to sabotage the measures of the SS.

1.
CERTIFICATE

ALSTER Benjamin (Recte Hasten)
born 3.6.1905 at Takinow

is employed by the Army Accommodation Administration, Lwow, as a foreman for urgent work.
Members of his family are ALSTER Hasten, Githa, Mother.
Valid until July 31st 1942
Extended until August 31st 1942

Lowo, 22.6.42
Army Billet Office
Signature
[Stamp]

The persons mentioned above are registered. They are to be exempted from evacuation.

2.

The Jewess ATLAS Rosa
Keeps house for the "A" Jew No. 20 008
employed by H.K.P. 547
whose identity card has been stamped by the SS and Police Leader. She is registered, and it is requested to leave her in Lwow.
Lwow, 10.8.1942
Army Car Park 547
Signature,
[Stamp.]

3.

Army Building Office Lwow.

C E R T I F I C A T E
For Family Members of Jews in Employment

The Jewess HIRSCHFELD Mina
born 1894, resident in Lwow, 2 Sonnen street, is the wife of the Jew provided with an employment Certificate by virtue of decree of 12.3.1942 HIRSCHFELD Oscar (No. 4181)

Valid until July 31st 1942
Signature
[Stamp.]

Lwow, July 1st 1942

There were cases when arrested Jews were in possession of 10 to 20 of such certificates.

Where Jews were arrested in the course of these check-ups most of their employers thought it necessary to intervene in favor of the Jews. This often happened in a manner which had to be called deeply shameful.

III - 27

An especially exaggerated example is the action of a certain Schmalz, a wholesale butcher working for the Army in Lwow, who sent from Berlin the following telegram to the Office of the SS and Police Leader:

"Urgent
SS Untersturmfuehrer Loehner
c/o SS Police Leader Lwow
District Office

The two certificate holders are craftsmen watchmakers; are resident in my future factory as night watchmen and watchmakers in day time. I should not wish to be guilty of their death; after my return you can have them both, they do not run away. I beg of you

Signature."

When steps were taken to investigate the actions of this butcher, it transpired that the fellow had carried on the most incredible black market business with the Jews. Schmalz was arrested and put at the disposal of the Public Prosecutor.

Despite all these measures concerning the employment of Jews their evacuation [Aussiedelung] from the district of Galicia was commenced in April 1942, and executed step by step.

When the Superior SS and Police Leader once again intervened in the solution of the Jewish problem by his Decree Concerning the Formation of Districts inhabited by Jews of 10.11.1942 already *254,989 Jews* had been evacuated [Ausgesiedelt], resp. resettled [umgesiedelt].

Since the Superior SS and Police Leader gave the further order to accelerate the complete evacuation [Aussiedelung] of the Jews, again considerable work was necessary to regulate the status of those Jews who, for the time being were permitted to be left in the armaments factories. The Jews in question were declared Labor Prisoners of the Superior SS and Police Leader and they were put into barracks, either within the factories or in camps established for this purpose. For the town of Lwow a Giant Camp was established at the borders of the town, in which at the time of writing 8,000 Jewish Labor Prisoners are confined. The agreement with the Army concerning the disposition and treatment of these Labor Prisoners was executed in writing. The decree which contained the measures now in force is attached herewith.

Lwow, October 23, 1942

The SS & Police Leader
   in the District of Galicia
   XIII-688/42 (g)
Re: Disposition of Jewish Labor
Your Ref: Letter of the Inspection
   of Armaments of 21.9.42 and letter of Command
   of Armaments of 19.10.42
To the Command of Armaments
                    Lwow
                                    SECRET

The Inspector of Armaments in the GG. and the Superior SS & Police Leader East, Secretary of State for Security in the GG. have issued special orders and rules for the uniform treatment of the Jewish laborers used in the armament factories. Following a conference between the Officer commanding the armaments enterprises Lwow, and the SS and Police Leader in the District of Galicia the ensuing agreement was reached on 17.10.1942:

I. Housing.

On principle the Jewish laborers are to be put into barracks and when in camps are subjected to control by the SS and Police Leader Galicia and in this respect the police offices under his orders. Since the establishment of Police Camps has not yet been completed everywhere the work administrations for the time being have themselves to place the Jewish laborers into camps. In case it should be impossible for a factory to provide housing in a camp, the Jewish laborers employed there are to be housed in certain blocks of the Jewish Quarter still remaining. With regard to this housing the work administrations will communicate with the local offices of the Security Police. It has to be emphasized that under no circumstances the relatives of the Jewish laborers may be allowed to find accommodation within the same block. With regard to the Jewish laborers employed in factories situated in Lwow, a separate order will be issued. For the time being they will be housed together in the Jewish Housing District in the same manner. (This question will be regulated by the SS & Pol. L.).

II. Food.

Feeding of the Jewish laborers has to be provided by the factories. It will take place within the factory without exception.

Besides a main meal, breakfast and supper will be provided. Full board will be provided also in case of illness. The factories will apply for provisions at, and receive them from, the GG., Principal Department, according to the rules issued by the Government. Feeding and agriculture department, Market Order IIIa 1a/100 18.8.42.

III. Clearing of Payments.

Commencing on 1 November 1942 the Jewish laborers will not receive any payment in cash. The factory administrations will pay to the SS and Pol. L. Galicia for each Jewish Laborer pro calendar day and shift 5 Zloty a man, 4 Zloty a woman. Salary tax and insurance contributions do not arise. From the above sums of 5, and 4 Zl. respectively, the expenses for feeding and the overhead expenses will be deducted. This amount to be deducted may not surpass Zl. 1.60 a day. The office of the SS & Pol. L. is entitled to examine accounts. The sums to be paid will be paid into the Account concerning payments of factories, maintained by the SS & Pol. L. Galicia at the Emission Bank in Lwow. Payment has to be competed the third of every month for the preceding month. For the purpose of proving the correctness, copies of the wage-lists for each day will be sent to the administration of the SS & Pol. L. Galicia, Lwow, Siegfriestreet 3.

IV. Clothing.

The Jewish laborers when sent to the camps will be permitted to take with them ample clothing, especially winter clothes. The local Police Offices have been especially informed of this order. With a view for supplementing and renewing, the factories may request supplementary clothing through the SS & Pol. L. but only for special reasons.

V. General Ruling.

The SS & Pol. L. Galicia and the Armament Command agree on the necessity of keeping the Jewish laborers fit for work, and that therefore appropriate housing, clothing, and medical care have to be provided. In case of difficulties, if any, the factory administrations are requested to agree with the local offices of the Security Police. The SS & Pol. L. Galicia and the Armaments Command, Lwow are to be informed in such cases. If difficulties should not be solved by such local discussions, application for a decision will have to be addressed without delay to the SS & Pol. L. of the District of Galicia.

Signed Hofmann
SS Brig. Leader and Gen. Maj. of Police

Distribution:
  Schwartz and Co., Lwow
  Textilia Lwow
  Metrawat AG. branch Lwow
  Training factories AW Lwow
  Hobag-Holzbau AG branch Lwow
  Barril Store factory in Bolechau
  Furniture Factory in Bolechau
  Carpathiaus Oil AG
For information to:
  Commander of the Security Police and SD in the Galicia District Lwow, with copies to the foreign agencies.
  Commander of the Order Police [Ordungspolizei] in the Galicia District Lwow with copies to the Military Police District Leaders.
  SS. Ustuf Fichtuer in the Staff.
  SS. Ustuf Loehnert in the Staff.
  SS. Ustuf Hildebrand in the Staff.

In the meantime further evacuation [Aussiedelung] was executed with energy, so that with effect from 23 June 1943 all Jewish Residence Districts could be dissolved. Therewith I report that the District of Galicia, with the exception of those Jews living in the camps being under the control of the SS & Pol. Leader, is
Free from Jews
Jews still caught in small numbers are given special treatment by the competent detachments of Police and Gendarmerie.
Up to 27 June 1943 altogether 434.329 Jews have been evacuated [ausgesiedelt].
Camps for Jews are still in existence in:

Lwow	Kosaki	Drohobycz
Weinbergen	Zborow	Boryslaw
Ostrow	Jezierna	Stryj
Kurowice	Tarnapol	Belechow
Jaktorow	Hluboczek	Broschniow
Lackie	Borki-Wielki	Njebelow
Pluhow	Kamienki	

containing altogether 21.156 Jews. This number is being reduced currently.
Together with the evacuated action, we executed the confiscation of Jewish property. Very high amounts were confiscated and paid over to the Special Staff "Reinhard". Apart from

Nazi Germany's War Against the Jews

furniture and many textile goods, the following amounts were confiscated and turned over to Special Staff "Reinhard":

As per 30.6.1943:

25,580 kg	Copper Coins
53,190 kg	Nickel Coins
97,581 kg	Gold Coins
82,600 kg	Necklaces—Silver
6,640 kg	Necklaces—Gold
432,780 kg	Broken Silver
167,740 kg	Silver Coins
18,490 kg	Iron Coins
20,050 kg	Brass Coins
20,952 kg	Wedding Rings—Gold
22,740 kg	Pearls
11,730 kg	Dental Gold—Dentures
28,200 kg	Powder Boxes—Silver or Metal
44,655 kg	Broken Gold
482,900 kg	Cutlery—Silver
343,100 kg	Cigarette Boxes—Silver or Metal
20,880 kg	Rings, Gold with stones
39,917 kg	Brooches, Ear Rings etc.
18,020 kg	Silver rings
6,166 kg	Watches, all kinds
3,133 kg	Watches, Silver
3,425 kg	Wrist Watches—Silver
1,256 kg	Wrist Watches—Gold
2,892 kg	Watches—Gold
68 kg	Cameras
98	Binoculars
7	Stamp Collections—complete
5	Trunks filled with loose stamps
100,550 kg	3 bags with rings, not genuine
3,290 kg	1 box with corals
460 kg	1 chest with corals
280 kg	1 chest with corals
7,495 kg	1 box with fountain pens and propelling pencils
	1 basket with fountain pens and propelling pencils
	1 suitcase with fire tongs
	1 suitcase with pocket knives
	1 suitcase with watch-parts

Banknotes: Paper—Metal

261,589.75	USA—Dollars—Paper

III - 32

The Documentary Evidence

	Gold Dollars: 3 a 5, 18 a 10, 28 a 20
2,515.75	Canadian Dollars
124	Argentine Pesos
18,766,64	Hungarian Pengoe
231,789	Roubles—Paper
	Gold Roubles: 1 a 7 ½, 11 a 10, 29 a 5
4316	Rouble—Paper
513	French Francs
2.460	Swedish Francs
52	Austrian Ducats—Gold
	Austrian Crowns 36 a 10, 25 a 20, 8 a 100
2,229,18,60	English Pounds
23	African Pounds
13,490	Roumanian Lei
25,671	Russian Cerwon
4,600,70	Czechoslovakian Crowns—Paper
185	Dutch Florins
5,277	Palastinian Pounds
9,300	Palastinian Mille
160	Lithuanian Oere
360	English Schillings
1	Irish Lst. Irish Pounds
1	Hungarian Pesos
2	Mexican Pesos
10	Norwegian Crowns
3,817,70	Slovakian Crowns
435	Karbowanez
16,795,000	Zloty

Following the "Fur-action" in December 1941 *35 Wagons of Furs* were handed over.

Earned Moneys from Forced Labor Camps and from W. and R. Factories

25.5.1943

1. *Forced Labor Camps*
   a. *Takings*
   Wages .... 11,511,606.98 Zl.
   Hidden money found
      in clothes ...... 1,232,143.71 Zl.
   Proceeds from use-
      less tools .... 807.93 Zl.
   ────────────────────
   12,744,558.62 Zl.

b. *Outgoings* (Board for Prisoners)
   1. Food, Clothes, Medicine .... 3,108,866.62 Zl.
   2. Wages, Custody by Ukrainian Police .... 47,358.51 Zl.
   3. Camp-sustenance Repairs, Rents . 118,063.15 Zl.
   4. Means of Conveyance
      Horses .... 1,448,863.57 Zl.
      Cars .... 83,324.14 Zl.
      Tools .... 3,037.10 Zl.
   5. Purchases of Furniture .... 2,410.15 Zl.
      Postage and Telephone .... 5,678.44 Zl.
      Office needs .... 29,005.59 Zl.
   6. Buildings ...... 220,000.00 Zl.

                                              5,066,607.27 Zl.

2. *W.&R. Factories Takings* .... 7,711,428.92 Zl.   7,711,428.92 Zl.
3. *Amount paid over to the SS Cashier*
   a. *Camps* .... 6,876,251.00 Zl.
   b. *W.&R. Factories*. 6,556,513.69 Zl.

                                             13,423,764.69 Zl.

Further payments to the SS-Cashier are effected every month. Owing to the great number of Jews and the vast area to be combed out these actions were performed with the assistance of detachments from the Security Police, the Order Police, the Gendarmerie, the Special Service, and the Ukrainian Police, all acting together in numerous single sweeps. Page 19 of this report contains a map intended to show how Jews lived scattered throughout the whole of the District, until the special Jewish residence districts were established. The detachments continually were exposed to serious physical and mental strains. Again and again they had to overcome the nausea threatening them when they were compelled to enter the dirty and pestilential Jewish holes. During the searches there has been found, moreover, a number of leaflets in the Hebrew language, inciting the Jews to breed lice carrying spotted fever, in order to destroy the Police Force. In fact several phials filled with lice were confiscated. Nothing but catastrophical conditions were found in the Ghettoes of Rawa-Ruska and Rohatyn. The Jews of Rawa-Ruska, fearing the evacuation, had concealed those suffering from spotted fever in underground holes. When evacuation was to start the Police found that 3000 Jews suffering from spotted fever lay about in this Ghetto.

* * * * * * *

[MAP]

From this map one is able to see how the Jews lived scattered throughout the whole of the district, until the special Jewish Residence Districts were established. The large dots refer to localities of more than 1000 Jews, the smaller ones where less than 1000 Jews lived.

At once every Police Officer innoculated against spotted fever was called into action. Thus we succeeded to destroy this plague-boil, losing thereby only one officer. Almost the same conditions were found in Rohatyn. Moreover our detachments again and again discovered smaller or larger centres of pestilence in many towns and villages. Despite all our precautionary measures 120 officers fell ill of spotted fever, of whom only 18 died, owing to the protective measures introduced by us.

Some photos of these dirt caves may give an idea of the degree of effort which every officer had to apply to force himself to merely enter these centres of dirt. [Photographs omitted.]

On the occasion of these actions, many more difficulties occurred owing to the fact that the Jews tried every means in order to dodge evacuation [Aussiedelung]. Not only did they try to flee, but they concealed themselves in every imaginable corner, in pipes, chimneys, even in sewers, etc. They built barricades in passages of catacombs, in cellars enlarged to dugouts, in underground holes, in cunningly contrived hiding-places in attics and sheds, within furniture, etc.

The smaller the number of Jews remaining in the district, the harder their resistance. Arms of all kinds, among them those of Italian make, were used for defense. The Jews purchased these Italian arms from Italian soldiers stationed in the District for high sums in Zloty currency. The ensuing photos give a small selection from the arms confiscated. Especially dangerous were the sawed-off carbines of all kinds. [Photographs omitted.]

Underground bunkers were found with entrances concealed in a masterly manner opening some times into flats, some times into the open. In most cases the entrances had only so much width that just one person could crawl through it. The access was concealed in such a manner that it could not be found by persons not acquainted with the locality. Here nothing succeeded but the assistance of some Jews to whom anything whatever was promised in exchange. What these dug-outs looked like will be shown by the ensuing photographs together with their comments: [Photographs omitted.]

In the course of the evacuation action we furthermore discovered that the Jews attempted more than ever to escape to foreign countries. These attempts were made by Jews in possession of considerable amounts of money, jewels, and of forged papers. They tried every means to effect their purpose and often approached members of the German and allied Forces with the request to transport them to or beyond the frontier by way of military cars. They offered in exchange disproportionally high amounts, in many cases up to 5,000 Zl. and more a person. Although in a few cases members of foreign forces, especially Hungarians, came to an agreement with them and fulfilled their part, in by far the most cases the Security Police was informed in time by V-men so that the necessary countermeasures were applied, the Jews caught, and the valuables confiscated. By way of illustration some cases are described:

In September 1942 the office of the SS & Police Leader was informed by an Italian soldier (of German blood resident in Switzerland) that some Jews were concealed within the Italian barracks in Lwow, who were to be smuggled across the frontier by members of the Italian Forces within the next days. Shortly before they intended to start, two leaders in mufti entered the barracks and succeeded in arresting a group of seven persons and confiscating 3,200 gold dollars and a large amount of diamonds and jewels. They made the interesting discovery that already 970 gold dollars had been paid for bribing 4 members of the Italian Forces. This money was confiscated also. The Italian soldiers thereupon were sent home.

On 13 May 1943 two German Drivers of the Luftwaffe Headquarters in Cracow reported that a Jew had approached them with the request to transport about 20 to 30 Jews from the Jewish camp Lwow to Brody; some of them were in possession of arms; they would provide forged transport orders; directed to these military drivers. In exchange they offered 20,000 Zl. The drivers were ordered to accept the offers, to load the Jews on the Luftwaffe car the 15 May at 5 p.m., to start in the direction of Brody, but to turn the car as soon as it passed the office of NSKK Lwow which was situated at this street, and to drive into the court yard of this office. In fact the car, manned with 20 Jews and one Pole, arrived in this court yard at 5:30 p.m. The Jews, some of whom were armed with charged pistols and sawed-off carbines with the safety devices released, were overwhelmed by a waiting detachment and disarmed. The following arms were confiscated:

    1. 1P. Beretta-pistol, Kal. pp
    2. do.
    9. further specifications.

The pistols, mentioned sub. 1. and 2. had been purchased by the Jews from members of the Italian Forces for 2,000 Zl. each. The names of the sellers could not be ascertained. After a diligent search, considerable valuables were found and confiscated. A diligent interrogation of the arrested Jews led to the discovery that a certain Jew by the name of Horowitz who was staying in the woods near Brody together with a larger group of Jews, used to organize such transports. As a result of this interrogation it was possible moreover to arrest those Jews who forged identity papers for fugitives. The Pole who was arrested at the same time, confessed to be a member of the Polish Resistance Movement "PPR". Furthermore he named the Jew Horowitz as the Chief Executive of the "PPR" in Lwow. The place of communication in the woods near Brody, having been discovered by these interrogations, the whole of this wood area was surrounded and combed out by detachments of the Gendarmerie and of the Ukrainian Police, and two companies of the German Army on the same day. These forces met smaller forces of armed bandits who had established themselves in several furnished dug-outs and trenches dating from the Russian occupation. The bandits in all cases used their arms, but they all were overwhelmed and rendered harmless.

33 Jewish bandits were shot. Some sawed-off carbines and some quick-firing rifles and pistols of Russian make were confiscated. Polish game-keeper taking part in the combing-out action was shot dead by the bandits. During the arrests in Lwow, one SS-man was wounded by a shot into the left shank. The 2 German drivers were paid as recompense for their exemplary conduct 2,000 Zl. each. The forged marching-orders and transport orders found in possession of the Jews are reproduced below. [Transport order omitted.]

In the same way we succeeded on May 21, 1943 in destroying a Jewish gang who again were armed with 0.8 cal. pistols of Italian origin. (In the meantime all Italian soldiers left the district of Galicia.)

Only some days later, the 31 May, we succeeded again, during a new comb-out, in destroying 6 dug-outs of major size containing 139 Jewish bandits.

On June 2, 1943, again some Jews who attempted to escape to Hungary by means of a military car owned by the Hungarian Army, were arrested and, since they resisted, shot. Here again considerable values were confiscated. The Hungarian soldiers participating in the action were adequately rewarded.

The evacuation having been completed, nevertheless, still minor actions are necessary in order to track Jews in hiding and concealment. This is proved by the fact that every day some persons are caught in possession of forged identity cards and passes. Some forged identity cards, passes, marching orders, and leave passes are enclosed herewith. [Cards and photographs omitted.]

Since we received more and more alarming reports on the Jews becoming armed in an ever increasing manner, we started during the last fortnight in June 1943 an action throughout the whole of the district of Galicia with the intent to use strongest measures to destroy the Jewish gangsterdom. Special measures were found necessary during the action to dissolve the Ghetto in Lwow where the dug-outs mentioned above had been established. Here we had to act brutally from the beginning, in order to avoid losses on our side; we had to blow up or to burn down several houses. On this occasion the surprising fact arose that we were able to catch about 20,000 Jews instead of 12,000 Jews who had registered. We had to pull at least 3,000 Jewish corpses out of every kind of hiding places; they had committed suicide by taking poison.

Our own losses suffered in these actions:
  Spotted Fever: dead—1 man
  Shot by Jews: dead—7 men
  Stabbed by Jews: dead—1 man
          fallen ill: 120 men
          wounded: 12 men

Lost by accident in evacuation action: dead: 2 men, wounded: 5 men.

Despite the extraordinary burden heaped upon every single SS-Police Officer during these actions, mood and spirit of the men were extraordinarily good and praiseworthy from the first to the last day.

Only thanks to the sense of duty of every single leader and

man have we succeeded to get rid of this PLAGUE in so short a time.

Copy of Document L-22 (USA 294). *Excerpt from report of War Refugee Board, Washington, D. C., estimating that 1,765,000 Jews were gassed in Birkenau (part of Auschwitz) between April 1942 and April 1944.*

* * *

Executive Office of the President
War Refuge Board
Washington, D. C.
Page 33.

German Extermination Camps—Auschwitz and Birkenau.

Careful estimate of the number of Jews gassed in Birkenau between April, 1942 and April, 1944 (according to countries of origin.)

Poland (transported by truck)	approximately	300,000
Poland (transported by train)	approximately	600,000
Holland	approximately	100,000
Greece	approximately	45,000
France	approximately	150,000
Belgium	approximately	50,000
Germany	approximately	60,000
Yugoslavia, Italy and Norway	approximately	50,000
Lithuania	approximately	50,000
Bohemia, Moravia and Austria	approximately	30,000
Slovakia	approximately	30,000
Various camps for foreign Jews in Poland	approximately	300,000
	approximately	1,765,000

Copy of Document L-26. *Excerpts from United Nations Information Organization Report No. 8, 14 June 1944, Conditions in Occupied Territories, pp. 14, 16, commenting upon deportation of Jews from Greece and the Netherlands.*

* * *

CONDITIONS IN OCCUPIED TERRITORIES

A Series of Reports Issued by the United Nations Information Organization.

(Formerly the Inter-Allied Information Committee) London, Pages 14, 16.

Greek Jews are in a special category. Many have been deported. Four-fifths of the Jewish population of Salonika are estimated to have been deported to Poland, many of them dying as a result of inhuman treatment.

The conditions under which the conscripts work vary according to where they are and who are their masters. Moreover, accurate information on this subject is scanty, but the following two examples give a fairly good picture.

Out of 400 Greeks conscripted to guard the Athens-Salonika railway ten froze to death within fifteen days. Their dependents received no compensation.

In a letter to his family a Greek conscript in Germany wrote on August 20, 1942: "Please send me money and clothes. We are working fourteen hours a day. Our salary is insufficient to buy food, even from the peoples' kitchens". A few days later the German authorities informed the family that this worker had suddenly disappeared.

* * * * * * *

According to the official statistics at the end of 1943, there were 380,000 Dutch workers in Germany and 40,000 in Belgium and Northern France.

These figures do not include those workers who have not returned for one reason or another, or those who have failed to come back from leave. They also do not include the 120,000 Jews who have been deported. Dr. Stothfang, one of Sauckel's closest collaborators, estimated the number of workers who have not returned from leave at 150,000.

The Germans have recently imposed a special regulation on Dutch workers in Germany for the purpose of putting an end to this "leave-vanishing" trick. As part of the routine, before a Dutch worker in the Reich can go home on leave, he has to submit, together with his application form, the names of two or more coworkers who will vouch for his return. If the worker fails to return, reprisals are taken against those who have stood surety. But even this unfair method has not succeeded in putting a stop to the practice or even in reducing the number of defaulters.

As a punishment for refusing to sign the pledge of loyalty, 4,000 students were sent to work in Germany. Efforts to conscript Dutch doctors for work in Germany failed as a result of the united stand which the whole medical profession took

The Documentary Evidence   L-26.

against such measures. Of the 120,000 Jews who were deported, tens of thousands are being employed in Labour Camps in the East.

Copy of Document L-31. *Excerpt from Communique of the Polish-Soviet Extraordinary Commission for Investigating the Crimes Committed by the Germans in the Majdanek Extermination Camp in Lublin, pp. 21, 26, in which reference was made to the wholesale murder of a vast number of Jews.*

* * *

COMMUNIQUE
of the
Polish-Soviet Extraordinary Commission for Investigating the Crimes Committed by the Germans in the Majdanek Extermination Camp in Lublin, Pages 21, 26.

"Last spring an incalculable number of corpses were exhumed and burnt in furnaces specially built for the purpose, evidently with the object of wiping out the traces of the crimes committed by Hitler's orders.

"These huge furnaces were built of bricks and iron and constituted a crematorium of a large capacity. Often the stench from the corpses reached the city, at least the east end of it, and consequently, even less informed people realized what was going on in that frightful place. * * *

"The fact that the activities of the 'Extermination Camp' were directed by the Hitler government is proved by the visit Himmler himself paid to the camp when he came to Lublin in the summer of 1943".

The Committee established the fact that in the crematorium alone over six hundred thousand bodies were burnt; on gigantic bonfires in the Krembecki Woods over three hundred thousand corpses were burnt; in the two old furnaces over eighty thousand corpses were burnt; on bonfires in the camp near the crematorium no less than four hundred thousand corpses were burnt.

With the object of covering up the traces of their crimes the Germans killed the attendants, prisoners in the camp, of the gas chamber and crematorium.

As a result of a thorough investigation of numerous affidavits by medical experts and material proof, the aforesaid Committee of Medical Experts under the chairmanship of Professor

Szyling-Syngalewicz, Professor of Medical Jurisprudence at the Lublin Catholic University, found that:

"During the whole period of four years that the Lublin Majdanek Camp was in existence, a deliberate and consistent system operated for the premeditated, wholesale extermination of people, both prisoners in the camp as well as people especially brought there for the purpose of extermination."

* * * * * * *

The Polish-Soviet Extraordinary Commission finds that during the four years the Majdanek Extermination Camp was in existence the Hitlerite butchers, on the direct orders of their criminal government, exterminated by means of wholesale shooting and wholesale asphyxiation in gas chambers of about one million five hundred thousand persons—Soviet prisoners of war, prisoners of war of the former Polish army, and civilians of different nationalities, such as Poles, Frenchmen, Italians, Belgians, Netherlanders, Czechs, Serbs, Greeks, Croatians, and a vast number of Jews.

Translation of Document L-53 (USA 291). Order from Commandant of the SIPO and SD (Security Police and Security Service) for the Radom District, 24 July 1944, on clearance of prisons, in which it was ordered that Jews were not to be liberated by the enemy or fall into their hands alive.

* * *

[Stamp:]
Commandant of the Sipo and SD for the
Radom District Branch Office Tomaschow.
Received 24.7.1944   1225
Dept. IVL Diary No. 22/44
Radom 21.7.44

Commandant of the Sipo and SD for the Radom District.
4143 TOP SECRET

To: The Branch Office for the attention of SS-Hauptsturmfuehrer Thiel—or acting deputy—in Tomaschow.

Subject: Clearance of Prisons.
Reference: None.

The Commander of the Sipo and SD in the General Government issued the following order in his teletype message No. 14002 dated 20.7.44, IV 6 No. 82/44 Top Secret:

I again stress the fact that the number of inmates of the Sipo

The Documentary Evidence   L-53

and SD prisons must be kept as low as possible. In the present situation, particularly those suspects, handed over by the Civil Police [Ordnungspolizei] need *only be subjected to a short, formal interrogation*, provided there are no serious grounds for suspicion. They are then to be sent by the quickest route to a concentration camp, should no court-martial proceedings be necessary or should there be no question of discharge. *Please keep the number of discharges very low.* Should the situation at the front necessitate it, early preparations are to be made for the total clearance of prisons. Should the situation develop suddenly in such a way that it is impossible to evacuate the prisoners, the prison inmates are to be liquidated and their bodies disposed of as far as possible (burning, blowing up the building, etc.). If necessary, *Jews* still employed in the armament industry or on other work are to be dealt with in the same way.

The liberation of prisoners or Jews by the enemy, be it the WB or the Red Army, must be avoided under all circumstances nor may they fall into their hands alive.

The above is to be noted and strictly complied with.
[signature illegible]

[Stamp:]
The Commandant of the Sipo and SD for the Radom District Branch Office Tomaschow IV L 22/44 Top Secret.
[in writing]
Tomaschow 25.7.44
Top Secret

SS-Obersturmfuehrer Pruess personally *within the office* for his information.
By order:
[signature illegible]
Information received 25/7
[signed] Preuss
[in writing]
Tomaschow 25.7.44

[Stamp:]
The Commandant Sipo and SD in the Radom District IV L 22/44 Top Secret.
   The
   1. Direction of depts. III, V and the technical direction of IV 1, IV 2, IV 3, and IV 6 have been informed.
   2. returned [?] I V L
By order:
[Signed] R.

III - 43

Translation of Document L-61 (USA 177). *Express letter from Sauckel to Presidents of Landes Employment Offices, 26 November 1942, concerning employment of Jews and exchange of Jews in essential employment by Polish labor.*

* * *

COPY

Saarlandstr. 96
Berlin S.W.11
26 November 1942

The Commissioner for the Four Year Plan.
The Plenipotentiary General for Manpower.

SECRET

Va 5431/7648/42 g   *Express letter*

To the Presidents of the "Landes" Employment Offices (Employment Office Brandenburg excepted)

Subject: Employment of Jews; here: Exchange of Jews in essential employment against Polish labor.

In agreement with the Chief of the Security Police and the SD, Jews who are still in employment are, from now on, to be evacuated from the territory of the Reich and are to be replaced by Poles, who are being deported from the General Government.

The Chief of the Security Police advises under the date of 26 October 1942 that it is anticipated that during the month of November the evacuation of Poles in the Lublin district will begin, in order to make room there for the settlement of persons of German race [Volksdeutsche].

The Poles who are to be evacuated as a result of this measure will be put into concentration camps and put to work where they are criminal or as social elements. The remaining Poles where they are suitable for labor, will be transported, without family, into the Reich, particularly to Berlin; there they will be put at the disposal of the labor allocation offices to work in armament factories instead of the Jews who are to be replaced.

The Jews who will become available as a result of the employment of Polish labor will be deported on a shuttle system. This will apply first to Jews engaged in menial work since they can be exchanged most easily. The remaining so-called "qualified" Jewish laborers will be left to the industries until their Polish replacements have been made sufficiently familiar with the work processes by a period of apprenticeship to be determined for each case individually. Loss of production in individual industries will thus be reduced to the absolute minimum.

I reserve the right to issue further instructions. Please inform the labor offices concerned accordingly.

To the President of the "Landes" Labor Office Brandenburg, Berlin W.62

I transmit the foregoing copy for your information. So far as the removal of Jews (still) in employment concerns your area [Bezirk] too, I request that you take the necessary measures in cooperation with the competent offices of the Chief of the Security Police and of the SD.

[Signed]: Fritz Sauckel

The Regierungs President Economics Admin Staff for War Economics Area XII [Wehrwirtschaftsbezirk XII].

Wilhelmstr. 48
Wiesbaden
12 Dec. 1942

III/11-B.E. 10. 23/3205/42 g   Tel. 5948

COPY
SECRET

to the Chambers of Commerce and Industry
and the Manual Workers' Guilds [Handwerkskammern]
in War Economics Area XII.
—address to individuals or acting deputy—

for your information:
By order:
[Signed]: Dr. Schneider
Certified:
Hellbach
Employee

[Stamp]
The Regierungspraesident
Landes Office of Economics
Coblenz
16 Dec. 1942
Diary No. 2627 Clerk

[Stamp]
The Regierungspraesident
Wiesbaden
Economics Admin Staff
for War Economics Area XII

For information:
  a. Chambers of Economics.
  b. "Landes" Master Mechanics.

c. "Landes" Economic Offices Koblenz and Saarbruecken for War Economics Area XII
—address to individuals or acting deputy.

Translation of Document L-152. Order, 3 November 1941, of Gestapo Office for Nurnberg-Fuerth area prohibiting friendly relations between Aryans and Jews.

* * *

COPY

Nr. 7479/41 II B 4

Nurnberg Nov.3.1941

Secret State Police
Gestapo Office Nurnberg-Fuerth
TO
   the Rural Councillors of Districts Oberfranken, Mittelfranken and Mainfranken
   the Police Direction Hof,
   the Police President in Wuerzburg
   the Mayors of the Cities of Ansbach, Aschaffenburg, Bayreuth, Coburg, Erlangen, Schweinfurt
   the Secret State Police-Detachment in Wuerzburg
   information to District Presidents in Ansbach & Wuerzburg

Subject: Attitude of persons of German blood toward Jews

For your information and attention I am publishing the following order of the RSHA of October 24, 1941. "Lately it has repeatedly become known here that, now as before, Aryans are maintaining friendly relations with Jews, and that they show themselves with them conspicuously in public. In view of the fact that these Aryans still do not seem to understand the elementary basic principles of National Socialism, and because their behavior has to be regarded as disrespect towards measures of the State, I order that in such cases the Aryan party is to be taken into protective custody temporarily for educational reasons; respectively, in serious cases, that they be put in a concentration camp, Grade I, for a period of up to three months. The Jewish party is in any case to be taken into protective custody until further notice and to be sent to a concentration camp.
  By order

signed: Dr. Grafenberger
a true copy
(S) signed: Martius
Clerk

Translation of Document L-156. Circular letter from Office of Commissioner for Four-Year Plan, 26 March 1943, concerning removal of Jews for forced labor.

* * *

SECRET
Copy

The Commissioner for the Four Years Plan
The Plenipotentiary General for Manpower
Berlin S.W.11, Saarlandstr. 96
26 March 1943

VI a 5431/2008/43 g
To the Presidents of the "Landes" Employment Offices
Re: Removal of Jews

At the end of February Reich Leader SS, in agreement with myself and the Reich Minister for Armaments and Munitions, for reasons concerning the security of the State, removed from their places of work all Jews who were still working freely and not in camps and either transferred them to a labor corps or collected them for removal [Fortschaffung]. So that the lightning character of the measure be protected, I have avoided to give you any prior notice and have informed only those Employment Offices in whose areas unattached Jewish labor was employed in larger numbers.

In order to gain an idea of the effect of this measure on the employment situation, I request you to report to me, as of 31 March 1943, to what extent Jews have been removed from employment and replacement through other forms of labor has become necessary. In supplying this information the number of firms and of Jews employed by these firms is to be based on the conditions which prevailed prior to evacuation. The enclosed form is to be used for the report. In so far as foreign labor has been requested and supplied as replacement, I request that this be noted in cols. 5 and 6 in red figures, distinct from the total figures.

Furthermore I request that I be informed of any special observations made in the course of this action, particularly concerning the effects it has had on the most important industries and the methods used by the firms themselves to compensate for their losses through internal reorganization.

Please, submit these reports by 10 April 1943.

Signed   [signature illegible]

Copy of Document L-161 (USA 292). *Excerpt from British War Office Report, Auschwitz Concentration Camp, 31 May 1945, concerning liquidation of 12,000 Hungarian Jews daily during July 1944.*

* * *

BRITISH WAR OFFICE REPORT
M. I 19 (R.P.S.)/2638 31 May 1945
Report
Poland

OSWIECIM (AUSCHWITZ) CONCENTRATION CAMP
Interrogation of—French student

"42. During July 1944 they were being liquidated at the rate of 12,000 Hungarian Jews daily, and, as the crematoria could not deal with such numbers, many bodies were thrown into large pits and covered with quick lime."

Copy of Document L-165 (USA 287). *Excerpt from The Jewish Food Situation, published in Polish Fortnightly Review of the Polish Ministry of Information, 15 December 1942, p. 7, describing food situation in the Warsaw Ghetto.*

* * *

POLISH
FORTNIGHTLY REVIEW,
Polish Ministry of Information
No. 58   London, Tuesday, December 15th, 1942, page 7.

THE JEWISH FOOD SITUATION

The Jewish section of the population, as we know, is subjected to general living conditions which are still worse than those of the Poles, and the uncertainty of life for them is increased by the continually changing orders and regulations affecting their day-to-day existence. In regard to food supplies, they are brought under a completely separate system, which is obviously aimed at depriving them of the most elemental necessities of life.

The separate and isolated quarters of towns which the German authorities have assigned as ghettoes for the Jewish inhabitants are theoretically autonomously administered and are completely cut off from the outside world. They are under the supervision of special German commissaries, who have unrestricted powers. Economic life inside the ghetto, and in particular the question of food supplies for its inhabitants, is in the hands of the Jewish Council [Judenrat]. All trade and commodity exchange, including the supply of foodstuffs, goes on through a special German organ known as the Transferstelle. This department is responsible for allocating and selling to the ghetto all kinds of goods, including food, as the respective German food or other departments allow at any moment. The goods thus obtained by the ghetto are distributed to the shops by the "Supplies Establishment," which is a special department under the Jewish Council.

As a rule, the ghetto receives foodstuffs of two main categories. The first group consists of rationed goods, which are allocated in accordance with the number of inhabitants and on a ration unit basis. It includes the main food articles such as bread, meat, sugar, fats, etc. The second category consists of goods which are not rationed in the strict sense of the word, but of which the sale to Jews is controlled and for which permission has to be given on each occasion by the German authorities. No article of food not included in either of these two categories can be sold to Jews, either outside or inside the ghettoes. In May, 1941, the German authorities gave permission for barely 154 tons of vegetables to be taken into the Warsaw ghetto, this amount working out at about two-thirds of a pound per person per month. And this was a comparatively high quota, for in the previous month only 48 tons had been allowed to come on to the ghetto market. In June, 1941, the quota of potatoes assigned to the ghetto was 67 tons and other vegetables 189.5 tons. In August there was some improvement in the situation, for the German authorities permitted the import of 100 tons of vegetables weekly into the ghetto, this working out at nine ounces per person.

The quantity allowed in the ration is continually changed, the tendency being to reduce the allotted quantities. The possession of a ration card is by no means a guarantee that a ration will be obtainable. From information received through neutral sources, the weekly rations of the most important articles of food in the Warsaw ghetto during a certain unspecified period of 1941 were as follows:

	Bread	Meat	Sugar	Fats
In grammes ...	420	125	45	25
In ounces (app.)	14 6/7	4½	1 3/5	9/10

Conditions were somewhat better in Cracow, where in March, 1941, the weekly ration for Jews was:

	Bread	Meat	Sugar	Fats
In grammes ..	1,000-1,090	None.	50	30
In ounces (app.)	36-39 1/5	....	1 4/5	1

The above figures call for no comment.

In such conditions the starving Jewish population has to resort to the purchase of food on the ghetto black market, which is supplied by smuggling over the walls at the danger of life, and by the extensive bribery of the German guards. Naturally, prices on the ghetto black market are considerably higher even by comparison with those on the Polish black market. The following figures relating to the autumn of 1941 (in Warsaw) illustrate this disparity:

	Per kilo. (2¼ lbs.)	
	Polish black market	Ghetto black market
Bread	15 zlotys.	32 zlotys.
Potatoes	4.31 zlotys.	8.50 zlotys.
Fats	45 zlotys.	90 zlotys.

(Pre-war exchange rate was about 25 zlotys to the pound.)

Thus, while the rations for Jews are only a half or a third of the rations for Poles, the prices on the black market are twice as high. A Jewish worker employed on forced labor, and receiving four zlotys a day (about 3s. 4d.) could at that time (autumn, 1941) buy for that amount only half a kilo (1⅛ lb.) of potatoes; a Jewish tailor earning 50 zlotys weekly could buy only half a kilo of fats.

Therefore the only hope of survival for the great majority of the Jews was in the communal assistance provided by the Jewish Council and various charitable organizations. In the summer of 1941 soup kitchens in the Warsaw ghetto were providing some 120,000 portions daily. This represented assistance to barely 25 percent of the total number of inhabitants, and only half the number actually needing help.

The terrible shortage of food, coupled with the serious overcrowding and insanitary conditions of the ghettoes, has led to a fearful increase in the mortality rate from month to month. In August, 1941, there were 5,620 deaths in the Warsaw ghetto, while in June, 1941 (the latest month for which figures have been available), there were only 396 births. The inevitable decline in ghetto population thus resulting was compensated for by the continual influx of Jews driven into the ghettoes by the German authorities, who rounded them up not only from all over Poland, but from almost all Europe.

In July, 1942, the German authorities started a process of wholesale extermination of the Jewish population of the ghettoes.

Translation of Document L-167. Order of Minister of Interior, 24 March 1942, restricting use of public transportation facilities by Jews, and covering letters.

* * *

Chamber of Industry and Commerce Koblenz District
Idar-Oberstein
Koblenz, 22 May 1942
43 Emil Schueller Str.
Tel. 2501

The Regierungspraesident,
Office of Economy for the
economic district of Moselland
B 3/18/1083/42 g
Vo/Li/Schl.

SECRET

Circular Order No. 279/42 IHK—251/42 HwK
To the Chambers of Industry and Commerce
and Chambers of Artisans
in the economic district of Moselland.
Personal Address or official deputy
Subject: Use of public transportation by Jews.

Forwarded enclosed is copy of an order of the Reichminister of the Interior of 24 March 1942 (Pol. S. IV B 4 b) (940/4-6-) 1155/41-33 for information.

By order
Signed: Dr. Vollweiler

For information
  Office of Economy Luxemburg
  Gauleitung (Gauwirtschaftsamt) Koblenz
                [Seal]   Certified:
                         [illegible]
                                  Clerk

Copy

The Regierungspraesident
Leadership Staff Economy
for the War Economy District XII
A/514/1116/42g Sch.
                Wiesbaden, 12 May 1942
                48 Wilhelmstrasse
                Telefon 5 94 81

SECRET

To the Chambers of Industry, Commerce and Artisans for the War Economy District [Wehrwirtschaftbezirk] XII.

III - 51

Subject: Use of public transportation by Jews.

Enclosed is forwarded the copy of an order of the Reichminister of the Interior on the use of public transportation by the Jews. The permits for the use of public transportation are to be issued exclusively by the local police authorities. Consideration is only to be given to the following:
1. when drafted for work.
2. for school children.
3. for Jewish legal counsels.

Jews, being employed, are requested by the Reichorganization of Jews in Germany to report at the office of the Employment Service for issue of the permits in question. Only such Jews will be permitted to use public transportation, who prove through a certificate from the Employment Service that they have to cover a distance of one hour or seven km (one way only). The certificates of the Employment Service will show place of work and residence of the Jews. The certificates of the Employment Service should in the case of shiftwork show corresponding entries. In the case of group employment of Jews the issue of a collective certificate is sufficient.

By order
Signed: SCHOENING (S)
Certified
[illegible signature]
Clerk

Copy of Copy

The Reichminister of the Interior   Berlin, 24 March 1942
Pol. S IV B 4 b (940/41–6–) 1155/41–33–Special Delivery

Subject: Use of public transportation by Jews.
Reference: Our circular orders of 15 September 1941
    and 16 February 1942—Pol. S IV B 4 b Kr.94041–6–
Enclosures: one of each (sample B)

With regard to the fact that complaints on disturbances through the use of public transportation (street cars, subways, buses, in Berlin also the S-railway) by Jews increase constantly, the following new traffic restrictions re use of public transportation by Jews *within their community* are issued in agreement with the Reichminister of Transportation and the Reichminister of Postal Services and under alteration of the current regulations, esp. the one cited in circular order referred to above, regarding police order re identification of Jews of 15 September 1941.—Pol. S. IV B 4b—No. 940/41–6.

1. According to the police order re identification of 1 September 1941 (RGBL. I. S.547) and in accordance with our respective circular orders of 15 September 1941 and 16 February 1942 —Pol. S IV B 4 b—No. 940/41—6, Jews are required to display the Jewish Star; in every case when travelling *within their community* these Jews are to carry with them a police permit, a smaller form of enclosed new sample B, issued for the use in that public transportation. In special cases, for instance when employed in groups, a collective permit can be issued.

2. The hitherto existing exclusive competence of the local police authorities for the issue of *these* permits is to be maintained.

3. Permits are to be issued only:

a. When drafted for work (inclusive work for officially recognized Jewish organizations), provided it is proved on the part of the Jew through an official certificate of the competent office of the Employment Service that one hour or seven km (one way only) is needed to reach the place of work (in the case of definitely permanent sick persons or invalids as well as disabled war veterans a relatively shorter distance is sufficient).

b. To schoolchildren, if it is proved through a certificate of the competent supervisory schoolboard that at least one hour *or* five km (one way only) are needed to reach the school (in the case of definitely permanent sick persons or invalids an accordingly shorter distance is sufficient).

c. and to Jewish legal counsel, medical technicians, and midwives who present their official authorization or concession.

4. As a rule only *one* specifically defined public means of transportation (for instance the street car) is to be free for use.

5. The permits for the use of public transportation are issued regularly with a time limit of one year in order to save work and paper as far as they do not concern specific trips. After expiration of this time limit a new permit is to be issued upon request, provided that the necessary requirements still exist, with the stipulation that the Jew has to return the last permit issued to him. In addition to that the Jews are under obligation generally to return the permits in case the circumstances under which the permit was originally issued no longer exist.

6. The necessary permits, according to enclosed sample B, are to be requested *not later* than 10 April 1942 from the intermediate authorities of the general inner administration of the RSHA, Dept. IV B 4, Berlin SW 11, Prinz-Albrechtstr.8.

7. Infractions of this order are to be punished with protective

custody by the competent authorities of the State Police [Staatspolizeileitstellen].

8. This regulation becomes effective 1 May 1942. Any different local regulations are herewith rescinded.

9. The eventual issue of detailed regulations through the Reichminister of Transport or the Reichminister of Postal Services is reserved.

10. The current prohibitions, restrictions, regulations, and executive orders remain in force. The above traffic regulations are to be brought to the attention of the Jewish organizations through the competent authorities of the state police in the Reichsgaue of Vienna, Carinthia, Lower-Danube, Upper-Danube, Salzburg, Styria, Tyrol and Vorarlberg, in the incorporated eastern territories (Danzig-West Prussia, Wartheland East-Upper Silesia, South East Prussia with Zichenau and district Bialistock) for strict compliance on the part of the Jews.

By order
signed Heydrich

Translation of Document L-179. *Letter from RSHA (Reichs Security Main Office) to police officials, 5 November 1942, concerning criminal procedure by the police against Poles, Jews and members of the Eastern peoples.*

* * *

Reich Security Main Main Office [RSHA]
II A 2 No. 567/42-176   Berlin, 5 November 1942
EXPRESS LETTER

To:
    a. The Higher SS and Police Fuehrer
    b. The Commanders and Inspectors of the Security Police and Security Service (SD)
    c. The Chiefs of the State Police (chief offices)
    d. The Supreme Commanders of the Security Police and the SD
    e. The Chiefs of the Criminal Police (Chief offices)
    f. The Chiefs of the SD-Sections (Chief Detachments)

Information to (Sections I, III, IV and V—5 copies each).

Subject: Criminal procedure against Poles and members of the Eastern peoples.

I. The Reichsfuehrer-SS has come to an agreement with the Reich Minister of Justice Thierack that the courts will forego the carrying out of regular criminal procedures against Poles and members of the Eastern peoples. These people of foreign extraction henceforth shall be turned over to the police. Jews and gypsies are to be treated likewise. This agreement was approved by the Fuehrer.

In pursuance of this agreement regulations are at present being worked out by the RSHA and the Reich Ministry of Justice to take effect possibly by 1 January 1943.

II. This agreement is based on the following considerations:

Poles and members of the Eastern peoples are persons of foreign extraction and racially of a lower value, residing in German Reich territory. This situation creates serious dangers for the German community which by necessity result in placing persons of foreign extraction under a criminal law different from the one concerning people of German-blood.

This necessity has not been fully taken into account so far. Only for Poles has there been a special regulation in the sphere of criminal law through the Ordinance concerning the Criminal Procedure against Poles and Jews in the incorporated Eastern territories of 4 December 1941 (Reich Law Gazette, "RGB1."—I page 759). But this special regulation also contains no basic solution of the questions which arise from the co-habitation of Germans with persons of foreign extraction. It only creates more severe penal regulations and a partly simplified criminal procedure for Poles. But the real question that persons of foreign extraction for reasons of national policy are to be treated entirely different from people of German blood is disregarded because basically, in spite of all aggravations, it applies to Poles the characteristics of the German criminal procedure.

In principle, therefore, the punishment of an offense committed by a Pole is still based on the same considerations which apply to the punishment of a German; this means the judge considers the personality of the offender and tries to find through a far-reaching appraisal of the personal motives of the offender a retribution for the crime which would do justice to the interests of the national community.

These considerations which may be right for the punishment of an offense committed by a German, are wrong with regard to the punishment of an offense committed by a person of foreign extraction. With regard to offenses committed by a person of foreign extraction the personal motives of the offender are to be disregarded entirely. Important is only that this offense endangers the order of the German community and that therefore measures must be taken to prevent further dangers. In other words the offense committed by a person of foreign extraction is not to be judged from the point of legal retribution by way of Justice, but from the point of view of preventing danger through police-action.

From this follows that the criminal procedure against persons of foreign extraction must be transferred from the courts to the Police.

III. The preceding statement serves for personal information. However, there are no objections to inform the Gauleiters accordingly should the need arise.

The Deputy
Signed: Streckenbach
Stamp of the Reich Fuehrer SS and Chief of the German Police in the Reich Ministry of Interior.
Certified: [signed] Kausch Clerk.

Translation of Document L-180 (USA 276). Excerpts from Report by SS Brigade Commander Stahlecker to Himmler, 15 October 1941, on activities of Action Group A in exterminating thousands of Jews in Latvia and Lithuania.

* * *

ACTION—GROUP A

[Pencilled] Personal property of SS-Obergruppenfuehrer Wv.31.1.1942

[Rubber-stamp] Secret matter of the Reich
40 copies   copy nr. 23

ACTION—Group A
Comprehensive Report up to 15 October 1941

	Page
I. *Table of Contents*	1
II. *Activities in police matters*	
A. Measures of organization	13
B. Cleansing and securing the action area	21
C. Counteraction against espionage	39
D. Control of persons and indexing	40
E. Criminal police work	41
III. *Report on the Situation*	
A. Situation before the invasion by German forces	
B. General conditions in the inhabited areas up to 1510.1941	47
C. Jewish influence on the general conditions of life in the Eastern territory	107
IV. *Nuisances and proposals for their removal*	134

Action-Group A, after preparing their vehicles for action proceeded to their area of concentration as ordered on 23 June 1941, the second day of the campaign in the East. Army Group North consisting of the 16th and 18th Armies and Panzer-Group 4 had left the day before. Our task was to hurriedly establish personal contact with the commanders of the Armies and with the commander of the army of the rear area. It must be stressed from the beginning that co-operation with the Armed Forces was generally good, in some cases, for instance with Panzer-Group 4 under Col. Gen. Hoeppner, it was very close, almost cordial. Misunderstandings which cropped up with some authorities in the first days, were cleared up mainly through personal discussions.

* * * * * * *

At the start of the Eastern Campaign it became obvious with regard to the *Security Police* that its special work had to be done not only in the rear areas, as was provided for in the original agreements, with the High Command of the Army, but also in the combat areas, and this for two reasons. On the one hand, the development of the rear area of the armies was delayed because of the quick advance and on the other hand, the undermining communist activities and the fight against partisans was most effective within the area of actual fighting—especially when the Luga sector was reached.

To carry out the duties connected with security police, it was desirable to move into the larger towns together with the armed forces. We had our first experiences in this direction when a small advance detachment under my leadership entered Kowne together with the advance units of the Armed Forces on 25 June 1941. When the other larger towns, especially Libau, Mitau, Riga, Dorpat, Reval, and the larger suburbs of Leningrad were captured, a detachment of the Security Police was always with the first army units. Above all, communist functionaries and communist material had to be seized, and the armed forces themselves had to be secured against surprises inside the towns; the troops themselves were usually not able to take care of that because of their small numbers. For this purpose the Security Police immediately after capture formed volunteer detachments from reliable natives in all three Baltic provinces; they carried out their duties successfully under our command. For example, it may be mentioned that the armed forces suffered not inconsiderable losses through guerillas in Riga, on the left of the Duena river; on the right bank of the Duena river, however, after these volunteer detachments had been organized in Riga not a single soldier was injured, although these Latvian detachments suffered some killed and wounded in fighting with Russian stragglers.

Similarly, native anti-Semitic forces were induced to start pograms against Jews during the first hours after capture, though this inducement proved to be very difficult. Following out orders, the Security Police was determined to solve the Jewish question with all possible means and most decisively. But it was desirable that the Security Police should not put in an immediate appearance, at least in the beginning, since the extraordinarily harsh measures were apt to stir even German circles. It had to be shown to the world that the native population itself took the first action by way of natural reaction against the suppression by Jews during several decades and against the terror exercised by the Communists during the preceding period. After reaching the Duena river and therewith Riga, the Action-Group detached itself at first from the further advance of the Army-Group North, and concentrated its forces on the pacification of the Lithouanian and Latvian area, and later of the old-Russian area which was reached at Opotschka. The work in this connection took on many shapes. In view of the constant changes in German troops and the fluctuation within the German authorities, which was caused by the transfer of the rear-area of the Wehrmacht to the rear-area of the Armies, and later to the civil administration and to the Commander of the Armed Forces the personnel and thus the opinions of the German authorities changed far too often and far too quickly. In the Security Police this had to be avoided, which led us to adopt the policy of keeping the same commanders in the same locality as far as possible. Thereby the Security Police gained a considerable advantage over all other comers, because it knew facts and people. As a matter of fact, they alone amongst all authorities may claim to have achieved a certain steadiness on the German side. The Lithouanians, Latvians, and the Esthonians, who have a fine feeling for such matters, came soon to acknowledge this fact and acted accordingly. Under these circumstances the Security Police tried to guide political, economic, and cultural matters according to definite policies, and to advise the other German authorities on these subjects. In the political sphere particularly the several competent authorities followed different viewpoints. It was regrettable that the Ministry for Eastern Affairs had not given clear directions from the beginning, so that up to date and in spite of our efforts the situation in the Baltic provinces is not clear. The example of Esthonia is significant for this fluctuation.

In agreement with the RSHA the Action-Group brought with them the Esthonian Dr. Mae as presumptive political adviser for the Esthonians. In order to avoid a pernicious muddle, as happened in Lithouania and Latvia, and in order to obtain the appointment of Dr. Mae or to avoid his removal, negotiations had to be carried out with, one after the other, the Army division capturing Reval, the Army Corps competent for Reval, the Garrison commander Reval, the Field Commandatura Reval, the 18. Army Group, North, the Commander of the Rear Army Area at the Army Group North, the General Commissioner and his deputy, and with the representative of the Ministry for Eastern Affairs. After the conquest of Lithouania and Latvia, the Action-Detachments 2 and 3 were separated from the Commander of the Rear-Area of the Armed Forces and were left in Lithouania and Latvia respectively for essential assignments. The Commanders of Action-Detachments 2 and 3 have been staying permanently in Kowno and Riga since the beginning of July. Contact was established also with the Reich Commissioner as soon as he was appointed and likewise with the General Commissioners, i.e. by the Action-Group and by the Action-Detachments. Co-operation with the Reich Commissioner depended on:

a. a delay in the inquiry addressed to the RSHA as to how the interpolation (sc. of the Security Police) at the Reich Commissioner's should be effected, and

b. on the negotiations of the Superior SS- and Police Fuehrer who on his own account had initiated negotiations with the Reich commissioner with regard to the interpolation of the police. No initiative of our own was admissible therefore until the questions to a) and b) had been settled. It was intended to get in touch with the Reich Commisioner with regard to this question at a convenient moment. There are plenty of special occasions. When the advance of the Army Group North was halted in Esthonia and at Luga and when heavy fighting and strong Russian attacks against the centre and the right wing ensued, the Action-Group again teamed up with the armies, in particular the 4. Panzer Group, because the struggle against the partisans who now began to appear in great numbers, was and still is a job for the Security Police. The area to the North of Pleskau and between the Peipus- and Ilmen- lakes with far extending forest and swamps was really an ideal area for Russian partisan warfare. The difficulties of the terrain further impeded activities even for the smaller units. After the failure of purely military activities such as the placing of sentries and combing through the newly occupied territories with whole divisions, even the Armed Forces had to look out for new methods. The Action-Group undertook to search for new methods. Soon therefore the Armed Forces adopted the experiences of the Security Police and their methods of combatting the partisans. For details I refer to the numerous reports concerning the struggle against the partisans. The activities of the Security Police were rendered more difficult during the further course of the struggle against the partisans because the vehicles either could not be used or were to be preserved for the advance on Leningrad, which was always expected at that time. Special difficulties arose for the Command of the Action-Group at this time. Whilst the larger parts of the Security Police, in action in Lithouania and Latvia, were 700 km to the rear, the other parts were in action against the partisans behind the frontline, extending for nearly 600 km. For the transmission of signals we had only a wireless truck stationed in Riga, and one medium and one light wireless truck for this vast area. Even the use of army telephones failed over distances of more than 200 km. The Action-Group as a whole could be led only by personal contacts, although the ways and roads, including the army highways, were in an extremely bad state. Even on the army highway an hourly average speed of 10 km could not be exceeded. In spite of this, my own motorcar had to do 15.000 km during this time. Similar difficulties because of the vast areas arose for the Commanders of the Action-detachments, so that even messenger trips became a serious problem. For some time this situation became even more difficult, when the further attack against Leningrad no longer followed the great road from Pleskau via Lungau, but had to bend far to the West, so that the centre of the counter-attacks against partisans was transferred to the forest and swamp areas East of the Peipus Lake and the areas to the West of the Ilmen Lake."

* * * * * * *

During the process of capturing Esthonia the Action-Group 1a was transferred definitely to Esthonia, except for the detachment with the 18th Army. The pacification of Esthonia had to be considered as especially important because of the good racial composition of the population. After Action-Group B had transferred parts of White Ruthenia to Action Group A, Action-detachment 1b reinforced by parts of Action-detachment 2 and

3 took over this area. For the investment of Leningrad, the Security Police aside from the heavily increased activities against the partisans, received the further assignment to observe carefully the population which was slowly returning from the woods. As trench warfare developed around Leningrad, it was recommended to the armies to evacuate wholly a zone around Leningrad, a measure which had been carried out already whenever possible by the Security Police together with units of Armed SS and the uniformed police. In this area a network for information is being established which is to be as complete as possible. From the very beginning, the Security Police systematically collected information about Leningrad in all aspects. The 18th Army asked us to take over in addition military reconnaissance of Leningrad of resp. the area of the 8th Russian Army which was invested in the area around Oranienburg. * * * This description of the over-all situation showed and shows that the members of the Stapo (the Secret State Police), Kripo and SD (Security Service) who are attached to the Action-Group, are active mainly in Lithouania, Latvia, Esthonia, White-Ruthenia and to a smaller part in front of Leningrad. It shows further that the forces of the uniformed police and the Armed SS are active mainly in front of Leningrad, in order to take measures against the returning population and under their own officers. This is so much easier because the Action detachments in Lithouania, Latvia and Esthonia have at their disposal native police units, as described in encl. 1, and because so far 150 Latvian reinforcements have been sent to White-Ruthenia. The distribution of the leaders of Security Police and SD during the individual phases can be gathered from encl. 2, the advance and the activities of the Action-Group and the Action-detachments from encl. 3. It should be mentioned that the leaders of the Armed-SS and of the uniformed police who are reserves have declared their wish to stay on with the Security Police and the SD.

A. *The Baltic Area.* I. *Organization Measures.* 1. *Formation of auxiliary police and of police.* In view of the extension of the area of operations and the great number of duties which had to be performed by the Security Police, it was intended from the very beginning to obtain the co-operation of the reliable population for the fight against vermin—that is mainly the Jews and Communists. Beyond our directing of the first spontaneous actions of self-cleansing, which will be reported elsewhere, care had to be taken that reliable people should be put to the cleansing job and that they were appointed auxiliary members of the Security Police. The difference of the situation in each part of the area of operations also had to be taken into account. In Lithouania activist and nationalist people formed themselves into so-called partisan-units at the beginning of the Eastern Campaign, in order to take active part in the fight against Bolshevism. According to their own report they suffered 4,000 casualties.

* * * * * * *

2. *Reconstruction of prisons*. The prisons in the Baltic countries were found to be either empty or occupied by Jews or Communists who had been arrested by Self-Protection Units.
* * *

Whenever the prisons were too small because of the large number of people who were to be arrested, provisional concentration camps were established. The construction of large concentration camps is in preparation. The schedules attached as encl. 5 show the present occupancy of the prisons.

II. *Cleansing and Securing the Area of Operations.* 1. *Instigation of self-cleansing actions.* Considering that the population of the Baltic countries had suffered very heavily under the government of Bolshevism and Jewry while they were incorporated in the USSR, it was to be expected that after the liberation from that foreign government, they (i.e. the population themselves) would render harmless most of the enemies left behind after the retreat of the Red Army. It was the duty of the Security Police to set in motion these self-cleansing movements and to direct them into the correct channels in order to accomplish the purpose of the cleansing operations as quickly as possible. It was no less important in view of the future to establish the unshakable and provable fact that the liberated population themselves took the most severe measures against the Bolshevist and Jewish enemy quite on their own, so that the direction by German authorities could not be found out.

In Lithouania this was achieved for the first time by partisan activities in Kowno. To our surprise it was not easy at first to set in motion an extensive pogrom against Jews. Klimatis, the leader of the partisan unit, mentioned above, who was used for this purpose primarily, succeeded in starting a pogrom on the basis of advice given to him by a small advanced detachment acting in Kowno, and in such a way that no German order or German instigation was noticed from the outside. During the first pogrom in the night from 25. to 26.6 the Lithouanian partisans did away with more than 1,500 Jews, set fire to several

Synagogues or destroyed them by other means and burned down a Jewish dwelling district consisting of about 60 houses. During the following nights about 2,300 Jews were made harmless in a similar way. In other parts of Lithouania similar actions followed the example of Kowno, though smaller and extending to the Communists who had been left behind.

These self-cleansing actions went smoothly because the Army authorities who had been informed showed understanding for this procedure. From the beginning it was obvious that only the first days after the occupation would offer the opportunity for carrying out pogroms. After the disarmament of the partisans the self-cleansing actions ceased necessarily.

It proved much more difficult to set in motion similar cleansing actions in *Latvia*. Essentially the reason was that the whole of the national stratum of leaders had been assassinated or destroyed by the Soviets, especially in Riga. It was possible though through similar influences on the Latvian auxiliary to set in motion a pogrom against Jews also in Riga. During this pogrom all synagogues were destroyed and about 400 Jews were killed. As the population of Riga quieted down quickly, further pogroms were not convenient.

So far as possible, both in Kowno and in Riga evidence by film and photo was established that the first spontaneous executions of Jews and Communists were carried out by Lithouanians and Latvians.

In *Estonia* by reason of the relatively small number of Jews no opportunity presented itself to instigate pogroms. The Esthonian self-protection units made harmless only some individual Communists whom they hated especially, but generally they limited themselves to carrying out arrests.

2. *Combating Communism*. Everywhere in the area of operation counteractions against communism and Jewry took first place in the work of the Security Police.

The Soviet officials and the functionaries of the Communist Party had fled with the Soviet Army. In view of the experiences made during the Bolshevist oppression which lasted more than one year, the population of the Baltic countries realized that all remainders of Communism left behind after the retreat of the Red Army had to be removed. Such basic opinion facilitated essentially the work of the Security Police with regard to cleansing in this sphere, especially since active nationalist people co-operated in this cleansing, viz. in Lithouania the partisans, in Latvia and Esthonia the self-protection units.

* * * * * * *

b. Search for and Arrest of Communists. Aside from these searching activities, a systematic search was made for Communist functionaries, Red-Army soldiers, and persons more seriously suspect because of their activities for Communism and who had been left behind. In some places the Self-Protection Units themselves had rendered harmless the most infamous Communists already spontaneously. Using all available units of the Detachments and Self-Protection Formations, and with the help of the German uniformed police, large scale actions were carried out in the larger towns resulting in many arrests and search actions.

* * * * * * *

3. *Action against Jewry.* From the beginning it was to be expected that the Jewish problem in the East could not be solved by pogroms alone. In accordance with the basic orders received, however, the cleansing activities of the Security Police had to aim at a complete annihilation of the Jews. Special detachments reinforced by selected units — in Lithouania partisan detachments, in Latvia units of the Latvian auxiliary police—therefore performed extensive executions both in the towns and in rural areas. The actions of the execution detachments were performed smoothly. When attaching Lithouanian and Latvian detachments to the execution squads, men were chosen whose relatives had been murdered or removed by the Russians.

Especially severe and extensive measures became necessary in *Lithouania*. In some places—especially in Kowno—the Jews had armed themselves and participated actively in franctireur war and committed arson. Besides these activities the Jews in Lithouania had collaborated most actively hand in glove with the Soviets.

The sum total of the Jews liquidated in Lithouania amounts to 71,105.

During the pogroms in Kowno 3,800 Jews were eliminated, in the smaller towns about 1,200 Jews.

In *Latvia* as well the Jews participated in acts of sabotage and arson after the invasion of the German Armed Forces. In Duensburg so many fires were lighted by the Jews that a large part of the town was lost. The electric power station burnt down to a mere shell. The streets which were mainly inhabited by Jews remained unscathed.

In Latvia up to now 30,000 Jews were executed in all. 500 were made harmless by pogroms in Riga.

Most of the 4,500 Jews living in Esthonia at the beginning of the Eastern Campaign fled with the retreating Red Army. About 200 stayed behind. In Reval alone there lived about 1,000 Jews.

The arrest of all male Jews of over 16 years of age has been nearly finished. With the exception of the doctors and the Elders of the Jews who were appointed by the Special Commandos, they were executed by the Self-Protection Units under the control of the Special Detachment 1a. Jewesses in Pernau and Reval of the age groups from 16 to 60 who are fit for work were arrested and put to peat-cutting or other labor.

At present a camp is being constructed in Harku, in which all Esthonian Jews are to be assembled, so that Esthonia will be free of Jews within a short while.

After the carrying out of the first larger executions in Lithouania and Latvia it became soon apparent that an annihilation of the Jews without leaving any traces could not be carried out, at least not at the present moment. Since a large part of the trades in Lithouania and Latvia are in Jewish hands and others carried on nearly exclusively by Jews (especially those of glaziers, plumbers, stovebuilders, cobblers) many Jewish partisans are indispensable at present for repairing installations of vital importance for the reconstruction of towns destroyed and for work of military importance. Although the employers aim at replacing Jewish labor with Lithouanian or Latvian labor, it is not yet possible to displace all employed Jews especially not in the larger towns. In co-operation with the labor exchange offices, however, all Jews who are no longer fit for work are being arrested and shall be executed in small batches.

In this connection it may be mentioned that some authorities of the Civil Administration offered resistance, at times even a strong one, against the carrying out of larger executions. This resistance was answered by calling attention to the fact that it was a matter of carrying out basic orders.

Apart from organizing and carrying out measures of execution, the creation of *Ghettos* was begun in the larger towns at once during the first days of operations. This was especially urgent in Kowno because there were 30.000 Jews in a total population of 152.400. Therefore, at the end of the first pogrom a Jewish Committee was summoned who were informed that the German authorities so far had not seen any reason to interfere in the quarrels between Lithouanians and Jews. The sole basis for creating a normal situation would be to construct a Jewish Ghetto. Against remonstrations made by the Jewish Committee, it was declared that there was no other possibility to prevent further pogroms. On this the Jews at once declared themselves ready to do everything in their power to transfer their co-racials to the town district of Viriampol which was intended as a Jewish Ghetto and with the greatest possible speed. This own district lies in the triangle between the Mamel river and a tributary; it is connected with Kowno by one bridge only and can, therefore, easily be locked off.

In Riga the so-called "Moskau suburb" was designated as a Ghetto. This is the worst dwelling district of Riga, already now mostly inhabited by Jews. The transfer of the Jews into the Ghetto-district proved rather difficult because the Latvians dwelling in that district had to be evacuated and residential space in Riga is very crowded. 24,000 of the 28,000 Jews living in Riga have been transferred into the Ghetto so far. In creating the Ghetto, the Security Police restricted themselves to mere policing duties, while the establishment and administration of the Ghetto as well as the regulation of the food supply for the inmates of the Ghetto were left to Civil Administration; the Labor Offices were left in charge of Jewish labor.

In the other towns with a larger Jewish population Ghettos shall be established likewise.

Marking of the Jews by a yellow star, to be worn on the breast and the back was ordered in the first instance by provisional orders of the Security Police, was carried out within a short time on the basis of regulations issued by the Commander of the Rear area and later by the Civil Administration.

The number of Jews executed up to the present may be seen in the schedule on encl. 8.

* * * * * * *

Copies of the latest experience reports are attached as encl. 9. [This enclosure reveals the name of the Commander of the Action-Group: Dr. Stahlecker, SS-Brigade Commander and Major-General of the Police.]

5. *Other jobs of the Security Police. 1.* Occasionally the conditions prevailing in the lunatic asylums necessitated operations of the Security Police. Many institutions had been robbed by the retreating Russians of their whole food supply. Often the guard and nursing personnel fled. The inmates of several institutions broke out and became a danger to the general security; therefore in Aglona (Lithouania), 544 lunatics; in Mariampol (Lithouania), 109 lunatics and; in Magutowo (near Luga) 95 lunatics were liquidated.

Sometimes authorities of the Armed Forces asked us to clean out in a similar way other institutions which were wanted as billets. However, as interests of the Security Police did not require any intervention, it was left to the authorities of the Armed Forces, to take the necessary action with their own forces.

2. The Action-Commandos dealt to a large extent with the search for persons who had been deported and with the exhumation of people who had been murdered by the Russians. For reasons of propaganda the propaganda squadrons of the Armed Forces and sometimes of the foreign press were made to participate.

In Esthonia the exhumation of Esthonians murdered by the Russians was organized more extensively. In view of the extent of the work which had been done here, a central office was established in Reval, in order to organize searches for the whereabouts of removed and murdered persons, under the systematic guidance of the Security Police.

The extent of this work is shown by the fact that from Reval alone 30,000 men had been reported missing.

* * * * * * *

V. *Work of the Police concerning Crime Detection.*

* * * * * * *

In order to eliminate the most heavy cases of crime until preventive measures can be introduced, professional criminals are being taken into the care of the Action-detachments and executed whenever the case warrants such measures.

* * * * * * *

Action-Group B liquidated so far 7,620 Jews in Borrissow.

* * * * * * *

III. *Report on the Situation*

* * * * * * *

A. *The Situation in Lithouania.* As the population did not receive any information with regard to their future fate, the national-minded part (sc. of the population) is still thinking of a future Lithouanian State of their own. No effort can be noticed to approach the Lithouanian people to the German peoples.

* * * * * * *

The active anti-Semitism which flared up quickly after the German occupation did not falter. Lithouanians are voluntarily and untiringly at our disposal for all measures against Jews, sometimes they even execute such measures on their own.

* * * * * * *

. The faculties of Arts and Sciences should be closed altogether. There is some need though for the Medical faculty and some of the technical branches. More than 60% of the dentists were Jews; more than 50% of the doctors as well. The disappearance of these brings about an extreme shortage of doctors which cannot be overcome even by bringing in doctors from the Reich.

* * * * * * *

B. *The Situation in Latvia.* In Courland the ordinance of the Naval Commander in Libau, Captain Dr. Kavelmacher of the German Navy had caused some unrest. This ordinance announced measures of reprisal against the population of Libau in case of attacks against German soldiers. It reads as follows:

'For each and every case of a known or unknown culprit firing on German soldiers, certain people of Libau shall be arrested and shot at once under Martial Law.' 'Similarly' runs the ordinance 'for each and every attempt of sabotage whether effective or not, part of the Latvian population living near the place of the act of sabotage shall be arrested and shot under Martial Law'. This ordinance was published in the Libau paper "Das Kurlaendische Wort". The Libau population is quite excited, as may be understood. The fear is abroad that further actions may be provoked by hostile people (Communist or Jewish).

* * * * * * *

Table of Enclosures

Enclosures:
1. a. Survey of the whole Personnel of the Action-Group A.
1. b. Map of Distribution of the Members of Action-Group A on action Commandos.
2. (Headquarters) of Commanders of Action-Group.
3. Line of Advance of Action-Group A.
4. Strength and Distribution of the Auxiliary Police.
5. Figures on Prison-Inmates.
6. Special Report on the GPU in Latvia.
7. Survey of the Supreme Authorities of the Esthonian Socialist Soviet-Republic.
8. Report on the Number of Executions.
9. Report on Experiences in Counteractions against Partisans.
10. Schedule concerning Organization and Distribution of departments of the Crime Detective Force in Latvia.
11. Report on the Work of the Crime Detective Force in Latvia.
12. Schedule of the Crime Detective Force in Esthonia.
13. The Peoples of the Baltic Countries.
14. Map showing Employees in the Baltic Countries according to Economic Branches.
15. Number of Employees of the Main Economic Groups in the Baltic Countries.
16. Number and Distribution of Jewish Population in the Areas.
17. Share of the Jews in the Economy.
18. Share of Jews in Number of Latvian Trade Establishments.

The Documentary Evidence

Encl. 1 a
Total Strength of Action Group A

Total:	990	
Waffen—SS	340	34.4%
Motor Bicycle-Riders	172	17.4%
Administration	18	1.8%
Security Service (SD)	35	3.5%
Criminal Police [Kripo]	41	4.1%
State Police [Gestapo]	89	9.0%
Auxiliary Police	87	8.8%
Order Police	133	13.4%
Female Employees	13	1.3%
Interpreters	51	5.1%
Teleprinter-Operators	3	0.3%
Wireless-Operators	8	0.8%

Enclosure 1 b

Composition of the Action-detachments

Action-detachments	1 b		1 b		2		3	
Interpreters	15	13.7%	6	5.4%	18	10.8%	8	5.6%
Wireless-Operators	2	1.9%	1	0.9%	2	1.2%	1	0.7%
Teleprinter-Operators						1.8%		
Reservists	25	24%	26	23.7%	41	23.6%	32	22.9%
Motorbicycle-Riders	23	22.1%	34	30.9%	50	29.4%	34	24.3%
Administration	3	2.9%	2	1.8%	4	2.4%	1	0.7%
Security Service	8	7.8%	3	2.7%	8	4.8%	10	7.%
Criminal Police	11	10.5%	6	5.4%	13	7.8%	10	7.%
State Police Gestapo	18	16.2%	12	11.%	26	15.6%	29	20.6%
Auxiliary Police			20	18.2%			15	10.5%
Female Employees	1	0.9%			4	2.4%	1	0.7%
Total	105		110		170	[sic]	141	

Enclosure 5. Occupation of Prisons.

Prisons in Lithouania. Action-detachment 3 at present in ascertaining the number of occupants of prisons in Lithouania.

In Kowno are under arrest:
in the central prison.................520 persons, including 50 Jews
in the police prison................. 69 persons, including 3 Jews

Enclosure 8. Survey of the number of executed persons.

Area	Jews	Communists	Total
Lithouania			
Kowno town and surroundings (land)	31.914	80	31.994
Schaulen	41.382	763	42.145
Wilna	7.015	17	7.032
	80.311	860	81.171
Latvia			
Riga town and surroundings (land)			6.378
Mitau			3.576
Libau			11.860
Wolmar			.209
Dueanaburg	9.256	589	9.845
	30.025	1.843	31.868
Esthonia	474	684	1.158
White-Ruthenia	7.620		7.620
Total:			
Lithouania	80.311	860	81.171
Latvia	30.025	1.845	31.868
Esthonia	474	684	1.158
White-Ruthenia	7.620	....	7.620
	118.430	3.387	121.817

To be added to these figures:

In Lithouania and Latvia Jews annihilated by pogroms	5.500
Jews, Communists and partisans executed in old-Russian area	2.000
Lunatics executed	748
	122.455
Communists and Jews liquidated by State Pol. and Security Service Tilsit during search actions	5.502
	135.567

The Documentary Evidence   L-180

Map showing "Number of persons liquidated in the Baltic countries as per 25.10.1941."
The following figures have been entered into the map:

District of Libau in area of Courland	11.860
District of Mitau in area of Semgslen	3.576
District of Riga town in area of	6.378
District of Riga town in area of Livland	209
District of Fellin	1.158
District of Dueanburg in area of Lettgslen	9.845
in area of Shcaulen	42.145
District of Kowno	31.994
in area of Wilna-land	7.032

Additionally pogrom
in Lithouania and Latvia about	5.500
border area Lithouania	5.502

Enclosure 9: Report on Activities and Experience in Counteractions against Partisans. First Report:

Action Group A of the Security Police and the Security Service. (Gen.) Staff 17.7.1941
Report on activities and Experiences in Counteractions against Partisans.

When it was decided to extend the German operations to Leningrad and also to extend the activities of Action Group A to this town, I gave orders on 18 July 1941 to parts of Action Detachments 2 and 3 and to the Staff of the Group to advance to Novosselje, in order to prepare these activities and to be able to advance as early as possible into the area around Leningrad and into the city itself. The advance of the forces of Action Group A which were intended to be used for Leningrad, was effected in agreement with and on the express wish of Panzer-Group 4.

The detachment which was formed for action towards Leningrad was trained for operations in Leningrad during the first days after the advance to Novosselje. However, as an advance to Leningrad is not to be expected at the time planned previously, the parts of Action detachments 2 and 3 which were concentrated in Novosselje were used for extensive operations of cleansing and pacifying in the area of Panzer-Group 4, in agreement with this Group. This is done mainly in the area limited by the connection-line between Pog-Gora-Novosselje-Osjerjewo.

In their operations it was intended to arrest in the first instance any remaining Communist functionaries, and other active Communists and Jews. As nearly all Jews and Communist functionaries had fled with the retreating Soviet forces, only 6 Jews and 10 Communists were arrested and executed."

* * * * * * *

At the start the following procedure was followed:

In villages, in the area where partisans had not been ascertained before, one behaved friendly towards the population. In view of the generally known shortage of bread one usually succeeded very quickly in finding one or several villagers who could be used as persons of confidence. They were promised to get bread provided they would give information concerning partisans or if they would inform the nearest units of the German Army or Police of any partisans appearing in the future. The network of information, thus built up yielded much information for the Action-Group, thus enabling them to surround more narrowly the quarters of the partisans.

There was especially information concerning villagers who had given good or provisional shelter to partisans. On the basis of these reports a great many villages were combed out. After a village had been surrounded, all the inhabitants were forcibly shepherded into one square. The persons suspected on account of confidential information and other villagers were interrogated, and thus it was possible in most cases to find the people who helped the partisans. These were either shot off-hand or if further interrogations promised useful information, taken to headquarters. After the interrogation they were shot.

In order to get a deterring effect, the houses of these who helped the partisans were burned down on several occasions. The population which had congregated was told of the reasons for the punitive measures. At the same time they were threatened that the whole village would be burned down if partisans were helped once more and if partisans appearing in the village were not reported as quickly as possible.

The tactics, to put terror against terror, succeeded marvelously. From fear of reprisals, the peasants came a distance of 20 km and more to the headquarters of the detachment of Action Group A on foot or on horseback in order to bring news about partisans, news which was correct in most of the cases. During the cleansing operations which were made on account of these reports, 48 helpers of partisans, including 6 women, were shot so far.

In this connection a single case may be mentioned, which proves the correctness of the principle "terror against terror". In the village of Jachnowa it was ascertained on the basis of a report made by the peasant Jemeljanow and after further interrogations and other searches that partisans had been fed in the house of Anna Prokoffjewa. The house was burnt down on 8 August 1941 at about 21 hours, and its inhabitant arrested.

Shortly after midnight partisans set alight the house of the informer Jemaljanow. A detachment sent to Jachnowa on the following days ascertained that the peasant woman Ossipowa had told the partisans that Jemaljanow had made the report which has caused our action.

Ossipowa was shot and her house burnt down. Further two 16 year old youths from the village were shot because according to their own confession, they had rendered information and courier-services to the partisans. Obviously, it was on account of these punitive measures that the partisans left the forest camp near the village. The camp was found during this operation.

*   *   *   *   *   *   *

Dr. Stahlecker
ss Brigade Commander and Maj Gen
of the Police.

(Second report)

The Commander of the Security Police and the Security Service
  Action-Group A.

Riga 29.9.1941

Report on Experiences in Counteractions against the Partisans

*   *   *   *   *   *   *

Action detachment of Action Group A of the Security Police participated from the beginning in the fight against the nuisance created by partisans. Close collaboration with the Armed Forces and the Exchange of experiences which were collected in the fight partisans, brought about a thorough knowledge of the origin, organization, strength, equipment and system used by the Red partisans as time went on.

*   *   *   *   *   *   *

IV. Counteractions against the Partisans.

As it was vitally necessary, though, to obtain hints and information concerning abode and direction of the partisans from the population, the latter had to be forced by the use of the most severe measures, to supply useful information and reports. In the knowledge that the Russian has been accustomed from old to ruthless measures on the part of the authorities, the most severe measures were applied. He who helped the partisans to obtain food and shelter, rendered them information services or who have knowingly false information, was shot or hanged. Houses where partisans obtained food or shelter were burnt down. Where a larger number of villagers helped the partisans in such a way, the whole village was burnt down as punishment and in order to create terror.

* * * * * * *

Escaped Red Armists who have found their way through the German lines procure civilian clothes as quickly as possible and get in touch with partisans. It has been ascertained that these Red-Armies form the fighting back-bone of the partisan units. It does not seem, therefore, expedient to treat Red-Armists found in civilian clothing as prisoners of war without further ado and to collect them in prisoner-of-war camps. But an interrogation and survey has to be carried out as thoroughly as possible. It has further to be considered in each and every case, whether Red-Armists found in civilian clothes should be separated from regular prisoners of war, and should be brought into the assembly camps for civilian internees. It seems further suitable to exhort escaped Red-Armists by posters to give themselves up at the nearest Army Unit within a short time after the posting of such posters, say within 3 days. Should they not comply with this order they should be dealt with as partisans, that means they should be shot, without making such exception dependent of proof that they actually knew of the order.

To conclude, attention should be drawn to the necessity of interrogating captured partisans thoroughly before they are liquidated so that we increase our knowledge on organization, abode, strength, armament and plans of the partisans. Sometimes it may become necessary to take advantage of the opportunity to use third degree interrogation methods.

Signed: Dr. Stahlecker
SS-Brigade Commander

Translation of Document L-185 (USA 484). *Excerpt from Organization Plan of the RSHA (Reich Security Main Office) showing function of SS Major Eichmann as concerned with Matters concerning Jews and Evacuations.*

* * *

Subject: Plan of the Division of Work of the Reich Security Main Office (RSHA)

Enclosed, the plan of the division of work of the RSHA is forwarded.

As far as plans are drawn up in the future for the inspectors of the Security Police, State police (Main) agencies, Criminal

Police (Main) agencies and the Security Service (Main) Sections (SD), they are to be adapted as far as possible to the plan of the division of work of the RSHA.
Certified: PRAMM, Chancellery Employee
By order: 1st Dr. NECKMANN

Group IV B

Group Chief: SS Major HARTL
Deputy: SS Major Regierungsrat ROTH

Section	Subject	Specialist	Participants
IV B 1	Political Catholicism	SS Major RR ROTH	
IV B 2	Political Protestant sects	SS Major RR ROTH	
IV B 3	Other churches—Freemasonry	at present vacant	
IV B 4	Matters concerning Jews Matters concerning evacuations	SS Major EICHMANN	

Translation of Document L-188 (USA 386). Report of 8 August 1944 on confiscation of Jewish homes, furniture, and possessions in France, Belgium and Holland up to 31 July 1944.

* * *

Copy

Office West
The Head of the Department

Paris, August 8th 1944
Progress Report up to July 31st 1944

The Office West achieved the following results up to July 31st 1944: 69 619 Jewish homes were confiscated.

Dispatched to the several towns, including special orders, were: 69 512 Sets of furnishings, each a complete house.

The sum total of furniture and fittings dispatched required a loading capacity of: 1 079 373 cbm.

The following were required to provide this capacity incl. additional deliveries: 26 984 railroad cars, equivalent to 674 trains.

Further during the action we confiscated for the use of the Reich and handed over to the Department for Foreign Exchange

[Devisenschutzkommando]: 11 695 516 RM Foreign currency and Securities.

The special purpose branches in France, Belgium and Holland furthermore dispatched: 2 191 352 kg Scrap Metal, Scrap Paper and textiles.

According to the report on Special Tasks [Sonderaufgaben] bombed-out persons accommodated in France, were presented with furniture and fittings valued at 1 516 186 RM

The above results were achieved by a staff of 30 female and 82 male

Officials and Employees of the Ministry for the Occupied Eastern Territories.

A True Copy (Signed) Deubelmann Employee

Office West   Paris, 7.8.44
                                           Schw/H

In carrying out the Fuehrer's orders for the M-action, the following results were achieved within the area of the Office West from invasion day (6th June 44) up to 1st August 44, by 30 female and 82 male officials and employees of the Ministry for the Occupied Eastern Territories.

1. Camoins (trucks) arrived (through confiscation of homes in Paris) 2006
2. Railroad cars arrived from Branch Offices 52
3. Railroad cars loaded and dispatched to Germany 372
4. Receipts from sale of Scrap Material .... 28 124 91 RM
5. Boxes received 20 154
6. Boxes handled, packed and dispatched 21 710
   Containing:
   China .... 199 boxes
   Glass .... 208 boxes
   Kitchen utensils .... 196 boxes
   Clothing .... 177 boxes
   Coat-hangers .... 120 boxes
   Tailors' materials .... 45 boxes
   Linen .... 128 boxes
   Curtains, for windows .... 8 boxes
   Curtains (heavy) .... 72 boxes
   Mirrors .... 24 boxes
   Clocks .... 73 boxes
   Vases .... 45 boxes
   Lamps .... 102 boxes
   Brushes .... 29 boxes
   Toys .... 99 boxes
   Sports gear .... 42 boxes
   Optical instruments .... 17 boxes
   Electrical appliances .... 48 boxes
   Tools .... 35 boxes
   Gasmasks .... 78 boxes
   Leather goods .... 253 boxes
   Medical goods .... 41 boxes
   Sanitary goods .... 119 boxes
   Household goods .... 115 boxes
   Scrap iron .... 1,503 boxes
   Scrap paper .... 1,714 boxes

The Documentary Evidence   L-188

Books	482 boxes
Copper, aluminum	266 boxes
Bottles	730 boxes
Rags	240 pressed bales
Scraps of furs	123 boxes
Silver goods	33 boxes

7. Special work:

SS-Garrison-Administration Munich	27 cars
SS-Directorats Central Office	51 wagons
116th Armoured Regiment, Dortmund	2 wagons
116th Armoured Regiment, Dortmund	2 wagons
47th Inf. Div.	3 wagons
Obersturmfuehrer Tychsen, Wearer of the Oak Leaves Medal [Eichenlaubtraeger]	1 wagon
Cptn. Ninnemann	1 wagon
Cptn. Adamy	1 wagon
Sturmbannf. Brehmer, Wearer of Nights' Cross [Ritterkreuztraeger]	1 wagon
Obergruppenf. Lorenz, Berlin	3 wagons
Reich Postal Director, Berlin, Cuilleaume	1 wagon
Pianos, Messrs H. Langner, Breslau	3 wagons
Division: "Das Reich"	1 wagon

The cabinet-makers' workshop set up in the camp repaired and restored:
30 Sideboards
23 Dining Room Tables
56 Dining Room Chairs
43 Chests of Drawers
65 Beds
10 Dressing Tables
30 Bedside-Tables and Washing-Stands
12 Book Cases
24 Writing desks
25 Easy Chairs
25 Kitchen Cabinets
15 Kitchen Tables
35 Kitchen Chairs
1 Couch
4 Easy chairs were upholstered and recovered.

Report on the M-Action

The fight against Jews, Freemasons and the forces allied to them or otherwise ideologically opposed to us, has always been a most urgent task of National Socialism, especially during the War which has been forced upon us. In order to secure, within the areas occupied by Germany, all research material and the cultural effects of the groups indicated and to dispatch them to Germany, the Fuehrer at the suggestion of Reichsleiter Rosenberg was ordered that libraries, archives, lodges and other ideological and cultural institutions of all kinds be searched for appropriate material and that this be secured for the ideological instruction of the National Socialist Party.

The same order applies to cultural effects which were either in the possession of or were the property of Jews and were unclaimed or originated from sources not clearly ascertainable.

The Special Purpose Staff [Einsatzstab] of Reichsleiter Rosenberg was charged with the carrying out of this task. In addition to this seizure of property, at the suggestion of the Director West of the Special Purpose Staff it was proposed to the Reichsleiter that the furniture and other contents of the unguarded Jewish homes should also be secured and dispatched to the Minister for the Occupied Eastern Territories, for use in the occupied Eastern Territories. The Fuehrer agreed to Reichsleiter Rosenberg's proposal by means of the letter of the Reich Minister and Chief of the Reich Chancellery dated 31.12.41. The Special Purpose Staff of Reichsleiter Rosenberg was charged with carrying out this task in the occupied territories. The amount of work to be done in this section forced the Special Purpose Staff of Reichsleiter Rosenberg to return the mandate of 14.1.1942 to the Minister for the Occupied Eastern Territories so that this might be executed by him, owing to personnel difficulties. The Minister for the Occupied Eastern Territories thereupon organized the Office West on 25.3.42 in Paris with local branches in France, Belgium and Holland. The Director West of the Special Purpose Staff of Reichsleiter Rosenberg E.R.R. was appointed Chief of this Office. At first all the confiscated furniture and goods were dispatched to administrations in the Occupied Eastern Territories. Owing to the terror attacks on German cities, which then began and in the knowledge that bombed-out people of Germany ought to have preference over the Eastern people, Reich Minister and Reichsleiter Rosenberg obtained a new order from the Fuehrer according to which the furniture etc. obtained through the M.-Action was to be put at the disposal of bombed-out people within Germany.

Copy of Document L-198. *State Department Dispatch by Consul General Messersmith, 14 March 1933, concerning physical attacks against American citizens in Berlin because they were Jews.*

* * *

No. 1184

        AMERICAN CONSULATE GENERAL
           Berlin, Germany, March 14, 1933

SUBJECT: Molestation of American citizens domiciled or temporarily in Berlin, by persons wearing the uniform of a political party.

THE HONORABLE
    THE SECRETARY OF STATE
        WASHINGTON

SIR:

I have the honor to inform the Department that since the last elections held in Germany on March 5, 1933, the Consulate General has been receiving visits from Americans domiciled or temporarily in Berlin who have made affidavits to the effect that they have been molested and maltreated in their homes or in the streets of this city by persons wearing the uniform of the National-Socialist party. A copy of the affidavits executed at this Consulate General and in one case at the Consulate General at Munich is transmitted herewith, but as a basis of the report to be made in this dispatch a resume of each case is given below:

Leon Jaffe, an American citizen, bearer of passport No. 217672, issued at Washington May 1, 1930, and residing at 914 Hoe Avenue, New York City, who is the manager of the Newbury Manufacturing Company of 68 Northampton Street, Boston, Massachusetts, and who is in Berlin on behalf of his firm, declares that on Saturday, March 4, about 1 a. m. he was returning home when at the corner of the Leibnitz and Bismarckstrasse he encountered six men dressed in the brown National-Socialist uniform who, without any provocation on his part, began to hurl epithets such as "verfluchter Jude" and struck him. He explained in English that he was an American and they allowed him to go without further molestation.

Henry H. Sattler, an American citizen, bearer of Departmental passport No. 495326, issued on May 13, 1932, is living with his father in Berlin who has an advertising business here at Helmstaedterstresse 16 and in New York at 220 Fifth Avenue, declares that on the morning of March 4 about 1 a. m. he was coming home from a restaurant in the company of two Germans when they were attacked at the Barbarossa-Platz by about 15 men belonging to the National-Socialist party. They were struck without provocation, the police were called, and their statement was taken.

Nathaniel S. Wollf, an American citizen, residing in Rochester, N. Y., declares that on March 6, about 5 a. m. there came into his room five or six National-Socialists with drawn revolvers. After abusing him he was taken from his room in an automobile to another house where in a bare room his hands and feet were tied and he was subjected to various indignities including blows and physical injuries. His hands and feet were later untied by what was evidently a National-Socialist officer who apologized for the conduct of his associates and treated him with some kindness, but compelled him to sign a paper that he would leave Berlin the next evening. The officer then told his associates to release Mr. Wollf and left, but his associates instead of releasing Mr. Wollf took him in an automobile to the Grunewald on the outskirts of the city where they made as though they would tie him to a tree and beat him with straps, and after having thoroughly terrorized him left him without money, going off in their automobile.

Edwin Franden Dakin, of Hannibal, Missouri, bearer of Departmental passport No. 546684 issued August 8, 1932, declares that he is in Germany for study and that on the morning of March 6 at 1.30 o'clock approximately five men entered his apartment and after threating him with pistols and inflicting physical injury evidently satisfied themselves that he was not the person they were looking for and left him without further molestation. He declares that several of the men who threatened him with revolvers were undoubtedly intoxicated.

Phillip Zuckerman, an American citizen, bearer of Departmental passport No. 74664, issued June 7, 1929, temporarily in Berlin, but whose place of business is in Leipzig, declares that on Tuesday, March 7, about 10.30 in the morning as he was leaving his office he was accosted on the Niederwallstrasse by two persons in National-Socialist uniform who suggested that he contribute to the funds of the "Hitler-Jugend" whereupon he offered one mark, but on being recognized as a Jew these persons demanded that he contribute at least twenty marks and threatened physical injury if he did not acquiesce.

Salomon Friedmann, included in the passport of his father, Joseph Salomon, who is the bearer of passport No. 2 issued at the Consulate General at Berlin on May 16, 1929, declares that on March 7 on the Potsdamer Platz he was attacked by three National-Socialists who called him a Jew and struck him with rubber clubs.

Max Schussler, an American citizen, bearer of Departmental passport No. 12877 issued April 13, 1929, temporarily residing in Berlin with his wife where he occupies an apartment, declares that he is in Berlin on business as he has considerable property here which he is looking after. He has among his properties a place occupied as a beer restaurant the occupant of which as soon as the present Hitler-Hugenberg Government came into power refused to continue to pay further rent. Mr. Schussler states that he took the usual steps legally to bring about the collection of the rent, and at 2 o'clock on the morning of March 7 his house was entered by two men in National-Socialist uniform and two others in civilian clothes who came into his bedroom and at the point of revolvers ordered him and his wife to dress. His wife was compelled to take off her nightgown and appear completely naked before the intruders. After they had dressed at the point of pistols and after continued threats he was compelled to sign several documents to the effect that he would not continue to proceed against his tenant either for eviction or for payment of rent. He was told that if he on the next day endeavored to change his decision he would be dead.

Louis Berman, an American citizen, bearer of Departmental passport No. 344925 issued February 28, 1931, declares that he is a medical student in the University of Berne and came to Berlin on March 8 for a brief holiday. That night while passing along the Liniestrasse at about 12.30 o'clock on his way to his lodgings he was accosted by four men in National-Socialist uniform who attacked him and in the scuffle he declares that his briefcase containing $285 and private papers disappeared.

Herman I. Roseman, an American citizen, bearer of Departmental passport No. 308868 issued August 27, 1930, declares that on March 10 about 4.30 in the afternoon he came out of the K.d.W. department store with his fiancee when a man in S.A. uniform stepped on his toe purposely which was the beginning of further molestation during which he was given various blows in the presence of policemen who did not interfere.

Julian Fuhs, bearer of passport No. 35 issued by the Consulate General at Berlin on January 6, 1931, states that he is a naturalized American citizen temporarily in Germany where he is writing a history of music while his wife, a German citizen, operates a restaurant in Nuernbergerstrasse 16. He declares that on Saturday, March 11, between 1 and 2 a. m. several S.A. men entered the restaurant of his wife and took him into a toilet room where he was physically assaulted. The police were called in and in this instance seem to have given certain protection to Mr. Fuhs and to his wife.

It is interesting to note that all of the above Americans are Jews with the exception of Mr. Dakin. The Consulate General is satisfied that in every one of these cases the attack upon the persons and homes of these Americans was unprovoked and brought about through the assumption that they were Jews. It is not believed that the attacks were made upon them as Americans or as foreigners, but on the ground that they were Jews.

The first cases reported to the Consulate General were those of Messrs. Wollf, Sattler and Dakin, and as the circumstances in the case of Mr. Wollf were particularly aggravated it was obvious that immediate and adequate steps would have to be taken in order to prevent further molestation of Americans. As the circumstances seemed to indicate that attacks on Jews were being made indiscriminately and upon those of other nationalities as well as Americans, it seemed advisable in the protection of the interests of the many Americans in Berlin of whom quite a number are Jews, that immediate steps should be taken to bring the case of Mr. Wollf to the attention of the highest authorities in the Reich. The ordinary procedure in these cases would have been for the Consulate General to take them up with the Police President of Berlin, but as the Police President has recently been appointed to his post by the National-Socialists and as Mr. Goering, one of the leaders of the National-Socialist movement, is also in charge of the Prussian Ministry of the Interior, there seemed to be much probability that if I reported the cases to the Police Praesidium and to the Prussian Ministry of the Interior they would be given routine investigation and that in the meantime attacks might continue. I had the very definite impression that in order to protect the interests of our people in Berlin the information with regard to these unjustified attacks on Americans should be brought to the highest authorities. I therefore on March 6 after discussing this with the Ambassador who was in agreement, addressed a letter to him transmitting copies of the affidavits in the cases of Messrs. Wollf, Sattler and Dakin. The Embassy immediately took up these cases with the Minister of Foreign Affairs and in a telegraphic report which it made to the Department it has already informed it that the cases were brought to the attention of the Chancellor, Mr. Hitler, and of the cabinet at a cabinet meeting by the Minister of Foreign Affairs.

On March 8 I again transmitted to the Embassy the case of Mr. Schussler.

On March 9 it seemed desirable to take these cases up directly with the Police President as well, and I therefore arranged to call on him that morning, accompanied by Mr. Geist of the staff. I left with the Police President a letter to which were appended the affidavits in the cases of Messrs. Wollf, Sattler, Dakin, Schussler, Jaffe and Friedmann. The Police President expressed appreciation that we had brought these cases to his attention, had furnished such complete data as that contained in the affidavits, expressed regret that the unprovoked attacks should have been made on American citizens, and declared that he would take immediate and appropriate steps to protect our citizens in Berlin from further attacks and molestation. I took the opportunity to express to the Police President the hope that as the fact these Americans had made affidavits would probably become known, he would see that these persons had adequate police protection as otherwise some of them might suffer serious injury from irresponsible and uncontrolled persons. The Police President indicated that he understood the circumstances and would take the necessary steps. I gathered the definite impression that the Police President was himself interested in seeing that Americans and other foreigners in Berlin were properly protected and that he would not fail to take energetic steps.

On March 9 I transmitted to the Embassy the affidavits of Mr. Friedmann and of Mr. Jaffe. On March 13 there were transmitted the affidavits of Messrs. Berman, Zuckerman, Roseman and Fuhs. On March 13 there were transmitted to the Police President the affidavits of Messrs. Berman, Zuckerman, Roseman and Fuhs, as well as a supplementary affidavit executed by Mr. Schussler, the original one having already been sent him.

These attacks on American citizens as well as the others which have been reported to the authorities on citizens of other nationalities, are undoubtedly the result of the propaganda against the Jews which has been a distinct part of the Hitler movement. In a speech made in the Sport-Palast by Mr. Goebbels, one of the principal lieutenants of the present Chancellor, Mr. Hitler, immediately before Mr. Hitler made his first speech as Chancellor, Mr. Goebbels indulged before an audience of some 12,000 people in unrestrained statements with regard to the Jewish newspapers and Jews generally as the enemies of Germany. I was present at this meeting and it was difficult to believe that a speech of this kind would be tolerated immediately preceding a speech by the responsible Chancellor of the German Government. Prior to the elections on March 5 the admirable police force of Germany was able to restrain the uniformed National-Socialists from excesses against the Jews and any breaches of the peace resulted in the arrest of the offenders. Discipline among the uniformed National-Socialists, however, was also apparently sufficiently strong to prevent them from these attacks on innocent, unarmed persons. The effect of the victory at the polls, however, on March 5 showed itself in the unrestrained actions which immediately followed, and it may be assumed I believe that the attacks which have been taking place against Americans and other Jews are due to this hatred which has been instilled into the young men of the National-Socialist movement.

That the representations of the Embassy had considerable effect is apparent from the fact that towards the middle of last week the Chancellor issued a statement addressed to National-Socialist adherents, that attacks on single persons must stop and that discipline and order among National-Socialist adherents must be maintained. He called upon the National-Socialists to see that these attacks on foreigners were stopped as they were being made by Communists masquerading in National-Socialist uniforms. He emphasized in his statement that these attacks on foreigners were creating a wrong impression concerning the National-Socialist movement in foreign countries.

The evening before Mr. Hitler made this statement in Berlin, Mr. Goering, however, had made a speech in Essen in which he declared that the police in Germany were not supported by the Government for the purpose of protecting Jewish stores. This statement was made in connection with the acts of uniformed National-Socialist adherents who interfered with the customers of Jewish department stores in Berlin and other cities in Germany and of chain stores, and in certain cases brought about their temporary closing.

While the statement of Mr. Hitler seemed to be quite reassuring to those who had the impression that the police had had their power taken away from them and that these excesses might be expected to continue on the part of uniformed National-Socialists, the speech of Mr. Goering was very disturbing. There was evidence that the police in Berlin and other cities whose discipline and effectiveness are well known had had their morale very much upset. In order to retain their places and not to be thrown among the unemployed, many of the police immediately before the elections and after joined the National-Socialist movement. Evidence which has come to the Consulate General not only through the affidavits herewith transmitted, but from other reliable sources, shows that the power had at least temporarily passed from the uniformed police to the so-called "Hilfs-Polizei" in National-Socialist uniform. This situation was exceedingly disturbing.

When I called upon the Police President on March 9 he was particularly anxious to know whether we had any evidence from Americans to the effect that they had called for the assistance of the police and that the police had failed to give it. He at that time gave the impression that the police retained their authority and that he would use all his influence, although a National-Socialist, to that end.

The further cases reported by the Embassy to the Foreign Office and by the Consulate General to the Police Praesidium, as already set forth in this dispatch, were undoubtedly also brought to the attention of the Chancellor and of the leaders of the National-Socialist movement, and on Sunday, March 12, Mr. Hitler again issued a statement over the radio addressed to the National-Socialist adherents in Germany in which he referred in even more emphatic terms than he had done earlier in the week to the necessity for the maintenance of discipline and order and of National-Socialists refraining from attacks of violence on individuals and from the performance of any acts which could bring the National-Socialist movement into discredit outside of the country. I can find no definite information pointing to the fact, but there is much reason to believe that during Saturday, March 11, strict orders were issued by the National-Socialist leaders to the district leaders throughout the country that attacks on stores, interference with persons going in and out of shops and attacks on individuals must cease and that disciplinary steps would be undertaken against National-Socialists who broke discipline. The quietness of Sunday and Monday, March 12 and 13, indicate that some such unmistakable orders must have been issued.

Vice Chancellor von Papen expressed in my hearing on Saturday evening a grave doubt as to whether the National-Socialist groups throughout the country were under control. It is a grave question, and one still open to a good deal of discussion, as to how much power is retained by the Chancellor and how much has passed to his more radical nominal subordinates, such as Goering, Goebbels and Roehm. Since the elections on March 5 some of the more important thinking people in various parts of Germany have allied themselves with the National-Socialist movement in the hope of tempering its radicalism by their action within rather than without the party. These are very useful to the National-Socialist party, and there are indications that in the last few days it has been brought strongly to the attention of the Chancellor and of leaders of the movement which he heads that these attacks on Jews, Communists and department stores, etc., are creating a situation not only in Germany, but outside of Germany, which is of real danger to the country as well as to the National-Socialist party.

The Consulate General has refrained from giving any information to the press with regard to these individual cases, but did on the occasion of my visit to the Police President state that I had been there to leave the affidavits of the Americans who had so far executed them. The press, however, has been able to get in touch with some of the individuals concerned, and European as well as I understand American newspapers have been carrying some of the stories of the Americans who have been molested. I am of the opinion that it was a good thing that some of these stories which are undoubtedly correct, receive publication in the press outside of Germany as their publication may have had something to do with the two declarations made to his party by Mr. Hitler, and the newspaper publicity undoubtedly strengthened the representations made by the Embassy to the Foreign Office and by this Consulate General to the Police President.

It is impossible to make any predictions as to what course events will take so far as the safety of lives and property is concerned. I believe, however, that for the present the excesses will have been largely curbed and that greater power again lies with the regular police. Whether the uncontrolled young men in National-Socialist uniform can be definitely and permanently restrained depends upon many factors which are still uncertain. Hatreds have been awakened and instilled over a period of years and it will be difficult for these young men to forget these hatreds unless new ideas displace them. Some occupation will have to be found for these men in uniform by the present Government or they will have to be taken out of the uniform. It is however, interesting that the developments within the last 48 hours show a definite exercise of restraint and renewed pressure of authority.

The Consulate General is giving very careful attention to this problem of the protection of the Americans in Berlin and in Germany, and there is transmitted herewith a copy of a memorandum dated March 6, 1933, which was sent to the consular officers in the country. So far only one case has been reported of an attack on an American citizen outside of Berlin. It is the case of Mrs. Jean Klauber of Munich, and a copy of her affidavit is transmitted herewith. The Consulate General will not fail to keep the Department informed of any developments in this connection of interest.

        Respectfully yours,

        /s/ George S. Messersmith
        /t/ George S. Messersmith
           American Consul General.

310/800

GSM:HP

Translation of Document L-199. *Excerpts from newspaper Berliner Tageblatt, 29 March 1933, concerning the Anti-Jewish Boycott.*

* * *

BERLINER TAGEBLATT, March 29, 1933
Boycott Manifesto of the National Socialist German Labor Party.
The Eleven Points
Point 9.

In tens of thousands of mass meetings, which shall reach to the smallest village, the action committees shall immediately put forward a demand for the introduction of a *numerous clauses* for Jews in all professions, corresponding to their proportion to the German population. In order to heighten the force of this action, the demand is to be restricted to three branches for the present: (a) to students attending the secondary schools and universities, (b) to the Medical profession, (c) to the legal profession.

* * * * * * *

Reasons for the Boycott Action

We see the distress and misery of our own compatriots and feel obligated not to leave anything undone that can prevent further damage to our own people. For, those responsible for these lies and vilifications are the Jews among us. From them emanates this campaign of hatred and lies against Germany. It is up to them to put the liars in the rest of the world in their proper place. Since they do not wish to do this, we shall see to it that this campaign of hate and lies against Germany shall not be directed against the innocent German people, but against the responsible instigators themselves. The boycott and atrocity agitation must not and will not hit the German people, but a thousand times more the Jews themselves.

Translation from Document L-201. *Excerpts from newspaper Berliner Boersen Zeitung, 12 April 1933, on the murder of a Jewish lawyer.*

* * *

BERLINER BOERSEN ZEITUNG, 12 April 1933, night issue
Disguised Criminals Murder Jewish Lawyer.
Horrible Murder in Chemnitz.

T. U. Chemnitz, 12th April.

On Monday night the Jewish Lawyer Dr. Weiner was visited at his home by several men, who wore S.A. bands and brown caps, and taken away by force in an automobile. Next morning Dr. Weiner was found on Wiedenauer Flur at Mittweida shot to death by a bullet through his head.

Police headquarters report the following:

"Here is no doubt that Dr. Weiner fell victim to a savage crime which obviously had been committed by enemies of the national movement. Here is no trace of the perpetrators. The following has been found so far: On 10th of April at 22:30 hours three men dressed in SA uniform demanded admittance to the lawyer's home in Chemnitz on Stollberg Strasse. Presenting an identification they declared that the lawyer was arrested and requested him to follow them. The lawyer checked the identification personally and remarked upon a question of his wife that it were in order. The behavior of the men was so confident that the wife of the lawyer and two of his friends who were then present failed to check with the police station, as repeatedly suggested by the press, although they had an emergency telephone in their home by which they could have called the riot squad.

The fact is that no warrant for protective custody for the lawyer Weiner existed, and no warrant for his arrest was issued to the SA. Weiner was not even listed on the boycott roster for Jewish lawyers because he was a veteran of the last war in which he became an officer. An automobile had not been noticed in front of his home. But it is to be supposed that one was parked nearby. The culprits probably drove later to Wiederau. It is established that the shooting took place there in a sand hole. The fatal shot, obviously 3 shots have been fired, was fired at close range into the back of the head by a 6.35 Millimeter calibre pistol. It was no murder for robbery. Passport, driver's license, gold watch and more than 400 marks cash were found in the pockets of the dead. Two of the culprits are between 25 and 28, and the third is between 28 and 30 years of age."

Copy of Document L-202. *State Department Dispatch from D. H. Buffum, American Consul General at Leipzig, 21 November 1938, on Antisemitic Onslaught in Germany as seen from Leipzig.*

* * *

Voluntary; political.

[Rubber Stamp]
ASSISTANT SECRETARY OF STATE
JAN. 4, 1939
MR. MESSERSMITH
ANTISEMITIC ONSLAUGHT IN GERMANY AS SEEN
FROM LEIPZIG

From: /s/   David H. Buffum
           David H. Buffum,
             American Consul

Date of Preparation: November 21, 1938
Date of Forwarding: To be carried to Berlin by trusted messenger as soon as practicable.
Approved: Ralph C. Busser,
            Ralph C. Busser,
             American Consul General.

The following resume of the antisemitic onslaught in Germany so far as this consular district is concerned, constitutes a narration of Leipzig angles as to this flagitious attack upon a helpless minority that very probably has had no counterpart in the course of the civilized world. The macabre circumstances that form the subject matter of this report had a fittingly gruesome prelude in Leipzig a few hours before they occurred in the form of rites held on one of the principal squares of the city on the night of November 9, 1938 in commemoration of fallen martyrs to the Nazi cause prior to the political take-over in 1933. To such end apparently anything in the corpse category that could be remotely associated with Nazi martyrdom, had been exhumed. At least five year old remains of those who had been considered rowdyish violators of law and order at the time, had been placed in extravagant coffins; arranged around a colossal, flaming urn on the Altermarkt for purposes of display, and ultimately conveyed amid marching troops, flaring torches and funeral music to the "Ehrenhain", Leipzig's National Socialistic burial plot. For this propagandistic ceremony the entire market place had been surrounded with wooden lattice work about ten yards high. This was covered with white cloth to form the background for black swastikas at least five yards high and broad. Flame-spurting urns and gigantic banners completed a Wagnerian ensemble as to pomposity of stage setting; but it can not be truthfully reported that the ceremony aroused anything akin to awe among the crowds who witnessed it. Judging from a few very guardedly whispered comments, the populace was far more concerned over the wanton waste of materials in these days when textiles of any kind are exceedingly scarce and expensive, rather than being actuated by any particularly reverent emotions. On the other hand for obvious reasons, there were no open manifestations of disapproval. The populace was destined to be much more perturbed the following morning during the course of the most violent debacle the city had probably ever witnessed.

The shattering of shop windows, looting of stores and dwellings of Jews which began in the early hours of November 10, 1938, was hailed subsequently in the Nazi press as "a spontaneous wave of righteous indignation throughout Germany, as a result of the cowardly Jewish murder of Third Secretary von Rath in the German Embassy at Paris." So far as a very high percentage of the German populace is concerned, a state of popular indignation that would spontaneously lead to such excesses, can be considered as nonexistent. On the contrary, in viewing the ruins and attendant measures employed, all of the local crowds observed were obviously benumbed over what had happened and aghast over the unprecedented fury of Nazi acts that had been or were taking place with bewildering rapidity throughout their city. The whole lamentable affair was organized in such a sinister fashion, as to lend credence to the theory that the execution of it had involved studied preparation. It has been ascertained by this office that the plan of "spontaneous indignation" leaked out in Leipzig several hours before news of the death of Third Secretary von Rath had been broadcasted at 10 P.M. November 10, 1938. It is stated upon authority believed to be reliable, that most of the evening was employed in drawing up lists of fated victims. Several persons known to this office were aware at 9 P.M. on the evening of November 9, 1938 that the "spontaneous" outrage was scheduled for that night, sometime after midnight and several of such persons interviewed, stayed up purposely in order to witness it.

At 3 a.m. November 10, 1938 was unleashed a barrage of Nazi ferocity as had had no equal hitherto in Germany, or very likely anywhere else in the world since savagery, if ever. Jewish dwellings were smashed into and contents demolished or looted. In one of the Jewish sections an eighteen year old boy was hurled from a three story window to land with both legs broken on a street littered with burning beds and other household furniture and effects from his family's and other apartments. This information was supplied by an attending physician. It is reported from another quarter that among domestic effects thrown out of a Jewish dwelling, a small dog descended four flights to a broken spine on a cluttered street. Although apparently centered in poor districts, the raid was not confined to the humble classes. One apartment of exceptionally refined occupants known to this office, was violently ransacked, presumably in a search for valuables that was not in vain, and one of the marauders thrust a cane through a priceless medieval painting portraying a biblical scene. Another apartment of the same category is known to have been turned upside down in the frenzied course of whatever the invaders were after. Reported loss of looting of cash, silver, jewelry, and otherwise easily convertible articles, have been frequent.

Jewish shop windows by the hundreds were systematically and wantonly smashed throughout the entire city at a loss estimated at several millions of marks. There are reports that substantial losses have been sustained on the famous Leipzig "Bruhl", as many of the shop windows at the time of the demolition were filled with costly furs that were seized before the windows could be boarded up. In proportion to the general destruction of real estate, however, losses of goods are felt to have been relatively small. The spectators who viewed the wreckage when daylight had arrived were mostly in such a bewildered mood, that there was no danger of impulsive acts, and the perpetrators probably were too busy in carrying out their schedule to take off a whole lot of time for personal profit. At all events, the main streets of the city were a positive litter of shattered plate glass. According to reliable testimony, the debacle was executed by S. S. men and Storm Troopers not in uniform, each group having been provided with hammers, axes, crowbars and incendiary bombs.

Three synagogues in Leipzig were fired simultaneously by incendiary bombs and all sacred objects and records desecrated or destroyed, in most instances hurled through the windows and burned in the streets. No attempts whatsoever were made to quench the fires, functions of the fire brigade having been confined to playing water on adjoining buildings. All of the synagogues were irreparably gutted by flames, and the walls of the two that are in the close proximity of the consulate are now being razed. The blackened frames have been centers of attraction during the past week of terror for eloquently silent and bewildered crowds. One of the largest clothing stores in the heart of the city was destroyed by flames from incendiary bombs, only the charred walls and gutted roof having been left standing. As was the case with the synagogues, no attempts on the part of the fire brigade were made to extinguish the fire, although apparently there was a certain amount of apprehension for adjacent property, for the walls of a coffee house next door were covered with asbestos and sprayed by the doughty firemen. It is extremely difficult to believe, but the owners of the clothing store were actually charged with setting the fire and on that basis were dragged from their beds at 6 A. M. and clapped into prison.

Tactics which closely approached the ghoulish took place at the Jewish cemetery where the temple was fired together with a building occupied by caretakers, tombstones uprooted and graves violated. Eye witnesses considered reliable report that ten corpses were left unburied at this cemetery for a week's time because all grave diggers and cemetery attendants had been arrested.

Ferocious as was the violation of property, the most hideous phase of the so-called "spontaneous" action, has been the wholesale arrest and transportation to concentration camps of male German Jews between the ages of sixteen and sixty, as well as Jewish men without citizenship. This has been taking place daily since the night of horror. This office has no way of accurately checking the numbers of such arrests, but there is very little question that they have gone into several thousands in Leipzig alone. Having demolished dwellings and hurled most of the moveable effects to the streets, the insatiably sadistic perpetrators threw many of the trembling inmates into a small stream that flows through the Zoological Park, commanding horrified spectators to spit at them, defile them with mud and jeer at their plight. The latter incident has been repeatedly corrobated by German witnesses who were nauseated in telling the tale. The slightest manifestation of sympathy evoked a positive fury on the part of the perpetrators, and the crowd was powerless to do anything but turn horror-stricken eyes from the scene of abuse, or leave the vicinity. These tactics were carried out the entire morning of November 10th without police intervention and they were applied to men, women and children.

There is much evidence of physical violence, including several deaths. At least half a dozen cases have been personally observed, victims with bloody, badly bruised faces having fled to this office, believing that as refugees their desire to emigrate could be expedited here. As a matter of fact this consulate has been a bedlam of humanity for the past ten days, most of these visitors being desperate women, as their husbands and sons had been taken off to concentration camps.

Similarly violent procedure was applied throughout this consular district, the amount of havoc wrought depending upon the number of Jewish establishments or persons involved. It is understood that in many of the smaller communities even more relentless methods were employed than was the case in the cities. Reports have been received from Weissenfels to the effect that the few Jewish families there are experiencing great difficulty in purchasing food. It is reported that three Aryan professors of the University of Jena have been arrested and taken off to concentration camps because they had voiced disapproval of this insidious drive against mankind.

Sources of information
Personal observation and interviews.
800
DHB/dhb

Copy of Document L-205 (GB 157). Telegram from Ambassador Kennedy at London to Department of State, Washington, 8 December 1938, reporting extremely violent statements against Jews by Ribbentrop, German Ambassador in London.

* * *

TELEGRAM RECEIVED
From London, Dated December 8, 1938
Rec'd 6:43 p.m.

Secretary of State,
Washington,
1414, December 8, 7 p.m.
PERSONAL FOR THE ACTING SECRETARY FROM RUBLEE.
My 1403, December 7, 3 p.m.

The representative of the German Embassy assured us that we would receive further explanation of the cancellation or postponement of the Brussels meeting in the course of yesterday. He said that this telegram was being deciphered and that undoubtedly he would have further details. However, late last evening he called merely to state that it was now understood that the meeting had had to be put off in view of the sudden illness of the principal negotiator on the German side. He regretted that he could tell us no more.

During the day we had a telephone call from Berenger's office in Paris. We were told that the matter of refugees had been raised by Bonnet in his conversation with von Ribbentrop. The result was very bad. Ribbentrop, when pressed, had said to Bonnet that the Jews in Germany without exception were pickpockets, murderers and thieves. The property they possessed had been acquired illegally. The German Government had therefore decided to assimilate them with the criminal elements of the population. The property which they had acquired illegally would be taken from them. They would be forced to live in districts frequented by the criminal classes. They would be under police observation like other criminals. They would be forced to report to the police as other criminals were obligated to do. The German Government could not help it if some of these criminals escaped to other countries which seemed so anxious to have them. It was not however willing for them to take the property which had resulted from their illegal operations with them. There was in fact nothing that it could or would do.

From our German contact we have information that the French raised the question of refugees not only in principle but concretely in respect to the financial aspects of the question. Berenger, while attending the officers meeting, gave a hint that his Government was preparing to take this line. We attempted to dissuade him from crossing wires with our negotiation and he assured us that he would do his best to keep the discussion of refugees on a general plane but he added Chamberlain had requested Daladier to take the matter up with Ribbentrop and so it would have to be taken up. Winterton denies this.

The British assured us this morning that they did not communicate to the French the details of the financial plan which they now tell us they have prepared but which they are holding back for the present. They say that they are as mystified as we are about the French move and do not know what specific financial proposals Bonnet may have raised with Ribbentrop. With regard to the visit of Schacht to London we have no conclusive information. The British will say no more than that the visit is imminent. The Germans say they are not at liberty to discuss the matter.

HPD   KENNEDY

Translation of Document L-217. Order, 20 November 1936, from Gestapo Office at Duesseldorf to effect that steps be taken to prevent the camouflage of Jewish businesses.

* * *

Secret State Police
State Police Office for the District [Regierungsbezirk] of Duesseldorf

Duesseldorf, 20.11.1936

II 1 E 1 1510/36

Subject: Camouflage of Jewish businesses.

It is evident from numerous recent reports that apart from the alleged national-socialist coordination, an increasing number of attempts are being made by Jewish owners of firms to camouflage the real nature of their firms by the most devious of ways. It has therefore been ascertained again that Jews dispatch their goods, not under their own names, but under the names of Aryan employees who agree to this. Even the representatives of Jewish firms are making a practice, more and more, of saying that the goods they offer are from Aryan firms. Furthermore, forwarding agents frequently send Jewish goods to customers under their own names so that, in this way, the delivery firms should remain unknown to the general public.

The blame for the circumvention lies not only with the Jewish owners of firms and their assistants, but also with the Aryan customers themselves. The latter often require that the goods they want be sent under the name of a neutral sender, so that they can buy them without any trouble.

I request that these and similar attempts at camouflage be stopped whenever they occur, if necessary in conjunction with the Commercial Police [Gewerbepolizei] and the competent industrial offices. No larger actions (interference in industry) are, however, to be carried out; in cases of doubt, a report is to be made here at once.

To conclude I request that a report be sent in, not later than 10 December 1936, on the observations made to date and on any measures that may have to be taken.

Additional note for District Councillors [Landraete]: I enclose copies for the Police Administration authorities.

By order

signed Hoehmann
Witnessed:
[signature illegible]
Police Officer Assistant

To:
The branch offices of the State Police,
The district councillors of the Bezirk,
The Chief burgomasters of Crefeld-Uerdingen,
Neuss and Viersen.

L-217   Nazi Germany's War Against the Jews

The District Councillor
No. 1098 P   Kleve, 23 November 1936
Copy to Chief Burgomaster at Goch for his information,
a report to be made before 5. 12. 36 for
and on behalf of
[signature illegible]
Stamp: for the files of the Burgomaster as local police authority

---

Translation of Document L-219 (USA 479). Excerpt from Organization Plan of RSHA (Reich Security Main Office) as of 1 October 1943, showing function of SS-O'Stubaf Eichmann in charge of Jewish affairs and matters of evacuation.

* * *

SECRET
ORGANIZATION PLAN
OF THE REICH MAIN SECURITY OFFICE
[RSHA-Reichssicherheitshauptamt]
1 October 1943

GROUP IV B
Political, Churches, Sects and Jews

Group Director:
At present unassigned
Deputy:
SS-Sturmbannfuehrer Regierungsrat ROTH
Tel: No. Ext 21, Post 21

Section	Function	Head	Telephone Central	Ext.	Post
IV B 1	Political Catholicism	SS-Stubaf. RR. Roth	Me	21	21
IV B 2	Political Protestantism Sects	SS-Stubaf. RR. Hahnenbruch	Me	20	
IV B 3	Other churches, Freemasonry	SS-O'Stuf. Wandesleben	Me	27	27
IV B 4	Jewish affairs, matters of evacuation, confiscation of means of suppressing enemies of the people and State, dispossession of rights of German citizenship	SS-O'Stubaf Eichmann	Eu	50	50

III - 96

Translation of Document M-1 (GB 178). *Excerpt from newspaper Fraenkische Tagezeitung, 24 June 1935, on Streicher's speech to the Hitler Youth on 22 June 1935 attacking the Jewish people.*

* * *

Report in the "Fraenkische Tageszeitung" dated 24th June 1935 on Streicher's speech to the Hitler Youth on the "Holy Mountain" near Nurnberg on the 22nd June 1935

Julius Streicher's speech to Youth:

"* * * Boys and girls, look back to a little more than 10 years ago. A great war — the World War — had whirled over the peoples of the earth and had left in the end a heap of ruins. Only one people remained victorious in this dreadful war, a people of whom Christ said its father is the devil. That people had ruined the German nation in body and soul. Then Adolf Hitler, unknown to anybody rose from among the people and became the voice which called to a holy war and battle. He cried to the people, for everybody to take courage again and to rise and give a helping hand to take the devil from the German people, so that the human race might be free again from these people that have wandered about the world for centuries and millenia, marked with the sign of Cain.

Boys and girls, even if they say that the Jews were once the chosen people, do not believe it, but believe us when we say that the Jews are not a chosen people. Because it cannot be that a chosen people should act among the peoples as the Jews do today.

A chosen people do not go into the world to make others work for them, to suck blood. They do not go among the peoples to chase the peasants from their homesteads. They do not go among the peoples to make your fathers poor and to drive them to despair. A chosen people do not rape women and girls. A chosen people do not slay and torture animals to death. A chosen people do not live by the sweat of others. A chosen people join the ranks of those who live because they work. *Don't you ever forget that.*

Boys and girls, for you we went into prison. For you we always suffered. For you we had to accept mockery and insult and became fighters against the Jewish people, against that organized body of world criminals, against whom already Christ fought the greatest anti-semite of all times * * *

* * * Look, today the Jews are trying again to drive the nations into war against us, which is supposed to bring the German nation to a definite end.

But we swear we will do all in our power to enlighten all Germans and humanity, that if ever war should come once more it can only be a crusade against the arch-enemy in all nations, the eternal Jew.

A world-wide court must be set up, a court that will judge these who are to blame for so much. We offer our hand to every people. We do not want to create hatred against other peoples. We offer our hand to every people. But you, boys and girls, shout it to the world:

Here stands German youth. We hate that people of whom Christ once said, "It is of the devil."

Translation of Document 001-PS (USA). Memorandum for the Fuehrer signed Rosenberg, 18 December 1941, concerning Jewish possessions in France and suggesting that 100 French Jews be executed.

* * *

Copy to Regional Leader of the NSDAP
Extract of par. 1 to DEGENHARD 15 April

SECRET

Documentary Memorandum for the Fuehrer
Concerning: Jewish Possessions in France

In compliance with the order of the Fuehrer for protection of Jewish, cultural possessions, a great number of Jewish dwellings remain unguarded. Consequently, many furnishings have disappeared, because a guard could, naturally, not be posted. In the whole East, the administration has found terrible conditions of living quarters, and the chances of procurement are so limited that it is not practical to procure any more. Therefore, I beg the Fuehrer to permit the seizure of all Jewish home furnishings of Jews in Paris, who have fled, or will leave shortly, and that of Jews living in all parts of the occupied West, to relieve the shortage of furnishings in the administration in the East.

2. A great number of leading Jews were, after a short examination in Paris, again released. The attempts on the lives of members of the armed forces have not stopped, on the contrary they continue. This reveals an unmistakable plan to disrupt the German-French cooperation, to force Germany to retaliate, and, with this, evoke a new defense on the part of the French against

Germany. I suggest to the Fuehrer that, instead of executing 100 Frenchmen, we substitute 100 Jewish bankers, lawyers, etc. It is the Jews in London and New York who incite the French communists to commit acts of violence, and it seems only fair that the members of this race should pay for this. It is not the *little* Jews, but the *leading* Jews in France, who should be held responsible. That would tend to awaken the Anti-Jewish sentiment.
BERLIN 18 Dec 1941
R/H
        signed: A. ROSENBERG

Copy of Document 001A-PS (USA 1). *Affidavit of Major William H. Coogan, Chief of Documentation Division of the Office of U.S. Chief of Counsel, 19 November 1945, describing manner in which captured German documents were collected, analyzed, numbered and translated in preparation for introduction in evidence before the International Military Tribunal sitting at Nurnberg, Germany.*

* * *

19 November 1945

I, Major William H. Coogan, O-455814, Q. M. C., a commissioned officer of the Army of the United States of America, do hereby certify as follows:

1. The United States Chief of Counsel in July 1945 charged the Field Branch of the Documentation Division with the responsibility of collecting, evaluating and assembling documentary evidence in the European Theater for use in the prosecution of the major Axis war criminals before the International Military Tribunal. I was appointed Chief of the Field Branch on 20 July 1945. I am now the Chief of the Documentation Division, Office of United States Chief of Counsel.

2. I have served in the United States Army for more than four years and am a practicing attorney by profession. Based upon my experience as an attorney and as a United States Army officer, I am familiar with the operation of the United States Army in connection with seizing and processing captured enemy documents. In my capacity as Chief of the Documentation Division, Office of the United States Chief of Counsel, I am familiar with and have supervised the processing, filing, translation and photostating of all documentary evidence for the United States Chief of Counsel.

3. As the Army overran German occupied territory and then Germany itself, certain specialized personnel seized enemy documents, books, and records for information of strategic and tactical value. During the early stages such documents were handled in bulk and assembled at temporary centers. However, after the surrender of Germany, they were transported to the various document centers established by Army Headquarters in the United States Zone of Occupation. In addition to the documents actually assembled at such document centers, Army personnel maintained and secured considerable documents "in situ" at or near the place of discovery. When such documents were located and assembled they were catalogued by Army personnel into collections and records were maintained which disclosed the source and such other information available concerning the place and general circumstances surrounding the acquisition of the documents.

4. The Field Branch of the Documentation Division was staffed by personnel thoroughly conversant with the German language. Their task was to search for and select captured enemy documents in the European Theater which disclosed information relating to the prosecution of the major Axis war criminals. Officers under my command were placed on duty at various document centers and also dispatched on individual missions to obtain original documents. When documents were located, my representatives made a record of the circumstances under which they were found and all information available concerning their authenticity was recorded. Such documents were further identified by Field Branch pre-trial serial numbers, assigned by my representatives who would then periodically dispatch the original documents by courier to the Office of the United States Chief of Counsel.

5. Upon receipt of these documents they were duly recorded and indexed. After this operation, they were delivered to the Screening and Analysis Branch of the Documentation Division of the Office of United States Chief of Counsel, which Branch re-examined such documents in order to finally determine whether or not they should be retained as evidence for the prosecutors. This final screening was done by German-speaking analysts on the staff of the United States Chief of Counsel. When the document passed the screeners, it was then transmitted to the Document Room of the Office of United States Chief of Counsel, with a covering sheet prepared by the screeners showing the title or nature of the document, the personalities involved, and its importance. In the Document Room, a trial identification number

The Documentary Evidence

001A-PS

was given to each document or to each group of documents, in cases where it was desirable for the sake of clarity to file several documents together.

6. United States documents were given trial identification numbers in one of five series designated by the letters: "PS", "L", "R", "C", and "EC", indicating the means of acquisition of the documents. Within each series documents were listed numerically.

7. After a document was so numbered, it was then sent to a German-speaking analyst who prepared a summary of the document with appropriate references to personalities involved, index headings, information as to the source of the document as indicated by the Field Branch, and the importance of the document to a particular phase of the case. Next, the original document was returned to the Document Room and then checked out to the photostating department, where photostatic copies were made. Upon return from photostating, it was placed in an envelope in one of several fireproof safes in the rear of the Document Room. One of the photostatic copies of the document was sent to the translators, thereafter leaving the original itself in the safe. A commissioned officer has been, and is, responsible for the security of the documents in the safe. At all times when he is not present the safe is locked and a military guard is on duty outside the only door. If the officers preparing the certified translation, or one of the officers working on the briefs, found it necessary to examine the original document, this was done within the Document Room in the section set aside for that purpose. The only exception to this strict rule has been where it has been occasionally necessary to present the original document to the defendants for examination. In this case, the document was entrusted to a responsible officer of the prosecution staff.

8. All original documents are now located in safes in the Document Room, where they will be secured until they are presented by the prosecution to the court during the progress of the trial.

9. Some of the documents which will be offered in evidence by the United States Chief of Counsel were seized and processed by the British Army. Also, personnel from the Office of the United States Chief of Counsel and the British War Crimes Executive have acted jointly in locating, seizing and processing such documents.

10. Substantially the same system of acquiring documentary evidence was utilized by the British Army and the British War

Crimes Executive as that hereinabove set forth with respect to the United States Army and the Office of the United States Chief of Counsel.

11. Therefore, I certify in my official capacity as hereinabove stated, to the best of my knowledge and belief, that the documents captured in the British Zone of Operations and Occupation, which will be offered in evidence by the United States Chief of Counsel, have been authenticated, translated, and processed in substantially the same manner as hereinabove set forth with respect to the operations of the United States Chief of Counsel.

12. Finally, I certify, that all Documentary evidence offered by the United States Chief of Counsel, including those documents from British Army sources, are in the same condition as captured by the United States and British Armies; that they have been translated by competent and qualified translators; that all photostatic copies are true and correct copies of the originals and that they have been correctly filed, numbered and processed as above outlined.

[Signed] WILLIAM H. COOGAN
Major, QMC, O-455814

Translation of Document 014-PS (USA 784). *Report by Rosenberg to the Fuehrer, 20 March 1941, concerning shipment of Jewish property.*

* * *

Report to the Fuehrer

I report the arrival of the principal shipment of ownerless Jewish "cultural property" [Kulturgut] in the salvage location Neuschwanstein by special train on Saturday the 15th of this month. It was secured by my staff for Special Purposes [Einsatztab] in Paris. The especial train, arranged for by Reichsmarschall Hermann Goering, comprised 25 express baggage cars filled with the most valuable paintings, furniture, Gobelins, works of artistic craftsmanship and ornaments. The shipment consisted chiefly of the most important parts of the collections Rothschild, Seligmann, Bernheim-Jeune, Halphen, Kann, Weil-Picard, Wildenstein, David-Weill, Levy-Benzion.

My Staff for Special Purposes started the confiscatory action in Paris during October 1940 on the basis of your order, my Fuehrer. With the help of the Security Police (SD) and the

Secret Field Police [Geheime Feldpolizei] all storage—and hiding-places of art possessions belonging to the fugitive Jewish emigrants were systematically ascertained. These possessions were then collected in the locations provided for by the Louvre in Paris. The art historians of my staff have itemized scientifically the complete art-material and have photographed all works of value. Thus, after completion, I shall be able to submit to you shortly a conclusive catalogue of all confiscated works with exact data about origin plus scientific evaluation and description. At this time the inventory includes more than 4000 individual pieces of art, partly of the highest artistic value. Besides this special train the masterpieces selected by the Reichsmarschall—mainly from the Rothschild collection—have been forwarded in two special cars to Munich already some time ago. They have been deposited there in the air raid shelters of the Fuehrer-building.

According to instruction the chief special train has been unloaded in Fussen. The cases containing pictures, furniture etc. have been stored in the castle Neuschwanstein. My deputies accompanied the special train and took care of the unloading in Neuschwanstein too.

First of all the paintings have to be unpacked to determine any possible damage suffered during the transport. Furthermore, the observation of climatic influences upon the paintings and their future careful maintenance necessitate their unpacking as well as their skillful setting-up. Due to lack of time a part of the shipment has not yet been fully inventoried in Paris. This has to be taken care of by my co-workers on the spot in Neuschwanstein to supplement the inventory in full. I have detached for Neuschwanstein the necessary technical and scientific personnel of my staff for the execution of this work. The required time for the unpacking and arranging in Neuschwanstein as well as the preparing of the exhibition rooms will take approximately 4 weeks. I shall report the completion of the work to you then, and request you, my Fuehrer, to let me show you the salvaged works of art at the spot. This will give you a survey over the work accomplished by my staff for Special Purposes.

Over and above the chief shipment there are secured in Paris a mass of additional abandoned Jewish art possessions. These are being processed in the same sense and prepared for shipment to Germany. Exact accounts about the extent of this remaining shipment are at the moment not available. However, it is estimated that the work in the Western areas will be fin-

ished entirely within two to three months. Then a second transport can be brought to Germany.
Berlin, 20 March 1941

Translation of Document 015-PS (USA 387). *Letter and Report of Rosenberg to Hitler, 16 April 1943, concerning seizure of ownerless Jewish art possessions.*

* * *

[Rosenberg Letter and Report to Hitler]

16 April 1943
673/R/Ma

Mr Fuehrer:

In my desire to give you, my Fuehrer, some joy for your birthday I take the liberty to present to you a folder containing photos of some of the most valuable paintings which my special purpose staff [Einsatzstab], in compliance with your order, secured from ownerless Jewish art collections in the occupied western territories. These photos represent an addition to the collection of 53 of the most valuable objects of art delivered some time ago to your collection. This folder also shows only a small percentage of the exceptional value and extent of these objects of art, seized by my service command [Dienststelle] in France, and put into a safe place on the Reich.

I beg of you, my Fuehrer, to give me a chance during my next audience to report to you orally on the whole extent and scope of this art seizure action. I beg you to accept a short written intermediate report of the progress and extent of the art seizure action which will be used as a basis for this later oral report, and also accept 3 copies of the temporary picture catalogues which, too, only show part of the collection you own. I shall deliver further catalogues which are now being compiled, when they are finished. I shall take the liberty during the requested audience to give you, my Fuehrer, another 20 folders of pictures, with the hope that this short occupation with the beautiful things of art which are nearest to your heart will send a ray of beauty and joy into your revered life.

Heil, my Fuehrer

Intermediate Report of the Seizure of Ownerless Jewish Art Possessions, by the Special Purpose Staff [Einsatzstab] of Reichsleiter Rosenberg in the Occupied Western Territories.

The seizure action began in compliance with the Fuehrer order of 17 Sept 1940. At first those art collections were seized which the Jews, fleeing from occupied territories, left behind in Paris. The seizure action was extended to all remaining cities and villages of the occupied French territory where it was thought that Jewish art collections might be hidden. By using all possible ways and means we discovered and seized all Jewish art collections which were hidden either in Jewish homes in Paris, in castles in the provinces or in warehouses and other storage places. The seizure action was in part very difficult and tedious and, up to now, not all completed. The escaped Jews knew how to camouflage the hiding places of these objects of art, and to find them was made more difficult by the Frenchmen originally charged with the administration of the hiding places. The special purpose staff [Einsatzstab] in connection with the security police [Sicherheitsdienst-SD], the squad for the protection of the foreign currency market [Devisenschutzkommando] and by using their own ingenuity succeeded in securing the main part of art collections, left behind by the escaped Jews, and bringing it safely to the Reich. The most important part of the action was the securing of 79 collections of well-known Jewish art collectors in France. The list of collections is attached hereto. Top place on the list is taken by the famous collections of the Jewish family of Rothschild. The difficulty of the seizure action is shown by the fact that the Rothschild collections were distributed over various places in Paris, in Bordeaux and in the Loire castles of the Rothschilds, and could only be found after a long and tedious search. Although the action covered the past 2 years, we discovered and secured, through the use of trusted agents, quite a large part of the Rothschild collection in 1942.

Besides the seizure of these complete Jewish art collections, we also searched all vacant Jewish apartments in Paris and other places for single art objects which might have been left behind. The main job in this action was to ascertain all addresses of Jews, escaped from the occupied territories, since we had to overcome quite a few difficulties on the part of the French police force which naturally tried their best to retard our progress. During this search through hundreds of single Jewish apartments a large amount of art objects were secured.

These in this manner secured collections and single pieces of art were transferred to central collecting points in Paris, located in the so-called Jeu de Paume and rooms of the Louvre. The art expert of the special purpose staff inventoried, photographed and packed all secured objects of art. Taking the inventory was made more difficult by the fact that all data pertaining to the collection were suppressed by the former owners. For this reason each art object had to be examined separately for origin, place where found, and period. The work is so designed that at its conclusion the finished inventory will represent an unimpeachable document, as far as the historical background of the art collection is concerned. It will show, on one side, the monetary, and on the other, the historical value. The Jewish owners and collectors only judged these collections by their material value. Consequently they did not recognize the historical value and therefore showed no inclination to make these collections available for research. However, this research has now been accomplished by the sorely understaffed special purpose staff. All their findings were incorporated into 3 temporary books which will serve as basis for one catalogue, soon to be compiled.

During the time from 17 Sept 1940 to 7 April 1943, 10 transports of 92 cars or a total of 2775 crates were sent to Germany. The contents of the crates were: paintings, antique furniture, Gobelins, objects of art, etc. Besides all this another special transport of 53 art objects was shipped to the Fuehrerbau in Muenchen, and 594 pieces (paintings, plastics, furniture, textiles) delivered to Reichs Marshal [Goering].

Castle Neuschanstein was designated as the first shelter. After this castle was filled, the Bavarian administration for state-owned castles and parks saw fit to relinquish several rooms in the castle Herrenchiemsee for further shipments.

Since these 2 shelters were not enough and since the Bavarian administration could not supply any more we rented 2 more in the neighborhood; it was made possible through the intervention of the State Treasurer [Reichsschatzmeister]. We rented several rooms in the former Salesianer monastery at Buxheim near Memmingen in Schwaben and the privately owned castle Kogl near Voecklabruck at Upper Austria [Oberdonau]. The location and condition of these 2 shelters is such that they are perfect in regards to safety against air attack and fire, and can easily be guarded. All art objects are so divided between the 4 shelters that it is possible to continue the inventory and care, and that no large collections of valuable art objects will be concentrated in any one place. All measures for safety are taken care of by the combined efforts of: 1. the Bavarian administration for castles and parks, 2. the central control of the fire prevention police, and 3. the local representatives of State and Party. In this way the highest degree of safety has been achieved.

9455 articles in the aforementioned shelters have been completely inventoried, as of 1 April 1943. The inventory is as follows:

    5255 Paintings
     297 Sculptures
    1372 Pieces antique furniture
     307 Textiles
    2224 Small objects of art, including East-Asiatic art

The inventory in addition to records of seizure and lists of seizure and transport, follows the pattern of the enclosed file card [Karteikarte]. On this file card is noted all information necessary to characterize all objects as to origin, master, technique, time, etc. These file cards together with the extended explanations of the men charged with taking the inventory constitute the basis for the editing of the master catalogue. Besides this there is in preparation a photo-library in one of the central offices in Berlin, as well as in Neuschwanstein. Since the number of technicians was small, the time short, and the necessity of a quick expert from Paris was paramount, only the most valuable objects were inventoried in Paris. Therefore the inventory has to be continued in the shelters. According to the latest count there are approximately 10,000 more objects to be inventoried.

At present there are 400 crates in Paris, ready for shipment which will be sent to the Reich as soon as necessary preliminary work in Paris is completed. Should the present 4 shelters not prove sufficient for consequent shipments, 2 more places, namely the castle Bruck near Linz and the camp Seisenegg near Amstetten on the lower Danube have been prepared.

For reasons of fire prevention all art objects in the shelters had to be unpacked skillfully. These measures were also necessary to accomplish the inventory and to continue with the care of the valuable art objects. Restoration has begun since many needed it when we acquired them. At present a repair shop with all necessary tools is being outfitted in Fuessen in which all paintings, pieces of furniture and other objects will be restored, to safeguard preservation. The unpacking, the continuation of the inventory, and the establishment of the photo-library, and too, the editing of the master catalogue, will take considerable time.

The action of seizure [Fassungaktion] in Paris and occupied Western territories will be continued, although on a reduced scale, since there are still new art objects of great value to be found. The administration of the East not only will seize furniture, but also the art objects which might yet be found there. Here too valuable art objects were found in the last months. These art objects, found during the collection of furniture, were also sent to the shelters and will receive the same treatment as the others. Besides these objects, whose art value is established, hundreds of modern French paintings were seized which from the German standpoint are without value as far as the national-socialist art conception is concerned. These works of modern French painters will be listed separately, for a later decision as to their disposition.

On orders from the Reichs Marshal some of the works of modern and degenerate French art were exchanged in Paris for paintings of known value. The exchange was of great advantage to us, since we received 87 works by Italian, Dutch and German masters, who are known to be of great value. We shall continue to trade whenever a chance presents itself. At the completion of the action a proposal as to the disposition of the modern and degenerate French paintings will be presented.
Berlin, 16 April 1943

Translation of Document 041-PS. *Memorandum, Rosenberg to Hitler, 3 October 1942, concerning seizure of 40,000 tons of Jewish household goods in the West.*

* * *

Memorandum for the Fuehrer

By a decision of the Fuehrer the Reichsminister for the occupied Eastern territories has received the authority to put to use for the support of government arrangements in the Eastern territories the available household goods of refugees, absent or deported Jews in the occupied Western areas. This is the so-called Action "M". For the execution of Action "M" the service office West [Dienststelle Westen] has been set up in Paris with directive authority in France, Belgium and the Netherlands. Up to the present time about 40,000 tons of household goods have been loaded on free transportation space (ship and railway) bound for the Reich.

In recognition of the fact that the requirements of bomb damaged persons in the Reich must take precedence over the demands of the East, the Reich Ministry has placed a major portion (over 19,500 tons) of the household goods at the disposal of the bomb damaged persons in the Reich. The goods have then been transported by the appropriate service office west in the occupied territory. Likewise, the Reich Ministry will place at the disposition of bomb-damaged persons the greatest portion, at least 80%, of the goods accruing from Action "N" [sic]. For its own purposes only these goods which are urgently needed in the East will be reserved.

The execution of Action "M" has resulted in two categories of difficulties up to the present time:

a. Transportation Question. The goods have been transported up to this point as Armed Forces goods by means of railway cars and ships. The transportation authorities [Kommandanturen] now wish to treat the transport requirements of Action "M" as the transport of the civilian sector. This would lead to unbearable delays and among other difficulties would require the export-approval of the French State. Because of this the following decree is required: Goods which the Reich Minister for the East-Service Office West [Dienststelle Westen] Paris or their directive authorities France, Belgium and the Netherlands, declare as goods accruing from Action "M", are to be transported as Armed Forces goods.

b. Distribution of furniture among bombed-out persons. The giving up of the furniture to bombed-damaged persons is being delayed in order that it may be submitted upon import into the Reich territory to handling by the customs. After time-losing determination of the value, the furniture in many cases is auctioned to the bomb-damaged persons by Chief Financial Commissioners [Oberfinanzpraesidenten]; to avoid these red-tape procedures the following decree is proposed:

1. Goods accruing from Action "M" are exempt from all customs handling. For such goods there are no obligations or duties to pay.

2. Bomb damaged districts announce their needs in household furnishing under the auspices of the competent Reich defense commissar to Reich Ministry for Occupied Eastern Territories—Central Section. The Reich Ministry instigates the immediate removal of the objects placed at its disposal by its service office West [Dienststelle Westen] and in accordance with the indications of the Reich defense commissar ships directly to the competent regional directorates [Gauleitungen]. These give the furniture to the persons suffering the bomb damage on a loan basis. The determination of the value of the furniture and the definitive acquisition by the person suffering the bomb damage remains in abeyance till a later accounting. Up to the time of reckoning the goods are Reich property, and are

subject to the evaluation right of the Reich Minister for the occupied Eastern territory.

By these proposals a type of management would be achieved whereby persons who have suffered bomb damage would have furniture and household goods at their disposal in the shortest possible time. And thereby also a portion of their most immediate difficulties would be eliminated.

Berlin, 3 October 1942

Signed: A. ROSENBERG

Translation of Document 053-PS. *Excerpt from Report by Hans Koch, deputy of Reichsminister for Occupied Eastern Territories, 5 October 1941, concerning political situation in Ukraine, describing execution of 3500 Jews in Kiev.*

* * *

The Deputy of the Reichs Ministry [Reichsministerium] for the Occupied Eastern Provinces with the Army Group South.—Captain Dr. Koch

REPORT 10
(Concluded on 5th October 1941)
SECRET
(See also the morale report which will be ready in a short time "Legacy of the Soviets in the Ukrainian Areas"—concluded at the end of September 1941)

---

f. The *fire of Kiev* (24-29 September 1941) destroyed the very center, that is the most beautiful and most representative part of the city with its two large hotels, the central Post Office, the radio station, the telegraph office and several department stores. An area of about 2 square kilometers was affected, some 50,000 people are homeless; they were scantily housed in abandoned quarters. As reconciliation for the obvious sabotage, the Jews of the city, approximately (according to figures from the SS-Commands for commitment) 3,500 [sic] people, half women, were liquidated on the 29th and 30th September. The population took the execution—as much as they found out about it— calmly, many with satisfaction; the newly vacated homes of the Jews were turned over for the relief of the housing shortage. Even if certain relief was created in a social respect, the care of the city of half a million is still in danger and one can already foresee food shortages and eventual epidemics.

Translation of Document 069-PS (USA 589). Letter from Bormann to Rosenberg, 17 January 1939, enclosing order of 28 December 1938, concerning decisions on Jewish question.

* * *

NATIONAL SOCIALIST GERMAN WORKERS PARTY
The Deputy of the Fuehrer, Staff Director
Munich 33, Brown House, January 17, 1939
SECRET
Regulation No 1/39 g

Subject: Jews

After a report of General Field Marshal Goering the Fuehrer has made some basic decisions regarding the Jewish question. The decisions are brought to your attention in the enclosure. Strict compliance with these directives is requested.

signed: M. BORMANN

1 enclosure
Distribution: III b
Official:
   [signed: signature illegible]
      Office Rosenberg, Rec'd Nr 5827 Jan 19, 39; filed Feb 2
         Submitted to
         RL Jan 19
         Urban Jan 20
         Schickedanz Feb 13

Copy

Berlin, Dec 28, 1938

Minister President General Field Marshal Goering, Commissioner for the Four Year Plan
SECRET

Pursuant to my report the Fuehrer has made the following decisions on the Jewish question.

A.

I: Housing of Jews

1. *a.* Protective regulations for tenants will not be generally revoked in the case of Jews. It is desirable, however, to proceed in individual cases in such a way that Jews will live together in one house, as much as feasible under rental conditions.

b. For this reason the arianization of real estate will be *the last step of the total aryanization*, that means that at present real estate is only to be arianized in individual cases where there are compelling reasons. An immediate concern is the

III - 111

aryanization of plants and business enterprises, farm property, forests, etc.

2. *The use of sleepers and dining cars is to be prohibited for Jews.* Apart from that no separate Jew-compartments must be arranged for. Neither should any bans be pronounced regarding the use of railways, streetcars, subways, buses and ships.

3. The ban for Jews is to be pronounced only for certain public establishments etc. This includes such hotels and restaurants which are mainly visited by Party members (for instance: Hotel Kaiserhof, Berlin; Hotel Vierjahreszeiten Munich; Hotel Deutscher Hof, Nurnberg; Hotel Drei Mohren, Augsburg, etc.) The ban can further be pronounced for swimming pools, certain public squares, resort towns, etc. Mineral baths may, in individual cases and if prescribed by a doctor, be used by Jews, but only in a manner not causing offense.

II. Pensions are not to be denied to Jews who have been civil servants and who have been pensioned. It is to be investigated, however, whether those Jews can manage on a smaller pension.

III. Jewish social care is not to be arianized or to be abolished, so that Jews will not become a public burden but can be cared for by Jewish institutions.

IV. Jewish patents are property values and therefore to be arianized too. (A similar procedure was used during the World War by America and other states pertaining to German citizens.)

B.
Mixed Marriages:

I. 1. *with children* (half-Aryans 1 class)

a. If the father is German and the mother Jewish the family is permitted to remain in their present apartment. No ban for Jews regarding housing is to be pronounced against these families.

The property of the Jewish mother may be transferred in such cases to the German husband respectively the half-Aryan children.

b. If the father is Jewish and the mother German these families are neither to be housed in Jewish quarters for the time being. This because the children (half-Aryan 1st class) are not to be exposed to the Jewish agitation as they will have to serve later in the labor service and the armed forces.

The property may for the time being be transferred partly or entirely to the children.

2. *without children*

a. If the husband is German and the wife Jewish par. 1 a holds true accordingly.

b. If the husband is Jewish and the wife German these childless couples are to be treated as pure Jews.

Property values of the husband cannot be transferred to the wife. Both can be lodged in Jewish houses or quarters. Especially in the case of emigration both spouses are to be treated like Jews as soon as the augmented emigration has been set into motion.

II. If the German wife divorces the Jewish husband she returns to the German blood-kinship. All disadvantages for her are dropped in this case.

signed: GOERING

Authenticated copy:
signed: JAHN

Translation of Document 078-PS. *Regulations issued by Heydrich, 28 June 1941, for treatment of political prisoners of war, providing for the execution of Jews.*

* * *

COPY

OFFICE IV

Berlin 28 June 1941

SECRET STATE MATTER!

Directives for the Chiefs of Security Police and Secret Service Teams Assigned to PW Camps

These teams are assigned after agreement has been reached between the chiefs of the Security Police, secret service and the Supreme Command of the Army and * * * (see annex). The Commands work upon the special authorization and according to the general directives in the Camp regulations which was given to them and is independently in close harmony with the AO.

The duty of the Commands is the political screening of prisoners and the segregation and further handling of undesirable elements among them with regard to political, criminal or similar respects.

Resources cannot be placed at the disposal of the Commands for the fulfillment of their missions. The "German penal code" [Fahndungsbuch], the "Temporary permit of Leave List"

[Aufenthaltsermittlungsliste], and "Special Penal Code USSR" will prove to be of little value; the Special Penal Code USSR therefore does not suffice as only a small part therein is dangerous to the designated Soviet Russians.

The Commands will therefore have to rely on their own specialty and ingenuity upon establishment and self-producing knowledge. Therefore they will only then be able to begin with the fulfillment of their mission when they have gathered an appropriate amount of material.

For their work, the Commands are to make as much use of the experiences of the Camp Commanders as possible, who in the meantime have profited by the observation and examination of prisoners.

Further, the Commands will have to take pains from the beginning to search among the prisoners for seemingly trustworthy elements, may they be communists or not, in order to make them useful for their intelligence purposes.

Through the establishment of such trusted personnel [V-Personen] and through the use of all other present possibilities among the prisoners, it must succeed to screen all elements.

In every case the Commands are to provide themselves with definite clarity over the encountered measures through the examination and eventual questioning of prisoners.

Above all it is important to find out:
1. all outstanding functionaries of the State and of the Party, especially
2. professional revolutionists,
3. the functionaries of the Comintern,
4. all leading Party functionaries of the Russian Secret Police [KPdSU] and their associated organizations in the Central, district, and county Committees,
5. all the Peoples' Commissars and their Assistants,
6. all the former Polit-Commissars in the Red Army,
7. all leading personalities of the Central and Middle Offices among the State authorities,
8. the leading economic personalities,
9. the Soviet Russian Intelligence agents,
10. all Jews,
11. all persons who are established as being instigators or fanatical communists.

Just as important is the finding of persons who are devoted to the reconstruction, the administration, and management of the conquered Russian provinces.

Finally, such persons must be secured who can be used to

transact further discoveries, whether of the Police or similar work, and for the clarification of universal interesting questions. In this category fall all the higher State and Party functionaries who are in the camp on the basis of their position and knowledge and who can give information on the measures and working methods of the Soviet State, the Communistic Party or the Cominterns.

In view of the pending decisions, considerations must also be given to the peoples' membership. At the end of the screening, measures, to be decided later, as to the transfer of prisoners from one command to another, will follow.

The Camp Commanders are directed by the Supreme Command of the Army to report such proposals.

Executions will not be carried out in the camps or immediate vicinity. Should the camps in the General Government be situated in the immediate vicinity of the border, then the prisoners for special handling are to be taken care of in former Soviet Russian Provinces.

The Commands are to keep records of the fulfillment of special handlings; which must include:
- Serial number
- Family and Surname
- Date of birth and place
- Military rank
- Profession
- Last residence
- Reason for special handling
- Day and place of special handling

Office IV

SECRET STATE MATTER

Supplement to the Directives for the Commands of the Security Police and Security Service assigned to P. W. camps

1. In the directives of the 17th July 1941, I have repeatedly pointed to the fact that it is the duty of the Special Purpose Command of the Security Police and Security Service to find not only the untrustworthy but also those trustworthy elements in general which can come into consideration for the reconstruction of the Eastern provinces.

I reemphasize that one duty is as important as the other.

In order to obtain a most extensive view of the co-activity of the Special Purpose Command, I order that the numeral 4 (number of those persons found to be trustworthy) will be especially heeded in the weekly reports.

The war prisoners who are found to be trustworthy and who were formerly in leading position in the Soviet Russian economic circles, are to be listed, if possible, according to branch their last employment, and by name.

2. I reemphasize again the fact that in view of the pending decisions, consideration must especially be given to the peoples' citizenship.

Ukranians, White Russians, Aserbeidschanians, Armenians, North Caucasians, Georgians, Turks are only to be designated as definitely untrustworthy and dealt with according to the directive when they are definitely proven to be Bolshevists, Polit-Commissars, or other dangerous functionaries.

One must be careful, in as much as the Turkish people frequently have a Jewish appearance and the circumcision alone does not denote a Jewish descent (for example, Mohammedans).

3. The conception "highbrow" [Intelligenzler] should not be interpreted along European viewpoints.

The simplest, most primitive Soviet-Russian illiterate can, in his political fanaticism, be more dangerous than, for instance, the Soviet-Russian engineer, who due to his ability, went to High School, even though, he only outwardly appeared to be in accord with the Bolshevistic system.

In this respect the highbrow are mainly the professional revolutionists, writers, editors, and persons in the Comintern.

4. Those Soviet Russians who are definitely found to be untrustworthy are to be forthwith reported—as designated in the directives of the 17th July 1941. Following the introduction of the execution authorization, further fulfillment of the designated measures are to begin *without further delay*.

A further custody in the camps in question are to be avoided for various reasons.

Finally I reemphasize that under no circumstances are the executions to be carried out either in the Camp or in the near vicinity.

It is self-understood that these executions are not public. It is a matter of principle not to admit spectators.

5. I again charge the leaders and members of the Special Service Staff with the following: exemplary behavior during

and after duty hours, top cooperation with camp commanders and careful checking of work.

                signed: Heydrich
                     (S)
                            Verified:
   signed: Wolfert, Member of the Chancellory

Translation of Document 090-PS (USA 372). *Letter from Rosenberg to Schwarz, 28 January 1941, concerning registration and collection of Jewish libraries and art treasures, and synopsis of correspondence on subject.*

          *   *   *

                        18 September 1940
                             2474—R/Dt.
     SECRET

To the Reich Treasurer of the NSDAP
Reich Director F. X. Schwarz,
Munich 33.

Dear Party Member Schwarz,
   Thanks for your helpfulness in regard to the safeguarding of scientific materials in the occupied territories. I deduce from this that you are interested in this work and would therefore like to inform you about several matters.
   It took some time until we found by and by the several treasures, and until we could ascertain that a lot had been abducted from Paris into other towns. Thus the treasures of the Rothschilds, robbed together from all parts of the world, are being secured by us not only in Paris but also in the various castles of the Rothschilds (Bordeaux, Deauville and so on). Legal doubts arose and I have discussed them with the Fuehrer. Subsequently he caused a new order to be issued by the Chief of the Supreme Command of the Armed Forces which I enclose in duplicate. Thus the Seminary (Hohe Schule) will still receive a Polish library of 130,000 volumes. This will include the complete history of the East, probably a large Slavic library and many other items. Together with a lot of scientific material many extremely valuable objects of art have been found in cases at the residence of the Rothschilds. This has been secured and the Fuehrer will decide at a later date as to the final disposal.

In Brussels and Amsterdam we are on the track of valuable objects too. I believe that we shall be able to bring quite some material from there to Germany.

You see that we are industrially endeavoring to exploit the present moment. Such an opportunity will hardly present itself again. I am trying to keep the Staff for Special Purposes down to a minimum. Nevertheless it is unavoidable that a number of experts have to work at various places. And the work takes longer than was anticipated in the beginning.

Once more many thanks. If I should come to Munich in the near future I hope to meet you.

                                      Heil Hitler!
                                   28 January 1941
                                     3581/R/dt
                                    [initials] Sch

To: The Reich Treasurer of the NSDAP
       Reich Director F. X. Schwarz
Munich 33

Subject: Staff for Special Purposes in Paris

Dear Party Member Schwarz,

About the work of my Staff for Special Purposes in France, Holland and Belgium I can inform you that the major part of the work in France will be finished by the end of February. Then only a few men have to remain in Paris.—However, in Belgium and Holland extensive research work has still to be carried out. I hope nevertheless to wind up the main part of the work there within a measurable space of time. The arrangement and registration of the large art treasures claimed a lot of special work. I had these treasures confiscated simultaneously with the scientific material. The Fuehrer is going to decide what to do with them shortly. As I informed you previously the values involved will come close to a billion dollars according to expert estimates.

I told you already verbally that the largest Jewish library of the world, consisting of 350,000 volumes, will be placed in the institution which is going to be opened at Frankfurt on the Main within a short time. Another 200,000 volumes will be added from Holland.

The library of the IInd International about the history of the social movements cannot be transferred for the moment to Germany due to lack of space. Two will have to take charge of it in Amsterdam where scientific work can start immediately. This library consists of 130,000 volumes.

The account of the expenditures up till now will be submitted to your deputy by the administrative branch of my office. However, I have to request that you put another amount of 100,000 Reichsmark at my disposal so that I can complete the work satisfactorily. At the same time I propose once more that you have parts of those sums reimbursed—be it from the Reich Marshal or from the Fuehrer's funds for cultural purposes. There is no doubt that I also have collected treasures which will not benefit the Seminary directly.

Once more I want to express my deepest thanks for letting us have the Schrenk-Notzing-Palais in Munich for our institution. Prof. Harder, the future director of this institution, is extremely pleased with it and will soon get in touch with your deputy.

A depiction of the situation regarding the branch offices of the Seminary in the various cities is just being completed and will be submitted to you within a short time.

Once more many thanks for your generous support.

Heil Hitler
Yours
[in pencil] Sch

[SYNOPSIS]
Letter of 22 May 1941, 4592/4863/R/Ma
To the Reich Treasurer of the NSDAP, Reich Director Schwarz, Munich 33.
Written by Rosenberg

Letter of 9 May 1941, K IV/te. 4363 H. [Initialed] Sch
To the Deputy of the Fuehrer for the supervision of the complete mental and doctrinal [Weltanschaulich] education of the NSDAP
Mr. Reich Director Alfred Rosenberg, Berlin W 35, 17 Margareten Str.
Written and signed by the Reich Treasurer of the Party Schwarz.

Letter 19 April 1941 from the Office for Jewish and Masonic Problems.
Frankfurt on the Main, 1 Schwindstrasse; Schi/Fl.
To the Deputy of the Fuehrer for the supervision of the complete mental and doctrinal training and education of the

NSDAP, attention Adjutant, Berlin W 35, 17 Margaretenstr., Party member Koeppin
Written by Chief Reich Director (Oberreichsleiter) Schimner and signed by him.

Letter of 3 April 1941, K IV/kr.
To the Deputy of the Fuehrer for the supervision of the complete mental and doctrinal education of the NSDAP,
Reich Director Alfred Rosenberg, Berlin W 35, 17 Margareten Str.
Written and signed by the Reich Treasurer of the Party Schwarz.

Copy of a letter of 28 March 1941, from the Reich Commissar for the occupied territories of the Netherlands, General Commissar for Special Purposes, Section ro. international organizations, Den Haag, Fluweelen Burgwal 22; SCH/R.
To F. J. M. Rehse, Munich 2 M, 1 Residenzstrasse (residence)
Written by Schwier, authenticated by Kretzer.

Copy of a letter from NSDAP, Collection FJM. Rehse, 2 April 1941, Munich, 1 Residenzstr.
To the Reich Treasurer Schwarz, Munich, Administration Building
Written by F. J. M. Rehse, Authenticated by Reigl

[The five previously enumerated letters all deal with the request of party member Rehse to obtain the furnishings, paraphernalia and books of a masonic lodge for the party collection Rehse. This was finally granted in the letter of 22 May 1941 by Rosenberg.]

---

11 June 1942
R./K. 1035/42

To the Reich Treasurer of the NSDAP,
Reich Director Franz Xavier Schwarz
Munich 33
Dear Party Member Schwarz,

The work of my staff for special purposes has been hampered through lack of personnel. Nevertheless, the tabulating of the cultural objects secured from France has progressed so far that an exhibition of selected paintings can be arranged in the castle Neuschwanstein. The overall catalogue will be ready for typesetting in a few weeks. I would enjoy it tremendously if the two of us could be the first ones to visit this exhibition. We could then decide which objects and tapestries to suggest to the Fuehrer to be used for the furnishing of the Seminary [Hohe Schule] respectively of my office. The Fuehrer will hardly be able to visit the exhibition due to the fact that he is presently overburdened with work. However I shall ask him to visit it later and shall inform you when the Fuehrer will be able to come.

Once more I thank you for your generous support extended to my staff for special purposes. I am convinced that a large number of most valuable cultural objects have been secured for the German people.

Translation of Document 136-PS (USA 367). *Hitler order, 29 January 1940, concerning establishment of "Hohe Schule", the center for Nazi ideological research.*

* * *

Copy

Information to all Sections of Party and State.

The "Hohe Schule" is supposed to become the center for national socialistic ideological and educational research. It will be established after the conclusion of the war. I order that the already initiated preparations be continued by Reichsleiter Rosenberg, especially in the way of research and the setting up of the library.

All sections of party and State are requested to cooperate with him in this task.

(Signed) ADOLF HITLER

Berlin, 29 January 1940
Certified a true copy
Berlin 15 Dec 1943
    Dr. Zeiss
Stabseinsatzfuehrer

Translation of Document 137-PS (USA 379). *Order from Keitel to Commanding General of Armed Forces in the Netherlands, 5 July 1940, to cooperate with the Einsatzstab Rosenberg (Rosenberg's staff for seizing Jewish property, libraries and art treasures).*

* * *

The Chief of the High Command of the Armed Forces, No. 2850/40 secret Adj. Chief OKW

137-PS　　　　　　　　　　Nazi Germany's War Against the Jews

(Please indicate above file number, the date and short contents in the answer)
                Berlin W 35, Tirpitzufer 72-76   5 July 1940
                                    Telephone: Local 218191
                                    Long distance   218091

To the Supreme Commander of the Army, the Supreme Commander of the Armed Forces in Holland.

Reichsleiter Rosenberg has requested from the Fuehrer to have:

1. The State libraries and archives searched for documents which are valuable for Germany.

2. The chanceries of the high church authorities and lodges searched for political activities which are directed against us, and to have the material in question confiscated.

The Fuehrer has ordered that this plan should be complied with and that the Secret State police—supported by the keepers of the archives of Reichsleiter Rosenberg—should be entrusted with the search. The Chief of the Security Police, SS Lt. General Heydrich, has been notified; he will get in touch with the responsible military commanders to carry out this order.

This measure should be carried out in all the territories of Holland, Belgium, Luxembourg and France which are occupied by us.

It is requested that the subordinate agencies should be notified.

                The Chief of the Supreme Command
                of the Armed Forces.
                                (Signed)   KEITEL

To Reich leader Rosenberg
Copy for information
(Signed) [Illegible]
Captain [Rittmeister] and executive officer.

Translation of Document 138-PS. Order from Keitel to Commanding General in Occupied France, 17 September 1940, to cooperate with the Einsatzstab Rosenberg (Rosenberg's staff for seizing Jewish property, libraries and art treasures).

*　　*　　*

Copy
The Chief of the Supreme Command of the Armed Forces
        Berlin W 35, Tirpitzufer 72-76, 17 Sept 1940

III - 122

038-PS

Tel: 21 81 91

2 f 28.14 W.Z. No. 3812/40 g

To the Chief of Army High Command for the Military Administration in Occupied France.

In supplement to the order of the Fuehrer transmitted at the time to Reichsleiter Rosenberg to search lodges, libraries and archives in the occupied territories of the west for material valuable to Germany, and to safeguard the latter through the Gestapo, the Fuehrer has decided:

The ownership status before the war in France, prior to the declaration of war on 1 September 1939, shall be the criterion.

Ownership transfers to the French state or similar transfers completed after this date are irrelevant and legally invalid (for example, Polish and Slovak libraries in Paris, possessions of the Palais Rothschild or other ownerless Jewish possessions). Reservations regarding search, seizure and transportation to Germany on the basis of the above reasons will not be recognized.

Reichsleiter Rosenberg and/or his deputy Reichshauptsellenleiter Ebert has received clear instructions from the Fuehrer personally governing the right of seizure; he is entitled to transport to Germany cultural goods which appear valuable to him and to safeguard them there. The Fuehrer has reserved for himself the decision as to their use.

It is requested that the services in question be informed correspondingly.

Signed: KEITEL

For information:
Attention: Reichsleiter Rosenberg

certified true copy
Berlin 15 December 43
(Dr. Zeiss)

[Rosenberg special purpose staff seal]

Translation of Document 139-PS. Order of Reinecke, Chief of the General Department of OKW, 10 October 1940, concerning instructions to be given to Military Administration in Belgium to cooperate with Einsatzstab Rosenberg (Rosenberg's staff for seizing Jewish property, libraries and art treasures).

* * *

139-PS   Nazi Germany's War Against the Jews

Copy
SUPREME COMMAND OF THE ARMED FORCES
Berlin W 35 Tirpitzufer 72-75 10 October 1940.
Tel: Local Service 21 81 91
Long Distance 21 80 91

Az 2 f 28 J (Ia).
No. 1838/40 g.
Reference: Chief Supreme Command Armed Forces
   No. 3812/40 g WZ of 17 September 1940.

To: Supreme Army High Commander.

   As supplement to the above-mentioned letter, addressed to the Military Administration of Occupied France, it is requested that corresponding directions be given also to the Military Administration in Belgium.

Chief of the Supreme Command
of the Armed Forces

   By Order

                          Signed: REINECKE

For Information:
Attention Reichsleiter ROSENBERG's Adjutant.
Reference: 2606/a.
                     Rosenberg's special purpose staff seal.
Certified true copy
Berlin 15 December 1943
    (Dr. Zeiss)
Chief special purpose Staff.

    Translation of Document 140-PS. Order of Reinecke, Chief of the General Department of OKW, 30 October 1940, supplementing order of 5 July 1940, on seizure of Jewish possessions by Einsatzstab Rosenberg (Rosenberg's staff for seizing Jewish property, libraries and art treasures).

SECRET
Copy

Supreme Command of the Armed Forces
Az.Zf.285 (G-3) Nr. 1838/40
        Berlin W 35, Tirpitzufer 72-76 30 Oct. 1940
            Tel. local 218191, long distance 218091
To: The Armed Forces Commander in the Netherlands

III - 124

In supplement to the order of the Fuehrer transmitted, under Nr 2850/40 secret Adj. Chief of the Supreme Command of the Armed Forces, of 5.7.1940, to Reichsleiter Rosenberg, to search lodges, libraries and archives of the occupied territories of the West, for material valuable to Germany, and to safeguard the latter through the Gestapo, the Fuehrer has decided:

The ownership status before the war in France, prior to the declaration of war on 1 Sept. 1939, shall be the criterion.

Ownership transfers to the French state or similar transfers completed after this date are irrelevant and legally invalid (for example, Polish and Slovak libraries in Paris, possessions of the Palais Rothschild or other ownerless Jewish possessions). Reservations regarding search, seizure and transportation to Germany on the basis of the above reasons will not be recognized.

Reichsleiter Rosenberg and/or his deputy Reichshauptstellenleiter Ebert has received clear instructions from the Fuehrer personally governing the right of seizure, he is entitled to transport to Germany cultural goods which appear valuable to him and to safeguard them there. The Fuehrer has reserved for himself the decision as to their use.

It is requested that the services in question be informed correspondingly.

           The Chief of the Supreme Command
              of the Armed Forces
                        By order
                  Signed: REINECKE
                  Certified a true copy
                  Berlin 15 Dec 1943
                    (Dr. Zeiss)
            Chief of special purpose staff

For information:
Attention Adj. of Reichsleiter Rosenberg
Re Nr 2606/Ma
    signed   Reinecke
       [Rosenberg's Special Purpose Staff SEAL]

Translation of Document 141-PS (USA 368). *Goering order, 5 November 1940, concerning seizure of Jewish art treasures.*

              *   *   *

In conveying the measures taken until now, for the securing of Jewish art property by the Chief of the Military Administration Paris and the special service staff Rosenberg (The Chief of the Supreme Command of the Armed Forces 2 f 28.14.W.Z.Nr 3812/40 g), the art objects brought to the Louvre will be disposed of in the following way:

1. Those art objects about which the Fuehrer has reserved for himself the decision as to their use.

2. Those art objects which serve to the completion of the Reichs Marshal's collection.

3. Those art objects and library stocks the use of which seem useful to the establishing of the higher institutes of learning and which come within the jurisdiction of Reichsleiter Rosenberg.

4. Those art objects that are suited to be sent to German museums, of all these art objects, a systematic inventory will be made by the special purpose staff Rosenberg; they will then be packed and shipped to Germany with the assistance of the Luftwaffe.

5. Those art objects that are suited to be given to French museums or might be of use for the German-French art trade, will be auctioned off at a date yet to be fixed; the profit of this auction will be given to the French State for the benefit of those bereaved by the war.

6. The further securing of Jewish art property in France will be continued by the special purpose staff Rosenberg in the same way as heretofore in connection with the Chief of the military administration Paris.

Paris, 5 November 1940

I will submit this proposal to the Fuehrer. Those instructions are in effect until he has reached a decision.

Signed: GOERING

Certified true copy:
Berlin 15 Dec. 1943
(Dr. Zeiss)
Chief of special purpose staff
[Rosenberg's special purpose staff seal]

Translation of Document 145-PS (USA 373). *Rosenberg order, 20 August 1941, concerning safeguarding the cultural goods in the Occupied Eastern Territories.*

* * *

The Reichs Minister for the Occupied Eastern Territories
Berlin W 35, Rauch Street 17/18, 20 Aug 1941
Tel: 21 95 15 and 39 50 46
Cable address: Reichminister East

The Documentary Evidence   145-PS

Na 369/R/H
Director of the Reichs Main Office UTIKAL [Reichshauptstellenleiter]
Berlin

Subject: Safeguarding the cultural goods in the occupied Eastern Territories

I have instructed the Reichs Commissioner for the Eastland and his subordinate general and district commissioners to secure all cultural goods in the Reichs Commissariat of the East which are appropriate in general for national-socialistic research as well as research of the activities of the opponents of National-Socialism. I delegate you to carry out with an "Einsatzstab" to be formed for this purpose this work of the Reichs Commissioner, the General, Main and Regional Commissioners, for their support. During the execution of this mission you will remain directly subordinate to Main Division II of my ministry whose directors will provide you with additional instructions. The orders issued by the Fuehrer for the "Einsatzstab" in the West remain also the same for the East.

The execution of your job will be financed, as in the occupied western territories, through the Reichs treasurer of the NSDAP. A later accounting between him and the ministry for the occupied eastern territories, respectively with the Reichs Commissariats, is held in reserve.

I am including a letter of mine to the Reichs Commissioner of the Eastland.

                                        Heil Hitler!
                                Signed: ROSENBERG
1 inclosure

Translation of Document 149-PS (USA 369). *Hitler Order, 1 March 1942, establishing authority of Einsatzstab Rosenberg to explore libraries and archives and confiscate material for the "Hohe Schule," Nazi center for ideological research.*

* * *

FUEHRER DECREE

Jews, freemasons and the ideological enemies of National Socialism who are allied with them are the originators of the present war against the Reich. Spiritual struggle according to plan against these powers is a measure necessitated by war.

I have therefore ordered Reichsleiter Alfred Rosenberg to accomplish this task in cooperation with the Chief of the High Command of the Armed Forces. To accomplish this task, his Einsatzstab for the occupation territories has the right to explore libraries, archives, lodges, and other ideological and cultural establishments of all kinds for suitable material and to confiscate such material for the ideological tasks of the NSDAP and for scientific research work by the university [Hohe Schule]. The same rule applies to cultural goods which are in the possession or are the property of Jews, which are abandoned or whose origin cannot be clearly established. The regulations for the execution of this task with the cooperation will be issued by the Chief of the High Command of the Armed Forces in agreement with Reichsleiter Rosenberg.

If necessary measures for the eastern territories under German administration will be taken by Reichsleiter Rosenberg in his capacity as Reich Minister for occupied eastern territories.

(Signed) A. HITLER

Fuehrers Headquarters, March 1942
To all Bureaus *of the Armed Forces, the Party and the State.*

Translation of Document 151-PS. Order from Reichsminister for Occupied Eastern Territories, 7 April 1942, concerning safeguarding of cultural goods, research material and Scientific Institutions in the East.

* * *

The Reichsminister for the occupied Eastern territory
Berlin W 35, Kurfuerstenstrasse 134 7 April 1942
Tel. 21 99 51

N. I/1/13/42

To: Reich Commissioner for the Ostland, Riga
Reich Commissioner for the Ukraine, Rowno

SUBJECT: Safeguarding of Cultural Goods, Research Material and Scientific Institutions in the Occupied Eastern Territories.

I

I have assigned Reichsleiter Rosenberg's Einsatzstab for the Occupied Territories with the seizure and uniform handling of cultural goods, research material and scientific apparatus from libraries, archives, scientific institutions, museums, etc., which are found in public, religious or private buildings. The Einsatzstab begins its work, as newly directed by the Fuehrer's decree of 1 March 1942, immediately after occupation of the territories by the combat troops, in agreement with the Quartermaster General of the Army, and completes it in agreement with the competent Reich Commissioners after civil administration has been established. I request all authorities of my administration to support as far as possible the members of the Einsatzstab in carrying out all measures and in giving all necessary information, especially in regard to objects which may have been already seized from the occupied Eastern territories and removed from their previous location, and information as to where this material is located at the present time.

Any activity for the purpose of safeguarding cultural goods can be permitted only if it is carried out in agreement with Reichsleiter Rosenberg's Einsatzstab. The Einsatzstab will be constantly informed concerning the method and extent of investigations, work projects and measures.

All authorities of my administration are hereby instructed that objects of the afore-mentioned type will be seized only by Reichsleiter Rosenberg's Einsatzstab, and to abstain from arbitrary handling as a matter of principle.

Insofar as seizures or transports have already taken place contrary to these provisions, Reichsleiter Rosenberg's Einsatzstab, Berlin-Charlottenburg 2, Bismarckstrasse 1, telephone: 34 00 18, will be informed without delay, with an exact list of the objects as well as indication of the current storage place and persons entitled to dispose of them.

II

In exceptional cases immediate measures may be taken to safeguard or transport objects to a safe place in order to avoid threatened danger (for example, danger of collapse of buildings, enemy action, damage by weather, etc.). In all cases a written report will be submitted immediately to my Einsatzstab.

Decision regarding exceptions lies with the Reich or General Commissioners in agreement with the commissioners of the staff.

III

I have sent copies of this order directly to the General Commissioners.   By order

Signed/t/ Dr. LEIBBRANDT
OFFICIAL:
/s/ [Illegible]
Office Employee

Authenticated copy
Berlin Dec 15, 1943
signed: ZEISS
    (Dr. Zeiss)
Leader of Stabseinsatz

Translation of Document 154-PS (USA 370). Letter from Lammers to high State and Party authorities, 5 July 1942, confirming Rosenberg's authority to seize material in connection with spiritual battle against Jews and Free-Masons.

*   *   *

The Reichminister and Chief of Chancellery.
    Berlin W 8, Voss-strasse 6, 5 July 1942
        Present Headquarters of the Fuehrer

To: The Highest Reich Authorities and
     The Services directly subordinate to the Fuehrer.

The Fuehrer has delegated Reichsleiter Rosenberg in his capacity of commissioner of the Fuehrer to supervise the total spiritual and philosophical indoctrination and education of the NSDAP in the spiritual battle against Jews and Free-Masons as well as against the affiliated philosophical opponents of National Socialism, who are the cause of the present war. For this purpose, the Fuehrer has ordered that Reichsleiter Rosenberg's Staff should be authorized, in the occupied territories under military administration and in the occupied Eastern territories under civil administration (exclusive of the General Gouvernement), to search libraries, archives, lodges and other philosophical and cultural institutions of all types for relevant material for the execution of his task and to request the competent Wehrmacht and police services to seize the material found in order to support the NSDAP in fulfillment of its spiritual task and for the later scientific research work of the "Hohe Schule", whereby police files concerning political activities will remain with the police, and all others be transferred to Reichsleiter Rosenberg's Staff. The staff is authorized to make the same request with regard to cultural goods that are ownerless goods or the ownership of which cannot be readily determined. The Chief of the Army High Command, in agreement with Reichsleiter Rosenberg, will issue regulations governing the cooperation with the Wehrmacht. The necessary measures within the Eastern territories under German administration will be taken by Reichsleiter Rosenberg in his capacity as Reichsminister for the occupied Eastern territories.

I inform you of this order of the Fuehrer and request you to support Reichsleiter Rosenberg in the fulfillment of his task.

/s/ Dr. Lammers

Translation of Document 155-PS. *Instructions to Army Commands throughout occupied Europe, 30 September 1942, to cooperate with units of the Einsatzstab Rosenberg (Rosenberg's staff for seizing Jewish property, libraries and art treasures).*

* * *

Army High Command,
General Staff of the General Headquarters
Headquarters Army High Command 30/9/1942.

Az. Dept. War Administration
No. II/11564/42

SUBJECT: Deployment of Special Units of the Special Service Staff of Reichsleiter Rosenberg, for the occupied Eastern areas.

I. *Tasks:*

The Fuehrer, in his decree of 1/3/1942, has delegated Reichsleiter Rosenberg in his capacity as "Commissioner for the supervision of the entire spiritual and philosophical indoctrination and education of the NSDAP", with the spiritual battle against Jews, Free-Masons and the affiliated philosophical opponents of National Socialism, who are the cause of the present war. The planned spiritual battle against these powers was declared essential to the war effort by the Fuehrer. For this purpose, the Fuehrer has ordered, among other things, that the "Special Purpose Staff of Reichsleiter Rosenberg for the occupied areas" should be authorized in the occupied areas under military administration and in the occupied Eastern territories under civil administration—exclusive of the General Government—to

a. Search libraries, archives, lodges, and other philosophical and cultural institutions of all kinds, for material suitable to the accomplishment of his task, and to have this material seized.

b. To cause the seizure of cultural goods which are owned by

Jews, or without ownership, or the owner of which cannot readily be determined.

c. The Reich minister of the occupied Eastern territories has established on 12/6/1942 a "Central Office for the seizure and safekeeping of cultural goods in the occupied Eastern Territories." Disregarding exceptional cases, in which the safeguarding of endangered cultural goods is urgent, it is desired to keep these goods in place for the present. This has been agreed upon, according to the agreement reached between Armed Forces High Command General Staff of the General Headquarters, and the Special Purpose Staff of Reichsleiter Rosenberg.

d. In the Eastern Theatre of operations, also such cultural goods as do not fall under §*b*—especially museum pieces—are to be concealed, respectively safeguarded, to save them from damage or destruction.

For the accomplishment of the missions named in I*a, b* and *c*, the "Special Purpose Staff Reichsleiter Rosenberg" employs special units. With the consent of Reichsleiter Rosenberg, the deployment of these special units is regulated as follows:

1. For the central steering of the Special Units, according to need, a delegate of the Special Purpose Staff of Reichsleiter is employed, who is director of the Special Units in the Army Group area, respectively the Army area. This man is obligated to inform the Supreme Commander of the Army Group respectively Army in time, of the directives he has received from Reichsleiter Rosenberg or from the staff leader. The Supreme Commander is authorized to give the delegate directives which are necessary to avoid disturbing the operations. These directives supersede all others. The delegates depend upon steady and close cooperation with the G-2 (Intelligence Officer). The Special Unit authorities can demand the furnishing of a liaison man by the delegate to the G-2. The G-2 has to coordinate, the missions of the Special Purpose Units with the military intelligence [Abwehr] and the secret field police. For the cooperation with the defense officers, respectively defense offices, the decisions reached in the talks between Special Purpose Staff Rosenberg and Armed Forces High Command/Foreign intelligence, will apply.

2. The Special Units of Reichsleiter Rosenberg carry out their work in their own responsibility and according to the directives given by Reichsleiter Rosenberg.

3. For the accomplishment of the missions described in I*a, b, c*, the Special Units Reichsleiter Rosenberg have the right to search buildings in the theater of operations for relevant mate-

rial and confiscate it. The secret field police is to be informed of the confiscations. The secret field police furnishes official aid to the Special Units if necessary.

4. The demarcation line between the working territory of the Special Units Reichsleiter Rosenberg and the Special Units of the Chief of the Security Police and the security service is regulated by direct agreement between both service offices.

5. *a.* The Special Units belong to the Armed Forces. They wear brown uniforms with the swastika insignia.

b. The Special Units have a strength of 20-25 men, their clothes and equipment, together with a corresponding number of vehicles, is secured by the Special Purpose Staff, Reichsleiter Rosenberg.

c. The Special Units are always subordinated to the service branches to which they are attached for the execution of their mission, with respect to care, march, accommodation and rations.

d. The members of the Special Units are identified by a "service-book" of the Special Purpose Staff Reichsleiter Rosenberg, which corresponds to the pay-book. This service-book is to contain always the rank of the owner. It is further noted there, how the owner is to be treated in comparison (E.M., NCO, Officer). The service branch, which receives a Special Purpose Unit, has to certify on a special sheet, provided for this purpose by the service office, the fact and duration of the deployment with this branch as members of the Armed Forces. The service-book counts as identity card.

e. The Special Units are eligible for medical care. They are to be vaccinated according to the orders given to the Army.

f. Distribution of a fuel contingent is always to be arranged with the chief quartermaster of the Army with which a special unit is placed. Vehicles are to be cared for by the H.K.P.

g. Field postal service of the Special Units during movement, is carried by way of the field post number of the service branch which has a Special Unit attached. By transformation to long, permanent work, application for their own field post number can be made with the army field postmaster concerned.

h. Under priority of military necessity the Special Units have the right to use Armed Forces telephone and telegraph lines forward, and, when possible, also to the rear. Within the area of the military administrations, connection with the Armed Forces telephone net is to be made possible.

i. With regard to the use of means of transportation, the rules decreed for the Army also apply to the Special Units. Armed

Forces driving licenses are to be furnished by the service branch, to which a Special Unit is attached.

It is to be made certain, that the above regulations are always made known to the commanding authorities, which receive Special Units for deployment.

The Special Units Reichsleiter Rosenberg are to be supported in every way in the execution of their mission. Particularly, insofar as operations permit, deployment directly with the fighting troops is to be made possible.

IV. Independent of the missions of the Special Units Reichsleiter Rosenberg, in accordance with paragraph I*a*, *b*, *c*, the troops and all military service offices employed in the theater of operations, are directed to save valuable art monuments whenever possible, and safeguard them from destructions or damages.

The preliminary safeguarding of cultural goods, museums, etc. by the troops and military service units under subsequent agreement, respectively yield to Special Units Reichsleiter Rosenberg, wins particular significance in the occupied Eastern territories where, in contrast to the West and South East, no organizations for the protection of art have been designated by Armed Forces High Command/General Staff of the Army/Generals' Quarters.

By direction

/s/ Wagner

Distribution

All High Commands of the Army Groups with signal co's [Nachrichtenabteilung] 5; each for all field commanders of the Army territory.

All Army High Commands and Panzer Army High Commands with signal co's [Nachrichtenabteilung] each, Staff Don with 3 signal co's [Nachrichtenabteilungen].

Military Commander in France, Paris

Military Commander in Belgium, and Northern France, Brussels

Army Territory (W.B.) South East

(with each 6 Signal co's [Nachrichtenabteilung])

With each 2 signal co's for Commander, General and
    Military Governor of Serbia
    Military Governor of Soloniki-Agnis
    Military Governor Southern Greece

With each 1 Signal co's for the Commander of the Fortress Crete, Foreign Branch Armed Forces High Command/Gen-

eral Headquarters South, Armed Forces High Command/ Armed Forces Command Staff.
With each 2 Signal Battalions for Military Governor Eastland, Military Governor Ukraine.
Reichsminister for the occupied Eastern territories, Berlin, with each 2 Signal co's [Nachrichtenabteilungen].
Special Purpose Staff Reichsleiter Rosenberg for the occupied territories, Berlin-Charlottenburg, Bismarckstr. 1.
Center—Force—East.

Translation of Document 158-PS (USA 382). Message, 1 June 1944, initialed Utikal, Chief of Staff of Einsatzstab Rosenberg (Rosenberg's staff for seizing Jewish property, libraries and art treasures), concerning a special unit dispatched to Hungary.

* * *

Berlin W 35, Margaretenstr. 17, 1 June 1944
22 95 51 St—U/Sz

MESSAGE

The Einsatzstab of Reichsleiter Rosenberg for the occupied territories has dispatched a Sonderkommando under the direction of Stabseinsatzfuehrer Dr. Zeiss, who is identified by means of his Service Book Number 187, for the accomplishment of the missions of the Einsatzstab in Hungary described in the Fuehrer's Decree of 1 March 1942.

According to the Fuehrer's Decree of 1 March 1942 (transmitted to the Supreme Reichs authorities by means of a letter of the Reichs Minister and Chief of the Reichs Chancellory RK 9495 B) in connection with the Army High Command Order #II 11564/42 General Army Staff (Gen d H)/General Quartermaster-Az (Gen Qu-Az) Section K Administration (Administration) of 30 Sept 42, all offices are requested to support and help the Sonderkommando.

initial: U [Utikal]

Translation of Document 159-PS (USA 380). Message, 6 June 1944, initialed Utikal, Chief of Staff of Einsatzstab Rosenberg (Rosenberg's staff for seizing Jewish property, libraries and art treasures), concerning special unit dispatched to Denmark and Norway.

* * *

159-PS   Nazi Germany's War Against the Jews

Berlin 6 June 1944

Movement Order

Colonel-Einsatzfuehrer H. W. Ebeling is traveling to Denmark and Norway in order to carry out a special mission of Reichsleiter Rosenberg in harmony with the person authorized by the Reich in Denmark and the Reichs Commissar in Norway in conjunction with the Fuehrer's decree of 1 March 1942 (distributed to the highest Reich authorities through correspondence of the Reichs Minister and the Chief of the Reich Chancellery RK 9495 B) and the Supreme Army Command Order Nr. II/11564/42, General Staff of the Army/General Quartermaster Az. Section K Administration of the 30th Sept. 42.

As long as it is necessary for him to stay, all the offices of the State and the Army are directed to support the activities of the person mentioned on the basis of the Fuehrer decree of 1 March 1942, the Supreme Army Command Order of 30 September 1942, and the Einsatz directive of the Head of the Security Police and Security Service of the 1st July 1942.

                       initialled: U [Utikal]
                       Chief of the Einsatzstab

Translation of Document 171-PS (USA 383). *Undated report on "Library for Exploration of the Jewish Question" by the Hohe Schule District Office.*

*   *   *

Library for Exploration of the Jewish Question

"Hohe Schule", District Office, Frankfurt/Main.
Institute for Exploration of the Jewish question

On 26 March 1941 Reichsleiter Alfred Rosenberg inaugurated as the first district office of the "Hohe Schule" in Frankfurt/Main the Institute for Exploration of the Jewish Question (Frankfurt/Main Bockenheimer Landstrasse 68).

According to the order of the Fuehrer from 29 Jan 1940 the "Hohe Schule" is supposed to represent "the center of the national-socialist doctrine and education." At the same time Reichsleiter Rosenberg was authorized to make all necessary preparations for the foundation of the "Hohe Schule" in the realm of research and organization of libraries.

The district office in Frankfurt/Main, activated under those

The Documentary Evidence　　　　　　　　　　　　　　171-PS

preparatory measures, competent for the domain of the Jewish question, contains besides a research-department and archives, a voluminous library whose stock shall be the subject of this article.

The basis for the library for exploration of the Jewish question is made up of the libraries from occupied territories, confiscated by the Einsatzstab Reichsleiter Rosenberg, in accordance with the orders of the Fuehrer from 5 July 1940, 17 Sept 1940 and 1 March 1942. This material is derived from Jewish property, now centrally collected to serve the research, doctrine and education of the German people.

The most significant book-collections today belonging to the stock of the "Library for exploration of the Jewish question", are the following:

1. The library of the *Alliance Israelite Universelle*. Among the approximately *40,000 volumes* of this library from Paris (mainly Judaica and Hebraica) are numerous volumes of magazines, voluminous pamphlet material, a very detailed literature and collection of clippings from newspapers regarding the affair Dreyfus, about 200 Hebrew manuscripts and 30 manuscripts in other languages, about 20 incunabula.

2. The stock of the *Ecole Rabbinique* consists mostly of Judaica and Hebraica, altogether about *10,000 volumes*. The Jewish texts of this Rabbi-school in Paris offers valuable Talmud-material and complete magazine series.

3. The library of the *Federation de Societe des Juifs de France* (about *4000 volumes*) contains besides general literature about Jewry mostly Russian literature about the Jewish question.

4. The stock of the Jewish bookstore in Paris *Lipschuetz* (about *20,000 volumes*) contains in its most valuable part bibliographical works, Hebraica and so on.

5. The various collections from former property of the *Rothschilds* of Paris generally are of no more than common interest, but they also show that the various members of the Rothschild family collected Jewish literature for their own orientation. The collections in question are the following:

    a. Collection *Edouard Rothschild* (about *6,000 volumes*)
    b. Collection *Edouard and Guy Rothschild* (about *3,000 volumes*)
    c. Collection *Maurice Rothschild* (about *6,000 volumes*)
    d. Collection *Robert Rothschild* (about *10,000 volumes*)
    e. Collection of the Rothschild family from hunting lodge *Armainvilliers* (about *3,000 volumes*)

These Rothschild collections contain, besides the valuable

book stock, important archive material which gives information on connections between Jews and non-Jews in France and abroad. In this connection it should be mentioned that the district office Frankfurt/Main also is in possession of the archives of the last 100 years of the Parisian bank of Rothschild (760 boxes).

6. The *Rosenthaliana* from Amsterdam with *20,000 volumes* (mostly German language literature on the Jewish question).

7. The library of the *Sefardic Jewish community in Amsterdam* with about *25,000 volumes* (mostly Hebraica).

8. The large amount of books secured in the *occupied eastern territories* (prevalent Soviet-Jewish and Polish-Jewish literature, voluminous Talmud literature) are from collecting points in Riga, Kauen, Wilna, Minsk and Kiev (about *280,000 volumes*).

9. Book collections from Jewish communities in *Greece* (about *10,000 volumes*).

10. Book material from a "Sonderaktion" in the Rhineland (collecting point *Neuwied*) with about *5,000 volumes*.

11. The book collections mentioned under 1-10 were turned over to the Library for Exploration of the Jewish Question by the Einsatzstab Reichsleiter Rosenberg and are constantly being filled up by new shipments from the Einsatzstab. Besides that, some 100,000 volumes which were obtained from other sources (finance offices and so on) by the district office, belong to the library for exploration of the Jewish question. Therefore, the library for exploration of the Jewish questions contains as of 1 April 1943:

Approximately *550,000 volumes* (about 3,300 book boxes) including 325 boxes (approx. 24,000 volumes) earmarked for the district office but still kept in Berlin with the Staff, and including approx. 220,000 volumes (about 650 boxes) prepared for shipment to Frankfurt/Main at the various collecting points of the Einsatzstab and partly packed.

In detail, these stocks deposited in Berlin cover the material of the above under Nos. 3, 5*b*, *d* and *e* mentioned libraries (about 17,000 volumes), furthermore parts of the collections mentioned under Nos. 5*a* and *c* (about 7,000 volumes); all the books at the collecting points ready for shipment to Frankfurt/Main cover the whole stock as the collections mentioned under Nos. 6 and 7 (about 50,000 volumes), part of that material secured in the East (compare No. 8 above; there are in Minsk about 20,000 volumes, in Wilna about 50,000 volumes and in Kiev about 100,000 volumes). The stocks mentioned here which are still in Berlin or at the collecting points, make up approximately another *240,000 volumes*. The district office in Frankfurt/Main has received so far approximately *300,000 volumes* (about 2,325 boxes).

Of these, approximately 2,325 book boxes which arrived at the library for exploration of the Jewish question, were so far unpacked and put on bookshelves:

- 567 boxes of the Alliance Israelite Universelle (out of 656 boxes)
- 165 boxes of the Ecole Rabbinique (out of 243 boxes)
- 50 boxes of the book store Lipschuetz (out of 197 boxes)
- 84 boxes of the collection Edouard Rothschild (the remaining 75 boxes are still in Berlin)
- 23 boxes of the collection Maurice Rothschild (the remaining 39 boxes are still in Berlin)
- 159 boxes of the collection point Riga (the whole stock)

Thus 1,048 book boxes (about 150,000 volumes) were unpacked that is half of the book boxes, so far received in Frankfurt/Main.

27,848 volumes were catalogued in Frankfurt/Main from 1 May 1941 (beginning of cataloguing) to 31 March 1943 (catalogued according to authors and subjects). According to the same principle the new publications which were put into the library for the exploration of the Jewish question since 1941, were catalogued—9,325 volumes.

Apart from the actual importance of the Jewish question, the library for the research of the Jewish question assumes a high position in the realm of German libraries with its present collection of about 550,000 volumes because this Frankfurt library could be brought to such a degree of completeness as regards the literature on the Jewish question as never before in Europe or elsewhere. In the New Order of Europe Organization *the* library for the Jewish question not only for Europe but for the world will arise in Frankfurt on the Main.

Translation of Document 176-PS (USA 707). *Report on Einsatzstab Rosenberg (Rosenberg's staff for seizing Jewish property, libraries and art treasures) Working Group Netherlands, signed Schimmer, listing lodges and Jewish libraries confiscated.*

* * *

REPORT

On the activities of the Einsatzstab of the Bureau of the Reichsleiter Rosenberg in the occupied Western Territories and The Netherlands. Working Group Netherland

The Working Group Netherland of the Einsatzstab Reichsleiter Rosenberg began its work in agreement with the competent representative of the Reichskommissar during the first days of September, 1940. The execution of the past, conforming with the Fuehrer's orders, coordinated itself with the liquidation, that is confiscation, according to civil law, of the various subversive institutions—as set forth in the circulars of the OKW (A2 Nr. 2850/40g Adj. Chief OKW), dated 5 July 1940, and of the Chief of the OKW to the Commander in Chief of the Wehrmacht in France (2 f 28.14WZ Nr. 3812/40g) dated 17 September 1940, as well as to the Commander in Chief of the OKW in the Netherlands. (Az 2 f 28 J (IA) Nr. 1338/40g) dated 30 October 1940. The screening of the material of the various Masonic lodges was taken care of primarily, and the library and the archives of the following lodges were sifted and all useful material was packed.

[List of Lodges Confiscated Follows in Original Document.]

All together 470 cases combining material from the here mentioned lodges and from organizations of a similar status were packed and transported to Germany. Furthermore, everything the temple of the lodge in Nijmegen and the temple of the I. O. O. F. in Haarlem contained, was sent to Germany. Also, steel-shelves for about 30,000 books were taken from the building belonging to the Grooten Oosten in Den Haag where they have so far been used for the Bibliotheka Klossiana, containing parts of one library of the Grooten Oosten, and the library of the Vrijmetselar-Stichting, Amsterdam, are of great value. And so are the archives of the Grooten Oosten in Den Haag, containing all the historical documents of the lodges affiliated with it.

To estimate the value of the Bibliotheka Klossiana, containing many rare pieces, it is to be remembered that in 1930 the Grooten Oosten der Nederlande was offered $5,000,000 for the Bibliotheka Klossiana by Freemasons in the U. S.

A particularly valuable discovery was made by the Working Group searching the altars in the building of the Grooten Oosten in Den Haag. The Master-Hammer of the Grooten Oosten, made of pure gold, which some of its members had presented to the Grooten Oosten on its 60th Anniversary, fell into our hands. It is a piece of high quality whose money-value alone is estimated to be 3,000 Reichsmark.

The Working Group took over the International Institute for Social History in Amsterdam with its library and archives, boxes of extraordinary value. It seems that this Institute was founded in 1934 with the intention of creating a center of intellectual resistance against National Socialism. Its employees were mainly Jewish refugees from Germany. The contents of its library and its archives with many very valuable items were brought together from all over the world. In the library, there are about 160,000 volumes, though most of them will have to be catalogued. Of particular interest is the German, French and Russian Department. According to the decision made by Reichsleiter Rosenberg, the Institute was taken over in its entity. A member of the Dienstelle was nominated as Director of the Institute—he, together with his collaborators, will arrange the books, catalogue the scientific material and get the Institute ready for the work of the Party. What may be said already is that the scientific value of the library and the archives is that they contain a complete collection of material on the social and socialist movements in certain countries.

The libraries of the Societas Spinozana in Den Haag and of the Spinoza-House in Rijnsburg also were packed. Packed in 18 cases, they, too, contain extremely valuable early works of great importance for the exploration of the Spinoza problem. Not without reason did the Director of the Societas Spinozana try, under false pretenses which we uncovered, to withhold the library from us.

Then the library of the Alliance Francaise, Den Haag, was packed (6 cases) as well as the German publication of the refugee-publishers Aller de Lange, Querido, Fischer-Beerman, Forum-Zeek, of the Kultura Bookshop and the publications of the Pegasus-Verlag, all in Amsterdam, a total of 17 cases. After that, the Working Group concentrated on packing the newspaper and magazine stocks of the International Institute for Social History. The very exclusive racks which had been brought together from all over the world were kept at the Institute in complete disorder and left to self-destruction; they were properly packed into 776 cases and stored, for the time being, in the Working Groups' storehouses. It is very strongly suggested that these newspapers and magazines be bound and the volumes be put up in proper libraries as fast as possible; otherwise, an irreparable loss will be the result since these newspapers and magazines are from all over the world.

A large unknown amount of material classified as "Enemy

Goods" and coming from the so-called "Overseas-Gifts", that is, household goods of Jewish refugees, is falling into our hands daily. These gifts are being kept at the so-called "House in Holland", and so far 43 cases were packed there, including the private library of the former Minister of the Eisner-Government, Neurath.

In agreement with the Commander-in-Chief of the Wehrmacht in the Netherlands, all libraries in houses of Jewish refugees and confiscated by the Wehrmacht, are being turned over to the Working Group. So far, the library of the Jew De Cat in Haarlem was packed into 4 cases.

An extremely valuable library, containing inestimable works in Sanskrit, was confiscated when the Theosophic Society in Amsterdam was dissolved, and packed into 96 cases.

A number of smaller libraries belonging to the Spiritists, Esperanto Movement, the Bellamy Movement, the International Biblical Research and various other minor international organizations were packed into 7 cases; texts belonging to various minor Jewish organizations were packed into 4 cases, and a library of the Anthroposophic Society in Amsterdam into three.

It is safe to say that the racks of books confiscated, packed and so far sent to Germany by the Working Group are of extraordinary scientific value and shall contribute an integral part of the library of the "Hohe Schule." The money-value of these libraries, as shown in the case of the "Klossiana", can only be estimated, but surely amount to 30-40,000,000 Reichsmark.

For the coming months, action is planned on the following, enumerated here in chronological order:

1. The libraries of the Theosophic Society and similar organizations in Den Haag, Rotterdam and several other places.

2. Continuous sifting of objects confiscated in the "House in Holland" and other buildings.

3. Screening of several archives with press-photos, consisting altogether of 2.6 million pictures which shall be turned over to us by the Reichskommissariat.

4. The Jewish private libraries in Amsterdam, particularly:

A. The Israelite Library Beth-Hamidrasch Etz Chaim, Amsterdam, Rapenburgerstraat 109. This library, founded in 1740, contains about 4,000 volumes, particularly Jewish theology.

B. Library of the Netherland Israelite Seminar, Amsterdam, Rapenburgerstraat 177. It contains 4,300 volumes of Hebraica and 2,000 volumes Judaica. At the time, it took over the library of the Jewish Society for Literature, Thoelet (1830-1837) and valuable Jewish private collections. Amongst other things, it contains precious old prints from the years 1480 to 1560 and some manuscripts.

C. The Portuguese-Israelite Seminar, Amsterdam, Jonas Daniel Meyerplein 5. There are 25,000 volumes, 450 manuscripts, 600 prints [Inkunablen] and numerous Exlibris, coins and the like and the famous material on Talmud Literature.

D. The so-called Rosentaliana, primarily a foundation by the Jew Rosenthal from Hannover. From there, it was at the time transferred and affiliated with the local university library. In the meantime, it has on account of donations, grown considerably. Technically, it belongs to the Municipality of Amsterdam, but in the Catalogue of Libraries in the Netherlands of 1931, it is designated as "Private". According to the catalogue, it contains 25,000 volumes and 300 manuscripts. However, the amount of volumes reaches 100,000 indeed.

The libraries mentioned under 4 ought to be of particular interest for the history of Western Europe. It is very likely that hitherto unknown facts may be brought into the open, on the era of Cromwell and that of the glorious Revolution of 1688 and the resulting personal union between England and the Netherlands. In particular, light may be thrown on Cromwell's attitude toward the Jews, possibly even on the Jewish influence on the development of the Secret Service.

The temple and the museum of the Grooten Oosten der Nederlande. At present, both are needed for exhibitions on behalf of the Dienstelle of the Reichskommissar. With the end of the exhibition temple furnishings and museum shall be turned over to us.

A very conservative estimate of the value of the objects enumerated in 1 to 5 may be about three times as much as that of the libraries already packed. Therefore, it is safe to say that the library of the "Hohe Schule" shall, with very little effort, receive an extraordinary amount of treasures which shall give it a unique position in the realm of questions regarding Judaism and Free-Masonism.

The Working Group, in executing the afore-mentioned tasks, is bound strictly to the pace set by the Reichskommissar for the handling of the Jewish questions and that of the international organizations. This pace again is determined by the political evolution which is taking shape according to decisions made on a higher level, and which must not be hampered by individual acts. Work that has been authorized to be done by the Working Group, but has not yet been accomplished should now, with twice as much personnel as before, be finished within 2 to 3 months. It may be mentioned that the Working Group has been working overtime for weeks now, and also is working, as is done on the battlefield, on Sundays.

The leader of the Working Group Netherland.

Schimmer
Oberbereichsleiter.

Translation of Document 212-PS (USA 272). *Memorandum from Rosenberg file concerning instructions for treatment of Jews in the East.*

* * *

COPY

Directions for the handling of the Jewish question

1. *In General.* The competency of the Chief of the Security Police and Security Service, who is charged with the mission of solving the European Jewish question, extends even to the occupied eastern provinces. Accordingly, the offices under the Security Police for the purpose of handling the Jewish question in the occupied eastern provinces are qualified for their present sphere of activity.

In the individual Reichs commissariats, and within these, in the General commissariats, Jewry represents a portion of the population which is very varied in strength. For example, millions of Jews live in White Russia and in the Ukraine who have lived here for generations. In the central province of the USSR, however, the Jews have moved in, for by far the greatest part, during Bolshevistic times. Those Russian Jews who followed in the wake of the invading Red Army of 1939 and 1940 to East Poland, West Ukraine, West White Russia, the Baltic lands, Bessarabia, and Buchenland are one particular group.

All measures for the Jewish question in the occupied eastern provinces must be met with the point of view that the whole Jewish question will be solved in general for all of Europe after the war at the latest. They are therefore to be instituted as preparatory partial measures and must be in agreement with those decisions which may otherwise be met in this field. This is especially true for the preparation of at least temporary reception centers for Jews from the Reich province.

An eventual act by the civilian population against the Jews is not to be prevented as long as this is compatible with the maintenance of order and security in the rear of the fighting troops. Namely, retaliatory measures are to be allowed against the Jews who come into the provinces which were newly occupied by the Red Army in the last few years. However, strict measures are to be taken against street mobs and other evil elements for whom it concerns only plunder of Jewish stores and stealing Jewish property for their own personal gain.

2. *Definition of the term "Jew".* The peaceful settlement of the Jewish question requires the previous determining as to who is to be considered a Jew in the occupied Eastern provinces. In reference to the solving of the European Jewish question and to the strong influence which Jewry had upon the remaining Russian population until the invasion of German troops, and which it still exercises at present, it appears necessary from a political, as well as from a popular point of view, for the purpose of avoiding a later regaining strength of the Jews, to grasp the term "Jew" in the most far-reaching sense.

Therefore, he is a Jew, who belongs to the Jewish religion, or has been recognized as Jewish by other circumstances; he who has a parent who is a Jew in accordance with the above sentence is also a Jew.

3. *Comprehension, mark of recognition, suspension of the rights of freedom and segregation.* The first main goal of the German measures must be strict segregation of Jewry from the rest of the population. In the execution of this, first of all is the seizing of the Jewish populace by the introduction of a registration order and similar appropriate measures. Soviet Jewry has, constantly, attempted, since the Bolshevistic Revolution, to disguise itself in order to unobtrusively move into leading positions, especially in the grain regions of the USSR. For this purpose many Jews have dropped their Jewish names and have taken Russian family names and Russian surnames. It is to be decreed, that the person who must register must report all changes of name by Jews during his lifetime, or as far as he knows during the time of his forefathers, to his superior and to make them retrogressive. The same goes for previous departure from the religious congregation and acceptance of other faiths (other manifold). The erasure of the Jewish deception will be easier in the Reichs commissariat Eastland and Ukraine, where the larger part of the Jews have been living for generations than in the other Reichs commissariats. The Soviet archive material, in so far as it is preserved, is to be brought to use for this.

. Then immediately, the wearing of the recognition sign consisting of a yellow Jewish star is to be brought about and all rights of freedom for Jews are to be withdrawn. They are to be placed in Ghettos and at the same time are to be separated according to sexes. The presence of many more or less closed Jewish settlements in White Ruthenia and in the Ukraine makes this mission easier. Moreover, places are to be chosen which make possible the full use of the Jewish manpower in case labor needs are present. These Ghettos can be placed under the supervision of a Jewish self-government with Jewish officials. The guarding of the boundaries between the Ghettos and the outer world is, however, the duty of the police.

Also in the cases in which a Ghetto could not yet be established, care is to be taken through strict prohibitions and similar suitable measures that a further intermingling of blood of the Jews and the rest of the populace does not continue.

4. *Removal of the Jewish influence in political, economical, cultural and social fields.* Relative with the measures to segregate the Jews physically from the rest of the populace, everything necessary is to be used in order to eliminate every influence of the Jewry upon the Russian people. This is to happen immediately in political and cultural fields, whereas in all other cases consideration is to be taken that the common interests are not impaired. This is especially true for the economic missions which are important due to the demands of the war and those which concern the national economy.

An entire reconversion of Jewish professional life must be brought about insofar as it does not deal with manual laborers. The group of State employees in the Russian government along with the strongest Jewish professional groups shall vanish entirely. Likewise, similar professional groups are to be divorced from the public life, whereby, however, the tempo of these measures must correspond with the general economical and social need.

The entire Jewish property is to be seized and confiscated with exception of that which is necessary for a bare existence. As far as the economical situation permits, the power of disposal of their property is to be taken from the Jews as soon as possible through orders and other measures given by the commissariat, so that the moving of property will quickly cease.

Any cultural activity will be completely forbidden to the Jew. This includes the outlawing of the Jewish press, the Jewish theatres and schools.

The slaughtering of animals according to Jewish rites is also to be prohibited.

5. *Forced Labor.* The present manpower shortage in the occupied eastern territories as well as the ideological-political considerations make the demand appear of basic significance to introduce forced labor commitment in the strictest form. This will have to take place move by move by the elimination of the Jews from their professional life although they are to be permitted to work in their own occupations if they fall within the scope of the labor commitment. Moreover, the Jewish manpower is to be used for heavy manual labor.

The standing rule for the Jewish labor employment is the complete and unyielding use of Jewish manpower regardless of age in the reconstruction of the occupied eastern territories. The missions, which are to be given to the Jews in their labor employment, are especially the highway, railroad and canal construction, as far as the ameliorations, etc. are considered. Also, it seems that agricultural employment above all, will be brought about under strict supervision. Nothing is to be done against the employment of the Jews in cutting of wood, production of straw shoes, brooms and brushes within the Ghettos.

In the employment of the Jews, care is to be taken that Jewish labor is only so used in those productions which will later suffer no noticeable interruption in case of a rapid withdrawal of these labor forces, and which excludes a specialization of Jewish workers. It is to be avoided in every case that Jewish workers become indispensable in essential production.

6. *Violations.* Violations against German measures, especially against the forced labor regulations, are to be punishable by death to the Jews. All violations are to be dealt with by courts-martial.

Translation of Document 342-PS. Decree, 13 October 1941, directing the confiscation of Jewish property in the Reichs Commissariat Ostland.

* * *

Reichs Commissioner for the East [Ostland] Sect. II h
Directions concerning the Treatment of Jewish Property in the Reichs Commissariat Ostland of 13 October 1941

Par. 1

The total, movable and immovable properties of the Jewish population in the territories governed by the Reichs Commissioner for Eastern areas are placed under confiscation by the administration for the commission and the seizure according to the following regulations.

Par. 2

Property is defined as movable and immovable objects along with all accessories, claims, commissions, rights and interests of all types.

Par. 3

1. The confiscation will be carried out by the Reich Commissioner for the East or those officers who have been authorized by him. It can be carried out by directives to individual persons or in general by a proclamation and can be limited to individual objects of wealth.

2. The following shall be excluded from confiscation:

a. That part of the household furniture which will take care of the basic essentials of life.

b. Cash, bank and savings credit, as well as bonds, up to a total value of one hundred Reichsmarks.

Par. 4

1. With the confiscation the previous owner loses all rights to dispose of the confiscated property.

2. Whoever has confiscated property in possession or custody, will administer it until further notice. The changing or disposal of the property or of its profits will only be allowed inside the bounds of orderly management. All other measures taken beyond this will need the approval of the Reichs Commissioner for the East or those agencies authorized by him.

Par. 5

1. The property that is placed under confiscation can be brought under the administration of the commission, so far as it is necessary for orderly management.

2. The assuming of control by the administrative commission will at the same time be looked upon as confiscation.

3. The Reichs Commission for the East will issue directives about the arrangement and management of this administration.

Par. 6

1. Confiscated property can be called in by the Reichs Commissioner for the East or by the agencies authorized by him.

2. The disposal of the confiscated property will be left to the authorized agencies.

3. These agencies will decide with finality, using administrative means, on the debts which belong to the confiscated property. The responsibility will be limited to the sales value of the confiscated property.

Par. 7

Bids for the purchase of the property which comes under confiscation can be publicly advertised.

Par. 8

The responsible authorities can demand information from everyone to carry out their task.

Par. 9

1. The following will be punished with a prison sentence and monetary fine or one of those punishments.

a. Those who will undertake to withdraw an object of value from the offices of the civil authorities or those installed with the authority for disposal, or in any other manner to thwart, to evade, or to impair the action of confiscation.

b. Those who intentionally or carelessly do not fulfill in due time or completely one of those directives imposed upon him, such as an order of execution or other directive of execution, and the report and information obligations concerning it.

2. In severe cases the punishment is penal servitude. If the accused is charged with willful disobedience or should it be any other especially severe case, the death sentence is authorized.

Par. 10

The Reichs Commissioner in the East will issue the necessary measures to carry out those directives.

Par. 11

The directive will go into effect on the day of its publication.

Riga, 13 October 1941
The Reichs Commissioner for the East
Signed: LOHSE

Translation of Document 404-PS (USA 256). *Excerpts from Hitler, Mein Kampf, pp. 456, 457, 675, on racial superiority and attacking international world finance Jewry.*

* * *

MEIN KAMPF
Adolf Hitler
German Edition, 1935

[Pages 456 to 457]

It is precisely our German people, that today, broken down, lies defenseless against the kicks of the rest of the world who need that suggestive force that lies in self-confidence. But this *self-confidence has to be instilled* into the young fellow-citizen from childhood on. His entire education and development has to be directed at giving him *the conviction of being absolutely superior to others*. With this physical force and skill he has again to win the belief in the invincibility of his entire nationality. For what once led the German Army to victory was the sum of the confidence which the individual and all in common had in their leaders. The confidence in *the possibility of regaining its freedom* is what will restore the German people. But this conviction must be the final product of the same feeling of millions of individuals.

* * * * * * *

[Page 475]

The racial State will have to see to it that there will be a generation which, by a suitable education, will be ready for the final and ultimate decision on this globe. The nation which enters first on this course will be the victorious one.

[Page 675]

MEIN KAMPF
Adolf Hitler
Munich, 1933, 39th Edition.

The trade union in national-socialist interpretation, has not the mission to gradually transform into one class, through condensation, all the various individuals among the people, thereby to take up the fight against other similarly organized structures within the nation. On the whole we cannot assign this mission to the trade union, rather it was first conferred on it at the moment in which it became the weapon of Marxism. It is not that the trade union is imbued with the spirit of the class struggle, directly, on the contrary, Marxism has made of it an instrument for its class war. It created the economic weapon which the international world Jew uses for the ruination of the economic basis of free, independent national states, for the annihilation of their national industry and of their national commerce, and thereby for the enslavement of free peoples in the service of international world finance Jewry.

Translation of Document 501-PS (USA 288). Collection of four documents on execution of Jews by gas, June 1942, one signed by Dr. Becker, SS Untersturmfuehrer at Kiev, 16 May 1942.

* * *

Field Post Office
No 32704
B Nr 40/42

Kiev, 16 May 1942

TOP SECRET

To: SS-Obersturmbannfuehrer Rauff
Berlin, Prinz-Albrecht-Str. 8

[Handwritten:]
pers.
R/29/5 Pradel n.R
b/R

[Handwritten:] Sinkkel [?] b.R, p 16/6

The overhauling of vans by groups D and C is finished. While the vans of the first series can also be put into action if the weather is not too bad, the vans of the second series *(Saurer) stop completely in rainy weather*. If it has rained for instance for only one half hour, the van cannot be used because it simply skids away. It can only be used in absolutely dry weather. It is only a question now whether the van can only be used standing at the place of execution. First the van has to be brought to that place, which is possible only in good weather. The place of execution is usually 10-15 km away from the highways and is difficult to access because of its location; in damp or wet weather it is not accessible at all. If the persons to be executed are driven or led to that place, then they realize immediately what is going on and get restless, which is to be avoided as far as possible. There is only one way left; to load them at the collecting point and to drive them to the spot.

I ordered the vans of group D to be camouflaged as house-trailers by putting one set of window shutters on each side of the small van and two on each side of the larger vans, such as one often sees on farm-houses in the country. The vans became so well-known, that not only the authorities, but also the civilian population called the van "death van", as soon as one of these vehicles appeared. It is my opinion, the van cannot be kept secret for any length of time, not even camouflaged.

The Saurer-van which I transported from Simferopol to Taganrog suffered damage to the brakes on the way. The Security Command [SK] in Mariupol found the cuff of the combined oil-air brake broken at several points. By persuading and bribing the H.K.P. [?] we managed to have a form machined, on which the cuffs were cast. When I came to Stalino and Gorlowka a few days later, the drivers of the vans complained about the same faults. After having talked to the commandants of those commands, I went once more to Mariupol to have some more cuffs made for those cars too. As agreed, two cuffs will be made for each car, six cuffs will stay in Mariupol as replacements for group D and six cuffs will be sent to SS-Untersturmfuehrer Ernst in Kiev for the cars of group C. The cuffs for the groups B and A could be made available from Berlin, because transport from Mariupol to the north would be too complicated and would take too long. Smaller damages on the cars will be repaired by experts of the commands, that is of the groups in their own shops.

Because of the rough terrain and the indescribable road and highway conditions the caulkings and rivets loosen in the course of time. I was asked if in such cases the vans should be brought to Berlin for repair. Transportation to Berlin would be much too expensive and would demand too much fuel. In order to save those expenses I ordered them to have smaller leaks soldered and if that should no longer be possible, to notify Berlin immediately by radio, that Pol. Nr..... is out of order. Besides that I ordered that during application of gas all the men were to be kept as far away from the vans as possible, so they should not suffer damage to their health by the gas which eventually would escape. I should like to take this opportunity to bring the following to your attention: several commands have had the unloading after the application of gas done by their own men. I brought to the attention of the commanders of those S.K. concerned the immense psychological injuries and damages to their health which that work can have for those men, even if not immediately, at least later on. The men complained to me about head-aches which appeared after each unloading. Nevertheless, they don't want to change the orders, because they are afraid prisoners called for that work could use an opportune moment to flee. To protect the men from these damages, I request orders be issued accordingly.

The application of gas usually is not undertaken correctly. In order to come to an end as fast as possible, the driver presses the accelerator to the fullest extent. By doing that the persons to be executed suffer death from suffocation and not death by dozing off as was planned. My directions now have proved that by correct adjustment of the levers death comes faster and the prisoners fall asleep peacefully. Distorted faces and excretions, such as could be seen before, are no longer noticed.

Today I shall continue my journey to group B, where I can be reached with further news.

                                          Signed: Dr. Becker
                                                     SS Untersturmfuehrer

Reich Security Main Office
Message Center

1900, 15 June 1942   [Handwritten:]
Riga E 2   II D 3a Maj Pradel
Message No. 152452   R 16/6
                                             Weiderhausen

Riga 7082—15–6–42—1855—BE
To Reich Security Main Office—Roem. 2D3A—Berlin

TOP SECRET

Subject: S-Vans

A transport of Jews, which has to be treated in a special way, arrives weekly at the office of the commandant of the Security Police and the Security Service of White Ruthenia.

The three S-vans, which are there, are not sufficient for that purpose. I request assignment of another S-van (5-tons). At the same time I request the shipment of 20 gas-hoses for the three S-vans on hand (2 Daimond, 1 Saurer), since the ones on hand are leaky already.

         The commandant of the Security Police and
                        the Security Service
                                      "Ostland"
                                 Roem IT—126/42 GRS

Stamp: Signed: Truehe, SS-Hauptsturmfuehrer
     No 240/42
     II D 3a 16 June 42
Procedure: [handwritten]
     1. When can we count on having another S-van ready?
     2. Are gas-hoses on hand, ordered or when to be delivered?
     3. Request answer.

                               R 16/6

                Reich Security Main Office
II D 3a B Nr 240/42   Berlin, 22 June 1942
                      TOP SECRET
                                     Stamped:
                                 Message Nr 107903
                             Sent by message center
                               2016, 22 June 42

1   FS [?]
     To the Commandant of the Security Police and
     Security Service Ostland

Riga
Subject: S-Van

The delivery of a 5-ton Saurer can be expected in the middle of next month. The vehicle has been at the Reich Security Main Office for repairs and minor alterations up to this time 100 meters of hose will be supplied.

By order of
[signature as in heading]

2. Dissemination at once by II D 3a (9)
By direction

Rauff

Handwritten note:

Berlin, 13 July 1942

II D 3a (9)

Nr I.Z. Widderhausen [?] for further action and attention to the note of 13 July 1942 on back page of telegram from Belgrad. For the reasons mentioned 5 sections of hose, each of 10 meters, can be supplied me.

By direction

[signature illegible]

Reich Security Main Office
Stamps: 1003 9 Jun 1942

handwritten:
After return
immediate repair

II D 3a No 964/42
10 June 1942

R 10/6
Notify about repair

ND. Nr 144702
Belgrad No. 3116 9.6.42 0950—SOM
To: Reich Security Office, Amt Roem 2 D 3 KL. A—Z. HD. V.
Major Pradel—Berlin.
Subject: Special-van-Saurer
Preceding messages: None

The Drivers SS-Scharfuehrer Goetz and Meyer have fulfilled their special mission and could be ordered back with the van mentioned above. In consequence of a broken rear-axle-half, transportation cannot be made by car.

Therefore I have ordered the vehicle loaded and shipped back to Berlin by railroad.

Estimated arrival between 11th and 12th June 1942. The drivers Goetz and Meyer will escort the vehicle.
The commandant of Security Police and Security Service Belgrad—Roem I—BNR 3985/42
Signed: Dr. Schaefer, SS-Obersturmbannfuehrer

[Handwritten note back page]

II D 3a (2)
T.O.S. a Dr. SUKKEL

Berlin, 11 June 1942

For further action and immediate start of repairs. I request to be informed about arrival of vans.
By direction:

signed: Just
Berlin, 16 June 1942

II D 3a (9)
Note

The vehicle arrived 6 June 1942 about 1300 h. After thorough cleaning the repairs will start immediately.
By direction

signed: [?]
Berlin, 13 July 1942.

II D 3a (9)
1. Note: The S-truck Pol 71463 is ready.
2. Sent to the *motor-pool management T. F. Niederhausen* for its information and further action.
By direction

signed: [?]

Translation of Document 502-PS (USA 486). Regulations dated 17 July 1941 on discovering all professional revolutionaries, functionaries of the Komintern, Jews, etc. from among Soviet Prisoners of War in camps and executing them.

* * *

TOP SECRET

B 101
Enclosures 2
Berlin, 17 July 1941

Office IV

Regulations (directives)
for the commandos of the Chief of the Security Police
and of the Security Service, which are to be activated
in Stalags.

The activation of commandos will take place in accordance with the agreement of the Chief of the Security Police and Security Service and the Supreme Command of the Armed Forces as of 16 July 1941 (see enclosure I). The commandos will work independently according to special authorization and in consequence of the general regulations given to them, in the limits of the camp organizations. Naturally, the commandos will keep close contact with the camp commander and the defense officers assigned to him.

The mission of the commandos is the political investigating of all camp-inmates, the elimination and further "treatment"

a. of all political, criminal or in some other way undesirable elements among them.

b. Of those persons who could be used for the reconstruction of the occupied territories.

For the execution of their mission, no auxiliary means can be put at the disposal of the commandos. The "Deutsche Fahndungsbuch", the "Aufenthaltsermittlungsliste" and the "Sonderfahndungsbuch UdSSR" will prove to be useful in only a small number of cases; the "Sonderfahndungsbuch UdSSR" is not sufficient, because it contains only a small part of Soviet-Russians considered to be dangerous.

Therefore, the commandos must use their special knowledge and ability and rely on their own findings and self-acquired knowledge. Therefore, they will be able to start carrying out their mission only when they have gathered together appropriate material.

The commandos must use for their work as far as possible, at present and even later, the experiences of the camp commanders which the latter have collected meanwhile from observation of the prisoners and examinations of camp inmates.

Further, the commandos must make efforts from the beginning to seek out among the prisoners elements which appear reliable, regardless if there are communists concerned or not, in order to use them for intelligence purposes inside of the camp and, if advisable, later in the occupied territories also.

By use of such informers and by use of all other existing possibilities, the discovery of all elements to be eliminated among the prisoners, must succeed step by step at once. The commandos must learn for themselves, in every case by means of short questioning of the informers and eventual questioning of other prisoners.

The information of *one* informer is not sufficient to designate a camp inmate to be a suspect, without further proof; it must be confirmed in some way if possible.

Above all, the following must be discovered:
> All important functionaries of State and Party, especially Professional revolutionaries.
> Functionaries of the Komintern.
> All policy-forming Party functionaries of the KPdSU and its fellow organizations in the central committees, in the regional and district committees.
> All Peoples-Commissars and their deputies.
> All former Political Commissars in the Red Army.
> Leading personalities of the State authorities of central and middle regions.
> The leading personalities of the business world.
> Members of the Soviet-Russian intelligence.
> All Jews.
> All persons, who are found to be agitators or fanatical communists.

It is not less important, as mentioned already, to discover all those persons who could be used for the reconstruction, administration and management of the conquered Russian territories.

Finally, all such persons must be secured who are still needed for the completion of further investigation, regardless if they are police investigations or other investigations, and for explanations of questions of general interest. Among them are all those especially, who because of their position and their knowledge are able to give information about measures and working methods of the Soviet-Russian State, of the Communist Party or of the Komintern.

In the final analysis, consideration must be given to the nativity in all decisions to be made. The leader of the Einsatz Kommando will give every week a short report by telephone or an express-letter to the Reich-Security-Main-Office, containing:

1. *Short* description of their activities in the past week.

2. Number of all definitely suspicious persons. (report of number sufficient)

3. Individual names of all persons found to be functionaries of the Komintern, leading functionaries of the Party, Peoples-Commissars, leading personalities and Political Commissars.

4. Number of all persons found not to be suspicious informers, with a short description of their position.
  A. Prisoners-of-war.
  B. Civilians.

On the basis of those activity reports the Reich-Security-Main-Office will issue immediately the further measures to be applied. For the measures to be applied on the basis of this successive directive the commandos are to demand the surrender of the prisoners involved from the camp command.

The camp commandants have received orders from the Supreme Command of the Armed Forces, to approve such requests (see enclosure I).

Executions are not to be held in the camp or in the immediate vicinity of the camp. If the camps in the General-Government are in the immediate vicinity of the border, then the prisoners are to be taken for special treatment, if possible, into the former Soviet-Russian territory.

Should execution be necessary for reasons of camp discipline, then the leader of the Einsatz Kommando must apply to the camp commander for it.

The commandos have to keep lists about the special treatments carried out and must contain:
  Current number.
  Family name and first name.
  Time and place of birth.
  Military rank.
  Profession.
  Last residence.
  Reason for special treatment.
  Day and place of special treatment
    (card file).

In regard to executions to be carried out and to the possible removal of reliable civilians and the removal of informers for the Einsatz-group in the occupied territories, the leader of the Einsatz-Kommando must make an agreement with the nearest State-Police-Office, as well as with the commandant of the Security Police Unit and Security Service and beyond these with the Chief of the Einsatz-group concerned in the occupied territories.

Reports of that kind are to be transmitted for information to the Reich-Security-Main-Office, IV. A 1. Excellent behavior during and after duty, the best cooperation with the camp-commanders, and careful examinations are the duty of all leaders and members of the Einsatz-Kommando.

The members of the Einsatz-Kommando must be constantly impressed with the special importance of the missions entrusted to them.

Translation of Document 579-PS. *Three letters, District Commissioner, Employment Director at Riga, and Economic Directorate in Latvia, 21 July 1941, 10 February 1942, and 6 July 1942, concerning forced Jewish labor in Riga and Latvia.*

* * *

Weimar, 5 January 1943
The District Commissar in Riga—Employment Office
Section [Fachgebiet] 2 (Commitment of work)
Riga, 6 July 1942
File note

Subject: Commitment of Jews.
here: cooperation with the administration offices of the armed forces.

For the last 10 days Jews have been picked up almost daily for commitment in the peat industry by units of the Armed Forces. While doing so, very considerable difficulties arose because the members of the Armed Forces who get the Jews from the ghetto daily do not want to comply with the regulations which are issued by the man responsible for work commitment.

It is agreed that the soldiers take over the Jews in columns at the exit of the ghetto. Actually, however, several soldiers enter the fenced-in ghetto and pick up the Jews in question without any permission. During the last week, government inspector Rottenberger and the undersigned were present, at an early hour, during the dispatching of the Jews. Some soldiers also did not follow the instructions of the Reich German workers, entered the ghetto, and themselves got the men who had worked so far for the units in question. It was pointed out to them that manpower had to be committed for specially urgent measures. These instructions were not followed by the soldiers, but they shouted around in the presence of more than 1000 Jews, and simply took the men away in spite of the order forbidding it. In one instance a soldier arrived the next morning in a steel helmet and again did not follow the instructions of the Reich-German manpower. A German police sergeant was charged with banishing the soldiers from the ghetto. The sergeant had hardly turned around when the soldier entered the ghetto again and again got Jews whom he was not supposed to get, and took them away. In another case, the undersigned was just in time to prevent a pfc. of the Air Force from beating a Jewish policeman. The Jewish policeman beat a Jew who did not want to report for a certain work. The Jewish police is doing well with the daily commitment of about 4000 Jews. Therefore it must be prevented that Germans attack Jewish policemen in the presence of thousands of Jews.

As soon as German soldiers who pick up the Jewish manpower daily from the ghetto, follow the instructions of the Reich-German manpower, and, above all, keep discipline, it will be possible to get the Jewish manpower ready for work considerably faster every day. According to my opinion it is at least necessary that one German policeman who can prevent the illegal seizures by the German soldiers, be placed at the entrance of the ghetto daily from 0530 to 0800 hours.

For information:

signed Lippmann.

The District Commissar in Riga
The Chief of The Employment Office
Riga Azsargu Iela 29/31

Riga, 10 February 1942

Department................
File No....................

To the Reich Commissar for the Baltic States
Work policies and social administration
Riga, through the Commissar General in Riga.

Subject: Transport of Jews from Kauen.
Ref.: Your letter of 6 February 1942.

The transport of Jews from Kauen arrived here on 8 February 1942. However, instead of the requested 500 males only,

222 males and
137 females

were sent.

Due to the fact that there exists a considerable need of Jewish manpower for transport and construction work, I am requesting an additional 1000 Jewish males from Kauen.

I was informed by the transport leader that the Jews in Kauen, as far as their commitment for work is concerned, are not under the jurisdiction of the employment office, but that the Jewish manpower is distributed by the German police.

For:

[signature illegible]
(Oberregierungsrat)

[ink note:]
To the Commissar General
[Initials illegible]

Command of Economic Affairs [Wirtschaftskommando] for the Territory of the former Latvia Department of Work

Riga, 21 July 1941

Subject: Work commitment of *Jews*.

File note

According to the Group Agriculture there is a considerable shortage of workers for farming in Latvia, which endangers especially the beet harvest. According to my findings and also those of the economy office North (Wi.-In. Nord) no prisoners of war are at present available for farming. It should be examined, therefore, to which extent and under which conditions other possibilities of commitment are available.

To clarify the possibility of committing Jews, a conference took place today between the economy office North and the chief war administration advisor (O.K.V.R.) Ellroth, from the department of work. Together with Mr. Ellroth we went to the *SS* and conferred with the leader of the *SD*, Sturmbannfuehrer Batz, as well as his deputy, Hauptsturmfuehrer Kirsten. Our proposal to earmark the Jews, to put them together in a ghetto, then to establish a council for Jews, and to effect with it the extensive commitment of Jews for work, was favorably accepted. It was also agreed upon that the commitment of Jews for work should be effected *only* through the special offices for commitment to be created by the employment office resp. offices, in order to make sure of leadership according to the necessities for war and state policies. The SS reserves only the right of the decision of political problems and the execution of political tasks. The earmarking of the Jews and their collection in a ghetto is being done. It was furthermore announced that conferences had already taken place between the SS - SD on the one hand and the military administration headquarters (Feldkommandatur) on the other hand, with the result that a registration of the Jews at the police precincts, a daily report of the Jews there, and the establishment of a special office should be instituted for the execution of the commitment of Jews for work through the military administration headquarters.

After that a conference with the war administration council [Kriegsverwaltungsrat] Nachtigall also took place at the *military administration headquarters*, which had the same result. The military administration headquarters (Fk.) agrees also that the commitment of Jews for work is done by the employment office after the registration of the Jews. While registering, a special index card can be put aside for this commitment of work.

The discussions at the Fk. resulted furthermore in the issuing by the commander of the rear army district of a decree on *ceiling prices and wages*, already last Wednesday, because it is his opinion that he alone can issue official decrees with effective penalties. Furthermore, the locally customary prices and wages are already established.

[signature illegible]

Distribution: O.K.V.R.
    Wi.-In. Nord, Dept. for work Commandant
    SS.-SD.
    Fk.

Translation of Document 654-PS (USA 218). *Excerpts from Notes of Thierack, Reich Minister of Justice, 18 September 1942, on discussion with Himmler concerning delivery of Jews to Himmler for extermination through work.*

*   *   *

U I *b*

Discussion with Reich Fuehrer of SS Himmler on 18.9.42 in his Field Headquarters in the presence of State Secretary Dr. Rothenberger, SS Gruppenfuehrer Streckenbach and SS Obersturmbannfuehrer Bender.

*   *   *   *   *   *

2. The delivery of anti-social elements from the execution of their sentence to the Reich Fuehrer of SS to be worked to death. Persons under protective arrest, Jews, Gypsies, Russians and Ukrainians, Poles with more than 3-year sentences, Czechs and Germans with more than 8-year sentences, according to the decision of the Reich Minister for Justice. First of all the worst anti-social elements amongst those just mentioned are to be handed over. I shall inform the Fuehrer of this through Reichsleiter Bormann.

*   *   *   *   *   *   *

14. It is agreed that, in consideration of the intended aims of the Government for the clearing up of the Eastern problems, in future Jews, Poles, Gypsies, Russians and Ukrainians are no longer to be judged by the ordinary courts, so far as punishable offenses are concerned, but are to be dealt with by the Reich Fuehrer of SS. This does not apply to civil lawsuits, nor to Poles whose names are announced or entered in the German Racial Lists.   Signed   Th.

Translation of Document 682-PS. Notes of Thierack, Reich Minister of Justice, on discussion with Goebbels, 14 September 1942, in Berlin, concerning groups to be exterminated, including Jews.

* * *

DISCUSSION OF THIERACK WITH DR. GOEBBELS ON SEPT. 14, 1942 IN BERLIN

1—2.15 p.m.

2. With regard to the destruction of asocial life, Dr. Goebbels is of the opinion that the following groups should be exterminated: Jews and Gypsies unconditionally, Poles who have to serve 3—4 years of penal servitude, and Czechs and Germans who are sentenced to death or penal servitude for life or to security custody [Sicherungsvorwahrung] for life. The idea of exterminating them by labor is the best. For the rest, however, except in the aforementioned cases, every case has to be dealt with individually. In this case, of course, Czechs and Germans have to be differently judged. There may be cases where a German sentenced to 15 years of penal servitude is not to be considered asocial, but in contrast to this, a person sentenced to penal servitude up to 8 years may be.

Translation of Document 701-PS (USA 497). Letter from Minister of Justice to public prosecutors, 1 April 1943, to effect that Jews who are released from a penal institution are to be sent to the concentration camps Auschwitz or Lublin for the rest of their lives.

* * *

The Reich Minister of Justice 4410 b-Vs 1 379/43 g
    Berlin W 8, Wilhelmstrasse 65 1 April 1943
                     Telephone 11 00 44
                     Long Distance 11 65 16
To The Public Prosecutors of the Courts of Appeal,

To the Commissioner of the Reich Minister of Justice for the penal camps in Emsland.

PAPENBURG (Ems)

Regarding: Poles and Jews who are released from the penal institutions of the Department of Justice.

Instructions for the independent penal institutions.

1. With reference to the new guiding principles for the application of Article 1, Section 2 of the decree of 11 June 1940 (Reich Legal Gazette I S. 877)—attachment I of the decree (RV) of 27 January 1943—9133/2 enclosure I-III a2 2629—the Reich Chief Security Office has directed by the decree of 11 March 1943—II A 2 number 100-43—176:

a. Jews, who in accordance with number VI of the guiding principles, are released from a penal institution, are to be taken by the State Police (Chief) Office competent for the district in which the penal institution is located, for the rest of their lives to the concentration camps Auschwitz or Lublin in accordance with the regulations for protective custody that have been issued.

The same applies to Jews who in the future are released from a penal institution after serving a sentence of confinement.

b. Poles, who in accordance with number VI of the guiding principles are released from a penal institution, are to be taken by the State Police (Chief) Office competent for the district in which the penal institution is located, for the duration of the war to a concentration camp in accordance with the regulations on protective custody that have been issued.

The same applies in the future to Poles who, after serving a term of imprisonment of more than 6 months, are to be discharged by a penal institution.

Conforming to the request of the Chief Office for Reich Security, I ask that in the future,

a. All Jews to be discharged,

b. All Poles to be discharged,

Who have served a sentence of more than 6 months be designated for further confinement to the State Police (Chief) Office competent for the district and are to be placed promptly at its disposal, before the end of sentence for conveyance.

2. This ruling replaces the hitherto ordered return of all Polish prisoners undergoing imprisonment in the Old Reich condemned in annexed Eastern territories. The decree (RV) of 28 July 1942—4410 *b* Vs *1* 1731—has lost its meaning. Imprisonment up to 6 months imposed within the incorporated

Eastern territories, excluding exceptions, is to be carried out in these territories, and not in the Old Reich.

By order of
Dr. Eichler

[Stamp: Reichministry of Justice, Office of the Ministry]

Certified:
[signed]   Freyer
Clerk of Justice

Translation of Document 710-PS (USA 509). Letter from Goering to Heydrich, 31 July 1941, concerning solution of Jewish question.

* * *

The Reich Marshal of the Greater German Reich
Commissioner for the Four Year Plan
Chairman of the Ministerial Council for National Defense

Berlin, 31 July 1941

To: The Chief of the Security Police and the Security Service; SS-Gruppenfuehrer Heydrich

Complementing the task that was assigned to you on 24 January 1939, which dealt with the carrying out of emigration and evacuation, a solution of the Jewish problem, as advantageous as possible, I hereby charge you with making all necessary preparation in regard to organizational and financial matters for bringing about a complete solution of the Jewish question in the German sphere of influence in Europe.

Wherever other governmental agencies are involved, these are to cooperate with you.

I charge you furthermore to send me, before long, an overall plan concerning the organizational, factual and material measures necessary for the accomplishment of the desired solution of the Jewish question.

signed: GOERING

Translation of Document 1012-PS. Teletype from OKW to Military Commander of France, 3 February 1942, concerning consultation of Hitler and Keitel about shooting of Jews and Communists.

* * *

Copy
SSD—TELEGRAM
Anna 4873   3 February 42   1650

1012-PS   Nazi Germany's War Against the Jews

SECRET

To the Military Commander of France
Attention of Infantry General Von Stuelpnagel, Paris.
Reference: Telegram of 1 Jan. 1942.

General Field Marshal *Keitel*, after a conference with the Fuehrer, refuses to consider the plan of sole judging and arbitrary final decision for measures in cases of assault and acts of violence with explosives which was proposed from there as long as the measures which are proposed from there do not take into consideration in their type and magnitude the fundamental attitude of the Fuehrer for assaults and violent acts with explosives which have been reported since Jan. 15, and which have not yet been clarified but are on the increase. Sharp and deterring punishment must be instituted by shooting a large number of arrested Communists and/or Jews and persons who have previously committed assault and by arresting at least one thousand Communists, and/or Jews for shipment. Field Marshal Keitel awaits corresponding instructions for submission to the Fuehrer.

OKW Gen QU (V) Nr. II 1887/42 SECRET
1830 1 B O M HRRXMV
France

Translation of Document 1015B-PS (USA 385). *Report on activities of special staff (Einsatzstab) for Pictorial Art, October 1940 to July 1944, to effect that 21,903 art objects, seized from Jews were inventoried.*

* * *

SPECIAL STAFF FOR PICTORIAL ART

Report of work during the period from October 1940 to July 1944

On the basis of the decree of the Fuehrer of 17 September 1940 relative to the seizure of ownerless works of arts formerly possessed by Jews in the occupied Western territories, the special staff for pictorial art commenced at the beginning of October 1940 in Paris with the seizure of the works of art abandoned by the internationally known Jewish Rothschild family, which was also famous as the possessor of great art collections. It was not possible for the various members of the Jewish Rothschild family, nor for many other rich French Jews, to take any con-

III - 166

siderable part of their art possessions to England and America in their precipitous flight before the German occupation. The staff has not only seized very great parts of the art treasures abandoned in the Paris City Palaces of the Rothschilds, but it also systematically searched the country-seats of the individual members of the Rothschild family, such as the famous Loire castle, for art treasures and thereby safeguarded for the Reich very important parts of the world famous Rothschild art collection. The art possessions of the Rothschild's were traced not only to cleverly hidden places in the individual castles but also to depots and warehouses, as for example in Bordeaux and other coastal cities, where these art treasures had already been packed for transport to America. In this same manner the art possessions of other French Jews famous as art collectors such as Kann, David-Wlil, Levy de Benzion and Seligmann were traced by the staff and seized in their entirety.

After the seizure of the most famous Jewish art collections in Paris, all abandoned dwellings of the wealthy Parisian Jews, as well as the warehouses of all shipping firms and many other art depots of emigrated Jews, which were very often camouflaged by French gentiles, were systematically searched by the special staff for pictorial art and very considerable art treasures found in this manner. These seizures were carried out on the basis of preliminary exhaustive investigations into the address lists of the French police authorities, on the basis of Jewish handbooks, warehouse inventories and order books for French shipping firms as well as on the basis of French art and collection catalogs. The clearly established Jewish origin of the individual owners was proved in each case in cooperation with the French police authorities and the Sicherheitsdienst (Security Service), as well as on the basis of the political secure material of the staff itself.

According to the same system, the seizure of ownerless Jewish works of art was gradually extended over the whole French territory. The investigations of the special staff for pictorial art were often made extraordinarily difficult by proven sabotage by French authorities, as well as by camouflaging of Jewish possessions by trusteeship of French gentiles covering up for the Jews. In spite of this, Jewish art possessions in the occupied French territories was seized to such an extent as to justify the assumption that, in spite of all opposition and camouflaging, the most important part of the art possessions which had been in the hands of Jews in France, insofar as these had not already been removed before the occupation, was safeguarded by the staff. *The wholesale removal of irreplaceable European art values was thereby prevented and the highest artistic products of all European nations assured for Europe.*

In the course of this art seizure by the staff in the occupied Western territories, the following were seized from 203 locations (collections).

21,903 art objects of all types, as counted and inventoried up to now.

A seizure record was made for each location, recording the origin of the objects with exact individual data. All seized art treasures were first taken to a collection warehouse at the former Jeau de Paume Museum and then to rooms of the Louvre which had been placed at their disposal. They were scientifically inventoried and photographed by scientific art workers of the special staff for pictorial art and carefully packed there by experts for transport to the Reich. These jobs were especially difficult, since the majority of the collections and individual art objects were taken over without any inventories or indications of origin, and the scientific cataloguing had to be carried out by the scientific art workers of the staff.

Since the beginning of 1943, art seizures of the staff have been extended to include also furniture seizures of the East Ministry, whereby a great number of individual valuable art works could be seized from individual dwellings and warehouses.

During the period from March 1941 to July 1944, the special staff for pictorial art brought into the Reich: *29 large shipments including 137 freight cars with 4174 cases of art works.*

These shipments were taken to 6 shelters in the Reich, unpacked and stored with observation of all conservation, air raid and fire protection precautions. At the shelters the inventories, which had served in Paris only for identification were supplemented according to scientific view-points, and the results of the scientific cataloguing were recorded on inventory lists and thoroughly indexed. With this scientific inventory of a material unique in its scope and importance and of a value hitherto unknown to art research, the special staff for pictorial art has conducted a work important to the entire field of art. *This inventory work will form the basis of an all-inclusive scientific catalog, in which should be recorded hstory, scope and scientific and political significance of this historically unique art seizure.*

A restoration work shop equipped with all technical aids was established by the special staff at one of the shelters, and has been occupied with the care and restoration of seized articles of artistic value as well as with their permanent observation at the shelters. Several hundreds of the works of art that had been neglected by their Jewish owners or had earlier been inexpertly restored were restored in this workshop and their preservation assured.

In addition, all seized articles of artistic value were photographed by the photography workshop of the special staff and included in a film library. Thereby not only the identity of each individual art work was recorded, but also material of permanent value for study and publication in the field of art was created.

Up to 15 July 1944 the following had been scientifically inventoried:

21,903 art works
- *5,281 paintings, pastels, water-colors, drawings.*
- *684 miniatures, glass and enamel paintings, books and manuscripts*
- *583 plastics, terra-cottas, medallions and plaques.*
- *2,477 articles of furniture of value to art history.*
- *583 textiles* (Gobelins, rugs, embroideries, Coptic materials).
- *5,825 hand-made art works* (porcelains, bronze, faiences, majolica, ceramics, jewelry, coins, art objects made with precious stones).
- *1,286 East Asiatic art works* (bronzes, plastics, porcelains, paintings, folding screens, weapons).
- *259 art works of antiquity* (sculptures, bronzes, vases, jewelry, bowls, cut stones, terra-cottas).

These figures will be increased, since seizures in the West are not yet completed, and it has not been possible to make a scientific inventory of part of the seized objects because of the lack of experts.

The extraordinary artistic and material value of the seized art works cannot be expressed in figures. The paintings, period furniture of the 17th and 18th centuries, the Gobelins, the antiques and renaissance jewelry of the Rothschilds are objects of such a unique character that their evaluation is impossible, since no comparable values have so far appeared on the art market.

A short report, moreover, can only hint at the artistic worth of the collection. Among the seized paintings, pastels and drawings there are several hundred works of the first quality, masterpieces of European art, which could take first place in any museum. Included therein are absolutely authenticated signed works of Rembrandt van Rijn, Rubens, Frans Hals, Vermeer van Delft, Velasquez, Murilio, Goya, Sebastiano del Piombo, Palma Vecchio, etc.

Of first importance among the seized paintings are the works of the famous French painters of the 18th century, with masterpieces of Boucher, Watteau, Algaud, Largielliere, Kattier, Fragonard, Pater, D Nloux and de Trcy.

This collection can compare with those of the best European museums. It includes many works of the foremost French masters, who up to now have been only inadequately represented in the best German museums. Very important also is the representation of masterpieces of the Dutch painters of the 17th and 18th centuries. First of all should be mentioned the works of van Dyck, Salomon and Jacob Ruisdar Wouvermann, Terborch, jan Weenix, Gabriel Metsu, Adrian van Ostade, David Teniers, Pieter de Hooch, Willem van der Velde, etc.

Of foremost importance also are the represented works of English paintings of the 18th and 19th centuries, with masterpieces of Reynolds, Romney and Gainsborough. Cranach and Amberger, among the German masters, should be mentioned.

The collection of French furniture of the 17th and 18th centuries is perhaps even more highly to be evaluated. This contains hnudreds of the best preserved and, for the most part, signed works of the best known cabinet-makers from the period between Louis XIV to Louis XVI. Since German cabinet-makers played an important part in this golden age of French cabinetry, now recognized for the first time in the field of art, this collection is of paramount importance.

The collection of Gobelins and Persian tapestries contains numerous world famous objects. The collection of handicraft works and the Rothschild collection of renaissance jewelry is valuable beyond comparison.

Very many works of art were seized by the staff from the luggage of Jewish emigrants in Holland as well as in the occupied territories of France and Belgium.

Work in the Eastern territories.

The activity of the special staff for pictorial art was limited in the occupied Eastern territories to a scientific and photographic recording of public collection and their safeguarding and care in cooperation with the military and civil services. In the course of the evacuation of the territory several hundred most valuable Russian Ikons, several hundred Russian paintings of the 18th and 19th centuries, individual articles of furniture and furniture from castles were saved in cooperation with the individual army groups, and brought to a shelter in the Reich.

A collection of degenerate Bolshevist art, as well as a collection of degenerate Western art, was also made for political study purposes. In addition, a rich collection of material concerning Soviet architecture was made.

25 portfolios of pictures with the most valuable works of the art collections seized in the West were presented to the Fuehrer on 20 April 1943, together with three volumes of a provisional catalog of paintings and an interim progress report. Additional portfolios of pictures are in preparation.

Robert SCHOLZ
Bereichsleiter
Chief of the Special Staff for Pictorial Art

Translation of Document 1015I-PS (USA 385). *Letter from Goering to Rosenberg, 30 May 1942, on activities of Einsatzstab Rosenberg (Rosenberg's staff for seizing Jewish property, libraries and art treasures).*

* * *

The Reich Marshal of the Greater German Reich
Berlin W8, 30 May 1942
Leipziger Str. 3

Dear Party member Rosenberg:

Your Einsatzstab for the seizure of cultural goods in Paris, I believe, has been wrongly reported to you as if it were dealing in works of art itself. I know the task of the Einsatzstab very well and must assert that there is no agency to which I am able to express such unrestricted praise for its continued work and readiness as to this agency proper with all its collaborators. Presumably I have given cause for the reputation of dealing in works of art because I have asked some especially experienced gentlemen if anywhere during their stay in Paris or France they should hear of any pictures or other art objects to be sold by art dealers or private individuals to look at those objects and to inform me if there should be anything of interest for me. Since the latter was often the case, I have then again asked the gentlemen to do me the favor to acquire the objects for me for which purpose I have kept a depot ready for them. If thus some gentlemen got very busy to make contacts with art dealers it was exclusively a personal favor which was done for me for the benefit of building up my collection. Since very many prospective buyers endeavor to seize art objects in the occupied territory, I can well imagine that perhaps out of ignorance of the circumstances, but perhaps also out of envy they have caused the gentlemen of your Einsatzstab to be suspected wrongly.

I feel it my duty to give you this information and to ask you that it may remain this way. On the other hand I also support personally the work of your Einsatzstab wherever I can do so, and a great part of the seized cultural goods can be accounted for because I was able to assist the Einsatzstab by my organization.

With best regards and Heil Hitler!

Yours

Signed: Hermann Goering

Translation of Document 1024-PS (USA 278). *Excerpts from Memorandum from Rosenberg file, 29 April 1941, concerning organization for handling problems in the Eastern Territories, suggesting that ghettos and forced labor will be lot of Jews.*

* * *

29 April 1941

General organization and tasks of our office for the general handling of problems in the Eastern territories

The Chief of this office under whom a personal expert plus the necessary office staff is to be placed, is to be assisted in all general problems of the office by his permanently assigned representative (Gauleiter Dr. Meyer). The permanent representative heads a main office which organizes the whole interior srvice as well as a number of departments which have to work on special problems. . . .

A general treatment is required for the Jewish problem for which a temporary solution will have to be determined (forced labor for the Jews, creation of Ghettos, etc.) The church problems of the whole East are of a varying nature (character) and require an intensive treatment in relation to the past, to the now existing laws and to the interested future relationship. . . .

Translation of Document 1028-PS (USA 273). *Memorandum from Rosenberg file, 7 May 1941, on decisive solution of Jewish problem through institution of ghettos or labor battalions.*

* * *

The Documentary Evidence   1028-PS

[Memorandum from Rosenberg file, 7 May 1941]
[Translation of Only Typewritten Material]

After the customary removal of Jews from all public offices, the Jewish question will have to have a decisive solution, through the institution of Ghettos. Insofar as the Jews have not been driven out by the Ukrainians themselves, the small communities must be lodged in large camps, in order to be kept busy by means of forced labor in the same way as it has already been the practice in Letzmanorstadt (Lodz).

[Translation of paragraph, excluding all crossed out words.]

After the customary removal of Jews from all public offices, the Jewish question will have to undergo a decisive solution through the institution of Ghettos or labor battalions. Forced labor is to be introduced.

Translation of Document 1061-PS (USA 275). Official report of Stroop, SS and Police Leader of Warsaw, entitled "The Warsaw Ghetto Is No More," describing destruction of Warsaw Ghetto in April/May, 1943.

* * *

THE WARSAW GHETTO IS NO MORE

For the Fuehrer and their country the following fell in the battle for the destruction of Jews and bandits in the former Ghetto of Warsaw:

[follow 15 names]

Furthermore, the Polish Police Sergeant Julian Zielinski, born 13 November 1891, 8th Commissariat * * * fell on 19 April 1943 while fulfilling his duty. * * * They gave their utmost, their life. We shall never forget them. The following were wounded:

[follow the names of—
   60 Waffen SS personnel.
   11 "Watchmen" from Training Camps, probably Lithuanians, to judge by their names.
   12 Security Police Officers in SS Units.
    5 men of the Polish Police.
    2 regular Army personnel engineers]

Units used in the action	Average number of personnel used per day
SS Staff & Police Leader	6/5
Waffen SS:	
SS Panzer Grenadier Training and Reserve Battalion 3, Warsaw	4/440

III - 173

SS Cav. Training and Res Bat. Warsaw.............. 5/381

Police:
SS Police Regiment 22   I. Bat.................. 3/94
                       III. Bat.................. 3/134
Engineering Emergency Service................ 1/6
Polish Police 4/363
Polish Fire Brigade 166

Security Police:
Wehrmacht
Light AA Alarm Battery III/8 Warsaw.... 2/22
Engineers Det. of Railway Armored Trains
  Res. Bat. Rembertow 2/42
  Res. Eng. 14 Gora-Kalwaria 1/34

Foreign Racial Watchmen:
1 Bat. "Trawniki" men 2/335

Total: 36/2054

[Translator's note: This obviously means 36 officers, 2054 men]

The creation of special areas to be inhabited by Jews, and the restriction of the Jews with regard to residence and trading is nothing new in the history of the East. Such measures were first taken far back in the Middle Ages; they could be observed as recently as during the last few centuries. These restrictions were imposed with the intention of protecting the aryan population against the Jews.

Identical considerations led us as early as February, 1940 to conceive the project of creating a Jewish residential district in Warsaw. The initial intention was to establish as the Ghetto that part of the City of Warsaw which has the Vistula as its Eastern frontier. The particular situation on prevailing in Warsaw seemed at first to frustrate this plan. It was moreover opposed by several authorities particularly by the City Administration. They pointed in particular that disturbances in industry and trade would ensue if a Ghetto were founded in Warsaw, and that it would be impossible to provide the Jews with food if they were assembled in a closed area.

At a conference held in March 1940, it was decided to postpone the plan of creating a Ghetto for the time being, owing to the above objections. At the same time a plan was considered to declare the District of Lublin the collecting area for all Jews within the Government General, especially for the evacuated or fugitive Jews arriving from the Reich. But as early as April 1940, the Higher SS and Police Leader, East, Cracow, issued a

III - 174

declaration that there was no intention of assembling the Jews within the Lublin District. In the meantime, the Jews had increasingly taken to crossing the frontiers without permission and illegally. This noted especially at the limits of the Districts of Lowicz and Skierniewice. Conditions in the town of Lowicz became dangerous from the point of view of hygiene as well as from that of the Security Police, owing to these illegal migrations of Jews. The District President of Lowicz, therefore, began to install Ghettos in his district in order to avoid these dangers.

The experiences in the district of Lowicz, after Ghettos had been installed, showed that this method is the only one suitable for dispelling the dangers which emanate repeatedly from the Jews.

The necessity of erecting a Ghetto in the City of Warsaw as well became more and more urgent in the summer of 1940, since more and more troops were being assembled in the district of Warsaw after termination of the French campaign. At that time the Department for Hygiene urged the speedy erection of a Ghetto in the interest of preserving the health of the German Forces and of the native population as well. The original plan of establishing the Ghetto in the suburb of Praga as intended in February 1940, would have taken at least 4 to 5 months, since almost 600,000 persons had to be moved. But since experience showed that greater outbreaks of epidemics might be expected in the winter months and since for this reason the District Medical Officer urged that the resettling action ought to be completed by 15 November 1940 at the latest, the plan of establishing a suburban ghetto in Praga was dropped; and instead, the area which hitherto had been used as a quarantine area for epidemics was selected for use as a Jewish residential area. In October 1940, the Governor ordered the Commissioner of the District, President for the City of Warsaw, to complete the resettlement necessary for establishing the Ghetto within the City of Warsaw by 15 November 1940.

The Ghetto thus established in Warsaw was inhabited by about 400,000 Jews. It contained 27,000 apartments with an average of 2½ rooms each. It was separated from the rest of the ctiy by partition and other walls and by walling-up of thoroughfares, windows, doors, open spaces, etc.

It was administered by the Jewish Board of Elders, who received their instructions from the Commissioner for the Ghetto, who was immediately subordinated to the Governor. The Jews were granted self-administration in which the German supervising authorities intervened only where German interests were touched. In order to enable the Jewish Board of Elders to execute its orders, a Jewish Police force was set up, identified by special armbands and a special beret and armed with rubber truncheons. This Jewish Police force was charged with maintaining order and security within the Ghetto and was subordinated to the German and Polish Police.

II

It soon became clear, however, that not all dangers had been removed by this confining the Jews to one place. Security considerations required removing the Jews from the city of Warsaw altogether. The first large resettlement action took place in the period from 22 July to 3 October 1942. In this action 310,322 Jews were removed. In January 1943 a second resettlement action was carried out by which altogether 6,500 Jews were affected.

When the Reichsfuehrer SS visited Warsaw in January 1943 he ordered the SS and Police Leader for the District of Warsaw to *transfer to Lublin the armament factories and other enterprises of military importance which were installed within the Ghetto including their personnel and machines.* The execution of this transfer order proved to be very difficult, since the managers as well as the Jews resisted in every possible way. The SS and Police Leader thereupon decided to enforce the transfer of the enterprises in a large-scale action which he intended to carry out in three days. The necessary preparations had been taken by my predecessor, who also had given the order to start the large-scale action. I myself arrived in Warsaw on 17 April 1943 and took over the command of the action on 19 April 1943, 0800 hours, the action itself having started the same day at 0600 hours.

Before the large-scale action began, the limits of the former Ghetto had been blocked by an external barricade in order to prevent the Jews from breaking out. This barricade was maintained from the start to the end of the action and was especially reinforced at night.

When we invaded the Ghetto for the first time, the Jews and the Polish bands succeeded in repelling the participating units, including tanks and armored cars, by a well-prepared concentration of fire. When I ordered a second attack, about 0800 hours, I distributed the units, separated from each other by indicated lines, and charged them with combing out the whole of the Ghetto, each unit for a certain part. Although firing commenced again, we now succeeded in combing out the blocks according to plan. The enemy was forced to retire from the roofs and elevated bases to the basements, dug-outs, and sewers. In order to prevent their escaping into the sewers, the sewerage system was dammed up below the Ghetto and filled with water, but the Jews frustrated this plan to a great extent by blowing up the turning off valves. Late the first day we encountered rather heavy resistance, but it was quickly broken by a special raiding party. In the course of further operations we succeeded in expelling the Jews from their prepared resistance bases, sniper holes, and the like, and in occupying during the 20 and 21 April the greater part of the so-called remainder of the Ghetto to such a degree that the resistance continued within these blocks could no longer be called considerable.

The main Jewish battle group, mixed with Polish bandits, had already retired during the first and second day to the so-called Muranowski Square. There, it was reinforced by a considerable number of Polish bandits. Its plan was to hold the Ghetto by every means in order to prevent us from invading it. The Jewish and Polish standards were hoisted at the top of a concrete building as a challenge to us. These two standards, however, were captured on the second day of the action by a special raiding party. SS Untersturmfuehrer Dehmke fell in this skirmish with the bandits; he was holding in his hand a hand-grenade which was hit by the enemy and exploded, injuring him fatally. After only a few days I realized that the original plan had no prospect of success, unless the armament factories and other enterprises of military importance distributed throughout the Ghetto were dissolved. It was therefore necessary to approach these firms and to give them appropriate time for being evacuated and immediately transferred. Thus one of these firms after the other was dealt with, and we very soon deprived the Jews and bandits of their chance to take refuge time and again in these enterprises, which were under the supervision of the Armed Forces. In order to decide how much time was necessary to evacuate these enterprises thorough inspections were necessary. The conditions discovered there are indescribable. I cannot imagine a greater chaos than in the Ghetto of Warsaw. The Jews had control of everything, from the chemical substances used in manufacturing explosives to clothing and equipment for the Armed Forces. The managers knew so little of their own shops that the Jews were in a position to produce inside these shops arms of every kind, especially hand grenade, Molotov cocktails, and the like.

Moreover, the Jews had succeeded in fortifying some of these factories as centers of resistance. Such a center of resistance in an Army accommodation office had to be attacked as early as the second day of the action by an Engineer's Unit equipped with flame throwers and by artillery. The Jews were so firmly established in this shop that it proved to be impossible to induce them to leave it voluntarily; I therefore resolved to destroy this shop the next day by fire.

The managers of these enterprises, which were generally also supervised by an officer of the Armed Forces, could in most cases make no specified statements on their stocks and the whereabouts of these stocks. The statements which they made on the number of Jews employed by them were in every case incorrect. Over and over again we discovered that these labyrinths of edifices belonging to the armament concerns as residential blocks, contained rich Jews who had succeeded in finding accommodations for themselves and their families under the name of "armament workers" and were leading marvelous lives there. Despite all our orders to the managers to make the Jews leave those enterprises, we found out in several cases that managers simply concealed the Jews by shutting them in, because they expected that the action would be finished within a few days and that they then would be able to continue working with the remaining Jews. According to the statements of arrested Jews, women also seem to have played a prominent part. The Jews are said to have endeavored to keep up good relations with officers and men of the armed forces. Carousing is said to have been frequent, during the course of which business deals are said to have been concluded between Jews and Germans.

The number of Jews forcibly taken out of the buildings and arrested was relatively small during the first few days. It transpired that the Jews had taken to hiding in the sewers and in specially erected dug-outs. Whereas we had assumed during the first days that there were only scattered dug-outs, we learned in the course of the large-scale action that the whole Ghetto was systematically equipped with cellars, dug-outs, and passages. In every case these passages and dug-outs were connected with the sewer system. Thus, the Jews were able to maintain undisturbed subterranean traffic. They also used this sewer network for escaping subterraneously into the Aryan part of the city of Warsaw. Continuously, we received reports of attempts of Jews to escape through the sewer holes. While pretending to build air-raid shelters they had been erecting dug-outs within the former Ghetto ever since the autumn of 1942. These were intended to conceal every Jew during the new evacuation action, which they had expected for quite a time, and to enable them to resist the invaders in a concerted action. Through posters, handbills, and whisper propaganda, the communistic resistance movement actually brought it about that the Jews entered the dug-outs as soon as the new large-scale operation started. How far their precautions went can be seen from the fact that many of the dug-outs had been skilfully equipped with furnishings sufficient for entire families, washing and bathing facilities, toilets, arms and munition supplies, and food supplies sufficient for several months. There were differently equipped dug-outs for rich and for poor Jews. To discover the individual dug-outs was difficult for the units, as they had been efficiently camouflaged. In many cases, it was possible only through betrayal on the part of the Jews.

When only a few days had passed, it became apparent that the Jews no longer had any intention to resettle voluntarily, but were determined to resist evacuation with all their force and by using all the weapons at their disposal. So-called battle groups had been formed, led by Polish-Bolshevists; they were armed and paid any price asked for available arms.

During the large-scale action we succeeded in catching some Jews who had already been evacuated and resettled in Lublin or Treblinka, but had broken out from there and returned to the Ghetto, equipped with arms and ammunition. Time and again Polish bandist found refuge in the Ghetto and remained there undisturbed, since we had no forces at our disposal to comb out this maze. Whereas it had been possible during the first days to catch considerable numbers of Jews, who are cowards by nature, it became more and more difficult during the second half of the action to capture the bandits and Jews. Over and over again new battle groups consisting of 20 to 30 or more Jewish fellows, 18 to 25 years of age, accompanied by a corresponding number of women kindled new resistance. These battle groups were under orders to put up armed resistance to the last and if necessary to escape arrest by committing suicide. One such battle group succeeded in mounting a truck by ascending from a sewer in the so-called Prosta, and in escaping with it (about 30 to 35 bandits). One bandit who had arrived with this truck exploded 2 hand grenades, which was the agreed signal for the bandits awaiting in the sewer to climb out of it. The bandits and Jews—there were Polish bandits among these gangs armed with carbines, small arms, and in one case a light machine gun, mounted the truck and drove away in an unknown direction. The last member of this gang, who was on guard in the sewer and was detailed to close the lid of the sewer hole, was captured. It was he who gave the above information. The search for the truck was unfortunately without result.

During this armed resistance the women belonging to the battle groups were equipped the same as the men; some were members of the Chalutzim movement. Not infrequently, these women fired pistols with both hands. It happened time and again that these women had pistols or hand grenades (Polish "pineapple" hand grenades) concealed in their bloomers up to the last moment to use against the men of the Waffen SS, Police, or Wehrmacht.

The resistance put up by the Jews and bandits could be broken only by relentlessly using all our force and energy by day and night. *On 23 April 1943 the Reichs Fuehrer SS issued through the higher SS and Police Fuehrer East at Cracow his order to complete the combing out of the Warsaw Ghetto with the greatest severity and relentless tenacity.* I therefore decided to destroy the entire Jewish residential area by setting every block on fire, including the blocks of residential buildings near the armament works. One concern after the other was systematically evacuated and subsequently destroyed by fire. The Jews then emerged from their hiding places and dug-outs in almost every case. Not infrequently, the Jews stayed in the burning buildings until, because of the heat and the fear of being burned alive they preferred to jump down from the upper stories after having thrown mattresses and other upholstered articles into the street from the burning buildings. With their bones broken, they still tried to crawl across the street into blocks of buildings which had not yet been set on fire or were only partly in flames. Often Jews changed their hiding places during the night, by moving into the ruins of burnt-out buildings, taking refuge there until they were found by our patrols. Their stay in the sewers also ceased to be pleasant after the first weeks. Frequently from the street, we could hear loud cries coming through the sewer shafts. Then the men of the Waffen SS, the Police or the Wehrmacht Engineers courageously climbed down the shafts to bring out the Jews and not infrequently they then stumbled over Jews already dead, or were shot at. It was always necessary to use smoke candles to drive out the Jews. Thus one day we opened 183 sewer entrance holes and at a fixed time lowered smoke candles into them, with the result that the bandits fled from what they believed to be gas to the center of the former Ghetto, where they could then be pulled out of the sewer holes there. A great number of Jews, who could not be counted, were exterminated by blowing up sewers and dug-outs.

The longer the resistance lasted, the tougher the men of the Waffen SS, Police, and Wehrmacht became; they fulfilled their duty indefatigably in faithful comradeship and stood together as models and examples of soldiers. Their duty hours often lasted from early morning until late at night. At night, search patrols with rags wound round their feet remained at the heels of the Jews and gave them no respite. Not infrequently they caught and killed Jews who used the night hours for supplementing their stores from abandoned dug-outs and for contacting neighboring groups or exchanging news with them.

Considering that the greater part of the men of the Waffen-SS had only been trained for three to four weeks before being assigned to this action, high credit should be given for the pluck, courage, and devotion to duty which they showed. It must be stated that the Wehrmacht Engineers, too, executed the blowing up of dug-outs, sewers, and concrete buildings with indefatigability and great devotion to duty. Officers and men of the Police, a large part of whom had already been at the front, again excelled by their dashing spirit.

Only through the continuous and untiring work of all involved did we succeed in catching a total of 56,065 Jews whose extermination can be proved. To this should be added the number of Jews who lost their lives in explosions or fires but whose numbers could not be ascertained.

During the large-scale operation the Aryan population was informed by posters that it was strictly forbidden to enter the former Jewish Ghetto and that anybody caught within the former Ghetto without valid pass would be shot. At the same time these posters informed the Aryan population again that the death penalty would be imposed on anybody who intentionally gave refuge to a Jew, especially lodged, supported, or concealed a Jew outside the Jewish residential area.

Permission was granted to the Polish police to pay to any Polish policeman who arrested a Jew within the Aryan part of Warsaw one-third of the cash in the Jew's possession. This measure has already produced results.

The Polish population for the most part approved the measures taken against the Jews. Shortly before the end of the large-scale operation, the Governor issued a special proclamation which he submitted to the undersigned for approval before publication, to the Polish population; in it he informed them of the reasons for destroying the former Jewish Ghetto by mentioning the assassinations carried out lately in the Warsaw area and the mass graves found in Catyn; at the same time they were asked to assist us in our fight against Communist agents and Jews (see enclosed poster).

The large-scale action was terminated on 16 May 1943 with the blowing up of the Warsaw synagogue at 2015 hours.

Now, there are no more factories in the former Ghetto. All the goods, raw materials, and machines there have been moved and stored somewhere else. All buildings etc., have been destroyed. The only exception is the so-called Dzielna Prison of the Security Police, which was exempted from destruction.

III

Although the large-scale operation has been completed, we have to reckon with the possibility that a few Jews are still living in the ruins of the former Ghetto; therefore, this area must be firmly shut off from the Aryan residential area and be guarded. Police Battalion III/23 has been charged with this duty. This Police Battalion has instructions to watch the former Ghetto, particularly to prevent anybody from entering the former Ghetto, and to shoot immediately anybody found inside the Ghetto without authority. The Commander of the Police Battalion will continue to receive further direct orders from the SS and Police Fuehrer. In this way, it should be possible to keep the small remainder of Jews there, if any, under constant pressure and to exterminate them eventually. The remaining Jews and bandits must be deprived of any chance of survival by destroying all remaining buildings and refuges and cutting off the water supply.

It is proposed to change the Dzielna Prison into a concentration camp and to use the inmates to remove, collect and hand over for reuse the millions of bricks, the scrap-iron, and other materials.

IV

Of the total of 56,065 Jews caught, about 7,000 were exterminated within the former Gretto in the course of the large-scale action, and 6,929 by transporting them to T.II, which means 14,000 Jews were exterminated altogether. Beyond the number of 56,065 Jews an estimated number of 5,000 tr 6,000 were killed by explosions or in fires.

The number of destroyed dug-outs amounts to 631.

Booty:
>7 Polish rifles, 1 Russian rifle, 1 German rifle
>59 pistols of various calibers
>Several hundred hand grenades
>Several hundred incendiary bottles
>Home-made explosives
>Infernal machines with fuses
>A large amount of explosives, ammunition for weapons of all calibers, including some machine-gun ammunition-

Regarding the booty of arms, it must be taken into consideration that the arms themselves could in most cases not be captured, as the bandits and Jews would, before being arrested, throw them into hiding places or holes which could not be ascertained or discovered. The smoking out of the dug-out by our men, also often made the search for arms impossible. As the dug-outs had to be blown up at once, a search later on was out of the question.

The captured hand grenades, ammunition, and incendiary bottles were at once reused by us against the bandits.

Further booty:
>1,240 used military tunics part of them with medal ribbons—Iron Cross and East Medal)
>600 pairs of used trousers
>Other equipment and German steel helmets
>108 horses, 4 of them still in the former Ghetto (hearse)

Up to 23 May 1943 we had counted:
4.4 million Zloty; furthermore about 5 to 6 million Zloty not yet counted, a great amount of foreign currency, e: g. $14,300 in paper and $9,200 in gold, moreover valuables, rings, chains, watches, etc.) in great quantities.

State of the Ghetto at the termination of the large-scale operation:

Apart from 8 buildings (Police Barracks, hospital, and accommodations for housing working-parties) the former Ghetto is completely destroyed. Only the dividing walls are left standing where no explosions were carried out. But the ruins still contain a vast amount of stones and scrap material which could be used.

Warsaw, 16 May, 1943.

>The SS and Police Fuehrer in the District of Warsaw.
>[Signed] Stroop
>SS Brigadefuehrer and Majorgeneral of Police.

Copy
Warsaw, 20 April 1943.
Journal No. 516/43 secret.
Daily Reports
SS Service Teletype message

From: The SS and Police Fuehrer in the District of Warsaw
Ref. No.: I ab/St/Gr—16 07
Re: Ghetto Operation.
To: The Higher SS and Police Fuehrer East, *Cracow*

Progress of Ghetto Operation on 19 April 1943:

Closing of Ghetto commenced 0300 hrs. At 0600 order to Waffen-SS (strength: 16/850) to comb out the remainder of the Ghetto. Hardly had the units fallen in, strong concerted fire-concentration by the Jews and bandits. The tank used in this action and the two heavy armored cars pelted with Molotov cocktails (incendiary bottles). Tank twice set on fire. Owing to this enemy counterattack, we had at first to take the units back. Losses in first attack: 12 men (6 SS-men, 6 Trawniki-men). About 800 hrs. second attack by the units, under the command of the undersigned. Although the counterattack was reported, this time we succeeded in combing out the blocks of buildings according to plan. We caused the enemy to retire from the roofs and elevated prepared positions into the cellars or dug-outs and sewers. During this combing-out we caught only about 200 Jews. Immediately afterwards raiding parties were directed to dug-outs known to us with the order to pull out the Jews and to destroy the dug-outs. About 380 Jews captured. We found out that the Jews had taken to the sewers. Sewers were completely inundated, to make staying there impossible. About 1730 hrs. we encountered very strong resistance from one block of buildings including machine-gun fire. A special raiding party invaded that block and defeated the enemy, but could not catch the resisters. The Jews and criminals resisted from base to base, and escaped at the last moment across lofts or through subterranean passages. About 2030 hrs. the external barricade was reinforced. All units were withdrawn from the Ghetto and dismissed to their barracks. Reinforcement of the barricade by 250 Waffen-SS men. Continuation of operation on 20 April 1943.

Units at my disposal:

SS-Panzer-Gren. Res. Batl. 6/400
SS-Cav. Res. Batl. 10/450
Police 6/165
Security Service 2/48

ceeded in causing the firms of W.C. Toebens, Schultz and Co. and Hoffman to be ready for evacuation with their entire personnel on 21 April 1943 at 0600 hrs. In this way, I hope to get the way free at last for cleaning out the Ghetto. The Trustee Toebens has pledged himself to induce the Jews, numbering about 4,000 to 5,000, to follow him voluntarily to the assembling point for being resettled. In case this has as little success as was attained in the case of the Army Accommodation Office, I am going to clean out this part of the Ghetto as well by force. I beg to acknowledge receipt of the order which the Obergruppenfuehrer communicated to me by telephone today, and of the powers granted to me.

Next report on 21 April 1943 at noon.

     The SS and Police Fuehrer in the
       District of Warsaw
        Signed: Stroop
  SS-Brigadefuehrer and Majorgeneral of Police.

       Copy
     Teletype message

Certified copy:
SS-Sturmbannfuehrer.
From: The SS and Police Fuehrer in the District of Warsaw
       Warsaw, 21 April 1943.
Ref. Nr. I ab/St/Gr—16 07 —Journal Nr. 527/43.
Re: Ghetto Operation.
To the Higher SS and Police Fuehrer East,
SS-Obergruppenfuehrer and General of Police, *Krueger*—or deputy.
Cracow

Progress of Ghetto Operation on 21 April 1943.

Supplementing the report which I made today about 1400 hrs. by telephone, I beg to report:
Forces at my disposal as of 20 April 1943.

Start of operation: 0700 hrs. The whole of the Ghetto has continued to be cordoned off since the start of the operations on 19 April 1943.

Inasmuch as the special operation concerning the block of buildings occupied by the Army Accommodation Office had to be interrupted yesterday because of darkness, one battle group reinforced by Engineers and heavy artillery was again sent into the block of buildings, which was found to contain an enormous quantity of dug-outs and subterranean passages firing from time to time. I resolved therefore to blow up these passages which we had discovered and subsequently to set the entire block on fire. Not until the building was well aflame did screaming Jews make their appearance, and they were evacuated at once. We had no losses in this operation. Precautionary measures were taken in order to ensure that the conflagration remained localized.

The main body of our forces was detailed to cleanse the so-called uninhabited, but not yet released, part of the Ghetto by proceeding from South to North. Before we started this action, we caught 5,200 Jews who had been employed in enterprises under the supervision of the Commissioner for Armament [Ru Ko-Betrieben] and transported them under armed guard to the Railway Station which had been chosen for use in the resettlement. I formed 3 search-parties to which were attached special raiding parties who had the duty to attack or blow up the dug-outs which were known to us. This operation had to be interrupted when darkness set in, after one-half of the area mentioned had been combed out.

Continued on 22 April 1943, 0700 hrs.

Apart from the Jews who were to be evacuated, 150 Jews or bandits were killed in battle and about 80 bandits were killed when their dug-outs were blown up. The enemy today used the same arms as on the previous day, particularly home-made explosives. Samples have been kept by the SS and Police Fuehrer. For the first time we observed the participation of members of the Jewish Women's Battle Association (Chalutzim Movement). We captured rifles, pistols, hand grenades, explosives, horses, and parts of SS uniforms.

Own losses: 2 policemen, 2 SS men, 1 Trawniki-man.
  (light wounds)

The SS and Police Fuehrer
in the District of Warsaw.
Signed: Stroop

Certified copy:
        SS-Brigadefuehrer and Majorgeneral of Police.
SS-Sturmbannfuehrer.

Copy
Teletype message

From the SS and Police Fuehrer in the District of Warsaw
Warsaw, 22 April 1943.

Ref. No. I ab St/Gr 16 07—Journal Nr. 530/43 secret.

April 1943 about 2100 hours, and had requested them to remove their goods by 1200 hours. Since the Wehrmacht did not start this evacuation until 1000 hours I felt obliged to extend the term until 1800 hours. At 1815 hours a search party entered the premises, the building having been cordoned off, and found that a great number of Jews were within the building. Since some of these Jews resisted, I ordered the building to be set on fire. Not until all the buildings along the street and the back premises on either side were well aflame did the Jews, some of them on fire, emerge from these blocks, some of them endeavored to save their life by jumping into the street from windows and balconies, after having thrown down beds, blankets, and the like. Over and over again we observed that Jews and bandits, despite the danger of being burned alive, preferred to return into the flames rather than risk being caught by us. Over and over again the Jews kept up their firing almost to the end of the action; thus the engineers had to be protected by a machine gun when toward nightfall they had to enter forcibly a concrete building which had been very strongly fortified. Termination of today's operation; on 25 April 1943 at 0145 hours, 1,660 Jews were caught for evacuation, 1,814 pulled out of dug-outs, about 330 shot. Innumerable Jews were destroyed by the flames or perished when the dug-outs were blown up. 26 dug-outs were blown up and an amount of paper money, especially dollars was captured; this money has not yet been counted.

Our forces; as on the preceding day, minus 50 men of the Waffen-SS.

Our losses: 2 SS men and 1 Trawniki man wounded.

Altogether there have now been caught in this action 25,500 Jews who lived in the former Ghetto. Since there are only vague estimates available of the actual number of inhabitants I assume that now only very small numbers of Jews and bandits still remain within the Ghetto.

Operation will be continued on 25 April 1943, 1300 hours.

I beg to ackowledge receipt of teletype messages Nos. 1222 and 1223 of 24 April 1943. As far as can be predicted, the present large-scale operation will last until Easter Monday inclusive.

Today large posters were affixed to the walls surrounding the Ghetto, announcing that everybody who enters the former Ghetto without being able to prove his identity will be shot.

The SS and Police Fuehrer
in the District of Warsaw.
Signed: Stroop
SS-Brigadefuehrer and Major General of Police.

number of Jews and bandits were buried under the ruins. In a number of cases it was found necessary to start fires in order to smoke the gangs out.

I must add that since yesterday some of the units have been shot at time and again from outside the Ghetto, that is, from the Aryan part of Warsaw. Raiding parties at once entered the area in question and in one case succeeded in capturing 35 Polish bandits, Communists, who were liquidated at once. Today it happened repeatedly when we found it necessary to execute some bandits, that they collapsed shouting "Long Live Poland," "Long live Moscow."

The operation will be continued on 23 April 1943, 0700 hrs.
The SS and Police Fuehrer
in the District of Warsaw.
Signed: Stroop
SS-Brigadefuehrer and Majorgeneral of Police.
Certified copy:
SS-Sturmbannfuehrer.

Copy
Teletype message

From the SS and Police Fuehrer in the District of Warsaw
Warsaw, 23 April 1943.
Ref. No.: I ab/st/Gr—16 07—Journal No. 538/43 secret.
Re: Ghetto Operation.
To: The Higher SS and Police Fuehrer East, SS-Obergruppenfuehrer and General of Police *Krueger*—or deputy.
Cracow

Progress of Ghetto Operation on 23 April 1943. Start: 0700 hrs.

The whole of the former Ghetto had been divided for the purposes of today's combing-out operations into 24 districts. One reinforced searching party was detailed to each district with special orders. These assignments had to be carried out by 1600 hours.

Result of this action: 600 Jews and bandits ferreted out and captured, about 200 Jews and bandits killed, 48 dug-outs, some of them of a quite elaborate character, blown up. We captured apart from valuables and money—some gas masks.

The units had been informed that we intended to terminate the operation today. In the morning the Jews had already become aware of this instruction. This is why a renewed search by the searching parties was undertaken after an interval of 1 to 1½ hours. The result was, as always, that again Jews and bandits were discovered to be in various blocks. From one block shots were even fired against the cordoning units. An attack by a special battle group was ordered and in order to smoke the bandits out, every building was now set on fire. The Jews and bandits held their fire up to the last moment and then concerted their fire against the units. They even used carbines. A number of bandits who were shooting from balconies were hit by our men and crashed down.

Furthermore, today we discovered a place said to have been the headquarters of the "P PR"; we found it unoccupied and destroyed it. It was on this 5th day of operations that obviously we found the worst of the terrorists and activists, who so far had always found ways and means to dodge every searching or evacuation action.

A racial German reported that again some Jews had escaped through the sewers into the Aryan part of the city. We learned from a traitor that there were some Jews in a certain house. A special motorized raiding party invaded the building and caught 3 Jews, 2 of them females. During this operation their motor-car was pelted with one incendiary bottle and one explosive; 2 policemen were wounded.

The whole operation is rendered more difficult by the cunning way in which the Jews and bandits act; for instance, we discover that the hearses which were used to collect the corpses lying around at the same time bring living Jews to the Jewish cemetery, and thus they are enabled to escape from the Ghetto. Now this way of escape also is barred by continuous control of the hearses.

At the termination of today's operation about 2200 hours, we discovered that again about 30 bandits had passed into a so-called armaments factory, where they had found refuge. Since the forces are storing goods of great value in this enterprise, this factory was requested to evacuate the building by noon on 24 April; this will enable us to cleanse that labyrinth of a building tomorrow.

Today 3,500 Jews were caught who are to be evacuated from the factories. A total of 19,450 Jews have been caught for resettlement or already evacuated up to today. Of these about 2,500 Jews are still to be loaded. The next train will start on 24 April 1943.

Strength as of 22 April 1943, without 150 Trawniki men;

these have already been put at the disposal of the Eastern Command as reinforcement for another assignment.
Our losses:
    2 Police corporals ("SB") wounded
    1 Trawniki man wounded.
    The operation will be continued on 24 April 1943, 1000 hours. This hour was chosen so that Jews who may still be in the Ghetto will believe that the operation was actually terminated today.

The SS and Police Fuehrer
in the District of Warsaw.
Signed: Stroop
SS-Brigadefuehrer and Major general of Police.

Certified copy:
SS-Sturmbannfuehrer.

Copy
Teletype message

From the SS and Police Fuehrer in the District of Warsaw
Warsaw, 24 April 1943.
Ref: Nr.: I ab/St/Wdt—16 07—Journal No. 545/43 secret.
Re: Ghetto operation.
The Higher SS and Police Fuehrer East, SS-Obergruppenfuehrer and general of the Police *Krueger*—or deputy.
Cracow

Progress of operation on 24 April 1943, start 1000 hours.
    Contrary to the preceding days, the 24 searching parties which had again been formed did not start at one end of the Ghetto, but proceeded from all sides at the same time. Apparently the Jews still in the Ghetto were deceived by the fact that the operation did not start until 1000 hours into believing that the action really had been terminated yesterday. The search action, therefore, had especially satisfactory results today. This success is furthermore due to the fact that the noncommissioned officers and men have meanwhile become accustomed to the cunning fighting, methods and tricks used by the Jews and bandits and that they have acquired great skill in tracking down the dugouts which are found in such great number. The raiding parties having returned, we set about to clean a block of buildings, situated in the northeastern part of the former Ghetto. In this labyrinth of buildings there was a so-called armaments firm which reportedly had goods worth millions for manufacture and storage. I had notified the Wehrmacht of my intentions on 23

Copy
Teletype message

From: The SS and Police Fuehrer in the District of Warsaw

Warsaw, 25 April 1943

Ref. No. I ab/St/Wdt—16 07—Journal No. 549/43 secret.

Re: Ghetto operation.

To: The Higher SS and Police Fuehrer East, SS-Obergruppenfuehrer and General of Police *Krueger*—or deputy.
Cracow

Progress of operation on 25 April 1943, start 1300 hours.

For today 7 search parties were formed, strength 1/70 each, each allotted to a certain block of buildings.

Their order was: "Every building is to be combed out once more; dug-outs have to be discovered and blown up, and the Jews have to be caught. If any resistance is encountered or if dug-outs cannot be reached, the buildings are to be burnt down." Apart from the operations undertaken by these 7 search parties, a special operation was undertaken against a center of bandits, situated outside the wall surrounding the former Ghetto and inhabited exclusively by Poles.

Today's operations of the search parties ended almost everywhere in the starting of enormous conflagrations. In this manner the Jews were forced to leave their hideouts and refuges. A total of 1,960 Jews were caught alive. The Jews informed us that among them were certain parachutists who were dropped here and bandits who had been equipped with arms from some unknown source. 274 Jews were killed. As in the preceding days, uncounted Jews were buried in blown up dug-outs and, as can be observed time and again, burned with this bag of Jews today. We have, in my opinion, caught a very considerable part of the bandits and lowest elements of the Ghetto. Intervening darkness prevented immediate liquidation. I am going to try to obtain a train for T II tomorrow. Otherwise liquidation will be carried out tomorrow. Today also, some armed resistance was encountered; in a dug-out three pistols and some explosives were captured. Furthermore, considerable amounts of paper money, foreign currency, gold coins, and jewelry were seized today.

The Jews still have considerable property. While last night a glare of fire could be seen above the former Ghetto, today one can observe a giant sea of flames. Since we continue to discover great numbers of Jews whenever we search and comb out, the operation will be continued on 26 April 1943. Start: 1000 hours.

Including today, a total of 27,464 Jews of the former Warsaw Ghetto, have been captured.

Our forces; as on the previous day.

Our losses; 3 members of the Waffen-SS and one member of the Security Police wounded.

Total losses up to date:

Waffen SS	27 Wounded
Police	9 Wounded
Security Police	4 Wounded
Wehrmacht	1 Wounded
Trawniki men	9 Wounded

50 Wounded

and 5 dead:

Waffen SS	2 Dead
Wehrmacht	2 Dead
Trawniki men	1 Dead

5 Dead

The SS and Police Fuehrer
in the District of Warsaw.
Signed: Stroop
SS-Brigadefuehrer and Majorgeneral of Police.

Certified copy:
SS-Sturmbannfuehrer.

Copy
Teletype message

From: The SS and Police Fuehrer in the District of Warsaw
Warsaw, 26 April 1943.

Ref. No.: I ab/St/Wdt—16 07—Journal Nr. 550/43 secret.

Re: Ghetto operation—supplementary report.

To: The Higher SS and Police Fuehrer East, SS-Obergruppenfuehrer and General of Police *Krueger*—or deputy.

Cracow

1. The operation on 25 April 1943, was terminated at 2200 hrs.

2. General effects of the execution of this operation.

The Poles resident in Warsaw are much impressed by the

toughness of our operations in the former Ghetto. As can be seen from the daily reports, the general situation has greatly calmed down since the beginning of that operation within the city area of Warsaw. From this fact one may conclude that the bandits and saboteurs resided in the former Ghetto, and that now all of them have been destroyed.

In this connection the fact may be of some interest, that an illegal ammunition store was seen to explode when we burned down a certain building in the dwelling area on which we were working at the time.

The SS and Police Fuehrer
in the District of Warsaw.
Signed: Stroop
SS-Brigadefuehrer and Majorgeneral of Police.

Certified copy:
SS-Sturmbannfuehrer.

Copy
Teletype message

From: The SS and Police Fuehrer in the District of Warsaw
Warsaw, 26 April 1943.

Ref. Nr.: 1 ab/St/Wdt—16 07 Journal Nr. 551/43 secret.

To: The Higher SS and Police Fuehrer East, SS-Obergruppenfuehrer and General of Police *Krueger*—or deputy.

Cracow

Start of operation: 1000 hrs.

The whole of the former Ghetto was once more combed through today by the same search parties, each of them allotted to the same district as before. In this way I tried to bring about that the leaders of these parties work in thoroughfares, blocks of buildings, and courtyards which they know already and that thus they are able to penetrate deeper and deeper into the maze of dug-outs and subterranean passages. Almost every search party reported resistance, which however they broke either by returning fire or by blowing up the dug-outs. It becomes clearer and clearer that it is now the turn of the toughest and strongest among the Jews and bandits. Several times dug-outs have been forcibly broken open, the inmates of which had not come to the surface during the whole of this operation. In a number of cases the inmates of the dug-outs were hardly in a condition, when the dug-out had been blown up, to crawl to the surface. The captured Jews report that many of the inmates of the dug-outs became insane from the heat, the smoke, and the explosions.

Several Jews were arrested who had kept close liaison with the group of Polish terrorists and collaborated with it. Outside the former Ghetto we arrested 29 Jews. During today's operation several blocks of buildings were burned down. This is the only and final method which forces this trash and subhumanity to the surface. We again captured arms, incendiary bottles, explosive charges and considerable amounts of cash and foreign currency. Today I also arranged that several so-called armament and defense enterprises will evacuate their stores from the buildings at once, so that these buildings in which the Jews now have taken refuge, under the protection of the army of the German Wehrmacht and police, can be combed out. In one case we again discovered, as previously, that in a building which had been said to contain a giant enterprise there existed in fact almost no stores or goods. One factory was closed without further ado, and the Jews were evacuated.

Result of today's operation:

30 Jews evacuated, 1,330 Jews pulled out of dug-outs and immediately destroyed, 362 Jews killed in battle. Caught today altogether: 1,722 Jews. This brings the total of Jews caught to 29,186. Moreover, it is very probable that numerous Jews have perished in the 13 dug-outs blown up today and in the conflagrations.

At the time of writing not one of the Jews caught still remains within Warsaw. The scheduled transport to T. II had no success. [Note of translator: This probably means that no Jews were available for regular transport to the extermination camp.]
Strength: as on preceding day.
Our losses: none.

End of today's operation at 2145 hrs. Will be continued on 27 April 1943 at 0900 hrs.

The SS and Police Fuehrer
in the District of Warsaw.
Signed: Stroop
SS-Brigadefuehrer and Majorgeneral of Police.

Certified copy:
SS-Sturmbannfuehrer.

Copy
Teletype message

From the SS and Police Fuehrer in the District of Warsaw

Warsaw, 27 April 1943.

Ref. No.: I ab/St/Gr—16 07—Journal No. 555/43 secret.

The Documentary Evidence 1061-PS

Re: Ghetto Operation.
To: The Higher SS and Police Fuehrer East, SS-Obergruppenfuehrer and General of Police *Krueger*—or deputy.

Cracow
Progress of operation on 27 April 1943. Start: 0900 hrs.

For today's operation I formed 24 raiding parties with the same task as on several days of last week; they had to search the former Ghetto in smaller groups. These search parties pulled 780 Jews out of dug-outs and shot 115 Jews who resisted. This operation was terminated about 1500 hrs.; some of the parties had to continue to operate because they had found more dug-outs.

At 1600 hrs. a special battle group, 320 officers and men strong, started cleansing a large block of buildings situated on both sides of the so-called Niska Street in the Northeastern part of the former Ghetto. After the search the entire block was set on fire, after having been completely cordoned off. In this action a considerable number of Jews were caught. As before, they remained in the dug-outs, which were either below the ground or in the lofts of the buildings until the end. They fired their arms to the last moment, and then jumped down into the street, sometimes from as far up as the fourth floor, having previously thrown down beds, mattresses, etc., but not until the flames made any other escape impossible. A total of 2,560 Jews were caught today within the former Ghetto, of whom 547 were shot. Moreover, Jews in a not ascertainable number perished when dug-outs were blown up, or in the flames. The sum total of Jews, formerly residing in the Ghetto caught in this action, now amounts to 31,746.

We learned from an anonymous letter that there were a considerable number of Jews in a block of buildings adjoining the Northeastern part of the Ghetto, but outside of it. A special raiding party under the command of 1st. Lt. of Police Diehl was dispatched to attack these buildings. The raiding party discovered a gang of about 120 men, strongly armed with pistols, rifles, hand grenades, and light machine guns, who resisted. They succeeded in destroying 24 bandits in battle and arresting 52 bandits. The remainder could not be caught or destroyed, since darkness intervened. The buildings, however, were surrounded at once, so that an escape will hardly be possible. This cleansing action will be continued tomorrow. Moreover, we arrested 17 Poles, among whom 2 Polish Policemen, who should have been aware, among other things, of the existence of this gang. In this operation we captured 3 rifles, 12 pistols, partly of heavier caliber, 100 Polish "pineapple" hand grenades, 27 German steel helmets, quite a number of German uniforms, tunics and coats which were even furnished with ribbon of the East medal, some reserve magazines for machine guns, 300 rounds of ammunition, etc. The leader of the raiding party had a difficult task because the bandits were disguised in German uniform, but despite this fact, he did his duty with great efficiency. Among the bandits who were caught or killed, there were some Polish terrorists who were identified with certainty. Today we succeeded furthermore in discovering and liquidating one of the founders and leaders of the Jewish-Polish resistance movement. The external appearance of the Jews whom we are catching now shows that it is now the turn of those Jews who were the leaders of the entire resistance movement. They jumped from the burning windows and balconies, abusing Germany and the Fuehrer and cursing the German soldiers.

SS-men who descended into the sewers discovered that a great number of corpses of perished Jews are being washed away by the water.

Our strength:

From 0700 to 1900 hrs.	288 German Police 200 Trawnikimen 140 Polish Police	Cordoning forces.
From 1900 to 0700 hrs.	288 German Police 250 Waffen-SS 140 Polish Police	

Strength in the operation:
- 3/115 German Police
- 4/400 Waffen-SS
- 1/6 Engineering Serv.
- 2/30 Security Police
- 2/21 Engineers

Our losses:
- 3 wounded:
- 2 Waffen-SS
- 1 Trawniki-man

Termination of operation: 2300 hrs. Will be continued on 28 April 1943 at 1000 hrs.

The SS and Police Fuehrer
in the District of Warsaw.
Signed: Stroop
SS-Brigadefuehrer and Majorgeneral of Police.

Copy

Teletype message

From the SS and Police Fuehrer in the District of Warsaw

Warsaw, 28 April 1943.

Ref. Nr. I ab/St/Gr—16 07—Journal Nr. 562/43 secret.

Re: Ghetto operation

To: The Higher SS and Police Fuehrer East, SS-Obergruppenfuehrer and General of Police *Krueger*—or deputy.

Cracow

Progress of operation on 28 April 1943. Start 1000 hrs.

Today, 10 raiding parties were formed for combing out the whole of the Ghetto. These raiding parties again discovered proceeding step by step, a number of dug-outs, which were found to have been prepared as far ago as the middle of last year for use in the resistance of the Jews. A total of 335 Jews were forcibly pulled out of these dug-outs. Apart from these operations, we continued to cleanse the resistance center used by the Jewish military organization, situated at the borders of the Ghetto. We succeeded in shooting 10 more bandits, and in arresting 9, beyond those caught yesterday, and in capturing more arms, ammunition, and military equipment. In the afternoon a battle group again was directed against a block of buildings which had already been combed out; the block was set on fire during this operation. As on previous days, masses of Jews emerged, forced out by the flames and the enormous clouds of smoke. At another point an Engineer officer, attached by the Wehrmacht to the units with great trouble opened a dug-out situated about 3 meters below ground. From this dug-out, which had been ready since October of last year and was equipped with running water, toilet and electric light, we pulled out 274 of the richest and most influential Jews. Today again we encountered very strong resistance in many places and broke it. It becomes clearer every day that we are now encountering the real terrorists and activists, because of the duration of the operation.

Result of today: 1,655 Jews caught for evacuation, of whom 110 were killed in battle.

Many more Jews were killed by the flames; moreover, Jews in an unascertainable number were destroyed by the dug-outs being blown up. By the results of today the number of Jews caught or destroyed rises to 33,401 altogether. This number does not include the Jews who were killed by fire or destroyed in the dug-outs.

Our strength: as on the previous day.

Our losses: 3 wounded (1 Police, 2 Waffen-SS)

Termination of operation: 2200 hrs. Will be continued on 29 April 1943. 1000 hrs.

The SS and Police Fuehrer
in the District of Warsaw.
Signed: Stroop
SS-Brigadefuehrer and Majorgeneral of Police.

Certified copy:
SS-Sturmbannfuehrer.

Copy
Teletype message

From: the SS and Police Fuehrer in the District of Warsaw

Warsaw, 29 April 1943.

Ref. Nr. I ab/St/Gr—16 07—Journal Nr. 566/43 secret.

Re: Ghetto Operation.

To: The Higher SS and Police Fuehrer East, SS-Obergruppenfuehrer and General of Police *Krueger*—or deputy.

Cracow

Progress of large-scale operation of 29 April 1943. Start 1000 hrs. As on the previous day I formed search parties, who had the special task of searching those blocks of buildings which had been recently separated. A larger raiding party was detailed to clean a certain block of buildings (formerly the Hallmann concern) and to burn this block down. 36 more dug-outs used for habitation were discovered altogether, and from them and other hideouts and from the burning buildings, 2,359 Jews were caught of whom 106 were killed in battle.

Captured are 2 rifles, 10 pistols, 10 kilograms of explosives, and ammunition of various types.

When a large dug-out was blown up, the entire building collapsed and everyone of the bandits perished. In the ensuing conflagration loud detonations and darting flames showed that the building must have contained large stores of ammunition and explosives. Some sewer entrances were blown up. Two exists discovered outside the Ghetto were also made unusable by blowing them up or walling them up.

The depositions of some of the inmates of the dug-outs are to the effect that these Jews have been unable to leave the dug-outs for the last 10 days and that their food, etc., is now beginning to grow short because the large-scale operations had lasted so long. Furthermore, the Jews testify that bandits appeared at night who were Jews or sometimes Poles, wearing black masks, who walled the dug-outs up from the outside and admonished them not to give any signs of life, so that they could continue to live in the Ghetto when the action was finished. Some of the armaments factories are being evacuated very slowly. In several cases one gains the impression that this is done intentionally. Thus I discovered with regard to one firm, Schulz and Co., which I had visited on Easter Monday and then instructed to start evacuation at once and to have it completed within 3 days, that up till today, Thursday, nothing had been done.

Our strength: as on the previous day.
Our losses: none.

Termination of operation at 2100 hrs. Will be continued on 30 April 1943, 0900 hrs.

Total caught or destroyed: 35,760.

The SS and Police Fuehrer in the
District of Warsaw.
Signed: Stroop
SS Brigadefuehrer and Majorgeneral of Police.

Certified copy:
SS-Sturmbannfuehrer.

Copy
Teletype message

From: The SS and Police Fuehrer in the District of Warsaw
Warsaw, 30 April 1943.
Ref. No.: I ab/St/Gr—16 07—Journal No. 579/43 secret.
Re: Ghetto Operation.
To: The Higher SS and Police Fuehrer East, SS-Obergruppenfuehrer and General of Police *Krueger*—or deputy.
Cracow

Progress of large-scale operation on 30 April 1943. Start 0900 hrs.

Combing out by search parties was continued. Although some giant blocks of buildings now are completely burned out, the Jews continue to stay in the dug-outs 2 to 3 meters below ground. In many cases we are not able to discover those dug-outs unless some Jew, whom we have already caught, gives us a hint as to their whereabouts. Repeatedly, during the last few days, Jews have testified that some armed Jews emerge at night from some hideouts or dug-outs and threaten the other Jews with shooting if they give any signs of life. We were able to ascertain beyond all doubt that several dug-outs had been closed from the outside by these bandits, who tried in this manner to prove that they meant business. Altogether, 30 dug-outs were discovered, evacuated, and blown up today. Again we caught a great number of bandits and subhumans. Apart from the bombing-out operations effected by small parties, two larger battle groups were occupied with bombing out and destroying by fire several interconnected blocks of buildings.

A total of 1599 Jews were caught today, of whom 179 were killed in battle. The sum total of Jews caught up to date thereby rises to 37,359. 3,855 Jews were loaded today. The number of Jews in possession of arms was much higher than before among the Jews caught during the last few days. Today, we again captured arms and particularly parts of German uniforms from them. The operation against Fort Traugutta did not have any positive results. So far as we were able to discover subterranean exits, we either occupied them or blew them up. In attacking one of the blocks we had to use a gun today.

Our strength:

Used in the operation:

Police	5/133
Security Police	3/36
Waffen SS	6/432
Engineer	2/40
Staff	3/7

Cordoning forces:

Waffen SS	3/318
German Police	2/89
Trawniki men	200

moreover some Polish Police

Our losses: 1 wounded (Police)

Termination of today's large scale action: 2100 hours. Will be continued on 1 May 1943, 0900 hours.

The SS and Police Fuehrer
in the District of Warsaw.
Signed: Stroop
SS-Brigadefuehrer and Majorgeneral of Police.

Copy

Teletype message

From: The SS and Police Fuehrer in the District of Warsaw

Warsaw, May 1, 1943.

Ref.: Nr.: I ab/St/Gr—16 07—Journal No. 583/43 secret.

Re: Large-scale Ghetto operation.

To: The Higher SS and Police Fuehrer East, SS-Obergruppenfuehrer and General of Police *Krueger*—or deputy.

Cracow

Progress of large scale operation on 1 May 1943. Start 0900 hrs.

10 searching parties were detailed, moreover a larger battle group was detailed to comb out a certain block of buildings, with the added instruction to burn that block down. Within this block of buildings there existed a so-called armament factory which had not yet been entirely evacuated, although it had had enough time to do so. It was not exempted from the operation. Today's operation a total of 1,026 Jews were caught, of whom 245 were killed, either in battle or while resisting. Moreover, a considerable number of bandits and ringleaders were also caught. In one case a Jew who had already been made ready for transport fired three shots against a 1st Lieutenant of Police, but missed his mark. All the Jews caught today were forcibly pulled out of dug-outs. Not a single one gave himself up voluntarily, after his dug-out had been opened. A considerable part of the Jews caught were pulled out of the sewers. We continued systematically blowing up or blocking up the sewer entrances. In one case the Engineers laid a strong concentrated charge and had to proceed to an adjoining entrance where they had something to do. In the meantime a Jew emerged from the sewer, removed the fuse from the concentrated charge, and appropriated the charge. In the further course of this operation we succeeded in catching the Jew, still in possession of the concentrated charge.

In order to ascertain the movements of the Jews during the night, today I used for the first time 5 scouting parties, each 1/9 strong, at irregular intervals during the night. In general, it has to be stated that our men need extraordinary diligence and energy to discover the Jews who are still in so-called dug-outs, caves, and in the sewerage system. It can be expected that the remainder of the Jews who formerly inhabited the Ghetto will now be caught. The sum total of Jews caught so far has risen to 38,385. Not included in this figure are those who died in the flames or in the dug-outs. One patrol discovered an unascertainable number of corpses floating in a main sewer under the Ghetto. Outside of the Ghetto, in the immediate vicinity of Warsaw, the gendarmerie has shot a total of 150 Jews who could be proved to have escaped from Warsaw.

Again we captured pistols and explosives.

Our strength, used in operation:

Police (German)	4/102
Waffen SS	7/350
Engineers (Wehrmacht)	2/38
Engineering Emergency Service	1/6
Security Police	2/1

Cordoning units:

Waffen SS	300
German Police	1/71
Trawniki	250

Our losses: 1 policeman — wounded yesterday, died from wounds.

Termination of today's large-scale action: 2200 hours. Will be continued on 2 May 1943, 1000 hours.

The SS and Police Fuehrer
in the District of Warsaw.
Signed: Stroop
SS-Brigadefuehrer and Majorgeneral of Police.

Certified copy:
SS-Sturmbannfuehrer.

Copy
Teletype message

From: The SS and Police Fuehrer in the District of Warsaw

Warsaw, 2 May 1943.

Ref. No.: I ab St/Gr—16 07—Journal No. 584/43 secret.

Re: Large-scale Ghetto operation.

To: The Higher SS and Police Fuehrer East, SS-Obergruppenfuehrer and General of Police *Krueger*—or deputy.

Cracow

Progress of large-scale operation on 2 May 1943, start 1000 hrs. 9 raiding parties combed out the whole area of the former

Ghetto; moreover a larger detachment was detailed to clean out or destroy one block of buildings grouped around the two armament enterprises Transavia and Wischniewski. To find more dug-outs, the raiding parties took along with them some Jews caught on the previous day to act as guides. In these operations the raiding parties pulled out 944 Jews from dugouts; 235 more Jews were shot on this occasion. When the block of buildings mentioned above was destroyed, 120 Jews were caught and numerous Jews were destroyed when they jumped from the attics to the inner courtyards, trying to escape the flames. Many more Jews perished in the flames or were destroyed when the dug-outs and sewer entrances were blown up. The Jews were removed from two armaments concerns and the managers were requested to evacuate within a short time.

Altogether we caught today: 1,852 Jews. The sum total of Jews caught thereby rises to 40,237 Jews. 27 dug-outs were discovered, forcibly opened and destroyed, arms and ammunition captured. When the external barricade was shot at and when some Jews who broke out from a sewer entrance outside the Ghetto made an attack, we suffered 7 losses, 4 Policemen and 3 Polish Policemen. The scouting parties used during the night encountered armed resistance from some Jews who under the protection of darkness ventured to emerge from their holes and dug-outs. We did not suffer losses thereby. On the other hand, a considerable number of Jews were killed or wounded in this operation.

Our strength, used in operation:
    German Police 3/98
    Engineering Em Service 1/6
    Security Police 3/12
    Engineers (Wehrmacht) 2/37
    SS-Gren 11/409
    SS-Cav. 3/7

Cordoning forces:
    German Police 2/9
    SS-Gren. 1/300
    Trawniki 200

Our losses:
    4 Policemen wounded
    3 Polish policemen wounded

Present at today's large-scale operation was the Higher SS and Police Fuehrer East, SS-Obergruppenfuehrer and General of Police Krueger.

Termination of operation: 2030 hours. Will be continued on 3 May 1943, 0900 hours.

The SS and Police Fuehrer
in the District of Warsaw.
Signed: Stroop
SS-Brigadefuehrer and Majorgeneral of Police.

Certified copy:
SS-Sturmbannfuehrer.

Copy
Teletype message

From: The SS and Police Fuehrer in the District of Warsaw

Warsaw, 3 May 1943.

Ref. Nr.: I ab-St/Gr—16 07—Journal Nr. 597/43 secret.
Re: Large-scale Ghetto operation.
To: The Higher SS and Police Fuehrer East, SS-Obergruppenfuehrer and General of Police *Krueger*—or deputy.
Cracow

Progress of large-scale operation on 3 May 1943, start 0900 hrs. In the combing-out operation of the former Jewish Ghetto today 19 more dug-outs were discovered and the result was as follows:

Pulled out of dug-outs	1,392 Jews
Shot	95
Evacuated from former armament factories	177

The sum total of Jews caught thereby rises to 41,806 Jews. In most cases the Jews offered armed resistance before they left the dug-outs. We had two casualties (wounded). Some of the Jews and bandits fired pistols from both hands. Since we discovered several times today, that Jewesses had pistols concealed in their bloomers, every Jew and bandit will be ordered from today on, to strip completely for the search. We captured among other things, one German rifle, model 98, two 08 pistols and other calibers, also home-made hand grenades. The Jews cannot be induced to leave their dug-outs until several smoke candles have been burned. According to depositions made yesterday and today, the Jews were asked during the second half of 1942 to erect air-raid shelters. At that time under the camouflage of erecting air-raid shelters, they began to build the dug-outs which they are now inhabiting, in order to use them for an anti-Jewish operation. Some of the scouting parties used in the

Ghetto were shot at last night. One casualty (wounded). These scouting parties reported that groups of armed bandits marched through the Ghetto.
Strength: as on the previous day.
Losses: 3 SS-men wounded.
　　Termination of today's operation: 2100 hrs. Will be continued on 4 May 1943. 0900 hrs.
3,019 Jews were loaded.
The SS and Police Fuehrer
in the District of Warsaw.
Signed: Stroop
SS-Brigadefuehrer and Majorgeneral of Police.
Certified copy:
SS-Sturmbannfuehrer.

Copy
Teletype message

From: The SS and Police Fuehrer in the District of Warsaw
　　　　　　　　　　　　　　　　Warsaw, 4 May 1943.
Ref. No.: I ab-St/Gr—16 07—Journal No. 603/43 secret.
Re: Large-scale Ghetto operation.
To: The Higher SS and Police Fuehrer East, SS-Obergruppen-
　fuehrer and General of Police *Krueger*—or deputy.
Cracow

Progress of large-scale operation on 4 May 1943, start 0900 hrs.
　For mopping up the dug-outs a raiding party was used, 1/60 strong and reinforced by an Engineer's detachment provided by the Wehrmacht. This raiding party pulled 550 Jews out of dug-outs and killed in battle 188 Jews. Discovering the dug-outs becomes more and more difficult. Often they can only be discovered by betrayal through other Jews. If the Jews are requested to leave their dug-out voluntarily, they hardly ever obey; they can only be forced to do so by the use of smoke-candles.
　The main forces were detailed about 1100 hours to comb out, mop up, and destroy two large blocks of buildings, containing the former firms Toebbens, Schulz and Co., and others. After these blocks had been completely cordoned off, we requested the Jews who were still within the buildings to come forward voluntarily. By this measure, we caught 456 Jews for evacuation. Not until the blocks of buildings were well aflame and were about to collapse did a further considerable number of Jews emerge, forced to do so by the flames and the smoke. Time and again the Jews try to escape even through burning buildings.

Innumerable Jews whom we saw on the roofs during the conflagration perished in the flames. Others emerged from the upper stories in the last possible moment and were only able to escape death in the flames by jumping down. Today we caught a total of 2,283 Jews, of whom 204 were shot and innumerable Jews were destroyed in dug-outs and in the flames. The sum total of Jews caught rises to 44,089.

As is learned from depositions made by the Jews, today we caught part of the governing body of the so-called "Party." One member of the committee which leads the gang will be used tomorrow for mopping up some more fortified dug-outs with armed Jews inside. When the armament enterprises were evacuated, we again observed that the goods carted away were by no means valuable military equipment, as had been pretended, but trifles, like used furniture and other requisitioned items. We took appropriate measures against this at once.

The scouting parties who patrolled during the night in the former Ghetto again reported movements of the Jews in the burned out and destroyed streets and courtyards. In order to be better able to take the Jews by surprise, the scouting parties at night tie rags and other stuff around their shoes. In skirmishes between the scouting parties and Jews, 30 Jews were shot.

We captured 1 carbine, 3 pistols, and some ammunition. During the conflagration a considerable amount of stored ammunition exploded.

Our strength, used in operation:

German Police	4/101
Engineering Em. Service	1/6
Security Police	2/14
Engineers	2/41
Waffen SS	11/407

Cordoning forces:

	Day	Night
German Police	2/87	1/11
Waffen SS	25	1/300
Trawniki	200	
Polish Police	1/180	1/180

Our losses: None.

Termination of operation: 2330 hours. Will be continued on 5 May 1943, 1000 hours.

The SS and Police Fuehrer in
the District of Warsaw.
Signed: Stroop
SS-Brigadefuehrer and Majorgeneral of Police.

Copy

Teletype message

From: The SS and Police Fuehrer in the District of Warsaw

Warsaw, 5 May 1943.

Ref. Nr.: I ab/St/Gr—16 07—Journal No. 607/43 secret.
Re: Large-scale Ghetto operation.
To: The Higher SS and Police Fuehrer East, SS-Obergruppenfuehrer and General of Police *Krueger*—or deputy.

Cracow

Progress of large-scale operation on 5 May 1943. Start 1000 hrs. In the beginning of today's operations the raiding parties seemed to have less results than on the preceding days. When the operation terminated, however, quite a number of dug-outs had again been discovered, owing to the tracking ability of the men and to betrayal; 40 of these dug-outs were destroyed. As far as possible, the Jews in these dug-outs were caught (1,070 altogether). The combing out patrols shot about 126 Jews. Today again the Jews resisted in several places until they were captured. In several cases the entrances (hatches) of the dug-outs were forcibly held or bolted from the inside, so that only by using a strong explosive charge could we force them open and destroy the inmates. Today, we again captured arms and ammunition, including one pistol. From one enterprise still in existence (so-called Prosta) 2,850 Jews were caught for evacuation. This figure was included in the sum total reported earlier, so that only 1,070 have to be added; the present sum total therefore is 45,159.

Our strength: as on the preceding day.
Our losses: 1 SS man wounded, 1 Policeman wounded.
  Sum total of losses to date: 8 dead, 55 wounded.
  Termination of operation: 2200 hrs. Will be continued on 6 May 1943, 0900 hrs.

The SS and Police Fuehrer in the
District of Warsaw.
Signed: Stroop
SS-Brigadefuehrer and Majorgeneral of Police.

Certified copy:
SS-Sturmbannfuehrer.

Copy
Teletype message
From: The SS and Police Fuehrer in the District of Warsaw
Warsaw, 6 May 1943.
Ref. No.: ab/St/Gr—16 07—Journal No. 614/43 secret.
Re: Ghetto large-scale operation.
To: The Higher SS and Police Fuehrer East, SS-Obergruppenfuehrer and General of Police *Krueger*—or deputy.
Cracow

Progress of large-scale operation on 6 May 1943, start 0930 hrs.

Today we combed especially those blocks of buildings which were destroyed by fire on 4 May 1943. Although it was hardly to be expected that any living person could still exist in those blocks, we discovered quite a number of dug-outs in which a burning heat had developed. From these dug-outs and from other dug-outs which we discovered in other parts of the Ghetto, we pulled out 1,553 Jews. While resisting, and in a skirmish, 356 Jews were shot. In this skirmish the Jews fired from 08 pistols and other calibers and threw Polish "pineapple" hand grenades. One SS Unterscharfuehrer was wounded and a total of 47 dug-outs were destroyed.

2 men of the external cordoning forces were wounded. The Jews who had broken out from the Ghetto seemed to be returning now with the intention of assisting the Ghetto Jews by force or liberating them. One Jew who had escaped from Lublin was caught just outside of the Ghetto wall. He was armed as follows: 1 08 pistol, ample reserve ammunition, 2 Polish "pineapple" hand grenades. It could not be reliably ascertained so far whether the so-called "Party Directorate" of the Jews ("PPR") have been caught or destroyed. We are on their traces. It is to be hoped that tomorrow we shall succeed in tracing down this so-called Party Directorate. In order to enable us to intercept more effectively the Jews and bandits who approach the Ghetto, covering detachments of the external barricade were shifted farther inside the Aryan part. The former miniature Ghetto "Prosta" was searched by raiding parties today. We caught some Jews who had stayed behind. The firm Toebbens was requested to evacuate this miniature Ghetto by noon on 10 May 1943. The so-called library, situated outside the Ghetto, was put at their disposal for temporary storage of their raw materials, etc.

The sum total of Jews caught so far rises to 47,068. The Polish Police take pains to deliver to my office every Jew who turns up within the city, because they are eager to win such premiums as have been paid in earlier cases. The undersigned received some anonymous letters in which he was notified of the fact that some Jews are staying in the Aryan part of the city. One anonymous letter draws a parallel between Katyn and the large-scale action within the Ghetto.

Our strength:
Used in operation:

German Police	4/101
Engineering Em. Service	1/6
Security Police	2/14
Engineers	3/72
Waffen SS	10/500

Cordoning forces:

	Day	Night
German Police	2/87	1/11
Waffen SS	25	1/300
Trawniki	200	—
Polish Police	1/180	1/180

Our losses:
  1 Policeman dead
  1 Policeman seriously wounded
  1 SS Unterscharfuehrer less seriously wounded

Termination of operation: 2100 hours. Will be continued on 7 May 1943, 0930 hours.

The SS and Police Fuehrer in the
District of Warsaw.
Signed: Stroop
SS-Brigadefuehrer and Majorgeneral of Police.

Certified copy:
SS-Sturmbannfuehrer.

Copy
Teletype message

From: The SS and Police Fuehrer in the District of Warsaw
Warsaw, 7 May 1943.
Ref. Nr.: I ab/St/Gr—16 07—Journal Nr. 616/43 secret.
Re: Large-scale Ghetto operation.
To: The Higher SS and Police Fuehrer East, SS-Obergruppenfuehrer and General of Police *Krueger*—or deputy.
Cracow

Progress of large-scale operation on 7 May 1943, start 1000 hrs.
  The combing-out parties today obtained the following results:

49 dug-outs discovered. Part of the Jews were caught. A considerable, not ascertainable, number of Jews who refused to leave the dug-outs and offered armed resistance were destroyed when the dug-outs were blown up. Altogether 1,019 Jews were caught alive today, 255 shot. The sum total of Jews caught so far rises to 48,342. Today we again encountered armed resistance in several cases, whereby we lost 1 SS man (wounded). We captured 4 pistols of various calibers and some stores of ammunition.

The location of the dug-out used by the so-called select "Party Directorate" is now known. It is to be forced open tomorrow. The Jews testify that they emerge at night to get fresh air, since it is unbearable to stay permanently within the dug-outs owing to the long duration of the operation. On the average the raiding parties shoot 30 to 50 Jews each night. From these statements it was to be inferred that a considerable number of Jews are still underground in the Ghetto. Today we blew up a concrete building which we had not been able to destroy by fire. In this operation we learned that the blowing up of a building is a very lengthy process and takes an enormous amount of explosives. The best and only method for destroying the Jews therefore still remains the setting of fires.

Our strength: as on the preceding day.
Our losses: 1 Waffen-SS man wounded.

Termination of operation: 2100 hours, will be continued on 8 May 1943 1000 hours.

The SS and Police Fuehrer in the
District of Warsaw.
Signed: Stroop
SS-Brigadefuehrer and Majorgeneral of Police.

Certified copy:
SS-Sturmbannfuehrer.

———

Copy
Teletype message
From: The SS and Police Fuehrer in the District of Warsaw
Warsaw, 8 May 1943.

Ref. No.: I ab/St/Gr—16 07—Journal No. 624/43 secret.
Re: Large-scale Ghetto operation.
To: The Higher SS and Police Fuehrer East, SS-Obergruppenfuehrer and General of Police *Krueger*—or deputy.
Cracow
Progress of operation on 8 May 1943, start 1000 hours.

The whole former Ghetto was searched today by raiding parties for the remaining dug-outs and Jews. As reported some days a number of subhumans, bandits, and terrorists still remain in the dug-outs, where heat has become intolerable by reason of the fires. These creatures know only too well that their only choice is between remaining in hiding as long as possible or coming to the surface and trying to wound or kill off the men of the Waffen-SS, Police, and Wehrmacht who keep up the pressure against them.

We continued today the operation against the dug-out of the so-called select "Party Directorate" which we had discovered yesterday, as reported in my teletype message yesterday. We succeeded in forcing open the dug-out of the Party Directorate and in catching about 60 heavily armed bandits. We succeeded in catching and liquidating Deputy Leader of the Jewish Military Organization "ZWZ" and his so-called Chief of Staff. There were about 200 Jews in this dug-out, of whom 60 were caught and 140 were destroyed, partly owing to the strong effect of smoke-candles, and partly owing to heavy explosive charges which were laid in several places. The Jews whom we caught had already reported that innumerable Jews had been killed by the effect of the smoke-candles. The fight of the first six days was hard, but now we are able to state that we are catching those Jews and Jewesses who were the ringleaders in those days. Every time a dug-out is forced open, the Jews in it offer resistance with the arms at their disposal, light machine guns, pistols, and hand grenades. Today we again caught quite a number of Jewesses who carried loaded pistols in their bloomers, with the safety catch released. Some depositions speak of 3 to 4,000 Jews who still remain in underground holes, sewers, and dug-outs. The undersigned is resolved not to terminate the large-scale operation until the last Jew has been destroyed.

A total of 1,091 Jews were caught today in dug-outs; about 280 Jews were shot in battle, innumerable Jews were destroyed in the 43 dug-outs which were blown up. The sum total of Jews caught has risen to 49,712. Those buildings which had not yet been destroyed by fire, were set on fire today and we discovered that a few Jews were still hiding somewhere within the walls or in the staircases.

Our strength:
  Used in operation:
    German Police 4/101
    Engineering Em Service 1/6

1061-PS Nazi Germany's War Against the Jews

Security Police		2/14
Engineers		3/69
Waffen SS		13/527

Cordoning forces:

	Day	Night
German Police	1/87	1/36
Waffen SS		1/300
Trawniki	160	
Polish Police	1/160	1/160

Our losses:
  2 Waffen SS dead
  2 Waffen SS wounded
  1 Engineer wounded

A policeman wounded on 7 May 1943 died today from wounds. We captured about 15 to 20 pistols of various calibers, considerable stores of ammunition for pistols and rifles, moreover a number of hand grenades, made in the former armament factories.

Termination of action: 2130 hours, will be continued on 9 May 1943 1000 hours.

The SS and Police Fuehrer
in the District of Warsaw.
Signed: Stroop
SS-Brigadefuehrer and Majorgeneral of Police.

Certified copy:
SS-Sturmbannfuehrer.

Copy
Teletype message

From: The SS and Police Fuehrer in the District of Warsaw
Ref. No.: I ab/St/Gr 1607 Journal No. 625/43.
Re: Large-scale Ghetto Operation.
To: The Higher SS and Police Fuehrer East, SS-Obergruppen-
  fuehrer and General of Police *Krueger*—or deputy.
Cracow

Progress of large-scale operation on 9 May 1943, start 1000 hours.

The operation carried out today had the following result: The raiding parties at work today discovered 42 dug-outs. From these dug-outs we pulled out alive 1,037 Jews and bandits. In battle 319 bandits and Jews were shot, moreover an uncertain number were destroyed when the dug-outs were blown up. The

III - 216

block of buildings which formerly contained the "Transavia" concern was destroyed by fire; in this operation we again caught a number of Jews, although this block had been combed through several times.

Again we captured some pistols and hand grenades.
Our strength:
    Used in operation:
        German Police 4/103
        Security Police 2/12
        Engineers 3/67
        Waffen SS 13/547
Cordoning Forces:

	Day	Night
German Police	1/87	1/36
Waffen SS	—	1/300
Trawniki	160	—
Polish Police	1/160	1/160

Our losses: None.

The total of Jews caught up to date has risen to 51,313. Outside the former Ghetto 254 Jews and bandits were shot.

Termination of operation: 2100 hours, will be continued on 10 May 1943, 1000 hours.
                The SS and Police Fuehrer
                in the District of Warsaw.
                      Signed: Stroop
        SS-Brigadefuehrer and Majorgeneral of Police.

Copy
Teletype message
From: The SS and Police Fuehrer in the District of Warsaw,
                      Warsaw, 10 May 1943.
Ref. Nr. I ab St/Gr 16 07 Journal No. 627/43 secret.
Re: Large-scale Ghetto Operation.
To: The Higher SS and Police Fuehrer East, SS-Obergruppen-
    fuehrer and General of Police *Krueger*—or deputy.
Cracow

Progress of large-scale action on 10 May 1943 start 1000 hrs.

Today raiding parties again combed out the area of the former Ghetto. As on preceding days we again pulled out of the dugouts, against all expectations, a considerable number of Jews. The resistance offered by the Jews had not weakened today. In contrast to the previous days, it seems that those members of the main body of the Jewish battle group who are still in existence and have not been destroyed have retired into the ruins still within their reach, with the intention of firing from there against our men and inflicting casualties.

Today we caught a total of 1,183 Jews alive, 187 bandits and Jews were shot. Again a not ascertainable number of Jews and bandits were destroyed in the blown-up dug-outs. The total of Jews caught up to date has risen to 52,693.

Today at 0900 hours a truck drove up to a certain sewer in the so-called Prosta. Someone in the truck exploded two hand grenades, which was the signal for the bandits who were standing ready in the sewer to climb out of it. The bandits and Jews —there are always some Polish bandits among them—armed with carbines, small arms, and one machine gun, climbed into the truck and drove away in an unknown direction. The last man of the gang, who stood sentry in the sewer and had the duty of closing the sewer lid, was captured. It was he who gave the above information. He testified that most of the members of the gang, which had been divided into several battle groups, had either been killed in battle or had committed suicide because they had realized the futility of continuing the fight. The search for the truck, which was ordered at once, had no results. The bandits testified further that the Prosta is now the refuge for the still existing Jews because the Ghetto has become too hot for them. For this reason, I resolved to deal with the Prosta in the same manner as with the Ghetto, and to destroy this miniature Ghetto.

Today, we again captured small arms and some ammunition. The Security Police yesterday succeeded in capturing a workshop outside the Ghetto which manufactured 10,000 to 11,000 explosive charges and other ammunition.

Our strength: as on the preceding day.

Our losses: 3 SS men wounded.

Owing to the excellent understanding between us and the Wehrmacht, the detachment of Engineers was reinforced. Moreover, a considerable amount of explosives was put at our disposal.

Termination of operation: 2200 hours. Will be continued on 11 May 1943, 0930 hours.

      The SS and Police Fuehrer in the
        District of Warsaw.
          Signed: Stroop
  SS-Brigadefuehrer and Majorgeneral of Police.

Copy
Teletype message

From: The SS and Police Fuehrer in the District of Warsaw

Warsaw, 11 May 1943.

Ref. No.: I ab-St/Gr—16 07 Journal No. 629/43 secret.
Re: Ghetto large-scale Operation.
To: The Higher SS and Police Fuehrer East, SS-Obergruppenfuehrer and General of Police *Krueger*—or deputy.

Cracow

Progress of large-scale operation on 11 May 1943, start 0930 hours.

The scouting parties sent out last night again reported that there must still be some Jews within the dug-outs, since some Jews were seen in the ruined streets. The scouting parties shot 12 Jews. On the basis of these reports, today I again formed raiding parties who in combing-out operations discovered, captured, and destroyed a total of 47 dug-outs. Today again we caught some Jews who had taken refuge in ruins which were still protected by a roof. The Jews and bandits are still seeking this new refuge, because staying in the dug-outs has become unbearable. One dug-out was discovered which contained about 12 rooms equipped with plumbing, running water, and separate bathrooms for men and women. Considerable amounts of food were captured or secured, in order to make it more and more difficult for them to get necessary food.

A total of 931 Jews and bandits were caught. 53 bandits were shot. More of them perished when dug-outs were blown up and when a small block of buildings was destroyed by fire. The total of Jews caught up to date has risen to 53,667. We captured several pistols, hand grenades, and ammunition.

We have not been able to smoke out the sewers systematically once more, since we are short of smoke-candles. "OFK" is ready to provide new smoke-candles.

Our strength:

Used in operation:
German Police	6/126
Engineering Em. Service	1/6
Security Police	2/14
Engineers	4/76
Waffen SS	12/308

Cordoning forces:

	Night	Day
German Police	1/112	1/86
Waffen SS	—	1/130
Trawniki	160	—
Polish Police	1/160	1/160

Our losses: 1 SS man wounded.

Total of losses up to date: 71 wounded, 12 dead.

Termination of today's operation: 2145 hours, will be continued on 12 May 1943, 0930 hours.

The SS and Police Fuehrer in the
District of Warsaw.
Signed: Stroop
SS-Brigadefuehrer and Majorgeneral of Police.

Certified copy:
SS-Sturmbannfuehrer.

Copy
Teletype message

From: The SS and Police Fuehrer in the District of Warsaw

Warsaw, 12 May 1943.

Ref. No.: I ab-St/Gr—16 07—Journal No. 637/43 secret.

Re: Large-scale Ghetto Operation.

To: The Higher SS and Police Fuehrer East, SS-Obergruppenfuehrer and General of Police *Krueger*—or deputy.

Cracow

Progress of large-scale operation on 12 May 1943, start 0930 hours.

When the raiding parties combed out the area for remaining dug-outs in which Jews were hiding, they succeeded in discovering 30 dug-outs. 663 Jews were pulled out of them and 133 Jews were shot. The sum total of Jews caught has risen to 54,463.

Furthermore today the units cordoning off the miniature Ghetto were reinforced and destroyed by fire. Probably a considerable number of Jews perished in the flames. No accurate information in this regard could be obtained since the fire was still burning when darkness set in. One concrete building in the Prosta, from which Jews had been removed, was heavily damaged by blowing-up operations in order to make it impossible for the bandits to use it as a base later.

It is noteworthy that the Poles, without having been warned, took appropriate measures for protecting their window-panes, etc., before the blowing-up started.

The transports of Jews leaving here will be directed to T.II beginning today.

Our strength:

Used in operation:
German police	5/126
Engineering Em. Service	1/6
Security Police	2/14
Engineers	4/74
Waffen SS	12/508

Cordoning forces:

	Day	Night
German Police	1/112	1/86
Waffen SS	—	1/300
Trawniki	160	—
Polish Police	1/160	1/160

Our losses: 1 Waffen SS man wounded.

Termination of today's operation: 2160 hours, will be continued on 13 May 1943, 1000 hours.

    The SS and Police Fuehrer
     in the District of Warsaw.
        Signed: Stroop
  SS-Brigadefuehrer and Majorgeneral of Police.

Certified copy:
SS-Sturmbannfuehrer.

Copy
Teletype message
From: The SS and Police Fuehrer in the District of Warsaw
       Warsaw, 13 May 1943.

Ref. No.: I ab/ St/Gr 16 07 Journal No. 641/43 secret.
Re: Large-scale Ghetto Operation.
To: The Higher SS and Police Fuehrer East, SS-Obergruppenfuehrer and General of Police *Krueger*—or deputy.
Cracow

Progress of large-scale operation on 13 May 1943, start 1000 hours.

In combing out the Ghetto and the miniature Ghetto (Prosta) today we found 234 Jews. 155 Jews were shot in battle. Today it became clear that the Jews and bandits whom we are catching now belong to the so-called battle groups. All of them are young fellows and females between 18 and 25 years of age. When we captured one, a real skirmish took place, in which the Jews not only fired from 08 pistols and Polish Vis pistols, but also threw Polish "pineapple" hand grenades at the Waffen-SS men. After part of the inmates of the dug-out had been caught and were about to be searched, one of the females quick as lightning put her hand under her shirt, as many others had done, and fetched from her bloomers a "pineapple" hand grenade, drew the safety-catch, threw the grenade among the men who were searching her, and jumped quickly to cover. It is only thanks to the presence of mind of the men that no casualties ensued.

The few Jews and criminals still staying in the Ghetto have for the last few days been using the hideouts they can still find among the ruins, retiring at night into the dug-outs whose location is known to them, to eat and get provisions for the next day. Lately we have been unable to extract information on the whereabouts of further dug-outs from the captured Jews. The remainder of the inmates of that dug-out where the skirmish took place were destroyed by using heavier explosive charges. From a Wehrmacht concern we evacuated 327 Jews today. The Jews we catch now are sent to T.II.

The total of Jews caught has risen to 55,179.

Our strength:
 Used in operation:
  German police 4/182
  Engineering Em. Service 1/6
  Security Police 2/14
  Engineers 4/74
  Waffen SS 12/517

Cordoning forces:

	Day	Night
German Police	2/137	1/87
Waffen SS	—	1/300
Trawniki	270	—
Polish Police	1/160	1/160

Our losses: 2 Waffen SS dead
     3 Waffen SS wounded
     1 Policeman wounded.

The 2 Waffen SS men lost their lives in the air attack against the Ghetto.

33 dug-outs were discovered and destroyed. Booty: 6 pistols, 2 hand grenades, and some explosive charges.

Termination of today's operation: 2100 hours, will be continued on 14 May 1943, 1000 hours.

My intention is to terminate the large-scale operation on 16 May 1943 and to turn all further measures over to Police battalion III/23. Unless ordered otherwise, I am going to submit to the conference of SS and Policefuehrers a detailed report of the operation, including an appendix containing photos.

The SS and Police Fuehrer
in the District of Warsaw.
Signed: Stroop
SS-Brigadefuehrer and Majorgeneral of Police.

Certified copy:
SS-Sturmbannfuehrer.

Copy
Teletype message

From: The SS and Police Fuehrer in the District of Warsaw
Warsaw, 14 May 1943.

Ref. No. I ab/St/G 16 07 Journal No. 646/43 secret.
Re: Large-scale Ghetto Operation.
To: The Higher SS and Police Fuehrer East, SS-Obergruppenfuehrer and General of Police *Krueger*—or deputy.
Cracow

Progress of large-scale operation on 14 May 1943, start 1000 hours.

The raiding parties formed today went to work within the areas allotted to each of them under orders to force open further dwelling dug-outs and to catch the Jews. In this way a considerable number of bandits and Jews were caught, especially as some traces had been discovered during the night which were now followed up with good results. The night patrols clashed with armed bandits several times. These bandits fired a machine gun and small arms. In this operation we had four casualties— 3 Waffen-SS Men and 1 Policeman. Repeatedly, shots were fired from the Aryan part against the external barricade. In the skirmishes about 30 bandits were shot and 9 Jews and bandits, members of an armed gang, were captured. One dug-out was taken during the night, the Jews captured, and some pistols, among them one of 12-mm caliber, were captured. In one dug-out inhabited by 100 persons, we were able to capture 2 rifles, 16 pistols, some hand grenades and incendiary appliances. Of the bandits who resisted, some again wore German military uniform, German steel helmets and "knobeloecher." Apart from the carbines, we captured 60 rounds of German rifle ammunition. One raiding party had a skirmish with a gang, 10 to 14 strong, on the roofs of a block of buildings at the border of the Ghetto (Aryan part). The bandits were destroyed; we suffered no losses.

The captured bandits repeatedly testify that still not all persons in the Ghetto have been caught. They confidently expect that the action will soon be over, and that they will then be able to continue to live in the Ghetto. Several bandits stated that they had long been in a position to kill off the leader of the action, the "General," as they call him, but that they would not do so, since they had orders to that effect to avoid the risk of a further intensification of the anti-Jewish measures.

Today again some concrete buildings in which the bandits find refuge time and again were blown up by the engineers.

In order to force the bandits in the sewers to come to the surface, 183 sewer entrances were opened at 1500 hours, and smoke-candles were lowered into them at an ordered x-time. Thereupon the bandits, seeking escape from what they supposed to be poison gas, crowded together in the center of the former Ghetto, and we were able to pull them out of the sewer entrances there.

I shall come to a decision after tomorrow's operations regarding termination of the action.

Today SS-Gruppenfuehrer and Lieutenant General of Waffen-SS von Horff was present during the operations.

Our strength:

Used in operation:

German Police	4/184
Engineering Em. Serv.	1/6
Security Police	2/16
Engineers	4/73
Waffen-SS	12/510

Cordoning forces:

	Day	Night
German Police	2/138	1/87
Waffen SS	—	1/300
Trawniki	270	—
Polish Police	1/160	1/160

Our losses: 5 wounded, 4 Waffen SS, 1 Police

A total of 398 Jews were caught today. Furthermore 154 Jews and bandits were shot in battle. The total of the Jews caught has risen to 55,731.

Booty: rifles, pistols, and ammunition. Further, a number of incendiary bottles (Molotov cocktails).

Termination of action; 2155 hours, will be continued on 15 May 1943 0900 hours.

The SS and Police Fuehrer
in the District of Warsaw.
Signed: Stroop
SS-Brigadefuehrer and Majorgeneral of Police.

Certified copy:
SS-Sturmbannfuehrer.

Copy
Teletype message

From: The SS and Police Fuehrer in the District of Warsaw
Warsaw, May 15th 1943.
Ref. No.: I ab/St/Gr 16 07 Journal No. 648/43 secret.
Re: Large-scale Ghetto Operation.
To: The Higher SS and Police Fuehrer East, SS-Obergruppenfuehrer and General of Police *Krueger*—or deputy.
Cracow

Progress of large-scale operation on 15 April 1943. Start 0900 hours.

The 5 scouting parties who patrolled the Ghetto last night reported that they encountered Jews only sporadically. In contrast to the preceding nights, they were able to shoot 6 or 7 Jews. The combing-out actions today also had little result. 29 more dug-outs were discovered, but part of them were no longer inhabited. A total of 87 Jews were caught today and 67 bandits and Jews were shot in battle. In a skirmish which developed around noon, and in which the bandits again resisted by using Molotov cocktails, pistols, and home-made hand grenades, the gang was destroyed; but subsequently a policeman was wounded by a shot through the right thigh. A special unit once more searched the last block of buildings which was still intact in the Ghetto, and subsequently destroyed it. In the evening the chapel, mortuary, and all other buildings on the Jewish cemetery were blown up or destroyed by fire.

The sum total of Jews caught has risen to 55,885.
Our strength:
    Used in operation:
        German Police 4/184
        Engineering Em. S. 1/6

Security Police	2/16
Engineers	4/74
Waffen-SS	12/510

Cordoning forces:

	Day	Night
German Police	2/138	1/87
Waffen-SS	—	1/300
Trawniki	270	—
Polish Police	1/160	1/160

Our losses: 1 Policeman wounded.

We captured 4 pistols of larger calibers, 1 infernal machine with fuse, 10 kilograms of explosives, and a considerable amount of ammunition. Termination of operation: 2130 hours. Will be continued on 16 May 1943, 1000 hours.

I will terminate the large-scale operation on 16 May 1943 at dusk, by blowing up the Synagogue, which we did not succeed in accomplishing today, and will subsequently charge Police Battalion III/23 with continuing and completing the measures which are still necessary.

The SS and Police Fuehrer
in the District of Warsaw.
Signed: Stroop
SS-Brigadefuehrer and Majorgeneral of Police.

Certified copy:
SS-Sturmbannfuehrer.

Copy
Teletype message
From: The SS and Police Fuehrer in the District of Warsaw
Warsaw, May 16th, 1943.
Ref. No.: I ab-st/Gr 16 07 Journal Nr. 652/43 secret.
Re: Large-scale Ghetto Operation.
To: The Higher SS and Police Fuehrer East, SS-Obergruppen-
    fuehrer and General of Police *Krueger*—or deputy.
Cracow

Progress of large-scale operation on 16 May 1943, start 1000 hours.

180 Jews, bandits, and subhumans were destroyed. The former Jewish quarter of Warsaw is no longer in existence. The large-scale action was terminated at 2015 hours by blowing up the Warsaw Synagogue.

The measures to be taken with regard to the established

III - 226

banned areas were handed over to the commander of police battalion III/23, whom I instructed carefully.

Total number of Jews dealt with 56,065, including both Jews caught and Jews whose extermination can be proved.

No losses today.

I will submit a final report to the Conference of SS Police Fuehrer on 18 May 1943.

The SS and Police Fuehrer in the
District of Warsaw.
Signed: Stroop
SS-Brigadefuehrer and Majorgeneral of Police.

Certified copy:
SS-Sturmbannfuehrer.

Copy
Teletype message

From: The SS and Police Fuehrer in the District of Warsaw
Warsaw, 24 May 1943.

Ref. No.: I ab-St/Gr 16 07 Journal Nr. 663/43 secret.
Re: Large-scale Ghetto Operation.
Ref: Your teletype message Nr. 946 or 21 May 1943.
To: The Higher SS and Police Fuehrer East, SS-Obergruppenfuehrer and General of Police *Krueger*—or deputy.
Cracow

I beg to reply to the above teletype message:
No. 1:

Of the total of 56,065 caught, about 7,000 were destroyed in the former Ghetto during large-scale operation. 6,929 Jews were destroyed by transporting them to T.II; the sum total of Jews destroyed is therefore 13,929. Beyond the number of 56,065 an estimated number of 5 to 6,000 Jews were destroyed by being blown up or by perishing in the flames.
No. 2:

A total of 631 dug-outs were destroyed.
No. 3 (booty):

    7 Polish rifles, 1 Russian rifle, 1 German rifle.
    59 pistols of various calibers.
    Several 100 hand grenades, including Polish and home-made ones.
    A few 100 incendiary bottles.
    Home-made explosive charges.
    Infernal machines with fuses.

Large amounts of explosives, ammunition for all calibers, including machine-gun ammunition.

With regard to the bag of arms one must take into consideration that in most cases we were not able to capture the arms themselves, since the Jews and bandits before they were captured threw them away into hidehouts and holes which we could not discover or find. The smoke which we had developed in the dug-outs also prevented our men from discovering and capturing the arms. Since we had to blow up the dug-outs at once we were not in a position to search for the arms later on.

The hand grenades, explosive charges, and incendiary bottles captured were used at once against the bandits.

Furthermore, we captured:
- 1,240 used uniform tunics (partly equipped with medal ribbons, Iron Cross, and East Medal).
- 600 pairs of used trousers.
- Pieces of equipment, and German steel helmets.
- 103 horses, 4 of them in the former Ghetto (hearse).

We counted up to 23 May 1943:
- 4.4 million Zloty. We captured moreover about 5 to 6 million Zloty, not yet counted, a considerable amount of foreign currency, including—
  - $14,300 in paper.
  - $ 9,200 in gold.
- Large amounts of valuables (rings, chains, watches etc.)

No. 4:

With the exception of 8 buildings (police barracks, hospital and accommodations for working parties) the former Ghetto has been completely destroyed. Where blowing-up was not carried out, only partition walls are still standing. But the ruins still contain enormous amounts of bricks and scrap material which could be used.

The SS and Police Fuehrer in the
District of Warsaw.
Signed: Stroop
SS-Brigadefuehrer and Majorgeneral of Police.

Certified copy:
SS-Sturmbannfuehrer.

Pictorial report

[Translator's note: captions of photos follow in order]
1. The building of the former Jewish Council.

The Documentary Evidence   1061-PS

2. Out of the factories.
3. Discussion of the evacuation of a factory.
4. The Jewish section chiefs of the armament factory Brauer.
5. Brauer Company!
6. Column marching to the railway station.
7. On the way to the transhipping place.
8. Search and interrogation.
9. Jewish Rabbis.
10. Jewish Rabbis.
11. A patrol.
12. Dregs of humanity.
13. Forcibly pulled out of dug-outs.
14. Just pulled out of a dug-out.
15. Just pulled out of a dug-out.
16. These bandits resisted by force of arms.
17. Bandits destroyed in battle.
18. A dug-out is opened.
19. Jewish traitors.
20. Bandits!
21. Smoking-out of the Jews and bandits.
22. A place which had been prepared for escape and jumping down.
23. Destruction of a block of buildings [2 photos].
24. Destruction of a block of buildings.
25. [no caption]
26. On the way to the transhipping place.
27. Jews are marched away.
28. On the way to the transhipping place.
29. Photos showing parts of so-called dwelling dug-outs.
30–33 [no caption]
34. Measures for covering a street.
35. They were found in underground dug-outs.
36. (1) These bandits are avoiding arrest by jumping down.
    (2) Bandits after having jumped down.
37. The radio car of the command post.
38. Ascaris who were used in the operation.
39. The C.O. of the large-scale action.
40. This is how the former Ghetto looks after having been destroyed.
41–48. [no caption]

Translation of Document 1104-PS (USA 483). Memorandum, 21 November 1943, enclosing copies of report concerning execution of Jews in Minsk.

III - 229

* * *

The Personal Reviewer of the Permanent Deputy of the Minister of the Reich

Berlin, 21 November 1941

Bi/T Nr 58 A/41 Secret
To Dr. Marquart

Enclosed herewith I transmit to you the copy of an incident regarding the measures against the Jews in the general-district of Minsk, with the request to submit the same to the Minister of the Reich.

On order of the Gauleiter I have sent one copy to Lieutenant General of the SS, Heydrich, with the request for investigation of the incident.

signed: BIGENWALD

3 enclosures

Copy /T

The Commissioner General for White Ruthenia
Dept Gauleiter/Ka

Minsk, 1 November 1941

To the Reich Commissioner for the Eastern Territories, Gauleiter Hinrich Lohse, Riga

Today, money, valuables and other objects were deposited at the cashier of my office against receipt, in the presence of Government Councillor Dr. Idelberger of the Police Battalion 11. These matters were from Sluzk and other regions which the Police Battalion 11 had included in its action without my order and without my knowledge. All objects and the money have been safely deposited by officials of Commissariat General with the Reich Credit Institute [Reichskreditanstalt] and are held at the disposal of the Reich Commissioner. Reserve officer 1st Lieutenant of the Police Brodeck attempted in the course of this incident to purchase gold for private purposes in order to use it for a personal affair, as witnessed by Government Councillor Dr. Idelberger, my adjutant, SS-2nd Lt Wildenstein and myself.

I have immediately reported the case to the responsible field command post at Minsk and requested the arrest of the police officer. 1st Lt Brodeck was immediately set free by the investigating court martial officer as the court martial officer did not find any basis for charges in this incident. This is contrary to the legal conception of my office. Any private dealing in gold is prohibited in the German Reich. Aggravating in this case is furthermore the fact that an officer of the same unit is involved which has effected the liquidation of the former possessors of gold.

The Commissioner General for White Ruthenia
　　　　　　　　　　　　　　signed: KUBE

SECRET
Copy/T

The Commissioner General for White Ruthenia
Dept Gauleiter/Ka

Minsk, 1 November 1941

Personal

To the Reich Commissioner for the Eastern Territories Gauleiter Hinrich LOHSE Riga

Enclosed I submit a report of the Commissioner for the territory of Sluzk, Party member Carl, with the request not to let this matter rest. Herewith I propose to prosecute the guilty officers commencing with the battalion commander of the security police to the last lieutenant.

For about the last three weeks, I have discussed the Sluzk action against the Jews with the responsible SS-Brigadier General and Brigadier-General of the Protection Police, Zenner, Member of the Reichstag, and I have pointed out that the tradesmen should be spared by all means and that the commissioner responsible for the territory should be contacted prior to the action. Above all, any act lowering the prestige of the German Reich and its organizations in the eyes of the White Ruthenian population should be avoided.

The Police Battalion No. 11 from Kauen has as a unit, directly subordinate to the armed forces, taken independent action without informing me, the SS-Brigadier-General or any other office of the Commissariat General, thereby impairing most seriously the prestige of the German nation. I request to have the commissioner of the territory Carl and all his officials and collaborators from Riga questioned under oath and to record the hearing. Then, in order to set an example, I request to grant my motion to prosecute the entire staff of officers of the Police Battalion 11.

I am submitting this report in duplicate so that one copy may be forwarded to the Reich Minister. Peace and order cannot be maintained in White Ruthenia with methods of that sort. To bury seriously wounded people alive who worked their way out of their graves again, is such a base and filthy act that this incident as such should be reported to the Fuehrer and Reich Marshal. The civil administration of White Ruthenia makes very strenuous efforts to win the population over to Germany in accordance with the instructions of the Fuehrer. These efforts cannot be brought in harmony with the methods described herein.

The Commissioner General
for White Ruthenia
signed: KUBE

Enclosures

Riga 11 November 1941
Original with two enclosures to the Reich minister for the Occupied Eastern Territories Berlin
with the request for consideration. It is deemed necessary that higher authority take immediate steps.
 By order of

The Reich Commissioner for
the Eastern Territories
signed: WICHMANN

Copy/T of the copy
The Commissioner of the Territory of Sluzk
Sluzk, 30 October 1941
SECRET
To the Commissioner General Minsk
Subject: Action against Jews

Referring to the report made by phone on 27 October 1941 I now beg to inform you in writing of the following:

On 27 October in the morning at about 8 o'clock a first lieutenant of the Police Battalion No. 11 from Kauen (Lithuania) appeared and introduced himself as the adjutant of the battalion commander of the security police. The first lieutenant explained that the police battalion had received the assignment to effect the liquidation of all Jews here in the town of Sluzk, within two days. The battalion commander with his battalion in strength of four companies, two of which were made up of Lithuanian partisans, was on the march here and the action would have to begin instantly. I replied to the first lieutenant that I had to discuss the action in any case first with the commander. About half an hour later the police battalion arrived in Sluzk. Immediately after the arrival the conference with the battalion commander took place according to my request. I first explained to the commander that it would not very well be possible to effect the action without previous preparation, because everybody had been sent to work and that it would lead to terrible confusion. At least it would have been his duty to inform me a day ahead of time. Then I requested him to postpone the action one day. However, he rejected this with the remark that he had to carry out this action everywhere and in all towns and that only two days were allotted for Sluzk. Within these two days, the town of Sluzk had to be cleared of Jews by all means. I immediately protested violently against it, pointing out that a liquidation of Jews must not be allowed to take place in an arbitrary manner. I explained that a large part of the Jews still living in the towns were tradesmen and families of tradesmen respectively. But these Jewish tradesmen were not simply expendable because they were indispensable for maintaining the economic life. Furthermore, I pointed out that White Ruthenian tradesmen are so to say non-existent, that therefore all vital plants had to be shut down all at once, if all Jews would be liquidated. At the end of our conference, I mentioned that all tradesmen and specialists, inasmuch as they were indispensable, had papers of identification and that these should not be pulled out of the factories. Furthermore, it was agreed that all Jews still living in the town should first be brought into the ghetto in order to segregate them, especially with regard to the families of tradesmen which I did not want to have liquidated either. Two of my officials should be assigned to segregate them. The commander did not in any way contradict my idea and I had therefore the firm belief that the action would be carried out accordingly. However, a few hours after the beginning of the action the greatest difficulties already developed. I noticed that the commander had not at all abided by our agreement. All Jews without exception were taken out of the factories and shops and deported in spite of our agreement. It is true that part of the Jews was moved by way of the ghetto where many of them were processed and still segregated by me, but a large part was loaded directly on trucks and liquidated without further delay outside of the town. Shortly after noon complaints came already from all sides that the factories could not function any more because all Jewish tradesmen had been removed. As the commander had proceeded on his way to Baranowitschi I got in touch with the deputy commander, a captain, after searching a long time, and demanded to stop the action immediately because my instructions had been disregarded and the damage done so far with respect to the economic life could not be repaired any more. The captain was greatly surprised at my idea and stated that he had received orders from the commander to clear the whole town of Jews without exception in the same manner as they had done in other towns. This mopping up had to be executed on political considerations and economic reasons had never played a role anywhere. However, due to my energetic intervention, he finally halted the action toward evening.

For the rest, as regards the execution of the action, I must point out to my deepest regret that the latter bordered already on sadism. The town itself offered a picture of horror during the action. With indescribable brutality on the part of both the German police officers and particularly the Lithuanian partisans, the Jewish people, but also among them White Ruthenians, were taken out of their dwellings and herded together. Everywhere in the town shots were to be heard and in different streets the corpses of shot Jews accumulated. The White Ruthenians were in greatest distress to free themselves from the encirclement. Regardless of the fact that the Jewish people, among whom were also tradesmen, were mistreated in a terribly barbarous way in the face of the White Ruthenian people, the White Ruthenians themselves were also worked over with rubber clubs and rifle butts. There was no question of an action against the Jews any more. It rather looked like a revolution. I myself with all my officials have been in it without interruption all day long in order to save what could yet be saved. In several instances I literally had to expel with drawn pistol the German police officials as well as the Lithuanian partisans from the shops. My own police was employed for the same mission but had often to leave the streets on account of the wild shooting in order to avoid being shot themselves. The whole picture was generally more than ghastly. In the afternoon a great number of abandoned Panje carriages with horses were standing in the streets so that I had to instruct the municipal administration to take care of the vehicles immediately. Afterwards it was ascertained that they were Jewish vehicles ordered by the armed forces to move ammunition. The drivers had simply been taken off the carriages and led away, and nobody had worried in the least about the vehicles.

I was not present at the shooting before the town. Therefore I cannot make a statement on its brutality. But it should suffice, if I point out that persons shot have worked themselves out of their graves some time after they had been covered. Regarding the economic damage I want to state that the tannery has been affected worst of all. 26 experts worked there. Of them, fifteen of the best specialists alone have been shot. Four more jumped from the truck during the transport and escaped, while seven others were not apprehended after they fled. The plant barely continues to operate today. Five wheelwrights worked in the wheelwright shop. Four of them have been shot and the shop has to keep going now with one wheelwright. Additional tradesmen such as carpenters, blacksmiths, etc. are still missing. Up till now it was impossible for me to obtain an exact survey. I have mentioned already in the beginning, that the families of tradesmen should be spared too. But now it seems that almost in all families some persons are missing. Reports come in from all over, making it clear that in one family the tradesman himself, in another family the wife and in the next one again the children are missing. In that way, almost all families have been broken up. It seems to be very doubtful whether under these circumstances the remaining tradesmen will show any interest in their work and produce accordingly, particularly as even today they are running around with bloody and bruised faces due to the brutality. The White Ruthenian people who had full confidence in us, are dumbfounded. Though they are intimidated and don't dare to utter their free opinion, one has already heard that they take the viewpoint that this day does not add to the glory of Germany and that it will not be forgotten. I am of the opinion that much which we have achieved during the last month has been destroyed through this action and that it will take a long time until we shall regain the confidence of the population which we have lost.

In conclusion I find myself obliged to point out that the police battalion has looted in an unheard of manner during the action, and that not only in Jewish houses but just the same in those of the White Ruthenians. Anything of use such as boots, leather, cloth, gold and other valuables, has been taken away. On the basis of statements of members of the armed forces, watches were torn off the arms of Jews in public, on the street, and rings were pulled off the fingers in the most brutal manner. A major of the finance department reported that a Jewish girl was asked by the police to obtain immediately 5,000 rubles to have her father released. This girl is said to have actually gone everywhere in order to obtain the money.

Also within the ghetto, the different barracks which had been nailed up by the civil administration and were furnished with Jewish furniture, have been broken open and robbed. Even from the barracks in which the unit was quartered, window frames and doors have been forcibly removed and used for campfires. Although I had a discussion with the adjutant of the commander on Tuesday morning concerning the looting and he promised in the course of the discussion that none of the policemen would enter the town any more, yet I was forced several hours later to arrest two fully armed Lithuanian partisans because they were apprehended looting. During the night from Tuesday to Wednesday the battalion left the town in the direction of Baranowitschi. Evidently, the people were only too glad when this report circulated in the town.

So far the report. I shall come to Minsk in the immediate future, in order to discuss the affair personally once again. At the present time, I am not in a position to continue with the action against the Jews. First, order has to be established again. I hope that I shall be able to restore order as soon as possible and also to revive the economic life despite the difficulties. Only, I beg you to grant me one request: "In the future, keep this police battalion away from me by all means."

signed: CARL

Translation of Document 1113-PS. *Excerpt from report of 6 November 1942 from Riga concerning action "Marshfever" noting that 8350 Jews were executed.*

* * *

Higher SS- and Police Leader for the East
2000/42 g

11 Jacobstr, Riga, November 6, 1942
SECRET

* * * * * * *

Final Report "Marshfever"

9. *Miciajewicze (p. 2479)*
9 Feb—9 Mar 1942

By motorized Gendarmery—patrols and a company from the 15th Latvian Police Battalion. Seventy bandits shot. By carrying out these actions the following successes were obtained:

a.—49 bandit camps, pill-boxes and strong points, as well as several villages in the swamp-areas which were used as hideouts were smoked out and destroyed.

b.— 389 armed bandits shot in combat.

The Documentary Evidence   1113-PS

1274 suspicious persons sentenced and shot.
   8350 Jews executed.
   c.—1217 persons evacuated.
   d.—3 antitank guns,
      2 heavy machine guns,
      3 light machine guns,
      1 radio set (sender and receiver),
      some radio equipment, rifles and other small arms,
      large amount of explosives and ammunition, hand grenades, Teller mines, pieces of equipment and other material, as well as
      1 truck, 1 passenger car,
      80 panji-carts (peasant carts),
      42 bicycles,
      62 horses,
      5 cows as well as food supplies have been captured.

Besides the above stated objects the enclosed 14 sketches were found during actions against bands in the territory of Smolewicze north-eastward of Minsk in a camp abandoned shortly before the two bandits whose portraits are enclosed were recognized by comparison with captured bandits and shot. One of them is the leader of the bandits, a Bolshevist commissar.

Translation of Document 1117-PS (USA 384). Goering order, 1 May 1941, directing all Party, State and Wehrmacht services to support Einsatzstab Rosenberg (Rosenberg's staff for seizing Jewish property, libraries and art treasures) in battle against Jews and Freemasons throughout all occupied territories.

* * *

The Reichs Marshal of the Greater German Reich
                              Headquarters, 1, May 1941

The battle against Jews, Freemasons and other affiliated forces of opposite "Weltanschauung" is a foremost task of National Socialism during the war.

I therefore welcome the decision of Reichsleiter Rosenberg to form staffs in all occupied territories for the purpose of safeguarding all research material and cultural goods of the above-mentioned groups, and transporting them to Germany.

III - 237

All Party, State and Wehrmacht Services are therefore requested to give all possible support and assistance to the Chief of Staff of Reichsleiter Rosenberg's staffs, Reichshauptstellenleiter Party Comrade Utikal, and his deputy DRK-Feldfuehrer Party Comrade von Beer, in the discharge of their duties. The above-mentioned persons are requested to report to us on their work, particularly on any difficulties that might arise.

signed: GOERING.

Translation of Document 1138-PS (USA 284). *Enclosure in letter from Reich Commissioner for Baltic States to Rosenberg, 13 August 1941, concerning provisional directives on treatment of Jews in area of Reichskommissariat Ostland (Baltic States and White Russia).*

* * *

SECRET

(II 1 d 3000)
THE REICH COMMISSAR FOR EASTLAND
RIGA   Riga, 13 August 1941
TO: The Reich Minister for Occupied Eastern Territories, Berlin
   W 35.

I beg to enclose an account of planned provsional directives for treatment of Jews in the Reichskommissariat Ostland. [Translator's note: Baltic States and White Russia.]

[Signed]   BANSE [?]

To Department [Hauptabteilung] II with request for opinion.
   (By order)
(Habs, 24 August)

(Gauleiter has taken cognizance)
(return to Dr. Runte)
(19 August 1941)

Enclosure:
(III a/13/ ei Grh)

[Translator's note: All lines enclosed in parentheses were added to the original typewritten document in pencil or ink. There is also a slip attached to the document, initialed by Dr. Runte, Gauleiter M. and R.]

Reich commissar for Eastland
   Kommissariat Ostland, 13 Aug. 41
   Habs 4 Sept.

SECRET!

Provisional directives on the treatment of Jews in the area of the Reichs-Kommissariat Ostland.

My instructions in my address of 27 July 1941 in Kowno determine the final settlement of the Jewish question in the area of the Reichskommissariat Ostland.

Insofar as further measures are taken, especially by the Security Police (SIPO), to carry out my oral instructions, they will not be affected by the following *preliminary* directives. It is merely the job of these preliminary directives to assure these, and for such length of time, minimum measures by the General or Regional Commissars, where and for as long as further measures are not possible in the direction of the final solution of the Jewish question.

I. *a.* For the time being only those Jews will be subject to these directives who are citizens of the German Reich, the Protectorate of Bohemia and Moravia, of the former Republics of Poland, Lithuania, Latvia, Estonia, of the USSR or of its component states, or stateless Jews.

b. Other Jews of foreign nationality, others of mixed blood and spouses of Jews who are not ready to share the fate of their Jewish spouses are to be denied permission to leave the area of the Reichskommissariat Ostland because it is a military area. They are to be watched. In addition they can be subjected to the following measures, among others: obligation to report daily, prohibition of moving, or assignment to specific dwelling, prohibition of leaving the municipal area limitations on circulation. In case of necessity they are to be taken into police custody until further decisions can be made.

II. A Jew is, whoever descends from at least 3 grandparents who were full Jews by race.

A Jew is also whoever descends from one or two grandparents who were full Jews by race, if he

a. belongs or belonged to the Jewish denomination, or

b. on 20 June 1941 or later was *married* to, or living in common-law marriage with, a person who is Jewish within the purview of these directives, or who now or in future enters into such a relationship.

III. In cases of doubt, the district (or municipal) Commissar decides, according to his best judgment, who is a Jew within the purview of these directives.

IV. General Commissars will immediately order the following measures, as soon as or insofar as civil administration has been introduced in their areas:

a. The Jews are to be listed, through imposition of the duty to report, by name, sex, age, and address. Furthermore the rosters of Jewish congregations, and the statements of trustworthy natives, will serve as bases for their listing.

b. It will be decreed that Jews distinctively mark themselves by prominently visible yellow hexagonal stars of at least 10 cm. in diameter worn on the left side of the breast and in the center of the back.

c. Jews are prohibited from:
1. Changing of their home town and their homes without permission of the area (municipal) Commissar.
2. Use of sidewalks, public means of transportation (i.e., railroad, streetcars, bus, steamer, horse-drawn taxis) and automobiles.
3. Use of public facilities and institutions serving the population (resorts and bathing facilities, parks, meadows, playgrounds, and athletic fields).
4. Attendance at theatres, movies, libraries, museums.
5. Attendance at schools of any type.
6. The possession of automobiles and radio sets.
7. Kosher slaughtering.

d. Jewish doctors and dentists may treat or advise only Jewish patients. If Ghettos or camps are erected, they are to be distributed among them for the care of their inmates. Jewish druggists are to be permitted practice of their profession according to need, but only in Ghettos or camps. Drug stores previously managed by Jews are to be transferred to trusteeship of Aryan druggists.

Practice of their profession is prohibited to Jewish veterinarians.

e. Jews are to be forbidden exercise of the professions and activities designated below:
1. Activity as attorney, notary-public or legal adviser.
2. Operation of banks, money-changing offices and pawn shops.
3. Activity as representative, agent, and intermediary.
4. Trade in real estate.
5. Migratory trade.

f. The following will be decreed for the handling of Jewish property:
1. *General.* The property of the Jewish population is to be confiscated and secured. The previous Jewish legal owner, from the moment of confiscation, is no longer authorized to dispose of his property. Legal

transactions which violate this provision are null and void.

2. *Duty to report.* The entire property of the Jewish population is to be reported. The deadline for reporting is determined by the General or area Commissars. It is mandatory for anyone who owns or stores Jewish property and anyone who, without being owner, proprietor, or custodian, legally or actually disposes of, or can dispose of, Jewish property, to report it.

The duty to report not only applies to the legal Jewish owner, but also to anyone who, for example, administers Jewish property, who has taken it into safe-keeping or obtained it in any other manner.

The reporting must be done on a form according to the attached model.

The General Commissars regulate reporting procedure with regard to local conditions and determine the officials to whom the reports are to be submitted. The reports should be submitted, if possible, to the area commissars. The area commissars are, however, empowered also to be in charge of the giving out and the receiving of forms; this applies also to government offices which are not supplied or equipped by the civil administration. These offices are to forward the forms handed in to the area Commissars.

3. *The duty of delivery.* Jewish property is to be delivered on special demand. The demand can take place by general proclamation or by order to definite individuals. The General Commissars order through proclamation immediate delivery of the following articles:

    a. Domestic and foreign currency.
    b. Securities and financial records of every sort, (i.e., stocks, promissory notes, exchange, debt records, bank and savings-bank books).
    c. All articles of value (coined and uncoined gold and silver, other precious metals, jewelry, precious stones, etc.).

Articles turned in are to be entered in a serially numbered receipt book in two copies (carbon) according to the attached model. The entries are to be signed for by the person delivering the article and by the receiving office. The carbon copy of the entry is to be transmitted immediately by the receiving office to the area Commissar. The delivered articles are to be transmitted to the fund of the area Commissar and to be safeguarded by the latter. A special order will be issued on their utilization.

4. *On the Question of Subsistence:* The Jewish popula- is left with the following:

    a. that portion of their household articles necessary for scanty subsistence (furniture, clothing and linen).

    b. A daily amount of money 0.20 RM (2 Rubles) for each Jewish member of the household, the amount of money for a month to be released in advance.

V. The following further measures are to be emphatically striven for, with due consideration for local and especially economic conditions:

  a. Jews are to be cleaned out from the countryside.

  b. The Jews are to be removed from all trade, especially from trade with agricultural products and other foodstuffs.

  c. The Jews are to be forbidden residence in resorts and spas, and in localities that are economically, militarily, or spiritually of importance.

  d. Jews are to be concentrated, as much as feasible, in cities or in sections of large cities, whose population is already predominantly Jewish. Ghettos are to be established there, and the Jews are to be prohibited from leaving these Ghettos. In the Ghettos they are to be given only as much food as the rest of the population can do without, but no more than suffices for scanty nourishment of the Ghetto inmates. The same applies to supply with other consumer goods. The inmates of the Ghetto regulate their internal conditions by self-administration which is supervised respectively by the city, area Commissar or his deputy. Jews can be assigned as police for internal order. They are to be equipped with rubber truncheons or sticks at most and are to be distinguished by the wearing of the white arm bands, with the yellow Jewish Star on the right upper arm. For the external hermetic sealing of the Ghettos, auxiliary police from among the natives are to be used as much as is feasible. Permission from the area Commissar must be obtained before anyone may enter the Ghetto.

e. Jews, capable of working, are to be drafted for forced labor according to the need for work. The economic interests of natives worthy of assistance must not be interfered with by Jewish forced labor. Forced labor can be performed in working parties outside the Ghettos or in the Ghettos or, where Ghettos are not yet established; also individually outside (i.e., in the workshop of the Jew). Pay need not correspond to work done; it need only correspond to the need for scanty subsistence for the forced laborer and the non-employable members of his family, taking due consideration to his present cash holdings. (cf. IV f 4 b). Those private establishments and persons, for whose account the forced labor is done, pay an appropriate fee to the pay office of the area Commissar which, in turn, disburses pay to the forced laborers. A special order will be issued for the accounting on amounts of money received.

6. It is left up to the General Commissars to order measures mentioned in par. 5 uniformly for their area or to turn over their promulgation in detail to the area Commissars. Likewise the General Commissars are authorized to issue more detailed orders within the framework of this policy or to authorize their area Commissars to do it.

DISTRIBUTION:
        Reichskommissariat   12
        Higher SS and Police leaders   20
        General Commissar:
            Estonia   10
            Lithuania   10
            Latvia   10
            White Ruthenia   60
        Surplus supply   28

Translation of Document 1189-PS. *Excerpt from Special Instructions No. 44, 4 November 1941, on Feeding of Civilian Population in the occupied Eastern Territories, in which it is provided that Jews are to receive one half the ration allowed "for population which does no work worth mentioning."*

* * *

1189-PS Nazi Germany's War Against the Jews

in the field 4/11/1941

Wi Stab Ost Fue/Ia, Az.B.NR. 6730/41
Special Instructions No. 44

Feeding of Civilian Population in the occupied Eastern Territories

Weekly Maximum in Grams

a. *For population which does no work worth mentioning.*

Meat and meat products	none
Fat	70
Bread	1500
Potatoes	2000

* * * * * * *

d. *Children under 14 years old and Jews:*
Half of the maximum according to a.

Translation of Document 1208-PS (USA 590). Goering order, 10 December 1938, concerning elimination of Jews from German economic life and confiscation of Jewish businesses and fortunes.

* * *

SECRET
1938
Reich Justice Ministry
[various numbers and notes]

The Commissioner of the Four Year Plan
[various illegible notations]
Reich Justice Ministry, 14 Dec 1938

To:
The Highest Reich authorities,
The leaders and heads of branches of the Party and the affiliated organizations,
The district leaders,
The Reich governors,
The state governments,
The Chief Presidents and Presidents of the governments,
The Reich commisars for the Saar territory
for the Reunion of Austria with the German Reich
for the Sudeten German districts.

To message: to the Reich leaders of the NSDAP.

In agreement with the representatives of the leader I hereby order the following:

III - 244

I

1. The elimination of Jews from the German economic life is the task of the state and therefore is exclusively the duty of the authorities and agencies expressly designated for that.

2. As far as special installations have been created for this purpose, they require the approval of the Reich minister of ecenomy or they are to be dissolved.

II

The taking over of Jewish businesses and other fortunes from Jewish possession has to be affected only on a strictly lawful basis according to the directives issued for this purpose. Transactions which were made since 1 Nov 1938 contradictory thereto, will be cancelled.

III

Only the Reich is entitled to the benefit from the elimination of the Jews from the German economic life.

Persons and agencies which have illegally benefited from the transfer of Jewish businesses or other fortunes from Jewish possession, may therefore be ordered to pay a compensation tax in favor of the Reich.

Berlin, 10 December 1938
The Commissar of the Four Year Plan
Signed: GOERING
General Fieldmarshall

To be circulated Dept. IV

Messrs:	Read	Messrs:	Read
DR. VOLKMAR*		DR. MERTEN	Initialed 11/1
ANZ	Initialed 10/1	DR. PAETZOLD*	
DR. BECKER	Initialed 11/1	DR. POHLE*	
BRAUNS	Initialed 14/1	DR. PRITSCH*	
DR. BREITHAUPT	Initialed	REINECK	Initialed 14/1
EPPING	Initialed 11/9	REINECKE	Initialed 13/1
FECHNER	Initialed 12/9	REXROTH	Initialed 11/1
DR. FICKER	Initialed 14/1	DR. SAAGE	Initialed 11/1
DR. HESSE*		SEBODE (since 9.1.39)	Initialed 16/1
HENSSLER, Vacation	18/1	DR VON SPRECK-	
HOFFMAN	Initialed 11/1	ELSEN	Initialed 11/1
HORNIG	Initialed 11/1	DR. SCHAEFFER,	
DR. JONAS*		GAss.	Initialed 11/1
DR. KOEHLER	Initialed 13/1	DR. SCHULTZE	Initialed 11/1
DR. KRAMER, AGR	Initialed 11/1	STAUD	Initialed 12/1
KUEHNEMANN	Initialed 11/1	STEMMLER*	
LAUTERBACH*		DR. VOGELS	Initialed 13/1
LENTZ	Initialed, date illegible	DR. WAITNAUER	Initialed 11/1
MASSFELLER	Initialed 13/1	ZIEGERT	Initialed 11/1

to V a 445/38 Secret

---

* Line drawn through name in original document.

Translation of Document 1347-PS (USA 285). *Extract of decree, 18 September 1942, Reich Minister for Nutrition and Agriculture, concerning food supply for Jews.*

* * *

The Reich Minister for Nutrition and Agriculture
Berlin W 8, Wilhelmstr. 72
18 September 1942.

To the State Governments [Landesregierungen] (State Nutrition offices) the Prussian Provincial Presidents (provincial nutrition offices) with the exception of the Eastern territories not incorporated into Upper Silesia.

For information of the district presidents [Regierungspraesidenten] and respective authorities

Re: food supply for Jews.

* * * * * * *

2. Rations.

Jews will no longer receive the following foods beginning with the 42nd distribution period (19 October 1942): meat, meat products, eggs, wheat products (cake, white bread, wheat rolls, wheat flour, etc.) whole fresh skimmed milk, as well as such foods as are distributed not on food ration cards issued uniformly throughout the Reich but on local supply certificates or by special announcement of the nutrition offices on extra coupons of the food cards. Jewish children and young people over 10 years of age will receive the bread ration of the normal consumer. Jewish children and young people over 6 years of age will receive the fat ration of the normal consumer, no honey substitute and no cocoa powder, and they will not receive the supplement of marmalade accorded the age classes of 6 to 14 years. Jewish children up to 6 years will receive ½ liter of fresh skimmed milk daily.

Accordingly no meat, egg or milk cards and no local supply certificates shall be issued to Jews. Jewish children and young people over 10 years of age will receive the bread cards and those over 6 years of age the fat cards of the normal consumer. The bread cards issued to Jews will entitle them to rye flour products only. Jewish children under 6 years of age shall be issued the supply certificate for fresh skimmed milk. "Good for ½ liter daily" shall be noted on it.

Jews cannot be self-providing in the sense of any decree.

3. Regulation for sick persons, etc.

The regulations for sick and infirm persons, expectant and nursing mothers and women in childbed do not apply to Jews.

The regulations of this decree apply also to Jewish inmates of hospitals.

4. Special allotments.

Jews are excluded from special allotments.

5. Exchange of food cards for travel and restaurant coupons.

The exchange of food cards for travel and restaurant coupons may be allowed to Jews only in urgent exceptional cases.

6. Ration-free food.

For the purchase of non-rationed food the Jews are not subject to restrictions as long as these products are available to the Aryan population in sufficient quantities. Ration-free foods which are distributed only from time to time and in limited quantities, such as vegetable and herring salad, fish, paste, etc., are not to be given to Jews. The nutrition offices are authorized to permit Jews to purchase turnips, plain kind of cabbage, etc.

7. Marking of ration cards.

Ration cards issued to Jews shall be printed over diagonally (i.e. over all individual coupons) with the repeated over-print "Jew". A color in contrast to the basic color of the cards shall be chosen for this. Cards and coupons overprinted "Jew" do not entitle the bearer to special allotments. Cancellation of these coupons before issue of the cards is therefore not necessary.

8. Special shopping time for Jews.

In order to avoid inconveniences in the supply of the Aryan population, it is recommended that the nutrition authorities establish special shopping times for Jews.

9. Food gift parcels for Jews.

The nutrition offices have to charge in full against the rations of the received all gift food parcels from abroad addressed to Jews. Should it be products which are rationed but not regularly distributed (such as coffee, cocoa, tea, etc.) the entire shipment or in case of a delayed report on the receipt of the package, the still unused part—will be made available to big consumers, such as hospitals and will be charged against their rations.

In the decree of 29 April 1941, of which a copy is enclosed, the Reich Minister of Finance instructed the Customs Office to report weekly to the competent nutrition offices all gift packages, regardless of the quantity of the incoming merchandise, when it is known or can suspect that the receiver is a Jew. In case the report of the Customs Office to the nutrition office is delayed until the food received in the gift package is consumed, it can still be charged against their rations.

Insofar as the State Police Offices are informed of these food parcels from abroad addressed to Jews, they will secure the packages and put them at the disposal of the nutrition offices [Ernaehrungs-Aemter.]

For the Secretary of State Reicke

Translation of Document 1397-PS. Law for the reestablishment of the Professional Civil Service, 7 April 1933, providing for the dismissal of officials of non-aryan descent.

* * *

1933 REICHSGESETZBLATT, PAGE 175, Art. 1-18, 7 April 1933

Law for the Reestablisment of the Professional Civil Service
7 April 1933

The Reichsgovernment has enacted the following law, which is hereby proclaimed:

Art. 1

1. For the reestablishment of a national professional civil service and for the simplification of administration, officials may be discharged from office according to the following regulations, even when the necessary conditions according to the appropriate laws do not exist.

2. Officials, as used in this law, means immediate [unmittelbare] and mediate [mittelbare] officials of the Reich, immediate and mediate officials of the federal states [Laender], officials of communes [Gemeinde] and communal associations, officials of public legal corporations as well as institutions and undertakings placed upon the same status as these public legal corporations (Third decree of the Reichspresident for the safeguarding of business and finance of 6 October 1931—RGBl. I P. 537, 3rd part, Chapter V, Section I, Art. 15, subparagraph 1). The stipulations apply also to employees of agencies supplying social insurance, who have the rights and duties of officials.

3. Officials as used in this law also includes officials in temporary retirement.

4. The Reichsbank and the German State Railway Co. are empowered to make corresponding regulations.

Art. 2

1. Officials who since 9 November 1918 have attained the status of officials without possessing the required or usual preparation or other qualifications are to be dismissed from service.

Their former salaries will be accorded them for a period of 3 months after their dismissal.

2. A right to waiting allowances, pensions, or survivors pension and to the continuance of the official designation, the title, the official uniform and the official insignia is not possessed by them.

3. In case of need a pension, revocable at any time, equivalent to a third of the usual base pay of the last position held by them may be granted them, especially when they are caring for dependent relatives; reinsurance according to the provisions of the Reich's social insurance law will not take place.

4. The stipulations of Section 2 and 3 will receive corresponding application in the case of persons of the type designated in Sec. 1, who already before this law became effective had been retired.

Art. 3

1. Officials, who are of non-aryan descent, are to be retired; insofar as honorary officials are concerned, they are to be removed from official status.

2. Section 1 is not in effect for officials who were already officials since 1 August 1914, or who fought during the World War at the front for the German Reichs or who fought for its allies or whose fathers or sons were killed in the World War. The Reichsminister of the Interior can permit further exceptions in understanding with the appropriate special minister or the highest authorities of the federal states in the case of officials abroad.

* * * * * * *

Berlin, 7 April 1933

The Reichschancellor
Adolf Hitler
The Reichsminister of the Interior
Frick
The Reichsminister of Finance
Count Schwerin von Krosigk

Translation of Document 1400-PS. *Excerpts from law changing the regulations in regard to public officers, 30 June 1933, providing that non-aryans may not be appointed Reich officials.*

* * *

1933 REICHSGESETZBLATT, PART I, PAGE 433
Law Changing the Regulations in regard to Public Officers,
June 30, 1933

Chapter 2
Article 1a

1. Only such persons may be appointed Reich officials who possess for their career the prescribed education or customary training or who have special qualifications for the office about to be given, and who guarantee that they will support the Reich at all times without reservation.

2. Women may only be appointed Reich officials for life when they have completed the 35th year.

3. Anyone of non-Aryan descent, or married to a person of non-Aryan descent, may not be appointed a Reich official. Reich officials of Aryan descent who marry a person of non-Aryan descent are to be discharged. The question of who is of non-Aryan descent is to be decided by regulations decreed by the Reich Minister of the Interior.

4. If urgent requirements of the administration so necessitate, the highest Reich officials may make exceptions in individual cases—exceptions from the provisions of (2) with the approval of the Reich Minister of Finance, exceptions from the provisions of (3) with the approval of the Reich Minister of the Interior.

* * * * * * *

The Reichschancellor
Adolf Hitler
The Reichsminister for Finance
Graf Schwerin von Krosigk
The Reichsminister of the Interior
Frick

Translation of Document 1406-PS. Decree for reporting of Jewish-owned property, 26 April 1938.

* * *

1938 REICHSGESETZBLATT, PART I, PAGE 414
Decree for the Reporting of Jewish Owned Property of 26 April 1938

On the basis of the Decree for the Execution of the Four Year Plan of 18 October 1936 (RGBl I, 887) the following is hereby decreed:

Article 1

1. Every Jew (Article 5 of the First Regulation under the Reich Citizenship Law of 14 November 1935 (RGBl I, 1333)) shall report and evaluate in accordance with the following in-

structions his entire domestic and foreign property and estate on the day when this decree goes into force. Jews of foreign citizenship shall report and evaluate only their domestic property.

2. The duty to report holds likewise for the non-Jewish marital partner of a Jew.

3. Every reporting person's property must be given separately.

Article 6

1. The administrative offices responsible under this regulation are in Prussia—Highest Administrative Officer [Regierungspraesident] (in Berlin the Police President); Bavaria — Highest Administrative Officer [Regierungspraesident]; Saxony — The District Head [Kreishauptmann]; Wurtemberg — The Minister of the Interior; Baden—The Minister of the Interior; Thueringen—Reich Governor [Reichsstatthalter]; Hessen —Reich Governor; Hamburg—Reich Governor; Mecklenburg— Ministry of the State, Interior Department; Oldenburg—Minister of Interior; Braunschweig—Ministry of Interior; Bremen —Senator for Administration of Interior; Anhalt—Ministry of State Interior Department; Lippe—Reich Governor (Land Government); Schaumburg-Lippe—Land Government; Saarland— The Reich Commissioner for the Saar.

2. Austria—The Reich Governor has jurisdiction. He may transfer his authority to another board.

* * * * * * *

Berlin, 26 April 1938
     The Deputy for the Four Year Plan
              Goering
           General Field Marshal
     The Reich Minister of the Interior
               Frick

Translation of Document 1409-PS. Order concerning utilization of Jewish property, 3 December 1938.

* * *

1938 REICHSGESETZBLATT, PART I, PAGE 1709
Order concerning the Utilization of Jewish Property of 3 December 1938

On the basis of Article 1 of the Second Regulation by the Administrator for the Four Year Plan based on the Decree of November 24, 1938 for the Reporting of Jewish-owned Property (RGBl. I, 1668), the following is decreed in cooperation with the competent Reich Ministers:

Chapter I *Industrial Enterprises*

Article 1

The owner of a Jewish industrial enterprise (Third Regulation under the Reich Citizenship Law of 14 June 1938, RGBl I 627) may be ordered to sell or liquidate the enterprise within a definite time. Certain conditions may be stipulated in the order.

Article 2

1. A trustee may be appointed for Jewish industrial enterprises, the owners of which have been ordered to sell or liquidate (Article 1), for the temporary continuation of the enterprise and for the completion of the sale or liquidation, especially if the owner of the enterprise has not complied with the order within the definite period and his application for an extension has been rejected.

2. The trustee is empowered to undertake all judicial and extra-judicial actions and legal measures, which the business of the enterprise, its liquidation or sale require. His authority replaces any legally required power of attorney.

3. The trustee must exercise the care of a responsible businessman and is subject to State control.

4. The owner of the enterprise is to pay the expenses of the trustee in connection with his work.

Chapter II *Land and Forest Enterprises Real Estate and other Property*

Article 6

A Jew (Article 5 of the First Regulation under the Reich Citizenship Law of November 14, 1935) (RGBl I, 1333), may be ordered to sell wholly or partly his land or forest enterprise, his other land or forest properties, his other real estate or other properties within a definite time. Certain conditions may be stipulated in the order. The regulations of Article 2 to 4 are to be applied accordingly.

Article 7

1. Jews cannot legally acquire real estate and mortgages.

2. The regulations of Article 2, 4, 5 and 6 of the Decrees based on the Decree of 26 April 1938, for the Reporting of Jewish-owned Property (RGBl I, 415) are to be applied accordingly.

* * *

Chapter III *Compulsory Deposit of Securities*
Article 11

1. Within a week after this decree goes into effect, Jews must deposit all their stocks, shares in mines, bonds, and similar securities at a foreign exchange bank. New securities must be deposited within a week after their acquisition. The holder of securities belonging to a Jew may not deliver them to anyone but a foreign exchange bank for the account of the Jew.

2. Insofar as securities are already deposited at a foreign exchange bank on behalf of Jews or titles registered or coupons deposited with an administrative authority for which preferred annuities will be granted, the Jews must immediately notify the said bank, the Administration of Public Loans or the administrative authority by a written declaration of the fact that they are Jews. In case of (1) Sentence 3, this declaration must be made to the said holder.

3. The deposits and the registered titles are to be marked as Jewish.

Article 12

The disposing of securities deposited as Jewish, as well as the release of such securities require the consent of the Reich Minister of economics or an authority named by him.

Article 13

The provisions of Articles 11 and 12 do not apply to foreign Jews.

Chapter IV *Jewels, Gems and Objects of Art*
Article 14

1. Jews are forbidden to acquire, pawn or sell objects of gold, platinum or silver as well as precious stones and pearls. Such objects, except in the case of existence of attachments on behalf of a non-Jewish creditor at the time when this decree goes into effect may only be acquired by public purchasing offices, established by the Reich. The same applies to other jewels and objects of art insofar as the price of the individual objects exceeds one thousand Reichsmarks.

2. The provisions of (1) does not apply to foreign Jews.

* * * * * * *

This decree goes into effect on the day of publication.
Berlin, 3 December 1938

Reich Minister of Economic Affairs
Walter Funk
Reich Minister of Interior
Frick

Translation of Document 1412-PS. *Decree imposing one billion Reichsmark fine upon Jews of German nationality, 12 November 1938.*

* * *

1938 REICHSGESETZBLATT, PART I, PAGE 1579
Decree relating to the payment of a fine by the Jews of German nationality of 12 Nov. 1938.

The hostile attitude of the Jewry towards the German people and Reich, which does not even shrink back from committing cowardly murder, makes a decisive defense and a harsh punishment (expiation) necessary. I order, therefore, by virtue of the decree concerning the execution of the 4-year Plan of 18 Oct. 1936 (RGBl I, page 887) as follows:

Section 1

On the Jews of German nationality as a whole has been imposed the payment of a contribution of 1,000,000,000 Reichsmark to the German Reich.

Section 2

Provisions for the implementation are issued by the Reich-Minister of Finance in agreement with the Reich-Ministers concerned.

Berlin, 12 November 1938.

The Commissioner for the Four Year Plan

Goering

General Field-Marshal.

Translation of Document 1415-PS. *Police regulation authorizing imposition upon Jews of restrictions on their appearance in public, 28 November 1938.*

* * *

1938 REICHSGESETZBLATT, PART I, PAGE 1676
Police Regulation of the Appearance of Jews in Public of 28 November 1938

On the basis of the Decree of 14 November 1938 Regarding the Police Decrees of the Reich Ministers (Reichsgesetzblatt I, P. 1582), the following is decreed:

ARTICLE 1

The Government Presidents in Prussia, Bavaria, and the Sudeten German areas, the proper authorities in the remaining provinces of the old Reich, the district captains (the Mayor in Vienna) in Austria and the Reich Commissar of the Saar district may impose upon Jews, both subjects of the German State and stateless Jews (Article 5 of the First Decree of 14 November 1935, Regarding the Reich Citizen Law, Reichsgesetzblatt I, p. 1333), restrictions as to place and time to the effect that they may not enter certain districts or may not appear in public at certain times.

ARTICLE 2

Whoever wilfully or negligently violates the regulations of Article I is to be fined up to 150 Reichsmarks or punished with imprisonment up to six weeks.

ARTICLE 3

This police decree goes into effect the day after its promulgation.

Berlin, 28 November 1938

The Reich Minister of Interior

By order:

Heydrich.

Translation of Document 1416-PS. Reich Citizenship Law of 15 September 1935.

* * *

1935 REICHSGESETZBLATT, PART 1, PAGE 1146

The Reich Citizenship Law of 15 Sept 1935

The Reichstag has adopted unanimously, the following law, which is herewith promulgated.

Article 1

1. A subject of the State is a person, who belongs to the protective union of the German Reich, and who, therefore, has particular obligations towards the Reich.

2. The status of the subject is acquired in accordance with the provisions of the Reich- and State Law of Citizenship.

Article 2

1. A citizen of the Reich is only that subject, who is of German- or kindred blood and who, through his conduct, shows that he is both desirous and fit to serve faithfully the German people and Reich.

2. The right to citizenship is acquired by the granting of Reich citizenship papers.

3. Only the citizen of the Reich enjoys full political rights in accordance with the provision of the laws.

Article 3

The Reich Minister of the Interior in conjunction with the Deputy of the Fuehrer will issue the necessary legal and administrative decrees for the carrying out and supplementing of this law.

Nurnberg, 15 Sept 1935 at the Reichsparteitag of Liberty

The Fuehrer and Reichs Chancellor

Adolf Hitler

The Reichs Minister of the Interior

Frick

Translation of Document 1417-PS (GB 258). *First Regulation to the Reich Citizenship Law, 14 November 1935, defining term "Jew" and providing that a Jew cannot be a citizen of the Reich.*

.*   *   *

1935 REICHSGESETZBLATT, PART 1, PAGE 1333

First Regulation to the Reich Citizenship Law of 14 Nov. 1935

On the basis of Article 3, Reich Citizenship Law, of 15 Sept. 1935 (RGBl I, page 146) the following is ordered:

Article 1

1. Until further issue of regulations regarding citizenship papers, all subjects of German or kindred blood, who possessed the right to vote in the Reichstag elections, at the time the Citizenship Law came into effect, shall, for the time being, possess the rights of Reich citizens. The same shall be true of those whom the Reich Minister of the Interior, in conjunction with the Deputy of the Fuehrer, has given the preliminary citizenship.

2. The Reich Minister of the Interior, in conjunction with the Deputy of the Fuehrer, can withdraw the preliminary citizenship.

Article 2

1. The regulations in Article 1 are also valid for Reichs subjects of mixed, Jewish blood.

2. An individual of mixed Jewish blood, is one who descended from one or two grandparents who were racially full Jews, insofar as does not count as a Jew according to Article 5, paragraph 2. One grandparent shall be considered as full-blooded if he or she belonged to the Jewish religious community.

Article 3

Only the Reich citizen, as bearer of full political rights, exercises the right to vote in political affairs, and can hold a public office. The Reich Minister of the Interior, or any agency empowered by him, can make exceptions during the transition period, with regard to occupying public offices. The affairs of religious organizations will not be touched upon.

Article 4

1. A Jew cannot be a citizen of the Reich. He has no right to vote in political affairs, he cannot occupy a public office.

2. Jewish officials will retire as of 31 December 1935. If these officials served at the front in the World War, either for Germany or her allies, they will receive in full, until they reach the age limit, the pension to which they were entitled according to last received wages; they will, however, not advance in seniority. After reaching the age limit, their pension will be calculated anew, according to the last received salary, on the basis of which their pension was computed.

3. The affairs of religious organizations will not be touched upon.

4. The conditions of service of teachers in Jewish public schools remain unchanged, until new regulations of the Jewish school systems are issued.

Article 5

1. A Jew is anyone who descended from at least three grandparents who were racially fully Jews. Article 2, par. 2, second sentence will apply.

2. A Jew is also one who descended from two full Jewish parents, if: (a) he belonged to the Jewish religious community at the time this law was issued, or who joined the community later; (b) he was married to a Jewish person, at the time the law was issued, or married one subsequently; (c) he is the offspring from marriage with a Jew, in the sense of Section 1, which was contracted after the Law for the protection of German blood and German honor became effective (RGBl. I, page 1146 of 15 Sept 1935); (d) he is the offspring of an extramarital relationship, with a Jew, according to Section 1, and will be born out of wedlock after July 31, 1936.

Article 6

1. As far as demands are concerned for the pureness of blood as laid down in Reichs law or in orders of the NSDAP and its echelons—not covered in Article 5—they will not be touched upon.

2. Any other demands on pureness of blood, not covered in Article 5, can only be made with permission from the Reich Minister of the Interior and the Deputy of the Fuehrer. If any such demands have been made, they will be void as of 1 Jan 1936, if they have not been requested from the Reich Minister

of the Interior in agreement with the Deputy of the Fuehrer. These requests must be made from the Reich Minister of the Interior.

Article 7

The Fuehrer and Reichs Chancellor can grant exemptions from the regulations laid down in the law.

Berlin, 14 November 1935

The Fuehrer and Reichs Chancellor
Adolf Hitler
The Reich Minister of the Interior
Frick
The Deputy of the Fuehrer
R. Hess
(Reich Minister without Portfolio)

Translation of Document 1419-PS. *Law concerning Jewish Tenants, 30 April 1939, providing that a Jew cannot invoke protection of tenancy laws, that a lease may be dissolved, where only one party to it is a Jew, by the other party.*

* * *

1939 REICHSGESETZBLATT, PART I, PAGE 864

Law concerning Jewish Tenants of 30 April 1939

The Reich Government has enacted the following law which is hereby promulgated:

Article 1 *Abatement of the Tenancy Protection Provisions*

A Jew cannot invoke the protection of the tenancy laws where the landlord in giving notice to vacate the premises can furnish him with a certificate from the communal authorities that his shelter is assured for the time subsequent to the expiration of the tenancy. This does not apply where the landlord is also a Jew.

Article 2 *Premature Dissolution of Lease*

A lease may be dissolved, where only one of the parties to it is a Jew, by the other party at any time within the legal term of giving notice, notwithstanding that the lease is signed for a specified time, or that the stipulated time of giving notice is longer than that fixed by law. The landlord, however, may not give notice for vacating the premises earlier than the term agreed upon, where he does not furnish certificate from the communal authorities that the shelter of the tenant has been assured elsewhere subsequent to the vacating of the premises.

Article 3 *Sub-Leases*

Sub-leases may be concluded only between Jews and Jews. Permission to sublet is not necessary where the house owner is also a Jew.

* * * * * * *

Berlin, 30 April 1939

The Fuehrer and Reich Chancellor
Adolf Hitler
The Reich Minister of Justice
Dr Guertner
The Reich Minister of Labor
His Deputy: Dr Krohn
The Deputy of the Fuehrer
R. Hess
The Reich Minister of the Interior
Frick

Translation of Document 1422-PS. *Thirteenth regulation under Reich Citizenship Law, 1 July 1943, depriving Jews of all protection of the law by providing that criminal actions committed by Jews shall be punished by the police.*

* * *

1943 REICHSGESETZBLATT, PART I, PAGE 372

Thirteenth Regulation under the Reich Citizenship Law of 1 July 1943

Under Article 3 of the Reich Citizenship Law of September 15, 1935 (RGBl I 1146) the following is ordered:

Article 1

1. Criminal actions committed by Jews shall be punished by the police.
2. The provision of the Polish penal laws of 4 December 1941 (RGBl I 759) shall no longer apply to Jews.

Article 2

1. The property of a Jew shall be confiscated by the Reich after his death.
2. The Reich may, however, grant compensation to the non-Jewish legal heirs and persons entitled to sustenance who have their domicile in Germany.
3. This compensation may be granted in the form of a lump sum, not to exceed the ceiling price of the property which has passed into possession [Verfuegungsgewalt] of the German Reich.

4. Compensation may be granted by the transfer of titles and assets from the confiscated property. No costs shall be imposed for the legal processes necessary for such transfer.

Article 3

The Reich Minister of the Interior with the concurrence of the participating higher authorities of the Reich shall issue the legal and administrative provisions for the administration and enforcement of this regulation. In doing so he shall determine to what extent the provisions shall apply to Jewish nationals of foreign countries.

Article 4

This regulation shall take effect on the seventh day of its promulgation. In the Protectorate Bohemia and Moravia it shall apply where German administration and German courts have jurisdiction; Article 2 shall also apply to Jews who are citizens of the Protectorate.

Berlin, 1 July 1943

The Reich Minister of the Interior
Frick
Chief of the Party Chancellery
M. Bormann
Reich Minister of Finance
Count Schwerin von Krosigk
Reich Minister of Justice
Dr. Thierack

Translation of Document 1472-PS (USA 279). Cable dated 16 December 1942, signed by SS Gruppenfuehrer Mueller, concerning transportation during January 1943 of 45,000 Jews from Bialystock District, Theresienstadt Ghetto, the occupied areas in the Netherlands, and Berlin to Auschwitz for forced labor.

* * *

[CABLE]

Date 16 December 1942

URGENT—SECRET

TEXT:

In accordance with the increased recruitment of manpower into the concentration camps, which was ordered by 30 January 1943, the following may be applied in the Jewish sector.

1. Total amount: 45,000 Jews.
2. Start of transportation 11 January 1943.
3. Completion of transportation 31 January 1943.

territories, is subject to confiscation, administration by commissioner and sequestration in accordance with the following regulations.

2. This does not apply to the property of persons who have gained German citizenship in accordance with Article 6 of the edict of the Fuehrer and Reich Chancellor concerning organization and administration of Eastern territories, dated 8 October 1939 (RGBl I, 2042). The competent authority (Article 12) may permit additional exceptions.

3. Nationals of the former Free City of Danzig who are of Polish nationality are considered as nationals of the former Polish State.

Article 2

1. Confiscation will be applied in case of property belonging to:

a. Jews.

b. Persons who have fled or who have absented themselves for longer than temporary period.

2. Confiscation may be applied:

a. If the property is needed for the public good, especially for purposes of national defense or the strengthening of German folkdom.

b. If the owners or other persons entitled to it immigrated into the, then, area of the German Reich after 1 October 1918.

3. Confiscation may be limited to individual articles of property.

4. As a rule the following articles are to be exempted from confiscation:

a. Movable articles destined exclusively for personal use.

b. Cash, bank and savings bank deposits as well as stocks and bonds up to a total value of one thousand marks.

*   *   *   *   *   *   *

Article 22

f. The decree of the Reich protector in Bohemia and Moravia on Jewish property of 21 June 1939 [Verordnungsblatt des Reichsprotektors in Boehmen und Maehren p. 45] and the decree of the Reich protector in Bohemia and Moravia on the removal of the Jews from the economy of the protectorate of 26 Jan 1940 [Verordnungsblatt des Reichsprotektors in Boehmen and Maehren P. 45] with the provision that the proceedings for the removal of Jews will also be carried out in regard to the property of subjects of the former Polish State according to these provisions, in agreement with the chief-trusteeship East;

for the sequestration and confiscation the agencies named in Article 12 remain competent.

* * *

Article 24

1. This decree becomes effective one week after its proclamation.

2. The commissioner for the four year plan will fix the time of its becoming invalid.

Berlin, 17 September 1940

>The chairman of the ministerial council for the defense of the Reich and commissioner for the four year plan

GOERING
Reichs Marshal

Translation of Document 1674-PS. Excerpts from Second decree for the execution of the law regarding the change of surnames and forenames, 17 August 1938, requiring that Jews may be given only such given-names as provided in Ministry of Interior directives.

* * *

1938 REICHSGESETZBLATT, PAGE 1044, 17 Aug. 1938

The second decree for the execution of the law regarding the change of the surnames and forenames of 17th August 1938.

On the basis of Article 13, of the law of 5 January 1938 (Reichsgesetzblatt I.S. 9) concerning the change of the surnames and given-names, the following is ordered:

Art. 1

1. Jews may be given only such given-names as are cited in the directives issued by the Ministry of Interior concerning the utilization of given-names.

2. Para. (1) is not applicable to Jews who are foreign citizens.

Art. 2

1. In so far as the Jews are still using some other given-names different from those which are at their disposal according to Art. 1,—they are obliged to assume by the 1st January, 1939, a second, additional given-name as follows; for males, the given-name Israel and for females the given-name Sara.

Art. 3

1. Whoever deliberately disobeys the directives of Art. 3 is to be punished by imprisonment of up to six months. Cases of negligent disobedience will be punished by imprisonment of no more than one month.

The Documentary Evidence 1674-PS

2. Whoever deliberately or carelessly neglects to give the proper notification according to Art. 2 is to be fined or punished by imprisonment of no more than one month.
Berlin, 17th, August 1938.
       Reichs Minister of the Interior:
        Representative, Dr. Stuckart.
       Reichs Minister of Justice:
         Dr. Guertner.

Copy of Document 1689-PS (USA 286). *Excerpt from "Czechoslovakia Fights Back," a document of the Czechoslovak Ministry of Foreign Affairs, 1943, describing elimination of Jewish life in Bohemia and Moravia.*

*   *   *

CZECHOSLOVAKIA FIGHTS BACK
A Document of the Czechoslovak Ministry of Foreign Affairs
Published by
American Council on Public Affairs
Washington, D. C., 1943
[Pages 110, 111, and 114]

On December 2, 1942, a special order issued by the "Protectorate" Ministry of Agriculture excluded the Jews not only from buying unrationed foods, but even from receiving them as a gift from any private citizen. The same order has left it to the discretion of the Ministry of Agriculture to exclude Jews entirely or partially from obtaining rationed food, thus exposing the remnants of the Jewish community to death by starvation.

One hour on five days a week has been allowed for shopping, this hour being fixed at a time when, after first the Germans and then the Czechs have done their buying, the small stocks are mostly exhausted.

After the occupation of Poland, Hitler designated Lublin and its immediate district as a reservation in which all Jews from the occupied countries were to be concentrated. Some 2,000 Jews of Moravska Ostrava were the first to be sent there. A year later, at the end of October 1941, 48,000 Czech Jews were already picked out for deportation. Men between the ages of sixteen to fifty were sent to labor camps, while their womenfolk and children were taken to special settlements in Eastern Poland.

At the end of June, 1942, deportation to Poland began on a large scale. The Gestapo was instructed to prepare by every

III - 265

Monday and Thursday contingents of a thousand Jews each. Those to leave were given a day or two's notice. The Nazi records of the Jewish registration were out of date and it often happened that the call-up cards were addressed to persons who had died years ago, had left the country or had already been deported. In such cases the daily quota of a thousand was made up by people simply picked up from the streets or dragged from their beds at night-time. The Gestapo took a delight in so selecting the deportees that families were split, wives separated from their husbands, and even small children from their mothers. Those left at home were never allowed to bid farewell to their relatives or friends. But sometimes, on early summer mornings, their Czech friends could watch those gloomy processions of the outlawed marching to the railway station and passing for the last time through the streets of Prague.

At the end of 1942, no Jewish life in Bohemia and Moravia was left. Out of the 90,000 Czech Jews more than 72,000 have been deported.

Although the deportations went on, leaving at the end of August, 1942, only some 20,000 Jews in Slovakia, most of them in ghettos, the Nazis were still not satisfied. At the end of November, 1942, a special committee was set up to consider the final expulsion of the remainder of the Jews. By then, out of the 95,000 Jews, 76,000 had already been deported.

Translation of Document 1708-PS (USA 255, USA 324). *The Program of the NSDAP. National Socialistic Yearbook, 1941, p. 153.*

* * *

National Socialistic Yearbook 1941
Edited by: Dr. Robert Ley
Published by: Central Publishing House of the NSDAP
Franz Eher, successor Munich
The program of the NSDAP

The program is the political foundation of the NSDAP and accordingly the primary political law of the State. It has been made brief and clear intentionally.

All legal precepts must be applied in the spirit of the party program.

Since the taking over of control, the Fuehrer has succeeded in the realization of essential portions of the Party program from the fundamentals to the detail.

The Party Program of the NSDAP was proclaimed on 24

February 1920 by Adolf Hitler at the first large Party gathering in Munich and since that day has remained unaltered. Within the national socialist philosophy is summarized in 25 points:

1. We demand the unification of all Germans in the Greater Germany on the basis of the right of self-determination of peoples.

2. We demand equality of rights for the German people in respect to the other nations; abrogation of the peace treaties of Versailles and St. Germain.

3. We demand land and territory (colonies) for the sustenance of our people, and colonization for our surplus population.

4. Only a member of the race can be a citizen. A member of the race can only be one who is of German blood, without consideration of creed. Consequently no Jew can be a member of the race.

5. Whoever has no citizenship is to be able to live in Germany only as a guest, and must be under the authority of legislation for foreigners.

6. The right to determine matters concerning administration and law belongs only to the citizen. Therefore we demand that every public office, of any sort whatsoever, whether in the Reich, the country or municipality, be filled only by citizens. We combat the corrupting parliamentary economy, office-holding only according to party inclinations without consideration of character or abilities.

7. We demand that the state be charged first with providing the opportunity for a livelihood and way of life for the citizens. If it is impossible to sustain the total population of the State, then the members of foreign nations (non-citizens) are to be expelled from the Reich.

8. Any further immigration of non-citizens is to be prevented. We demand that all non-Germans, who have immigrated to Germany since the 2 August 1914, be forced immediately to leave the Reich.

9. All citizens must have equal rights and obligations.

10. The first obligation of every citizen must be to work both spiritually and physically. The activity of individuals is not to counteract the interests of the universality, but must have its result within the framework of the whole for the benefit of all. Consequently we demand:

11. Abolition of unearned (work and labour) incomes. Breaking of rent-slavery.

12. In consideration of the monstrous sacrifice in property

and blood that each war demands of the people personal enrichment through a war must be designated as a crime against the people. Therefore we demand the total confiscation of all war profits.

13. We demand the nationalization of all (previous) associated industries (trusts).

14. We demand a division of profits of all heavy industries.

15. We demand an expansion on a large scale of old age welfare.

16. We demand the creation of a healthy middle class and its conservation, immediate communalization of the great warehouses and their being leased at low cost to small firms, the utmost consideration of all small firms in contracts with the State, county or municipality.

17. We demand a land reform suitable to our needs, provision of a law for the free expropriation of land for the purposes of public utility, abolition of taxes on land and prevention of all speculation in land.

18. We demand struggle without consideration against those whose activity is injurious to the general interest. Common national criminals, usurers, Schieber and so forth are to be punished with death, without consideration of confession or race.

19. We demand substitution of a German common law in place of the Roman Law serving a materialistic world-order.

20. The state is to be responsible for a fundamental reconstruction of our whole national education program, to enable every capable and industrious German to obtain higher education and subsequently introduction into leading positions. The plans of instruction of all educational institutions are to conform with the experiences of practical life. The comprehension of the concept of the State must be striven for by the school [Staatsbuergerkunde] as early as the beginning of understanding. We demand the education at the expense of the State of outstanding intellectually gifted children of poor parents without consideration of position or profession.

21. The State is to care for the elevating national health by protecting the mother and child, by outlawing child-labor, by the encouragement of physical fitness by means of the legal establishment of a gymnastic and sport obligation, by the utmost support of all organizations concerned with the physical instruction of the young.

22. We demand abolition of the mercenary troops and formation of a national army.

III - 268

23. We demand legal opposition to known lies and their promulgation through the press. In order to enable the provision of a German press, we demand, that: a. All writers and employees of the newspapers appearing in the German language be members of the race: b. Non-German newspapers be required to have the express permission of the State to be published. They may not be printed in the German language: c. Non-Germans are forbidden by law any financial interest in German publications, or any influence on them, and as punishment for violations the closing of such a publication as well as the immediate expulsion from the Reich of the non-German concerned. Publications which are counter to the general good are to be forbidden. We demand legal prosecution of artistic and literary forms which exert a destructive influence on our national life, and the closure of organizations opposing the above made demands.

24. We demand freedom of religion for all religious denominations within the state so long as they do not endanger its existence or oppose the moral senses of the Germanic race. The Party as such advocates the standpoint of a positive Christianity without binding itself confessionally to any one denomination. It combats the Jewish-materialistic spirit within and around us, and is convinced that a lasting recovery of our nation can only succeed from within on the framework: common utility precedes individual utility.

25. For the execution of all this we demand the formation of a strong central power in the Reich. Unlimited authority of the central parliament over the whole Reich and its organizations in general. The forming of state and profession chambers for the execution of the laws made by the Reich within the various states of the confederation. The leaders of the Party promise, if necessary by sacrificing their own lives, to support the execution of the points set forth above without consideration.

Adolf Hitler proclaimed the following explanation for this program on the 13 April 1928:

Explanation

Regarding the false interpretations of Point 17 of the program of the NSDAP on the part of our opponents, the following definition is necessary:

Since the NSDAP stands on the platform of private ownership it happens that the passage "gratuitous expropriation" concerns only the creation of legal opportunities to expropriate if necessary, land which has been illegally acquired or is not administered from the view-point of the national welfare. This is directed primarily against the Jewish land-speculation companies.

Translation of Document 1724-PS (USA 266). Announcement in Press Conferences, 4 August 1938, of breaking up of synagogue.

* * *

Press conference on August 4, 1938 headed by Regional Leader [Gauamtsleiter] Schoeller

Duration: 1 hour

[Page 1, par. 4]

The breaking up of the synagogue (information must still be secret).

On August 10, 1938 at 10 o'clock A. M. the breakup of the synagogues will commence. Gauleiter Julius Streicher will personally set the crane into motion with which the Jewish symbols (Star of David etc.) will be torn down. This should be arranged in a big way. Closer details are still unknown.

Translation of Document 1752-PS (GB 159). Memorandum, dated 15 June 1944, concerning preparations for International Anti-Jewish Congress.

* * *

SECRET

Preparations already made for the International Congress

Reichsleader Alfred Rosenberg received the order from the Fuehrer to stage an anti-Jewish congress. The date for this congress was fixed at 11.7. after a discussion, and after the corresponding preparations had been made.

The following preparations for the congress have been undertaken:

1. In Germany.
2. abroad.

1. *Preparations in Germany.*

a. The financing of the congress has been taken on by the Reich Treasury of Chief, Schwarz. Further, after the Fuehrer had decided on Cracow as the site of the congress, Reich Minister and General Governor Frank has taken over all the costs that arise within his General Government.

b. *The site of the meeting.*

All negotiations concerning billeting, feeding and welfare of the guests, the lecture rooms etc. have been readily settled with the offices of the General governor. (Instead of Cracow, a place that is safe from air raids, for instance Zakopane, can be selected at any time.)

c. The program of lectures has been discussed with the appropriate offices,

1. Foreign Office
2. Propaganda Ministry
3. Head Office for internal security

and has met with general approval. The Reich Foreign Minister as well as Reich Minister Dr. Goebbels have given their assent to the program.

d. German speakers and lecturers have been visualized, among others three German Ministers. The promise of these three gentlemen to attend seems certain. Some lectures are already on hand.

The final preparations, those for the cultural extra items on the programme, have been taken in hand. (See the letter from Reichsleader Rosenberg to Reichsleader Bormann concerning the appearance of the Berlin Philharmonic Orchestra, with Furtwaengler as conductor.)

Even the formation of international organisations for investigating and combatting Jewry, which have been provided for in connection with the congress, have been brought about, and scientific presidents of the organisations have been earmarked. Some individual personalities have already been approached. Amonst others we already have the promise of Geheimrat Professor Dr. Eugen Fischer to be president of the European organisation for the "racial-biological questions of Jewry".

e. The following have been entered as honorary members:
    Reich Foreign Minister Joachim von Ribbentrop
    Reich Minister of the Interior and Reichsleader of the SS Heinrich Himmler
    Reich Minister Dr. Goebbels
    Reich Minister and Governor Dr. Frank

2. *Preparations abroad*

The Foreign Office has accepted the task of contacting the prominent European people, with the exception of a few of the occupied territories in Europe, via its representatives abroad.

The German representatives abroad have received several official instructions, according to which they are
  a. to propose delegates to be invited,
  b. nominate lecturers,
  c. approach the representatives of governments with a view to their participating at the congress.

In the course of these instructions being carried out, the following have promised their participation, or membership of the congress-committee and membership of the honorary committee:

Italy: Minister for National Enlightenment Mezzasoma (honorary committee)
The former Minister of State Preziosi (congress-committee and congress lecturer)
France: Minister for Education Abel Bonnard (Honorary committee)
Secretary of State Paul Marion (congress-committee)
Hungary: Minister for the Interior van Jarossh (honorary committee and congress lecturer)
Holland: The leader of the NSB, Mussert (Personally invited by Reichsleader Rosenberg during the latter's stay in Holland)
Arabia: The Grand Mufti of Jerusalem (honorary committee and congress lecturer)
Iraq: Prime Minister Gailani (honorary committee)
Norway: At the present moment a representative of Reichsleader Rosenberg has arrived here, in order personally to convey an invitation to Prime Minister Quisling to attend the congress.

Contacts have also been established with countless other countries. For the time being the promises to attend of the prominent representatives are not yet at hand. On the other hand promises have been received from delegates from Sweden, Roumania, Slovakia and illegal delegates from Switzerland, Spain and Portugal. Further the office of General in the SS Berger has undertaken to invite renowned leaders of the Germanic volunteers in the SS to take part in the congress. Amongst others, Britons and Americans are visualized in this connection, who are also willing to speak.

The occupied eastern territory is included via the Ministry for the East. A number of promises to attend have been received from renowned personalities in this territory. Lectures have already been received from foreign speakers, amongst others from the former Minister of State Preziosi.

3. Reason for the importance of the Congress at the present time. The reports from outside Germany and the anti-German allied propaganda tries to make believe beyond all doubt that the whole war is being kindled by the other side more and more

as a crusade, because the German nation plans to destroy the "Jewish People".

The Soviet Union: We refer to the pro-semitic Molotov-congress in Moscow.

U.S.A.: We refer to permanent session of the Jewish Congress. The *last new* beginning 6. 5. 1944.

England: We refer to the English failure to pay attention to their own White Paper regarding Palestine problem.

At the same time, we point out the slowly rising anti-Semitic feeling in the countries of our opponents. It seems necessary that the feeling caused by enemy propaganda that National Socialism is retreating on all fronts, be refuted by this great anti-Jewish Congress.

The invasion army is not fighting against the barbarian Germany of annihilation of Jews but it is fighting for world Jewry!

What kind of propaganda is being duly turned out on the German side?

To give up this plan or to postpone this International Congress *to an indefinite date*, after half of Europe has already been won for this plan would support or strengthen the propaganda conducted against us.

It must be borne in mind that not a German authority but an international assembly is responsible for the Congress and issues invitations to it.

The preparations for the Congress have so far progressed with the greatest possibilities of disguise.

An arrangement, which has been made on general lines, mentions only an International historic and scientific congress taking place in a Town in the East of the Reich.

Berlin, 15th June 1944.
Hg/We

/s/ Hans Hagemeyer,
Head of the Department.

Translation of Document 1757-PS (GB 175). *Excerpts from Report of Goering's Commissioners for investigation of Aryanisations carried out in Franconia between 9/11/38 and 9/2/39 and the irregularities connected therewith.*

* * *

REPORT OF GOERING'S COMMISSION
for the investigation of the Aryanisations carried out
in the Gau of Franconia between 8.11.38 and 9.2.39

and the irregularities connected therewith which have been established.

[P.9] k. By an order of the Reich Chancellor of the Exchequer of the 2nd September 1938, No. 57/38, issued with the agreement of the Fuehrer's deputy, all party offices, including organisations and attached formations, are forbidden to accept administrative dues, donations, gifts, bequests or material payments of any other kind for the participation of the party in economic tasks, including the transfer of Jewish firms to persons of German race, nor are they allowed to make the fulfillment of such tasks dependent on the payment of contributions, etc. The order was addressed to all Gau treasurers and reached the Gauleaders as well, among others.

[P.12] From the course of events one can only assume that the Reich Chancellor of the Exchequer's order of the 2nd September 1938 No. 57/38 about the ban on financial payments for the cooperation of the Party in Aryanisation and other economic tasks was considered in Franconia to be superseded, and that they thought themselves entitled to obtain considerable sums of money for the Gau of Franconia in connection with Aryanisation.

[P.13] 1. Following upon the November demonstrations, the deputy Gauleader, Holz, took up the Jewish questions. His * * * reason can be given here in detail on the basis of his statement of the 25th March 1939:

"*The 9th and 10th November 1938.* In the night of the 9/10 November and on the 10th November 1938 events took place throughout Germany *which I considered to be the signal for a completely different treatment of the Jewish question in Germany*. Synagogues and Jewish schools were burnt down and Jewish property was smashed both in shops and in private houses. Besides this, a large number of particular Jews were taken to concentration camps by the police. Towards midday we discussed these events in the Gauleiter's house. All of us were of the opinion *that we now faced a completely new state of affairs on the Jewish question*. By the great action against the Jews, carried out in the night and morning of the 10th November, *all guiding principles and all laws on this subject had been made illusory*. We were of the opinion (particularly myself) that we should now act on our own initiative in this respect. I proposed to the Gauleiter that, in view of the great existing lack of houses, the best thing would be to put the Jews into a kind of *internment camp*. Then the houses would become free in a twinkling and the housing shortage would be relieved, at least in part. Besides that, we would have the Jews under control and supervision. I added "The same thing happened to our prisoners of war and war internees." The Gauleiter said that this suggestion was, for the time being, impossible to carry out. Thereupon, I made a new proposal to him: I said to him *that I considered it unthinkable that, after the Jews had had their property smashed they should continue to be able to own houses and land*. I proposed that these houses and this land ought to be taken away from them, and declared myself ready to carry through such an action. I declared that by the Aryanisation of Jewish land and houses *a large sum could accrue to the Gau out of the proceeds*. I named some millions of marks. I stated that in my opinion, this Aryanisation could be carried out as legally as the Aryanisation of shops. The Gauleiter's answer was something to this effect: *"If you think you can carry this out, do so. The sum gained will then be used to build a Gau school."* The very same afternoon I began to organize the Aryanization of land. I stated here as in my memorandum, too, *that I considered this Aryanisation of Jewish land as a logical continuation of the events of the 9th and 10th November*. I was of the opinion that I was doing a service to the Party by trying to bring it money. I was further of the opinion *that the transfer of the land and houses from Jewish to German hands was a National-Socialist action."*

[P.16] Holz appointed commissioners for Nurnberg and Furth to carry out the Aryanisation of Jewish landed property * * *

[P.18] 2. The Aryanisation was accomplished by the alienation of properties, the surrender of claims, especially mortgage claims, and reductions in buying price.

The payment allowed the Jews was basically 10% of the nominal value or nominal sum of the claim. As a justification for these low prices, Holz claimed at the Berlin meeting of the 6th February 1939 that the Jews had mostly bought their property during the inflation period for a tenth of its value. As has been shown by investigating a large number of individual cases selected at random, this claim is not true.

[P.70] Favoritism shown to third parties and irregularities during the Aryanization of properties.

[P.72] *Schoeller case.* c. Gauamtsleiter Fritz Schoeller bought *Grimmstrasse 3, Nurnberg* by a contract of the 15th November 1938. The house has a nominal value of RM 43,300 and an exchange value of RM 50,000. The buying price was fixed at RM 5,000. Holz admitted (statement of the 27th March

1939) that he was in agreement with the buying of the property. He based his agreement on the fact that Schoeller was an old and deserving party member and deserved particular consideration owing to his family circumstances.

Report of German Commission to Goering on Streicher.
[Extract from Part II]

[P. 139] On the other hand, the minority of the shares of the Mars-Werke, Nurnberg, with a face value of Reichsmark 112,500, were acquired through publishing house manager Fink for the Gauleiter according to the latter's instructions at the instigation of the deceased SA Brigadier General Koenig. These shares were in the possession of the Jewish banking house Kohn, the proprietor of which was at the time in protective custody. Verlagsdirektor Fink, as agent for the Gauleiter, acquired the parcel of Mars-Werke shares from this Jew at 5 per cent of the face value, i.e., the sum of Reichsmark 5,600.

In the presence of Fink, Koenig informed the Gauleiter in detail of the completed transaction. The Gauleiter gave his complete assent and, in addition, gave the order to transfer the parcel of shares from the account of the banking firm Kohn to the account of Fink at the Dresdner Bank. He further ordered that his name should not be mentioned at all in connection with the transaction.

By order of the Gauleiter, Fink withdrew Reichsmark 5,600 from a Stuermer account, and later, also acting for the Gauleiter, he bought the remainder of the shares of the Mars-Dresdner Bank, at 60 per cent for the Gauleiter with Stuermer funds.

After Fink learned of the investigating commission he discussed the matter with Gauleiter Streicher. Streicher told Fink that he would keep the shares, because they had no connection with the Aryanization of estates, and if the purchase of the Mars shares should be contested he would simply pay over the required sum to the Reich.

After the investigating commission had started to work Gauleiter Streicher sent for Fink and told him the following: "The police have found out about the Mars shares. We will simply say that the shares were not bought for me but for the Fraenkische Tageszeitung!!" [P. 145] Thanks to the efforts of the district economic adviser and president of the chamber of commerce Strobl, it was possible to persuade the Hungarian consul Pfaller to buy the estate of the Gauleiter on Lake Constance without ever having seen it, for a price of Reichsmark 240,000. It is noteworthy that the Gauleiter and people close to him had a very bad opinion of Consul Pfaller, but after the purchase of the estate the Gauleiter sent him a picture. In order to avoid the Gauleiter's appearing personally as the seller, a sham contract was made with publisher Willmy, so that the latter would appear to the outside world as the seller of the estate.

[P. 152] Gauleiter Streicher likes to beat people with a riding whip, but only if he is in the company of several persons assisting him. Usually the beatings are carried out with sadistic brutality.

The best known case is that of Steinruck, whom he beat bloodily in the prison cell, together with deputy Gauleiter Holz and SA Brigadier General Koenig. After returning from this scene to the "Deutscher Hof" he said: "Now I am relieved. I needed that again!" Later he also stated several times that he needed another Steinruck case in order to "relieve" [erloesen] himself.

In August 1938 he beat editor Burker at the district house, together with district leader Schoeller and his adjutant Koenig.

On 2 December 1938 he asked to have three youthful criminals (15 to 17 years old) who had been arrested for robbery brought to the room of the director of the criminal police office in Nurnberg-Fuerth. Streicher, who was accompanied by his son Lothar, had the youths brought in singly and questioned them about their sex life and in particular, through clear and detailed questioning, he laid stress on determining whether and since when they masturbated. One of the youths did not know the word, whereupon Streicher gave him a vivid description. The last one of these three boys he beat with his riding whip, with blows on the head and the rest of the body.

[P. 151] From 1934 to 1938 Gauleiter Streicher employed the Jew Jonas Wolk as contributor to the Stuermer. Wolk wrote for the Stuermer under the pseudonym of "Fritz Brandt". In addition, Wolk did spy work for the Gauleiter abroad. From February 1937 to August 1938 the Stuermer paid the Jew Wolk a fee of Reichsmark 8,262.39. Wolk was previously convicted six times, among other things with loss of civic rights. It is especially significant that Streicher had the Jew Wolk paid by the Fraenkische Tageszeitung from 1934 to 1937. The Fraenkische Tageszeitung paid Wolk the sum of Reichmark 9,623.65.

[P. 160] According to the statement of the district treasurer [Gauschatzmeister], his financial adviser, and several other persons, Streicher is regarded as extremely brutal. The statements made by Verlagsdirektor Fink are especially significant. He declared that he was convinced that the Gauleiter would have him bumped off one of these days, as soon as he found out that Fink had told the truth to the investigating commission.

[P. 161] According to reports of reliable witnesses, Gauleiter Streicher is in the habit of pointing out on the most varied occasions that he alone gives orders in the district of Franconia. For instance, at a meeting in the Collosseum in Nurnberg in 1935 he said that nobody could remove him from office. In a meeting at Herkules Hall, where he described how he had beaten Prof. Steinruck, he emphasized that he would not allow himself to be beaten, *not even by an Adolf Hitler*.

[P. 166] For, this also must be stated here, in Franconia the Gau acts first and then orders the absolutely powerless authorities to approve.

[P.172] In general it is to be said that Koenig was regarded as the evil spirit in Franconia. In an unheard-of-manner he tyrannized the Gau leader, the authorities and the population, and he knew how to make the influence of his power felt everywhere. Koenig's word carried the weight of that of the Gauleiter.

[P. 174] In favor of Strobl [pencil note: Director of the AEG, Gau economic adviser, and president of the Chamber of Industry and Commerce] it must be said that he, in contrast to almost all other defendants, immediately told the truth on all points in his interrogations. It is primarily thanks to him that clearness was quickly reached in many cases which could be verified.

As an excuse for his incorrect acts Strobl states that he like all others persons in the Gau of Franconia was to such an extent under the pressure of Gauleiter Streicher and his adjutant Koenig that he would never have dared to do anything against the orders of the two men mentioned.

[P.179] By the law of April 1938 it is decreed that all applications for Aryanization shall be submitted to the competent Gauleiter. From that time on Strobl submitted the applications which he had up to that time handled by himself, to the adjutant of the Gauleiter, SA Brigadier General Koenig for approval. He makes the excuse that it had been the practice in Franconia for the adjutant to take care of almost all matters as agent for and deputy of the Gauleiter. Every order of Brigadier General Koenig was equivalent to an order of the Gauleiter.

Copy of Document 1759-PS (USA 420). Portion of affidavit of Raymond H. Geist, formerly American Consul and First Secretary of Embassy in Berlin, Germany, 1929-1939, dated 28 August 1945, describing Nazi Germany's anti-Jewish activities 1933-1938.

* * *

United Mexican States
Mexico, Federal District } ss
Embassy of the United States of America

Mexico City, D. F. } ss
Mexico

Raymond H. Geist, being first duly sworn, deposes and says:

I came to Berlin in December, 1929, as Consul and continued in that capacity, exercising my official functions until the end of 1939. In 1938 I was appointed First Secretary of the Embassy and continued in that office discharging at the same time my duties as consul.

As I have stated, my frequent contacts with this entire Gestapo organization began with the first wave of terrorist acts in the week of March 6-13, 1933. That wave was accompanied by universal mob violence. Since 1925, one of the cries of the Nazi party had been "Jude Verrecke" (Death to the Jews) and when the Nazi party won the elections in March, 1933, on the morning of the sixth, the accumulated passion blew off in wholesale attacks on the Communists, Jews, and those who were suspected of being either. Mobs of S.A. men roamed the streets, beating up, looting, and even killing persons.

No American citizen, so far as I am aware, was killed, but a number of them were assaulted and injured and appealed to the Consulate General for aid and protection. For example, Nathaniel Wolff, an American citizen, who resided in Rochester, New York, made an affidavit which stated:

This morning, March 6, at 5 o'clock, there came into my room five or six Nazis with drawn revolvers. They abused me, called me a dirty Russian Jew and started going through my belongings. They asked me what remarks I had made. I replied that I had made none that I knew of and that I am not interested in politics. One of them shouted "Do you call throwing bombs not being interested in politics?" Another asked at the same time, "Are you the Wolff who lived in the Pension Stephanie?" Having left the Stephanie on account of difficulties with the Portier regarding the price of the room and his behavior, I whistled very softly, intimating that I understood the source of the denunciation. Thereupon one of the Nazis remarked: "Du Scheiss Jude, warum pfeiffst du?" and hit me in the jaw. They said that they would take me to the police station, whereupon I answered, "The quicker, the better, because my conscience is absolutely clear." One of them said, "Do you call throwing bombs having a clear conscience?" The intruders were not accompanied by an officer, nor did they carry "Hilfspelizei" armbands. They took me in an automobile to an address in the Knewbeck Strasse beyond the Kant Strasse (I believe No. 67 or 76, Gartenhaus left, I think three or four flights up the stairs). I was conducted to a bare room in which the shutters were closed and the windows boarded, evidently to prevent sounds from getting out, where, after my possessions were taken away including my keys, I was left with two guards who spent the time abusing the Jews. At five minutes before seven, the group who had arrested me returned with two or three members including one who was apparently a leader when I was again abused, that is, they gave me to understand that they imagined I was implicated in communistic activities. I remarked that I should like to send a telegram to my cousin, Alan Steyne at the Hamburg American Consulate, and asked if I had the right to do so, whereupon the leader replied: "As a foreigner you have no right, and especially not as a Jew." One of the men then proceeded to bind my hands and feet as closely and as painfully as possible. I still bear the marks of the bruises on my wrists. I was questioned about various English and French letters which had been found in my room and taken along with them and then I was left about half an hour alone because they evidently discussed my fate. After some time one of the group returned and advised me that every one had a right to his own political opinions as long as no attempt was made to mix into politics. He remarked that nothing was to be gained by brutality, undid the rope and freed my hands and feet and gave me a cup of coffee and said, "Probably the thing isn't so bad because women chatter a great deal" and that I was denounced by a girl. After a few minutes he elaborated the statement that the girl, Paula, of the Pension, had denounced me as having the intention of throwing bombs at the Nazi parade. I expressed my astonishment and told him the facts of the case. He appeared to laugh it off and asked me if I would be willing to sign a paper on the condition that they would release me. I said "yes." They then said I would have to go to the police to have my signature attested to and one of the men who had come in, in the meanwhile, went out to draft the paper I was to sign. He returned with the paper which read: (1) "I am a Jew," (2) "I will leave tonight for Paris," (3) "I promise never again to set my foot on German soil." "I attest that no physical violence was done to me and that none of my property was stolen." This paper I signed. They told me to put on my coat and come to the police. Instead of taking me to the police station they took me to Charlottenburg towards the Gruenwald. When I asked to which police station they were taking me, they replied "You'll get there soon enough." When we were near the Heer Strasse they pretended that the automobile was broken down and informed me that I would have to walk through the woods to get to the police station. We proceeded into the woods where three members drew their pistols and the other two brought straps out of their pockets and informed me that they were going to teach me a lesson and made as if they were about to tie me to a tree. They said that they intended to beat the life out of me and "You can walk back afterwards." I replied that I hoped I would be able to walk. This was probably about eight o'clock and we were entirely alone as nobody had followed us. I took off my coat myself and remarked "If one can't help oneself, one may as well make the best of it." One of them threw my coat to the ground and said "Get ready" and after making a threatening gesture, said "You can go home now!" pointing to the wrong direction, whereupon they walked rapidly to the automobile and disappeared yelling after me, "Keep your mouth shut." I was also threatened that if they ever caught me in Germany again, they would know how to get me out of the way. * * *

Another American, Herman I. Roseman, made an affidavit which stated:

Yesterday, March 10, 1933, in the afternoon at about 4:30, I came out of "KDW" with my fiancee, Fraulein Else Schwarzlose, residing in Wilmersdorf, Kaiser-Allee 172, and proceeded to walk along Tauentzien Strasse. A man in S. A. uniform stepped on my toe purposely, obviously offended me and said "Pardon." I said "bitte," and walked ahead. He followed me and kicked me saying; "Na und?" A policemen saw this and walked ahead, paying no attention to attacks made on me. Then I took my passport out of my pocket, showed it to the second policeman, and said that I was an American citizen, but he walked ahead, obviously not able to afford me protection, or at least being unwilling. The S. A. man continued to attack me, struck me in the face, wounded me over the eye, and continued to do me bodily harm. During this attack, all the time my walking along, we reached another policeman, and I applied to him, showng my passport and said: "I am an American and am entitled to protection." He shrugged his shoulders and said "What can I do?" By this time the S. A. man had obviously inflicted enough attack upon me and walked away.

Upon my appeal the policeman brought my fiancee and me to the station house at 13 Bayreuther Strasse. My fiancee and I reported to the officer in charge. He heard the story and said that he was sorry, but that there was nothing to do. My face was bleeding. The policeman said that he had had orders not to interfere in any affair in which an S. A. man took part. I then asked him what I could do to protect myself. He said that there was nothing to do but to wait until the situation was better. He added that the police were absolutely powerless, and were under the direction of the S. A., and that there were S. A. [Sturm-Abteilung] in the police itself. Thereupon I departed * * *

Another American, Mrs. Jean Klauber, made an affidavit which stated:

That on the night of Friday, March 10, 1933, she and her husband had retired for the night when they were awakened by a prolonged ringing of their apartment bell. They heard pounding upon the street door and a demand for immediate entry, and a concurrent threat to break the door down. The street door was opened by the janitor's wife, and a party of four or five men entered and went at once to the apartment of the deponent where they again rang and pounded on the door. Mr. Klauber asked who was there, and was answered—"The police." He opened the door and a party of four or five men in brown uniforms, one wearing a dark overcoat and carrying a rifle, pushed in, jostling Mr. and Mrs. Klauber aside. One asked Mrs. Klauber where the telephone was and she indicated the room where it was to be found and started to go there. Thereupon, she was knocked down by one of them. They went on to the bedroom where Mr. and Mrs. Klauber followed them, and there they demanded their passports. Mr. Klauber went to the wardrobe to get his, and was stopped, being asked by the intruders whether he was carrying any weapons. Being clothed only in pajamas, his denial was accompanied by a gesture indicating his garb. He then turned to the wardrobe, opened it, and reached for one of his four suits hanging there in which he thought the passport was, and was immediately attacked from behind by all but one of the intruders, who beat him severely with police clubs, the one with the overcoat and rifle standing by. Remarks were shouted such as "Look. Four suits, while for fourteen years we have been starving." Mrs. Klauber tried to inquire the reason for their actions, and was answered—"Jews. We hate you. For fourteen years we have been waiting for this, and tonight we'll hang many of you."

When the intruders stopped beating Mr. Klauber he was unconscious, and they demanded the passports again of Mrs.

Klauber. Mrs. Klauber found her American passport and her German passport (required by local authorities as the wife of a German citizen, and issued by the Police at Munich after her arrival here), and the intruders took both in spite of Mrs. Klauber's protests that she was American. She then searched for her husband's passport, laid hold of his pocket-book, and in her excitement offered it to them. Though full of money they refused it, and again demanded the passport. Mrs. Klauber then found it and handed it over.

Then the intruders returned to the unconscious Mr. Klauber, saying "He hasn't had enough yet," and beat him further. Then they left, saying "We are not yet finished," and just as they departed, one of them said to Mrs. Klauber "Why did you marry a Jew? I hate them" and struck her on the jaw with his police club * * *

I personally can verify that the police had been instructed not to interfere; that is that there was official sanction for these activities. Affidavits taken from numerous victims attest this fact. I had become acquainted with the two police officers stationed at the corner of Bellevuestrasse and Tiergartenstrasse near where the Consulate General was located; these officers told me that they and all the other police officers had received definite instructions not to interfere with the S.A., the S.S. or the Hitler Youth.

For the Germans who were taken into custody by the Gestapo, chiefly Communists at that time, there was, from my experience and from the information that I had from all sources, a regular pattern of brutality and terror. Upon arrest, the victims would be systematically subjected to indignities and brutalities such as beatings, kicking, pushing downstairs, deprivation of food and all comforts, and threats of much worse. After the victims had been imprisoned—usually in cellars, since both the headquarters at No. 8 Albrechtstrasse and the S.A. meeting places usually had them—they would be beaten with various degrees of severity. If the Gestapo believed that the victim—particularly Communist leaders—had information as to other alleged accomplices they would give systematic beatings, usually when stripped and tied on a table. This would go on often for many days until they had extracted the information they wanted or killed the victim.

Based on all of the reports which I had from many sources, my judgment is that the victims were numbered in the hundreds of thousands all over Germany. Many of them were ultimately released. I can state with certainty that the contemporaneous accounts in foreign newspapers, such as the London Times and the American newspapers which I have seen, are accurate.

The second wave of terror was not so systematic nor so concentrated as to point of time. It was directed chiefly against the Jews, and was chiefly the result of the ruthless and occasionally violent enforcement of numerous decrees and orders, such as the Nurnberg Decrees. After the initial outbreak in March, 1933, and all through that year and the next, the Jews still in Germany had, in many cases, come to believe that things might become a little better and that they could live in some sort of peaceable relationship with the Nazis, even though they were reduced to the status of second or third class citizens. In 1935, however, the pressure on them began to increase and they began to be excluded completely from certain civil activities. The terrorism was continued all the time to some degree; but the enforcement of the new decrees in 1935 was characterized by such brutality and ruthlessness that it warrants special attention. Inadvertent violators were dealt with, for example, with great severity.

The 1938 wave of terror was a very pronounced and definite one. Again the object was the Jews, particularly the wealthy ones. The ostensible occasion was the murder of the German diplomat, von Reith, by a French Jew, but the violence was in no sense spontaneous. Dr. Best, the Administrative Officer of the Gestapo, told me that the terror had been decided upon and ordered by Hitler himself, and that he, Dr. Best, could, therefore, do nothing about it. Actually that statement corroborated what everyone knew. Innumerable persons with whom I talked and who witnessed the violence told me that at all of the synagogues, which had been set on fire by the Nazis, the fire departments were always present, but never acted except to prevent the fires from spreading to neighboring non-Jewish properties. Nor did the police interfere with any of these acts of vandalism and incendiarism.

I personally did not see any of the violence nor the burning of the synagogues while the acts were being perpetrated, as the mobs throughout Germany commenced to work at midnight on November 8, 1938, and carried through their activities during the early morning hours of November 9. At that time I was on my way to the Wartburg Castle, and on the day of November 9 I saw the burned synagogues and the looted and smashed shops in Eisennach, and later in Berlin. I also know that at this time many of the wealthy Jews, who had previously escaped attack, were arrested, among whom were relatives of American citizens. Pursuant to requests from the United States, some of which were transmitted through the Department of State, I personally intervened with the Gestapo through Dr. Best, and secured the return of nearly twenty victims from the Saxonhausen Concentration Camp. Among these victims were Fritz Warburg and Eugene Garbaty. I think that many, perhaps most of these people, were released in the space of ten days or two weeks with the warning that if they remained in Germany they would have cause to regret it. In all cases the victims were subjected to rough treatment. Those who returned from the concentration camp and whom I saw in my office had their hair closely clipped, a common outward sign that they had been at Saxonhausen.

The Gestapo authorities with whom I spoke on my frequent, and often daily visit to the Gestapo headquarters did not hesitate to state that they regarded Communists in particular as subversive and as an element dangerous to the State, and that it was necessary to wipe them out. Diehls, the first chief of the Gestapo, in particular, whom I saw nearly every day of the March wave of terror in 1933, made no attempt to conceal the systematic character of the roundups of what he called "subversive persons"; though he did attempt to justify it to me as necessary to the safety of the State. While denying that any violence against American citizens was contemplated, he admitted that it was being undertaken against Germans. Terroristic tactics, however, in all their various forms, were so completely and thoroughly the actuating policy, that it would have been wholly redundant to discuss it. They and I both understood that it was the mainspring of all Gestapo activity—indeed of all activity—and that it was beyond discussion.

On one occasion I received a clear and definite admission of the Nazi terroristic policy with respect to many of their victims. In 1938 I was making strenuous efforts to free a young man from a concentration camp. He had been arrested in March, 1933, for aiding certain of his comrades to escape Germany, and had been sentenced by regular courts to a sentence of 2½ years. When he was released from the Brandenburg Prison at the end of that time, he was taken into custody by the Gestapo and sent to Dachau, the notorious concentration camp, and from there to Buchenwald. I had tried over a long period of time to secure his release by appeals personally to Himmler, Heydrich and Best, and had failed. In 1938, however, I was told by Ministerialraet Krohne, in the Ministry of Justice, that if I could reach Gruppenfuehrer Eiche of the Todtenkopfverbaende (Death's Head Regiments) I might be successful. Eiche was then head of all German concentration camps. After having first been told officially by the Gestapo that no such person existed, I was finally able by a ruse to secure his telephone number whereupon, through the recommendation of Krohne, I was able to make an appointment with Eiche at the Saxonhausen Concentration Camp near Berlin. He told me that with respect to Communists and any other persons who were suspected of holding views contrary to the Nazi conception of the State, such persons were "Asociale", that is, impossible of social assimilation and, therefore, they must be physically eliminated from society or destined to perpetual confinement. Thaelman, the leader of the Communists in the Reichstag, was, as is well known, kept during the Hitler regime in perpetual confinement. His ultimate fate has never been revealed.

On another occasion I was given considerable information by a high official of the Gestapo as to the policy of the Nazis with respect to the Jews. I had had considerable contact with the head of the Jewish section of the Gestapo, known as the "Judische Abteilung der Gestapo", one Dr. Hasselbacher, in connection with making arrangements for official representatives of the American Joint Distribution Committee to visit certain Jewish centers throughout Germany, for which visits, of course, the permission of the Gestapo was necessary. These negotiations brought me frequently in touch with Dr. Hasselbacher, whom I came to know very well. He told me that Germany will be made "Judenrein", that is, clean of Jews. He said that all Jews who failed to leave Germany would be exterminated. That statement was made in 1938 before the extermination camps were established, but the statement of Hasselbacher clearly indicated the eventual emergence of extermination camps in accordance with the general Nazi plan; for certainly the Jews were unable to leave Germany, even if they had been permitted to do so by the Nazis, as no worldwide arrangement had been made to receive them in other countries.

I had a great deal of experience with the systematic measures which were taken to confiscate property of non-Nazis, particularly Jews. Force of circumstance and a settled governmental policy made this campaign a more gradual one. Drastic and sudden action would have led to the alienation of a great deal of ready assets owned by the Jews and would have tended to destroy the economic value of Jewish-owned property. It would also have resulted in the physical destruction or hiding by Jews of things of value, as indeed did happen to a great extent. Consequently, the Nazis permitted many Jews, particularly those of wealth and position, to remain unmolested for many years, giving the Jews the faithless and false assurance that they were exempted from the general repressive program for various reasons. For example, I knew well the leading German cigarette manufacturer, Eugene Garbaty. Until September, 1938, he was in complete control of his fortune. During that month, however, he was compelled to sell his factory, worth between seven million and ten million marks for the sum of one million marks. In October, 1938, his country estate near Dresden, valued probably over two million marks, was simply confiscated with no payment at all. It was to be used, as the authorities stated, for a welfare center for German Youth. After his experience in the Pogrom of November 8, 1938, Garbaty applied for a passport and received one only after paying a bribe of 500,000 marks to the corrupt Count Heldorf, Chief of Police in Berlin, and enough other fines to equal the million marks that he had received for his factory. He left Germany with nothing, except that earlier, by bribing the customs officials with approximately 250,000 marks, he had been able to get valuable art treasures out of Germany. Garbaty is now a citizen of the United States and is living in Connecticut.

Another instance of the same nature occurred with respect to my landlord, Mr. Franz Rinkel, who told me the entire story of his persecution at the hands of the Nazis. He had a fine house at No. 2 Bruckenalle in Berlin, in which I lived. Rinkel was one of the victims sent to Saxonhausen and whom, after the space of a week, I was able to rescue. One Dr. Lilienthal, a fanatical Nazi lawyer practicing in Berlin, coveted Rinkel's house. The general system of expropriating the property of the Jews was illustrated in this particular case. My landlord was approached by Dr. Lilienthal and told the price the latter desired to pay, a mere fraction of the value of the estate. He was given a few days to make up his mind to sell at that price. He sold because he knew that if he did not, he would be accused of some trumped-up crime and taken away to the concentration camp. Dr. Lilienthal took possession of Rinkel's house. I know that on many occasions where it was thought necessary to increase the pressure, the prospective purchaser or his agent would be accompanied by a uniformed S.A. or S.S. man. I know because I lived in the immediate neighborhood and know the individuals concerned, that Baron von Neurath, one time Foreign Minister of Germany, got his house from a Jew in this manner. Indeed, he was my next door neighbor in Dahlem. Von Neurath's house was worth approximately 250,000 dollars. I know too that Alfred Rosenburg, who lived in the same street with me, purloined a house from a Jew in similar fashion. There were, of course, innumerable instances in which Nazis used their positions in the Party to void debts and the like. An illustration of this were the cases of the persons who came to the Consulate in Berlin and informed us of the circumstances. For example, Max Schussler, an American citizen, made an affidavit which states:

* * * I own several apartment houses in Berlin, one situated at Ring Strasse 11, Berlin-Steglitz. On the property at Ring Strasse 11 resides a tenant by the name of Hans Zink, who owns and operates a restaurant in those premises. He has been in arrears in his rent for about a year. Since the first of February of this year, that is, since the new Government came into power, he has refused to pay his rent. I gave instructions to the Sheriff to have him put out. Yesterday two uniformed men came to my office and spoke to my secretary and said that if I do not recall the order to the Sheriff to have Zink evicted, something will happen to me. I did not see these men. My secretary received them. She stated they wore black trousers and brown shirts. She referred them to my attorney, Felix Szkolny, Charlottenstrasse 17, Berlin S. W. 68. They went to the attorney, but he refused to give the order. They came to my office again and said to my secretary that if I did not give the order in writing and hand it over to a certain address within an hour's time, something would happen. I then called the police station at Alexandrinenstrasse 134, Revier No. 113, and a police officer came to my office and accompanied me to a taxi, when I went home.

About a week before, it may be noted, Zink had come to my office and insisted on my rescinding the order of eviction, and said, "I care nothing about law; we are now in power, remember that. Do anything you please, I am not going out of the office until you cancel the order". I called the police and an officer came. Zink said, "I do not care what you say". After about ten minutes the officer put him out.

At two o'clock Tuesday morning, March 7, I was awakened and faced by two men with pistols, who had come into the house. They were allowed to enter by the janitress, as they claimed to be "Hilfspolizei", and also by my maid. These two men were accompanied by two others in civilian clothes, the former wearing the brown National Socialist uniforms. They said, "Here, dress yourselves, quick too". My wife asked them to turn about while she dressed, but they refused. She was compelled to stand naked before the intruders. When she protested they said, "Don't be theatrical". My wife then wanted to telephone, but they said, "No, sit down. Do not touch the telephone", while they kept their pistols pointed at us all the time. I sat down. One of them said, "Have you got a fountain pen? You sign that". I had to sign the order to the Sheriff cancelling the order of eviction, and had to sign another letter to the tenant Zink, stating that the order of eviction was called off. I hesitated to sign and they drew their revolvers on me, and my wife in terror fell to her knees, and then I signed. I asked if they had credentials, and they pointed to the "Hakenkreuz" on their sleeves and said that was their credentials. They then said, "If you recall that order tomorrow, you will be dead". After I signed, they left * * *

Actually, all Nazis used their positions in the Party as a means of enriching themselves. I have already spoken of the bribe to the customs officials and the Foreign Office officials, which Mr. Garbaty was compelled to pay. Another instance of the venality of the Nazi officials was illustrated in the case of Mendelssohn Bartholdy, who owned a house near me and whom I knew well. He was told by Count Heldorf, Chief of Police in Berlin, through his stooge, one Herr Schmidt, that his passport would cost him 250,000 marks. Bartholdy told me the facts and asked me if he should pay. Knowing the Nazi practices and the danger which he ran as a Jew in Germany, I advised him to pay. He did, got his passport and visa, and left Germany. This happened in November, 1938.

I was informed by a personal friend, a Jewish banker in Berlin, Herr Kempner, whom I believed to be qualified to make an accurate estimate, that the total confiscations from Jews in Germany was between seven and eight billion marks.

I had less experience with the manner in which the Nazis operated in industrial firms. However, from the accounts of numerous American businessmen with manufacturing plants in Germany, accounts which agreed with the information which I had with respect to similar activities in German factories, I know that the Nazis used their Party position to obtain authority and power. Many American businessmen told me that they had serious troubles operating their factories because the Nazi officials in the establishment, usually recruited from the workmen, attempted to take over the management themselves, and engaged consistently and ruthlessly in acts of persecution against non-Nazi workmen. Many German firms were actually dominated by fanatical Nazis, usually persons who had had no previous position of importance, such as janitors, timekeepers and the like. Their position in the Nazi hierarchy gave them importance in the enterprise out of all proportion to their standing and position.

[Signed]   Raymond H. Geist

Subscribed and sworn to before me, William L. Brewster, Vice Consul of the United States of America, duly commissioned and qualified, in Mexico, D. F., Mexico, this 28th day of August 1945.

[Signed]   William L. Brewster
Vice Consul of the United States of America
Service No. 6684
Tariff No. 38
No fee prescribed.

Translation of Document 1778-PS (USA 257). Book "The Poisonous Mushroom" published in Nurnberg, 1938, concerning Jews.

* * *

THE POISONOUS MUSHROOM [Der Giftpilz]

A Stuermer book for young and old Fables by Ernst Hiemer
Pictures by Fips
Published by Der Stuermer—Nurnberg copyright 1938

* * * * * * *

[P.6] "It is almost noon," he said, "now we want to summarize what we have learned in this lesson. What did we discuss?"

All children raise their hands. The teacher calls on Karl Scholz, a little boy on the first bench. "We talked about how to recognize a Jew."

"Good! Now tell us about it!"

Little Karl takes the pointer, goes to the black board and points to the sketches.

"One usually recognizes a Jew by his nose. The Jewish nose is crooked at the end. It looks like the figure 6. Therefore it is called the "Jewish Six". Many non-Jews have crooked noses, too. But their noses are bent, not at the end but further up. Such a nose is called a hook nose or eagle's beak. It has nothing to do with a Jewish nose."

"Right!" says the teacher. "But the Jew is recognized not only by his nose . . ." The boy continues. The Jew is also recognized by his lips. His lips are usually thick. Often the lower lip hangs down. That is called "sloppy". And the Jew is also recognized by his eyes. His eyelids are usually thicker and more fleshy than ours. The look of the Jew is lurking and sharp.

[P.9] Then the teacher goes to the desk and turns over the black board, on its back is a verse. The children recite it in chorus:

> From a Jew's countenance—the evil devil talks to us,
> The devil, who in every land—is known as evil plague.
> If we shall be free of the Jew—and again will be happy and glad,
> Then the youth must struggle with us—to subdue the Jew devil.

[P.32] Inge sits in reception room of the Jew doctor. She has to wait a long time. She looks through the journals which are on the table. But she is most too nervous to read even a few sentences. Again and again she remembers the talk with her mother. And again and again her mind reflects on the warnings of her leader of the BDM [League of German Girls]: "A German must not consult a Jew doctor! And particularly not a German girl! Many a girl that went to a Jew doctor to be cured, found disease and disgrace!"

When Inge had entered the waiting room, she experienced an extraordinary incident. From the doctor's consulting room she could hear the sound of crying. She heard the voice of a young girl: "Doctor, doctor leave me alone!"

Then she heard the scornful laughing of a man. And then all of a sudden it became absolutely silent. Inge had listened breathlessly.

"What may be the meaning of all this?" she asked herself and her heart was pounding. And again she thought of the warning of her leader in the BDM.

Inge was already waiting for an hour. Again she takes the journals in an endeavor to read. Then the door opens. Inge looks up. The Jew appears. She screams. In terror she drops the paper. Frightened she jumps up. Her eyes stare in to the face of the Jewish doctor. And this face is the face of the devil. In the middle of this devil's face is a huge crooked nose. Behind the spectacles two criminal eyes. And the thick lips are grinning. A grinning that expresses: "Now I got you at last, you little German girl!"

And then the Jew approaches her. His fleshy fingers stretch out after her. But now Inge has her wits. Before the Jew can grab hold of her, she hits the fat face of the Jew doctor with her hand. Then one jump to the door. Breathlessly Inge runs down the stairs. Breathlessly she escapes the Jew house.
[P.61]

The pimpf [Hitler boy between 10-14] so far has not said anything. Suddenly he stops. Then he grasps his two friends by the arm and pulls them away. They stop in front of a billboard. They read a large poster. It says Julius Streicher makes an address in the People's Hall about "The Jews are our misfortune".

"That is where we go!" shouts Konrad, "I wanted to hear him speak for a long time." "I have heard him once before at a meeting two years ago," says Erich. "Do tell us all about it!" the two pimpfs beg.

The Hitler youth recounts:

"The meeting was overcrowded. Many thousands of people attended. To begin with, Streicher talked of his experiences in the years of struggle, and of the tremendous achievements of the Hitler Reich. Then he began to talk about the Jewish question. All he said was so clear and simple that even we boys could follow it. Again and again he told about examples taken from life. At one time he talked most amusingly and cracked jokes, making all of us laugh. Then again he became most serious, and it was so quiet in the hall that one could hear a needle drop. He talked of the Jews and their horrible crimes. He talked of the serious danger which Judaism is for the whole world.

"Without a solution of the Jewish question there
    will be no salvation of mankind".

That is what he shouted to us. All of us could understand him. And when, at the end, he shouted the "Sieg-Heil" for the Fuehrer, we all acclaimed him with tremendous enthusiasm. For two hours Streicher spoke at that occasion. To us it appeared to have been but a few minutes.

Translation of Document 1816-PS (USA 261). *Stenographic report of the meeting on the Jewish question, under the Chairmanship of Fieldmarshal Goering, 12 November 1938.*

* * *

STENOGRAPHIC REPORT OF THE MEETING ON "THE JEWISH QUESTION" UNDER THE CHAIRMANSHIP OF FIELD MARSHALL GOERING IN THE REICHS AIR FORCE
(12 November 1938—11 o'clock)

Part I

Goering: Gentlemen! Today's meeting is of a decisive nature. I have received a letter written on the Fuehrer's orders by the Stabsleiter of the Fuehrer's deputy Bormann, requesting that the Jewish question be now, once and for all, coordinated and solved one way or another. And yesterday once again did the Fuehrer request by phone for me to take coordinated action in the matter.

Since the problem is mainly an economic one, it is from the economic angle that it shall have to be tackled. Naturally a number of legal measures shall have to be taken which fall into the sphere of the Minister for Justice and into that of the Minister of the Interior; and certain propaganda measures shall be taken care of by the Minister for Propaganda. The Minister for Finance and the Minister for Economic Affairs shall take care of problems falling in their respective resorts.

In the meeting, in which we first talked about this question and came to the decision to aryanize Germany economy, to take the Jew out of it, and put him into our debit ledger, was one in which, to our shame, we only made pretty plans, which were executed very slowly. We then had a demonstration, right here in Berlin, we told the people that something decisive would be done, but again nothing happened. We have had this affair in Paris now, more demonstrations followed and this time something decisive must be done!

Because, gentlemen, I have enough of these demonstrations! They don't harm the Jew but me, who is the last authority for coordinating the German economy.

If today, a Jewish shop is destroyed, if goods are thrown into the street, the insurance company will pay for the damages, which the Jew does not even have; and furthermore goods of the consumer goods belonging to the people, are destroyed. If in the future, demonstrations which are necessary occur, then I pray that they be directed so as not to hurt us.

Because it's insane to clean out and burn a Jewish warehouse then have a German insurance company make good the loss. And the goods which I need desperately, whole bales of clothing and what-not, are being burned; and I miss them everywhere.

I may as well burn the raw materials before they arrive. The people of course, do not understand that; therefore we must make laws which will show the people once and for all, that something is being done.

I should appreciate it very much if for once, our propaganda would make it clear that it is unfortunately not the Jew who has to suffer in all this, but the German insurance companies.

I am not going to tolerate a situation in which the insurance companies are the ones who suffer. Under the authority invested in me, I shall issue a decree, and I am, of course, requesting the support of the competent Government agencies, so that everything shall be processed through the right channels and the insurance companies will not be the ones who suffer.

It may be, though, that these insurance companies may have insurance in foreign countries. If that is the case, foreign bills of exchange would be available which I would not want to lose. That shall have to be checked. For that reason, I have asked Mr. Hilgard of the insurance company, to attend, since he is best qualified to tell us to what extent the insurance companies are protected against damage, by having taken out insurance with other companies. I would not want to miss this, under any circumstances.

I should not want to leave any doubt, gentlemen, as to the aim of today's meeting. We have not come together merely to talk again, but to make decisions, and I implore the competent agencies to take all measures for the elimination of the Jew from German economy and to submit them to me, as far as it is necessary.

The fundamental idea in this program of elimination of the Jew from German economy is first, the Jew being ejected from the Economy transfers his property to the State. He will be compensated. The compensation is to be listed in the debit ledger and shall bring a certain percentage of interest. The Jew shall have to live out of this interest. It is a foregone conclusion, that this aryanizing, if it is to be done quickly, cannot be made in the Ministry for Economy in Berlin. That way, we would never finish.

On the other hand, it is very necessary to have safety precautions so that the lower echelons, Statthalter, and Gauleiter will not do things unreasonably. One must issue correction directives, immediately.

The aryanizing of all the larger establishments, naturally, is to be my lot—the Ministry for Economy will designate which and how many there are—it must be done by a Statthalter or his lower echelons, since these things reach into the export trade, and cause great problems, which the Statthalter can neither observe, nor solve from his place.

It is my lot, so that the damage will not be greater than the profit, which we are striving for.

It is obvious gentlemen, that the Jewish stores are for the people, and not the stores. Therefore, we must begin here, according to the rules previously laid down.

The Minister for Economic Affairs shall announce which stores he'll want to close altogether. These stores are excluded from aryanizing at once. Their stocks are to be made available for sale in other stores; what cannot be sold, shall be processed through the "Winterhilfe" or taken care of otherwise. However, the sales values of these articles shall always be considered, since the State is not to suffer but should profit through this transformation. For the chain and department stores—I speak now only of what can be seen, certain categories have to be established, according to the importance of the various branches.

The trustee of the State will estimate the value of the property and decide what amount the Jew shall receive. Naturally, this amount is to be set as low as possible. The representative of the State shall then turn the establishment over to the "Aryan" proprietor, that is, the property shall be sold according to its real value.

There begins the difficulties. It is easily understood that strong attempts will be made to get all these stores to party-members and to let them have some kind of compensations. I have witnessed terrible things in the past; little chauffeurs of Gauleiters have profited so much by these transactions they have now about half a million. You, gentlemen, know it. Is that correct?

(Assent)

Of course, things like that are impossible. I shall not hesitate to act ruthlessly in any case where such a trick is played. If the individual involved is prominent, I shall see the Fuehrer within two hours and report to him.

We shall have to insist upon it, that the Aryan taking over the establishment is of the branch and knows his job. Generally speaking he is the one who must pay for the store with his own money. In other words, an ordinary business transaction is to be sought—one merchant selling, the other one buying a business. If there are party members among the contenders, they are to be preferred, that is if they have the same qualifications: first shall come the one who had the most damage, and secondly, selection should be according to length of Party membership.

Of course, there may be exceptions. There are party-members who, as may be proven, lost their business concessions by action of the Schuschnigg or Prague Government, and so went bankrupt. Such a man has naturally first option on a store for sale, and he shall receive help if he does not have the means to help himself. The trustee of the State can justify this help, if he is more businesslike in the transfer. This party-member should have the chance to buy the store for as cheap a price as possible. In such a case the State will not receive the full price, but only the amount the Jew received. Such a buyer may even receive a loan besides, so that he will get off to a good start.

I wish to make it clear that such a proceeding shall only be legal if the party-member has once owned such a store. For example, a party-member was the owner of a stationery store, and Schuschnigg took away the concession to operate it so that the man lost the store and went bankrupt. Now, if a Jewish stationery store is being aryanized, this party-member should get the store on conditions which he'll be able to fulfill. Such a case shall be the only exception though, in all other cases the procedure shall be of a strictly businesslike nature whereby the party-member, like I said before, shall have the preference, if he has the same qualifications as any other candidate, who is not a member of the party.

When selling for the actual value we shall find only about 60 Aryans ready to take over 100 Jewish stores. I don't think that we have a German for every Jewish store. You must not forget that the Jew sees his main activity in the field of trade, and that he owns 90% of it. I doubt that we'd have a demand big enough. I even doubt that we'd have enough people, particularly now since everybody has found his field of work.

Therefore, I ask the Minister for Economy to go beyond what we think ought to be done for the sake of the principle, in liquidating the establishments. I ask him to go further, even though there won't be any candidates. That'll be perfectly alright.

The transfer of stores and establishments shall have to be executed by the lower echelons, not through Berlin but through the Gaue and through the Reichsstatthalterschaft. Therein shall be the seat of the members of the Board of Trustees, even if it consists of a few people only. The Statthalter and his people cannot do this job; the trustees will have to tackle it. But the Statthalter shall be the authority which supervises, according to the regulations given him, the trustees, particularly in dealings such as the transfer to party-members.

Naturally, these establishments cannot disappear all at once but we'll have to start by Monday, in a manner that shall make it obvious that a change has begun to materialize. Besides that, cerain stores could be closed which willl make things here easier.

Another point! I have noticed that Aryans took over a Jewish store and were then so clever to keep the name of the Jewish store as "formerly," or kept it altogether. That must not be; I cannot permit it. Because it may happen—what has just happened—stores were looted because their signboards bore Jewish names—because they had once been Jewish, but had been "aryanized" a long time ago. Names of former Jewish firms shall have to disappear completely, and the German shall have to come forward with his or his firm's name. I ask you to carry this out quite definitely. That much then regarding aryanizing the stores and wholesale establishments, particularly in regard to signboards and of all that is obvious!

Of the consequences resulting from this for the Jew, I shall speak later, because this is connected with other things.

Now for the factories. As for the smaller and medium ones, two things shall have to be made clear.

1. Which factories do I not need at all—which are the ones where production could be suspended? Could they not be put to another use? If not, the factories will be razed immediately.

2. In case the factory should be needed, it will be turned over to Aryans in the same manner as the stores. All these measures have to be taken quickly, since Aryan employees are concerned everywhere. I'd like to say right now that Aryan employees shall have to be given employment immediately after the Jewish factory is closed. Considering the amount of labor we need these days, it should be a trifle to keep these people, even in their own branches. As I have just said; if the factory is necessary, it will be aryanized. If there is no need for it, it being abandoned shall be part of the procedure of transforming establishments not essential for our national welfare into one that is essential for it—a procedure that shall take place within the next few weeks. For it, I shall still need very much space and very many factories.

If such a factory is to be transformed or razed, the first thing to be done is check the equipment. The questions arising will be: Where can this equipment be used? Could it be used after the place is transformed? Where else might it be needed badly? Where could the machinery be set up again? It follows that aryanizing factories will be an even more difficult task than the aryanizing of stores.

Take now the larger factories which are run solely by a Jewish owner, without control by a Board of Directors; or take corporations where the Jews might be in the Supervisory Council or Board of Directors. There the solution is very simple: the factory can be compensated in the same manner as in the sale of stores and factories; that is, at a rate which we shall determine, and the trustee shall take over the Jew's interest as well as his shares, which he in turn may sell or transfer to the State, which will then dispose of them. So, if I have a big factory, which belonged to a Jew or a Jewish corporation, and the Jew leaves, perhaps with his sons who were employed there, the factory will still continue to operate. Maybe a director will have to be appointed because the Jew has run the factory himself. But otherwise, particularly if the maintenance of the establishment is very essential everything will run smoothly.

Everything is very simple. I now have his shares. I may give them to some Aryan or to another group or I may keep them. The State takes them over and offers them at the stockmarket, if they are acceptable there and if it so desires, or it makes use of them in some other way.

Now, I shall talk of the very big establishments, those in which the Jew is in the Board of Directors, in which he holds shares etc., and so is either the owner or one of the coowners; in any case in which which he is greatly interested. There too, things are comparatively simple; he delivers all of his shares which shall be bought at a price fixed by the trustee. So the Jew gets into the account book. The shares shall be handled like I've just explained. These cases cannot be taken care of by the Gaue and Reichsstatthalter, but only by us here on top; because we are the ones to decide where these factories are to be transferred to, how they may be affiliated with other establishments or to what an extent the State shall keep them or hand them over to another establishment belonging to the State. All this can only be decided here. Of course, the Gauleiter and Statthalter will be glad to get hold of the shares, and they'll make great promises to beautify our capital cities, etc. I know it all! It won't go! We must agree on a clear action that shall be profitable to the Reich.

The same procedure shall be applied where the Jew has a share in, or owns property of German economy. I am not competent enough to tell off hand in what forms that might be the case, and to what an extent he'll have to lose it. Anyway, the Jew must be evicted pretty fast from German economy.

Now, the foreign Jews. There we'll have to make distinctions between the Jews who have always been foreigners—and who shall have to be treated according to the laws we arranged with their respective countries. But regarding those Jews who were Germans, have always lived in Germany and have acquired foreign citizenship during the last year, only because they wanted to play safe. I ask you not to give them any consideration. We'll finish with these. Or have you any misgivings? We shall try to induce them through slight, and then through stronger pressure, and through clever maneuvering—to let themselves be pushed out voluntarily.

Woermann: I'd like the Foreign Office to be included, since a generally valid decision could hardly be made.

Goering: We cannot consult you in every case, but on the whole we will.

Woermann: Anyway, I'd like to make known the claim of the Foreign Office to participate. One never knows what steps may become necessary.

Goering: Only for important cases! I do not like to take this category under special consideration. I have learned only now to what extent that has been done, particularly in Austria and Czechoslovakia. If somebody was a Czech in Sudetenland, we do not have to consider him at all, and the Foreign Office doesn't have to be consulted because that person now belongs to us. And in Austria and also in Sudetenland, too many become all of a sudden Englishmen or Americans or what-not—and generally speaking we cannot consider that a great deal.

[Part II is missing]

PART III

Funk: That is quite a decisive question for us: should the Jewish stores be reopened?

Goebbels: If they will be reopened is another question. The question is will they be restored? I have set the deadline for Monday.

Goering: You don't have to ask whether they'll be reopened. That is up to us to decide.

Goebbels: Number 2. In almost all German cities synagogues are burned. New, various possibilities exist to utilize the space where the synagogues stood. Some cities want to build parks in their places, others want to put up new buildings.

Goering: How many synagogues were actually burned?

Heydrich: Altogether there are 101 synagogues destroyed by fire; 76 synagogues demolished; and 7,500 stores ruined in the Reich.

Goering: What do you mean "destroyed by fire?"

Heydrich: Partly, they are razed, and partly gutted.

Goebbels: I am of the opinion that this is our chance to dissolve the synagogues. All these not completely intact, shall be razed by the Jews. The Jews shall pay for it. There in Berlin, the Jews are ready to do that. The synagogues which burned in Berlin are being leveled by the Jews themselves. We shall build parking lots in their places or new buildings. That ought to be the criterion for the whole country, the Jews shall have to remove the damaged or burned synagogues, and shall have to provide us with ready free space.

Number 3: I deem it necessary to issue a decree forbidding the Jews to enter German theaters, movie houses, and circuses. I have already issued a decree under the authority of the law of the chamber for culture. Considering the present situation of the theaters, I believe we can afford that. Our theaters are overcrowded, we have hardly any room. I am of the opinion that it is not possible to have Jews sitting next to Germans in movies and theaters. One might consider, later on, to let the Jews have one or two movie houses here in Berlin, where they may see Jewish movies. But in German theaters they have no business anymore.

Furthermore, I advocate that the Jews be eliminated from all positions in public life in which they may prove to be provocative. It is still possible today that a Jew shares a compartment in a sleeping car with a German. Therefore, we need a decree by the Reich Ministry for Communications stating that separate compartments for Jews shall be available; in cases where compartments are filled up, Jews cannot claim a seat. They shall be given a separate compartment only after all Germans have secured seats. They shall not mix with Germans, and if there is no room, they shall have to stand in the corridor.

Goering: In that case, I think it would make more sense to give them separate compartments.

Goebbels: Not if the train is overcrowded!

Goering: Just a moment. There'll be only one Jewish coach. If that is filled up, the other Jews will have to stay at home.

Goebbels: Suppose, though, there won't be many Jews going on the express train to Munich, suppose there would be two Jews in the train and the other compartments would be overcrowded.

These two Jews would then have a compartment all themselves. Therefore, Jews may claim a seat only after all Germans have secured a seat.

Goering: I'd give the Jews one coach or one compartment. And should a case like you mention arise and the train be overcrowded, believe me, we won't need a law. We'll kick him out and he'll have to sit all alone in the toilet all the way!

Goebbels: I don't agree. I don't believe in this. There ought to be a law. Furthermore, there ought to be a decree barring Jews from German beaches and resorts. Last summer * * *

Goering: Patricularly here in the Admiralspalast very disgusting things have happened lately.

Goebbels: Also at the Wannsee beach. A law which definitely forbids the Jews to visit German resorts!

Goering: We could give them their own.

Goebbels: It would have to be considered whether we'd give them their own or whether we should turn a few German resorts over to them, but not the finest and best, so we cannot say the Jews go there for recreation.

It'll also have to be considered if it might not become necessary to forbid the Jews to enter the German forests. In the Grunewald, whole herds of them are running around. It is a constant provocation and we are having incidents all the time. The behavior of the Jews is so inciting and provocative that brawls are a daily routine.

Goering: We shall give the Jews a certain part of the forest, and the Alpers shall take care of it that various animals that looked damned much like Jews,—the Elk has such a crooked nose—get there and become acclimated.

Goebbels: I think this behavior is provocative. Furthermore, Jews should not be allowed to sit around in German parks. I am thinking of the whispering campaign on the part of Jewish women in the public gardens at Fehrbelliner Platz. They go and sit with German mothers and their children and begin to gossip and incite.

Goebbels: I see in this a particularly grave danger. I think it is imperative to give the Jews certain public parks, not the best ones—and tell them: "You may sit on these benches" these benches shall be marked "For Jews only." Besides that they have no business in German parks. Furthermore, Jewish children are still allowed in German schools. That's impossible. It is out of the question that any boy should sit beside a Jewish boy in a German gymnasium and receive lessons in German history. Jews ought to be eliminated completely from German schools; they may take care of their own education in their own communities.

Goering: I suggest that Mr. Hilgard from the insurance company be called in; he is waiting outside. As soon as he'll be finished with his report, he may go, and we can continue to talk. At the time Gustloff died, a compensation for the damage Germany had suffered was prepared. But I believe that at present we should not work it through raised taxes but with a contribution paid only once. That serves my purpose, better.

(Hilgard appears)

Mr. Hilgard, the following is our case. Because of the justified anger of the people against the Jew, the Reich has suffered a certain amount of damage. Windows were broken, goods were damaged and people hurt, synagogues burned, etc. I suppose that the Jews, many of them are also insured against damage committed by public disorder, etc.

(Hilgard: "Yes")

If that is so, the following situation arises; the people, in their justified anger, meant to harm the Jew; but it is the German insurance companies that will compensate the Jew for damage. This situation is simple enough; I'd only have to issue a decree to that effect that damage, resulting from these risks, shall not have to be paid by the insurance companies. But the question that interests me primarily, and because of which I have asked you to come here, is this one: In case of reinsurance policies in foreign countries, I should not like to lose these, and that is why I'd like to discuss with you ways and means by which profit from reinsurance, possibly in foreign currency will go to the German economy, instead of the Jew. I'd like to hear from you, and that is the first question I want to ask: In your opinion, are the Jews insured against such damage to a large extent?

Hilgard: Permit me to answer right away. We are concerned with three kinds of insurances. Not with the insurance against damage resulting from revolt or from risks. But wtih the ordinary fire insurance, the ordinary glass insurance, and the ordinary insurance against theft. The people, because of their contracts, who have a right to claim compensation are partly Jews, partly Aryans. As for the fire insurance, they are practically all Jewish, I suppose. As for the department stores, the victim is identical with the Jew, the owner and that applies more to the synagogues, except for neighbors to whose places the fire may have spread. Although the damage done to the latter's property seems to be rather slight, according to the inquiries I made late last night.

As for the glass insurance which plays a very important part in this, the situation is completely different. The majority of the victims, mostly the owners of the buildings are Aryans. The Jew has usually rented the store, a procedure which you may observe all over, for example on Kurfuerstendamm.

Goering: That is what we've said.

Goebbels: In these cases, the Jew will have to pay.

Goering: It doesn't make sense, we have no raw materials. It is all glass imported from foreign countries and has to be paid for in foreign currency! One could go nuts.

Hilgard: May I draw your attention to the following facts: the glass for the shop windows is not being manufactured by the Bohemian, but by the Belgian glass industry. In my estimation, the approximate money-value to which these damages amount is $6,000,000 — that includes the broken glass, glass which we shall have to replace, mainly to Aryans because they have the insurance policies. Of course I have to reserve final judgment in all this, Your Excellency, because I have had only one day to make my inquiries. Even counting on about half of the $6,000,000 being spent in transacting the business, specialists from the industry itself are more confident in this matter than I am, we might well have to import glass for approximately $3,000,000. Incidentally, the amount of damage equals about half a whole year's production of the Belgian glass industry. We believe that half a year will be necessary for the manufacturers to deliver the glass.

Goering: The people will have to be enlightened on this.

Goebbels: We cannot do this right now.

Goering: This cannot continue! We won't be able to last with all this. Impossible! Go on then! You suggest that the Aryan is the one who suffers the damage; is that right?

Hilgard: Yes, to a large extent, as far as the glass insurance goes.

Goering: Which would have to replace the glass.

Hilgard: Yes. Of course there are cases in which the Aryan, the owner of the store is identical with the owner of the building. That is so with all department stores. In the case of the department store Israel, the owner is the Jew.

Goering: And now the third category.

Hilgard: Under this fall the victims of thievery.

Goering: I have to ask you a question. When all kinds of goods were taken from the stores and burned in the streets, would that also be thievery?

Hilgard: I don't think so.

Goering: Could that be termed as "Riot"?

Hilgard: That is just the question which we are unable to decide at this moment. Is it ordinary theft if entry into a dwelling or a contained of any kind is forced and something is taken away?

Goering: That is a case of "Riot."

Hilgard: Riot does not mean much since we have very little insurance against damage caused by riots—these were discarded by us long ago.

Goering: But this here is "Rioting." That is the legal term. There was no theft, and no individual broke into any place. But a mob rushes in and knocks everything to pieces, or "Public Disturbances."

Hilgard: Public disturbance. It is no riot.

Goering: Are they insured against damages caused by public disturbances?

Hilgard: No, no more. May I show this by an example. The most remarkable of these cases is the case Margraf Unter Den Linden. The Jewelry store of Margraf is insured with us through a so-called combined policy. That covers practically any damage that may occur. This damage was reported to us amounting to $1,700,000 because the store was completely stripped.

Goering: Daluege and Heydrich, you'll have to get me this jewelry through raids, staged on a tremendous scale!

Daluege: The order has already been given. The people are being controlled all the time. According to reports, 150 were arrested by yesterday afternoon.

Goering: These things will otherwise be hidden. If somebody comes to a store with jewels and claims that he has bought them, they'll be confiscated at once. He has stolen them or traded them in all right.

Heydrich: Besides that, looting was going on in the Reich in more than 800 cases, contrary to what we supposed; but we have already several hundred people who were plundering and we are trying to get the loot back.

Goering: And the jewels?

Heydrich: That is very difficult to say. They were partly thrown into the street and picked up there. Similar things happened with furriers, for example, in Friedrichstrasse, district C. There the crowd was naturally rushing to pick up minks, skunks, etc. It'll be very difficult to recover that. Even children have filled their pockets, just for fun. It is suggested that the Hitler Youth is not to be employed and to participate in such actions without the Party's consent. Such things are very easily destroyed.

Daluege: The Party should issue an order to the effect that the police will immediately receive a report in case the neighbor's wife, (everybody knows his neighbor) has a fur coat altered or in case somebody appears wearing new rings or bracelets. We'd like the Party to support us here.

Hilgard: These damages are not covered by the policy, I believe. May I say a word in general about our liabilities and a "Petidum" of the Versicherungswirkschaft report. We'd like to make it our point, Mr. General Field Marshall, that we shall not be hindered in fulfilling the obligations for which our contracts call.

Goering: But I have to. That is important for me.

Hilgard: If I may give reasons for this request, I'd like to say that it simply has to do with the fact that we carry out, to a large extent, quite a number of international transactions. We have a very good international basis for our business transactions, and in the interest of the equilibrium of the Foreign exchange in Germany, we have to make sure that the confidence in the German insurance shall not be ruined. If we now refuse to honor clear-cut obligations, imposed upon us through lawful contract, it would be a black spot on the shield of honor of the German insurance.

Goering: It wouldn't the minute I issue a decree—a law sanctioned by the State.

Hilgard: I was leading up to that.

Heydrich: The insurance may be granted, but as soon as it is to be paid, it'll be confiscated. That way we'll have saved face.

Hilgard: I am inclined to agree with what General Heydrich has just said. First of all, use the mechanism of the insurance company to check on the damage, to regulate it and even pay, but give the insurance company the chance to   *   *   *

Goering: One moment! You'll have to pay in any case because it is the Germans who suffered the damage. But there'll be a lawful order forbidding you to make any direct payments to the Jews. You shall also have to make payment for the damage the Jews have suffered, but not to the Jews, but to the Minister of Finance.

(Hilgard: Aha!)

What he does with the money is his business.

Schmer: Your Excellency, I should like to make a proposal. A certain rate should be fixed, say 15% or maybe a little higher, of all the registered wealth. I understand one billion is to be confiscated so that all Jews shall pay equally, and from the money raised this way, the insurance companies shall be refunded.

Goering: No. I don't even dream of refunding the insurance companies the money. The companies are liable. No, the money belongs to the State. That's quite clear. That would indeed be a present for the insurance companies. You make a wonderful Petidum there. You'll fulfill your obligations, you may count on that.

Kerl: It seems that in one respect, we'll have to arrange this somewhat differently. As far as the glass insurance goes, the fact of the matter is that the owners of the buildings will definitely have to be paid for the damage, as stipulated. The majority of these companies, with the exception of one Joint Stock Company in Cologne, are all very small reciprocity companies [Gegenseitsvereine]. They won't be able to make up for the damage. We'll have to find out how far they are covered by reinsurance which I cannot tell at the moment.

Hilgard: In this connection, the reinsurance plays a relatively small role, except for the large fire-insurance policies taken out by department stores. There is not reinsurance in the glass insurances, for the simple reason that, under normal conditions glass insurance is one of our best branches in the insurance business; and therefore does not need reinsurance. I have to add, though, that the amount of this damage is approximately twice as high as the amount of damage for an average year. It makes all our calculations wrong and completely wipes out our chance for profit.

(Interrupted by Kerl)

No, sir, that is the way it is. The whole premium of the German glass insurance amounts to $14,000,000, if I am not wrong. Under normal conditions it amounted to 4 or 5 million. The glass insurance is our greatest asset. So far, the greatest profits were made in it. But now, the amount of this damage is alone twice as high as the amount for one ordinary year. With the various special glass insurances, it is altogether different.

Goering: One moment! 4 to 5 millions normally. Twice as much would be about 10 million. You suggested 14 million. There are still 4 million left.

Hilgard: We'll also have to pay for the expenses. No, it is a very great catastrophe for us. Let me point out that the damage in the whole of Germany, in my estimation, shall amount to approximately 25 million mark. I wanted to be careful.

Heydrich: We estimate that the damage to property, to furniture and to consumer-goods amounts to several hundred million; although that includes the damage the Reich shall suffer from loss of taxes—sales taxes, taxes on property, and on income. I assume that the Minister of Finance too, has been informed of all this.

V. Krosigk: I have no idea about the extent.

Heydrich: 7,500 destroyed stores in the Reich.

Daluege: One more question ought to be cleared up. Most of the goods in the stores were not the property of the owner but were kept on the books of other firms, which had delivered them. Then there are the unpaid for deliveries by other firms, which definitely are not all Jewish but Aryan, those goods that were delivered on the basis of commission.

Hilgard: We'll have to pay for them, too.

Goering: I wished you had killed 200 Jews, and not destroyed such values.

Heydrich: There were 35 killed.

Kerl: I think we could do the following: Jews we don't pay anyhow. As for Aryans, payment shall have to be made. The insurance company may contact us through the "Reichsgruppe" and we shall investigate each case. I am thinking of the small reciprocity companies; it should be easy to find out whether they are capable of paying or not. In their cases, the amounts involved are not too large. We may find an arrangement for this later on; I am thinking of one in which the insurance companies arrange for recompensation exclusively to Aryans, and once they know the results of their inquiries, contact us. We shall then find a way out for these small companies. Of course only in cases where it is absolutely necessary.

Funk: That is not necessary. I'd like to refer to what I've said before about the decree. That seems to be the easiest solution.

Goering: We cannot do that. These people make a point of their ability to pay.

Funk: If the Jews pay for it, the insurance companies don't have to pay.

Goering: Right, well, gentlemen, this is all very clear. We'll stick to it. At this moment every insurance company, except Mr. Hilgard who is here, counts on having to pay for the damage. They want to pay too, and I understand this very well. They'll have to want that, so they cannot be reproached for not being secure enough to pay. The glass insurance, and a point was made of that, has brought the highest profits so far. That means they'd have enough surplus money, and if they haven't divided it all up in dividends, they'll have savings enough for the compensation. Such an insurance company will have to be in a position to pay for a damage of 10, 12, 15 million, that is three times the amount paid in the normal year. If they are unable to do that, then we'll have to wonder whether we should let small companies live at all. It would be insane to keep insurance companies which would be unable to pay for such a damage. To permit an insurance company like that to exist would simply mean to cheat the people. I suggest now the following. The damage shall be determined in each case. And for the time being, the insurance companies shall have to honor their contract in every respect and shall have to pay.

[Part IV is missing]

Part V

Goering: Now for the damage the Jew has had. At Margraf's the jewels disappeared, etc. Well, they are gone, and he won't get them refunded. He is the one who has to suffer the damage. As far as the jewels may be returned again by the police, they belong to the State. Now for the consumer foods which were thrown into the street, stolen, or burned. There too, the Jew will be the one who has the damage.

As for the goods that were kept on the basis of commissions, the Jew shall have to make good for the damage.

Goering: That doesn't have to be put in the decree, though. This decree is quite sufficient the way it is.

Hilgard: I wonder to what an extent insurance companies in foreign countries might be involved in this.

Goering: Well, they'll have to pay. And we'll confiscate that.

Hilgard: As for this merchandise sold on the basis of commissions, I can imagine that the American supplier of fur coats, shipping them from England or from America would in many cases insure it with English or American insurance companies!

Goering: Then they'll pay him for the damage. The question merely is the following: do you think there are reinsurances for all this damage in foreign countries?

Hilgard: Very few, amounting to very little.

Goering: Of course, the Aryan cannot report any damage because he hasn't had any. The Jew will make good.

The Jew shall have to report the damage. He'll get the refund from the insurance company but the refund will be confiscated. After it's all said and done, there will remain some profit for the insurance companies since they can't have to make good for all the damage. Mr. Hilgard, you may enjoy yourself.

Hilgard: I have no reason for that—the fact that we won't have to pay for all the damage is called profit!

Goering: Just a moment! If you are compelled under the law to pay 5 million and all of a sudden there appears an angel in my somewhat corpulent form before you, and tells you: you may keep 1 million — why, cannot that be called making a profit? I should actually split with you, or whatever you'd call it. I can see it, looking at you. Your whole body grins. You made a big profit.
(Remark: Let's initiate a tax for damages, resulting from public disturbance, to be paid by the insurance companies)
Hilgard: For me it goes without saying that the honorable German merchant cannot be the one who suffers. I have discussed this matter with the enterprises and I have spoken for it that the Aryan must not be the one who has the damage. But it is decidedly he who has it, because all the insurance companies, not one insurance company, are the ones that shall have to pay higher rates and at the same time shall receive lower dividends. Therefore, all the insurance companies are the losers. That is so, and that'll remain so, and nobody can tell me differently.
Goering: Then why don't you take care of it that a few windows less are being smashed! You belong to the people too! Send your representatives out. Let them instruct the people. If there should be any more questions speak to Mr. Lange.
(Reichsgruppenleiter Hilgard leaves the meeting)
Gentlemen, let us continue.
Woermann: I think that the foreign Jews are left out completely in Article 1. They are covered only by Article 2. But they should also be taken care of in Article 1. Otherwise they can be dealt with only if they are insured, and not if they are not insured.
Goering: Well, they'll have to insure themselves—or what else do you mean?
Woermann: As for insurance, the foreign Jews are, to my understanding, mentioned only in Article 2 and 3, and not in Article 1. If I remember correctly, you were going to say in Article 1: "Jews inside the country." Well, we'll have plenty of complaints then.
Goering: Pardon me. According to Article 2, they'll receive their compensation.
(Woermann: If they are insured!)
The number of those who are not insured is negligible.
Heydrich: I'd like to say one more thing of primary importance. In the decree we should not mention the confiscation. We can do that easily.

Goering: No, you cannot do that tacitly. A clear legal procedure will have to be employed there. But that is not what Mr. Woermann means, he is talking about these foreign Jews who are not insured. As far as they are insured, they are covered. This here concerns those who are not insured. That may be the case here and there.

Woermann: We shall then have plenty of complaints.

Goering: I'd like to avoid paying too much attention to the foreign Jews.

Woermann: But if Article 2 contains that provision, Article 1 may as well have it. The first draft by the Minister for Justice covered it all very nicely.

Guertner: Now, if I don't misunderstand Mr. Woermann, he is primarily concerned with the obligation for restoration which shall be valid generally while only Jews who have German citizenship are mentioned regarding the insurance.

I'd like to know whether there are any objections against compelling also the foreign Jew to restore the damage, and to inform him that he shall not be paid the money from the insurance.

Goering: He is quite able to do that.

Woermann: Even if he is not insured?

Guertner: Oh!

Goering: There should hardly be such instances. Let's take a chance on it.

Stuckart: If he is not insured, he'll have to have the damage restored anyway. How can he then make claims against anybody?

Goering: He cannot.

Woermann: He can file claims against the State.

Stuckart: According to which law? Damage caused by riots? We won't recognize riots.

Goering: Perfectly right.

Woermann: Generally speaking, may I say: regarding foreign Jews, the reservation that the contract is to be taken into consideration was made only for the organization. That is valid for all branches which we have discussed today, and also for the expropriation.

Goering: Like the Fuehrer says, we'll have to find a way to talk this over with the countries which also do something against their Jews. That every dirty Polish Jew has a legal position here and we have to stand him—that ought to cease. The Fuehrer was not very happy about the agreement that was made with the Poles. He thinks we should take a few chances and just tell the Poles; all right, we are not going to do that; let's talk over what we may be able to accomplish together; you are doing something against your own Jews in Poland; but the minute the Itzig has left Poland, he should suddenly be treated like a Pole! I'd like to disregard these stories from foreign countries a little.

Woermann: It ought to be considered wether or not the U S might take measures against German property. This question cannot be handled equally for all countries. I have to make a formal and general reservation.

Goering: I have always said and I'd like to repeat it that our steamship companies and German companies in general should finally catch on and liquidate their investments in the U S, sell them, etc. That country of scoundrels does not do business with us according to any legal rules. Once before they stole everything from us, that is why I don't understand how we could do it again, just for some temporary profit. It is dangerous. You can do it with a regular country but not with one that cares for the Right as little as the U S. The other day I had the American ambassador with me. We talked about the zeppelin and I told him: "We don't need any helium, I fly without helium but the prerequisites will have to be that this ship will be flying to civilized countries where the Right prevails. It goes without saying that one cannot fly to such gangster-states." He had a rather silly look on his face. One ought to tell these Americans. But you are right, Mr. Woermann, it ought to be considered.

Woermann: In other words, the foreign office is granted the right to be consulted.

Goering: Granted, but I'd like to avoid mentioning the foreign Jews as long as we can help it. We'd rather have the foreign office take part in these cases where that question becomes acute, so that some compromise can be reached.

Woermann: Generally, and in particular cases.

Funk: The decisive question is: Are the Jewish stores to be reopened or not?

Goering: That depends on how big a turnover these Jewish stores have. If it is big, it is an indication that the German people are compelled to buy there, in spite of its being a Jewish store, because a need exists. If we'd close all Jewish stores which are not open right now, altogether before Christmas, we'd be in a nice mess.

Fishboeck: Your Excellency, in this matter we have already a very complete plan for Austria. There are 12,000 Jewish artisan and 5,000 Jewish retail shops in Vienna. Before the National Revolution, we had already a definite plan for tradesman, regarding this total of 17,000 stores. Of the shops of the 12,000 artisans, about 10,000 were to be closed definitely and 2,000 were to be kept open. 4,000 of the 5,000 retail stores should be closed and 1,000 should be kept open, that is, were to be aryanized. According to this plan, between 3,000 and 3,500 of the total of 17,000 stores would be kept open, all others closed. This was decided following investigations in every single branch and according to local needs, in agreement with all competent authorities, and is ready for publication as soon as we shall receive the law which we requested in September; this law shall empower us to withdraw licenses from artisans, quite independently from the Jewish question.

Goering: I shall have this decree issued today.

Fishboeck: It was granted us in connection with the economic plan for Austria. I believe the only reason why it was not yet published was that negotiations between the Reich Ministry for Economic Affairs and the National Food Corporation were going on. A basic agreement had already been reached. We'll be able to close these 10,000 stores as a matter of mere routine as soon as the decree will be issued. As for the actual execution of the matter, somebody will have to take care of the merchandise in these stores. Until last week we had intended to more or less leave it up to the Jews themselves to liquidate the warehouses. We cannot do that anymore. We intend to create a central agency which shall take care of the merchandise to be used. Generally, the best procedure might be to turn the merchandise over to the particular branch which in turn shall divide it up among the Aryan stores. These, in turn, shall resell it on the basis of commissions or for a fixed price.

If this is carried out as planned, it'll concern only the approximately 3,000 remaining stores which shall be aryanized, according to the investigations made in the various branches. Actual buyers for about half of these stores are waiting: their contracts have been checked and are ready to be approved. If many of these cases were not approved sooner, it is only because the decision on the planning had not yet been made. As for the remaining 15,000 stores, negotiations have also gone rather far in many cases. We think that a deadline should be set, say until the end of the year. If, by the end of the year, definite buyers for the stores designated for Aryans, cannot be found, it'll have to be examined once more whether the stores should not be liquidated. In most cases that will be possible; an artisan's shop is of a rather individual character. As for retail stores, it would never be urgent enough, so as to say that the economic worth was too big. The very few stores which would still remain and found to be necessary but for which no buyer was available, could be taken over by trustees. This way, I believe that fewer than 100 stores would be left, and by the end of the year we would have liquidated all the Jewish-owned businesses which so far have been obvious as such in the eyes of the public.

Goering: That would be excellent.

Fishboeck: Out of 17,000 stores 12,000 or 14,000 would be shut down and the remainder aryanized or handed over to the bureau of trustees which is operated by the State.

Goering: I have to say that this proposal is grand. This way, the whole affair would be wound up in Vienna, one of the Jewish capitals, so to speak, by Christmas or by the end of the year.

Funk: We can do the same thing over here. I have prepared a law elaborating that, effective 1 January 1939, Jews shall be prohibited to operate retail stores and wholesale establishments as well as independent artisan shops. They shall be further prohibited from keeping employees or offer any ready products on the market. Wherever a Jewish shop is operated, the police shall shut it down. From 1 January 1939, a Jew can no longer be employed as an enterpriser as stipulated in the law for the Organization of National Labor from 20 January 1934. If a Jew holds a leading position in an establishment without being the enterpriser, his contract may be declared void within 6 weeks by the enterpriser. With the expiration of the contract all claims of the employee, including all claims to maintenance, become obliterated. That is always very disagreeable and a great danger. A Jew cannot be a member of a corporation; Jewish members of corporations shall have to be retired by 31 December 1938. A special authorization is unnecessary. The competent Ministers of the Reich are being authorized to issue the provision necessary for the execution of this law.

Goering: I believe that we can agree with this law.

(Remark: Yes)

Of course there remain a few things to be straightened out even after 1 January. We shall be able to handle them with these general methods which we shall have to employ for handling all other Jewish property. As for the Jewish stores, we may proceed vigorously; we believe that by Christmas enough buyers shall be found to take over the stores which from now on shall be entirely under pressure. Also the merchandise may be taken the way you have proposed it. To me, all this seems to be prepared in an excellent manner.

Funk: In every single store everything is there.

Schmer: Everything is there, except that we have no control, anymore, over this business with the trustees. I personally am of the opinion that we don't need it at all; so far we have managed quite well with the aryanization. For those few stores that are to be kept open, we shall easily find buyers. All other rooms shall be rented without much ado. There is a great need for this right here in Berlin.

Goering: But my dear friend, that way the Jew will receive the full amount.

Schmer: He will receive the amount that is far below the value, and the aryanizing shall have to be authorized, as before.

Goering: The Jew will receive the amount which won't be put into the account book.

Schmer: No. We can arrange that later. He cannot swallow the money. The amount is fixed, and under the law the Jew is compelled to report every change in his financial status, so that it can easily be controlled. He won't run away; we'll keep it in the Reich. The only thing you'd have to do is to issue a decree, or to transfer the provisions of Article 7 on to the Ministry for Economic Affairs in order to confiscate the Jewish property. He cannot run away from us.

Goering: Mr. Schmer, could not the following be done: Somebody will become aryanized and get 300,000 marks into his hands. He runs into the next best jewelry store around the corner and buys one piece of jewelry after another, and on the same day disappears across the border.

Schmer: In that case, we'll have to report this change in his property.

Goering: But if he wants to scram!

Fischboeck: The OK on the aryanizing is not being given the minute the price for the purchase is being paid. We do that the following way. The aryanizing is being authorized only under the condition that the price for the purchase is to be paid in installments lasting over a long period of time, in case the buyer is unable to pay; or, in case payment is being made, that the amount is to be put in the bank of a frozen account.

Goering: We could do the same thing here.

Schmer: In the provisions for the execution of the law we may stipulate that from a certain level on, payment shall have to be made in bonds of the Reich or something similar. That would have to be a decree made by the authorities which OK the aryanizing.

Daluege: The number of Jewish stores is unknown. Until yesterday, 7,500 were reported to us and the number does not increase.

Fischboeck: Because of what has happened the day before yesterday in Vienna, 5,000 were shut down there. There were 40,000 altogether.

Schmer: Shall the arrangement made in Austria remain?

Goering: Nothing will be changed there.

Fischboeck: Everything can be shut down at any time.

Heydrich: I know that a very high limit has been set for registering, 3,000 I believe.

Fischboeck: More than 5,000.

Goering: Is that the same in the Reich?

Fischboeck: Yes, in the Reich too. In this connection, I'd like to make a few more remarks. What we are very much concerned with, is the situation regarding the Jewish apartment houses which contribute a large percentage of Jewish wealth. Surprisingly enough, the Jewish national wealth in Austria is reported to amount to 320 million marks only; the value of the apartment houses alone amounts to 500 million. We should appreciate it very much if the regulation which makes it possible to requisition Jewish property would be made to be valid also for the apartment buildings; thus we would be enabled to have these houses administered by a board of trustees and to give the Jews the right to have a claim on the debit ledger of the Reich. That could also be an occasion to cash the contribution, which might be deducted this way in advance. The administration of these blocks of apartment buildings wouldn't be a problem at all. The only thing we'd need for it would be managers, and there'd be plenty of them. We'd like to requisition the apartment buildings and also any bonds that way. This question of the bonds has been left open so far. In Austria, a very large part of Jewish wealth, 266 billion Reichsmarks, is invested in bonds of all kinds, in shares or simply in bonds bringing a fixed rate of interest. In my opinion, a danger for the market does not exist because the Ministry for Economic Affairs would have control over these bonds. We'll pay by handing out claims, on the debit-ledger of the Reich. Therefore, the finances of the Reich won't be affected, the Minister for Finance shall only pay 3% for the claims on the debit-ledger of the Reich. He in turn receives internal loans, that means saves money. And if the bonds are not being sold, one might keep them 30 years until those claims on the debit-ledger of the Reich shall be expired.

Funk: Why should Jews not be allowed to keep bonds?

Goering: Because that way he would actually be given a share.

Funk: That is entirely new.

Goering: No. I said very clearly before; bonds and shares.

Funk: Shares yes, but not internal loans.

Fischboeck: It is certainly better to pay the Jew 3% instead of 4%. We'd have no possibility to control Jewish wealth the minute we'd let him have shares.

Goering: Gentlemen, no arguments. It is out of the question that he'd keep the shares. He'll have to turn them in.

Fischboeck: In that case I'd like you to arrange this by calling the shares in so that the stock market won't be ruined. That can very easily be done. They'll be turned in. Administering the shares is also much simpler. The trustee turns the shares over to the depot and receives claims on the debit-ledger of the Reich in their place. With this, the whole affair is settled. The only question is whether you want to recall the shares or not.

Funk: This way, the Reich will become possessor of half a billion shares.

Goering: Yes, yes.

Goebbels: He'll be able to get rid of them according to its needs.

Fischboeck: But it is a business based on profits.

V. Krosigk: I am wondering, first whether it will bring us profits. I grant you that, though. But secondly, an entirely new point of view has to be entered here. I can very well see the point in what the Minister, Mr. Fischboeck, says. As for the values that otherwise bring fixed rates of interest, it is an entirely new idea to expropriate the Jew also in this, though the intention had been to retain his status as the owner of the shares.

Fischboeck: The reason why this is so very important is that our whole action shall remain without success as long as the Jews shall be in possession of values, which they may realize quickly and employ for any other undertaking.

Goering: That's it. We want to prevent the Jews from again secretly manipulating against us.

Fischboeck: For example, if we don't want the Jews to possess jewelry we can prevent them from having it by allowing them to possess only Internal Loan bonds, that means that they could acquire the jewelry only by paying with bonds.

Goering: Nobody would pay them claims on the debit-ledger.

Fischboeck: They are not transferable.

Goering: Only if authorized.

Heydrich: Is it not possible to issue an order forbidding the Jew to invest his money in certain values, such as art treasures?

Goering: The arrangement with the registration in the debit-ledger is much simpler. Claims on the debit-ledger are not transferable. He cannot do anything with them, and he cannot do much with those $3\frac{1}{2}\%$.

Heydrich: But we'll also have to find an arrangement for confiscation of valuable objects in Jewish possession.

Goering: What he has now in his possession, that'll come.

Schmer: Article 7 of the decree states that the use of Jewish wealth in German economy shall be regulated through the Four Year Plan.

Goering: I think Fischboeck's proposal is very good. We should give it the form of a draft now, find the apartment buildings, the shares, etc.

Fischboeck: I should like also to have a decision made on the following question. In Austria, individuals, not institutions, owe the Jews 184 billion Reichsmarks. This way the Jews certainly have invested money in a way we don't like. That is money which they have loaned out to other Jews, oftener enough to an Aryan. This way, a dependency of the Aryan artisan from the Jewish creditor is created which we do not want. Now the question arises, and I would answer yes. Should trustees not be created to administer these debts and then pay with claims on the debit-ledger, according to demand coming in. The goal of this procedure would be to make the debtor independent from the Jewish creditor, to insert Aryan trusteeship and pay the Jew, as far as his demands could actually be met. Therefore it does not have to be paid. So we should have to insert trusteeship in this case also, but the difference to that in the case of the bonds would be that we won't simply pay but leave the decision for payment to the trusteeship.

Funk: If a word of this debate should reach the public, we'd have a run on the capital market tomorrow.

Fischboeck: That's why we have postponed these ideas all the time. We have examples for it that the Jews have sold, head over heel, bonds of internal loans, shares and everything they had.

Goering: I could stop that with a single decree, ordering the immediate stoppage of traffic of Jewish capital. He is punishable who buys from Jews, and his purchase shall be confiscated. I would not do it any other way.

[Part VI is missing]

Part VII

Frick: The Ministry of the Interior shall have to take part in it.

Goering: I have said so before.

(Shout by Goebbels)

* * * that is a misunderstanding., That is now the committee which is elaborating on nothing but on this problem which is being tackled. How are the shares, how are the claims on the debit-ledger to be handled? Therefore, I shouldn't like to have anybody else in the Committee, in order to keep it as small as possible.

Buerkel: Is the plan for the aryanizing to be discussed also?

Goering: Mr. Fischboeck shall bring that up. This place is the crux of the matter. I hope you have listened properly so that you know exactly what is to be valid for the Sudetengau! Of course, I too am of the opinion that these economic measures ought to be strengthened by a number of Police-action-Propaganda-measures and cultural displays so that everything shall be fixed now and the Jewry will be slapped this week right and left.

Heydrich: In spite of the elimination of the Jew from the economic life, the main problem, namely to kick the Jew out of Germany, remains. May I make a few proposals to that effect?

Following a suggestion by the Commissioner of the Reich, we have set up a center for the Emigration of Jews in Vienna, and that way we have eliminated 50,000 Jews from Austria while from the Reich only 19,000 Jews were eliminated during the same period of time; we were so successful because of the cooperation on the part of the competent Ministry for Economic Affairs and of the foreign charitable organizations.

Goering: The main thing is, you cooperated with the local leaders of the "Green Frontier."

Heydrich: That amounted to a very small number, your excellency. Illegal * * *

Goering: This story has gone through the whole world press. During the first night the Jews were expulsed into Czechoslovakia. The next morning, the Czechs grabbed them and pushed them into Hungary. From Hungary, they were returned to Germany and from there into Czechoslovakia. They traveled around and around that way. They landed finally on an old Barge in the Danube. There they lived, and wherever they tried to go ashore, they were barred.

Heydrich: That was the report. There weren't even 100 Jews.

Goering: For practically two weeks, a number of Jews left every midnight. That was in the Burgenland.

Heydrich: At least 45,000 Jews were made to leave the country by legal measures.

Goering: How was that possible?

Heydrich: Through the Jewish Kulturgemeinde, we extracted a certain amount of money from the rich Jews who wanted to emigrate. By paying this amount, and an additional sum in foreign currency, they made it possible for a number of poor Jews to leave. The problem was not to make the rich Jew leave but to get rid of the Jewish mob.

Goering: But children, did you ever think this through? It doesn't help us to extract hundreds of thousands from the Jewish mob. Have you ever thought of it that this procedure may cost us so much foreign currency that in the end we won't be able to hold out.

Heydrich: Only what the Jew has had in foreign currency.
(Goering: agreed)
This way. May I propose that we set up a similar procedure for the Reich, with the cooperation of the competent government agencies, and that we then find a solution for the Reich, based on our experiences, after having corrected the mistakes, the General Field Marshall has so rightly pointed out to us.
(Goering: agreed)
As another means of getting the Jews out, measures for Emigration ought to be taken in the rest of the Reich for the next 8 to 10 years. The highest number of Jews we can possibly get out during one year is 8,000 to 10,000. Therefore, a great number of Jews will remain. Because of the aryanizing and other restrictions, Jewry will become unemployed. The remaining Jews gradually become proletarians. Therefore, I shall have to take steps to isolate the Jew so he won't enter into the German normal routine of life. On the other hand, I shall have to restrict the Jew to a small circle of consumers, but I shall have to permit certain activities within professions; lawyers, doctors, barbers, etc. This question shall also have to be examined.

As for the isolation, I'd like to make a few proposals regarding police measures which are important also because of their psychological effect on public opinion. For example, who is Jewish according to the Nurnberg laws shall have to wear a certain insignia. That is a possibility which shall facilitate many other things. I don't see any danger of excuses, and it shall make our relationship with the foreign Jew easier.

Goering: A uniform?

Heydrich: An insignia. This way we could also put an end to it that the foreign Jews who don't look different from ours, are being molested.

Goering: But, my dear Heydrich, you won't be able to avoid the creation of ghettos on a very large scale, in all the cities. They shall have to be created.

Heydrich: As for the question of ghettos, I'd like to make my position clear right away. From the point of view of the police, I don't think a ghetto in the form of completely segregated districts where only Jews would live, can be put up. We could not control a ghetto where the Jews congregate amidst the whole Jewish people. It would remain the permanent hideout for criminals and also for epidemics and the like. We don't want to let the Jew live in the same house with the German population; but today the German population, their blocks or houses, force the Jew to behave himself. The control of the Jew through the watchful eye of the whole population is better than having him by the thousands in a district where I cannot properly establish a control over his daily life through uniformed agents.

Goering: We'd only have to forbid long-distance calls.

Heydrich: Still I could not completely stop the Jews from communicating out of their districts.

Goering: And in towns all of their own?

Heydrich: If I could put them into towns entirely their own, yes. But then these towns would be such a heaven for criminals of all sorts that they would be a terrific danger. I'd take different steps. I'd restrict the movement of the Jews and would say; in Munich, the governmental district and the district

* * *

Goering: Wait a minute! I don't care so much for it that the Jews don't appear in spots where I don't want them. My point is this one; if one Jew won't have any more work, he'll have to live modestly. He won't be able to go far on his $3\frac{1}{2}\%$—to restaurants, etc. He'll have to work more. That'll bring about a concentration of Jewry which may even facilitate control. You will know that in a particular house only Jews are living. We shall also have concentrated Jewish butchers, barbers, grocers, etc., in certain streets. The question is of course whether we want to go on tolerating that. If not, the Jew will have to buy from the Aryan.

Heydrich: No, I'd say that for the necessities in daily life, the German won't serve the Jew anymore.

Goering: One moment. You cannot let him starve. But there'll be the following difficulty. If you say that the Jews will be able to have so and so many retail stores, then they'll again be in business, and they'll have to sell for the wholesaler.

Schmer: In a small town that wouldn't work at all.

Goering: It could only be worked out if you'd reserve in advance whole districts or whole towns for the Jews. Otherwise, you'll have to have only Germans do business, and the Jew shall have to buy from them. You cannot set up a Jewish barbershop. The Jew will have to buy food and stockings.

Heydrich: We'll have to decide whether we want that or not.

Goering: I'd like to make a decision on that right now. We cannot make another subdivision here. We cannot argue: so and so many stores will remain for the Jew because then again no control will be possible since these stores in turn would have to work with wholesale stores. I'd say, all stores should be Aryan stores, and the Jew may buy there. One may go one step further and say that these and these stores will probably be frequented mostly by Jews. You may set up certain barbershops operated by Jews. You may make concessions in order to channel certain professions into certain streets for certain tasks. But not stores.

Heydrich: What about the ghetto? Would the Jews have to go to an Aryan district to buy.

Goering: No. I'd say that enough German storekeepers would love to dwell in the ghetto if they could do some business there. I wouldn't alter the principle that the Jew shall have no more say in German economy.

Heydrich: I shouldn't like to comment on that. Now a few things which are important also from a psychological angle.

Goering: Once we'd have a ghetto, we'd find out what stores ought to be in there, and we'd be able to say; you, the Jew so and so, together with so and so, shall take care of the delivery of goods. And a German wholesale firm will be ordered to deliver the goods for this Jewish store. This store would then not be a retail shop but a cooperative store, a cooperative one for Jews.

Heydrich: All these measures would eventually lead to the institution of the ghetto. I'd say one shouldn't want to build a ghetto. But these measures, if carried through as outlined here, shall automatically drive the Jews into a ghetto.

Funk: The Jews will have to move quite close together. What are 3 million? Everyone will have to stand up for the next fellow. The individual alone will starve.

Goering: Now, as to what Minister Goebbels has said before, namely compulsory renting. Now, the Jewish tenants will be together.

Heydrich: As an additional measure, I'd propose to withdraw from the Jews all personal papers such as permits and drivers licenses. No Jew should be allowed to own a car, neither should he be permitted to drive because that way he'd endanger German life. By not being permitted to live in certain districts, he should be furthermore restricted to move about so freely. I'd say the Royal Square in Munich, the Reichsweihestatte, is not to be entered any more within a certain radius by Jews. The same would go for establishments of culture, border fences, military installations. Furthermore, like Minister Dr. Goebbels has said before, exclusion of the Jews from public theaters, movie houses, etc. As for cultural activities, I'd like to say this; cultural activities in holiday resorts may be considered an additional feature, not absolutely necessary for the individual. Many German Volksgenessen are unable to improve their health through a stay at a resort town. I don't see why the Jew should go to these places at all.

Goering: To health spas, no.

Heydrich: Well, then I'd like to propose the same thing for hospitals. A Jew shall not lie in a hospital together with Aryan Volkgenossen.

Goering: We'll have to manage that gradually.

Heydrich: The same applies to public conveyances.

Goering: Are there no Jewish Sanatoriums and Jewish hospitals?

(Remarks—Yes!)

We'll have to finagle all this. These things will have to be straightened out one right after another.

Heydrich: I only meant to secure your approval in principle so that we may start out on all this.

Goering: One more question, gentlemen: What would you think the situation would be if I'd announce today that Jewry should have to contribute this 1 billion as a punishment?

Buerckel: The Viennese would agree to this whole-heartedly.

Goebbels: I wonder if the Jews would have a chance to pull out of this, and to put something on the side.

Brinkmann: They'd be subject to punishment.

V. Krosigk: Mr. Fischboeck, one question: Could this authorization be ordered without their closing out their securities?

Funk: They are all registered. They'll also have to register the money.

V. Krosigk: But for the time being they may dispose of it.

Goering: It won't help them to cash them all. They can't get rid of the money.

Funk: They'll be the ones to have the damage if they sell their stocks and bonds.

Fischboeck: There is a certain danger, but I don't think it is very great. But only then, when all the other measures shall definitely be carried out during next week.

V. Krosigk: They have to be taken during the next week at the latest.

Goering: I would make that a condition.

Fischboeck: Maybe it is good that we put ourselves under pressure this way.

Goering: I shall close the wording this way; that German Jewry shall, as punishment for their abominable crimes etc., etc., have to make a contribution of 1 billion. That'll work. The pigs won't commit another murder. Incidentally, I'd like to say again that I would not like to be a Jew in Germany.

V. Krosigk: Therefore, I'd like to emphasize what Mr. Heydrich has said in the beginning; that we'll have to try everything possible, by way of additional exports, to shove the Jews into foreign countries. The decisive factor is that we don't want the society-proletariat here. They'll always be a terrific liability for us.

(Frick: "and a danger!")

I don't imagine the prospect of the ghetto is very nice. The idea of the ghetto is not a very agreeable one. Therefore, the goal must be, like Heydrich said, to move out whatever we can!

Goering: The second point is this. If, in the near future, the German Reich should come into conflict with foreign powers, it goes without saying that we in Germany should first of all let it come to a showdown with the Jews. Besides that, the Fuehrer shall now make an attempt with those foreign powers which have brought the Jewish question up, in order to solve the Madagascar project. He has explained it all to me on 9 November. There is no other way. He'll tell the other countries. "What are you talking about the Jew for?—Take him!" Another proposal may be made. The Jews, gotten rid of may buy territory for their "coreligionists" in North America, Canada, or elsewhere.

I wish to summarize: The Minister of Economic Affairs shall direct the committee and he shall in one form or another, take all steps necessary within the next few days.

Blerning: I fear that during the next few days, beginning Monday, the Jews will start to sell bonds on internal loans for hundreds of thousands, in order to provide themselves with means. Since we control the course of the internal loan in order to sell more bonds, the Reich-Treasury, Loan-Committee or the Reich Minister for Finance should have to back this internal loan.

Goering: In what way could the Jew bring his bonds on the market?

(Remark: "Sell them")

To whom?

(Remark: "on the stock market—he orders a bank to do it.")

Well, I'll prohibit selling internal loan bonds for three days.

Blerning: That could be done only through a decree.

Goering: I can't see any advantage for the Jew. He won't know himself how and he'll have to pay. On the contrary, I believe he won't move.

Goebbels: For the time being he is small and ugly and stays at home.

Goering: I don't think it would be logical. Otherwise we'll have to do it. The reason why I want this decree in a hurry is that for the time being we have peace but who can guarantee that there won't be new trouble by Saturday or Sunday. Once and for all I want to eliminate individual acts. The Reich has taken the affairs in its own hand. The Jew can only sell. He can't do a thing. He'll have to pay. At this moment, the individual Jew won't think of throwing anything on the market. There'll be some chatter first, and then they will begin to run to us. They'll look for those great Aryans with whom they'll think they may have some luck, the so-called various mailboxes of the Reich with whom they can lodge their protests. These people will run my door in. All that takes some time, and by then we'll be ready.

Daluege: May we issue the order for confiscating the cars?

Goering: Also the Ministry of the Interior and the Police will have to think over what measures will have to be taken. I thank you.

[Conference closed at 2.40 PM]

Translation of Document 1919-PS (USA 170). *Excerpts from Himmler's speech to SS Gruppenfuehrers, 4 October 1943.*

* * *

Speech of the Reichsfuehrer—SS
at the meeting of SS Major-Generals at Posen
October 4th, 1943

The 1941 attack

In 1941 the Fuehrer attacked Russia. That was, as we can well see now, shortly—perhaps 3 to 6 months—before Stalin prepared to embark on his great penetration into Central and Western Europe. I can give a picture of this first year in a few words. The attacking forces cut their way through. The Russian Army was herded together in great pockets, ground down, taken prisoner. At that time we did not value the mass of humanity as we value it today, as raw material, as labour. What after all, thinking in terms of generations, is not to be regretted, but is now deplorable by reason of the loss of labour, is that the prisoners died in tens and hundreds of thousands of exhaustion and hunger [p. 3]. . . .

The Clearing out of the Jews

I also want to talk to you, quite frankly, on a very grave matter. Among ourselves it should be mentioned quite frankly, and yet we will never speak of it publicly. Just as we did not hesitate on June 30th, 1934 to do the duty we were bidden, and stand comrades who had lapsed, up against the wall and shoot them, so we have never spoken about it and will never [p. 65] speak of it. It was that tact which is a matter of course and which I am glad to say, is inherent in us, that made us never discuss it among ourselves, never to speak of it. It appalled everyone, and yet everyone was certain that he would do it the next time if such orders are issued and if it is necessary.

I mean the clearing out of the Jews, the extermination of the Jewish race. It's one of those things it is easy to talk about—"The Jewish race is being exterminated", says one party member, "that's quite clear, it's in our program—elimination of the Jews, and we're doing it, exterminating them." And then they come, 80 million worthy Germans, and each one has his decent Jew. Of course the others are vermin, but this one is an A-1 Jew. Not one of all those who talk this way has witnessed it, not one of them has been through it. Most of *you* must know what it means when 100 corpses are lying side by side, or 500 or 1000. To have stuck it out and at the same time—apart from exceptions caused by human weakness—to have remained decent fellows, that is what has made us hard. This is a page of glory in our history which has never been written and is never to be [p. 66] written, for we know how difficult we should have made it for ourselves, if—with the bombing raids, the burdens and the deprivations of war—we still had Jews today in every town as secret-saboteurs, agitators and trouble-mongers. We would now probably have reached the 1916/17 stage when the Jews were still in the German national body.

We have taken from them what wealth they had. I have issued a strict order, which SS-Obergruppenfuehrer Pohl has carried out, that this wealth should, as a matter of course, be handed over to the Reich without reseve. We have taken none of it for ourselves. Individual men who have lapsed will be punished in accordance with an order I issued at the beginning, which gave this warning; Whoever takes so much as a mark of it, is a dead man. A number of SS men—there are not very many of them—have fallen short, and they will die, without mercy. We had the moral right, we had the duty to our people, to destroy this people which wanted to destroy us. But we have not the right to enrich ourselves with so much as a fur, a watch, a mark, or a cigarette or anything else. Because we have exterminated a bacterium we do not want, in the end, to be infected by the bacterium and die of it. I will not see so much as a small area of sepsis appear here or gain a [p. 67] hold. Wherever it may form, we will cauterize it. Altogether however, we can say, that we have fulfilled this most difficult duty for the love of our people. And our spirit, our soul, our character has not suffered injury from it.

Translation of Document 1948-PS (USA 680). Letter from Governor in Vienna, 7 November 1940, evidencing RSHA (Reich Main Security Office) instructions to recruits Jews for forced labor.

* * *

The Reichsstatthalter in Vienna
I a Pol.—VIII—136/40   Vienna 7 November 1940
Subject: Compulsory Labor of Ablebodied Jews.

1. Notice:

On 5 November 1940 telephone conversation with Colonel [Standartenfuehrer] Huber of the Gestapo. The Gestapo has received directions from the Reich Security Main Office [RSHA], as to how ablebodied Jews should be drafted for compulsory labor service. Investigations are being made at present by the Gestapo, to find out how many ablebodied Jews are still available in order to make plans for the contemplated mass projects. It is assumed that there are not many more Jews available. If some should still be available, however, the Gestapo has no scruples to use the Jews even for the removal of the destroyed synagogues.

SS Colonel Huber will report personally to the "Regierungspraesident" in this matter.

I have reported to the "Regierungspraesident" accordingly. The matter should further be kept in mind.

2. Presented anew: 25 November 1940
Presented anew: 20.12.40

[Initialed]

By order:

[Signed] Dr. Fischer

Translation of Document 1949-PS. *Report of Statistical Office for Reich Gau Ostmark, 15 December 1939, on reduction in numbers of Jews especially in Vienna districts.*

* * *

State Administration of Reich Gau Vienna
Statistical Office for Reich Gau Ostmark
Zl. 3305/I 39

Vienna, 15 December 1939
1. Heldenplatz, Neue Burg
Tel. R 27-5-65

To the Reich Commissar for the Reunion of the Austrian Nation
 with the German Reich
through channels via the Governor [Regierungspraesident] of
 Vienna

The Statistical Office for Reich Gau Ostmark has the honor to submit herewith, in the enclosure, an initial compilation of early results of this year's census relative to the number and reduction in number of Jews and part Jews in Reich Gau Ostmark, especially in the Vienna districts, together with a brief commentary.

[Signature illegible]

1 file of the Statistical Office for the Reich Districts (Gaue) of the Ostmark, together with a summary of 15 December 1939
Zl. 3305/I 39

---

*Jews and Part Jews
in the Reich Districts [Gaue] of the Ostmark*

In the census of 17 May 1939, the question was put for the first time whether one of an individual's grandparents was full

Jew by race. The declarations were to be made by the people on the "Supplementary Card for Data on Descent and Education" in full and to the best of their ability; this supplementary card was to be given to the honorary census taker in a sealed, opaque envelope, which was opened only when the statistical count was made. No check has yet been made as to the correctness of the information submitted. In the compiling of the statistics, everyone who reported that three or four of his grandparents were full Jews was counted as a full Jew himself, everyone with two Jewish grandparents as a part Jew, Grade I, and correspondingly everyone with only one Jewish grandparent as a part Jew, Grade II. The resulting slight deviation from the pertinent legal definitions of full Jew and part Jew was occasioned by formulation of the question in the simplest possible way.

According to the initial results of this year's census, there were 91,480 full Jews and 22,344 part Jews of Grades I and II in Vienna as of 17 May 1939. In the remaining Reich Districts of the Ostmark there were 3,073 full Jews and 4,241 part Jews. According to this, there were altogether 121,138 Jews in the Ostmark, of whom 113,824, i. e. 94%, lived in Vienna, 3% in Niederdonau, 1% in the Steiermark, and less than 1% in each of the remaining Gaus.

While 80% of all the Jews in Vienna were full Jews and only 14% were part Jews, Grade I, and 6% part Jews, Grade II, in the other Reich Gaus the part Jews predominated, totaling 58%, as against 42% who were full Jews. Only in Niederdonau were the full Jews, with a total of almost 2,000, approximately as numerous as the part Jews.

These varying proportions of full Jews and part Jews are explained primarily by the emigration of Jews following the political change over. This emigration had reduced the number of *full* Jews in the Reich Gaus of the Ostmark, excluding Vienna and Niederdonau, to a small remainder of 1,103 by the time of the census.

The extent of the emigration of full Jews can be estimated approximately by comparison with the number of persons of Jewish faith reported in the census of 1934. It must be remembered, however, that in 1934 the number of those of Jewish faith did not include all full Jews and that, on the other hand, a small number of those of Jewish faith were part Jews, Grades I and II.

With this reservation, it can be stated that the number of Jews in the Ostmark (not including the annexed Sudeten-German regions) has diminished from 191,528 Jews by faith to 94,384 full Jews. At the same time the number of Jews in the Reich Districts (Gaus), excluding Vienna, decreased by 13,000 i.e. approximately 82% to 3,000. In Vienna alone, the decrease amounted to 84,000 persons, i. e. 48%.

The ratio of the sexes among full Jews has become so greatly dislocated that there are 100 male full Jews to every 136 female full Jews in Vienna, which can probably be ascribed to the earlier emigration of the Jewish males. The ratio among the part Jews, comparatively few of whom are thought to have emigrated, is 100:112, more nearly the average surplus of women in the population of Vienna.

According to data furnished by the Central Office for Jewish emigration, Vienna IV., about 100,000 Jews emigrated from the Ostmark in the period between the change over [Umbruch] and the census. This number is very close to the figure of 97,000 given above as the reduction in Jews since the census of 1934. Some 26,000 persons of Jewish faith emigrated from the Ostmark in the months succeeding the census.

While the problem of full Jews is almost completely solved, therefore, in the Reich Districts of the Ostmark, with the exception of Vienna, from a numerical standpoint the problem of part Jews still plays a relatively large role. For example, almost half of the approximately 1,000 Jews in Oberdonau are part Jews, Grade I, and more than one quarter are part Jews, Grade II. Similar conditions prevail in the remaining Reich Gaus, particularly in Salzburg, in Carinthia, and in the Tyrol.

Nevertheless the problem of part Jews in the Ostmark is first and foremost a problem for the Reich District of Vienna, where there are 86% of the part Jews Grade I and 80% of the part Jews Grade II. Gau Niderdonau takes second place, with a large interval, but has only 6% of the part Jews Grade I and 8% of the part Jews Grade II.

Out of all the part Jews in the Ostmark, 68% had two Jewish grandparents and 32% had one Jewish grandparent. It is worth noting that 70% of all Jews in Vienna were half-Jews, whereas less than 60% were half-Jews in the remaining Gaus of the Ostmark.

At the present time the problem of part Jews in Vienna is still numerically overshadowed by the large number of full Jews of whom there are estimated in round figures to be 70,000, since approximately 4,000 persons of Jewish faith have emigrated from the Ostmark every month since the census—with the exception of September.

[Signature illegible]
15.12.39.

***

Translation of Document 1950-PS (USA 681). *Secret letter from Lammers to von Schirach, 3 December 1940, reporting Hitler's decision to deport 60,000 Jews from Vienna.*

* * *

COPY

The Reichsminister and Chief of the Reich Chancellory
RK. 789 B secret

Berlin, W8 3 Dec. 40
Voss Str. 6

SECRET

To the Reich Governor in Vienna Gauleiter von Schirach
VIENNA

Dear Mr. von Schirach,

As Reichleiter Bormann informs me, the Fuehrer has decided after receipt of one of the reports made by you, that the 60,000 Jews still residing in the Reichsgau Vienna, will be deported most rapidly, that is still during the war, to the General Gouvernement because of the housing shortage prevalent in Vienna. I have informed the Governor General in Cracow as well as the Reichsfuehrer-SS about this decision of the Fuehrer, and I request you also to take cognizance of it.

HEIL HITLER!
Yours Obedient
/s/ Dr. LAMMERS.

Translation of Document 1965-PS (GB 176). *Article by Streicher, 4 November 1943, published in newspaper Der Stuermer, on disappearance of Jews from Europe.*

* * *

EXTRACT FROM "DER STUERMER", 4 November 1943

"It is really the truth that the Jews 'so to speak' have disappeared from Europe and that the Jewish 'reservoir' of the East, from which the Jewish plague has for centuries beset the peoples of Europe, has ceased to exist * * * However, the Fuehrer of the German people at the beginning of the war prophesied what has now come to pass * * *

Translation of Document 2012-PS. *First regulation for administration of the law for the restoration of professional Civil Service, 11 April 1933, defining non-Aryans and prohibiting them from holding civil service positions.*

* * *

1933 REICHSGESETZBLATT, PART I, PAGE 195

First Regulation for Administration of the Law for the Restoration of the Professional Civil Service
of 11 April 1933

On the basis of Article 17 of the Law for the Restoration of the Professional Civil Service of 7 April 1933 (RGBl I, 175), the following regulation is issued:

1

To Article 2:
Unfit, are all civil servants who belong to the communist party or communist aid- or supplementary organization. They are, therefore, to be discharged.

2

To Article 3:
1. A person is to be regarded as non-Aryan, who is descended from non-Aryans, especially Jewish parents or grandparents. This holds true even if only one parent or grandparent is of non-Aryan descent. This premise especially obtains if one parent or grandparent was of Jewish faith.
2. If a civil servant was not already a civil servant on 1 August 1914, he must prove that he is of Aryan descent, or that he fought at the front, or that he is the son or the father of a man killed during the World War. Proof must be given by submitting documents (birth and marriage certificate of the parents, military papers).
3. If Aryan descent is doubtful, an opinion must be obtained from the expert on racial research commissioned by the Reich Minister of the Interior (Sachverstaendiger fuer Rasseforschung).

3

To Article 4:
1. In determining whether the suppositions of Article 4, sentence (1) are given, the whole political career of the official is to be considered, particularly from 9 November 1918 on.
2. Every official is required on request to attest to the highest Reich or country authority (Article 7) as to what political party

III - 331

he has been a member of until the present. As political parties in the sense of this definition reference is made to the Reichsbanner, Black-Red-Gold, the Republican Judges' Union and the League for the Rights of Man.

4

All negotiations, documents and official certificates which are requisite for the fulfillment of this law, are free of duty and stamping (gebuehren-und stempelfrei).

Berlin, 11 April 1933

> The Reich Minister of the Interior
> Frick
> The Reich Minister of Finance
> Count Schwerim von Krosigk

Translation of Document 2022-PS. *Law against overcrowding of German schools and higher institutions, 25 April 1933, reducing number of non-Aryans.*

* * *

1933 REICHSGESETZBLATT, PART I, PAGE 225
Law against overcrowding of German Schools and Higher Institutions
of 25 April 1933

The Reich Government has enacted the following law that is promulgated herewith:

* * * * * *

Article 3

In those special schools and faculties where the number of pupils and students is greatly disproportionate to professional demand, the number of registered students must be reduced during the school year 1933 as far as it is, without excessive rigor, consistent with a proper proportion.

Article 4

The number of non-Aryan Germans, within the meaning of the Law for the Restoration of the Professional Civil Service, of 7 April 1933 RGBl I, p 175), who may be admitted to schools, colleges and universities, must not exceed a number proportionate to the Aryan students in each school, college or university compared to the percentage of non-Aryans within the entire German population. This proportion is fixed uniformly for the whole Reich.

If, in accordance with Article 3, the number of pupils and students is to be reduced, there is likewise a proper proportion to be established between the total number of students and the number of non-Aryans. In doing so a somewhat higher proportion may be fixed.

Clauses 1 and 2 do not apply in the case of nonAryans whose fathers have fought at the front during the World War for Germany or her allies, or to children whose parents were married before the enactment of this law, if the father or mother or two of the grandparents are of Aryan origin. The number of these students is not to be included when calculating the quota of non-Aryans.

* * * * * * *

Article 7

The decree is valid upon promulgation.
Berlin, 25 April 1933

The Reich Chancellor
Adolf Hitler
The Reich Minister of the Interior
Frick

Translation of Document 2083-PS. *Editorial Control Law, 4 October 1933, prohibiting non-Aryans from admission to the profession of editor.*

* * *

1933 REICHSGESETZBLATT, PART I, PAGE 713

Editorial Law
4 October 1933

The Reich Government has resolved upon the following law, which is hereby published:

Part One
The Editorial Profession

Section 1

The cooperative work carried on as main employment or based upon appointment to the position of chief editor in the shaping of the intellectual contents by written word, dissemination of news or pictures of the newspapers or political periodicals, which are published within the area of the Reich, is a public task, which is regulated as to its professional duties and rights by the state through this law. Its bearers are called editors. Nobody may call himself an editor who is not entitled to do so, according to this law.

Part Two
Admission to the Profession of Editor

Section 5

Persons who can be editors are only those who:
1. possess the German citizenship,
2. have not lost the civic rights [buergerliche Ehrenrechte] and the qualification for the tenure of public offices.
3. are of Aryan descent, and are not married to a person of non-Aryan descent.
4. have completed the 21st year of age,
5. are capable of handling business,
6. have been trained in the profession,
7. have the qualities which the task of exerting intellectual influence upon the public requires.

Section 6

For the requirement of the Aryan descent and the Aryan marriage, section 1a of the Reich Law for Officials [Reichsbeamtengesetz] and the provisions issued for its implementation will be applied.

* * * * * *

Section 47

The Reich Minister for Public Enightenment and Propaganda will set the date on which this law becomes valid.

Berlin, 4 October 1933
        The Reich Chancellor
        Adolf Hitler
    The Reich Minister for Public
    Enlightenment and Propaganda
        Dr. Goebbels

Translation of Document 2112-PS. *Order of the Reich Commissioner for Occupied Netherlands Territories concerning Jewish Real Estate—providing for its registration and confiscation, 11 August 1941.*

* * *

1941 VERORDNUNGSBLATT, PAGE 655

Order of the Reich Commissioner for the Occupied Netherlands Territories concerning Jewish Real Estate—11 August 1941

By virtue of article 5 of the decree of the Fuehrer concerning the exercise of Governmental authority in the Netherlands, of May 18, 1940 (RGBl. I, p. 778) I order as follows:

Part I
DEFINITION

Section 1

(1) Jewish real estate, as defined in this order is any real estate which belongs in whole or in part:
    1. To a Jew, as defined in Section 4 of Order No. 189/1940, concerning the registration of enterprises:
    2. To an enterprise which is required to register by virtue of Order No. 189/1940;
    3. To a private corporation, an association, an institution, a foundation or any other endowment, if one of the conditions of Section 2 of Order No. 189/1940 is fulfilled, although the organization in question is not an enterprise within the meaning of that order.

(2) Jewish real estate for the purpose of this order is, further, any right in real estate, as well as any mortgage, to which a person, an enterprise, an association, an institution, a foundation or any other endowment, as defined in paragraph (1), is entitled in its entirety or in part.

(3) The owner or beneficiary, for the purpose of this order, is the holder of title to the property, the possessor of a right in the real estate, or the mortgage creditor.

Section 2

The provisions of this order shall not apply to real estate covered by the provisions of Order No. 102/1941, concerning the registration and treatment of agricultural real estate in Jewish hands (Order for the Exclusion of Jews from Agriculture).

Part II
REQUIREMENT OF REGISTRATION

Section 3

(1) Jewish real estate must be registered in writing with the Netherlands Real Estate Administration, The Hague, Juliana

van Stolberglaan 45, by the use of a form which may be obtained from the Chambers of Industry and Commerce.

(2) Registration must be made before September 15, 1941. Any real estate acquired only after this order has become effective, must be registered within one month after such acquisition.

(3) The owner or beneficiary of real estate must register it. Any person who is entitled to represent the owner or beneficiary, or who is entitled to administrate such real estate, must also register it.

Section 4

(1) A person required to register must fill out the registration form completely and truthfully.

(2) Copies of the following documents must be filed with registration form, if they are in the possession of the person registering:

1. Excerpts from the Land-Register and the Mortgage-Register;
2. Contracts of sale and other documents concerning the acquisition of the real estate;
3. Contracts of lease or tenancy, or other documents showing an existing use.

(3) The Netherlands Real Estate Administration is empowered to require further information and the production of books, vouchers, and any other documents.

Section 5

(1) Every parcel of real estate, every right in real estate and every mortgage which on or before May 9, 1940, belonged to a person, an enterprise, an association, an institution, a foundation or any other endowment, as defined in Section 1, paragraph 1, or to which such person, enterprise, association, institution, foundation or other endowment was entitled, and which, before this order has become effective, has been transferred to any other person must likewise be registered.

(2) The owner or beneficiary as defined in paragraph I, and his representative, as well as his immediate successor in title and the representative of the latter, are required to perform this registration.

(3) Registration must be filed in writing before September 15, 1941, with the Netherlands Real Estate Administration. The registration must be accompanied by excerpts from the Land-Register and the Mortgage-Register, as well as by the contracts of sale and other documents concerning the legal transfer to

which reference was made in paragraph 1. Section 4, paragraph 3, shall not be applicable.

Section 6
The registration requirements shall not apply to real estate:
1. Which has been registered pursuant to Order No. 26/1940, concerning the handling of enemy property;
2. Which belongs or did belong to an association or foundation which has been registered by virtue of Order No. 145/1940, concerning the registration of non-commercial associations and endowments;
3. Which has been reported in the registration of an enterprise, pursuant to Section 6 of Order No. 189/1940.

* * * * * * *

PART VII
FINAL PROVISIONS

Section 20
(1) The Reich Commissioner for the Occupied Netherlands Territories (Commissioner General for Finance and Economic Affairs) shall carry out all measures necessary for the enforcement of this order. He is authorized to delegate his powers.

(2) The Reich Commissioner General for the Occupied Netherlands Territories (Commissioner General for Finance and Economic Affairs) shall have general power to make legally binding final decisions, in doubtful cases arising from the application of the provisions of this order.

Section 21
This order shall become effective on the day of publication.

THE HAGUE
   August 11, 1941
            Reich Commissioner for the Occupied
                   Netherlands Territories
                        SEYSS-INQUART

Translation of Document 2120-PS. Law invalidating all German passports of Jews residing in the Reich area, 5 October 1938.

* * *

1938 REICHSGESETZBLATT, PART I, PAGE 1342
Law on Passports of Jews on 5 October 1938

Based on the law on passport, alien police and registration affairs as well as on identification affairs of 11 May 1934 (Reichsgesetzblatt I, Page 589) the following is ordered in agreement with the Reich Minister of Justice:

Article 1

(1) All German passports of Jews (Article 5 of the first law to the Reich citizenship of 14 November 1935—Reichsgesetzblatt I, Page 1333), who reside in the Reich area, become invalid.

(2) The holders of the passports, mentioned in Section (1), are obliged to hand in these passports to the passport authority within Germany, in whose district the holder of the passport has his permanent residence or in lieu of such sojourns temporarily, within 2 weeks after this law becomes effective. For Jews who are staying abroad at the time of publication of this law, this period of two weeks begins with the day of their re-entry into the Reich area.

(3) The passports, made out to be valid abroad, will become valid again if they are marked with a sign designated by the Reich Minister of the Interior, which will mark the holder as a Jew.

Article 2

Whoever carelessly or willfully does not comply with the obligation described in article 1, section 2 will be punished with prison and fined up to 150 marks or with either one of them.

Article 3

The law becomes effective with its promulgation.

Berlin, 5 October 1938.

The Reich Minister of the Interior

By order
Dr. Best.

Translation of Document 2124-PS (GB 259). Decree introducing the Nurnberg Racial Laws into Austria, 20 May 1938.

* * *

1938 REICHSGESETZBLATT, PART I, PAGE 594

Decree Introducing the Nurnberg Racial Laws into the Land of Austria 20 May 1938

Pursuant to Article II of the law relating to the re-union of Austria with the German Reich, 13 March 1938 (Reichsgesetz Bl. I, p. 237), the following is ordered:

ARTICLE I
LAW RELATING TO CITIZENSHIP OF THE REICH

Section 1
The following are applicable to the Land of Austria:
1. The Law Relating to Citizenship of the Reich of 15 September 1935 (Reichsgesetz Bl. I, p. 1146).
2. Section 2, Sub-Section 2, Section 4, Sub-Sections 1, 3 and 4, Sections 5 and 6, Sub-Section 1, and Section 7 of the First Decree under the Law Relating to Citizenship of the Reich of 14 November 1935 (Reichsgesetz Bl. I, p. 1333).

Section 2
The effective date of Section 1, Sub-Section 2, of the Reich Citizenship Law will be determined by the Reich Minister of the Interior.

Section 3
The elimination of Jews from public offices which they hold on the effective date of this decree will be specially regulated.

Section 4
For the application of Section 5, Sub-Section 2, of the First Decree under the Reich Citizenship Law; 16 September 1935 will be considered the effective date of the Reich Citizenship Law in Austria also, and 17 September 1935 will be considered the day on which the law for the Protection of German Blood and Honor came into effect.

ARTICLE II
THE LAW FOR THE PROTECTION OF THE BLOOD

Section 5
The Law for the Protection of German Blood and Honor of 15 September 1935 (Reichsgesetz Bl. I, p. 1146) and the First Decree for the implementation of this Law of 14 November 1935 (Reichsgesetz Bl. I, p. 1334) are applicable to the Land of Austria.

Section 6
Section 3 of the Law for the Protection of the Blood will become effective on 1 August 1938.

Section 7
For the application of Section 12, paragraph 3, of the First Decree for the implementation of the Law for the Protection of the Blood, 16 September 1935 is also to be considered the effective date of the Law for the Protection of the Blood in Austria.

Section 8

1. A marriage cannot be entered into unless it is proved by the testimony of the local Burgermeister of the bride's permanent residence that there is no obstacle to the marriage according to the provisions of the Law for the Protection of the Blood and of the First Decree for the implementation of this law. If the bride has no permanent residence in Austria, the competence of the Burgermeister is determined by the further Provisions of Sction 3 of the General Administrative Procedure Law (Austrian BG. BL. #274/1925).

2. If the Burgermeister has any doubt about the existence of a marriage obstacle in the sense of Section 6 of the First Decree for the implementation of the Law for the Protection of the Blood, he must demand a Marriage Fitness Certificate from the bride and groom of the official physician.

Section 9

In the application of Section 15, sentence 2, of the First Decree for the implementation of the Law for the Protection of the Blood, the former possession of Austrian citizenship is equivalent to the former possession of German citizenship.

ARTICLE III
PROCEDURE REGULATIONS

Section 10

In annulment proceedings, the provisions of the Austrian Law relating to the jurisdiction and the procedure of the courts in lawsuits relating to the annulment of marriages are applicable, subject to the following limitations:

1. The suit is to be made against both spouses. If the public prosecutor or one of the spouses files an appeal, then in the first case both spouses and in the second case the public prosecutor and the other spouse are to be considered as adverse parties.

2. The regulations relating to compulsory representation by counsel are not applicable to the public prosecutor.

3. If the public prosecutor is defeated, the Treasury is obliged to refund the expenses incurred by the spouses, according to Sections 40 et seq., of the Austrian Civil Law.

4. No counsel for the defense of the marriage bond will be appointed.

5. The suit can only be filed, if both spouses are alive. If one of the spouses should die before the sentence is executed, the case is to be considered in the main as closed.

Section 11

The court of first instance has jurisdiction over violations of

Section 5, Sub-Sections 1 and 2, of the Law for the Protection of the Blood.

ARTICLE IV
CONCLUDING PROVISIONS

Section 12

If regulations introduced into Austria by this decree cannot be applied according to the letter, they are to be applied according to the spirit.

Section 13

This decree comes into effect on the day after its promulgation.

Berlin, 20 May 1938.

The Reichsminister of the Interior
Frick
The Deputy of the Fuehrer
Hess
The Reich Minister for Justice
per Dr. Schlegelberger.

Translation of Document 2154-PS (GB 167). Additional orders of the Central Committee for defense against Jewish horror and boycott agitation, 31 March 1933, signed by Streicher.

* * *

NATIONAL SOCIALIST PARTY CORRESPONDENCE

NSK No. 359   31 March 1933

Additional orders of the Central Committee for defense against Jewish horror and boycott agitation.

NSK. The following additional orders are issued by the Central Committee for defense against Jewish horror and boycott agitation:

Order No. 3

In enforcing the defensive boycott, the closing of Jewish business or the use of violence against their customers is to be avoided under all circumstances.

If such an establishment closes its doors voluntarily, no higher power is involved, and the proprietors have no excuse for discharges without notice or for the refusal to pay wages and salaries or for reductions.

Order No. 4

Numerous reports are received by the Central Committee saying that Jewish proprietors are transferring their establishments to German figureheads in order to avoid the effects of the defensive propaganda.

Therefore it is decreed that: Establishments transferred to German figureheads by the Jewish proprietors after 28 March 1933 will be considered as Jewish establishments for the duration of the defensive boycott.

Signed: Streicher

Order No. 5

Concerning the defensive action against the Jewish horror and boycott agitation beginning Saturday, 1 April at 10 AM, the local action committees are again reminded to see to it most strictly:

1. That any use of force is to be avoided. Establishments cannot be closed by the committee or by its agents. On the other hand, closing by the proprietor himself is not to be prevented.

Entering of Jewish establishments is strictly forbidden to SA or SS members or other agents of the action committee.

The only duty of the defensive guards is to inform the public that the proprietor of the establishment is a Jew.

2. That boycotting of establishments is refrained from if it has not been definitely proved that the proprietor is a Jew.

3. That provocateurs cause no property damage which is counter to the purpose of the defensive action.

4. That the action committee be kept informed of all details of the course of the defensive action by the SA and SS controllers so as to be constantly well posted.

5. Posters with provocative contents are forbidden.

Central Committee for defense against the
Jewish horror and boycott agitation.

Streicher.

Translation of Document 2156-PS (USA 263). Announcement of *Central Committee for defense against Jewish horror and boycott agitation, 29 March 1933, published in National Socialist Party Correspondence No. 357.*

* * *

NATIONAL SOCIALIST PARTY CORRESPONDENCE

NSK No. 357　　　　　　　　　　　　　　29 March 1933

The central committee for defense against Jewish horror and boycott agitation

NSK. The central committee for defense against Jewish horror and boycott agitation announces:

Julius Streicher, member of the Reichstag, commissioned with the task of creating and directing the central committee for defense against Jewish horror and boycott agitation, began nis work on Wednesday, 29 March. As presiding deputy of the central committee he appointed Karl HOLZ (Nurnberg), the editor of the anti-Semitic weekly "Der Stuermer". The other members of the central committee are:

> Robert Ley, Reichstag member, staff leader of the Fuehrer, in the supreme leadership of the party organization.
>
> Adolf Huehnlein, Major, Reichstag member, deputy chief of staff of the S. A.
>
> Heinrich Himmler, Reichstag member, Reich Fuehrer of the S. S.
>
> Reinhold Muchow, deputy head of the National Socialist factory cell leadership [Nationalsozialistische Betriebszellenleitung]
>
> Hans Oberlindober, Reichstag member, head of the National Socialist list organization for the care of war victims.
>
> Jakob Sprenger, Reichstag member, head of the National Socialist league of public officials.
>
> Walter Darre, Reichstag member, head of the agrarian-political Dept. of the N. S. D. A. P.
>
> Dr. von Renteln, Reichstag Fuehrer of the fighting league [Kampfbund] of the trade middle class
>
> Dr. Hans Frank II, Reichstag member, head of the National Socialist jurist's league
>
> Dr. Gerhard Wagner, head of the National Socialist league of physicians
>
> Willy Koerber, deputy of the Reich youth leader
>
> Dr. Achim Gercke, head of the National Socialist information department of the Nazi party executive board [Reichsleitung].

The office of the central committee for defense against Jewish horror and boycott agitation is located in Munich, Hotel "Reichsadler", 32 Herzog Wilhelm Street, Room 56. (Telephone Munich 90-0-12.)

Copy of Document 2171-PS. Excerpt from U. S. Government report B-2833 on Numerical Expansion of Buchenwald Concentration Camp, during years 1937-1945, with reference to substantial increase in November 1938.

* * *

Report B-2833

THE NUMERICAL EXPANSION OF THE CONCENTRATION CAMP BUCHENWALD DURING THE YEARS 1937-1945

(Based on the complete records of the competent service units)

PREFACE

The following figures are compiled from authentic material that the SS in their flight from the camp were unable to destroy. Particular attention is called to the fact that every number can be substantiated by the personal records of the prisoners in question.

In November 1938 the notorious great movement against the Jews in the Third Reich was carried through, which Hitler tried to justify by referring to the attempt on the life of the official of the German Embassy in Paris, von Rath. In a very short time the camp strength doubled itself. Whereas on 9 November 1938 it still amounted to 9,842, it had grown to 19,676 on 13 November 1938. No lodging facilities were available for such an increase. Temporarily the new arrivals were camped on the roll call ground and in the half completed sheep stable, until very primitive wooden barracks without any sanitary installations were erected alongside the roll call grounds, which later became famous as the Blocks 1a-5a. During the first few days the SS had no clear survey. The keeper of the records would announce over the loudspeaker, "If another Jew hangs himself, will he kindly stick a piece of paper with his name on it in his pocket, so that one knows who he is."

Where the Jews came from is given in the survey in Table 3.

Table 3

Place of Origin	Number	Place of Origin	Number
Giessen	138	Darmstadt	169
Mainz	97	Frankfurt a/M	2,621
Kassel	693	Eisenach-Gotha	99
Breslau	2,471	Offenbach	197
Dresden	151	Worms	124
Magdeburg	375	Nordhausen	316
Chemnitz	171	Aachen	89
Leipzig	270	Wuerzburg	135
Oppeln	703	Friedberg	103
Bielefeld	406	Erfurt	112
Meiningen	91	Halle/Saale	82
Dessau	85	Hannover	87
Various small places in Thueringen			689

This increase in the camp strength not only resulted in a definite but also in a greater percentage number of death cases, as indicated in Table 4.

Table 4

Period	Number of deaths	Average Camp Strength	Deaths in % Camp Strength
Oct. 10-Nov. 9, '38	53	10 156	0.52%
Nov. 10-Dec. 12, '38	244 +	17 262	1.41%

+ Among them 3 unknown dead and 3 suicides.

At that time the first construction work of the concentration camp and the necessary troop billets were finished in the rough. The SS sent their prophylactic prisoners to new places for the erection of other camps and SS barracks. The first professional criminals were sent to Camps Mauthausen and Flossenburg on 3 November 1938. Other Transports followed shortly. The "Actions-Juden" (Jews arrested during the movement or campaign against them) were also discharged after a comparatively short time, that is to say, after plundering them and requisitioning their property, they were for the greater part expelled from the Third Reich and upon leaving the camp had to immediately board a ship or cross the frontier. Through these proceedings and the inclusion of death cases the camp strength went down to 8,650 in round figures by the end of February 1939 and stayed at this level, for the time being.

Translation of Document 2233A-PS (USA 173). *Diary of Hans Frank, Governor General of Poland, Meetings of Department Chiefs in 1939/40, in which reference is made to shootings of Jews and forced labor for Jews.*

* * *

FRANK DIARY, Meetings of Departmental Chiefs in 1939/40
[Abteilungsleitersitzungen 1939/40]
Minutes of the 1st conference of the Department Chiefs on the 2nd December 1939.

[Page 3, line 4-13]

The condemning to death of an archbishop and bishop gives cause to the fundamental observation that a total war against any kind of resistance is being waged in the Government General. The two bishops have been condemned quite rightly, because arms were found in their possession. If, despite that, they were pardoned to hard labor, then certain other considerations were the cause for that. Reports by the press concerning the shooting of Jews are not desirable because such reports would intimidate the Jews.

Minutes of the 2nd conference of the Departmental Chiefs on the 8th December 1939.
[Page 4, par. 1 and 2]
The question of forced labor for the Jews could not be solved satisfactorily from one day to the other. Prerequisite for this would be the card indexing of the male Jews from 14 to 50 years of age. In this it had to be ascertained which trade the Jews had so far carried on, because just in those territories the Jews had various skilled trades, and it would be a loss if this manpower would not be usefully exploited. To do this, sweeping planning is necessary. For the time being the Jews had to be gathered in columns and had to be employed wherever there was a pressing need. It is the task of the chief of the district to determine these needs.

Translation of Document 2233C-PS (USA 271). *Diary of Hans Frank, Governor General of Poland. Tagebuch, 1940. Part IV. October-December, containing statement that Jews in Poland will be eliminated.*

* * *

FRANK DIARY, 1940.
Vol. IV, October-December

[Page 943, 4th-6th lines]
10/7/40
The Governor-General than addresses the assembly with the following words:
My dear Comrades!

* * * * * * *

[Pages 1158-1159]
I am very happy about this hour of the Armed Forces, for it joins us all together. Some of you left your mothers, your parents at home, others their wives, their brides, their brothers, their children. In all these weeks, they will be thinking of you, saying to themselves: my God, there he sits in Poland where there are so many lice and Jews, perhaps he is hungry and cold, perhaps he is afraid to write. It would not be a bad

idea then to send our dear ones back home a picture, and tell them: well now, there are not so many lice and Jews any more, and conditions here in the Government General have changed and improved somewhat already. Of course, I could not eliminate all lice and Jews in only one year's time. (public amused) But in the course of time, and above all, if you help me, this end will be attained. After all, it is not necessary for us to accomplish everything within a year and right away, for what would otherwise be left for those who follow us to do?

Translation of Document 2233D-PS (USA 281). *Diary of Hans Frank, Governor General of Poland, 1941 October-December. Speech of the Governor General 16 December 1941 to effect that Jews, of whom there are over 2,500,000 in general government, must be annihilated.*

* * *

FRANK DIARY, 1941 Oct-Dec.
CABINET SESSION

Tuesday 16 December 1941 in the Government
Building at Krakow

Speech of the Governor General
Closing the Session

[Page 76, line 10 to page 77 line 33]

As far as the Jews are concerned, I want to tell you quite frankly, that they must be done away with in one way or another. The Fuehrer said once: should united Jewry again succeed in provoking a world-war, the blood of not only the nations, which have been forced into the war by them, will be shed, but the Jew will have found his end in Europe. I know, that many of the measures carried out against the Jews in the Reich, at present, are being criticized. It is being tried intentionally, as is obvious from the reports on the morale, to talk about cruelty, harshness, etc. Before I continue, I want to beg you to agree with me on the following formula: We will principally have pity on the German people only, and nobody else in the whole world. The others had no pity on us. As an old National-Socialist, I must say: This war would only be a partial success, if the whole of Jewry would survive it, while we would have shed our best blood in order to save Europe. My attitude towards the Jews will, therefore, be based only on the expectation that they must disappear. They must be done away with. I have entered negotiations to have them deported to the East. A great discussion concerning that question will take place in Berlin in January, to which I am going to delegate the State-Secretary Dr. Buehler. That discussion is to take place in the Reich-Security Main-Office with SS-Lt. General Heydrich. A great Jewish migration will begin, in any case.

But what should be done with the Jews? Do you think they will be settled down in the "Ostland", in villages [Siedlungdoerfer]? This is what we were told in Berlin: Why all this bother? We can do nothing with them either in the "Ostland" nor in the "Reichkommissariat". So, liquidate them yourself.

Gentlemen, I must ask you to rid yourself of all feeling of pity. We must annihilate the Jews, wherever we find them and wherever it is possible, in order to maintain there the structure of the Reich as a whole. This will, naturally, be achieved by other methods than those pointed out by Bureau Chief Dr. Hummel. Nor can the judges of the Special Courts be made responsible for it, because of the limitations of the frame work of the legal procedure. Such outdated views cannot be applied to such gigantic and unique events. We must find at any rate, a way which leads to the goal, and my thoughts are working in that direction.

The Jews represent for us also extra-ordinarily malignant gluttons. We have now approximately 2,500,000 of them in the general government, perhaps with the Jewish mixtures and everything that goes with it, 3,500,000 Jews. We cannot shoot or poison those 3,500,000 Jews, but we shall nevertheless be able to take measures, which will lead, somehow, to their annihilation, and this in connection with the gigantic measures to be determined in discussions from the Reich. The general government must become free of Jews, the same as the Reich. Where and how this is to be achieved is a matter for the offices which we must appoint and create here. Their activities will be brought to your attention in due course.

Translation of Document 2233E-PS (USA 283). *Diary of Hans Frank, Governor General of Poland. Conference Volume, Cabinet session in Cracow, 24 August 1942, on necessity of sending food to Germany from Poland even at expense of starving 1.2 million Jews.*

* * *

FRANK DIARY, Conference Volume,
Cabinet session in Cracow on 24 August 1942
Cabinet session in the Great Conference Room of the
Government Building in Cracow
Monday, 24 August 1942

Subject: A new Plan for seizure and for food [Ernaehrung] of the General Gouvernement

written in 3 Copies:
1. Office of the Governor General
2. State Secretary Dr. Boepple
3. District Court Judge [Oberlandesgerichtsrat] Dr. Weh

Beginning of the Session at 4 p.m.

The *Governor General* opens the meeting with the following words:

Gentlemen,

I have called you together today with special speed and emphasis in order to acquaint you with a measure which is unusually important and decisive for all the work in the General Government in the year to come. What I tell you, I tell you in strictest confidence. I call your attention to the fact that every word which leaks out of this meeting, unofficially, might mean a tremendous damage to our country.

Under these circumstances you probably will not be surprised that the saying now has become true: Before the German people are to experience starvation, the occupied territories and their people shall be exposed to starvation. In this movement, therefore, we here in the General Government must also have the iron determination to help the Great German people, our fatherland.

Germany had almost sufficient rye to tide them over until the new harvest, but not sufficient wheat. In large parts of Germany, therefore, no more wheat can be distributed in the near future. We therefore must aid the fatherland until the beginning of the new wheat harvest.

The General Government therefore must do the following: The General Government has taken on the obligation to send 500,000 tons bread grains to the fatherland in addition to the foodstuffs already being delivered for the relief of Germany or consumed here by troops of the armed forces, Police or SS. If you compare this with our contributions of last year, you can see that this means a six-fold increase over that of last year's contribution of the General Government.

The new demand will be fulfilled exclusively at *the expense of the foreign population*. It must be done cold-bloodedly and without pity; for this contribution of the General Government is still more important this year since the occupied Eastern territories—Ukraine and Ostland—will not yet be able to make an important contribution toward the relief of Germany's food problem. Even if a million tons of bread grains could be delivered from Ostland and Ukraine, it would in the face of Germany's food situation be only a "drop in the bucket".

For this reason I wanted to acquaint you, Gentlemen, here in this governmental session with the decisions which I have made known today to Party member Naumann. You will essentially find an additional *increase* of the *quota* of foodstuffs to be shipped to Germany and *new regulations for the feeding of the population*; especially of the Jews and of the Polish population, whereby, if possible, the provisioning of the working people, especially of those working for German interests, shall be maintained.

The feeding of a *Jewish population*, estimated heretofore at 1.5 million, drops off to an estimated total of 300,000 Jews, who still work for German interests as craftsmen or otherwise. For these the Jewish rations, including certain special allotments which have proved necessary for the maintenance of working capacity, will be retained. The other Jews, a total of 1.2 million, will no longer be provided with foodstuffs.

State Secretary *Dr. Boepple* points out that by reason of the attendance list the names of all who took part in the meeting were known. Should rumors about the measures decided on today eventually seep through to the public, he would, as representative of the government, have them traced to their source, and bring the responsible parties to account.

End of the meeting: 1640 hrs

* * * * * * *

Not unimportant manpower has been taken from us in form of our old proven Jewish communities. It is clear that the working program is made difficult when in the middle of this program, during the war, the order for complete annihilation of the Jews is given. The responsibility for this cannot be placed upon the government of the General Government. The directive for the annihilation of the Jews comes from higher quarters. We have to be content with the consequences and can only report that the Jew has caused tremendous difficulties with regard to the work-program. I was able to prove, the other day, to Staatssekretaer Ganzenmueller, who was complaining that a big building project in the General Government came to a halt, that this would not have happened if the many thousands of Jews working at it had not been deported. Now the order is given that the Jews will have to be removed from the armament projects. I hope that this order, if not already cancelled, will soon be cancelled, for then the situation will be still worse.

Translation of Document 2233F-PS (USA 295). *Diary of Hans Frank, Governor General of Poland, Speech by Frank in Berlin 25 January 1944 in which he made statement that perhaps 100,000 Jews were left in the General Government.*

* * *

FRANK DIARY, 1944

Loose Leaf Volume covering period from 1 January 1944 to 28 February 1944—speech delivered by Hans Frank in Berlin 25 January 1944 before the Representatives of the German Press [Page 5]

At the present time we still have in the General Government perhaps 100,000 Jews.

* * * * * * *

Translation of Document 2233G-PS (USA 302). *Diary of Hans Frank, Governor General of Poland, 25 October to 15 December 1939 referring to resettlement of 1,000,000 Jews and institution of forced labor for the Jews.*

* * *

FRANK DIARY, 1939, from 25 October to 15 December

[Page 44].

* * * By spring 1,000,000 Poles and Jews from East and West Posen, Danzig, Poland and Upper Silesia must be received by the General Government. The resettlement of the ethnic Germans and the taking on of Poles and Jews (10,000 daily) must be accomplished according to plan. Especially urgent is the instituting of *forced labor for the Jews*. The Jewish population if possible must be extracted from the Jewish cities and be put to *work on roads*. The critical questions of housing and feeding are still to be cleared up * * *

[Page 19]. 11:00 o'clock.
* * * The Governor General received SS Lieutenant General Krueger, General Becker, SS Brigadier General Streckenbach, and Lieutenant Colonel Gudewill.
Brigadier General Streckenbach reported:
The Reichsfuehrer SS wishes that all *Jews* be evacuated from the newly gained Reich territories. Up to February approximately 1,000,000 people are to be brought in this way into the General Government. The families of good racial extraction present in the occupied Polish territory (approximately 4,000,000 people) should be transferred into the Reich and individually housed and thereby be uprooted as a people. The deadline provided for the migration transport is the 15th of November. The Governor General points out that better and greater transport ways be made ready for both the West-East as well as the East-West movements. SS Lieutenant General Krueger explained that, starting 15 November, the entire railroad net of the General Government will be at the disposal of the resettlement transports. The general governor gave SS Lieutenant General Krueger the assignments to organize these refugee transports * * *

Translation of Document 2233Q-PS. *Diary of Hans Frank, Governor General of Poland, Government Meetings, October-December 1941. Meeting of 16 December 1941 in which Frank stated that death sentences must be imposed upon Jews leaving the ghettos.*

* * *

FRANK DIARY, Government Meetings, Oct.-Dec., 1941
Meeting of the Government of General Government
Cracow, in the Government Building, 16 December 1941
[Page 35, lines 22-29].
Dr. Frank: Severe measures must and will be adopted against Jews leaving the ghettos. Death sentences pending against Jews for this reason must be executed as quickly as possible. This order, according to which every Jew found outside the ghetto is to be executed, must be carried out without fail. * * *
[Page 66, lines 13-22].

The Documentary Evidence   2233Q-PS

Chief of Office in Warsaw, Dr. Hummel: * * * In Warsaw, in spite of the setting up of a third court chamber, we have been able to decree only 45 death sentences, only 8 of which have been carried out since in each individual case, the Pardon Commission [Gnadenkommission] in Cracow has to make the final decision. A further 600 sentences were demanded and are under consideration. An effective isolation of the ghetto is not possible by way of the Special Court Procedure. The procedure to be followed up to liquidation takes too much time. It is burdened with too many formalities and must be simplified.

Translation of Document 2237-PS. Letter from Reich Commissioner for the Reunion of Austria with the German Reich to Goering, 18 November 1938, concerning actions against the Jews in Vienna on 9/10 November 1938.

* * *

SECRET

File on actions against the Jews in November 1938
1120
Action against the Jews on 9 and 10 November 1938
Legal Regulations
Reich Commissioner for the Re-Union of Austria with the
  German Reich
                                    Vienna I,-18 November 1938
                                                       Parliament
                                                  phone R, 50-5-60
To the Minister President,
  Generalfieldmarshal Goering
    Berlin
Sir!
The action in Vienna which took place during the night from 9 to 10 November was finished up completely by Tuesday.

The following is what happened substantially:

A decree of Dr. Goebbels, the Reichsminister for Propaganda, but above all his speech which he delivered in Berlin on the evening of 9 Oct 1938 as well as the contents of the speech he made in Munich were preludes for this so-called action. Though the hint was somehow indefinite, no different conclusion could be drawn since it said: "The fire-department has to be notified". This order was not given in the first place to the district leaders, but the lower echelons [Gliederungen] were notified first so that the district-leader had no chance to possibly take

III - 353

counter-measures. Besides there existed a few orders which were farther reaching than the hint by Dr. Goebbels. Here in Vienna in many cases even the schools were closed in the morning so that the youth could participate—"according to the order"—in the demonstrations. As always happens in such cases, the disorderly elements soon were leading and 40 different places were on fire. Around noontime the Major reported that the fire-department was no more in the position to control the situation. Simultaneously, the tumult against the Jewish stores began. That, one may say, was the signal for the day and the night of the long fingers. How did the Party act in this situation, and especially the political leaders?

Fieldmarshal, I assure you, that after thorough investigation I am able to state today that the political leaders, and that is the district leaders and their Kreis-leaders, are the ones who have prevented chaos in Vienna. Enormous quantities of stolen merchandise, above all jewelry and values, were safeguarded immediately by the Kreis-leaders, and at this moment an inventory is being made. Gold, silver and valuables will be brought to a safe in a bank today. There is no question of returning the goods which were taken away from the Jews because one does not know their original owners and also because the Jews make the most outrageous and untruthful statements. Therefore I am forced, my Fieldmarshal, to safeguard an extremely high quantity of valuables. The rest of the goods will be checked, and shall be sold to retail-shops for the purchase-value, since we have to expect a scarcity of goods on account of the protective measures for our territory which we had to take [Gebietsschutzmassnahmen].

Especially the enclosed orders will be necessary, for the restoration of normal conditions and of a legal status.

Fieldmarshal, please do examine the enclosures. In case you have no objections, I would like to enforce them immediately.

I may refer again to my request for support as for the introduction of the laws on organization and also for the execution of the Fuehrer-order.

Heil Hitler!
sign.: [illegible]

Telephone-message of the Kripo D.D.

State Police Vienna, Reg. Rat Dr. Pifrader gives the following information via phone at 07,30:

Since the Kripo-agencies [Kripostellen] of the "POl.-Aemter" are constantly making inquiries at the state police (Stapo), they will have to be informed by phone of the following:

Influential and rich male Jews of German nationality of not too high an age and who are healthy have to be arrested.

The owners of the fire-arms are to be treated especially severely and a special notation has to be made about them.

The police agencies [Po. Amtsdienststellen] have to be informed (as top secret) that the property of all native Jews has to be razed entirely. Therefore the police is not supposed to come to the aid of Jews in such cases.

Fires may be started only where there is no danger that the fire may spread. Therefore, as a rule, not in narrowly built parts of the city.

On a whole about 3,000 Jews are to be arrested.

Dr. Bayer D.D. of the Kripo

Translation of Document 2273-PS (USA 487). *Excerpt from a top secret report of Einsatz Group A on execution of 229,052 Jews in the Baltic Provinces.*

* * *

Draft
TOP SECRET
[Geheime Reichssache]
SPECIAL PURPOSE GROUP "A"
[Einsatzgruppe A]

* * * * * * *

III
Jews

The systematic mopping up of the Eastern Territories embraced, in accordance with the basic orders, the complete, removal if possible, of Jewry. This goal has been substantially attained—with the exception of White Russia—as a result of the execution up to the present time of 229,052 Jews (see Appendix). The remainder still left in the Baltic Provinces is urgently required as labour and housed in Ghettos.

To attain this object various kinds of measures were necessary in the different areas of the [Ostland].

In the three Baltic States of Estonia, Latvia and Lithuania, Jewry did not make itself decisively felt until the Bolsheviks had come into power there. But even before that the Jewish influence on the one hand and the anti-Jewish feeling of the population on the other hand, were very strong.

In the following the various areas of the Eastern Territories will be dealt with separately:

1. *Estonia*

As Estonia, until the middle of the last century, was part of a closed zone of the Russian Empire, into which it was forbidden for Jews to immigrate, the number of Jews in the country has always been insignificant.

At the beginning of 1940 there were living in Estonia about 4,500 Jews out of a total population of 1.2 millions. Their influence on the economic life of the country was considerably stronger than the proportion of Jews to the whole population. For instance 11% of Estonian industry was in Jewish hands. During the Bolshevik time it is true Jewish private property was nationalized, but nevertheless the Jews themselves were almost everywhere left as Directors of their former enterprises. By means of connections with the NKWD the Jews got themselves into a very strong position. They controlled the Press, cultural institutions, forced their way into the open professions, and were the only minority besides the Germans to have the right to cultural autonomy.

With the advance of the German troops the majority of the Jews, together with the Soviet-Russian authorities, left the country. Approx. 2,000 Jews remained behind in the country. Out of these almost 1,000 lived in Reval alone.

The Estonian Self Protection Movement [Selbstschutz], formed as the Germans advanced, did begin to arrest Jews, but there were no spontaneous pogroms. Only by the Security Police and the SD were the Jews gradually executed as they became no longer required for work.

Today there are no longer any Jews in Estonia.

2. *Latvia*

The total number of Jews in Latvia amounted in June 1935 to 93,479 or 4.79% of the total population.

When the Bolsheviks came into power in Latvia in June 1940, their Soviet-Russian racial comrades succeeded in obtaining authoritative influence for the Latvian Jews, who previously had been predominantly Zionist. Whereas before 1940 there were no Jews as State officials in Latvia, in fact there were no Jews in the State Administration at all, in the Soviet Russian Republic all the influential State positions were quickly in the hands of the Jews. Half of the total number of Judges were Jewish. The number was up to 80% in the Higher Courts and in particular on the Tribunal. Equally strong was the influence of the Jews on the economy and cultural life.

far more people have given "Yiddish" as their mother tongue than there were supposed to be Jews counted in the same area. Quite half of the Jews in the White Russian Settlement Area lived at the beginning of the war in the larger towns. Minsk was occupied to a very particular extent by Jews. In 1939 there were approximately 100,000 out of a total population of 238,000.

The social structure of the Jews shows a broad lower stratum of very poor Jews, both in the area formerly Polish, and in the White Russian Sector which was Bolshevik before the Russo-Polish war.

The proportionately thin upper stratum dominated simply every sphere of life in the former Polish sector, mainly as a result of its strong economic position, and in the former Soviet-Russian sector as a result of their influence in the leading Party positions. The Jew in the area formerly Polish is a particularly dangerous element, because of his intelligence and activity. But even the Soviet-Russian Jew has during the 25 years of Bolshevik domination assumed a very self-sufficient and arrogant air, which he has even retained after the entry of the German troops.

The final and fundamental elimination of the Jews remaining in the White Russian sector after the entry of the Germans is fraught with certain difficulties. Just in this place the Jews form an extremely high percentage of the specialized workers, who are indispensable because of the shortage in other reserves in this area.

Furthermore Einsatzgruppe A did not take over this area until after the heavy frost had set in, which made mass executions much more difficult. A further difficulty is that the Jews live widely scattered over the whole country. In view of the enormous distances, the bad conditions of the roads, the shortage of vehicles and petrol and the small forces of Security Police and SD, it needs the utmost effort in order to be able to carry out shootings in the country. Nevertheless 41,000 Jews have been shot up to now. This number does not include those shot in operations by the former Einsatzkommandos. From estimated figures about 19,000 partisans and criminals, that is in the majority Jews, were shot by the Armed Forces [Wehrmacht] up to December 1941. At the moment approximately 128,000 Jews must still be reckoned with in the area of the Commissariat-General. In Minsk itself — exclusive of Reich Germans — there are about 1,800 Jews living, whose shooting must be postponed in consideration of their being used as labour.

The Commander in White Russia is instructed to liquidate the Jewish question as soon as possible, despite the difficult situation. However a period of about 2 months is still required —according to the weather.

The shutting up of all the remaining Jews in special Ghettos is also almost completed in the towns in White Russia too. They will be used for work to the fullest extent by the authorities of the Armed Forces, the Civil Administration and German Authorities.

The feeding of the Jews in the Ghettos causes considerable difficulty, especially in White Russia but also in Lithuania. Together with the general decrease in working capacity, there is increased susceptibility to all contagious diseases.

5. *Jews from the Reich.*

Since December 1940 transports containing Jews have arrived at short intervals from the Reich. Of these 20,000 Jews were directed to Riga and 7,000 Jews to Minsk. The first 10,000 Jews evacuated to Riga were housed partly in a provisionally erected reception camp and partly in a newly established hut encampment near Riga. The remaining transports have for the time being been directed into a separate part of the Riga Ghetto.

The building of the hut encampment, as a result of the employment of all Jews fit for work, is so advanced that all evacuated Jews who survive the winter can be put into this camp in the spring.

Only a small section of the Jews from the Reich is capable of working. About 70-80% are women and children or old people unfit for work. The death rate is rising continually, also as a result of the extraordinarily hard winter.

The amount done by those few Jews from the Reich who are fit for work is satisfactory. They are preferred as labour to the Russian Jews, because they are German speaking and because of their *comparatively* greater cleanliness. Worthy of note is the adaptability of the Jews, with which they attempt to form their life in accordance with the circumstances.

The crowding together of the Jews into the smallest space, which occurs in all the Ghettos, naturally causes greater danger of epidemics, which is being combatted as much as possible by the employment of Jewish doctors. In isolated instances sick Jews with contagious diseases were selected under the pretext of putting them into a home for the aged or a hospital and executed.

CHART.......................... Judenfrei—free of Jews
Jewish Executions carried out by Special Purpose Group A.
Estimated number of Jews still remaining—128,000.

Translation of Document 2311-PS. *Decree of Hitler on Administration of the Oath to the Officials of the Province of Austria, 15 March 1938, with provision that Jewish officials shall not be sworn in.*

* * *

1938 REICHSGESETZBLATT, PART I, PAGE 245
Decree of the Fuehrer and Reich Chancellor concerning the Administration of the Oath to the Officials of the Province of Austria, March 15, 1938.

By virtue of Article II of the law of March 13, 1938, concerning the reunion of Austria with the German Reich (RGBl I, p. 237), I issue the following order:

SECTION 1. Public officials of the province of Austria shall take an oath of office upon entrance into service.

SECTION 2. The oath of office of public officials reads: "I swear that I shall be loyal and obedient to Adolf Hitler, the Fuehrer of the German Reich and People, and that I shall observe the laws and conscientiously fulfill the duties of my office, so help me God."

SECTION 3. The officials at present in office shall be sworn in forthwith in accordance with Section 2.

Jewish officials shall not be sworn in.

SECTION 4. A person is Jewish if he is descended from at least three racially full-blooded Jewish grandparents. A grandparent is automatically considered a full-blooded Jew if he belonged to the Jewish congregation.

A Jewish half-breed descended from two full-blooded Jewish grandparents is considered a Jew:

a. If he belonged to the Jewish congregation on September 16, 1935, or became a member of it thereafter.

b. If he was married to a Jew on September 16, 1935, or entered into marriage with one thereafter.

SECTION 5. Anyone who refuses to take this oath shall be removed from office.

SECTION 6. The legal and administrative regulations necessary for the implementation of this law shall be issued by the Reich Governor (Austrian Provincial Government).

SECTION 7. This decree shall enter into force on the day of its proclamation.

Vienna, March 15, 1938.

ADOLF HITLER, Fuehrer and Reich Chancellor.

Translation of Document 2326-PS. *Reich Principles Regarding Recruiting, Appointment and Promotion of Reich and Provincial Officials, 14 October 1936, providing that only an official of German blood may be promoted.*

* * *

1936 REICHSGESETZBLATT, PART I, PAGE 893

Reich Principles Regarding Recruiting, Appointment, and Promotion of Reich and Provincial Officials, October 14, 1936.

* * *

PROMOTION
Article 8

Only that official can be promoted who, besides absolutely fulfilling his general duties;

a. In consideration of his former political attitude offers absolute guarantee therefor, and has proved since January 30, 1933, that he takes the part of the National Socialist State at all times and represents it effectively.

b. Has given documentary proof that he and his spouse are of German or related blood (Article 1 a. paragraph 3 of the Reich officials law).

c. In his official achievements and abilities, completely fulfills the demands of the higher office. Length of service alone does not justify promotion in any case.

* * * * * * *

Berchtesgaden, 14 October 1936.

The Fuehrer and Reich Chancellor
ADOLF HITLER
The Reich Minister of Interior
FRICK
For the Reich Minister of Finance
REINHARDT
The Deputy of the Fuehrer
R. HESS
Minister without Portfolio

Translation of Document 2340-PS. *Excerpts from German Public Officials law of 27 January 1937 providing, among other things, that only a person of German blood may become an official.*

* * *

1937 REICHSGESETZBLATT, PART I, PAGE 41
German Public Officials Law
of 27 January 1937

A career as a public official, rooted in the German people and permeated by National Socialist ideology and loyalty bound to the Fuehrer of the German Reich and people, forms a foundation pillar of the National Socialist State. Therefore the Reich Government has enacted the following law, which is hereby promulgated.

CHAPTER I
Official Relationship [Beamtenverhaeltnis]
ARTICLE 1.

(1) The German official stands in a public service and trust relationship to the Fuehrer and to the Reich.

(2) He carries out the will of the state, which is based on the National Socialist German Labor Party.

(3) The state demands of the official absolute obedience and complete fulfillment of duty; in return it guarantees him a position for life.

* * * * * * *

CHAPTER II
Duties of Officials
1. General

* * * * * * *

ARTICLE 25.

(1) Only a person who is of German or related blood and who, if he is married, has a spouse of German or related blood can become an official. If the spouse is a mixed-blood second degree, an exception may be made.

(2) An official may marry only a person of German or related blood. If the betrothed is a mixed-blood second degree, the marriage may be approved.

(3) For the admission of an exception under subdivision 1, 2nd sentence, and the approval under subdivision 2, 2nd sentence, the supreme office authority in agreement with the Reich Minister of the Interior and the Deputy of the Fuehrer are the competent authorities. The same authorities may also permit

exceptions to subdivision 1, 1st sentence and subdivision 2, 1st sentence, in individual cases.
Berlin, 26 Jan. 1937

      The Fuehrer and Reichs Chancellor
          Adolf Hitler
      The Reichs Minister of the Interior
           Frick
      The Reich Minister of Finance
      Count Schwerin von Krosigk

Translation of Document 2375-PS. Affidavit of Rudolf Mildner, Commander of the Sipo and SD (Security Police and Security Service) in Denmark, dated 16 November 1945, concerning anti-Jewish actions in Denmark.

*   *   *

I, Dr. Rudolf Mildner, Colonel of the Police, being first duly sworn, declare:

I was made the commander of the Sipo and SD in Denmark on 15 September 1943. A few days after I arrived in Copenhagen an order from RF SS Himmler to the Reich plenipotentiary in Denmark, Dr. Best, arrived demanding the arrest of all Danish citizens of Jewish faith and their shipment to Stottin by ship and thence on to Theresienstadt. As commander I was subordinated to Reichplenipotentiary Dr. Best.

Immediately, with the approval of Dr. Best, I sent a telegram to the RSHA Gruppenfuehrer Mueller, asking to have the Jewish persecutions stopped. As reasons for this I mentioned that the Jews in Denmark had not yet shown themselves unfriendly toward the Reich, that the whole Danish nation would reject measures taken against the Jews, that action would have an unfavorable effect in Scandinavia, England, and the U. S., that the trade relationship between Germany and Sweden would be disturbed, as well as that with Denmark. In Denmark one could then expect political strikes and the amount of sabotage would increase, etc. The position of the Reich plenipotentiary and the Sipo would be made much more difficult and cooperation of the Danish police—I had an agreement partly worked out—would not become effective, etc. The answer to my telegram was an order by RF SS Himmler through Chef der Sipo and SD Kaltenbrunner that the anti-Jewish actions were to be carried out.

I flew to Berlin to talk personally with the Chef der Sipo and SD Kaltenbrunner personally. He was absent. I went to the head of Section IV, Gruppenfuehrer Mueller, who in my presence wrote a telegram to RF SS Himmler with my request (protest against the persecutions of Jews).

Shortly after my return to Copenhagen a direct order by RF SS Himmler sent through Chef der Sipo and SD Dr. Kaltenbrunner arrived saying, "The anti-Jewish actions are to be started immediately."

For the carrying out of this action RF SS Himmler had sent the special command Eichmann, directly subordinated to the Chief of Section IV SS Gruppenfuehrer Mueller, from Berlin to Copenhagen. This command had chartered two ships for the deportation of the Jews. This action failed, however, and there was great bitterness in Berlin from the head of Section IV, Gruppenfuehrer Mueller, towards Dr. Best and me. Eichmann and Sturmbannfuehrer Gunther, Eichmann's deputy, told me that Hitler and Himmler had raged when they received the report. One thought Dr. Best and I were to blame for the miscarried action.

Gruppenfuehrer Mueller gave me the mission of making a report about the causes of the miscarried plan. I sent the report directly to the Chef der Sipo and SD Obergruppenfuehrer Dr. Kaltenbrunner.

I swear under oath that the foregoing is correct and true.

[Signed]   R. Mildner

Subscribed and sworn to before me at Nurnberg, Germany, on 16 November 1945.

[Signed]   Whitney R. Harris,
Lieut., USNR.

Translation of Document 2376-PS. Affidavit of Rudolf Mildner, Commander of the Sipo and SD (Security Police and Security Service) in Denmark, dated 16 November 1945, concerning the official channels through which passed the orders for the deportation for forced labor and extermination of Jews throughout German occupied Europe.

* * *

I, Dr. Rudolf Mildner, Colonel of the Police, being first duly sworn, declare:

After the entry of the U.S.A. into the European war, Hitler put into execution the threat he once made in a speech in the West, "The Jews will be exterminated for that".

Out of the whole Reich territory and the Protectorate Bohemia and Moravia, the General Government Poland, as well as from the countries of Norway, Denmark, Holland, Belgium, France, Italy, Croatia, Serbia, Greece, Hungary, Slovakia, and from the German occupied Russian territory, under what was called "Arbeitseinsatz" [labor employment], the Jews were taken into concentration camps and camps for the armament industry.

The order for the deportation of the Jews in the Reich and in the countries occupied by German troops to labor and concentration camps were issued by RF SS Himmler. The orders had his signature and were classified "top secret" [Geheime Reichsache]. They passed through the Chef der Sicherheitspolizei and SD Dr. Kaltenbrunner, formerly Heydrich, to the Amtschef IV RSHA, Gruppenfuehrer Mueller, who orally talked over the execution of the matter with the head of action IV A 4, SS Obersturmbannfuehrer Eichmann, member of the SD and transferred from Department III to Department IV. The orders also went directly from RF SS Himmler to the local competent Hoeheren SS and Polizeifuehrer, with the Chef der Sipo and SD, Dr. Kaltenbrunner being informed.

Orders of the RF SS Himmler concerning the type of labor employment of the prisoners and the extermination of the Jews, so far as I could gather from conversations with a comrade of the Sipo, went directly through Obergruppenfuehrer Pool, Gruppenfuehrer Glucks, head of the Amtsgruppe D and the head of the concentration camps as "top secret" [Geheime Reichssache], either written or orally. SS Obersturmbannfuehrer Eichmann held the following positions: adviser to RF SS Himmler, the Chief of the Security Police and SD, SS Gruppenfuehrer, Dr. Kaltenbrunner, and the Amtschef of Section IV on all Jewish questions; deputy of RF SS Himmler in all deportations to camps and conversations with other countries concerning the evacuation of the Jews; and liaison man with all Hoeheren SS and Polizeifuehrer in matters concerning the Jews.

The orders for the carrying out of measures against the Jews Eichmann received (either orally from RF SS Himmler or in an order signed by Himmler) orally or on written orders from Chef der Sipo and SD, Dr. Kaltenbrunner, and from the Amtschef IV RSHA, Gruppenfuehrer Mueller, in Berlin. The channels for the issuing of orders on Jewish matters in the Sipo were known to me from cconversations with Gruppenfuehrer Mueller and comrades in the Sipo. I also got some information from the working plan and the business directions of the Sipo.

I swear under oath that the foregoing is correct and true.
[Signed] R. Mildner.

Subscribed and sworn to before me at Nurnberg, Germany, on 16 November 1945.

[Signed]   Whitney R. Harris
            Lieut., USNR.

Translation of Document 2402-PS. *Guide for the Party Courts, 17 February 1934.*

* * *

GUIDE FOR THE PARTY COURTS
[Richtlinien fuer die Parteigerichte]

17 February 1934

[Page VI]

Therefore party judges are responsible only to their national socialistic conscience and subordinates of no political leader, and they are subordinate only to the Fuehrer.

Walter Buch

[Page 1] Directives for the Party Courts of the NSDAP

1

Purpose of the Party Courts

Par. 1

The Party Courts have the purpose of preserving the collective honor of the party and of the individual party member, as well as settling differences of individual members in an amicable manner.

Their task is:

1. To take measures in the manner prescribed by existing directives against those party members whose behavior does not correspond to the sense of honor and to the ideology of the NSDAP, and, where it appears necessary for the preservation of the honor and good repute of the party, to propose the removal of unworthy members from the party;

2. To clear party members of unjustified suspicion of their integrity, as well as,

3. To work out an amicable settlement of quarrels between party members.

From the jurisdiction of party Courts are excepted S.A.-matters, i.e. breaches of discipline and complaints of S.A.-members, as well as differences of opinion and quarrels among S.A.-members. S.A.-members are all leaders, men, and candidates of organizations subordinated to the Supreme S.A.-leadership (S.A., S.S., S.A.R.I., S.A.R.II, and N.S.K.K.).

In cases of differences of opinion (No. 3) between a party member and a member of the S.A. who is not a party member;

a. The S.A. courts and offices, resp., have jurisdiction when the S.A.-member is the defendant,

b. The party courts have jurisdiction when the party member is the defendant or when both sides accuse each other.

Translation of Document 2405-PS. *Excerpts from German Publications, Speeches by Hitler, 1922-1923, on Jewish Question.*

* * *

"Is it not these criminals, this Jewry, who are the real foes of the Republic, these men who from the day of its birth burdened it with the lie that this people was guilty of the World War? And have they not undermined the Republic and thereby given to the foreign powers the spiritual arms with which these Powers for the last three years shower blows upon us and oppress us and say to us 'You deserve it, for you yourselves have confessed your guilt!' And have they not opposed the Republic, who have so reduced all power of resistance that today every Hottentot State is in a position to lord it over Germany? And do they not ceaselessly oppose Germany, who have brought us, once the people of honour, so low that we have a reputation for the meanest economic corruption and the most debased political outlook?" [Gesinnungslumperei]

  Hitler, Speech on "Free State or Slavery," 28 July 1922.
  Adolf Hitler's Reden, Munich 1925, p. 39.

"Clear away the Jews! Our people has genius enough—we need no Hebrews. If we were to put in their place intelligences drawn from the great body of our people, then we have found anew the bridge which leads to the community of the people."

  Hitler, Speech 27 April 1923 on "The Paradise of the Jew or the State of the German People."
  Adolf Hitler's Reden, Munich 1925 (Pamphlet), p. 77.

Translation of Document 2409-PS (USA 262). *Excerpts from the book "From the Imperial House to the Reich Chancellory" by Joseph Goebbels, concerning the anti-Jewish boycott of 1933.*

* * *

FROM THE IMPERIAL HOUSE TO THE REICH CHANCELLORY
[Vom Kaiserhof zur Reichskanzlei]
By Dr. Joseph Goebbels
Published by
"Zentralverlag der NSDAP, Franz Eher Nachf."
Munich, 1934. Pages 208, 290-292.

Diary Entry 21 November 1932

"In a conversation with Dr. Schacht I assured myself that he absolutely represents our point of view. He is one of the few who accepts the Fuehrer's position entirely."

* * *

The call for the boycott was approved by the entire cabinet. The Ministry has also been reorganized. Now we can start the work on a large scale.

30 March 1933.

The organization of the boycott is perfected. We now need only to press a button and it will start.

31 March 1933.

Many are downcast and are seeing ghosts. They believe that boycott would lead to war. If we offer resistance, we will but gain respect for us.

We are having a last discussion among a small circle and resolve that the boycott shall start tomorrow with all severity. It will be sustained for one day and then halted by an interval until Wednesday. If the agitation abroad will come to an end, then the boycott will be stopped; if not, the struggle will continue to the bitter end. Now the German Jews shall influence their racial comrades in the whole world, in order to save their own necks here.

I deliver an explanation with reference to this at the press conferences; there is breathless silence. There the slogan fits: The Jews have a Jew's fear.

In the evening I speak before the deputies at the Tennis Halls. The speech is transmitted over the radio by all broadcasting stations. I explain once again the entire situation and the necessity, which forces the boycott on us almost irrevocably.

This speech will enlighten the whole country. And tomorrow the boycott will start.

1 April 1933.

The boycott against the world atrocity propaganda has incited Berlin and the entire Reich to the fullest extent. For my own information I drive through the Taucutzien Street. All

Jewish stores are closed. At their entrances SA sentries are standing. The public has declared its solidarity everywhere. An exemplary discipline prevails. An imposing spectacle! Everything takes its course in the utmost tranquillity, within the Reich too.

2 April 1933.

The effects of our boycott are already plainly to be felt. The foreign countries are slowly coming to reason. The world will learn to understand, that it does not do any good to try to learn facts about Germany through Jewish emigrants.

We are facing campaign to conquer with intellect, which will have to be carried out in the world in exactly the same manner as we have carried it out inside Germany herself.

In the end, the world will learn to understand us.

3 April 1933.

Today, they had better give up Germany and make no such ado of their sorrows. For, the more they talk about it, the more acute the Jewish question will grow, and as soon as the world will begin to concern itself with it, then this problem will always be solved to the disadvantage of the Jews.

Translation of Document 2410-PS. *Article by Julius Streicher on the "coming popular action" (anti-Jewish boycott), under banner headline "Beat the World Enemy" from the South German edition of the newspaper Voelkischer Beobachter, 31 March 1933.*

* * *

VOELKISCHER BEOBACHTER, SOUTH GERMAN EDITION,
Friday, 31 March 1933
No. 90 Vol. 46. Munich
[Article by Julius STREICHER on the "coming popular action" under banner headline, "Beat the World Enemy"]

The same Jew who plunged the German people into the blood-letting of the World War and who committed on it the crime of the November Revolution, is now engaged in stabbing Germany, recovering from its shame and misery, in the back. It should be accomplished with the same methods with which World Jewry [Alljuda] committed the crime of the World War. The Jew is again engaged in poisoning the public opinion. World Jewry is engaged again in slandering the German people as a people of Huns and barbarians. For weeks the Jewish press in France, England, America and Poland spread its lies to the world that the eyes of the Communists who are captured in Germany are being gouged out, that protective-custody prisoners [Schutzhaeftlinge] are being tortured to death and that Jewish pogroms are carried out. And again the Jew stirs up the foreign nations, who are thus deceived and cheated, against Germany. And in order that the awakening Germany, the Germany of Adolf Hitler, should collapse at the very start, the racial comrades of the Jews who live in Germany conduct a shameless boycott campaign abroad against German products. "Do not buy German merchandise!" yells the Jewish press-clique to the world. And: "Judah declares war against Germany!"

Why is all this? Why the hate of the Jews against the new Germany? A new Germany was heralded by the bells of Potsdam. A Germany which shattered the hopes of the Jews that they would be able to continue their lives as drones and bloodsuckers on the German people without being checked. The Marxist and bourgeois parties protecting the Jews [Judenschutzpartei] lie battered on the ground and with them the Jewish hope is shattered that they will be able to reconquer their lost power over the German people from within. Hence the Jewish fury. Hence the Jewish hatred. Hence the Jewish atrocity accusations and boycott agitation abroad.

But even this last hope of theirs shall be frustrated! Millions of Germans longed to see the day on which the German people would be shaken up in its entirety to recognize at last the world enemy in the Jew. World Jewry intended to do harm to the German people and has done good. At 10 A.M. Saturday 1 April, the defensive action of the German people against the Jewish world criminal will begin. A defensive fight begins, such as never has been dared before throughout the centuries. World Jewry asked for the fight, is to have it! It is to have it until it shall have recognized that the Germany of the brown battalions is not a Germany of cowardice and of a submission. World Jewry is to have the fight until victory shall be ours!

National Socialists! Strike the world enemy! And if the world were full of devils, still we must succeed!

Translation of Document 2432-PS. Excerpts from Rosenberg's "Writings From the Years 1921-1923" urging adoption of measures against the Jews.

* * *

ALFRED ROSENBERG
WRITINGS FROM THE YEARS 1921–1923
1943
Hoheneichen Publishing Co./Munich, Page 497.

The "seething" force is in fullest motion in Germany. Silence has become senseless. But it is perhaps not yet too late to gather all Germans into a steel-hard racial united front. Ahead lies Bolshevistic chaos, the death of half the German nation. With this prospect before our eyes there can be no hesitation. This one challenge must go through the whole country: get the Jews out of all parties, institute measures for the repudiation of all citizenship rights of all Jews and half Jews, banish all eastern Jews, exercise strictest vigilance over the native ones, break up Zionism, which is involved in English-Jewish politics, confiscate its money, and banish its members to their English protector or to the Promised Land. Possible "Jew Strikes" must be dealt with accordingly.

With a firm will, this is possible. Hungary has proved it in part. If this is not done, none of the generations living today will have the opportunity to live in the German Fatherland again.

German, awake!

17 and 24 July, 4 and 21 August 1921

Translation of Document 2536-PS. Speech by Hans Frank, President of Academy of German Law and later Governor General of Poland, 3 October 1936, on the elimination of Jews from German jurisprudence.

* * *

DOCUMENTS OF GERMAN POLITICS
Dokumente der Deutscher Politik Vol. IV, Pages 225-230.

Speech by Dr. Frank on "The Jews in Jurisprudence" delivered at the Congress of the Reich Group of University Professors on the National Socialists Jurist League in Berlin on October 3, 1936.

" * * * this topic embraces all that which in our opinion will contribute to establishing National Socialism in the field of jurisprudence thus eliminating any alien racial spirit therefrom. * * *

"We National Socialists have started with anti-Semitism in our fight to free the German people, to re-establish a German Reich and to build our entire German spiritual, cultural and social life on the indestructible foundation of our race. We started a gigantic battle in 1919 * * * It took all the self confidence of German manhood to withstand and to triumph—in this fight to substitute the German spirit for Jewish corruption—over the concerted attacks of powerful world groups of which Jewry is a representative.

"Particularly we National Socialist Jurists have a mission of our own to accomplish in this batle. We construct German law on the foundations of old and vital elements of the German people. * * * It is obvious that it hardly needs mentioning that any participation whatsoever of the Jew in German law—be it in a creative, interpretative, educational or critical capacity—is impossible. The elimination of the Jews from German jurisprudence is in no way due to hatred or envy but to the understanding that the influence of the Jew on German life is essentially a pernicious and harmful one and that in the interests of the German people and to protect its future an unequivocal boundary must be drawn between us and the Jews.
* * *

"I would like to ask you to recognize the fact and to be thankful that the National Socialist movement alone, and, in it, each and every SA and SS man has enabled you to act independently of the Jewish hegemony. The spirit of National Socialist willingness to sacrifice—the achievement of the National Socialists and the beginning of this revolutionary era of Germandom—should also live in your universities."

Translation of Document 2540-PS. *Excerpts from decree concerning sequestration of private property in the General Government of Poland, 24 January 1940.*

* * *

VERORDNUNGSBLATT DES GENERAL GOUVERNEURS, No. 6, Jan. 27, 1940, Page 23.

3. PROPERTY

Decree concerning Sequestration of Private Property in the Government General, January 24, 1940.

In pursuance of subsection 1 of Section 5 of the decree of the Fuehrer and Reich Chancellor concerning the administration of the occupied Polish territories of October 12, 1939 (RGBl I, p. 2077), I hereby order as follows:

SECTION 8. Seizure of Abandoned Property. (1) Abandoned property shall be seized by the District Chief or Town Prefect and handed over for administration to the Director of the Trustee Administration of the Government General. Such seizure shall be ordered in writing.

(2) The rights of third parties in the seized property, including legal title transferred or reserved for the purpose of securing the payment of obligations, shall abate upon seizure. The Director of the Trustee Administration of the Government General may grant exemptions from such abatement.

SECTION 16. Restrictions of Property Rights heretofore Imposed. (1) Order No. 4 of the head of the Foreign Exchange Section of the office of the Governor General of November 20, 1939 (VBl.GGP., p. 57) shall not be affected by the provisions of this order.

(2) Debtors in respect of obligations owed to a Jew which are subject to an order of sequestration may terminate their obligation by paying the amount due into a blocked bank account of such Jewish creditor.

Cracow, January 24, 1940

FRANK
Governor General of the Occupied Polish Territories

Translation of Document 2542-PS (USA 489). Affidavit of SS-Sturmbannfuehrer Kurt Lindow, 30 September 1945, in which statement is made concerning execution of Jewish soldiers on the eastern front by screening teams of the Gestapo.

* * *

Statement
of
SS-Sturmbannfuehrer Kurt LINDOW

I, Kurt Lindow, having been duly sworn, make the following statement under oath:

1. I was Kriminaldirektor in Section IV of the RSHA (Chief Reich Security Office) and head of the subsection [Referat] IV A 1, from the middle of 1942 until the middle of 1944. I have the rank of SS-Sturmbannfuehrer.

2. From 1941 until the middle of 1943 there was attached to subsection IV A 1 a special department that was headed by the Regierungsoberinspektor, later Regierungsamtmann, and SS-Hauptsturmbannfuehrer Franz Koenigshaus. In this department were handled matters concerning prisoners of war. I learned from this department that instructions and orders by Reichsfuehrer Himmler, dating from 1941 and 1942, existed, according to which captured Soviet Russian political commis-

sars and Jewish soldiers were to be executed. As far as I know proposals for execution of such PWs were received from the various PW camps. Koenighaus had to prepare the orders for execution and submitted them to the chief of section IV, Mueller, for signature. These orders were made out so that one order was to be sent to the agency making the request and a second one to the concentration camp designated to carry out the execution. The PWs in question were at first formally released from PW status, then transferred to a concentration camp for execution.

3. The department chief [Sachbearbeiter] Koenigshaus was under me in disciplinary questions from the middle of 1942 until about the beginning of 1943 and worked, in matters of his department, directly with the chief of group IV A, Regierungsrat Panzinger. Early 1943 the department was dissolved and absorbed into the departments [Laenderreferate] in subsection IV B. The work concerning Russian PWs must then have been done by IV b 2a. Head of department IV b 2a was Regierungsrat and Sturmbannfuehrer Hans-Helmut Wolf.

4. There existed in the PW camps on the Eastern front small screening teams [Einsatzkommandos] headed by lower-ranking members of the secret police [Gestapo]. These teams were assigned to the camp commanders and had the job to segregate the PWs who were candidates for execution, according to the orders that had been given, and to report them to the office of the secret police [Geheimes Staatspolizeiamt].

5. I also know that in cases of sexual relationships between Poles and German women and girls the Poles, according to an order from Reichsfuehrer Himmler, were to be hanged. The execution of the Poles and the punishment by a court of German women depended upon the opinion of the "racial expert" [Rassereferant] at the HSSPF [Chief SS and Police leader] concerned. If the Poles had serious intentions of marriage, the racial expert would examine if the Pole was, on basis of his entire appearance, racially unobjectionable and therefore capable of being Germanized. If the opinion of the "racial expert" was positive, nothing happened, that is to say, the Pole was permitted to marry the German girl and was Germanized. But if the judgment was negative, then the Pole would be hanged and the German girl turned over to the courts for trial. Each individual case had to be reported, by the addition of photos, to the Reichsfuehrer Himmler, who had apparently reserved the decision for himself and who alone gave the order for the hanging. These cases must have been handled by department IV B 2b;

head of department IV B 2b was Regierungsrat and Sturmbannfuehrer Tomsen.

That the facts stated above are true; that this declaration is made by me voluntarily and without compulsion; that after reading over the statement I have signed and executed the same at Oberursel/Germany this 30th day of September 1945.

      [signed] KURT LINDOW
         Kurt LINDOW
         SS-Sturmbannfuehrer

Subscribed and sworn to before me at Oberursel/Germany this 30th day of September 1945.

  [signed] B. D. SILLIMAN, MAJOR JAGD
     B. D. SILLIMAN, Major JAGD

Translation of Document 2583-PS. *Quotation from speech made by Streicher on 31 October 1939.*

* * *

[Quotation from speech made by Streicher on 31 Oct. 1939]

This is our mission at home, to approach these future decisions without hesitation, to do our duty and to remain strong. We know the enemy, we have called him by name for the last twenty years: he is the World Jew. And we know, that the Jew must die.

Translation of Document 2602-PS. *Excerpt from telegram, Wilson, U. S. Ambassador, to Secretary of State, Washington, 10 November 1938, reporting breaking of Jewish owned shop windows and burning of synagogues.*

* * *

CONFIDENTIAL
TELEGRAM RECEIVED
——————— GRAY

FROM Berlin
Dated November 10, 1938
Rec'd 10:35 a.m.

Secretary of State,
 Washington
 605, November 10, 2 p. m.
 My 600, November 8, 4 p. m. and 603, November 9, 5 p. m.

In the early hours of this morning systematic breaking of Jewish owned shop windows throughout the Reich and the

burning of the principal synagogues in Berlin was carried out.
* * *

WWC:CSB
                                            WILSON

Translation of Document 2603-PS. Report from Kemp, U. S. Consul General in Bremen, Germany, to Secretary of State, Washington, 10 November 1938, concerning anti-Jewish demonstrations in Bremen.

* * *

Report by: Edwin C. Kemp
U. S. Consul General in Bremen

To the Secretary of State
  Washington, D. C.
Date: 10 November 1938
Subject: Anti-Jewish Demonstrations in Bremen

I have the honor to report that on the night of November 9th the Jewish synagogue and cemetery chapel in Bremen were burned, and the show windows of all the Jewish shops were smashed to pieces. Large notices written in red and black reading "Revenge for the murder of vom Rath", "Death of international Jewry" and similar phrases were left conspicuously in sight.

During the early hours of the 10th a number of arrests of Jews were made, and about nine o'clock in the morning about fifty Jewish men, some of decrepit age or health, were paraded along the main street under guard of about six S.A. men.

The attitude of the population, the presence of the many written notices which were done by the same hand and must have required some time to prepare are sufficient evidence that the destruction was not the work of a spontaneous mob enthusiasm, as claimed by some official authorities.

Translation of Document 2604-PS. Report of Honaker, American Consul General to U. S. Ambassador Wilson in Berlin, 12 November 1938, on anti-semitic persecution in the Stuttgart Consular District.

* * *

Report by Samuel W. Honaker, American Consul General
  to U. S. Ambassador Hugh R. Wilson, Berlin
Date: 12 November 1938

Subject: Antisemitic Persecution in the Stuttgart Consular District.

I have the honor to report that the Jews of Southwest Germany have suffered vicissitudes during the last three days which would seem unreal to one living in an enlightened country during the twentieth century if one had not actually been a witness of their dreadful experiences, or if one had not had them corroborated by more than one person of undoubted integrity.

Early on the morning of November 10th practically every synagogue — at least twelve in number — in Wuerttemberg, Baden and Hohenzollern was set on fire by well disciplined and apparently well equipped young men in civilian clothes. The procedure was practically the same in all cities of this district, namely, Stuttgart, Karlsruhe, Freiburg, Heidelberg, Heilbronn, et cetera. The doors of the synagogues were forced open. Certain sections of the buildings and furnishings were drenched with petrol and set on fire. Bibles, prayer books, and other sacred things were thrown into the flames. Then the local fire brigades were notified. In Stuttgart, the city officials ordered the fire brigades to save the archives and other written material having a bearing on vital statistics. Otherwise, the fire brigades confined their activities to preventing the flames from spreading. In a few hours the synagogues were, in general, heaps of smoking ruins.

Copy of Document 2605-PS (USA 242). Affidavit, 13 September 1945, of Dr. Rudolf Kastner, former President of the Hungarian Zionist Organization, describing German persecution of Hungarian Jews.

* * *

Dr. Rezsoe (Rudolph) Kastner, being duly sworn deposes and says:

I was born in 1906 at Kolozsvar, (now Cluj, Rumania), solicitor and journalist, residing at Chemin Krieg, 16, Pension Sergey, Geneva, now temporarily at 109, Clarence Gate Gardens, London.

I was in Budapest until November 28, 1944; as one of the leaders of the Hungarian Zionist organization I not only witnessed closely the Jewish persecution, dealt with officials of the Hungarian puppet government and the Gestapo but also gained insight into the operation of the Gestapo, their organization and witnessed the various phases of Jewish persecution. The following biographical data of mine might be of interest:

Between 1925–1940: Political Editor of "Uj Kelet" Jewish daily newspaper published in Koloszvar; Secretary-General of the Parliamentary Group of the Jewish Party in Rumania.

Between 1929–1931: Worked in Bucharest; member of the Executive of the Palestine Office of the Jewish Agency.

In Dec. 1940: Being a Jew I was excluded from the Chamber of Lawyers; "Uj Kelet", the daily, was closed down by the Hungarian authorities: I moved to Budapest.

Between 1943–1945: Associate President of the Hungarian Zionist Organization.

July 1942: I have been called up for Labor Service; together with 440 other Jewish intellectuals and citizens we worked in South-Eastern Transylvania on fortifications along the Hungarian-Rumanian border.

In Dec. 1942: I was demobilized. Returned to Budapest. Some time before being drafted I have begun to organize relief work for refugee Slovakian Jews. After my demobilization I succeeded in establishing—through diplomatic couriers — contact with the Relief Committee of the Jewish Agency, working in Istanbul. On their instructions I have taken over the leadership of the Relief Committee in Budapest. Our task was—

1. To help to smuggle Jews from Slovakia and Poland into Hungary to save them from the threat of the gas chamber.

2. To feed and clothe them and to assist in their emigration to Palestine.

3. To forward the minutes based on the declaration of the refugees on the question of deportation and annihilation of Jews to Istanbul, later to Switzerland, to the hands of the representatives of the Jewish Agency and the Joint Distribution Committee.

4. To cooperate with the Relief Committee of Bratislava in matters concerning saving, hiding of refugee Jews and exchange of information. After German occupation of Hungary, on the 19th March 1944, the Relief Committee concentrated its efforts on the saving of Hungarian Jewry.

5. The Relief Committee of the Jewish agency of which I was a president was engaged in helping Allied prisoners of war. Moreover we sent confidential reports to the Allies through Istanbul and Switzerland about our connections with officials of the German government. We helped to hide and supported leaders of the Hungarian underground and gave a wealth of information to those Hungarian authorities which were working against the Germans. During the siege of Budapest, when I

was already out of the country, other members of the Relief Committee participated in street fights against the Germans.

On 15 May 1944: One of my collaborators, Eugen Brand, was sent by the Germans to Istanbul to pass on certain business proposals in connection with saving of the Hungarian Jews.

On 21 August 1944: I traveled from Budapest under German escort to the Swiss frontier and acted as intermediary for the first conversation between Kurt Becher and Saly Mayer, Swiss representative of the Joint D. C., to discuss the price of abandoning the gassing. The conversation took place between St. Margareten and Hoechst on the bridge. From there I returned to Budapest.

On 14 October 1944: I traveled for the second time to St. Margarethen.

On 30 October 1944: I traveled to St. Gallen, accompanied by Kurt Becher and Kr. Wilhelm Billitz, director of the Manfred Weiss Works. On this occasion an interview took place between Becher and McClelland, Swiss representative of the War Refugee Board, in the Savoy Hotel, at Zurich. I returned to Budapest.

On 28 November 1944: I left on German instructions to the Swiss border.

On 20 December 1944: I entered Switzerland.

On 27 December 1944: I started out to travel back to Budapest, but could only get to Vienna. The Red Army encircled Budapest.

On 29 December 44–28 March 1945: I remained in Vienna. Afterwards toured Bratislava-Spitz an der Donau — Berlin — Bergen Belsen Hamburg—Berlin—Theresianstadt.

On 19 April 1945: I crossed the Swiss border.

The Germans entered into discussion with leaders of the Jewish community for reasons of administrative efficiency. We conducted the discussion in the hope that we might be able to save some human lives. By holding the ax over our heads they made us responsible for financial contributions and other exactions imposed on the Jewish community. Ultimately the leaders of the "Jewish council" and other intermediaries were also scheduled for extermination. The SS and the Gestapo was particularly intent on liquidating those who had direct knowledge of their operations. I escaped the fate of the other Jewish leaders because the complete liquidation of the Hungarian Jews was a failure and also because SS Standartenfuehrer Becher took me under his wings in order to establish an eventual *alibi* for himself. He was anxious to demonstrate after the fall of 1944 that

On 9 April 1944 the military authorities, with headquarters at Munkacs began the rounding-up of 320,000 Jews into Ghettos within the operational area. In order to prevent any armed resistance by the Jews, they were concentrated in brick factories (as at Kassa, Ungvar, Kolozsvar) or under the open sky (as at Nagybanyam, Marosvasarhely, Des), in a few cases they were allowed to retired into some sections of the cities (as in Nagyvarad, Maramorossiziget), Food allocations: daily 1/5th of a pound of bread and two cups of soup. From the Jews sent into the Ghettos even matches were taken away.

While an agreement was arrived at between Wesenmayer, German Minister and a representative of Sauckel on the one hand, and Prime Minister Sztojay, on the other, that Hungary would place 300,000 Jewish workers at the disposal of the Reich (who were to be selected by a mixed Hungarian-German committee), total deportation of all Jews was decided by Endre, Baky and Eichmann at a meeting in the Ministry of the Interior on the 14 April 1944.

Novak and Lullay left on the next day for Vienna to discuss the question of transport facilities with the management of the German railways.

A levy of 2,000,000 pengoes each was imposed by the Gestapo on the Jews of Novisad and Ungvar. Jewish shops were looted by Germans. Despite a German protest, the Hungarian Government ordered the closing down of all Jewish shops. The Jews resisted in the Ghetto of Munkacs. The Gestapo shot 27 of them, including the entire executive of the Jewish Community.

On 28 April 1944 the first deportation takes place; 1,500 persons suitable as laborers were taken from the Kistarcsa internment camp to Oswiecim. There, they were compelled to write encouraging notes to their relatives with datelines from "Waldsee." The notes were brought by an SS Courier to Budapest and were distributed by the Jewish Council.

In the meantime the Budapest Relief Committee received two messages from the Bratislava Committee. One message said that there was feverish work going on in Oswiecim to restore the gas chambers and crematoriums there, which were not working for months and a remark made by a SS-NCO that "soon we will get fine Hungarian sausages" was reported. The other message was to the effect that an agreement was reached, between the Hungarian, Slovakian, and German railway managements that, for the time being, 120 trains would be directed, via Presov, towards Oswiecim [Auschwitz]. This information was passed on to the Bratislava Relief Committee by an anti-

Nazi Slovakian railway official. It was obvious that it concerned deportation trains.

The delegate of the International Red Cross, to whom I have appealed for intervention, stated that in view of the Geneva Convention this was impossible for him. The Swedish and Swiss Legations promised that they would report to their Governments and ask for instructions. After repeated appeals the Primate of the Catholic Church promised an intervention on behalf of the converted Jews. But Sztojay refused to listen.

After consulting with all Jewish leaders we turned to the Germans. At first Grumey, Wisliczeny, and Hunsche negotiated with us; later Eichmann took over the negotiations. Eichmann arrived at Budapest on the first day of the German occupation, 19 March, 1944. Wisliczeny arrived there on March 22. The first time we negotiated was 3 April. At first the Germans demanded a compensation of 2,000,000 dollars and promised that in return for this sum they would not deport anyone. Later Eichmann declared: "I can only sell the Hungarian Jews as from Germany. Brand should leave at once for Istanbul and inform the Jews there and the Allies that I am prepared to sell 1,000,000 Hungarian Jews, for goods, primarily vehicles. I would transport them to Oswiecim and 'put them on ice.' If my generous offer is accepted I will release all of them. If not, they will all be gassed."

In the meantime the organization of the Ghettos had been directed by Wisliczeny, who had been traveling from town to town. The Hungarian police and gendarmerie was at his disposal everywhere. Officially he only acted as an "Advisor" to the Hungarian authorities; in reality everything took place on German orders.

15 May 1944 General and total deportation begins. One day before the evacuation all hospital cases, newly born babies, blind and deaf, all mental cases and prison inmates of Jewish origin were transferred to the Ghettos. About 80-100 Jews were placed in each cattle-car with one bucket of water; the car was then sealed down. At Kassa the deportation trains were taken over from the escorting Hungarian gendarmerie by the SS. While searching for "hidden valuables" the gendarmerie squads tortured the inmates with electric current and beat them mercilessly. Hundreds committed suicide. Those who protested or resisted were shot at once (as for instance Dr. Rosenfeld, solicitor of Marosvasarhely).

The Hungarian press and radio kept quiet about the deportations. The Hungarian government denied in the foreign press that Jews were tortured.

Between 5 June and 8 June 1944 Eichmann told me: "We accepted the obligation toward the Hungarians that not a single deported Jew will return alive!"

Up to 27 June 1944 475,000 Jews were deported.

The Pope and the King of Sweden intervened with Horthy. Then followed the ultimatumlike appeal of President Roosevelt to stop the brutal anti-Jewish persecutions. Thereupon Horthy has forbidden the deportation of the Jews from the capital which was already fixed to take place on July 5.

Endre, Baky, and the Germans protested against this decision and a further 30,000 Jews were deported from Transdanubia; the outer suburbs of Budapest were also emptied. Horthy dismissed Endre. But Eichmann, Endre, and Baky continued to try to liquidate the Jews of the capital with the collaboration of the gendarmerie. Liberators bombed Budapest and the railway junctions which were to be used by the deportation trains. Horthy has ordered the mobilization of the Army against an attempted coup d' etat (8 July). The gendarmerie thereupon went over to Horthy's side. But Eichmann emptied the camp of Kistarcsa by secretly collaborating with the Camp Commander and another 1,700 Jews were transported off in the direction of Oswiecim. On Horthy's orders the train was stopped at the frontier and the people were brought back. But Eichmann repeated his coup after 3 days and prevented any information reaching Horthy in time.

On 15 July 1944 an ultimatum was handed over by Wesenmayer, German Minister to the Hungarian Minister of Foreign Affairs demanding the deportation of the Budapest Jews. The Hungarian Government replied in a note to the effect that it was prepared to transfer the Budapest Jews to satisfy demands of military security, but only within the borders of the country. (27 July).

Allied successes have strengthened the position of the Hungarian Government against the Germans. Lakatos, new Hungarian Prime Minister sent a note to the German Government demanding the recall of Eichmann and his staff from Hungary, the transfer of the German-controlled internment camps to Hungarian authorities and the handing over of Hungarian politicians and high-ranking officers in German captivity to the Hungarians.

On 25 August 1944 the following instructions received from

Himmler, Wesenmayer informed the Hungarian Government that its demands would be fulfilled by the Germans.

But on 15 October 1944 a German coup ended the Horthy regime and Szalasy took over power. On 17 October Eichmann returns to Budapest by air. On his order the Arrow-Cross Party and the police began the deportation of all Jews locked into the houses marked by yellow stars; 25,000 Jewish people, mostly women were made to walk over 100 miles in rain and snow without food to the Austrian border; hundreds died on the way, more died in Austria through exhaustion and dysentery. On the border the transports were taken over by Wisliczeny; 20,000 Labor Service men shared the same fate.

The German authorities were the same as before; the most active Hungarian collaborators were: Minister Emil Kovarcz, Solymosi, Under-Secretary of State, and Ladislas Ferenczi, Lt. Col. of the gendarmerie.

On 8 December the deportations from Budapest stopped. According to Wisliczeny, Eichmann refused to carry out Himmler's order to stop deportations until he received written instructions from Himmler himself. Until 11 February 1945 the Arrow-Cross party-men did not stop to hunt down Jews in hiding, living on false papers; 10-15,000 Jews were shot on the shores of the Danube or in the streets during these 2 months. Thousands have died in the Ghettos, as well as in the "protected houses" of the Swedish and Swiss Legations, as a result of enemy action, sickness or starvation.

The losses of Hungarian Jewry

The 1940-41 census found 762,000 persons of Jewish persuasion within what was then Hungarian territory. But the persecution was extended to the Converted Jews, as well as to mixed marriages, of whom there were no official figures. Their numbers were estimated generally at 60,000.

According to figures estimated in August 1945:

There are at present in Budapest	150,000 Jews
In the provinces	40,000 Jews
In Transylvania (returned to Rumania), in Ruthenia (attached to Russia), in Upper Hungary (attached to Slovakia), and in the Backa (returned to Yugoslavia), there are estimated to be	50,000 Jews
Total	240,000 Jews
In territory occupied by the Allies and in Russia, Sweden and Switzerland approx.	50,000 Jews
Total	290,000 Jews

The Documentary Evidence   2605-PS

Of the 10,000 or so Slovakian, Polish, Yugoslav, and German Jews who were in Hungary at the time of the German occupation only about 750 are still alive, according to a reliable estimate.

Therefore, a total of 540,000 Hungarians and 10,000 refugee Jews perished, of them—

> The Germans were responsible for the death of. .450,000
> The Hungarians were responsible for the death of 80,000
> Suicides, sickness, enemy (allied) action. 20,000
>   ———
>   550,000

The figures concerning the deported Jews originate from Wisliczeny, who directed the deportations and was fully competent to give these figures.

It may be added that the objective of the new wave of deportations which started at the end of October 1944 was no longer Oswiecim. On this occasion older people, children, and the sick were not deported. Those who remained alive after the long journey on foot were — in the majority — employed on fortifications works along the Austro-Hungarian border; a lesser number were sent to Oranienburg, Dachau, and Bergen-Belsen.

General History of the Annihilation of the Jews Section IV.B. and the Annihilation of the Jews

Pogroms and the creation of the Ghettos organized in various centers in Poland during 1939-40 represented a period of hesitation. At that time the extinction of all European Jews was planned, but it was not finally decided upon. The Lublin "reservation," the playing of the Nazis with the idea of a Jewish center were expressions of this period of hesitation. The decision to exterminate the Jews was probably reached in 1941. In the occupied Baltic countries and in the Ukraine the SS formation working jointly with the Wehrmacht annihilated nearly all Jews (in the Baltic countries they were helped by the Latvians and Lithuanians). The mass-murder was carried out with the aid of bullets. The victims often dug their own tombs. Frequently they were buried alive. Then began the use of gas. The victims were killed by gas bursting out inside hermetically sealed lorries.

In the fall of 1941—according to a statement of Wisliczeny—made to me in January 1945 in Vienna—Kaltenbrunner commissioned SS Standartenfuehrer Blobl to work out the plan of the gas chambers. In the opinion of Wisliczeny the initiative came from Eichmann. Hitler approved of the plan at once. The

III - 387

execution was entrusted to the Eichmann-Himmler-Kaltenbrunner trio.

In December 1941 the first tests were carried out in Belzecz. According to a statement of Wisliczeny made to me in Vienna in February '45 it was a complete success. Thereupon three more death-camps were set up in Treblinka, Majdanek and Oswiecim [Auschwitz]. (Later a smaller camp was set up in Kalkini.)

According to statements of Krumey and Wisliczeny in February or March 1945 a conference of the officers of IV.B. was called to Berlin by Eichmann in the spring of 1942. He then informed them that the Government decided in favor of the complete annihilation of the European Jews and that this will be carried out silently in the gas chambers. "Victory is ours" declared Eichmann. "The end of the war is near. We must hurry as this is the last chance to free Europe of the Jews. After the war it will not be possible to utilize such methods."

Wisliczeny claims that he interjected the following remark to Eichmann's statement: "God help us that this method should never be possible against us."

Krumey confirmed this statement of Wisliczeny. He maintained that until the secret—which had to be kept strictly—was revealed by Eichmann, none of the officers of IV.B. knew anything about it.

The entire machinery of the German State supported Section IV.B. in this work. In occupied countries the Commanders of the Wehrmacht and the Gauleiters (Seyss-Inquart, Frank, Heydrich, etc.) in countries allied to Germany the German diplomats (Killinger in Bucharest, Wesenmayer in Zagreb, later in Budapest) supported the work.

The plan of operation was almost identical in all countries; at first Jews were marked, then separated, divested of all property, deported and gassed.

The Officers of IV.B. traveled from country to country. Wisliczeny—according to his own admission—directed the deportation in Slovakia and Greece.

> Brunner II. in Poland and Slovakia.
> Krumey, Seidl directed the work in Hungary, Austria, and Poland.
> Seidl was the first commander of Theresienstadt.
> Guenther directed deportations in Austria and Czechoslovakia.
> Danegger, Brunner in France.

Almost everywhere the local Quisling authorities and even part of the civilian populations assisted them.

Commanders of the death-camps gassed only on direct or indirect instructions of Eichmann. The particular Officer of IV.B. who directed the deportations from some particular country had the authority to indicate whether the train should go to a death camp or not, and what should happen to the passengers. The instructions were usually carried by the SS-NCO escorting the train. The letters "A" or "M" on the escorting instruction documents indicated Auschwitz (Oswiecim) or Majdanek; it meant that the passengers were to be gassed.

In case of doubt instructions by wire were asked from Eichmann in Berlin.

Regarding Hungarian Jews the following general ruling was laid down in Oswiecim: children up to the age of 12 or 14, older people above 50, as well as the sick, or people with criminal records (who were transported in specially marked wagons) were taken immediately on their arrival to the gas chambers.

The others passed before an SS doctor who, on sight, indicated who was fit for work, and who was not. Those unfit were sent to the gas chambers, while the others were distributed in various labor camps.

In September 1944 Slovakian partisans engineered the revolt in Banska-Bystricza. The Jewish youth joined the revolution enthusiastically. Eichmann thereupon sent SS Hauptsturmfuehrer Brunner to Bratislava with instructions to deport all the 17,000-odd Jews still left behind after the deportations of 1942. They were to go to Oswiecim.

SS and Hlinka-Guards arrested the Jews. They were transported from Sered. About 13,500 Jews were caught, the rest were in hiding. Following my appeal the A.D.C. of Becher Capt. Grueson journeyed to Bratislava and tried to intervene with SS Obersturmbannfuehrer Vitezka, Slovakian Gestapo Chief to stop the deportations. Vitezka's reply was: "As far as I am concerned I will agree readily if I get telegraphic authority from Kaltenbrunner to this effect." Becher said on 2 November 1944, in the Hotel Walhalla, St. Gallen, Switzerland, in the presence of the representative of the Joint D.C.: " We have militarily annihilated the Slovakian Jews."

In the first half of November 1944 about 20,000 Jews were taken from Theresienstadt to Oswiecim and were gassed, on instructions from Eichmann. As far as I could ascertain this was the last gassing process.

According to Becher, Himmler issued instructions—on his advice—on 25 November 1944 to dynamite all the gas-chambers and crematoria of Oswiecim. He also issued a ban on further murdering of Jews.

Wisliczeny confirmed the existence of such an order. But he maintained that Eichmann sabotaged this order and was supported in this by Mueller and Kaltenbrunner.

Following the advance of the Russian Army it was necessary to evacuate the Polish and Silesian camps. Some of the Jewish prisoners were sent to Bergen-Belsen or other camps. Most of the Jews found in these camps by the Allies arrived there either at the end of 1944 or at the beginning of 1945. Other Jews in the extermination camps were shot, or were frozen dead on the way.

There were no mass-murders in the months preceding the German surrender but owing to starvation—due partly to the collapse of the German transport system and the general lack of food—the sick and weakened Jews died by the thousands.

After the fall of 1944 Himmler granted several concessions. Thus he permitted the departure for Switzerland of 1,700 Hungarian Jews deported to Bergen-Belsen and also agreed to suspend the annihilation of the Jews of the Budapest Ghetto. Himmler permitted the handing over to the Allies the Jews of Bergen-Belsen and Theresienstadt without a shot being fired, which in his eyes and eyes of his colleagues was such a generous and colossal concession that he certainly hoped some political concession in return. In the hope of establishing contact with the Allies Himmler made some concessions even without expecting economic returns. To this desire of Himmler may be ascribed the general prohibition dated 25 November 1944; concerning the further killing of Jews. On 27 November 1944 Becher showed me a copy of Himmler's order on this subject. Eichmann at first did not obey this order.

In accordance with my above described activities I had dealings among others with the following individuals:

Germans: Special Section Commando (for the Liquidation of Jews):

    Adolf Eichmann, SS-Obersturmbannfuehrer, head of section IV.B. in the Reich Security Head Office and the following officers of his staff:

        SS Obersturmbannfuehrer Guenther; Danegger; Hermann Krumey.

        SS Hauptsturmfuehrer Dieter Wisliczeny; Dr. Seidl; Novak; Hunsche; Schmiedsieffen.

    Several NCO's, among them:

        Hauptsturmfuehrer Richter.

Oberscharfuehrer Nuemann.
Special Staff (Economic Staff):
    SS Standartenfuehrer Kurt Becher, and some officers of his staff.
SS Standartenfuehrer Wesenmayer, German Minister in Budapest (after 19 March 1945).

Hungarians:
    Nicholas Mester, Under-Secretary of State in the Ministry of Education.
    Ladislas Vitez Ferenczy, Lt. Col. of the Gendarmerie.
    Leo Lullay, Captain of the Gendarmerie.
    Dr. Stephen Olah, Counselor of the Ministry.
    Ladislas Baky, Under-Secretary in the Ministry of Interior.

Hungarian Resistance Workers:
    Henry Lazar, present Hungarian Under-Secretary of State to the Ministry of Agriculture.
    Nicholas Kertesz, former Social-democratic member of Parliament.
    Bela Zsolt, journalist.
    A. Bereczky, Trustee of the Calvinist Church.

Neutrals:
    Prof. Waldemar Langlet, Cultural Counselor of the Swedish Legation.
    Count Tolstov) Representatives of the Swedish Red
) Cross;
    Paul Wallenberg) Head of the protection of foreign in-
    Consul Lutz   ) terests Section of the Swiss Lega-
) tion.
    Freidrich Born, delegate of the International Red Cross.
    The Charge d'Affaires of the Swiss Legation.
    The Charge d'Affaires of the Spanish Legation.

Jews:
    All members of the Jewish Council, especially Samuel Stern (Court Counselor), Chairman of the Pest Jewish Community.
    Dr. Charles Wilhelm; Dr. Ernest Petoe, Dr. Boda (Chief Government Counselor), Vice-chairman.
    Philip Freudiger, President of the Orthodox Jewish Community and members of the council of that Community.
    Otto Komoly, President of the Zionist Organization.
    Nicholas Krausz, head of the Palestine Office of the Jewish Agency.

[signed] DR. KASTNER REZSOE
DR. REZSOE (RUDOLF) KASTNER

Subscribed and sworn to before me this 13th day of September 1945 at the Office of the United States Chief of Counsel, 49 Mount Street, London W.1, England.

[signed] WARREN F. FARR
WARREN F. FARR
Major, Judge Advocate General's
Dept., Office U. S. Chief of Counsel

Copy of Document 2613-PS. *Excerpts from "The Black Book of Poland" describing ghettos in Poland and forced labor for Jews.*

* * *

THE BLACK BOOK OF POLAND
[Page 236]

The Lublin Reservation

In a speech on 10 October 1939, Hitler hinted at a general solution of the Jewish problem as one of his war aims, but he did not go into details. Soon afterwards, the establishment of a so-called "Jewish reservation" in the Lublin area was begun. It is significant that the Nazis themselves have written almost nothing about this "reservation." Only through neutral sources did it leak out that large numbers of Jews were being transferred from Western Poland, Bohemia, and Austria to the Lublin area.

"The haste with which the reservation has been established out of nothing is leading to desperate situations. Sometimes trains drive on for 40 kilometers beyond Lublin and halt in the open country, where the Jews alight with their luggage and have to find themselves primitive accommodations in the surrounding villages. Up to November 10 about 45,000 Jewish men, women, and children from Cieszyn, Bogumin, Moravska Ostrava, Prague, Pilzno, other towns of the Protectorate, and from Vienna and the new Reich provinces, Danzig-Westpreussen and Posen-Warthegau, have been sent to the reservation. Under the supervision of men of the SS-Death's-head Corps, the Jews are compelled to work at road-building, draining marshes, and rebuilding the damaged villages. There is compulsory labour service for men up to seventy years and for women up to fifty-five." (Luxemburger Wort, 21 November 1939.)

"Up to now some 8,000 persons, one-third of them women

and children, have been transported to the resettlement camps in the Jewish reservation. These camps are about 15-20 km. from Niske, a Polish town on the San which suffered severely in the war. These camps are completely isolated behind high barbed wire fences and the Gestapo maintains a strict control over them." (National-Zeitung, Basle, 7 November 1939.)

The methods adopted when Jews are transported to this reservation can be gathered from a letter sent by the Israelitische Kultusgemeinde Wien to those of the Viennese Jews who were chosen by the authorities to be transported to Lublin. It runs:

"By order of the authorities a large transport of Jews, fit to work, up to fifty years of age, will go to Poland on October 18, 1939, to start colonizing work. You have been chosen by the authorities to go with this transport and you have to appear on October 17, 1939, at 6 AM in * * *. Every person in this transport is permitted to take with him clothes and equipment up to 50 kg in weight. Every person is allowed to take money up to 300 marks. It is of the greatest importance that all concerned should take builders' tools with them, such as mallets, saws, planes, hammers, and nails, and when reporting, an exact statement must be made as to which of these tools you can provide. Should you disobey this summons, which has been issued by the State authorities, you will have to face the consequences." (See photograph No. 54.)

[Page 241]

The Ghetto in Warsaw

When the ghetto idea was adopted finally, it was carried out with German thoroughness. At first, a few weeks after the occupation, the German authorities had tried to drive all the Jews in Warsaw into a ghetto.

The Warsaw Jews, by payment of a heavy fine, were able to avoid the overhasty establishment of the ghetto, which would have created very difficult problems. This fine, however, did not achieve anything more than postponement.

Already in April 1940, the area destined for the ghetto was called "the closed, contaminated area" and was surrounded by walls. In October last the Governor of Warsaw, Fischer, and his delegate, Leist, issued a series of orders defining the limits of the ghetto, ordering the concentration of Jews from all over Warsaw within these limits, and the expulsion from the newly formed ghetto of all Aryans. These migrations had to take place before 31 October 1940. Thus 110,000 Jews and 80,000 Poles were given 12 days in which to move. Both Poles and Jews hurried to migrate, although the removals were very difficult and expensive in view of the many houses destroyed and of the lack of means of transport. The time limit had to be postponed until 15 November 1940. Meanwhile the limits of the ghetto were twice changed, on one occasion being reduced, on the other enlarged. For various reasons the most fantastic enclaves were made. For instance, the market halls, the Law Courts in Leszne Street, and many works under German direction were not included in the ghetto, although they are in the heart of the old Jewish district. As a result, both Poles and Jews had to move several times. The Jews who were removed to the ghetto were forbidden to take anything with them with the exception of hand luggage.

On 16 November, the ghetto was closed without any warning. An 8-foot high concrete wall was built to enclose the district. The supplies of food to the ghetto were stopped. The German police confiscated the food carried to the ghetto by Poles, and also the food, transported by Poles in tramcars, passing through the ghetto. Food prices in the ghetto soared. When the ghetto was closed the German police started practicing endless chicanery towards the Jews. The Jews had to take off their hats to German policemen. They were ordered to exercise with bricks or concrete slabs in their hands, to climb telephone poles, to wash in the gutters, etc. The police shot at sight Poles or Jews who tried to get food into the ghetto (about 20 Jews and Poles were killed). Germans in uniform rob the homes of the richer Jews (in the Leszne and Ogrodowa Street), taking away furniture, money, and even food.

[Page 243]

The Ghetto in Lodz

Warsaw is by no means the only place where the Jews have been herded into a ghetto. The same process took place in many other towns with large Jewish populations, although it was not tackled everywhere with the same thoroughness as in Warsaw.

A very similar position to that in Warsaw has developed at Lodz. This big industrial town of Central Poland was formally annexed by Germany and even given a new name "Litzmannstadt."

[Page 244]

On 30 April the Jewish quarter in the northern part of Lodz was finally barred off. Here all the Jews of the town were compelled to live. Again, of course, hygienic reasons were given for this step. But it is admitted that economic reasons too had influenced the Germans to introduce this measure. Jews had played an important part in the economic life of Lodz and had contributed to the importance of this town as an industrial center.

In order to get hold of businesses founded by Jews and to rob them of the raw material in their possession, the ghetto plan proved very convenient. This is openly admitted in the Deutsche Allgemeine Zeitung of 13 October 1940.

[Page 246]

The Ghetto of Cracow

At the beginning of 1941 the German authorities decided to organize a ghetto in Cracow. Originally, as already said, the Germans intended to expel the Jews from Cracow altogether, and in fact a large number were expelled. Later a decision was taken to leave some 20,000 Jews in the city. Part of a suburb of Cracow, Podgozre, situated on the right bank of the river Vistula, has been assigned as the ghetto area. The Poles living in this area have been ordered to shift to other parts of the city. The general order issued by Dr. Frank was applied to Cracow in a decree issued by the Chief of the Cracow district on 3 March and published in the Krakauer Zeitung of 6 March 1941. This decree provides for the creation of a special closed ghetto district in Cracow.

[Page 247]

Health in the Ghetto

No official figures have been published relating to the hygienic conditions in occupied Poland, but occasionally notes and articles in the German press reveal that health conditions, particularly in the Jewish quarters, are anything but good. Considering that the Jews are all but starving, this is hardly surprising. According to the Hamburger Fremdenblatt of 29 October 1940, 98 percent of the cases of typhoid and spotted fever in Warsaw were in the ghetto. The delegation of the American Joint Distribution Committee reported that all but 8 percent of the typhoid cases in Warsaw were among the Jewish population. Diseases due to malnutrition and overcrowding are used by the Nazis as a pretext for slandering the Jews and for further restrictions. The head of the Health Department in the "Government General," for instance, issued an order in March 1940, to the effect that in future Jews could only be attended by Jewish doctors.

The catastrophic condition of food supplies and terrible housing and sanitary conditions in the ghetto are causing a very high mortality, which is increasing with every month. In May 1941, the figure was 5,000, which is equal to 120 per thousand per annum. This is a twelvefold increase over the prewar rate.

As the birthrate has fallen to a minimum, there is not only no annual increase, but even a decline in the population. But this is more than offset by the continual influx of Jews compulsorily deported from the provincial towns, where the Germans do not propose to set up separate Jewish quarters.

[Page 571]

Decree Concerning the Introduction of Compulsory Labor for the Polish Population of the "Government General"

Dated October 26, 1939

Section 1

(1) All Polish inhabitants of the "Government General" between the ages of 18 and 60 years are subject to compulsory public labor with immediate effect.

Section 3

(2) Compulsory public labor comprises, in particular, work in agricultural concerns, the building and maintenance of public buildings, the construction of roads, waterways and railways, the regulation of rivers and land work.

[Page 572]

Section 4

(1) The payment of persons subject to compulsory labor shall be effected at rates that may be fair.

(2) The welfare of persons subject to compulsory labor and their families shall be secured as far as possible.

Section 5

The regulations required for the execution of the present Decree shall be issued by the Director of the Department of Labor in the office of the "Government General."

Warsaw, October 28, 1939.

[Page 573]

Decree Concerning the Introduction of Compulsory Labor for the Jewish Population of the "Government General"

Dated October 26, 1939

Section 1

Compulsory labor for the Jews domiciled in the "Government General" shall be introduced with immediate effect. The Jews shall for this purpose be formed into forced labor groups.

Section 2

The prescriptions required for the execution of the present Decree shall be issued by the higher SS and police leader. He may define territories east of the Vistula in which the execution of the present Decree shall be waived.

Warsaw, October 26, 1939.

The Documentary Evidence   2613-PS

The Governor-General for the Occupied Polish Territories
                                                    Frank
                        ─────────

Translation of Document 2620-PS (USA 919). *Affidavit of Otto Ohlendorf, Chief of the Security Service (intelligence and counter-intelligence agency of the SS), 5 November 1945, concerning his participation in liquidation in the East of 90,000 men, women and children, of whom the majority were Jews.*

* * *

AFFIDAVIT

I, Otto Ohlendorf, being first duly sworn, declare:

I was chief of the Security Service (SD), Amt III of the main office of the chief of the Security Police and the SD (RSHA), from 1939 to 1946. In June 1941 I was designated by Himmler to lead one of the special commitment groups [Einsatzgruppen], which were then being formed, to accompany the German armies in the Russian campaign. I was the chief of the Einsatzgruppe D. Chief of the Einsatzgruppe A was Stahlecker, department chief in the foreign office. Chief of Einsatzgruppe B was Nebe, chief of Amt V (KRIPO) of the Main Office of the chief of the security police and the SD (RSHA). Chief of Einsatzgruppe C was first Rasch (or Rasche) and then Thomas. Himmler stated that an important part of our task consisted of the extermination of Jews—women, men, and children—and of communist functionaries. I was informed of the attack on Russia about 4 weeks in advance.

According to an agreement with the armed forces high command and army high command, the special commitment detachments [Einsatzkommandos] within the army group or the army were assigned to certain army corps and divisions. The army designated the areas in which the special commitment detachments had to operate. All operational directives and orders for the carrying out of executions were given through the chief of the SIPO and the SD (RSHA) in Berlin. Regular courier service and radio communications existed between the Einsatzgruppen and the chief of the SIPO and the SD.

The Einsatzgruppen and Einsatzkommandos were commanded by personnel of the Gestapo, the SD, or the criminal police. Additional men were detailed from the regular police [Ordnungspolizei] and the Waffen SS. Einsatzgruppe D consisted of approximately 400 to 500 men and had about 170 vehicles at its disposal.

III - 397

When the Germany army invaded Russia, I was leader of the Einsatzgruppe D in the Southern sector, and in the course of the year, during which I was leader of the Einsatzgruppe D, it liquidated approximately 90,000 men, women, and children. The majority of those liquidated were Jews, but there were among them some communist functionaries too.

In the implementation of this extermination program the special commitment groups were subdivided into special commitment detachments, and the Einsatzkommandos into still smaller units, the so-called Special Purpose Detachments [Sonderkommandos] and Unit Detachments [Teilkommandos]. Usually, the smaller units were led by a member of the SD, the Gestapo, or the criminal police. The unit selected for this task would enter a village or city and order the prominent Jewish citizens to call together all Jews for the purpose of resettlement. They were requested to hand over their valuables to the leaders of the unit, and shortly before the execution to surrender their outer clothing. The men, women and children were led to a place of execution which in most cases was located next to a more deeply excavated antitank ditch. Then they were shot, kneeling or standing, and the corpses thrown into the ditch. I never permitted the shooting by individuals in the group D, but ordered that several of the men should shoot at the same time in order to avoid direct, personal responsibility. The leaders of the unit or especially designated persons, however, had to fire the last bullet against those victims who were not dead immediately. I learned from conversations with other group leaders that some of them demanded that the victims lie down flat on the ground to be shot through the nape of the neck. I did not approve of these methods.

In the spring of 1942 we received gas vehicles from the chief of the security police and the SD in Berlin. These vehicles were made available by Amt II of the RSHA. The man who was responsible for the cars of my Einsatzgruppe was Becher. We had received orders to use the cars for the killing of women and children. Whenever a unit had collected a sufficient number of victims, a car was sent for their liquidation. We also had these gas vehicles stationed in the neighborhood of the transient camps into which the victims were brought. The victims were told that they would be resettled and had to climb into the vehicles for that purpose. Then the doors were closed and the gas streamed in through the starting of the vehicles. The victims died within 10 to 15 minutes. The cars were then driven to the burial place, where the corpses were taken out and buried.

I have seen the report of Stahlecker [document L-180] concerning Einsatzgruppe A, in which Stahlecker asserts that his group killed 135,000 Jews and communists in the first 4 months of the program. I know Stahlecker personally, and I am of the opinion that the document is authentic.

I was shown the letter which Becher has written to Rauff, the head of the technical department of Amt II, in regard to the use of these gas vehicles. I know both these men personally, and am of the opinion that this letter is an authentic document.

[signed] Ohlendorf

Subscribed and sworn to before me this fifth day of November 1945 at Nurnberg, Germany.

[signed] Smith W. Brookhart
Lt. Col. IGD

Ex O—Ohlendorf
   Nov. 5, 45
   R. R. Kerry, Reporter.

Translation of Document 2622-PS. Affidavit of Otto Ohlendorf, Chief of the Security Service (intelligence and counter-intelligence agency of the SS) concerning execution of Jewish prisoners of war on eastern front.

* * *

DECLARATION UNDER OATH

I, Otto Ohlendorf, being first duly sworn, declare:

I was chief of the Security Service (SD), Amt III in the main office of the chief of the security police and of the SD (RSHA) from 1939 to 1943.

In 1941, shortly after the start of the campaign against Russia, an agreement was entered into between the chief of the Security Police and of the SD and the OKW (supreme command of the armed forces) and OKH (supreme command of the army) to the effect that operative detachments [Einsatzkommando] of the Security Police and SD were to go to the prisoner of war camps on the Eastern front to screen the prisoners of war. All Jews and communist functionaries were to be removed from the prisoner of war camps by the operative detachments and were to be executed outside of the camps. To my knowledge, this action was carried out throughout the entire Russian campaign.

In the other occupied territories and in the Reich—to my knowledge—the Gestapo had been made responsible for this program in the Russian prisoner of war camps. This action was, to my knowledge, carried on throughout the greater part of the war.

[signed] OHLENDORF

Translation of Document 2662-PS (USA 256). *Excerpt from Mein Kampf, 39th Edition, 1939, pp. 724-725 on the subject of the Jew as the evil enemy of mankind.*

* * *

MEIN KAMPF, Adolf Hitler
[Pages 724-725]

And again it is the National Socialist Movement which has to fulfill its most tremendous task:

It must open the eyes of the people with regard to foreign nations and must remind them again and again of the true enemy [the Jew] of our present-day world. In the place of the hate against Aryans — from whom we may be separated by almost everything, to whom however, we are tied by common blood or the great tie of a common culture—it must dedicate to the general anger the evil enemy of mankind, as the true cause of all suffering.

It must see to it, however, that, at least in our country, he be recognized as the most mortal enemy and that the struggle against him may show, like a flaming beacon of a better era, to other nations too, the road to salvation for a struggling Aryan mankind.

Translation of Document 2663-PS (USA 268). *Hitler's speech to the Reichstag, 30 January 1939, prophesying the annihilation of the Jewish race in Europe.*

* * *

VOELKISCHER BEOBACHTER, Munich Edition,
1 February 1939

Hitler speech to Reichstag of 30 January 1939

Once more I will assume the part of a prophet:

If the international Jewish financiers within and without Europe succeeded in plunging the nations once more into a world war, then the result will be not the Bolshevisation of the world and thereby the victory of Jewry—but the annihilation of the Jewish race in Europe. * * *

Translation of Document 2665-PS (USA 270). *The Jewish Question Past and Present, from "World Battle", April-September 1941, p. 71.*

* * *

WORLD BATTLE
[Weltkampf]
The Jewish Question Past and Present
[Die Judenfrage in Geschichte und Gegenwart]
Publisher: Wilhelm Grau; Editor: Peter-Heinz Seraphim
No. 1/2 April-September 1941, Page 71

"The Jewish question will be solved for Europe only when the last Jew has left the European continent."

Translation of Document 2668-PS (USA 269). *"And Don't Forget the Jews", from the Black Corps, 8 August 1940, No. 32, p. 2.*

* * *

THE BLACK CORPS [Das Schwarze Korps]
8 August 1940, No. 32, Page 2
* * * And Don't Forget The Jews

Just as the Jewish question will be solved for Germany only when the last Jew has been deported, the rest of Europe should also realize that the German peace which awaits it must be a peace without Jews.

Translation of Document 2673-PS. *Extract from "The Archive", No. 90, 30 October 1941, p. 495, concerning police decree requiring Jews to wear Jewish star in public.*

* * *

THE ARCHIVE
[Das Archiv]
No. 90, 30 October 1941, Page 495.

The Reich Minister of the Interior issued a police decree concerning marking of Jews, dated 1 September 1941 (RGBl. I, p. 547), according to which Jews, effective 19 September 1941, are allowed to appear in public only if they wear a yellow Jewish star, which has to be worn visibly on the left breast side of the upper garment.

Translation of Document 2682-PS. *Excerpts from newspaper Voelkischer Beobachter, 5 December 1938, No. 339, p. 5, concerning repeal of drivers' licenses and registration papers of Jews and restrictions against Jews prohibiting them from appearing in public in certain places in Berlin.*

* * *

VOELKISCHER BEOBACHTER
5 December 1938, No. 339, Page 5
NO MORE JEWISH DRIVERS

Immediate repeal of drivers' licenses and registration papers.

Heinrich Himmler, the Reichfuehrer SS and Chief of the German Police in the Reich Ministry of the Interior, issued the following preliminary police ordinance on the repeal of drivers' licenses and registration papers of mechanized vehicles issued to Jews.

The dastardly murder by the Jew Gruenspan which aimed at the entire German people makes the Jews appear as unreliable and unfit for owning and driving of mechanized vehicles. Subject to a definitive regulation the following is decreed:

1. For general security and police reasons and for the protection of the public I herewith prohibit all Jews of German nationality living in Germany from driving mechanized vehicles of all kinds and herewith repeal their drivers' licenses, effective immediately.

2. Jews of German nationality living in Germany are prohibited from owning cars and motorcycles (with and without sidecar). As to trucks additional regulation is reserved.

3. Jews of German nationality living in Germany must deliver up their drivers' licenses of all grades as well as the registration cards for cars and motorcycles without delay by 31 December 1938 at the latest to the respective police precincts or registration offices. The official plates are to be submitted with the registration cards for being destamped.

4. The competent police and administrative offices have to take the necessary measures.

5. Offenses will be punished in accordance with existing laws.

This police ordinance becomes effective immediately upon its publication by the press. No further communication will be made officially to the authorities in question.

RESTRICTION AGAINST JEWS IN BERLIN
BEGINNING 6 DECEMBER

In accordance with Reichs-Police-Decree [Reichspolizeiverordnung] of the 28 November 1938, Berlin, 4 December in regard to the appearance of Jews in public the President of the Police [Polizeipraesident] for the state police district [Landespolizeibezirk] of Berlin has issued a first order, which will become effective on the 6 December, 1938. It decrees, that streets, squares, parks, and buildings, which are affected by the restriction against Jews, are not to be entered or driven through in vehicles by Jews of German citizenship or by Jews without citizenship.

If such Jews are still residents of a district, which is affected by the restriction against Jews, at the time when this decree becomes effective, they will have to use a permit issued by the police station of this residential district in order to cross the border of the restricted area. Effective July 1939 and thereafter permits for residents of the restricted area will not be issued anymore.

The restriction against Jews in Berlin includes:

1. All theaters, cinemas, cabarets, public concert and lecture halls, museums, amusement places, the exhibition halls at the Messedamm including the exhibition area and radio-tower, the Deutschlandehalle and the Sports-place, the Reichs-sports-field [Reichssportsfeld], and all sports-places including the ice-skating rinks.

2. All public and private bathing establishments and indoor baths as well as open-air baths [Freibaeder].

3. The Wilhelmstrasse from the Leipziger Strasse up to Unter den Linden including the Wilhelmplatz.

4. The Vossstrasse from the Hermann-Goering-Strasse up to the Wilhelmstrasse.

5. The Reich-Honor-Monument [Reichsehrenmal] including the sidewalk on the north side of Unter den Linden from the university to the Zeughaus [Military Historical Museum].

Exempted from articles 1-2 are the institutions and events, which have been opened to Jewish visitors in accordance with properly authorized permission. Intentional or neglectful violation will be punished with a fine of up to 150 Reichsmark or confinement up to 6 weeks.

In addition it is announced among other things, that still more thorough orders of execution [Durchfuehrungsverordnungen] will be issued. This restriction against Jews does not apply to foreign Jews. It is probable that the restriction against Jews which has no time limits will soon be extended to include a large number of Berlin streets. In this respect the main streets and thoroughfares of Berlin especially come into consideration, because in these streets in particular Jewry even today more or less dominates the street scene. The rows of streets in the center and the north of Berlin, where the Jewish element has predominated for centuries already, as for example the Muenz-Linien-, and Grenadier-Strasse, will probably not be included in the districts restricted against Jews. It is therefore to be recommended that the Jews start right now looking for another residence in one of the above-mentioned parts of Berlin, and perhaps effect an exchange of residence with one of the blood Germans [Volksgenossen] residing there.

Furthermore, the Jews can figure on being restricted to purely Jewish inns in the future.

Translation of Document 2683-PS. *Newspaper report in Voelkischer Beobachter, 15/16 November 1938, of decree barring Jews from German universities.*

* * *

VOELKISCHER BEOBACHTER
15/16 November 1938
UNIVERSITIES BARRED FOR JEWS

A decree of the Reich Minister for Education taking immediate effect.

It is known that the Reich Minister for Science, Training, and Education for a long time has admitted Jews to the German universities to a very modest extent only. The draft of a bill now in preparation provides that in future no more Jews will be admitted to German universities.

The indignation of the German people aroused by the infamous crime of the Jew Gruenspan called for immediate action as German students cannot be expected to work along with Jews in the universities and their installations any longer. Reich Minister Rust therefore has ordered the rectors of German universities by telegraph to prohibit Jews from participating in the lectures and exercises as well as from entering the university buildings.

Translation of Document 2697-PS (USA 259). *Article: "The Chosen People of the Criminals" from newspaper Der Stuermer, No. 2, January 1935.*

* * *

DER STUERMER, No. 2, January 1935, Page 4.
THE CHOSEN PEOPLE OF THE CRIMINALS

The history book of the Jews which is usually called the "Holy Scriptures" impresses us as a horrible criminal romance

* * *

This "holy" book abounds in murder, incest, fraud, theft, and indecency. * * *

Translation of Document 2698-PS (USA 260). Article: "Two Little Talmud Jews" from newspaper Der Stuermer, No. 50, December 1938.

* * *

DER STUERMER, No. 50,
December 1938, Page 1.
TWO LITTLE TALMUD JEWS

The Thora is the old testament law book of the Jews. It contains:

The five books of Moses and all the oaths, curses, the criminal recipes and provisions of the God Jehovah for the Jewish people.

The Talmud is the great Jewish book of crimes that the Jew practices in his daily life.

Translation of Document 2699-PS (USA 258). Article: "Ritual Murder" from Der Stuermer, No. 14, April 1937.

* * *

DER STUERMER, Nurnberg, April 1937, No. 14,
Vol. 15, Pages 1-2.
RITUAL MURDER

The murder of the 10 year old Gertrud Lenhoff in Quirschied (Saarpfalz) * * * The Jews are our MISFORTUNE!

* * *

Also the numerous confessions made by the Jews show that the execution of ritual murders is a law to the Talmud Jew. The former Chief Rabbi (and later monk) Teofiti declares, f. i., that the ritual murders take place especially on the Jewish Purim (in memory of the Persian murders) and Passover (in memory of the murder of Christ).

The instructions are as follows:

The blood of the victims is to be tapped by force. On Passover, it is to be used in wine and matzos; thus, a small part of the blood is to be poured into the dough of the matzos and into the wine. The mixing is done by the Jewish head of the family.

The procedure is as follows: the family head empties a few

drops of the fresh and powdered blood into the glass, wets the fingers of the left hand with it and sprays (blesses) with it everything on the table. The head of the family then says: "Dam Izzardia chynim heroff dever Isyn porech harbe hossen maschus pohorus" (Exod. VII, 12) ("Thus we ask God to send the ten plagues to all enemies of the Jewish faith.") Then they eat, and at the end the head of the family exclaims: "Sfach, chaba, moscho kol hagoyim!" ("May all Gentiles perish—as the child whose blood is contained in the bread and wine!")

The fresh (or dried and powdered) blood of the slaughtered is further used by young married Jewish couples, by pregnant Jewesses, for circumcision and so on. Ritual murder is recognized by all Talmud Jews. The Jew believes he absolves himself thus of his sins.

Translation of Document 2700-PS. Article: "The Ritual Murder" from newspaper Der Stuermer, No. 28, July 1938.

* * *

DER STUERMER
Edited by Julius Streicher
Nurnberg, July 1938, Nr. 28, vol. 16, Page 5.
The ritual murder Jews slaughter [schaechten] men

Whoever had the occasion to be an eyewitness during the slaughtering of animals or to see at least a truthful film on the slaughtering, will never forget this horrible experience. It is atrocious. And unwillingly, he is reminded of the crimes, which the Jews have committed for centuries on men. He will be reminded of the ritual murder. History points out hundreds of cases, in which non-Jewish children were tortured to death. They also were given the same incision through the throat as is found on slaughtered animals. They also were slowly bled to death while fully conscious.

Translation of Document 2704-PS. Decree concerning Prohibition of Jewish Religious Slaughter of animals, in General Government of Poland, 26 October 1939.

* * *

VERORDNUNGSBLATT OF THE GOVERNOR GENERAL FOR THE OCCUPIED POLISH TERRITORY, 1939 Page 7.

Decree Concerning the Prohibition of Jewish
Religious Slaughter
By the virtue of Section 5, paragraph 1, of the decree of the

Fuehrer and Reichschancellor concerning the administration of the occupied Polish territories of 12 October 1939, I decree as follows:

Section 1

Cruelty to animals in any form is untenable in an area under German sovereignty. Therefore, effective immediately, I forbid Jewish ritual slaughter [Schaechten], that is, the painful killing of animals by slow bleeding, for the purpose of consumption of so-called kosher meat.

Section 2

(1) A person who is guilty of Jewish ritual slaughter shall be punished by internment in a penitentiary for a term of not less than 1 year.

(2) The same punishment that applies to the person committing the crime shall apply to an accessory, instigator, and accomplice.

(3) The attempt shall be punished in the same manner as the accomplished crime.

(4) Sentence to internment in a penitentiary can be executed by internment in concentration camps.

Warsaw, 26 October 1939
The Governor General for Occupied Polish Territories
FRANK

Translation of Document 2705-PS. Decree of Reich Commissioner for Occupied Netherland Territories for the avoidance of cruelty to animals in slaughtering, 3 August 1940.

* * *

OFFICIAL GAZETTE [VERORDNUNGSBLATT] FOR THE OCCUPIED NETHERLAND TERRITORIES

Article 16 published on August 3, 1940.
80.

Decree of the Reich Commissioner for the Occupied Netherland Territories for the Avoidance of Cruelty to Animals in Slaughtering

On (the basis of Article 5 of the Fuehrer's decree re executory powers of the government in the Netherlands of May 18, 1940 (RBGl. I S.788) I decree:

Article 1

(1) In slaughtering, warm-blooded animals are to be stunned before beginning the drawing of blood.

(2) During forced slaughterings (Article 3 of the law re

2705-PS Nazi Germany's War Against the Jews

Inspection of shambles [Fleischschaugesetz] Official Gazette [Staatsblatt] 1919 Nr.524) in which the situation does not permit the stunning of the animal, the rule of paragrah 1 is not applied.

Article 2

(1) The stipulations necessary for the execution of this decree will be issued jointly by the Secretary General in the Ministry of Social Affairs and the Secretary General in the Ministry of Agriculture and Fisheries.

(2) They will be published in the "Nederlandsche Staatscourant."

Article 3

(1) Whoever violates premeditatedly the rules of this decree or the stipulations necessary to its execution, will be punished with imprisonment up to the maximum of 6 months or with a fine up to 10,000 guilder.

(2) These violations are crimes.

Article 4

This decree will be effective as of 5 August 1940.

The Hague, 31 July 1940
The Reich Commissioner for the Occupied
Netherland Territories:
Seyss-Inquart

Copy of Document 2709-PS (USA 265). Report of Ralph C. Busser, American Consul-General in Leipzig, 5 April 1933, concerning anti-Jewish movement in central Germany.

* * *

PRESENT OPERATION AND EFFECT OF THE
ANTI-JEWISH MOVEMENT IN CENTRAL GERMANY,
Pages 23, 40-41.

From
Ralph C. Busser, American Consul, Leipzig, Germany.
Date of Completion: April 5, 1933.
Date of Mailing: April 10, 1933.

In Dresden several weeks ago uniformed "Nazis" raided the Jewish Prayer House (Bethaus), interrupted the evening religious service, arrested 25 worshippers, and tore the holy insignia or emblems from their head covering worn while praying.

Eighteen Jewish shops, including a bakery, mostly in Chemnitz, had their windows broken by rioters led by uniformed "Nazis."

Five of the Polish Jews arrested in Dresden were compelled to each drink one-half liter of castor oil. As most of the victims of assault are threatened with worse violence if they report the attacks, it is not known to what extent fanatical "Nazis" are still terrorizing Jews, communists, and Social Democrats, who are considered as favoring the old Parliamentary regime in Germany.

Some of the Jewish men assaulted had to submit to the shearing of their beards, or to the clipping of their hair in the shape of steps. One Polish Jew in Chemnitz had his hair torn out by the roots.

Translation of Document 2711-PS (USA 267). Article: "Symbolic Action" published in newspaper Fraenkische Tageszeitung—Nurnberg, 11 August 1938, concerning destruction of the Synagogue in Nurnberg.

* * *

FRAENKISCHE TAGESZEITUNG—NURNBERG
No. 186, Thursday, 11th August 1938, Pages 1-2, 4.
Symbolic action

In Nurnberg the Synagogue is being demolished! Julius Streicher himself inaugurates the work by a speech lasting more than an hour and a half. By his order then—so to speak as a prelude of the demolition—the tremendous Star of David came off the cupola. * * *

[Caption for picture]

Julius Streicher thanks the mayor of the city of the Reich Party Rallies [Reichsparteitage], Willy Liebel, for his energetic support.

[Caption for picture]

The crown of the cupola, the Jewish Star of David, disappears forever.

Translation of Document 2712-PS. Account of spontaneous anti-Jewish demonstrations throughout Germany, from newspaper Voelkischer Beobachter, 11 November 1938.

* * *

VOELKISCHER BEOBACHTER, Friday, 11 November 1938,
No. 315, Page 2, Column 2
ANTI-JEWISH DEMONSTRATIONS THROUGHOUT THE REICH

Berlin 10, November.

On the announcement of the death of the German diplomat, von Rath, who was killed at the hands of a cowardly Jewish assassin, spontaneous anti-Jewish demonstrations have developed throughout the Reich.

Translation of Document 2738-PS (USA 296). Affidavit of Wilhelm Hoettl, a member of the Security Service (intelligence and counter-intelligence agency of the SS), 26 November 1945, in which proof is given that 6 million Jews were killed by the Germans.

* * *

AFFIDAVIT OF DR. WILHELM HOETTL
26 November 1945

I, Wilhelm Hoettl, state herewith under oath:

My name is Dr. Wilhelm Hoettl, SS-Sturmbannfuehrer (Major of the SS). My occupation until the German collapse was that of a reporter and deputy Gruppenleiter in Amt VI (Office VI) of the Reichs Security Office [Reichssicherheitshauptampt].

Amt VI of the RSHA was the so-called Foreign Section of the Security Service and it was engaged in the Intelligence Service in all countries in the world. It corresponded somewhat to the English Intelligence Service. The group to which I belonged was occupied in the Intelligence Service of Southeastern Europe (the Balkans).

At the end of August 1944 I was talking to SS-Obersturmbannfuehrer Adolf Eichmann, whom I had known since 1938. The conversation took place in my home in Budapest.

According to my knowledge Eichmann was, at that time, Abteilungsleiter in Amt IV (the Gestapo) of the Reich Security Office [Reichssicherheitshauptampt] and in addition to that he had been ordered by Himmler to get a hold of the Jews in all the European countries and to transport them to Germany. Eichmann was then very much impressed with the fact that Rumania had withdrawn from the war in those days. Therefore, he had come to me to get information about the military situation which I received daily from the Hungarian Ministry of War and from the Commander of the Waffen-SS in Hungary. He expressed his conviction that Germany had now lost the war and that he, personally, had no further chance. He knew that he would be considered one of the main war criminals by the United Nations since he had millions of Jewish lives on his conscience. I asked him how many that was, to which he answered that although the number was a great Reich secret, he would tell me since I, as a historian, would be interested and that he would probably not return anyhow from his command in Rumania. He had, shortly before that, made a report to Himmler, as the latter wanted to know the exact number of Jews who had been killed. On the basis of his information he had obtained the following result:

Approximately four million Jews had been killed in the various extermination camps while an additional two million met death in other ways, the major part of which were shot by operational squads of the Security Police during the campaign against Russia.

Himmler was not satisfied with the report since, in his opinion, the number of Jews, who had been killed, must have been more than six million. Himmler had stated, that he would send a man from his Office of Statistics to Eichmann, so that he could make a new report on the basis of Eichmann's material, in which exact figures should be worked out.

I have to believe that this information, given to me by Eichmann, was correct, as he, among all the persons in question, certainly had the best survey of the figures of the Jews who had been murdered. In the first place, he "delivered" so to speak the Jews to the extermination camps through his special squads and knew, therefore, the exact figure and, in the second place, as Abteilungsleiter in Amt IV (the Gestapo) of the RSHA, who was also responsible for Jewish matters, he knew indeed better than anyone else the number of Jews who had died in other ways.

In addition to that, Eichmann was at that moment in such a state of mind as the result of the events, that he certainly had no intention of telling me something that was not true.

I, myself, know the details of this conversation so well because I was, naturally, very much affected and I had already, prior to the German collapse, given detailed data about it to American Quarters in a neutral foreign country with which I was in touch at that time.

I hereby swear, that the above statements have been made by me voluntarily and without duress or compulsion, and that the above statements are true according to my best knowledge and belief.

                [signed]   Dr. Wilhelm Hoettl

Signed and sworn to before me in Nurnberg, Germany this 26th day of November 1945.

[signed] Frederick L. Felton
Lieutenant USNR
#253345

Translation of Document 2746-PS. Decree concerning organization of Criminal Jurisdiction against Poles and Jews in the Incorporated Eastern Territories, 4 December 1941.

* * *

1941 REICHSGESETZBLATT, PART I, PAGES 759-761
ORGANIZATION OF CRIMINAL JURISDICTION

Decree concerning the Organization of Criminal Jurisdiction against Poles and Jews in the Incorporated Eastern Territories, 4th December 1941

The Council of Ministers for the Defense of the Reich herewith decrees:

1. CRIMINAL LAW

I

(1) Poles and Jews in the Incorporated Eastern Territories are to conduct themselves in conformity with the German laws and with the regulations introduced for them by the German authorities. They are to abstain from any conduct liable to prejudice the sovereignty of the German Reich or the prestige of the German people.

(2) The death penalty shall be imposed on any Pole or Jew if he commits an act of violence against a German on account of his being of German blood.

(3) A Pole or Jew shall be sentenced to death, or in less serious cases to imprisonment, if he manifests anti-German sentiments by malicious activities or incitement, particularly by making anti-German authorities or offices, or if he, by his conduct, lowers or prejudices the prestige or the well-being of the German Reich or the German people.

(4) The death penalty or, in less serious cases, imprisonment shall be imposed on any Pole or Jew:

1. If he commits any act of violence against a member of the German armed forces or associated services, of the German police force or its auxiliaries, of the Reich labor service, of any German authority or office or a section of the N.S.D.A.P.;

2. If he purposely damages installations of the German authorities or offices, objects used by them in performance of their duties or objects of public utility;

3. If he urges or incites to disobedience to any decree or regulation issued by the German authorities;

III - 412

4. If he conspires to commit an act punishable under subsections (2), (3) or (4), paragraphs 1 to 3, or if he seriously contemplates the carrying out of such an act, or if he offers himself to commit such an act, or accepts such an offer, or if he obtains credible information of such act, or of the intention of committing it, and fails to notify the authorities or any person threatened thereby at a time when danger can still be averted;

5. If he is in unlawful possession of firearms, hand-grenades or any weapon for stabbing or hitting, of explosives, ammunition or other implements of war, or if he has credible information that a Pole or a Jew is in unlawful possession of such object, and fails to notify the authorities forthwith.

II

Punishment shall also be imposed on Poles or Jews if they act contrary to German criminal law or commit any act for which they deserve punishment in accordance with the fundamental principles of German criminal law and in view of the interests of the state in the Incorporated Eastern Territories.

III

(1) Penalties provided for Poles and Jews are: imprisonment, fine or confiscation of property. The term of imprisonment is to be not less than three months and not more than ten years in a penal camp; for more serious offenses from two to fifteen years in a penal camp in which a more severe regimen is enforced.

(2) The death sentence shall be imposed in all cases where it is prescribed by the law. Moreover, in those cases where the law does not provide for the death sentence, it shall be imposed if the offense points to particularly objectionable motives or is particularly grave for other reasons; the death sentence may also be passed upon juvenile offenders.

(3) The minimum penalty or a fixed penalty prescribed by the German criminal law cannot be reduced unless the criminal act is directed against the offender's own people exclusively.

(4) If a fine cannot be recovered, imprisonment in a penal camp from one week to one year shall be imposed in lieu.

2. CRIMINAL PROCEDURE

IV

The state prosecutor shall prosecute a Pole or a Jew if he considers that punishment is in the public interest.

V

(1) Poles and Jews shall be tried by a special court or by the district judge.

(2) The state prosecutor may institute proceedings before a special court in all cases. Proceedings may be instituted by him before a district judge if the punishment to be imposed is not likely to be heavier than five years in a penal camp, or three years in a more rigorous penal camp.

(3) The jurisdiction of the people's court remains unaffected.

VI

(1) Every sentence will be enforced without delay. The state prosecutor may, however, appeal from the sentence of a district judge to the court of appeal. The appeal has to be lodged within two weeks.

(2) The right to lodge complaints which are to be heard by the court of appeals is reserved exclusively to the state prosecutor. The appeal is decided by the Oberlandesgericht.

VII

Poles and Jews cannot challenge a German judge on account of alleged partiality.

VIII

(1) Arrest and temporary detention are allowed whenever there are good grounds to suspect that an offense has been committed.

(2) During the preliminary inquiry, the state prosecutor may order the arrest and any other coercive measures permissible.

IX

Poles and Jews are not sworn in as witnesses in criminal proceedings. If the unsworn deposition made by them before the court is found false, the provisions as prescribed for perjury and false depositions on oath shall be applied accordingly.

X

(1) Only the state prosecutor may apply for the reopening of a case. In a case tried before a special court, the decision concerning an application for the reopening of the proceedings rests with this court.

(2) The right to lodge a plea of nullity rests with the state prosecutor general. The decision on the plea rests with the court of appeal.

XI

Poles and Jews are not entitled to act as prosecutors either in a principal or a subsidiary capacity.

XII

The court and the state prosecutor shall conduct proceedings within their discretion and according to the principles of the German law of procedure. They may, however, dispense with the provisions of the German law on the organization of courts and on criminal procedure, whenever this may appear to them advisable for the rapid and more efficient conduct of proceedings.

3. MARTIAL LAW
XIII

(1) Subject to the consent of the Reich Minister of the Interior and the Reich Minister of Justice, the Reich governor [Oberpraesident] may, until further notice, enforce martial law in the Incorporated Eastern Territories, either in the whole area under his jurisdiction or in parts thereof, against Poles and Jews guilty of grave excesses against the Germans or of other offenses which seriously endanger the German work of reconstruction.

(2) The courts established under martial law impose the death sentence. They may, however, dispense with punishment and refer the case to the secret state police.

(3) Subject to the consent of the Reich Minister of the Interior, the constitution and procedure of the courts established under martial law shall be regulated by the Reich governor [Oberpraesident].

4. EXTENT OF APPLICATION OF THIS DECREE
XIV

(1) The provisions contained in sections I-IV of this decree apply also to those Poles and Jews who on 1st September, 1939, were domiciled or had their residence within the territory of the former Polish state, and who committed criminal offences in any part of the German Reich other than the Incorporated Eastern Territories.

(2) The case may also be tried by the court within whose jurisdiction the former domicile or residence of the offender is situated. Sections V-XII apply accordingly.

(3) Paragraphs 1 and 2 do not apply to offenses tried by the courts in the Government General.

5. SUPPLEMENTARY PROVISIONS
XV

Within the meaning of this decree the term "Poles" means Schutzangehoerige or those who are stateless.

XVI

Article II of the decree of 6th June, 1940, concerning the introduction of German criminal law in the Incorporated Eastern Territories (Reichsgesetzblatt, Part I, p. 844) no longer applies to Poles and Jews.

XVII

The Reich Minister of Justice, in concurrence with the Reich Minister of the Interior, is authorized to issue rules and administrative regulations concerning the execution and implementation of this decree and to decide in all cases of doubt.

XVIII

This decree shall come into force on the fourteenth day after its publication.

Berlin, 4 December 1941

The president of the ministerial
council for Reich defense
Goering, Reich Marshal

The plenipotentiary for Reich administration
Frick

The Reich minister and chief of
the Reich Chancellery
Dr. Lammers

Translation of Document 2752-PS. Affidavit of Willy Litzenberg, a member of the Gestapo, 8 November 1945, concerning activities of Einsatz groups in executing Jews in the East.

* * *

AFFIDAVIT

I, Willy Litzenberg, being first duly sworn, declare:

I was head of sub-section IV A 1b from 1938 until the end of the war and served under Heinrich Mueller, Chief of Amt IV.

During a short period—to the best of my recollection it was during the occupation of, or the withdrawal from, the Crimea—I came across extracts from the reports of Einsatz groups operating in occupied territories on the Eastern front. These reports were mimeographed and were sent to a number of people in the RSHA, as well as—as far as I can remember—to offices outside the RSHA. I myself was not on the distribution list for these reports. On the occasion of a visit to the then head of the section of the RSHA dealing with Communists, Regierungskriminalrat Vegt, I saw there a map of Russia on which the German front was marked with little flags. I observed that this front was traced more exactly than could be ascertained from reports of the armed forces. I asked according to what viewpoint he had placed these pins. He replied that he followed the reports of the Einsatz groups. Up till then I had not known of such reports. I asked whether he could not let me have such reports too, whereupon I actually received such extracts from reports for some time. The sending of these reports to me ceased one day for reasons unknown to me.

I have examined document L-180, which is a copy of the report made by Stahlecker who commanded Einsatz group A. The extracts from reports received by me included information about persons killed. These persons were referred to as being "liquidated." The reports also dealt with military and political, as well as cultural and economic questions.

The report shown to me today, (Activity and situation report number 6) R-102 OCC Document, is similar to reports which came to my attention.

To my knowledge, the Einsatz groups which operated on the Eastern front during the period Heydrich was Chief of the RSHA, continued to operate under Kaltenbrunner.

[signed]   Willy Litzenberg

Subscribed and sworn to before me this 8 day of November 1945 in Nurnberg, Germany.

[signed]   Smith W. Brookhart, Jr.
Lt. Col. IGD.

Translation of Document 2801-PS (USA 109). *Minutes of discussion between Goering and Slovak Minister Durkansky (undated, but probably late fall or early winter 1938-39) in which statement appears that Jewish problem will be solved in Slovakia as in Germany.*

* * *

DISCUSSION
General-Fieldmarshal Goering with the Slovak Minister
Dr. Durkansky

Also present: the Head of the Propaganda Section of the Slovak Government Mach; Leader of the Germans in Slovakia, Karmasin; Reichsstatthalter Seyss-Inquart.

To begin with Durkansky (Deputy Prime Minister) reads out declaration. Contents:—"Friendship for the Fuehrer; gratitude that through the Fuehrer autonomy has become possible for the Slovaks." The Slovaks *never* want to belong to Hungary. The Slovaks want *full independence* with strongest political, economic and military ties to Germany. Bratislava to be capital. The execution of the plan only possible if the army and police are Slovak.

An independent Slovakia to be proclaimed at the meeting of the first Slovak Diet. In the case of a plebiscite the majority would favor a separation from Prague. Jews will vote for Hungary. The area of the plebiscite to be up to the March, where a large Slovak population lives.

The *Jewish problem* will be solved similarly to that in Germany. The Communist party to be prohibited.

The *Germans* in Slovakia do not want to belong to Hungary but wish to stay in Slovakia.

The *German influence* with the Slovak Government is considerable; the appointment of a German Minister (member of the cabinet) has been promised.

At present negotiations with Hungary are being conducted by the Slovaks. The Czechs are more yielding towards the Hungarians than the Slovaks.

The Fieldmarshal considers: that the Slovak negotiations towards independence are to be supported in a suitable manner. Czechoslovakia without Slovakia is still more at our mercy.

Air bases in Slovakia are of great importance for the German Air Force for use against the East.

Translation of Document 2840-PS. Excerpt from "Dr. Wilhelm Frick and His Ministry", 1937, pp. 180-181, on subject of early attempts (1924-25) by Nazi Party to eliminate the Jew from the German national body.

* * *

DR. WILHELM FRICK AND HIS MINISTRY.
[Dr. Wilhelm Frick und sein Ministerium] edited by
H. Pfundtner, 1937, Zentralverlag der
NSDAP, Muenchen, Pages 180-181

In the field of racial policy the National Socialists and Nationalists have, for the purpose of eliminating the Jew from the German national body, in the very first days of their parliamentary activity, on May 27, 1924, introduced the motion "to place all members of the Jewish race under special laws."

On 25 August, 1924, the National-Socialist freedom movement made the first motion in the Reichstag to "exclude members of the Jewish race from all public offices in Reich, countries, and autonomous bodies and to cause their immediate removal from office."

Soon afterwards Dr. Frick personally voiced his opinion on matters pertaining to civil service officials. On July 17, 1925, he declared: "Never before have the rights of the civil service officials been violated more than in this republic. The best proof for this is the 'Reduction of Personnel Decree'. We, however, demand that a beginning be made particularly in the reduction of two civil service categories. The first we refer to are the so-called officials of the Revolution. The other category consists of the members of the Jewish Race. We deem it below our dignity to be governed by people of that race."

Translation of Document 2841-PS. *Excerpt from "Care for Race and Heredity in the Legislation of the Reich", Leipzig, 1943, p. 14, to effect that racial legislation prepared way for final solution of Jewish problem.*

* * *

THE CARE FOR RACE AND HEREDITY IN THE LEGISLATION OF THE REICH,

[Rassen und Erbpflege in der Gesetzgebung des Reiches]
Stuckart and Schiedermair, Leipzig, 1943, p. 14

The aim of the racial legislation may be regarded as already achieved and consequently the racial legislation as essentially closed. It led, as already mentioned above, to a temporary solution of the Jewish problem and at the same time essentially prepared the final solution. Many regulations will lose their practical importance as Germany approaches the achievement of the final goal in the Jewish problem.

Translation of Document 2842-PS. *Excerpt from "Writings of the Years 1917-1921", by Alfred Rosenberg, Munich 1943, pp. 320-321, advocating national-political measures against the Jews.*

* * *

Alfred Rosenberg, WRITINGS OF THE YEARS 1917-1921, Munich 1943, pages 320-321.

The following national-political measures must be taken:

(1) The Jews are to be recognized as a nation living in Germany, irrespective of the religion they belong to.

(2) A Jew is he whose parents on either side are nationally Jews. Anyone who has a Jewish husband or wife is henceforth a Jew.

(3) Jews have no right to speak and write on or be active in German politics.

(4) Jews have no right to hold public offices, or to serve in

the Army either as soldiers or as officers. However, their contribution of work may be considered.

(5) Jews have no right to be leaders of cultural institutions of the state and community (theaters, Galleries, etc.) or to be professors and teachers in German schools and universities.

(6) Jews have no right to be active in state or municipal commissions for examinations, control, censorship, etc. Jews have no right to represent the German Reich in economic treaties; they have no right to be represented in the directorate of state banks or communal credit establishments.

(7) Foreign Jews have no right to settle in Germany permanently. Their admission into the German political community is to be forbidden under all circumstances.

(8) Zionism should be energetically supported in order to promote the departure of German Jews—in numbers to be determined annually — to Palestine or generally across the border.

Translation of Document 2843-PS. Excerpt from *Documents of German Politics, Vol. VII, pp. 728-729,* on Race Politics, commenting on Rosenberg's speeches, January and February 1939, advocating the elimination of Jews from Europe.

* * *

DOCUMENTS OF GERMAN POLITICS
[Dokumente der Deutschen Politik]
Junker und Duennhaupt Verlag/Berlin—1940
Events of the Reich 1939, Volume 7, Part 2, Pages 728-729.

II. RACE POLITICS

In this spirit Reich leader Alfred Rosenberg stated on 15 January 1939 in his speech at Detmold on the occasion of the sixth anniversary of the Landtag elections in Lippe: "For Germany the Jewish problem is solved only when the last Jew has left Germany."

The solution of the Jewish question is a problem not limited to Germany, but represents an international problem of the greatest importance. And so Reichsleiter Alfred Rosenberg, in his speech to the foreign diplomats and press in Berlin on 7 February 1939 ("Must theological fights result in enmity between states?"), "the necessity to gather the hundreds of thousands (of Jews) from Germany and later the millions of Jews from central and eastern Europe and settle them not in a disposed way, but compactly", and the further necessity "that a suggestion, organically justified, politically feasible and guaranteed for the future, be submitted for the benefit of all."

Translation of Document 2844-PS. *Excerpt from "The Program of the Nazi Party" by Gottfried Feder, August 1927, Munich, p. 17, commenting on anti-semitism.*

* * *

THE PROGRAM OF THE NAZI PARTY
[Das Programm der NSDAP]
by Gottfried Feder, Verlag F. Eher Nachf.,
G.m.b.H., Muenchen 2, N.O.—August 27, page 17.

Anti-Semitism is in a way the emotional foundation of our movement. Every National-Socialist is an anti-Semite, but not every anti-Semite will become a National-Socialist. Anti-Semitism is something purely negative; the anti-Semite has recognized the carrier of the plague of the nations, but this recognition is mostly transformed only into personal hatred against the individual Jew, and their successes in the economic life. At best anti-Semitism rises to the still negative demand to eliminate the Jew from our political and economic life. The anti-Semite as a rule does not worry over the "how" and "what then".

Translation of Document 2868-PS. *Excerpt from law relating to admission to profession of Patent-Agent and Lawyer, 22 April 1933, providing that non-aryan patent-agents may be taken off roster.*

* * *

1933 REICHSGESETZBLATT, PART I, NO. 41,
PAGES 217-218

Law Relating to the Admission to the Profession of Patent-agent and Lawyer of 22 April 1933

The Government of the Reich has resolved the following law which is promulgated herewith:

Section 1

Patent-agents who are of non-aryan descent pursuant to the law relating to the reestablishment of the Professional Civil Service [Weiderherstellung des Berufsbeamtentums] of 7 April 1933 (Reichsgesetzblatt, I, p. 175) may be taken off the roster of patent-agents kept by the Reich Patent Office up to 30 September 1933.

The provision of subsection 1 does not apply to patent agents, who have been entered into the roster since 1 August 1914 or who have fought in the front lines for the German Reich or its allies in the World War, or to those patent agents the fathers or sons of whom were killed in the World War. As to the question, who is to be regarded as a frontline fighter, the corresponding implementation regulations are applicable which were issued pursuant to Section 17, subsection 1 of the law relating to the Reestablishment of the Professional Civil Service of 7 April 1933 (Reichsgesetzblatt I, p. 175).

Signatures:

                                              The Reich President
                                                  von Hindenberg
                                           The Reich Chancellor
                                                      Adolf Hitler
                            The Reich Minister of the Interior
                                                          Frick

---

Translation of Document 2869-PS. *Excerpt from Law Relating to the Admission of Tax Advisors, 6 May 1933, providing that non-aryans should not be admitted and that admissions already granted to such persons are to be withdrawn.*

* * *

1933 REICHSGESETZBLATT, PART I, NO. 49, PAGE 257
Law Relating to the Admission of Tax Advisors
of 6 May 1933
Art. 1
Section 1

Persons who are of non-Aryan descent pursuant to the law relating to the reestablishment of the professional Civil Service [Berufsbeamtentums] are not generally to be admitted as tax-advisors. Admissions already granted to such persons are to be withdrawn.

Lawyers or notaries, even of non-Aryan descent, are admitted as plenipotentiaries or assistants [Beistand, i.e., person assisting the party other than counsel] in tax matters from case to case. Other persons of non-Aryan descent are not to be permitted on principle as plenipotentiaries or assistants (a.b.) in tax matters, not even from case to case. Exceptions thereof are admissible only insofar as such other persons will act as plenipotentiaries

or assistants for relatives pursuant to section 67, subsection 1, figures 2 and 3 of the Reich Tax Code.
Signatures:
>
> The Reich Chancellor
> Adolf Hitler
> The Reich Minister of Justice
> Dr. Guertner

Translation of Document 2870-PS. *Excerpts from executory decree for the law about the Repeal of Naturalization, 26 July 1933, providing for the repeal of the naturalization of Eastern Jews.*

* * *

1933 REICHSGESETZBLATT, PART I, PAGE 538.
Executory decree for the law about the Repeal of Naturalizations and the Ajudication of German Citizenship
of 26 July 1933.

On the basis of Article 3 of the law concerning the Repeal of Naturalizations and the Ajudication of German Citizenship of 14 July 1933 (Reichsgesetzblatt I, page 480), it is herewith decreed in agreement with the Reich Foreign Minister and the Minister of Finances:

Re Article I.

I.

Whether a naturalization is to be considered undesirable shall be ajudicated in accordance with racial national [voelkisch-national] principles. In the foreground are the racial, civic and cultural viewpoints regarding an increase of the German population compatible with the interests of Reich and folk by naturalization. Not only are facts preceding the date of naturalization to be taken into consideration, but especially also circumstances appearing subsequent to the date of naturalization.

Accordingly the repeal of naturalization is especially to be contemplated in the case of:

(*a*) Eastern Jews, unless they have fought on the German side at the front in the World War, or have rendered extremely meritorious services to the German interests.

(*b*) Persons who are guilty of a grave offense or a crime, or otherwise have acted in a way detrimental to the welfare of the state and the people.

II.

The repeal, unless particular reasons do make it advisable, shall not be pronounced in the case of:

(*a*) Naturalized citizens who possessed German citizenship

before 9 November 1918 and lost it due to the provisions of the Treaty of Versailles and its executory agreements without any action on their part.

(*b*) Persons who have been naturalized on account of their right to be naturalized in accordance with the provisions of the law on Reich's and State's Citizenship of 22 July 1913. (Reichsgesetzblatt, page 584).

* * * * * *

Berlin, 26 July 1933.

The Reich Minister of the Interior
By direction
Pfundtner

Translation of Document 2872-PS. Fourth Decree *relative to the Reich Citizenship Law, 25 July 1938, prohibiting Jews from practicing medicine.*

* * *

1938 REICHSGESETZBLATT, PART I, PAGE 969.
4th Decree relative to the Reich Citizen Law of 25 July 1938.
By virtue of Section 3 of the Reich Citizen Law of 15 Sept. 1935, (RGBl. I. p. 1146), the following is ordered:

Section I.

Appointment approvals of Jewish physicians expire on Sept. 30, 1938.

Section II.

The Reich Minister of the Interior or the Authority appointed by him, may authorize, on the recommendation of the Reich Chamber of Physicians [Reichsartsekammer]—the practice of medicine physicians until further notice whose appointment has expired by virtue of Section I. The permission may be granted by imposing taxes.

Section III.

1. Jews, whose appointment approval has expired and who have not received an authorization by virtue of Section II, are forbidden to practice medicine.

2. A Jew who has received an authorization by virtue of Section II must, with the exception of his wife and legitimate children, only treat Jews.

3. Whoever violates the regulations of Subsection I or II, either deliberately or carelessly, will be sentenced to one year of prison and a fine, or to either one of those punishments.

Section IV.

A Jew cannot be licensed as a physician.

Section V.
1. Physicians, whose appointment expired, according to the regulations of this decree, may be given, revocable at any time, a maintenance subsidy by the chamber of Reich physicians, in the case of want and worthiness, if they have been frontline soldiers. * * *
2. The chamber of Reich-physicians will decide upon further details in agreement with the Reich-Minister of the Interior and the Reich Minister of Finance. Bayreuth July 25, 1938.

  The Fuehrer and Reich Chancellor, Adolf Hitler
  The Reich Minister of the Interior, Frick
  The Deputy of the Fuehrer, R. Hess
  The Reich-Minister of Justice, Dr. Guertner.
  The Reich-Minister of Finance by order: Reinhardt.

Translation of Document 2874-PS. *Fifth Decree to the law relating to the Reich Citizenship Law, 27 September 1938, eliminating Jews from the bar in Germany and Austria.*

* * *

1938 REICHSGESETZBLATT, PART I, NO. 165, PAGE 1403.
Fifth Decree to the law relating to the Reich Citizenship of 27 September 1938.
Article I.
Elimination of the Jews from the Bar (Attorneyship).
Section 1.

Jews are excluded from the profession of a lawyer. In as much as Jews are still lawyers they are to be eliminated from the bar pursuant to the following provisions:

Old Reich—

a. Within the Territory:

The admission of Jewish lawyers to the bar is to be discontinued as from 10 November 1938.

b. Within the country of Austria:

 1. On order of the Reich-Minister of Justice Jewish lawyers have to be taken off the roster of lawyers until 31 December 1938 at the latest.

 2. Jews, however, who are entered on the roster of the Chamber of Lawyers [Reichs-anwaltskammer i.e. Bar Association] in Vienna, whose family has been resident in Austria at least 50 years and who have been fighting in the front-line may be exempted from the deletion for the time being. In this case the movement of deletion will be determined by the Minister of Justice.

3. The Reich Minister of Justice may forbid a lawyer to exercise his profession for the time being, until it will be decided, whether a deletion from the roster of lawyers will be effected.

Signatories:　　　　　The Fuehrer and Reich-Chancellor
　　　　　　　　　　　　　　　　Adolf Hitler
　　　　　　　　　　　The Reich Minister of Justice
　　　　　　　　　　　　　　　　Dr. Gursner
　　　　　　　　　　　The Reich Minister of Interior
　　　　　　　　　　　　　　　　Frick
　　　　　　　　　　　The Deputy of the Fuehrer
　　　　　　　　　　　　　　　　R. Hess
　　　　　　　　　　　The Reich Minister of Finance
　　　　　　　　　　　　(in the name of Reinhardt)

Translation of Document 2875-PS. Decree relating to the Exclusion of Jews from the German Economic Life, 12 November 1938.

* * *

1938 REICHSGESETZBLATT, PART I, PAGE 1580.
Decree Relating to the Exclusion of Jews from the German Economic Life of November 12, 1938

Pursuant to the decree for the execution of the four year plan of 18 October 1936 (Reichsgesetzblatt I, p. 887), the following is being decreed:

Section 1

(1) Jews (sec. 5 of the first decree relating to the Reich citizenship law of 14 November 1935—Reichsgesetzbl. I, p. 1333) are excluded from the operation of individual retail shops, exporting firms, sales agencies [Bestell Kontoren], as well as the independent operation of a trade, effective 1 January.

(2) Furthermore, effective the same day, they are prohibited to offer merchandise or business services on markets of all types, fairs or exhibitions, to advertise for such or accept orders for such.

(3) Jewish business establishments (third decree pursuant to the Reich citizenship law of 14 June 1938, Reichsgesetzbl. I, p. 627) which are being operated in violation of this decree are to be closed down by the police.

Section 2.

(1) Effective 1 January 1939, a Jew can no longer be manager of an establishment as defined by the law relating to the

organization of national labor of 20 January 1934 (Reichsgesetzbl. I, p. 45).

(2) If a Jew is employed as an executive in a business enterprise, he may be dismissed with 6 weeks' notice. After the expiration of this notice, all claims of the employee derived from the denounced contract become invalid, especially claims for retirement or dismissal pay.

Section 3

(1) No Jew may be a member of a cooperative [Genossenschaft].

(2) Jewish members of cooperatives will be separated effective 31 December 1938. No special notice is required.

Section 4

The minister of economics is empowered to issue regulations necessary for the implementation of this decree with the approval of the Reich ministers concerned. He may allow exceptions where, due to the transfer of Jewish business establishments into non-Jewish hands or due to the liquidation of Jewish business establishments or in special cases, this is required in order to safeguard the requirements of the public.

The Plenipotentiary for the Four Year Plan
Goering
Field Marshal

Berlin, November 12, 1938.

Translation of Document 2876-PS. *Tenth Decree relating to the Reich Citizenship Law, 4 July 1939, authorizing Reich Minister of Interior to abolish or take over all Jewish organizations and foundations.*

* * *

1939 REICHSGESETZBLATT, PART I, PAGE 1097
Tenth Decree Relating to the Reich Citizenship
Law of July 4, 1939.

On the basis of section 3 of the Reich citizenship law of 15 September 1935 (Reichsgesetzblatt, Part I, p. 1146) the following is hereby decreed:

Article 1.

Reich Association of the Jews.

Section 1.

(1) The Jews will be united into a Reich Association.

(2) The Reich association is an organization endowed with legal personality. It bears the name "Reich Association of the Jews", and has its headquarters in Berlin.

(3) The Reich association uses the Jewish worship congregations as local branch offices.

Section 2.

(1) The Reich association has the purpose of promoting the emigration of the Jews.

(2) The Reich association is likewise:

a. Supporter of the Jewish school instruction.

b. Supporter of the voluntary Jewish welfare administration.

(3) The Reich Minister of the Interior may transfer other missions to the Reich association.

Section 3.

(1) All Jewish citizens and stateless Jews belong to the Reich association, who have their residence or their customary abode in Reich territory.

(2) In case of a mixed-marriage, the Jewish partner is a member only,

a. If the man is the Jewish partner and there are no offspring from the marriage, or,

b. If the offspring are considered as Jews.

(3) Jews of foreign nationality and those Jews living in mixed marriage, who are not members by virtue of provision 2, are permitted to join the Reich association.

Section 4.

The Reich association is subject to the supervision of the Reich Minister of the Interior; its statutes require his approval.

Section 5.

(1) The Reich Minister of the Interior may dissolve Jewish clubs, organizations and foundations or decree their incorporation in the Reich association.

(2) In case of dissolution, the regulations of the civil law are valid for the liquidation. The Reich Minister of the Interior can however appoint and recall administrators and regulate the type of liquidation in departing from the provisions of civil law. After the liquidation is carried out, the property of the dissolved Jewish organizations is to be transferred to the Reich association.

(3) In case of incorporation, the property of the affected Jewish organizations devolves to the Reich association. A liquidation does not take place in these cases. The Reich association is responsible with all its property for the obligation incurred by the incorporated organization (institution).

(4) The Reich Minister of the Interior may abolish and change statutory provisions and resolutions of Jewish organizations and foundations, if they have decided upon regulations

concerning the disposal of the property in departing from these provisions. Jews who have profited in some manner as a result of the subsequently repealed statutory provisions or resolutions, are obliged to give it up to the Reich association in accordance with the fundamentals of unjustifiable enrichment.

The Reich Minister of the Interior
FRICK
The Deputy of the Fuehrer
HESS
The Reich Minister of Education
RUST
The Reich Minister of Church Affairs
KERRL

Translation of Document 2877-PS. *Police Decree concerning the "marking" of Jews, 1 September 1941, providing that Jews in Bohemia and Moravia may not travel without permission and may not appear in public without a Jewish star.*

* * *

1941 REICHSGESETZBLATT, PART I, NO. 100, PAGE 547
Police decree concerning the "marking" of the Jews of September 1, 1941.

Based upon the decree relating to the police decrees of the Reich minister of November 1938 (Reichsgesetzblatt I S 1582) and the decree concerning the legislative power in the Protectorate Bohemia and Moravia of June 7, 1939 (Reichsgesetzblatt I S 1039) it is ordered hereby in agreement with the "Reichsprotektor" in Bohemia and Moravia as follows:

Section 1

1. Jews (Section 5 of the first decree to the Reich citizen law of November 1935—Reichsgesetzblatt I S 1333) who finished the sixth year of their age are prohibited to appear in public without a Jewish star.

2. The Jewish star consists of a "Six Star" with black contours in the size of the palm of the hand of yellow material with the black inscription "Jew". It has to be worn on the left side of the chest of the clothing tightly sewed on.

Section 2

Jews are forbidden

a. to leave the boundary of their residential district without carrying a written permission of the local police authority.

b. to wear medals, decorations, and other badges.

Section 3
The sections 1 and 2 will not apply

a. to the Jewish spouse living in a mixed marriage, as far as descendants of the marriage are existent and these are not considered as Jews, and even then, if the marriage does not exist anymore or the only son has been killed in the present war.

b. to the Jewish wife of a childless mixed marriage for the duration of the marriage.

Section 4
1. Who contravenes against the prohibition of Sections 1 and 2, deliberately or carelessly, will be punished with a penalty up to 150 Reichsmark or with imprisonment up to six weeks.

2. Further reaching police security measures and also penal provisions, according to which a higher penalty is incurred, remain effective.

Section 5
The police decree is also effective in the Protectorate Bohemia and Moravia with the provision that the Reichsprotektor in Bohemia and Moravia may adopt the instruction of section 2 to the local conditions in the Protectorate Bohemia and Moravia.

Section 6
The police decree will be effective 14 days after its promulgation.

Berlin, September 1, 1941

The Reich Minister of the Interior
by order
Heydrich.

Translation of Document 2889-PS (USA 595). Speech by Alfred Rosenberg on "The Jew Question as World Problem", 28 March 1941, published in newspaper Voelkischer Beobachter, Munich edition, 29 March 1941, advocating elimination of Jews from Germany and Europe.

* * *

VOELKISCHER BEOBACHTER MUNICH EDITION
54th year, 1941
Editions No. 60-90.

No. 88

Saturday, 29 March 1941.

By Reichleader *Alfred Rosenberg*.

The Jew question as World Problem.

A speech at conclusion of demonstration in Frankfurt on Main.

Berlin, 28 March.

III - 430

At the concluding ceremony for the opening of the institute for exploration of the Jew question in Frankfurt on Main, Reich leader Rosenberg spoke from Berlin over the radio on the theme "The Jew question as World Problem." This speech was listened to jointly by the participants of the session. Reich leader Rosenberg stated essentially the following: * * *

The war which is being waged today by the German armed forces under the highest command of Adolf Hitler is therefore a war of an immense reform. It does not only overcome the world of ideas of the French revolution, but it also exterminates directly all those racially infecting germs of Jewry and its bastards, which now since over a hundred years could develop without check among the European nations. The Jew question, which for 2000 years was a problem for the European nations which was not solved, will now find its solution through the national socialistic revolution for Germany and whole Europe.

And if one asks in which form, then we have to say the following to this: During these decades a lot has been talked about a Jewish state as solution, and Zionism appears to some harmless people perhaps even today as an honest attempt to contribute on the part of the Jews also something toward the solution of the Jewish question.

In reality there never was nor will there ever be a Jewish State.

Contrary to the other nations on this globe, Judaism is no vertical organization which comprises all professions, but has been always a horizontal class among the different nations, that class which carried on material and spiritual intermediate trade. Secondly, the space being considered in Palestine is in no way suitable for any Jewish state. It is too small to absorb what was formerly 10 and is now 15 million Jews; in other words, therefore impractical for solving the Jewish question. The purpose of Zionism, in reality, was not to solve the Jewish question in the sense of the coordination of the whole Jewish people, but lay in an entirely different direction.

It was intended to build in Palestine a purely Jewish center, a real legitimate Jewish state in order to be able, at first, to be represented at all diplomatic conferences with full rights as national Jew.

Secondly, it was intended to make Palestine into a huge, economic staging area against the entire Near East. Thirdly, this Jewish state should have been an asylum for all those Jewish adventurers in the world who were evicted from the countries in which they acted. And, finally, nobody was even thinking of limiting, even in the slightest, the so-called state civil rights of the Jews in Germany, England, America, and also France. The Jews, therefore, would have maintained the rights of the Germans, Englishmen, Frenchmen etc., and the spaceless Jewish world state would have come constantly closer toward its realization, that is, an all-Jewish center without any interference of non-Jews and the Jewish high finance at the state rudder in all other countries of the world.

This dream is now finished. Now, just the reverse, we have to think of how and where to put the Jews. This can, as mentioned, not be done in a Jewish state, but only in a way which I shall call the Jewish reservation.

It is to be hoped that future statesmen will get together in order to gradually institute a settlement of Jews who, under experienced police supervision, now should do such useful work as they wanted to see done until now by non-Jews.

From an almost unlimited Jewish rule in all European countries to such a radical reverse, to an evacuation of this same Jewish race after 2000 years of parasitism on the European continent, then only can one conceive through this an idea of what an enormous philosophical and political revolution is in the making in Europe today.

Today the Jewish question is somewhat clear before our eyes. It is the problem of a simple national purity. It means the necessity for defense of inherent national tradition for all nations which still value culture and future. It is still a problem of economy for all those who cannot solve the social questions under the Jewish financial dictatorship. It is a political problem of power, because in many states the will has not yet been found to break this financial dictatorship of the Jewry. And, lastly, it is a historically ideological problem, given to the Europeans since the days when the first Jews immigrated to Rome. As national socialists we have but one clear answer for all these questions:

For Germany the Jewish Question is only then solved, when the Last Jew has left the Greater German space.

Since Germany with its blood and its nationalism has now broken for always this Jewish dictatorship for all Europe, and has seen to it that Europe as a whole will become free from the Jewish parasitism once more, we may, I believe, also say for all Europeans: For Europe the Jewish question will be solved only when the last Jew has left the European continent.

At that, it does not matter whether such a program can be realized in five, ten or twenty years. The transportation facilities in our time, if all nations join, would be strong enough to institute and to execute such a resettlement to a great extent. But the problem must and will one day be solved as we have visualized it from the first day of our fight — then accused utopists—and now proclaim it as strict realistic politicians. All nations are interested in the solution of this question, and we must declare here with all passion:

In this cleaning-up even Mr. Roosevelt with his Baruchs and his trophy film Jews will not be able to hamper us, but wholly to the contrary, just this proclamation, that the Jewish parasitical spirit shall represent today the freedom of the world, will especially awaken all resistance of the German character, and the strongest military instrument which history has seen, the German Armed forces of Adolf Hitler, will take care of it that this last furious attempt to let the white race once more march against Europe for the benefit of the Jewish financial dominion will find an end for all times.

We are of the opinion that this great war constitutes also a cleansing biological world revolution and that also those nations which are still opposed to us will recognize, at the end of the war, that Germany's business is today the business of the whole European continent, the business of the whole Jewish race, but also the business of all other cultured races on this globe who fight for a safe national cultural and state life. Thus we hope that one day, in a reasonable distribution of the great living spaces of this globe the nations will find that peace, that work and that prosperity which for decades have been harassed by never-tiring parasitical activity. Thus, we consider today the Jewish question as one of the most important problems among the total politics of Europe, as a problem which must be solved and will be solved, and we hope, yes, we know already today, that all nations of Europe will march behind this cleansing at the end.

Translation of Document 2894-PS. *General Decree of 10 September 1935 issued by Rust, Reichsminister of Education, on establishment of separate Jewish schools.*

* * *

DOCUMENTS OF GERMAN POLITICS
[Dokumente der Deutschen Politik] Published by Reg-Rat Paul Meier, Berlin, 1937, page 152.

General decree of September 10, 1935, issued by Reichsminister, Rust, on the establishment of separate Jewish schools:

"* * * The establishment of public and private Jewish schools has indeed led to a certain separation of those Jewish school children who belong to the Hebraic [Mosaischen] religion. The separation according to religions is however insufficient for a national socialist school system. The establishment of National Socialist class communities as a basis of a youth education, based on the idea of Germanism [Volkstungedanken] is possible only if a clear separation of the children is carried through according to the races they belong to.

"Therefore, from the school year of 1936 on, I intend to separate according to race, as completely as possible, all German subjects attending any type of school * * *."

Translation of Document 2904-PS. "The Racial Problem and the New Reich", published in The National Socialist Monthly, No. 38, May 1933, pp. 196-7, indicating that legislation is mainly educational and gives direction to the solution of the Jewish question.

* * *

NATIONAL SOCIALIST MONTHLY, ISSUE 38,
edited by Adolf Hitler
The Racial Problem and the New Reich
by
Dr. Achim Gercke
1933
Publishing House, Franz Eber Successors Co.
Munich, Pages 196-197

THE SOLUTION OF THE JEWISH QUESTION

The laws are mainly educational and give direction. This aspect of the laws should not be underestimated. The entire nation is enlightened on the Jewish problem; it learns to understand that the national community is a blood community; it understands for the first time the racial idea, and is diverted from a too theoretical treatment of the Jewish problem and faced with the actual solution.

Nevertheless the laws published thus far cannot bring a final solution of the Jewish problem, because the time has not yet come for it, although the decrees give the general direction and leave open the possibility of further developments.

It would be premature in every respect to work out and publicly discuss plans now to achieve more than can be achieved for the time being. However, one must point out a few basic principles so that the ideas which one desires to ripen will contain no mistakes.   *   *   *

All suggestions aiming at a permanent situation, at a stabilization of the status of the Jews in Germany do not solve the Jewish problem, because they do not detach the Jews from Germany.   *   *   *

Plans and programs must contain an aim pointing to the future and not merely consisting of the regulation of a momentarily uncomfortable situation.

Translation of Document 2907-PS. Notes of conference of Reich Ministers on 12 September 1933 concerning forthcoming session of the League of Nations Conference in Geneva where attacks against the Reich Government are to be reckoned with on account of the Jewish Question in Germany.

*   *   *

Notes Concerning the Conference of Ministers of 12 September 1933.

2. Report concerning the forthcoming session of the League of Nations Conference in Geneva.

The Minister of Foreign Affairs (von Neurath): The members of the League of Nations will come together in the near future for the regular annual meeting which he will also attend. The first session of the League is set for the 22nd September 1933. In this annual meeting of the League special interests will stress minority questions, which will in part be concerned with the fate of the German minorities and in part will also be directed against the Reich Government. Attacks against the Reich Government are to be reckoned with on account of the Jewish Question in Germany. In this year's meeting the basic relationship of Germany toward the International Workers' Office will inevitably, among other things, come to a discussion. The various fields of work of the League of Nations are entrusted to special commissions. One of these commissions works the refugee welfare program which has been organized by the League of Nations. It has become known that applications from Jewish commissions are pending in Geneva asking to extend this welfare program of the League to emigrants from Germany. Should this come under discussion it will be said on behalf of Germany that refugees from Germany will at all times be permitted to return to that country. The only exception to this are those refugees whose citizenship had been cancelled. In addition, the German representatives may refer to the actions of the Austrian Government in a similar question.

According to available reports from the Foreign Office, the state of mind toward Germany in League of Nations circles in Geneva is at present particularly displeasing. By the use of widespread propaganda there are hopes of bringing the Jewish question to discussion before the Political Commission. Our counter-propaganda should not hesitate, on its part, to bring the Jewish question to a head. Attention is to be paid thereby to the special position of the Jews in Eastern Upper Silesia in accordance with the League of Nations Agreement. It has become known that the Jewish Community in Gleiwitz has filed a complaint with the League of Nations. It would be stressed in the League of Nations Conference that there existed in Germany a Jewish minority without rights which needed protection. In answer to that it is to be emphasized that any altercations with Jews in Germany was the Reich's own affair. In order to formulate the most effective counter-propaganda the permission of the Reichs Chancellor is requested in order to permit the Reich Minister of Propaganda and Public Enlightenment to become a member of the delegation. Moreover, the experts in the Reich Ministry of the Interior and the Prussian Ministry of the Interior should hold themselves in readiness to be called.

The accomplishments of the League of Nations were never as futile as at present. In spite of that it would be a mistake to leave the field of political influence afforded by the League to one's opponents without a fight. The proper moment to leave the League of Nations would only come after a complete collapse of the demobilization conference and after a final settlement of the Saar Question. Furthermore, the Italian Government has, in spite of its basically opposed position toward the League of Nations, used the League as a means of attaining Italian political goals, and with success. If, to be sure, the League of Nations should come to decisions which were unbearable to the German way of life, then the Reich Government would reserve the right for itself to withdraw the German delegation from Geneva.

You are asked to voice any protests against the version of the Summaries contained herein to Dr. Thomsen, Oberregierungsrat in the Reich Chancellery, within twenty-four hours.

The Documentary Evidence   2907-PS

to RK 11152/33
         For the report to the Reich Chancellor
              on 19th September 1933:
         Inquiry of the Minister for Foreign Affairs
   1. Whether Rosenberg should go to Geneva.
   2. Whether a representative of Pass should be admitted as
defense counsel in the case of the Reichstag fire.
   Information by telephone, that there was no hesitation concerning an unofficial trip of Herr Rosenberg to Geneva.
   The Reichs Chancellor declared himself against the admittance of a representative of Pass as a defense counsel in the case of the Reichstag fire.
   AA 5 (R Tag 11)   B., 19 September 1933

Translation of Document 2916-PS. *Excerpt from Survey of deportations of Jews and Poles up to 15 November 1940, from collection of restricted intra-office documents on Commitment of Manpower, Doctrines—Orders—Directives, edited December 1940 by Reich Commissioner for the Strengthening of the National Character of the German People.*

* * *

                                        for departmental use only
Restricted
              The Reichsfuehrer SS
    Reich Commissioner for the Strengthening of the
       National Character of the German People
              COMMITMENT OF MANPOWER
              DOCTRINES-ORDERS-DIRECTIVES
Edited by the Department I Office of the Reich Commissioner
   for the Strengthening of the National Character of the
         German People. December 1940; Printed in
              the "Reich" printing office.

* * *

Survey of the accomplished evacuations. (Compiled by the Chief of the Security Police and the SD). [Page 117].
   Up to 15 November, 1940, the following were evacuated to the Government General:

From the "Reichsgau" Wartheland	234,620 Poles
From East Prussia	14,636 Poles
From East Upper Silesia	14,322 Poles
From Danzig-West-Prussia	30,758 Poles
	294,336 Poles

III - 437

The evacuations were carried out in 303 special trains.

From May 14, 1940 onwards the Poles were given on their journey 1,401,774 kg food as maintenance for 14 days by order of the General Governor. Besides that, each Pole received 20 Zloty (a total of 5,947,780 Zloty=2,973,890 RM).

Up to the 15 November, 1940, the following were evacuated to the General Government:

From Prague, Vienna, and Moravian Ostrau	5,035 Jews
From Stettin	1,000 Jews
From the West Zone of the Reich	2,800 Gypsies

In the West 6,504 Jews from Baden and the Pfalz were deported into the unoccupied part of France up to 15 November, 1940; from Lorraine 47,187 who spoke French (Destination Lyon).

Total Number of Evacuees up to 15 November, 1940

To the Government General	303,171
To Unoccupied France	53,691
Total	356,862

Translation of Document 2917-PS. Excerpts from decree concerning German people's list and German nationality in the Incorporated Eastern Territories, 4 March 1941, Introducing Citizenship Legislation.

* * *

1941 REICHSGESETZBLATT, PART I, PAGE 118

Decree re the German people's list and German nationality in the incorporated Eastern territories, of 4th March 1941.

By virtue of the Fuehrer's and Reich Chancellor's decree of 8th October 1939 (RGB I, p. 2042) about the organization and administration of the Eastern territories, the following is ordered:

* * * * * * *

Section III.
Introduction of citizenship legislation.
Para 8.

In the incorporated Eastern territories the following come into force with effect from the 1st December 1940:

(*a*) The law regarding Reich and State citizenship of the 22nd July 1913 (RGBl. p.583), and Para 3, Para 4, sub-para 1, sub-para 2, No. 2 and 4, and sub-para 3 of the decree regarding German citizenship of the 5th February 1934 (RGBl. I, p. 85) and the law for the alteration of the Reich and State citizenship law of the 15th May 1935 (RGBl. I, p.593).

(*b*) The regulations in para 2, sub-paras 1, 3, & 5 and para 3 of the law for the cancellation of naturalizations and the deprivation of German citizenship of the 14th July 1933 (RGBl, I, p. 480) and under Nos. I & II of para 2 of the decree of the 26th July 1933 (RGBl. I, p.538) for the execution of the said law.

Para 9.
[deals with dues and payments].
Section IV
FINAL REGULATION
Para 10.

The Reich Minister of the Interior will issue the legal and administrative regulations necessary for the execution and completion of this decree in agreement with the Fuehrer's Deputy and the Reich Fuehrer SS, Reich Commissar for the consolidation of German race and culture.

The Reich Minister of the Interior
FRICK
The Fuehrer's Deputy
R. HESS.
The Reich Fuehrer SS,
Reich Commissar for the consolidation
of German race and culture.
H. HIMMLER.

Translation of Document 2953-PS (GB 136). Letter, 29 June 1939, from Heydrich to Ribbentrop, with enclosure concerning instigation of pogroms against Jews in Lithuania.

* * *

29th June 1939

The Reichs Fuehrer-SS
Chief of Security HQ.
III 1123 AZ: g.Rs.
/39 POS./Kt.
[Stamp]
Foreign Office
Rm 38 g. Rs.
received 29th June 1939
1 Encl.
[Stamp] Most Secret

To the Reich Foreign Minister
SS Major General [Gruppenfuehrer] v.Ribbentrop
Wilhelmstrasse 63.
Berlin W. 8.

Dear Party comrade v. Ribbentrop.

Enclosed please find a further report about the "Woldemaras Supporters". As already mentioned in the previous report the *"Woldemaras Supporters" are still asking for help from the Reich*. I therefore ask you to examine the question of financial support, brought up again by the "Woldemaras Supporters", set forth on page 4 para 2 of the enclosed report, and to make a definite decision.

The request of the "Woldemaras Supporters" for financial support could, in my opinion, be granted. Deliveries of arms should not, however, be made, under any circumstances.

Heil Hitler!
Yours
Heydrich.
F 12 348.

Enclosure.

A/L/2

Translation of Extract to RM 33 Most Secret

In the middle of May it was decided to form a secret Lithuanian national socialist party. Its leaders are the most trustworthy members of the "Woldemaras Supporters". The direction of the work within the Officer's Corps is said to be in the hands of old members of the "Woldemaras Supporters". Besides that, they are said to have one assistant who is on the personal staff of President Smetana. In order to make full use of anti-semitic feeling in Lithuania it is intended to stage pogroms against the Jews. The sum of 100,000 Lit (about 41,000 Mark) is required for this illegal work. Besides that a leading "Woldemaras Supporter" is enquiring whether the Reich would send weapons as well. The reply was given to the effect that money would possibly be provided but weapons, however, would definitely not be delivered.

The fight against the Jews would result in a further increase in the escape of Jewish capital, causing Lithuania to be more dependent than ever on the German market.

Translation of Document 2960-PS (USA 406). Excerpt from "The Reich Ministry of Interior," Berlin, 1940, p. 62, discussing the three "Nurnberg Laws".

* * *

PUBLICATIONS ON THE STATE STRUCTURE
[Schriften zum Staatsaufbau]

The Documentary Evidence   2960-PS

New series of publications of the University of Politics, Part II
         Edited by von Paul Meier-Bennekenstein
Volume 41/42
             The Reich Ministry of Interior.
                  History and Structure
               By Dr. Franz A. Medius
             Published by Junker and Dunnhaupt
              Publishers, Berlin 1940, Page 62.

The work of the Reich Ministry of Interior forms the basis for the three "Nurnberg Laws" passed by a resolution of the Reichstag on the occasion of the Reich party meeting of Freedom.

The "Reich Citizenship Law" as well as the "Law for the protection of German blood and German honor (Blood Protection Law)" opened extensive tasks for the Ministry of Interior not only in the field of administration. The same applies to the "Reich Flag Law" that gives the foundation for the complete reorganization of the use of the flag * * *

Translation of Document 2984-PS. Excerpt from Law concerning Armed Forces, 21 May 1935, providing that Aryan descent is a prerequisite for active military service.

* * *

1935 REICHSGESETZBLATT, PART I, PAGES 609, 611, 614
        Law concerning Armed Forces of 21 May 1935,
                 Chapter II, Section 15.
                     Aryan Descent.

(1) Aryan descent is a prerequisite for active service in the Armed Forces.

(2) An examining committee will determine whether and to what extent exceptions may be permitted in accordance with directives which the Reich Minister of the Interior sets forth, in agreement with the Reich Minister of War.

(3) Only persons of Aryan descent may become officers in the Armed Forces.

(4) Members of the Armed Forces and of the reserve who are of Aryan descent, are prohibited from marrying persons of non-Aryan descent. Contraventions will result in the loss of any military rating.

(5) The service of non-Aryans during war remains subject to special regulations. * * *

The Fuehrer and Reich Chancellor
Adolf Hitler
The Reich Minister of Defense
von Blomberg
The Reich Minister of the Interior
Frick.

Translation of Document 2992-PS (USA 494). Three affidavits of Hermann Friedrich Graebe, 10 and 13 November 1945, giving eye-witness accounts of slaughter of all Jews in Dubno, Ukraine, in October 1942 and slaughter of 5000 Jews in the Rowno Ghetto, Ukraine, on 13 July 1942, and order of Area Commissioner of Rowno, 13 July 1942, exempting Jewish workers of Jung firm from the pogrom.
* * *

I, Hermann Friedrich Graebe, declare under oath:

At Wiesbaden, on 10 November 1945 I made two statements describing as an eye-witness the execution of Jews on the former airport near Dubno, Ukraine, and the herding together, ill-treatment and killing of men, women and children of the former Ghetto at Rowno, Ukraine.

By way of corollary to these statements I depose as follows:

1. The SS-man acting as the executioner on the edge of the pit during the shooting of Jewish men, women and children on the airport near Dubno, wore an SS-uniform with a grey arm-band about 3 cm wide on the lower part of his sleeve with the letters "SD" in black on it, woven in or embroidered.

2. SS-Sturmbannfuehrer Dr. Puetz was in charge of the carrying out of the operation (Aktion) at Rowno during the night of 13th July 1942. I knew Dr. Puetz personally as the "Kommandeur der SP u. SD" [commander of the Security Police and Security Service] of Rowno, for I had had several discussions with him with a view to preventing a pogrom against the Jews [Judenaktion] at Sdolbunow, Misotsch and Ostrog. Dr. Puetz was introduced to me by the Area Commissioner Georg Marschall. In addition I definitely remember that a nameplate was fixed on the outside of the door to his office bearing his name and rank.

On the morning of 14 July I recognized three or four SS-men in the Ghetto, whom I knew personally and who were all members of the Security Service in Rowno. These persons also wore the armband mentioned above. I cannot recall their names, but, in my opinion, the foreman Fritz Einsporn must know their names, as, to my knowledge, he corresponded with them.

I make the foregoing statement in Wiesbaden, Germany, on 13 November 1945. I swear before God, that this is the absolute truth.

(S) Fr. Graebe
(t) HERMANN FRIEDRICH GRAEBE

Before me, Homer B. Crawford, being authorized to administer oaths, personally appeared Hermann Friedrich Graebe, who being by me duly sworn through the interpreter Elisabeth Radziejewska, made and subscribed the following statement:

I, Hermann Friedrich Graebe, declare under oath:

From September 1941 until January 1944 I was manager and engineer-in-charge of a branch office in Sdolbunow, Ukraine, of the Solingen building firm of Josef Jung. In this capacity it was my job to visit the building sites of the firm. Under contract to an Army Construction Office, the firm had orders to erect grain storage buildings on the former airport of Dubno, Ukraine.

On 5 October 1942, when I visited the building office at Dubno, my foreman Hubert Moennikes of 21 Aussenmuehlenweg, Hamburg-Haarburg, told me that in the vicinity of the site, Jews from Dubno had been shot in three large pits, each about 30 meters long and 3 meters deep. About 1500 persons had been killed daily. All of the 5000 Jews who had still been living in Dubno before the pogrom were to be liquidated. As the shootings had taken place in his presence he was still much upset.

Thereupon I drove to the site, accompanied by Moennikes and saw near it great mounds of earth, about 30 meters long and 2 meters high. Several trucks stood in front of the mounds. Armed Ukrainian militia drove the people off the trucks under the supervision of an SS-man. The militia men acted as guards on the trucks and drove them to and from the pit. All these people had the regulation yellow patches on the front and back of their clothes, and thus could be recognized as Jews.

Moennikes and I went directly to the pits. Nobody bothered us. Now I heard rifle shots in quick succession, from behind one of the earth mounds. The people who had got off the trucks —men, women, and children of all ages—had to undress upon the order of an SS-man, who carried a riding or dog whip. They had to put down their clothes in fixed places, sorted according to shoes, top clothing and underclothing. I saw a heap of shoes of about 800 to 1000 pairs, great piles of under-linen and clothing.

Without screaming or weeping these people undressed, stood around in family groups, kissed each other, said farewells and waited for a sign from another SS-man, who stood near the pit, also with a whip in his hand. During the 15 minutes that I stood near the pit I heard no complaint or plea for mercy. I watched a family of about 8 persons, a man and woman, both about 50 with their children of about 1, 8 and 10, and two grown-up daughters of about 20 to 24. An old woman with snow-white hair was holding the one-year old child in her arms and singing to it, and tickling it. The child was cooing with delight. The couple were looking on with tears in their eyes. The father was holding the hand of a boy about 10 years old and speaking to him softly; the boy was fighting his tears. The father pointed toward the sky, stroked his head, and seemed to explain something to him. At that moment the SS-man at the pit shouted something to his comrade. The latter counted off about 20 persons and instructed them to go behind the earth mound. Among them was the family, which I have mentioned. I well remember a girl, slim and with black hair, who, as she passed close to me, pointed to herself and said, "23". I walked around the mound, and found myself confronted by a tremendous grave. People were closely wedged together and lying on top of each other so that only their heads were visible. Nearly all had blood running over their shoulders from their heads. Some of the people shot were still moving. Some were lifting their arms and turning their heads to show that they were still alive. The pit was already 2/3 full. I estimated that it already contained about 1000 people. I looked for the man who did the shooting. He was an SS-man, who sat at the edge of the narrow end of the pit, his feet dangling into the pit. He had a tommy gun on his knees and was smoking a cigarette. The people, completely naked, went down some steps which were cut in the clay wall of the pit and clambered over the heads of the people lying there, to the place to which the SS-man directed them. They lay down in front of the dead or injured people; some caressed those who were still alive and spoke to them in a low voice. Then I heard a series of shots. I looked into the pit and saw that the bodies were twitching or the heads lying already motionless on top of the bodies that lay before them. Blood was running from their necks. I was surprised that I was not ordered away, but I saw that there were two or three postmen in uniform nearby. The next batch was approaching already. They went down into the pit, lined themselves up against the previous victims and were shot. When I walked back, round the mound I noticed another truckload of people which had just arrived. This time it included sick and infirm people. An old, very thin woman with terribly thin legs was undressed by others who were already naked, while two people held her up. The woman appeared to be paralyzed. The naked people carried the woman around the mound. I left with Moennikes and drove in my car back to Dubno.

On the morning of the next day, when I again visited the site, I saw about 30 naked people lying near the pit—about 30 to 50 meters away from it. Some of them were still alive; they looked straight in front of them with a fixed stare and seemed to notice neither the chilliness of the morning nor the workers of my firm who stood around. A girl of about 20 spoke to me and asked me to give her clothes, and help her escape. At that moment we heard a fast car approach and I noticed that it was an SS-detail. I moved away to my site. 10 minutes later we heard shots from the vicinity of the pit. The Jews still alive had been ordered to throw the corpses into the pit—then they had themselves to lie down in this to be shot in the neck.

I make the above statement at Wiesbaden, Germany, on 10th November 1945. I swear before God that this is the absolute truth.

Hermann Friedrich Graebe

Subscribed and sworn to before me at Wiesbaden, Germany, this 10 day of November 1945.

Homer B. Crawford
Major, AC
Investigator Examiner, War Crimes Branch

I, Elisabeth Radziejewska, being first duly sworn, state: That I truly translated the oath administered by Major Homer B. Crawford to Hermann Friedrich Graebe and that thereupon he made and subscribed the foregoing statement in my presence.

Elisabeth Radziejewska
Interpreter

Subscribed and sworn to before me at Wiesbaden, Germany, this 10 day of November 1945.

Homer B. Crawford, Major, AC
Investigator Examiner, War Crimes Branch

SECRET

The Area Commissioner [Gebietskommissar]
ROWNO

Ref * * *

Messrs. JUNG, Rowno

The Jewish workers employed by your firm are not affected by the pogrom [Aktion]. You must transfer them to their new place of work by Wednesday, 15 July 1942 at the latest.

13/7.42
For the Area Commissioner

Beck
[Stamp]
Area Commissioner
Rowno

Before me, Homer B. Crawford, being authorized to administer oaths, personally appeared Hermann Friedrich Graebe, who, being by me duly sworn through the interpreter Elisabeth Radziejewska, made and subscribed the following statement:

I, Hermann Friedrich Graebe, declare under oath:

From September 1941 until January 1944 I was manager and engineer-in-charge of a branch office in Sdolbunow, Ukraine, of the Solingen building firm of Josef Jung. In this capacity it was my job to visit the building sites of the firm. The firm had, among others, a site in Rowno, Ukraine.

During the night of 13th July 1942 all inhabitants of the Rowno Ghetto, where there were still about 5000 Jews, were liquidated.

I would describe the circumstances of my being a witness of the dissolution of the Ghetto, and the carrying out of the pogrom [Aktion] during the night and the morning, as follows:

I employed for the firm, in Rowno, in addition to Poles, Germans, and Ukrainians about 100 Jews from Sdolbunow, Ostrog, and Mysotch. The men were quartered in a building,—5 Bahnhofstrasse, inside the Ghetto, and the women in a house at the corner of Deutsche Strasse,—98.

On Saturday, 11 July 1942, my foreman, Fritz Einsporn, told me of a rumor that on Monday all Jews in Rowno were to be liquidated. Although the vast majority of the Jews employed by my firm in Rowno were not natives of this town, I still feared that they might be included in this pogrom which had been reported. I therefore ordered Einsporn at noon of the same day to march all the Jews employed by us—men as well as women—in the direction of Sdolbunow, about 12 km from Rowno. This was done.

The Senior Jew [Judenrat] had learned of the departure of the Jewish workers of my firm. He went to see the Commanding Officer of the Rowno SIPO and SD, SS Major [SS Sturmbannfuehrer] Dr. Puetz, as early as Saturday afternoon to find out whether the rumor of a forthcoming Jewish progrom—which had gained further credence by reason of the departure of Jews of my firm—was true. Dr. Puetz dismissed the rumor as a clumsy lie, and for the rest had the Polish personnel of my firm in Rowno arrested. Einsporn avoided arrest by escaping from Sdolbunow. When I learned of this incident I gave orders that all Jews who had left Rowno were to report back to work in Rowno on Monday, 13 July 1942. On Monday morning I myself went to see the Commanding Officer, Dr. Puetz, in order to learn, for one thing, the truth about the rumored Jewish pogrom and secondly to obtain information on the arrest of the Polish office personnel. SS Major [SS—Sturmbannfuehrer] Puetz stated to me that no pogrom (Aktion) whatever was planned. Moreover such a pogrom would be stupid because the firms and the Reichsbahn would lose valuable workers.

An hour later I received a summons to appear before the Area Commissioner of Rowno. His deputy, Stableiter and Cadet Officer [Ordensjunker] Beck, subjected me to the same questioning as I had undergone at the SD. My explanation that I had sent the Jews home for urgent delousing appeared plausible to him. He then told me—making me promise to keep it a secret—that a pogrom would in fact take place on the evening of Monday 13 July 1942. After lengthy negotiation I managed to persuade him to give me permission to take my Jewish workers to Sdolbunow—but only after the pogrom had been carried out. During the night it would be up to me to protect the house in the Ghetto against the entry of Ukrainian militia and SS. As confirmation of the discussion he gave me a document, which stated that the Jewish employees of Messrs. Jung were not affected by the pogrom [Original attached.]

On the evening of this day I drove to Rowno and posted myself with Fritz Einsporn in front of the house in the Bahnhofstrasse in which the Jewish workers of my firm slept. Shortly after 22:00 the Ghetto was encircled by a large SS detachment and about three times as many members of the Ukrainian militia. Then the electric arclights which had been erected in and around the Ghetto were switched on. SS and militia squads of 4 to 6 men entered or at least tried to enter the houses. Where the doors and windows were closed and the inhabitant did not open at the knocking, the SS men and militia broke the windows, forced the doors with beams and crowbars and entered the houses. The people living there were driven on to the streets just as they were, regardless of whether they were dressed or in bed. Since the Jews in most cases refused to leave their houses and resisted, the SS and militia applied force. They finally succeeded, with strokes of the whip, kicks and blows with rifle butts in clearing the houses. The people were driven out of their houses in such haste that small children in bed had been left behind in several instances. In the street women cried out for their children and children for their parents. That did not prevent the SS from driving the people along the road, at running pace, and hitting them, until they reached a waiting freight train. Car after car was filled, and the screaming of women and children, and the cracking of whips and rifle shots resounded unceasingly. Since several families or groups had barricaded themselves in especially strong buildings, and the doors could not be forced with crowbars or beams, these houses were now blown open with hand grenades. Since the Ghetto was near the railroad tracks in Rowno, the younger people tried to get across the tracks and over a small river to get away from the Ghetto area. As this stretch of country was beyond the range of the electric lights, it was illuminated by signal rockets. All through the night these beaten, hounded and wounded people moved along the lighted streets. Women carried their dead children in their arms, children pulled and dragged their dead parents by their arms and legs down the road toward the train. Again and again the cries "Open the door!" "Open the door!" echoed through the Ghetto.

About 6 o'clock in the morning I went away for a moment, leaving behind Einsporn and several other German workers who had returned in the meantime. I thought the greatest danger was past and that I could risk it. Shortly after I left, Ukrainian militia men forced their way into 5 Bahnhofstrasse and brought 7 Jews out and took them to a collecting point inside the Ghetto. On my return I was able to prevent further Jews from being taken out. I went to the collecting point to save these 7 men. I saw dozens of corpses of all ages and both sexes in the streets I had to walk along. The doors of the houses stood open, windows were smashed. Pieces of clothing, shoes, stockings, jackets, caps, hats, coats, etc., were lying in the street. At the corner of a house lay a baby less than a year old, with his skull crushed. Blood and brains were spattered over the house wall and covered the area immediately around the child. The child was dressed only in a little shirt. The commander, SS Major Puetz, was walking up and down a row of about 80 to 100 male Jews who were crouching on the ground. He had a heavy dog whip in his hand. I walked up to him, showed him the written permit of Stabsleiter

Beck and demanded the seven men whom I recognized among those who were crouching on the ground. Dr. Puetz was very furious about Beck's concession and nothing could persuade him to release the seven men. He made a motion with his hand encircling the square and said that anyone who was once here would not get away. Although he was very angry with Beck, he ordered me to take the people from 5 Bahnhofstrasse out of Rowno by 8 o'clock at the latest. When I left Dr. Puetz, I noticed a Ukrainian farm cart, with two horses. Dead people with stiff limbs were lying on the cart. Legs and arms projected over the side boards. The cart was making for the freight train. I took the remaining 74 Jews who had been locked in the house to Sdolbunow.

Several days after the 13th of July 1942 the Area Commissioner of Sdolbunow, Georg Marschall, called a meeting of all firm managers, railroad superintendents, and leaders of the Organization Todt and informed them that the firms, etc., should prepare themselves for the "resettlement" of the Jews which was to take place almost immediately. He referred to the pogrom in Rowno where all the Jews had been liquidated, i.e., had been shot near Kostolpol.

I make the above statement in Wiesbaden, Germany, on 10 November 1945. I swear by God that this is the absolute truth.

Hermann Friedrich Graebe

Subscribed and sworn to before me at Wiesbaden, Germany this 10 day of November 1945.

Homer B. Crawford
Major, AC
Investigator Examiner,
War Crimes Branch

I, Elisabeth Radziejewska, being first duly sworn, state: That I truly translated the oath administered by Major Homer B. Crawford to Herman Friedrich Graebe and that thereupon he made and subscribed the foregoing statement in my presence.

Elisabeth Radziejewska
Interpreter

Subscribed and sworn before me at Wiesbaden, Germany, this 10th day of November 1945.

Homer B. Crawford
Major, AC
Investigator Examiner
War Crimes Branch, US Army

Translation of Document 3047-PS (USA 80). *Excerpt from notes made by Lahousen (Assistant to Admiral Canaris, Head of Intelligence Section OKW) for the diary of Admiral Canaris, 19 September 1939; and complete report, dated 24 October 1941, on the execution of 6500 Jews in Borrisow received by Lahousen in his official capacity as a German intelligence officer.*

* * *

Participants in trip
Lt. Col. Lahousen Piekenbrock
Captain Jary, retired
19 September 1939, 12:15 Departure Berlin
19:15 Arrival Gleiwitz

Stayed overnight at Hotel "Hausoberschlesien." 20 September 5:00 Departure Gleiwitz, via Katowice, Cracow, Tarnow, to the headquarters of Army High Command 14 in Rzeszow. 12:15-14:00 Conference in Rzeszow with G2 (IC) and Major Dehmel. G2 (Major Schmidt-Richtberg) explains situation as well as military action in Lwow. G2 further reports about unrest in that army area arising from the partly illegal measures taken by Special Purpose Group [Einsatz Gruppe] of Brigadier General Woyrsch. (Mass shooting especially of Jews.) It was especially annoying to the troops that young men instead of fighting at the front, were testing their courage on defenseless people.

Major Dehmel reports on measure taken by him in the area of the Ukrainian settlement area. (Advance territory of the 18th Army Command).

14:00 continuation of trips to Przemysl. Stayed overnight in the archbishop's palace of the Greek Catholic (Ukrainian) Bishop Josef Korzelowski. Excellent impression of the personality of this church dignitary. I discussed with him and his chancellor, a married Greek Catholic priest, the Ukrainian question and our cooperation with the Ukrainians. Great apprehension in the bishop's palace that Przemysl would be turned over to the Russians.

[Report received by Lahousen in his official capacity as a German intelligence officer.]
Copy

24 October 1941
Report on the execution of Jews in Borrisow.
From Friday 17 October to Monday 20 October I had official

business in Borrisow. Upon arrival there on Friday I was informed by the head of the Russian security police there, Ehof, who had been installed in this post some time ago by the SD, that on the night from Sunday to Monday all Jews of Borrisow were to be shot. To my astounded question, that it would be impossible to dispatch 8000 persons into Eternity in the course of a single night in a fairly orderly manner, he replied that it was not the first time that he did this and he would be able to finish the job with his men; he was no longer a layman at this. On this occasion I also learned that about 1500 Jews were to be spared temporarily, since they were specialists, such as cobblers, tailors, blacksmiths, locksmiths, in other words artisans who were urgently needed for building up the country. The said Ehof at this time presented me with an invitation, signed by him, to the "Celebration of the German Police" which was to take place in a Borrisow restaurant on Sunday 19 October at two o'clock.

I had known Ehof in my Borrisow days. He was at one time made Komm. [Communist?] mayor of Zembin, a town about 25 kilometers from Borrisow, by some army high command. Before the outbreak of the war he was, as a Volga German, employed as a teacher for the German language in the Russian School in Zembin.

Although the shootings of Jews were to be kept secret, they were already known in the Ghetto early on Saturday. I gave my own boots for repair to a Jewish cobbler who lived on the street leading to the airport. There I learned that a delegation was on its way to the mayor, Dr. Stankewitsch, and the Chief of the Russian Security Police, Ehof, in order to obtain a temporary reprieve of these executions so that they might present a petition to the general. However, the cobbler could not tell me which general was meant.

He only told me that the Jews consider it altogether impossible that Adolf Hitler or the general could have given the order to shoot these 6500 Jews. I learned further that the mayor, Dr. Stankewitsch, had promised them to speak to the general about it and that he added that he himself could only say that the conduct of the Jews residing in his official district had been exemplary in every respect. By "conduct" he meant the order in the Ghetto, the performing of the work imposed on the Jews, the raising of 300,000 Rubles in taxes imposed on them a few weeks ago, the turning in of gold, silver, etc., which they fulfilled completely.

On Saturday I visited the already mentioned "Celebration of

the German Police", not so much in order to drink beer or liquor there, but because I knew beforehand to what an unworthy extent this celebration would develop, in other words, to look the affair over.

Of the so-called prominent citizens there were present: a commissioner of the SD—a squire [Ordensjunker] Burg Vogelsang —with his wife, a lieutenant of the GFP, the mayor, Dr. Stankewitsch, the Chief of the Russian Security Police, Ehof.

In addition there were present the assistant chief of the Russian Security Police, Kowalewski, a large number of Security Policemen and their wives, fiancees, or girl friends, a number of German non-coms, and men, and a lot of people.

There was a lot of talk and still more drinking. I started a conversation with the above mentioned Russian—Kowalewski— an old policeman of the time of the Czars. He is a very sympathetic, quiet, and discreet man of 62, and he informed me among other things that this celebration was to be ended by 9 o'clock because a "welikoje deld", a big affair, was scheduled for tomorrow. K asked me to go home with him after the celebration because he had the urge to speak his mind. After reprimanding a few members of our Wehrmacht for disorderly conduct and because no one could expect me to witness these disgusting excesses any longer, I left this place at about 5 o'clock in the afternoon and returned about 8 o'clock in order to pick up K and to accompany him to his home. I spent two hours with K in lively conversation, we exchange reminiscences of Czarist days, of the time of the White Russian battles against Bolshevism, and then we also talked of present conditions. The point of view of K, who is a great admirer of everything German, especially of Adolf Hitler and the German Wehrmacht, coincided wholly with mine; a man who really has his heart in it.

After leaving K, I returned to my quarters and talked to my Russian landlord until bedtime. Here I learned among other things that a few days previously "Buessing Hall" had burned down and the next night "Opel Hall", and in addition another hall in which the kitchen, etc., of a German Wehrmacht unit was stationed. Of course we also talked of the impending shooting of Jews, for this was also known to the civilian population. My hosts said verbatim, and this was probably the attitude of all non-Jews living in Borrisow on that evening: "Pustj oni pogibajut: oni mnogo plochogo nam nadelali!" In German: "Let them perish; they did us a lot of harm!"

This is what happened on the following morning: The shootings were begun at 3 am. First the men were brought out. They were driven to the place of execution in Russian cars, escorted by men of the Russian Security police of Borrisow who were detailed for this purpose. Because there were not enough of these men, however, reinforcements were brought from the neighboring Russian Security Police offices, such as Zembin, etc. They were provided with the well-known red and white armband and armed with rifles or automatic pistols. On the Polotzkaja Uliza road leading to the airport I saw these cars, at considerable intervals, loaded with women and children. These cars were guarded by men of the Russian Security Police. On the roof sat among others a Russian policeman with an automatic pistol in readiness. The women and children of all ages in these cars cried and whimpered and screamed for help as soon as they saw a German Wehrmacht member. In this manner one car followed the other during the whole day in the direction of the place of execution, which was located in the woods near the former staff headquarters of the army group "Center". Besides, since there were apparently not sufficient cars and the time was drawing short, groups of women and children were constantly being herded down the already mentioned road, partly with iron rods. On the periphery of the Ghetto, that is on this same street, groups of Jewish women and children, even babies in their mother's arms, were standing ready to be picked up. In the distance the noise of rifles could be heard all day, the women and children cried and screamed, cars raced through the streets and the Ghetto and kept bringing new victims—all before the eyes of the civilian population and the German military personnel that happened to come along.

A blockade may have been intended but could not be carried out because the other side of the street as well as the side streets were inhabited by non-Jews. The eyes of the latter expressed either complete apathy or horror, because the scenes which took place in the streets were ghastly! The non-Jews may have believed on the evening preceding the executions that the Jews deserved their fate, but on the following morning their sentiment was: "Who ordered such a thing? How is it possible to kill off 6500 Jews all at once? Now it is the Jews' turn, when will it be ours? What did these poor Jews do? All they did was work! The really guilty ones are surely in safely!" The executions continued all day Monday! Late in the evening the shooting could not only be heard from the woods but also spread to the Ghetto and nearly all the streets of the city since, in order to escape their fate, many Jews had broken out of the Ghetto and tried somehow to save themselves. On that evening and during that night it was not advisable even for a member of the Wehrmacht to venture on the streets, in order to avoid the danger of being killed or at least wounded by the Russian policemen, due to a generally prevalent nervousness. About 10 o'clock in the evening a fire was raging in the city and mild shooting was going on. A few houses were burning in the Ghetto and in the vicinity of the Ghetto—the cause is not known to me.

It must be added that German soldiers were summoned toward evening to blockade the Ghetto and to prevent the Jews' escaping. As I learned from a noncommissioned officer, a few Jews were said to have been caught and turned over to the Russian Security Police for execution. The shooting continued throughout the night. On Tuesday, about 8 o'clock in the morning, I was again a witness of the same occurrences as on the previous day. By no means all the Jews had been shot. Many escorted Russian cars returned from the woods. Piled high on these cars was the clothing of the victims. Thus everybody could see what was going on. The clothing was brought to city warehouses. At many places in the Ghetto and along the street already described groups of Jews cowered, awaiting their execution.

As I heard, some Jews are said to have committed suicide in the nearby Beresina. The most gruesome scenes are said to have taken place in the Ghetto during this operation. According to report all specialists were shot, at least the majority of them. That may be so, for, escorted by two Russian policemen, I entered the homes of a tailor and a cobbler on the main street; the barbed wire had been torn down and I found the house abandoned. It is hard to describe the appearance of these homes! In order to obtain details of the executions, I struck up a conversation with these two Russian Security men, and I was told the following:

A few days earlier Russian prisoners of war had dug in the woods some huge mass graves about 100 meters long, 5 meters wide, and 3 meters deep. According to the reports of these eyewitnesses, the executions were performed as follows:

The first delinquents, about 20 men, were made to jump into the pits after taking off all but their underwear. They were then shot from above! Of course these dead and half-dead people were lying pell-mell. The next victims had to line them up so as to gain as much space as possible. Then it continued as above. When the bottom row of the mass grave was full, the Jews had to put a layer of sand over the bodies and had to trample upon both sand and bodies. The most horrible scenes are said to have taken place in these two mass graves! Shortly before my departure for the front I met two German soldiers, a private first class and a corporal, who, for curiosity's sake, had witnessed these executions from very close by. They fully confirmed the information sought by me. They added that the Russian policemen were given a great deal of liquor, otherwise they would hardly have been able to perform their difficult task! The population of Borrisow is of the opinion that the Russian Security men would enrich themselves with the valuables left behind by the Jews, such as gold, silver, furs, cloth, leather, etc., as they were said to have done during previous executions. These security men, moreover, are said to consist largely of old Communists, but nobody dares to report them because they are feared. The population generally desires the occupation of all important posts by German nationals!

      Signed: Soennecken
      Master sergeant and interpreter
      for the Russian language with
      Intelligence Command B

Postscript: There is a rumor in Borrisow that the now vacant houses of the Jews shall be prepared for Jews from Germany, who in turn shall be liquidated in the same manner as were the Jews of Borrisow.

Translation of Document 3048-PS (USA 274). Excerpt from Speech by von Schirach before European Youth Congress in Vienna, on deportation to the Ghetto of the East tens of thousands of Jews from Vienna, published in newspaper Voelkischer Beobachter, 15 September 1942.

*   *   *

VOELKISCHER BEOBACHTER
Vienna Edition
15 September 1942

Baldur von Schirach's speech before the European Youth Congress held in Vienna on 14 September 1942

The Jew a danger to culture.

*   *   *

Every Jew who exerts influence in Europe is a danger to European culture. If anyone reproaches me with having driven from this city, which was once the European metropolis of Jewry, tens of thousands upon tens of thousands of Jews into the ghetto of the East, I feel myself compelled to reply: I see in this an action contributing to European culture.

Translation of Document 3050AE-PS. *Excerpts from series of articles designed to create and foster an anti-Jewish attitude, published in "The SA Man."*

* * *

[Articles Designed to Create and Foster an Anti-Jewish Attitude]

Article entitled: "Finish up with the Jews", with subtitle: "We want no women to buy from Jews, and no Jewish girl friends." 27 July, 1935, p. 4. [This article reads in part as follows:]

"German women finally wake up and do not buy any more from Jews. And you, German girl, also finally wake up and do not go with Jews any longer.

"The Jew is also a person? Quite right! Nobody has ever argued that point. The only question is: What kind of a person is he? Oh, I know German women, your groceryman is such an obliging and decent Jew, and your friend, German girl, is such a nice and polite person! Yes, I understand.

To the devil finally with this nursery tale.

Snake remains a snake, and
Jew remains a Jew! * * *

* * * "German women, if you buy from Jews, and German girl, if you carry on with Jews, then both of you betray your German Volk and your Fuehrer, Adolf Hitler, and commit a sin against your German Volk and its future! Finally, wake up German woman, aren't you ashamed to give your household money to Jews? Do you know what you are doing thereby? You give the deadly enemy of the German Volk as well as your own and your children's deadly enemy the weapons into his hands for the fight against Germany. Must that be? Can't you really go two or three houses further and obtain your needs from a German national?

"And you, German girl, you give your best, your honor and your blood to one of a strange race?

"Aren't you ashamed of yourself?" * * *

Article entitled: "The Jewish World Danger." 2 February, 1935, p. 5.

The Documentary Evidence   3050AE-PS

Article entitled: "Jewish Worries" (defending the practice of excluding Jews from certain resorts). 20 July, 1935, p. 4.

Article entitled: "Jews Aren't Wanted Here," with pictures posted on outskirts of villages showing signs bearing the same message. 1 June, 1935, p. 1. [The last portion of this article reads as follows:]

"Since the day when National Socialism unrolled its flag and the march began for the Germany for Germans, our battle also included the Jewry * * * Let the Jew continue with his methods against New Germany. We know that at the end we will remain the victor, for every day and every National Socialist deed brings out the Jewish lies and horror system more and more, and by waking up the people and their knowledge of the Jewish world danger, the last hope of the Jewry for the undermining of Germany will suffer shipwreck.

"But the high point of Jewish impudence and arrogance is, on the one side, to wage the war against Germany to the last, and on the other side, to expect that the German working people should carry their money into Jewish stores. Here our explanation and our battle must be employed.

"It does not do for innumerable citizens to daily buy from Jews and to fill the pockets of our enemies with their money, who find their work and bread through the National Socialist Germany, and who are citizens of the National Socialist Reich, and benefited by the National Socialist battle. He who buys from Jews takes goods and wages from his citizens.

"The greatest part of our people have given the right answer to his lies and boycott campaign. In thousands of towns and villages signs and posters say: "Jews are not wanted here!" Many thousands of new citizens have become anti-Semitic because of Jewish dealings. However, the whole German folk must realize and grasp the Jewish world danger.

"We break no windows of Jewish stores, we do not carry out any program or any demonstrations in front of Jewish stores. We only elucidate or explain to our blood brothers regarding the methods of the Jew, his fight against us and against all peoples of the earth. Then, also, outside of the last German village, the sign will stand "Jews are not wanted here!" and then, finally, no German citizen will again cross the threshold of a Jewish store. To achieve this goal is the mission of the SA man as political soldier of the Fuehrer. Next to his word and his explanations stands his example."

Article entitled: "God Save the Jew." 17 August, 1935, p. 1.
Photograph showing SA men gathered around trucks upon which are pasted signs reading: "Read the Stuermer and you will know the Jew." 24 August, 1935, p. 3.
Photograph apparently representing public SA rally showing large sign which reads: "He who knows a Jew knows a devil." 24 August, 1935, p. 3.
Article entitled: "The Face of the Jew" (with portrait of a Jew holding the hammer and sickle). 5 Oct., 1935, p. 6.
Article entitled: "Jews, Blacks and Reactionaries." 2 November, 1935, p. 2.
Article entitled: "The Camouflaged Benjamin — Jewish Cultural Bolshevism in German Music." 23 November, 1935, p. 2.
Article entitled: "The Jewish Assassination." 15 February, 1936, p. 1.
Article entitled: "Murder—the Jewish Slogan." 4 April, 1936, p. 11.
Series of articles entitled: "The Jewish Mirror." 8 weekly installments beginning 22 May, 1936, p. 17.
Series of articles entitled: "Gravediggers of World Culture." beginning 5 December, 1936, p. 6 and continuing weekly to 13 March, 1937.
Article entitled: "Rumania to the Jews?" 2 January, 1937, p. 6.
Article entitled: "Bismark's Position on Jews." 2 January, 1937, p. 7.
Article entitled: "Jewry is a Birth Error." 13 February, 1937, p. 5.
Article entitled: "The Protection of the German Blood." 24 April, 1937, p. 1.
Article entitled: "Crooked Ways to Money and Power." 24 April, 1937, p. 1.
Article entitled: "The Camouflage of Jewry — Beginning or End?" 22 May, 1937, p. 14.
Article entitled: "How come still German Jews?" 18 June, 1938, p. 2.
Article entitled: "Westheimer Jew Servants." 22 January, 1938, p. 2.
Article entitled: "The Poor Jew — Well! Well!" 19 March, 1938, p. 15.

Article entitled: "Jewish Methods, Churchly Parallel." 9 September, 1938, p. 4.
Article entitled: "Jewish World Revolution — out of the U.S.A." 30 December, 1938, p. 4.
Article entitled: "Jews and Free Masons." 13 January, 1939, p. 15.
Article entitled: "Friends of the World Jewry—Roosevelt and Ickes." 3 February, 1939, p. 14.
[Anti-Masonic Articles]
Article entitled: "The World Polyp of Free Masonry," with subheading: "A Dangerous Enemy must be made Powerless." 23 February, 1935, p. 2.
Article entitled: "Revolts and Disturbances—the Work of the Free Masons." 28 March, 1936, p. 11.
Article entitled: "5 Million Free Masons—a World Threat." 5 March, 1938, p. 6.

December 1936

GRAVE-DIGGERS OF WORLD CULTURE

The way of Jewish sub-humanity to world Supremacy

"The 'SA-Mann' has made it its mission to function representatively in the clarification of the true face of Bolshevism. We begin today a series of articles which should bring out the dark paths upon which the Jewry wanted to achieve world supremacy by historical facts and material from reliable sources. Another purpose of this publication is to show that every time and in all States in which Bolshevism was at work, the Jews occupied the spiritual and organizational leadership and that Jewry and Bolshevism are one and the same in the end. For this purpose we suggest the comrades to especially take notice of this series of articles and to see that they are further circulated."

Translation of Document 3051-PS (USA 240). Three teletype orders from Heydrich to all stations of the State Police, 10 November 1938, on measures against the Jews, and one order terminating the action.

* * *

[First Document: Sheet of paper approximately 4 inches by 6 inches, containing pencil notes as follows:]
General Field Marshal has noted.

I.A. (by order)
[initials illegible]
15 Nov 38

[initials illegible] 20 Nov.

[Second Document:]
COPY

II
I. Teletype

Berlin, 10 November 1938

1. To all Headquarters and Stations of the State Police.
2. To all Sections and Sub-sections of the SD.

Urgently to be submitted!
Re: Measures against Jews.

Following my order of tonight, I explicitly point out that looting will be barred under all circumstances by using corresponding measures.

Looters are to be arrested. For more details, instructions will be given by me.

The Reich "Ministry of Justice" [Reichsjustizministerium] has instructed all Public Prosecutors to put at the disposal of the State Police the prisons to hold the arrested Jews.

In addition, the Reich Ministry of Justice asks that in no case are orders to be issued against persons who may have been arrested during the action.

Finally, the Reich Ministry of Justice has instructed the Public Prosecutors not to proceed in any interrogation on matters of the Jewish actions [Judenaktionen].

All this exclusively for your information.

The Chief of the Security Police
/s/ Heydrich

[Third Document:]
COPY

Berlin, 10 November 1938.

Chief of the Security Police
I. Teletype

To all Headquarters of the State Police.

Referring to my teletype instructions, I instruct you once more that whenever, during the protest action, looting has occurred, you should proceed ruthlessly, by intensive interrogations, to establish the persons guilty and to secure the objects of the looting.

I ask you to inform me by 11 November 1938, at 8 AM, by

telegram, all cases of looting known to you, indicating just the facts and the guilty persons if found.

Before turning over these persons to the examining judge, you must get my instructions.

If necessary, the Kripo can be used to clear up the facts.

Chief of the Security Police
/s/ Heydrich

[Fourth Document:]

SECRET

Copy of Teletype from Munich, 10 November 1938, 1:20 AM.

To all Headquarters and Stations of the State Police.
To all Districts and Sub-districts of the SD.
Urgent! Submit immediately to the Chief or his deputy!
Re: Measures against Jews tonight.

Because of the attempt on the life of the Secretary of the Legation von Rath in Paris tonight, 9-10 November 1938, demonstrations against Jews are to be expected throughout the Reich. The following instructions are given on how to treat these events:

1. The Chiefs of the State Police, or their deputies, must get in telephonic contact with the political leaders [Gauleitung oder Kreisleitung] who have jurisdiction over their districts and have to arrange a joint meeting with the appropriate inspector or commander of the Order Police [Ordnungspolizei] to discuss the organization of the demonstrations. At these discussions the political leaders have to be informed that the German Police has received from the Reichsfuehrer SS and Chief of the German Police the following instructions, in accordance with which the political leaders should adjust their own measures.

a. Only such measures should be taken which do not involve danger to German life or property. (For instance synagogues are to be burned down only when there is no danger of fire to the surroundings).

b. Business and private apartments of Jews may be destroyed but not looted. The police is instructed to supervise the execution of this order and to arrest looters.

c. On business streets, particular care is to be taken that non-Jewish business should be protected from damage.

d. Foreigners, even Jews, are not to be molested.

2. The demonstrations which are going to take place should not be hindered by the police provided that the instructions quoted above in section 1 are carried out. The police has only to supervise compliance with the instructions.

3. Upon receipt of this telegram, in all synagogues and offices of the Jewish communities the available archives should be seized by the police, to forestall destruction during the demonstrations. This refers only to valuable historical material, not to new lists of taxes, etc. The archives are to be turned over to the competent SD offices.

4. The direction of the measures of the Security Police concerning the demonstrations against Jews is vested with the organs of the State Police, inasmuch as the inspectors of the Security Police are not issuing their own orders. In order to carry out the measures of the Security Police, officials of the Criminal Police as well as members of the SD of the "Verfuegungstruppe" and the allgemeinen SS may be used.

5. Inasmuch as in the course of the events of this night the employment of officials used for this purpose would be possible, in all districts as many Jews, especially rich ones, are to be arrested as can be accommodated in the existing prisons [Haftraeumen]. For the time being only healthy men not too old are to be arrested. Upon their arrest, the appropriate concentration camps should be contacted immediately, in order to confine them in these camps as fast as possible. Special care should be taken that the Jews arrested in accordance with these instructions are not mistreated.

6. The contents of this order are to be forwarded to the appropriate inspectors and commanders of the Ordnungspolizei and to the districts of the SD [SD-Oberabschnitte und SD-Unterabschnitte], adding that the Reichsfuehrer SS and Chief of the German Police ordered this police measure. The Chief of the Ordnungspolizei, has given the necessary instructions to the Ordnungspolizei, including the fire brigade. In carrying out the ordered measures, the closest harmony should be assured between the Sicherheitspolizei and the Ordnungspolizei.

The receipt of this telegram is to be confirmed by the Chiefs of the State Police or their deputies by telegram to the Gestapo, care of SS Standartenfuehrer Mueller.

/s/ Heydrich,
SS Gruppenfuehrer.

[Fifth Document:]
COPY
Teletype
To all Headquarters of the State Police
To all Districts and Sub-districts of the SD.
Protest actions are stopped (see information of press and radio).

III - 462

- An increased patrol activity is to be instituted for the coming night in cooperation with the Order Police [Ordnungspolizei].

Actions still taking place should be barred. However, the justified indignation of the population should be taken into consideration.

Ruthless proceedings should be taken against looters.

The arrests should be continued without restriction and exclusively by the State Police [Staatspolizei] stations.

Chief of the Security Police
/s/ Heydrich

Translation of Document 3058-PS (USA 508). Letter from Heydrich to Goering, 11 November 1938, reporting results of the action against the Jews.

* * *

The General Field Marshal has been informed. No steps are to be taken.

By Order
Roe [?]
15. 11. 38

The Chief of the Security Police
LL B 4—5716/38 g

Berlin SW 11, 11 Nov. 1938
Prinz-Albrecht Strasse 8
Tel. A 2 Flora 0040.
SECRET

Express letter

To: The Prime Minister General Field Marshal Goering. For the attention of Dr. Gritzbach Secretary to the Ministry,
Berlin W 8,
Leipzieger Str. 3.

Subject: Action against the Jews.

Reports of the State Police offices which have been received up to 11.11.1938 give the following general impression:

In numerous cities, looting of Jewish shops and business premises has occurred. In order to avoid further looting, strong action was taken in all cases. 174 persons were arrested for looting.

The extent of the destruction of Jewish shops and houses cannot yet be verified by figures. The figures given in the reports: 815 shops destroyed, 171 dwelling-houses set on fire or destroyed, only indicate a fraction of the actual damage caused, as far as arson is concerned. Due to the urgency of the reporting, the reports received to date are entirely limited to general statements such as "numerous" or "most shops destroyed". Therefore the figures given must have been exceeded considerably.

191 Synagogues were set on fire, and another 76 completely destroyed. In addition 11 parish halls [Gemeindehauser] cemetery chapels and similar buildings were set on fire and 3 more completely destroyed.

20,000 Jews were arrested, also 7 Aryans and 3 foreigners. The latter were arrested for their own safety.

36 deaths were reported and those seriously injured were also numbered at 36. Those killed and injured are Jews. One Jew is still missing. The Jews killed include one Polish national, and those injured include 2 Poles.

(Signed) Heydrich K.

Translation of Document 3063-PS (USA 332). Letter of transmittal, 13 February 1939, and report about the events and the judicial proceedings by the Supreme Nazi Party Court against persons who killed Jews during the course of the anti-Jewish demonstrations of 9 November 1938.

* * *

National Socialist German Labor Party
The Chief Party Judge   Munich 33
         Telephone: 50812-50815, 50825
         [illegible pencil notations]
         Munich 13 February 1939
         Sch/L.

To the General Field Marshal Hermann Goering
Berlin W. 8, Leipzieger Street 3
         FILE
Dear Party Member Goering!

I enclose the report of my special senate about the procedure hitherto concluded concerning the excesses on the occasion of the anti-Jewish operations of 9 and 10 November 1938.

         Heil Hitler!
         (signed) Walter Buch
Enclosures

SECRET
National Socialist German Labor Party
Supreme Party Court [Oberstes Parteigericht]

The Chief of the Central Office   Munich 33
                                    Telephone 50812-50815, 50825
File no. 47   (Dictation) Symbol—Sch/R
SECRET

Report about the events and judicial proceedings in connection with the anti-semitic demonstrations of 9 November 1938

On the evening of 9 November 1938, Reich propaganda director Party Member Dr. Goebbels told the party leaders assembled at a social evening in the old town hall in Munich, that in the districts [Gauen] of Kurhessen and Magdeburg-Anhalt it had come to the hostile Jewish demonstrations, during which Jewish shops were demolished and synagogues were set on fire. The Fuehrer at Goebbels's suggestion had decided that such demonstrations were not to be prepared or organized by the Party, but so far as they originated spontaneously, they were not to be discouraged either. In other respects, Party Member Dr. Goebbels carried out the purport of what was prescribed in the teletype of the Reich propaganda administration of 10 Nov. 1938 (12:30 to 1 o'clock).

(Enclosure 2)

It was probably understood by all the Party leaders present, from the oral instructions of the Reich propaganda director, that the Party should not appear outwardly as the originator of the demonstrations but in reality should organize and execute them. Instructions in this sense were telephoned immediately (thus a considerable time before transmission of the first teletype) to the bureaus of their district [Gau] by a large part of the Party members present.

On 10 November 1938 at 01:20 there was issued to the State police and to the State police main offices [Leitstellen] the enclosed teletype (enclosure 1) of the secret state police; at 01:40, the circular of the Reich propaganda director (enclosure 2); at 02:56, a circular of the staff of the deputy of the Fuehrer (enclosure 3) prohibiting setting fire to Jewish shops; the circular of 10 November 1938 of the staff of the deputy of the Fuehrer (enclosure 4); at 15:15 confirmed that the Party carries no responsibility for drives [Aktionen] and makes it the duty of Party bureaus to proceed accordingly and to issue necessary directions only after reaching an understanding with the qualified Gauleiter.

At the end of November 1938 the chief Party Court through reports from several district [Gau] courts heard that these demonstrations of the 9 November 1938 had gone as far as plundering and killing of Jews to considerable extent and that they had already been the object of investigation by the police and the state prosecutor.

The deputy of the Fuehrer agreed with the interpretation of the chief Party Court, that known transgression in any case should be investigated under the jurisdiction of the party:

1. Because of the obvious connection between the events to be judged and the instructions which Reich propaganda director, Party Member Dr. Goebbels gave in the town hall at the social evening. Without investigation and evaluation of this connection, a just judgment did not appear possible. This investigation, however, could not be left to innumerable state courts, especially as the demonstrations had meanwhile been presented to the public as being the spontaneous expression of the sentiments of the people.

2. According to the conception of the Supreme Party Court [Oberstes Parteigericht] it must, as a matter of principle, be impossible for political offenses, which primarily concern the interests of the Party and which even though this be only from the viewpoint of the perpetrator are desired by the Party as illegal measures should be determined and judged by the state courts without the Party having the possibility of first obtaining clarification about the happenings and matters pertaining to them so that, if occasion arises, the Fuehrer could be asked in good time to cancel the proceedings at the state court. Due to such considerations General of the Army [Generalfeldmarschall] Party Member Goering, as deputy of the Fuehrer, has entrusted the secret state police and the Party jurisdiction with the investigation of excesses.

The Supreme Party Court has reserved for itself the investigation of killings, severe mistreatment and moral crimes. On the basis of state police inquiries the judges of the Supreme Party Court, who were present with their alternates [zweifacher Besetzung], held and completed quick trials of those cases about which facts were ascertained up to 17 January 1939. Gau leaders and Group leaders of the branches served as jurors at the trials and decisions. The decisions which, for reasons to be discussed later, contain in part only the statements of the facts, are attached.

1. Party Member Frey Heinrich, Party Member since 1932, residing in Rheinhausen, Horst-Wessel-Strasse 23, was ejected from the Party because of a moral crime and race violation perpetrated upon the thirteen-year-old school girl Ruth Kalter. Frey is in custody and has been handed over to the criminal court. (Enclosure 5).

2. Party Member *Gerstner* Gustav, Party membership number 3,135,242, SA-sergeant [Oberscharfuehrer], residing at Niederwern, at present district court prison Wuerzburg, was expelled from the NSDAP and SA because of theft. Gerstner is in custody and has been handed over to the public [staatlich] court because suspected of race violation (enclosure 6).

3. Party Members *schmidinger* Friedrich, SA-2nd Lt. [Sturmfuehrer], residing at 36 Eisenhand Street, Linz and *Hintersteiner Hans*, Party membership number 434,332, SA-captain, [Sturmhauptfuehrer] residing at 74 Haupt Street, Linz, was expelled from the NSDAP for moral crimes against the Jewess Unger and are now in protective custody (enclosure 7).

4. Party Member *Norgall* Franz, Party membership number 342,751, SA-2nd Lt. [Sturmfuehrer], residing at 58 Neuhoefer Street, Heilsberg (East Prussia), was given a warning and sentenced to three years deprivation of ability to hold public office because of disciplinary violation, namely killing of the Jewish couple Seelig in Heilsberg contrary to orders (enclosure 8).

5. Party Member *Rudnik* Rudolf, Party membership number 162,948, SA-major [Sturmbannfuehrer], residing at 3/0 Zerber Street, Dessau, was given a warning and sentenced to three years deprivation of ability to hold public office because of shooting of the sixteen-year-old Jew Herbert Stein contrary to orders after completion of the drive (enclosure 9).

In the following cases of killing of Jews, proceedings were suspended or minor punishments were pronounced:

6. Party Member *Fruehling* August, Party membership number about 4,188,000, SA-sergeant [Sharfuehrer], residing at 132 Deichweg, Lesum, and *Mahlstedt* Bruno, SA-corporal [Rottenfuehrer] living at Lesum, because of shooting of the Jewish couple Goldberg and because of shooting of the Jew Sinasohn (enclosure 10).

7. Party Members *Behring* Willi, Party membership number 209,620, SA-sergeant [Truppfuehrer], living at 40 York Street, Bremen, and *Heike* Josef, Party membership number 678,884, SA-1st Lt. [Obersturmfuehrer], residing at 73 Sedan Street, Bremen, because of shooting the Jew Rosenbaum and the Jewess Zwienicki (enclosure 11).

8. Party members *Uhlig* Max, Party membership number 2,473,540, SA-2nd Lt. [Sturmfuehrer] residing at 39 Maurer Street, Neidenburg, *Schudwitz* Emil, Party membership number 2,473,425, SA-sergeant [Truppfuehrer], residing at 6b Bruecken Street, Neidenburg, and PA. *Rueckstein* Fritz, SA-corporal [Rottenfuehrer], living at 8 Heimstaetten Street, Nei-

denburg, because of killing the Jew Zack, injuring the Jews Aron, Kurt and Helmuth Zack.

PA. *Tybussek* Max, SA-sergeant [Scharfuehrer], living at 4 Kurze Street, Neidenburg, PA. *Kubin* Ernst, SA-Pfc [Sturmmann], living at 5 Bruecken Street, Neidenburg, and PA. [Party aspirant] *Strysio* Wilhelm, SA-corporal [Rottenfuehrer], residing at 10 Ziegler Street, Neidenburg, because of killing the Jew Naftali and injuring the Aryan, Duscha (enclosure 12).

9. Party Member *Oesterreich* Fritz, Party membership number 489,020, local group leader [Orstgruppenleiter], residing at 56b Preussen Street, Luen-Horstmar, because of shooting the Jew Kniebel, Party Member *Gutt* Heinrich a member since 1 March 1933, special county section administrator [Kreisfachabteilungswalter] for division "plain and fancy foods" [Nahrung und Genuss], living at 80 Horst-Wessel Street, Luenen-Sued, because of shooting the Jew Bruch (enclosure 13).

10. Party Member *Frey* Adolf, Party membership number 1,829,915, local group leader [Ortsgruppenleiter], residing at 1 Robert Wagner Street, Eberstadt, because of shooting the Jewess Susanne Stern (enclosure 14).

11. Party Members *Schmidt* Heinrich, Party membership number 746,215, SS-1st Lt. [Obersturmfuehrer], residing at 22 Kirch Street, Luenen, and *Meckler* Ernst, Party membership number 2,792,904, block warden [Blockleiter], residing at 46 Kirch Street, Luenen, because of drowning the Jew Elsoffer (enclosure 15).

12. Party Members *Puchta* Werner, Party membership number 481,785, SA-major [Sturmbannfuehrer], residing at 11 Gravelott Street, Chemnitz, *Goerner* Werner, Party membership number 321,146, SA-1st Lt. [Obersturmfuehrer], residing at 130 Planitz Street, Chemnitz, *Immerthal* Guido, Party membership number 406,588, SS-Corporal [Rottenfuehrer], residing at 20 Geitel Street, Chemnitz, *Mueller* Kurt, party membership number 5,333,545, SS-corporal [Rottenfuehrer], residing at 4 Planetta Street, Chemnitz, for killing the Jew Fuerstenheim enclosure 16).

13. Party Member *Taudte* Heinrich, Party membership number 172,517, SS-man, residing at 23 Herrlein Street, Aschaffenburg, for killing the Jew Vogel (enclosure 7).

14. Party Member *Heinke* Werner, Party membership number 9,135, SS-Lieutenant Colonel [Obersturmbannfuehrer], residing at 12 Schiffbauer Street, Kuestrin, for killing the Jew Jakoby enclosure (enclosure 18).

15. Party Member *Schenk* Hans, Party membership number

246,109, SA-technical sergeant [Obertruppfuehrer], residing at 208 Tegernseerland Street, Munich, for killing the Jew of Polish nationality Chaim Both (enclosure 19).

16. Proceedings against the Party Members *Aichinger* Hans, SS-captain [Hauptsturmfuehrer], residing at 9 Seilergasse, Innsbruck, and *Hopfgartner* Walter, SS-Untersturmfuehrer residing at 21 Gabelsberger Street, Innsbruck, for killing the Jews Graubart, Dr. Bauer, and Berger, have already been quashed on the basis of inquiries on the part of the State Police and individual interrogations of the Supreme Court of the Party (enclosure 20).

In regard to cases 3-16 the Supreme Party Court asks the Fuehrer to quash the proceedings in the State Criminal Courts

The Reich Minister of Justice has been informed of this petition and the decisions on which it was based handed down by the Supreme Party Court.

Cases 4-16 are killings committed by order, committed on the basis of a vague or presumed order, committed without orders but motivated by hatred against Jews or in the opinion that vengeance ought to be taken for the death of Party Member von Rath upon the wish of the leaders, or killings motivated by a resolution suddenly formed in the excitement of the situation, whereby here too the professed object of the entire action was the innermost reason, as well as the thought that reprisals had to be made in some form or other, on behalf of Party Member von Rath.

If a clearly defined order is at hand (enclosures 10, 11, and 20) the request to quash the proceedings against the immediate perpetrator needs no further argument. The order must shift the responsibility from the person who acted to the person who gave the order. Furthermore the men often had to fight down strongest inner restraints in order to carry out the order. As was repeatedly expressed by the culprits, it is not our SA and SS men's affair to force their way into bedrooms by night dressed in civilian clothes in order personally to do away with the hated political foe by his wife's side or together with his wife.

The verification of the circumstances under which the orders were given has shown that in all these cases a misunderstanding arose in some link or other, of the chain of orders [Befehlskette] especially due to the fact that it was a matter of course to the National Socialist who was active in the days of the Party struggle that in drives in which the Party does not wish to appear as the organizer orders are not given with final clarity and with all details. He is therefore used to deduce more from what he reads in such an order than is said literally, just as it had frequently become the practice on the part of the person issuing the order in the interest of the Party to refrain from saying everything and merely to hint what he meant to achieve with the specific order — especially when it concerned illegal political demonstrations. Therefore Party Member Dr. Goebbels' instruction that the Party was not to organize this demonstration was most likely interpreted by each Party leader present in the town-hall to mean that the Party should not appear as the organizer. Party Member Dr. Goebbels probably meant it in that way, for politically interested and active circles who might participate in such demonstrations are members of the Party and its branches. Naturally they could be mobilized only through offices of the Party and its branches. Thus a series of subordinate leaders understood some unfortunately phrased orders which reached them orally or by phone, to mean that Jewish blood would now have to flow for the blood of Party Member von Rath, that at any rate the leadership did not attach importance to the life of a Jew, for example, not the Jew Gruenspan but all Jewry was guilty of the death of Party Member von Rath, the German people were therefore taking revenge on all Jewry, the synagogues were burning in the entire Reich, Jewish residences and businesses were to be laid waste, life and property of Aryans had to be protected, foreign Jews were not to be molested, the drive was being carried out by order of the Fuehrer, the police were withdrawn, pistols were to be brought, at the least resistance the weapon was to be used without consideration, as an SA man each one would certainly know what to do, etc.

(Enclosure 10, pages 5 ff, enclosure 20 and enclosure 11 pages 5 ff.)

It is a matter of course that, under the circumstances described, even an ambiguous order must direct the responsibility upwards. The same is true of a misunderstood order. (Enclosure 11 Heike case, and enclosure 12.)

It is another question, whether an intentionally ambiguous order, given with the expectation that the receiver of the order would recognize the intention of the one who gave it and would act accordingly, is not an example of the discipline of the past. In times of struggle such an order may, in individual cases, be necessary, in order to achieve a political success without giving the government any possibility of discovering the origin of the Party. This viewpoint is now obsolete. The public, down to the last man, realizes that political drives like those of 9 November were organized and directed by the Party, whether this is admitted or not.

When all the synagogues burn down in one night, it must have been organized in some way and can only have been organized by the Party. But the soldiers should never be put in a position of having any doubts in regard to the intention of the commander—whether the order really means what it says; for there is a possibility that such doubts may lead to the wrong results in important matters, or there might be doubts in a case when the commander wants to be certain that his order is understood and carried out literally. In any case, soldierly discipline and with it the National Socialist concept of discipline is undermined thereby.

Also in such cases as when Jews were killed without an order (enclosures 13, 14 and 15) contrary to orders (enclosures 8 and 9), ignoble motives could not be determined. At heart the men were convinced that they had done a service to their Fuehrer and to the Party. Therefore, exclusion from the Party did not take place. The final aim of the proceedings executed and also the yardsticks for critical examination must be according to the Policy of the Supreme Party Court [Oberstes Parteigericht]; on the one hand, to protect these party comrades who, motivated by their decent National Socialist attitude and initiative, had overshot their mark and, on the other hand, to draw a dividing line between the Party and these elements who for personal reasons basely misused the Party's national Liberation battle against Jewry or, beyond that, acted with criminal motives. For this reason, even in cases of acts contrary to orders, only disciplinary violation has been punished by punishment classed as exclusion [Ausschluss].

In the Schenk case (enclosure 19) Chaim *Both*, the Jew who was killed was a Polish citizen. The Supreme Party Court [Oberstes Parteigericht] accepted the defendant's plea that he was under the impression he had acted in self defense and quashed the proceedings. After conclusion of the proceedings the case was immediately referred back to the Secret-State Police Office [Geheimes Staatspolizeiamt] for revision of the notes in the files.

The report of the results of the proceedings so far is submitted (1) because police investigations in the other cases (all together 91) of killings have not been concluded, (2) because the results so far (especially in regard to motives and circumstances) should give an example and a general view, but, in particular, because in the future the Senate might refrain from carrying out proceedings in regard to killings of Jews within the framework of the drive of 9 November 38, in case there is no suspicion, based on police investigations, of selfish or criminal motives. The content of this report confirms this opinion. Beyond this, the last main session in the Schenk case showed that the first known case of the killing of a Jew, i.e., the Polish citizen, was reported to Reich Propaganda Leader, Party Member Dr. Goebbels on 10 November 1938 at about 2 o'clock and in this connection the opinion was expressed that something would have to be done in order to avoid having the entire drive take a dangerous turn. According to the statement by the deputy district leader [Gauleiter] of Munich — Upper Bavaria, Party Member Dr. Goebbels replied that the informer should not get excited about one dead Jew, that in the next few days thousands of Jews would perforce see the point. At that time most of the killings could still have been prevented by a supplementary decree. Since this did not happen it must be deduced from this fact as well as from the remark itself that the final success was intended, or at least considered as possible and desirable. The individual active agent carried out not only the assumed, but also the vaguely expressed and correctly understood will of the leaders. For that he cannot be punished.

[signature]   Schneider
              Schneider

[Seal]
Nat.Soc.Ger.Worker Party
Supreme Party Court.

Berlin, 22 February 1939.
[illegible pencil notation]

Dear Party Member Buch!

I thank you for forwarding the *report* of your special senate about the *procedure hitherto concluded concerning the excesses on the occasion of the anti-Jewish operations of 9 and 10 November 1938*, of which I have taken cognizance.

Heil Hitler!
                              your
                    (signed)   GOERING

To the Chief Party Judge
   Mr. Walter Buch
      Munich

Translation of Document 3085-PS. *Himmler's ordinance of 3 July 1943 charging Gestapo with execution of Thirteenth Ordinance under Reich Citizenship Law.*

* * *

MINISTERIAL GAZETTE OF THE REICH AND PRUSSIAN MINISTRY OF THE INTERIOR

Number 27

Berlin, 7 July 1943

8th (104th) year

Published by the Reich Ministry of the Interior, Page 1085.

General Tasks of the Police

Punishable acts by Jews.

Notice of the Reichsfuehrer of the SS and Chief of the German Police in the Reichsministry of the Interior of 3 July, 1943. -S-III A 5 b No. 22 IV/ 43-176-3.

All punitive reports which are made as well as all punitive and investigation procedures instigated by the authorities against Jews are to be referred for further processing without delay to the State Police main agency [Staatspol.(Leit-)Stelle] located in the permanent or temporary residence of the Jew concerned. If the Jew is suspected of trying to escape or if the danger exists that the course of law may be prejudiced, he is to be arrested and to be turned over without delay to the State Police main agency with the available documentary evidence.

To all police authorities.   —MBliV. S. 1085.

Translation of Document 3179-PS. *Law for the Protection of German Blood and Honor, 15 September 1935.*

* * *

1935 REICHSGESETZBLATT, PART I, PAGE 1146

Law for the Protection of the German Blood and of the German Honor

of 15 September, 1935.

Permeated by the knowledge that the purity of the German blood is the hypothesis for the permanence of the German people and animated by the inflexible determination to safeguard the German nation for all time, the Reichstag has unanimously decreed the following law which is hereby published:

1.

(1) Marriages between Jews and citizens of German or similar blood are forbidden. Contracted marriages are invalid even

if they are contracted abroad within the scope of this law.

(2) The proceedings for annulment can only be brought by the Public Prosecutors.

2.

Extra marital intercourse between Jews and citizens of German and similar blood is forbidden.

3.

Jews may not employ female citizens of German and similar blood under 45 years of age in their households.

4.

(1) Jews are forbidden to hoist the Reich and national flag and to display the colors of the Reich.

(2) On the other hand, the display of the Jewish colors is permissible. The practice of this authorization is under State protection.

5.

(1) Whoever acts contrary to the prohibition of 1 will be punished by penitentiary.

(2) The man who acts contrary to the prohibition of 2 will be punished by imprisonment or penitentiary.

(3) Whoever acts contrary to the terms of 3 or 4 will be punished by imprisonment up to 1 year and by fine or by one of these penalties.

6.

The Reich Minister of the Interior issues in agreement with the Fuehrer's Deputy and the Reich Minister of Justice the legal and administrative regulations necessary for the execution and supplementing of the law.

7.

The law comes into force on the day of publication.

"3" however only on 1 January 1936.

Nurnberg, 15 September 1935.

on the day of the Reich Party Rally of Freedom.

The Fuehrer and Reich Chancellor
ADOLF HITLER
The Reich Minister of the Interior
FRICK
The Reich Minister of Justice
DR. GUERTNER
The Fuehrer's Deputy
R. HESS
Minister without portfolio

The Documentary Evidence   3240-PS

Translation of Document 3240-PS. *Excerpt from Order signed by M. Bormann, 8 January 1937, refusing financial assistance to civil service employees to pay for services by Jewish doctors, dentists, lawyers, etc.*

* * *

DECREES OF THE DEPUTY OF THE FUEHRER
[Anordnungen des Stellvertreters des Fuehrers] Pages 383-385.
Decree Nr. 5/37
SUBJECT: Refusal of financial assistance etc. to patients of Jewish physicians etc.

At my instigation the Reich and Prussian Minister of the Interior has issued the following circular decree, which I transmit to you herewith for your information:

"(1) Financial assistance [Notstandsbeihilfen], including payments on account, or relief payments [Unterstuetzungen] will no longer be paid to civil service employees [Behoerdenangehoerige] for expenses that have arisen because they employed the services of Jewish physicians, dentists, pharmacies, medical personnel, hospitals, sanitoria, lying-in hospitals, funeral parlors, lawyers, etc. Exceptions will only be made in very exceptional individual cases (i.e., when imminent danger to life made the calling-in of a Jewish physician inevitable)."

* * * * * * *

In this connection I would like to remark that negotiations concerning further-reaching stipulations are already progressing.
Munich, 8 January 1937
  The Chief of Staff to the Deputy of the Fuehrer
                              (signed)   M. Bormann

Translation of Document 3244-PS (GB 267). *Preparatory Measures for the Solution of the Jewish Problem in Europe— Rumors about the Position of the Jews in the East, 9 October 1942.*

* * *

DECREES, REGULATIONS, ANNOUNCEMENTS
[Verfuegungen, Anordnungen, Bekanntgaben]
Vol. 2, Pages 131-132.
Preparatory Measures for the Solution of the Jewish Problem in Europe—Rumors About the Position of the Jews in the East.
V.I. 66/881 of the 9 Oct., 1942

In the course of the work on the final solution of the Jewish problem discussions about "very strict measures" against the Jews, especially in the Eastern territories, have lately been taking place within the population of the various areas of the Reich. Investigations showed that such discussions—mostly in a distorted and exaggerated form—were passed on by soldiers on leave from various units committed in the East, who had the opportunity to eye-witness these measures.

It is conceivable that not all "Blood Germans" are capable of demonstrating sufficient understanding for the necessity of such measures, especially not those parts of the population which do not have the opportunity of visualizing bolshevist atrocities on the basis of their own observations.

In order to be able to counter-act any formation of rumors in this connection, which frequently are of an intentional, prejudiced character, the following statements are issued for information about the present state of affairs:

For approx. 2000 years, a so-far unsuccessful battle has been waged against Judaism. Only since 1933 have we started to find ways and means in order to enable a complete separation of Judaism from the German masses.

The work toward a solution which has previously been accomplished can in the main be divided as follows:

1. The repulsion of Jews from the individual spheres of living of the German people. The laws issued by the lawmakers are hereby to be the basis, which guarantees that future generations will also be protected from a possible new overflooding by the enemy.

2. The attempt to completely drive out the enemy from the area of the Reich. In view of the only very limited living space [Lebensraum] at the disposal of the German people it was hoped this problem could be solved in the main by speeding up the Jewish emigration.

Since the outbreak of war in 1939 these possibilities of emigration decreased to an ever greater extent. On the other hand, in addition to the living space [Lebensraum] of the German people, their economic space [Wirtschaftsraum] grew steadily, so that in view of the large numbers of Jews residing in these territories a complete repulsion of the Jews by emigration is no longer possible.

Since even our next generation will not be so close to this problem and will no longer see it clearly enough on the basis of past experiences and since this matter, which has now started rolling, demands clearing up, the whole problem must still be solved by the present generation.

A complete removal or withdrawal of the millions of Jews residing in the European economic space [Wirtschaftsraum] is therefore an urgent need in the fight for the security of existence of the German people.

Starting with the territory of the Reich and proceeding to the remaining European countries included in the final solution, the Jews are currently being deported to large camps which have already been established or which are to be established in the East, where they will either be used for work or else transported still farther to the East. The old Jews as well as Jews with high military decorations [Kriegsauszeichnungen]: Iron Cross 1st Class [E.K.I.], Golden Medal for Valor [Goldene Tapferkeitsmedaille], etc., are currently being resettled in the city of Theresienstadt which is located in the Protectorate of Bohemia and Moravia.

It lies in the very nature of the matter that these problems, which in part are very difficult, can be solved only with ruthless severity in the interest of the final security of our people.

Translation of Document 3257-PS (USA 290). *Letter from Armament Inspector in the Ukraine to General Thomas, Chief of the Industrial Armament Department, OKW, 2 December 1941, enclosing report by Prof. Seraphim on the execution of 150,000 to 200,000 Jews in the Ukraine.*

* * *

Vol. 226-3
Armament in the Ukraine
    Inspector
                                 In the field, 2 December 1941
                                             Secret

To General of the Infantry, Thomas,
   Chief of the Industrial Armament Department [Wi Rue Amt]
Berlin W
Kurfurstenstr. 63-67
—1— enclosure

For the personal information of the Chief of the Industrial Armament Department [Wi Rue Amt] I am forwarding a total account of the present situation in the Reichskommissariat Ukraine in which the difficulties and tensions encountered so far and the problems which give rise to serious anxiety are stated with unmistakable clarity.

Intentionally I have desisted from submitting such a report through official channels or from making it known to other departments interested in it because I do not expect any results that way but, to the contrary, am apprehensive, that the difficulties and tensions and also the divergent opinions might only be increased due to the peculiarity of the situation.

Only the department authorized in the matter if it sees clearly can order a stoppage within the possibilities.

The report has been drafted by OKV Rat Prof. Seraphim and has no official but a definitely personal character.

I agree with his statements in all respects.

I wish to add, that the departments in question receive reports of the situation which state the existing material difficulties with complete frankness and that moreover nothing has remained untried by me to point out the existing difficulties and mistakes also to the gentlemen of the Reichskommissar Ukraine again and again in order to have them checked.

I would be obliged if the enclosed report were used only for the information of the Chief of the Industrial Armament Department [Wi Rue Amt] himself and his closest workers and if it were left *exclusively to the decision* of the Chief of the Industrial Armament Department to forward information on the essential facts which primarily might induce a change in the situation which gives rise to serious anxiety.

Jewish problem.

Regulation of the Jewish question in the Ukraine was a difficult problem because the Jews constituted a large part of the urban population. We therefore have to deal—just as in the General Government [gg.]—with a mass problem of policy concerning the population. Many cities had a percentage of Jews exceeding 50%. Only the rich Jews had fled from the German troops. The majority of Jews remained under German administration. The latter found the problem more complicated through the fact that *these Jews represented almost the entire trade* and even *a part of the manpower in small and medium industries* besides the business which had in part become superfluous as a direct or indirect result of the war. *The elimination therefore necessarily had far-reaching economic consequences and even direct consequences for the armament industry* (production for supplying the troops).

The attitude of the Jewish population was anxious—obliging from the beginning. They tried to avoid everything that might displease the German administration. That they hated the German administration and army inwardly goes without saying and cannot be surprising. However, there is no proof that Jewry as a whole or even to a greater part was implicated in acts of sabotage. Surely, there were some terrorists or saboteurs among them just as among the Ukrainians. But it cannot be said that the Jews as such represented a danger to the German armed forces. The output produced by Jews who, of course, were prompted by nothing but the feeling of fear was satisfactory to the troops and the German administration.

The Jewish population remained temporarily unmolested shortly after the fighting. Only weeks, sometimes months later, specially detached formations of the police [Ordnungspolizei] executed a planned shooting of Jews. This action as a rule proceeded from east to west. It was done entirely in public with the use of the Ukrainian militia and unfortunately in many instances also with members of the armed forces taking part voluntarily. The way these actions which included men and old men, women and children of all ages were carried out was horrible. The great masses executed make this action more gigantic than any similar measure taken so far in the Soviet Union. So far about 150,000 to 200,000 Jews may have been executed in the part of the Ukraine belonging to the Reichskommissariat [RK]; no consideration was given to the interests of economy.

Summarizing, it can be said that the kind of solution of the Jewish problem applied in the Ukraine which obviously was based on the ideological theories as a matter of principle had the following results:

a. Elimination of a part of the superfluous eaters in the cities.

b. Elimination of a part of the population which undoubtedly hated us.

c. Elimination of badly needed tradesmen who were in many instances indispensable even in the interests of the armed forces.

d. Consequences as to foreign policy—propaganda which is obvious.

e. Bad effects on the troops which in any case have indirect contact with the executions.

f. Brutalizing effect on the formations which carry out the executions—regular police—[Ordnungspolizei].

Scooping off the agricultural surplus in the Ukraine for the purpose of feeding the Reich is therefore only feasible if traffic in the interior of the Ukraine is diminished to a minimum. The attempt will be made to achieve this:

1. by annihilation of superfluous eaters (Jews, population of

the Ukrainian big cities, which like Kiev do not receive any supplies at all);

2. by extreme reduction of the rations allocated to the Ukrainians in the remaining cities;

3. by decrease of the food of the farming population.

It must be realized that in the Ukraine eventually only the Ukrainians can produce economic values by labor. If we shoot the Jews, let the prisoners of war perish, condemn considerable parts of the urban population to death by starvation and also lose a part of the farming population by hunger during the next year, the question remains unanswered: Who in all the world is then supposed to produce economic values here? In view of the manpower bottleneck in the German Reich there is no doubt that the necessary number of Germans will not be available either now or in the near future. However, if the Ukrainian is supposed to work he has to be maintained physically not due to sentiments but due to very sober economic considerations. Part of these is also the creation of an orderly correlation between currency, prices of goods and wages.

(Summary)

Population.

The attitude of the Ukrainian population is still obliging in spite of the deterioration of its economic situation during the last few months. A change of attitude is to be expected with continued deterioration which is certainly to be anticipated.

The Germans [Volksdeutsche] in the Ukraine do not constitute an element on which the administration and the economy of the country can lean.

A considerable proportion of the Jews who partly represented more than half of the population in the cities of the RK. has been executed. Thereby the majority of tradesmen has been eliminated, thus hurting also interests of the armed forces (supplies for troops, billets).

Billeting, food, clothing and health of the prisoners of war is bad, mortality very high. The loss of tens of thousands even hundreds of thousands during this winter is to be expected. Among them is manpower which could have been utilized successfully for the Ukrainian economy, also skilled specialists and tradesmen.

Copy of Document 3311-PS (USA 293). Charge No. 6 against Hans Frank, submitted by Polish Government to International Military Tribunal, dated 5 December 1945, describing operation of extermination camp "Treblinka B" where several hundred thousands of Jews were slaughtered.

* * *

CHARGE No. 6

[Seal of Main Commission for the Investigation of German Crimes in Poland]

In accordance with article 6 of the Charter the Polish Government indicts Dr. Hans Frank, Governor General of Poland, of the following crime:

The German authorities acting under the authority of Governor General Dr. Hans Frank established in March 1942 the extermination-camp at Treblinka, intended for mass killing of Jews by suffocating them in steam-filled chambers.

Particulars of the alleged Crime

In 1940 the German authorities established in the village of Treblinka, near Malkinia close to the railway line Warsaw-Bialystok, a concentration camp for Poles who refused to deliver contingents of agricultural products ordered by the German administrative authorities. In November 1941, the District Governor of Warsaw, Dr. Fischer, proclaimed this camp as a general concentration camp for the whole district of Warsaw and ordered all Poles to be deported there who some way or other contravened against the orders or prohibitions of the German authorities. Later on this camp was named "Treblinka A".

In March 1942, the Germans began to erect another camp "Treblinka B",/in the neighbourhood of "Treblinka A"/, intended to become a place of torment for Jews.

The erection of this camp was closely connected with the German plans aiming at a complete destruction of the Jewish population in Poland which necessitated the creation of a machinery by means of which the Polish Jews could be killed in large numbers. Late in April 1942, the erection of the first three chambers was finished in which these general massacres were to be performed by means of steam. Somewhat later the erection of the real "death-building" was finished which contains ten death chambers. It was opened for wholesale murders early in autumn 1942.

It may be mentioned here that there were several phases in the development of the persecution of the Jews in Poland. During the first period/till October 1940/the Germans were aiming only at the moral degradation and complete pauperization of the Jews by all kinds of restrictions of their rights, by the confiscation of their property etc., but later on they turned to their gradual annihilation and destruction as a nation. This change of policy is apparent in their treatment of the ghettos, first they had only to isolate the Jews from the Aryans but later on they were/the ghettos/the very means of the physical annihilation of the Jews.

Healthier and stronger Jews were deported for forced labor while those who remained in the Ghettos were decimated by starvation and epidemics. As these methods did not produce the desired results more drastic measures were adopted. Wholesale massacres were organized in the Ghettos and, finally, a complete annihilation of the ghettos was decided upon.

The Jews had simply ceased to exist. Special camps were established for this purpose where the destruction of human lives was carried on by mechanized means. The best known of these death camps are those of Treblinka, Belzec and Sobiber /in the Lublin district/. In these camps the Jews were put to death in their thousands by hitherto unknown, new methods, gas and steam chambers as well as electric current employed on a large scale. The victims were recruited chiefly from the General Government, and particularly from the following districts: Warsaw, Radom, Lublin, Krakow and Lwow, but Jews from outside the General Government were also sent there, particularly from the Bialystok district where the Ghettos were maintained for a long time and where in the summer months of 1943 about 10,000 Jews were rounded up and transported to Treblinka for extermination.

The main part of the "work" was done in summer and autumn 1942. Winter 1942 and the year 1943 were used for "mopping up operations", i.e. for the extermination of those who managed to dodge the main round-up and, of those younger Jews who were employed in war industry. To indulge in their lust for destruction the Germans did not hesitate to put to death even those younger Jews although their man-power was badly needed and their loss—as admitted by the Germans themselves —was a serious handicap for the war effort.

The Camp B of Treblinka is situated in hilly, wooded country. It covered an area of about 5,000 ha /8 square miles/ and was fenced off by hedges and barbed wire. It is bordered in the north by a young forest, in the west by a railway embankment while low hills shut it off from the East and South. There are several observation posts in the camp for the camp guard, as well as searchlights needed for securing the camp during the hours of darkness. A side track leads from the main railway track on to a loading platform adjoining a large open place fenced off by barbed wire, where several thousand persons can be accommodated at the same time. To the north stands a large barrack and in the southwestern corner an observation post. The place to the south of the barbed wire fence was used for sorting out pieces of clothes of the victims which were fit for further use [Lumpensortierungsplatz]. Further to the south is the place of execution and a mass grave. A gate opens from the place to a road leading to the buildings and one of them is divided by a narrow corridor into two parts and measures approx. 40 yards by 25 yards. On each side of the corridor are situated five chambers whose height is about 6 and a half feet. There are no windows. The doors can be shut hermetically.

The second building consists of three chambers and a boiler-room. The steam generated in the boilers is led by means of pipes to the chambers. There are terraceta floors in the chambers which become very slippery when wet. Along the southern wall of the building runs a long platform where the bodies of the victims were piled up after execution. A well is situated near the boiler-room.

Behind this building and separated from the rest of the camp by barbed wire stands a barrack and a kitchen destined for the grave diggers. On both sides of these buildings are situated observation posts. As the executions grew in numbers, mass graves were dug out by motor driven machines and not by hand and shovel as in the beginning.

The camp was guarded by Germans of the SS-detachments and by Ukrainians. The officer to whom this guard was subordinated was the SS-Capt. Sauer. This garrison [Legerschuiz] performed also duties of executioners, while menial services had to be performed by the inmates of the camps themselves, so e.g. the unloading of the trucks, stripping of the victims and sorting out of their clothes and shoes [Lumpensortierung], the emptying of the death chambers and the burying of the bodies. When a new transport arrived some of the Jews were picked out to do this work so long till they broke down morally under the impression of this organized and mechanized mass murder. Then they had to dig their own graves and take up their position at them, whereupon they were shot one by one by Sauer personally. Their last duty before dying was to push the body of the preceding victim into its own grave. A new party was then chosen to continue their work in the camp. The sadism of Sauer in enjoying the shooting personally sounds incredible, but his guilt has been established beyond any doubt.

The average number of Jews dealt with at the camp in summer 1942 was about two railway transports daily, but there were days of much higher efficiency. From autumn 1942 this number was falling.

After unloading in the siding all victims were assembled in one place where men were separated from women and children. In the first days of the existence of the camp the victims were made to believe that after a short stay in the camp, necessary for bathing and disinfection, they would be sent farther east, for work. Explanations of this sort were given by SS men who assisted at the unloading of the transports and further explanations could be read in notices stuck up on the walls of the barracks. But later, when more transports had to be dealt with, the Germans dropped all pretences and only tried to accelerate the procedure.

All victims had to strip off their clothes and shoes, which were collected afterwards, whereupon all victims, women and children first, were driven into the death chambers. Those too slow or too weak to move quickly were driven on by rifle butts, by whipping and kicking, often by Sauer himself. Many slipped and fell, the next victims pressed forward and stumbled over them. Small children were simply thrown inside. After being filled up to capacity the chambers were hermetically closed and steam was let in. In a few minutes all was over. The Jewish menial workers had to remove the bodies from the platform and to bury them in mass graves. By and by, as new transports arrived, the cemetery grew, extending in eastern direction.

From reports received it may be assumed that several hundred thousands of Jews have been exterminated in Treblinka. Exact figures are impossible to obtain as the Germans did not bother to keep any records concerning the number of Jews deported to this camp and killed there. It will be even impossible to establish some correct figures because as early as spring 1943 the Germans began to exhume the bodies and to burn them so as to destroy all evidence of the crimes perpetrated. These exhumations continued until summer 1943, when the victims were able to start a mutiny and to kill some of the guards enabling thus several hundred Jews to escape from the camp.

The above description of the mass murders in Treblinka gives only a faint idea of the horrors which prevailed in the camp. It is practically impossible to imagine the sufferings of the victims in the camp and to grasp the full extent of the atrocities. For the victims transported to the camp in cattle trucks and exposed for several days to the most cruel sufferings of body and soul, death in the steam chambers must have almost come as a welcome relief. Their only crime consisted in the fact of belonging to a race condemned by Hitler to death.

The responsibility of Dr. Hans Frank for the setting up of the camp at Treblinka and for the mass killings described above is inherent to his official position as Governor General of Poland.

The camp could not be set up without either his direct order or, at least, his approval, and the numbers of people killed there clearly indicate, that these atrocities were elements of a systematic policy of extermination. All those connected with the "liquidation" of ghettos and of the Jews themselves took their orders from the Governor General.

[Seal of Main Commission for the Investigation of German Crimes in Poland]

CERTIFICATE

This will certify that the document entitled "Charge No. 6, Camp of Treblinka", concerning the extermination of Jews in this camp, is hereby officially submitted by the Polish Government to the International Military Tribunal by the undersigned under the provisions set forth in Article 21 of the Charter.

/S/ Dr. Cyprian
Dr. Tadeusz Cyprian
Polish Deputy Representative of the United
Nations War Crimes Commission in London

[Seal of Main Commission for the Investigation of German Crimes in Poland]

Nurnberg, the 5th December, 1945

Translation of Document 3319-PS (GB 287). Foreign Office Correspondence, August 1941 to April 1944, giving reports and notes on conferences on anti-Jewish action in foreign countries.

* * *

Foreign Office
Inf. XIV
Anti-Jewish action abroad
Number 137 secret
1 enclosure

Berlin, April 28th, 1944
Am Karlsbad 8

SECRET

Subject: Anti-Jewish action in foreign countries.
In conjunction with wired circular [Drahterlass] Multex number 196 of February 17th, 1944.

To the German Embassy in Ankara, Madrid, Paris, the Office of the Reich Plenipotentiary for Italy, Fasano
the German Legation in Agram, Bern, Budapest, Bukarest, Helsingfors, Lisbon, Sofia, Stockholm
the Office of the Reich Plenipotentiary in Denmark in Kopenhagen
the German Consulate General Tangiers
the Athens Office of the Special Plenipotentiary of the Foreign Office for the Southeast
the Belgrad Office of the Special Plenipotentiary of the Foreign Office for the Southeast
the Office of the Foreign Office in Brussels
the Representative of the Foreign Office with the staff of the Reich Commissionar for the occupied Dutch territories in The Hague
the VAA. at the Reichs Commissionar Eastland in Riga

—each separately—

1. The Reich Foreign Minister has ordered the creation of the Inf. Stelle XIV (Anti-Jewish action abroad under the leadership of the Envoy I. K. Schleier). Its task is to deepen and to strengthen the anti-Jewish information in foreign countries.

This will be done by the collection of all experts of the departments and working units of the Foreign Office who are interested and take part in the anti-Jewish information in foreign countries. It will also be done in close cooperation with all offices which are engaged with anti-Jewish work, but are outside the Foreign Office, and with German missions in Europe.

Besides the co-workers who are directly assigned to the Inf.-Stelle XIV:

Commercial political department,
Cultural political department,
News and press department,
Radio political department,
Inland II
America-Committee,
England-Committee,
Deputy for the information system,
furthermore
one permanent representative of the Reich Main Security Office
one representative of the office of Reichsleiter Rosenberg and the provisional Director of the Institute for the Research of the Jewish problem, Frankfurt.

It is intended that other offices engaged or interested in anti-

Jewish work will also send permanent representatives to Inf. XIV.

2. It is necessary for the execution of the task charged to Inf. XIV that the missions send on *all material available to them, about Jewish or anti-Jewish occurrences as completely as possible and by the quickest means.* Not only material from the concerned country is wanted, but special emphasis must also be put on the procurement of documents which concern the countries with whom Germany is at war. This material must and can be procured almost exclusively via neutral countries.

The material collected at Inf. XIV will be edited in an appropriate way and will be put at the disposal *of the missions for the best and greatest possible utilization.*

It is the duty of the missions to make use of the material they receive in any and every possible way:
as basis for discussions for the members of the mission,
in the press,
in the radio of the country concerned, with measures which are at the disposal of the current information. (Activ-Information)

3. Individual reports about certain incidents of Jewish or anti-Jewish nature which come in from foreign countries will be forwarded by Inf. XIV to the departments of the office which are concerned with suitable suggestions for the purpose of further propagation.

The press department utilizes this material as much as possible in the news agency reports, such as the German News Buro (DNB), TO-EP and National Press Service (NPD).

The radio political department utilizes the reports in German and foreign language news broadcasts directed to foreign countries.

It is the task of the press and radio consultants of the missions to check all material coming in to them in order to find out, whether there are any anti-Jewish reports and whether and how these might be utilized in the press and in the radio of their respective country.

Inf. XIV will draw the special attention of the missions to reports where special emphasis is put on their propagation; this will be done from time to time by wired circular.

Besides these current news reports over press and radio, the mission will, from time to time, receive a collection of the material which comes in from all missions and which has a certain value and possibility for utilization, beyond the present moment.

Besides reports about actual individual incidents, the missions will currently receive documents from Inf. XIV on certain subjects, either as unfinished documents or as finished comments and articles. This material is also to be utilized in the best possible way.

The missions are asked to report soon how many copies of the material they want to receive each time, so that the material leaving by courier will be sent off from the beginning with the number of copies which are necessary for the practical work of the missions.

4. *Current reports are to be made about the practical utilization of the material in foreign countries; corroborating documents are to be enclosed, as far as this is possible.*
Special value is placed by the Reich Foreign Minister on this way of reporting.

5. In order to collect within the missions all questions connected with the anti-Jewish action in foreign countries, *a member of the mission is to be appointed consultant for Jewish questions; however, this should not be the consultant for culture, if possible.* (compare wired circular Multex number 196 of February 17th.) A wired report is requested as to who has finally been appointed consultant for Jewish questions of the mission. It is the task of the consultants for Jewish questions to put the material which arrives from Inf. XIV at the disposal of all those consultants of the missions who might be able to utilize it; furthermore, to take care of the collecting of the Jewish or anti-Jewish material in the domain of the mission and conveying it to Inf. XIV, as well as to supervise the collection and conveying of the reports and documents about the execution, and/or success to Inf. XIV.

6. An *archive* will be created at Inf. XIV, where all documents about Jewish and anti-Jewish happenings which are within reach of the Foreign Office and of the missions will be received, collected, and evaluated, according to plan.

It is a special duty of the missions to convey the complete material collected in their office district to the archive. Details about the material to be collected can be taken from the enclosure. Of course, the material collected in the archive is also to be utilized for the purposes of the missions. On the basis of the documents, Inf. XIV will send to the missions from time to time, evaluation reports about individual personalities or incidents.

7. Financial means necessary for the procurement of Jewish

or anti-Jewish material must be taken from the funds put at the disposal of the missions.

8. The missions are asked to inform the consular authorities under them appropriately and to incorporate them into the work. [signed] STEENGRACHT

Enclosure to decree number 137
(secret) of 28 April, 1944, Inf. XIV

Jewish and anti-Jewish archive of the Foreign Office.
 (Inf. XIV, anti-Jewish action abroad)
 I. The archive is organized in the following way:
 1. Personnel archive: containing all documents about Jewish and anti-Jewish personalities, including articles and reproductions of speeches of these circles of persons.
 2. Archive of objects: containing all incidents concerning the Jewish question, assorted according to individual incidents. The reports of the missions about the Jewish question and about anti-Jewish measures in the individual countries belong here; reports or documents about certain individual questions, for instance
  Jews in economy,
  Jews in cultural life,
  Palestine White-book, and similar things.
 3. Pictorial archive:
II. The following material may be used for this archive:
From the press: All newspaper and agency reports (the latter even then if not utilized in the press) about all incidents of Jewish and anti-Jewish nature.
Speeches of Jews and antisemites. General articles and reports about Jews. National measures against the Jews and against antisemites.
Jewish newspapers and magazines. Anti-Jewish newspapers and magazines.
Comic papers with anti-Jewish tendencies.
Pictures: Photographs (if possible, original copies with glossy surface, but reproductions from newspapers, magazines, and books, too, if necessary of Jews and antisemites). Photographs about incidents of Jewish and anti-Jewish nature (Jewish manifestations, celebrations, etc, anti-Jewish manifestations, demonstrations and others).
Radio: Listening reports of the national sender of the country concerned, as far as they touch Jewish or anti-Jewish incidents.
Cultural politics: All magazines, books, posters, leaflets, stickers

with Jewish and anti-Jewish tendencies. Discussions of Jewish and anti-Jewish books and movie pictures, Jewish or anti-Jewish quotations from the literature of the concerned country with exact specification from which book and from which spot these quotations have been taken.

Besides these sources which are the most important ones for the procurement of material for the archive, the following might be taken into consideration:

Notes of members of the missions, of other Reich Germans and of foreigners about discussions which are about Jewish or anti-Jewish personalities or incidents; reports of other offices to which the missions have access about such occurrences.

Procurement of personal statements of Jewish and anti-Jewish personalities (complete life history, if possible). Incidents about Jews in the economical life of the country concerned.

Provided it is possible and not connected with special expenses, it is requested to send in *the material in at least two copies.*

However, *reports* and *notes of the missions* are to be sent in five-fold, so that the necessary working copies can be forwarded to the interested departments without any further loss of work and time.

Foreign Office	[Receipt Stamp]	Berlin W 8
Inf. XIV	German Legation	Wilhelmstr. 74-76
No. 118/44	Bucharest	20 April, 1944
1 Enclosure	3 May 1944	
	No. 2803	

Contents: Work conference of specialists for Jewish questions of the German missions on 3 and 4 April 1944.

There is enclosed for your information a copy of the minutes of the work conference of the consultants for Jewish questions of the missions which was held at Krummhuebel on 3 and 4 April of this year. On account of their secret nature, the statements made by Counselor of Legation v. Thadden and SS Hauptsturmfuehrer Ballensiefen of the Reich Security Main Office (RSHA) have not been entered in the minutes.

In accordance with Multex No. 246 of 28 Feb. 1944, most of the missions sent in for the conference, sometimes with request for their return, collections of anti-Jewish propaganda material from the countries concerned, such as books, periodicals, posters, handbills, etc. It is planned not to return this material, but, rather, to include it in the comprehensive Jewish archives that are being built up and that are also at the disposal of the mis-

sions. The archives are being set up in Krummhuebel in order to insure their safety from war damage. In view of the importance to the anti-Jewish information work of a complete collection of all pertinent material, it is requested that the return of the material furnished by your office be dispensed with.
[signed] Schleier

To
German Embassy, Ankara
Office of the Plenipotentiary of the Greater German Reich for Italy in Pasano
German Embassy, Madrid
German Embassy, Paris
German Legation, Lisbon
German Legation, Bratislava
German Legation, Sofia
German Legation, Stockholm
German Legation, Zagreb
German Legation, Bern
German Legation, Bucharest
German Legation, Copenhagen

Confidential
Work-session of the consultants on Jewish questions of the German missions in Europe
Krummhuebel, 3 and 4 April 1944.

Greetings by ambassador Prof. Dr. Six, who gives the chairmanship to *ambassador Schleier*. In his opening-speech he deals with the tasks and aims of the anti-Jewish action abroad. Ambassador Schleier points to the faith of the Fuehrer in the racial principle of the people. This means repudiation of all foreign influences, and therefore the fight of National Socialism against the disintegrating and destructive activity of Jewry.

The hatred of Jewry for us was the result of this fight. Ambassador Schleier commemorates the first victims of the fight of international Jewry against the German people, Wilhelm Gustloff and Ernst v. Rath. That fight represents a considerable part of the great struggle of the German people. The Fuehrer therefore gave instructions to take up the fight against Jewry at an intensified rate and to explain its part in the present war. He said, that roots of anti-Jewish tendencies existed in England and America.

The question was, what possibilities existed for the European German Missions for the conduct of anti-Jewish activity. The work to be done would have to take place from the inside to the outside and vice-versa. Reports about the behaviour of Jewry in the country in question and about existing anti-Jewish tendencies in the country, would be necessary. Anti-Jewish propaganda in neutral countries was particularly difficult, but of the utmost importance, as there were possibilities that they might spread from there to England or America. The neutral countries, though, were also important as observation-posts. Press-excerpts, radio reports, notes about events in enemy countries and the Jewish camp, which are reported by subjects of the host-countries, as well as beginnings of anti-Jewish tendencies must be carefully collected and registered. Those reports must include all the spheres of life, which are influenced by the Jews.

This material would be collected and worked out by "Inf. XIV" and then handed over to the missions for exploitation through the press and radio, by handbills, pamphlets and through the channels of whispering-propaganda. The publication would be done by the Press, Radio and Culture-political department.

Ambassador Schleier then developed a few concrete projects. So, for instance, the idea was being entertained to organize a travelling exhibition on rails or motorized. He planned, furthermore, the publication of an anti-Jewish sheet-calendar, particularly for the States of South-Eastern Europe, as well as the creation of a great archive about all the problems of the Jewish question from the personal and factual viewpoint, which was to be accompanied by a collection of pictures.

Ambassador Six speaks then about the political structures of world-Jewry, which he explains as an ideological and historical result of social development since the French Revolution. The figures available in 1933 showed 17,000,000 confessional Jews. The real source of strength of Jewry in Europe and America was the Jewry of the East. It constituted the starting-point of the migration-movement from the European to the American area. Eastern Jewry advanced slowly from the East to the West and showed in that connection not only a religious but also a social inclination. Jewry had ceased to play its biological and at the same time its political role in Europe. Jewry occupied a leading position in the countries of the enemy-powers in their fight against National-Socialism and against the German people. The Jewish question had not been accentuated in Soviet-Russia, we know, however, by experiences made in the conduct of war, that the Jew now as before plays an important part in the hierarchy of Bolshevism.

Jewish infiltration maintained itself in the Soviet Union.

The second important country in this connection was England. There Jewry played a traditional part. Because of the plutocratic structure of England it had been possible to place Jews within the leading class, which influenced to a large extent the policy of the leading class during the 19th century. That interrelation step was an important factor for the evaluation of the present situation.

The cooperation of English and American Jewry played a decisive part at the outbreak of the war. There are about 7,000,000 Jews in the United States. Their position was founded on an economic basis. The democratic ideology proved to be fertile soil for the progressive influence of Jewry. The strong Jewish infiltration into the leading classes of the 3 powers fighting against Germany was a factor of the greatest importance.

Ambassador Six turns then to Zionism. Zionism meant the return of all Jews into their homeland and land of origin, Palestine. The idea was to assemble them there politically and biologically. The whole question of that return was, however, politically overshadowed by the Arabian question. The creation of a homeland [Heimstaette] had been promised to the Jews after the war by the Balfour Declaration of 1917. The Jewish element had spread itself in Palestine at the cost of the Arabs.

The physical elimination of Eastern Jewry would deprive Jewry of its biological reserves. Its present structure was characterized by its association with the three World-Powers. That association became obvious in the Soviet-Union through the ideological combination of Jewry and Bolshevism, in England by the penetration of the leading class and in the United States by the occupation of decisive key-positions in high-finance. The Jewish question must be solved not only in Germany but also internationally.

Embassy-counsellor v. Thadden speaks about the Jewish-political situation in Europe and about the state of the anti-Jewish, executive measures. The speaker gave an outline why the Zionist Palestine solution or other similar solutions must be rejected and the deportation of the Jews to the Eastern-territories carried out. Then he sketched the present state of anti-Jewish measures in all European countries.

The speaker then relates the countermeasures taken by world-Jewry against the German anti-Jewish measures in Europe.

The talks closed with the following request to the representatives of the missions:

1. Suppression of all propaganda even camouflaged as anti-

Jewish, liable to slow down or handicap the German executive measures.

2. Preparation for the comprehension among all nations of executive measures against Jewry.

3. Constant reports about the possibility of carrying out more severe measures against Jewry in the various countries by using diplomatic channels.

4. Constant reports about signs of opposition actions by world-Jewry, in order to enable us to take countermeasures in time.

(As the details of the state of the executive measures in the various countries, reported by the consultant, are to be kept secret, it has been decided not to enter them in the protocol.)

SS Captain [Haupstuormfuehrer] Dr. Ballensiefen reports about experiences made during the execution of the anti-Jewish measures in Hungary in connection with the political events there.

Prof. Dr. Mahr deals in his speech with the anti-Jewish action abroad conducted on the radio. He demands the intermingling of German radio broadcasts to foreign countries with anti-Jewish propaganda-material, as well as the influencing of radio installations of countries near to us or allied with us, in the same spirit; at the same time safeguarding the sovereignty of the countries in question. Good material must be procured for the internal German radio.

Miss Hauhsmann (Dr.) speaks about the anti-Jewish action abroad in the press and about the importance of press-pictures in the service of the anti-Jewish action abroad. The need of photographs for the press at home and abroad was great. The cooperation of the missions was necessary in the procurement of anti-Jewish pictures. Important also was the discussion of anti-Jewish films in the press. Dr. Hauhsmann then points out the practical possibilities for publicizing anti-Jewish material in the foreign press, in which activity the main weight would have to be borne by the Press-consultants of the missions.

Dr. Walz treats current anti-Jewish information. Real peace among the nations was impossible, as long as the Jewish problem was not solved, one way or the other. Information-activity had to take into consideration the prevailing mentality of the nations, which were to be influenced in an anti-Jewish sense. In the case of pamphlets, foreign examples should be initiated. Until now there was lacking an anti-Jewish film, which did not deal with known Jewish personalities, but which treated the little Jewish merchant and the Jewish intellectual in their daily activities.

Embassy-secretary (LS) Dr. Kutscher speaks about propaganda-theses within the frame-work of the anti-Jewish action abroad. Every propaganda must be ruled by certain directives. Those theses were to be considered as such directives for the information activity. They had to be adapted to the currently prevailing local circumstances. They were intended for internal use. LS. Dr. Kutscher then formulates a few fundamental principles: The Jews are the instigators of this war. They drove the nations into the war, because they are interested in it. The Jews are the misfortune of all the peoples. —A Jewish victory would mean the end of all culture (Example Soviet Union)—Germany does not only fight the Jews for itself, but for all European culture. —The Jew dug his own grave by causing this war. The aim of those phrases was to bring certain facts to the attention of the people until they were finally convinced of them.

Service leader Dienstleiter Haegmeyer speaks about the international anti-Jewish congress and its tasks. His aim was to collect all the European Forces, which had occupied themselves with the Jewish question. The congress must be set up politically. The composition of the guests was a decisive factor. Particular value must be attached to the attendance of European scientists. The speaker asked the mission to help him select the guests, who should be invited to the congress.

Now follow the reports of the representatives of the various missions about the Jewish-political situation in their countries and the possibilities of: a.) the procurement of anti-Jewish material, b.) the execution of anti-Jewish information by radio, press, general means of information (pamphlets, posters, leaflets, stickers, post-cards, whispering propaganda) and the executors of that kind of work.

Dr. Klassen (France) next presents a lengthy historical resume of the development of the Jewish problem and of anti-Semitism in France, and points out differences in the treatment of Jews in the Northern and Southern zones. In the Northern zone steps had been taken toward the Aryanization of Jewish concerns, and Jewish publications had been suppressed. According to French legislation for Jews, Jewish writers and actors were not forbidden to work but they could not own or manage a newspaper or a theater. Jews had vanished from Government positions. An Institute for Jewish Questions was founded in France in 1940. An anti-Jewish exhibition met with great success. Apart from a few anti-Semitic clericals, the Catholic Church gave far-reaching support to Jewry in the sense of the democratic ideology. A few anti-Semitic films had a discouraging effect. The film medium should therefore be more widely used. The information activity must stem from the French tradition and be represented as the affair of the French. Useful starting points might be found among the followers of Diat and of French Fascism. The situation in French North Africa was well suited to exploitation.

Dr. Beinert (Spain) reports that in Spain the Jewish question is not regarded as of present consequence from a racial standpoint. After the expulsion of the Jews in the Fifteenth Century, the Jewish question was regarded as a closed historical problem. The scope of anti-Jewish information is very closely limited therefore. It must not appear as German propaganda and can not appear as a large-scale campaign. It would be effective, on the other hand, to bring to the fore specific, impressive instances, especially with reference to economic aspects.

Dr. Matthias (Portugal), too, stresses the difficulties faced by anti-Jewish information activity in Portugal. There is no Jewish problem in our sense of the term, in Portugal. For one thing, the migration of the Jews from central Europe, which began before 1933 and was particularly strong after 1933 and during the French Campaign, did not essentially alter the picture in Portugal, since Portugal was primarily merely country of transit for the Jewish emigration. Secondly, the original Jewish problem, that is to say, the difficulties that resulted from immigration of Jews into Portugal in very early times, found its solution, in the course of centuries, in a way that does not represent a clearing up of the Jewish problem in our sense, but that wiped out the traces of Jewry as a racial component of the people.

The procurement of anti-Jewish material from the U.S.A. would be possible, but involved high costs.

Vice Consul Dr. Janke (Switzerland) points out that while the majority of all Swiss are anti-Semitic by healthy instinct, there is lacking a realization of the actuality of the Jewish question. The influence of Jews is much less than in the other countries under democratic-plutocratic regimes. An anti-Jewish information activity would have to be handled with great care and without revealing its German origin, in order not to challenge the severe statutory restrictions and evoke mistrust of Germany. The sharp censorship, also, must be taken into account. For this reason, the work must be camouflaged. Possibilities to be considered are anti-Jewish tracts, which should be constantly altered in format; also the exploitation of Jewish scandals, compilation of a list of all Jewish persons playing a leading role in the enemy countries, and the spreading of jokes about Jews. The inviting of Swiss personalities to attend the anti-Jewish congress would meet with difficulties.

Consul Dr. Meissner recommends, in connection with the anti-Jewish information work in *Italy*, exposure of the strong Jewish participation in illegal transactions (black market, sabotage, etc.), stating that, for the rest, the activity should appeal to Italian intelligence and should have a serious basis. It might be effective to publish an illustrated pamphlet objectively presenting Jewry as the catalytic agent of decay. Consideration could be given to Preziosi and Farinacci for an invitation to the congress.

Mr. Delbrueck (Sweden) points out the difficulties of anti-Jewish information activity in Sweden. There had been no Jewish problem in this country before the campaign against the Jews in Denmark and the resultant heavy migration of Jews to Sweden. The Jewish immigration had led, however, to a reaction of distaste. It could therefore be taken as the starting point for anti-Jewish information activity. Care would have to be taken, certainly, to avoid in this anything that would smack of German propaganda. Only a few pro-German newspapers were available. Anti-Semitic propaganda literature must be printed in Sweden exclusively. Placards could not be used there because there are no organizations at hand for it. Nor could postcards with anti-Jewish witticisms be used. No anti-Semitic propaganda could be made over the Swedish radio. The participation of fanatic idealists in the congress was certainly feasible.

Mr. Christensen (Denmark) states that the collection of material is possible now without more ado. Pictorial material could be obtained from the Royal Library in Copenhagen. As concerns information activity, the press can be used for "press release" [Auflageartikel] articles. This would make it, however, obvious that it was German propaganda material. The propaganda in Denmark must be carried out by the Danes and not by a central Germany agency.

Mr. Weilinghaus (Rumania) reports that the Jewish question in Rumania has been approached only from the economic and the general political standpoint, with the racial and ideological aspects consistently neglected. The Rumanian Government is taking a cautious attitude toward the Jewish question. It depends a great deal upon the military situation. It is therefore necessary for us to proceed cautiously with our work. The Rumanian Government has informed us that propagandistic handling of the Jewish question would be undesirable. So that the whispering campaign remains our chief tool. Because anti-

Jewish articles are not accepted by the rest of the press, "Porunca Vremii" remains our only anti-Semitic organ. The material used in this newspaper is then printed separately in a large number of copies for distribution. There is, in addition, the possibility of falling back on old material that was approved before the more stringent censorship provisions went into effect. Finally, articles could be introduced in the provincial press, since the provincial censorship officials are generally less alert. The anti-Bolshevist propaganda, which the Rumanians desire and support, furnishes an effective opportunity to it. In view of the present political situation, the speaker [Referent] does not recommend, for the present, the issuing of an invitation to Rumanians to attend the anti-Jewish congress.

Superior Govt. Councillor [Ob. Reg. Rat] *Dr. Hoffman (Bulgaria)* declares that the procurement of anti-Jewish material is entirely feasible. The information activity could not be based on ideological grounds. Bulgarians should be approached in regard to the Jewish question by appealing to their acquisitive instinct and their nationalist feeling. The Bulgarian Government has adopted a completely loyal attitude in the Jewish question. It is to be made clear to the Bulgarians that the Bulgarian Jews have no understanding of Bulgarian aspirations. The radio can be utilized to a limited extent. Leaflets should not arouse suspicion by too exaggerated a format. It is recommended that Sobranje deputy Andrejeff be invited to the congress.

Mr. Korselt (Slovakia) emphasizes that the anti-Jewish information activity can be continued only after resumption of the measures against racial Jews [Rassejuden], since otherwise the people would get the impression that the government was acting inconsistently. The anti-Jewish and anti-Bolshevist campaigns of enlightenment must be combined. Anti-Semitism must be employed to counteract the well-advanced Pan-Slavism, by pointing out that not the Slav, but the Jew rules Russia. To the Slovak intellect the Jew appears as an intelligent and congenial representative of urban life. As a countermeasure, the international ramifications of Jewry must be demonstrated by means of convincing statistics and factual reports. It would seem to the purpose to depict the Jews in moving pictures and in children's literature. There is a possibility that a representative may be sent to the congress.

Mr. Posemann (Turkey): Early last year the Turkish Government carried out a blow against the Jews in connection with an attempt to solve the problem of minorities. Very vigorous procedures were used in the carrying out of this action. Suspicions of Allied circles that anti-Jewish measures alone were concerned were countered by Turkey with references to simultaneous measures against the minorities. At any rate, Turkey abandoned further measures toward a solution of the problem of minorities and therewith of the Jewish problem. For this reason, no anti-Jewish propaganda can be carried out under our direction at the present moment, since it is not desired and would be a burden on Turkey's present foreign policy. There are no anti-Jewish publications in Turkey, aside from caricatures and comic books about Jews. A dawning realization of the extent of international Jewish domination can be seen in the translation of the "Protocol of the Elders of Zion" and of Ford's book, *The International Jew*. The marketing of these brochures and their distribution has been promoted by the Embassy. For the time being, only work within this narrow range is possible, since, as has already been emphasized, anti-Jewish propaganda that was obviously German-inspired might give rise to unfavorable political complications for us. In closing, Mr. Posemann made reference to the increasing difficulty with which any foreign propaganda could be introduced into Turkey. It was entirely out of the question that a leading Turkish personage would take part in the projected international congress.

In conclusion *Dr. Schickert* discussed the topic, "Science and the Jewish Question". Propaganda alone, he said, was not enough. One must bring out facts that are not generally known. The Jewish problem must become, in its full seriousness and depth, a subject for discussion in polite circles. This was dependent upon a scientific treatment of the Jewish question. It is necessary that scientists abroad be influenced in that direction.

After the representatives of the missions had presented their reports, *Minister Schleier* gave a resume of the results of the work conference, making special reference again to the question of procurement of material and to the work of the experts on Jewish questions attached to the missions as distributors of material to the representatives of press, radio, education, politics and business. It was important for the work of Inf. XIV that all speeches and expressions of opinion of a fundamental nature concerning the Jewish problem be brought together. Such collected material must also include, among other things, anti-Jewish comic papers, photographs of Jewish personalities, pictures of events and publications and pictures of Jewish life. A regular reporting of success achieved and tasks accomplished was indispensable to assure control of the work and to stimulate it constantly. As concerned the anti-Jewish international world congress, the specialists on Jewish questions [Referenten] would soon have to make up their minds about the question of inviting official and prominent representatives. A study should be made of the advisability of inviting outstanding foreign personages living in Germany.

Some words addressed to the specialists on Jewish questions:

Prof. Mahr suggests that duplicates of handbooks and reference books be obtained and sent to Krummhuebel for the projected archives. He recommends, further, the addition of lists of Freemasons of high degree, journalists, writers and business men who had Jewish relatives. Finally, he urges publication of a diplomatic handbook of Jewish world politics, which might also be published in the English and French languages. Consul Meissner alludes to the Jewish problem in Japan and East Asia, referring particularly to the numerous German Jews in Shanghai, and Minister Schleier adds a few supplemental observations and corrections. Legation Counsellor v. Thadden expresses three wishes to the mission: *a.* in making reports on the Jewish question, proper limits should be observed, *b.* reports are of no value unless they specify names and places, *c.* in regard to delivery of materials, all special desires must be made known. Vice Consul Janke expresses the wish that the list proposed by Prof. Mahr be limited to England, the U.S.A., and the Soviet Union. He also brings up the question of financing the anti-Jewish information work abroad. Mr. Hagemeyer desires to support the setting up of the lists, in particular with regard to the Soviet Union. SS-Hauptsturmfuehrer Ballensiefen suggests that the lists be supplemented by the inclusion of Jewish organizations. Mr. Posemann requests that anti-Jewish reports relative to Turkey be very carefully handled in the German press, in order not to break any political porcelain. Mr. Richter makes reference to the Union of South Africa and Australia as sources of material. Vice Consul Janke refers to the influence of Jews upon the International Red Cross in Geneva.

Minister Schleier speaks the final words and brings the conference to a close with a Siegheil! to the Fuehrer.

Inf. XIV
Anti-Semitic Work Abroad
WORKING CONFERENCE
of the Specialists for Jewish Questions With German Diplomatic Mission in Europe on 3 and 4 April 1944
in Hotel Sanssouci, at Krummhuebel
[Riesengebirge Mountains]

The Documentary Evidence   3319-PS

                        Daily Agenda
3 April:
0900 hours
                    Minister Prof. Dr. Six:
                          Welcome
            Minister Schleier, head of Inf. XIV:
                  Opening of the conference
          Mission and goals of anti-Semitic work
                     in foreign countries
                    Minister Prof. Dr. Six:
            The political structure of World Jewry.
             Legation Councillor Dr. v. Thadden:
        The political situation in Europe with regard to
           the Jewish question: a survey of the current
              position with regard to anti-Semitic
                   governmental measures.
            [Marginal note: HPTSTF. Ballenstein]
                       Prof. Dr. Mahr:
         Anti-Semitic work in foreign countries by radio
                    Dr. (Miss) Haussmann:
            a. Anti-Semitic work in foreign countries
                      through newspapers
             b. Newspaper photographs as a means of
              anti-Semitic work in foreign countries
                         Dr. Walz:
            Information about anti-Semitic activity
       Superior Legation Councillor (VLR) Tannenber
           Economies and anti-Semitic work abroad
      [Note of translator: this item has been crossed out]
              Legation Secretary Dr. Kutscher:
          Propaganda themes within the scope of anti-
                     Semitic work abroad.
                       Dr. Colin Ross:
             Anti-Semitic work abroad and in America
                        Dr. Berber:
          Anti-Semitic work abroad and in Great Britain
   [Note of translator: the last two items have been crossed out]
            Chief of Service [Dienstleiter] Hagemeyer:
       The international anti-Semitic Congress and its Mission.
1300 hours .... Breakfast together
1350 hours .... Reports of the Specialists for Jewish
            Questions with diplomatic mission about the
                         possibilities of
       a. procuring anti-Semitic propaganda material

                                                          III - 501

b. Carrying out anti-Semitic propaganda via radio, newspapers, general media of propaganda pamphlets, posters, leaflets, stickers, post cards, rumor propaganda, and the agents for carrying out this work.

Country:	Name:
France	Dr. Klassen
Spain	Mr. Juretschke

[Note of translator: above name crossed out, and the following hand-written notation substituted: "Beinert, Head(?) of the German Labor Front, Madrid"]

Portugal	Dr. Matthias
Switzerland	Vice-Consul Dr. Janke
Italy	Consul Dr. Meissner
Sweden	Mr. Delbrueck
Denmark	Mr. Vogler

[Note of translator: above name crossed out and "Christiansen" substituted]

Rumania	Mr. Weilinghaus
Bulgaria	SS-Obersturmbannfuehrer Bierman

[Note of translator: above name crossed out and "O. R. B. Hoffman" substituted]

Croatia	Prof. Dr. Walz (President of the German Scientific Institute)
Slovakia	Mr. Korselt
Turkey	Mr. Posemann

4 April:
0830 hours .... Movie:
      a. Newsreel
      b. Les Corrupteurs
(Place of movie show will be announced later!)

Immediately afterward
about 1030 hours....... Inspection of anti-Semitic propaganda
  Material mailed by the diplomatic missions
    in the various countries.

Immediately afterwards
about 1100 hours.......... General discussion about addresses
            delivered the previous day

Minister Schleier:

Final words and summary of the results of the Working Conference.

The afternoon will be available for individual Discussion between the Specialists of the Foreign Office, the guests and the Specialists for Jewish Questions of the Diplomatic Mission.

1930 hours .... Supper together

immediately afterwards .... comradely get-together

Miss Stein will be available at the hotel to participants in the conference for receiving telephone calls or other communications, and for making telephone calls out of town.

The Chief of the Security Police
and of the Security Service (SD)
IV B 4 b-2314/43 secret (82)

SECRET

Berlin 23 Sept. 1943

Special Delivery Letter
To
    a. All (administrative) offices of the state police.
    b. The commander of the Security Police, and the security Service, Central Office for the regulation of the Jewish question in Bohemia and Moravia, *in Prague.*
    c. The Commander of the Security Police and of the Security Service, *in Prague.*
    d. The Commander of the Security Police and of the Security Service in the occupied Dutch territories, *in the Hague.*
    e. The commander of the Security Police and of the Security Service for the domain of the Military Commander in France, *in Paris.*
    f. The Deputy of the Chief of the Security Police and of the Security Service for the domain of the Military Commander in Belgium and Northern France, *In Brussels.*
    g. The Commander of the Security Police and of the Security Service *in Metz.*
    h. The Commander of the Security Police and of the Security Service *in Strassborg.*
    i. The Commitment Command [Einsatzkommando] Luxembourg. *In Luxembourg.*
    j. The Commander of the Security Police and of the Security Service, in *Oslo.*
    k. The Commander of the Security Police and of the Security Service of the General Government, in *Cracow.*
    l. The Commander of the Security Police and of the Security Service East [Ostland] *in Riga.*
    m. The Commander of the Security Police and of the Security Service Ukraine *in Kiev.*
    n. The Chief of the Commitment group B, in *Smolensk.*
    o. The Commanders [Kommandeur] of the Security Police and of the Security Service in Carinthia(Kaernten) and Carnioia (Krain) *in Veldes.*

p. The Commander [Kommandeur] of the Security Police and of the Security Service in Lower Styria, *in Marburg.*
By way of information
To
   a. The Superior SS-and Police Leaders in the Reich and in Bohemia and Moravia.
   b. The Superior SS-and Police Leaders with the Reich Commissioner for the Occupied Dutch territories in *The Hague.*
   c. The Superior SS-and Police leader in France, *In Paris.*
   d. The Superior SS-and Police Leader with the Reich Commissioner for the occupied Norwegian territories, *in Oslo.*
   e. The Superior SS-and Police Leader, State Secretary for the Security system, *in Cracow.*
   f. The Superior SS-and Police Leader North (101) *in Riga.*
   g. The Superior SS-and Police Leader Niddle (102), in *Minsk.*
   h. The Superior SS-and Police Leader South (103) *in Kiev.*
   i. The investigator of the Security Police and of the Security Service.
Subject: Treatment of Jews with Foreign citizenship in the sphere of German power.
Reference: Decree of 5 March 1943, wired decree number 53579 of 24 March 1943 and wired decree number 91535 of 18 May 1943 — IV B 4 b 2314/43 secret (82)

In agreement with the Foreign Office, all Jews who remain in the sphere of German power after the end of the so-called home bringing action [Heimschoffungsaktion] and who have the citizenship of the following countries might now be included in the evacuation measures:

    1. Italy   6. Sweden
    2. Switzerland   7. Finland
    3. Spain   8. Hungary
    4. Portugal   9. Roumania
    5. Denmark   10. Turkey

Since the evacuation of these Jews to the East cannot yet take place at the present time, a temporary stay is provided in the concentration camp Buchenwald for male Jews over 14 years of age and in the concentration camp Ravensbruck for Jewesses as well as children.

The necessary measures are to be carried out on the following dates:
   a. For Jews with citizenship immediately,
   b. For Jews with Turkish citizenship on 20 October 1943,

c. For Jews with citizenship of other countries mentioned above on 10 October 1943

Roumania
[in pencil on right side]

A special application for protective custody is not requested for the transfer to the concentration camp, but the concentration camp headquarters are to be notified that the transfer to the concentration camp is taking place in the frame of the evacuation measures.

The regulation of the above mentioned decree of 5 March 1943 are in force for the management of the property and for the taking along of baggage.

As far as the evacuation of Jews with foreign citizenship which has already been ordered in the decree mentioned above has not yet been carried out, it is to be made up for immediately.

Concluding I want to point out the fact that Jews who are married to spouses with German or German related (artverwandt) blood are to be excepted from all measures now as before. After the execution of all measures a final report is requested (latest date November 1st 1943)

Additional remark for the commander of the Security Police and of the Security Service for the occupied Dutch territories:

Attention is drawn to the special regulation of the same day, as far as those Jews in Holland are concerned who have Roumanian citizenship.

By order
[signed] MULLER
[Stamp:] Foreign Office
Inl II 2777 Secret.
[in pencil]
Received October 5th 1943
Endorse

[Stamp:]
The ReichsfuehrerSS
and Chief of the
German Police
in the Reich Ministry
of the Interior

Certified:
[signed] RASENACK
Chancellery Clerk

Inl II 9947 Secret [in pencil]
The Chief of the Security Police and of the Security Service
VI B 4 b-2314/43 Secret (82)—

3319-PS — Nazi Germany's War Against the Jews

Copy

The Reich Minister for the Occupied Eastern territories
No. I/602/41 Secret
DIII 238
To the Foreign Office
Berlin W8
Wilhlmstr. 72-76

Berlin W35 Mar, 42
Rauchstr. 17/18
Secret!
Receipt stamp
Foreign Office
D III 260 g
Received 13 Mar. 42

Subject: Deportation of Rumanian Jews on the Bug.

With reference to the conference with Legationsrat Rademscher and Lieutenant Colonel [Obersturmbannfuehrer] Eichmann and my expert Amtsgerichsrat Dr. Wetzel, I send you in the enclosure a copy of the agreements of Tighina of 30 Aug 1941 with the request for acknowledgment. I point out especially number 7 of the agreements. I have already taken a position in my letter of 5 Mar. 1942.

By Direction
/s/ Dr. Draeutigam
Seal Authenticated
/s/ signature
Government inspector
Enclosure to Gen Qu II/1542/41
Top Secret

Copy
Secret

COPY

Agreements
about the security, administration, and economic exploitation of territories between
The Dniester and the Bug (Transnistria) and the Bug and the Dnieper (Bug-Dnieper-territory).

The following serve as a basis for the *agreements:*

The Fuehrer's letter of 14 Aug 41 to Chief of State [Staatschef] Antonescu.

The answering letter of the Chief of State of 17 Aug 41.

The letter of the Chief of the German Army mission to the Royal Rumanian General Staff of 24 Aug. 41.

To the mutual German Rumanian Agreements in the town hall at Tighina and the necessity of examining all questions to be treated from the viewpoint of the *Mutual* waging of the war which was emphasized there as an introduction by Major General Hauffe.

* * * * * * *

7. Deportation of Jews from Transnistria. Deportation of Jews across the Bug is not possible at present. They must, therefore, be collected in concentration camps and set to work, until a deportation to the east is possible after the end of operations.

8. The Rumanian border line agreed upon remains on the Dniester. Army Group South takes over the closing of the Eastern and Northern boundaries of Transnistria.

9. Accounting of deliveries. The accounting of deliveries of all kinds from Transnistria will be clarified by the Rumanian and German agencies competent for this.

It is essential at present to register all achievements carefully and to request receipts.

For the Royal
Rumanian Grand
General Staff
/s/ Tatarnu
Brigadier General

For the High Command
of the German Army
/s/ Hauffe
Major General

File memo

According to information today from director General Lecca, 110,000 Jews are being evacuated from Bukovina and Bessarabia into two forests in the Bug River Area. As far as he could learn, this action is based upon an order issued by Marshal Antonescu. Purpose of the action is the liquidation of these Jews.

Bucharest, October 17, 1941
[Signature illegible]

1. To be discussed with Vice Minister President Antonescu.

Confidential
Bucharest, October 16, 1943

Consultant for Jewish Questions
1. To the Chief of the Economic office
of the Auslandsorganisation (AO) of the NSDAP
party member Musmacher
Bucharest.

Subject: Expulsion of Jews from firms owned by citizens of the German Reich
Previous correspondence: known
Inc.: 1 To be returned.

1. With the request that it be returned, I am sending inclosed herewith a statement prepared by the Government Com-

missioner for Jewish Questions concerning Jews employed in firms owned by citizens of the German Reich. At my instigation, the Reich Commissar for Jewish Question had undertaken, on the basis of this list, to invalidate the labor books of all Jews working for these firms.

Please return this list when finished with it.

[signature illegible]
(Richter)
SS-Hauptsturmfuehrer

2. forwarded 5, Nov.
[initial] W
carbon copy to SS-Hauptsturmfuehrer Party Member Richter

Confidential
Note for Landesgruppenleiter Party Member Kohlhammer
Bucharest, August 2, 1943

Subject: Removal of Jews from firms owned by citizens of the German Reich.

In the sense of our understanding concerning the immediate removal of Jews still employed in Bucharest firms owned by citizens of the German Reich, I have determined, in collaboration with Party Member Richter of the German Legation, upon the following:

By referring to the lists at his disposal, Party Member Richter will immediately demand, through the Rumanian authorities, the withdrawal of the labor book from every Jew still active in Reich-German firms. The action itself will be started by the Legation and will thus be lent an official character and coordinated with the intentions of the Economic Counselor of the National Group [Landesgruppe].

[initialed]
M
/H. Musmacher/
Economic Counselor of the National
group [Wirtschafteberater der Landesgruppe]

Carbon Copy from the
National Group in Rumania
SS-Hauptatumfuehrer Richter
German Legation, Bucharest

The Documentary Evidence   **3319-PS**

6 August 1943

National Group Leader
[Landesgruppenleiter]   (Strictly confidential)
Office II
of the organization of the NSDAP abroad [Auslands-Organisation der NSDAP]

Dear Party Member Stempel,

    I am forwarding to you, inclosing herewith, a confidential circular addressed to my closest collaborators and should like to ask that you bring it to the attention of Party Member Christian, also. I have given my Economic Counselor strict injunctions to desist unconditionally from the tolerance heretofore practiced and to take the sternest measures against German firms which still employ Jews. We have named these firms for years, now, and they always find ways and means to postpone the removal of the Jews. Upon my recommendation, the Consultant for Jewish Questions in the German Legation, SS-Hauptsturmfuehrer Richter, will cooperate very closely with my Economic Adviser, so that the goal may be reached as soon as possible.

    The German Envoy, v. Killinger, is at any rate, one hundred percent in accord with my action and I hope that we can have the German firms free of Jews in Rumania within a very short time.

    I greet you with

                                          Heil Hitler
                                    Yours Kohlhammer
                     [signed]   Ludwig Kohlhammer
                                National Group Leader
Inc. as mentioned   [Landesgruppenleiter]

                                      Copy
National Group Leader [Landesgruppenleiter]
                              Bucharest, Aug. 5, 1943
For cognizance
To my colleagues of the Offices and to the ranking
Party representatives in Temeschburg, Arad, Hermannstadt, Kronstadt, Galatz, Braila, Gzernowitz.

Subject: Removal of Jews from firms owned by citizens of The
            German Reich.

    I pointed out at length, at last week's roll-call, that I no longer have any understanding, in the fourth year of the war and under total mobilization for war, for the case;

a. if a German firm continues to employ a single Jew or

b. if it requests from German agencies permission to continue to employ one or more Jews.

As a person well acquainted with economic conditions here, I can not think of a single case where a German firm would any way jeopardize its existence by an immediate removal of Jews. If a German firm did lose some business or other now through the immediate discharge of its Jewish employees, that is really a very small sacrifice compared to the tremendous difficulties overcome and sacrifices made by those firms who had to carry out the dismissal of Jewish employees during the Jewish era of King Carol-Lupescu.

In almost all cases actual experience has shown that the earlier and more thoroughly Aryanization is carried out, the more quickly a reliable and sound business development sets in.

I can only give the following advice to anyone who still employs a Jew: Make up your mind to this: your Yid either became very ill yesterday, or he was drafted for the labor service.

Do, now, that which you will have to do anyway.

Whoever fails to carry out the removal of Jews immediately can no longer claim, in the fourth year of the war, the right to be considered, treated, or addressed as the head of a German enterprise.

We dare not forget that untold thousands of our fellow Germans have lost all their property and become homeless because of Jewish criminal instincts and Jewish capital instigated, organized and are carrying out the despicable terror raids. We owe it to our sorely tried fellow countrymen in the heavily bombed regions to sever at once any connection we have with Jews.

Cases of so-called German firms which fail ruthlessly to get rid of the remaining Jewish connections within the next one or two months are to be reported to me.

Heil Hitler!
[signed] Ludkig Kohlhammer
National Group Leader

Top Secret

Ministerial Presidium
No. 311   256/R   Bucharest, Nov. 25, 1943
Directorate of the
Section for Liaison
with the ministries

Mr Commissar General!

With reference to your letter, no. 1126, of 24 November this year, we take pleasure in forwarding to you an extract from the stenographic record of the meeting of the council of Ministers on 17 November this year regarding the problem of the evacuation of the Jews from Transnistria.

Please be assured, Mr Commissar General, of our most favorable regard.

Secretary General:
By direction
signed   Basarabeanu
To the Commissar General for Jewish Questions
Deputy Director General
by direction
Signed with signature.

Translation of Document 3323-PS. *Excerpts from Decree concerning the obligations of Jews in the Netherlands to register, 10 January 1941.*

* * *

OFFICIAL GAZETTE FOR THE OCCUPIED DUTCH TERRITORIES, YEAR 1941
[Verordnungsblatt fuer die besetzten Niederlandischen Gebiete, Jahrgang 1941] part 2, page 19

Decree by the Reich Commissioner for the occupied territories of the Netherlands concerning the obligation to register persons who are entirely or partly of Jewish race.

By virtue of article 5 of the Fuehrer's decree dated 18 May 1940 (RGBl-page 77) relative to the exercise of governmental powers in the Netherlands I decree as follows:

Article 1

Persons who are entirely or partly of Jewish race and who are residing in the occupied territories of the Netherlands are to be registered in accordance with the following regulations.

Article 2

(1) In this decree a person is considered to be entirely or partly of Jewish race if he is descended from even one grandparent of full Jewish blood.

(2) A grandparent is automatically considered as being fully Jewish if he belongs or has belonged to the Jewish religious community.

Article 3

(1) If there should be any doubt as to whether a person should be considered to be entirely or partly of Jewish blood as given in article 2, the decision will be made, on request, by the Reich Comissioner for the occupied territories of the Netherlands or the office indicated by him.

(2) The following are entitled to make the request—
   1. every German office in the occupied territories in the Netherlands.
   2. the registration authorities
   3. the person in question

(3) The decision referred to in article 1 is final.

Article 4

(1) A person to be registered in accordance with articles 1 to 3, is compelled to register.

(2) If the person who is to be registered is unable to deal with business matters or limited in his ability to deal with business matters, his legal representative or those who actually look after him are compelled to make the registration.

*   *   *   *   *   *   *

Article 11

(1) This decree comes into force on the 14th day after it has been announced.

(2) The general secretary of the ministry of the Interior will issue the regulations necessary for its execution.

The Hague, 10th January 1941

The Reichs commissioner for the occupied territories in the Netherlands.

Seyss-Inquart.

Translation of Document 3325-PS. *Decree of the Reich Commissioner for the Occupied Dutch Territories restricting the enrollment of Jews at Dutch Universities, 11 February 1941.*

*   *   *   *   *   *   *

OFFICIAL GAZETTE FOR THE OCCUPIED DUTCH TERRITORIES, YEAR 1941

[Verordnungsblatt fuer die besetzten Niederlaendischen Gebiete] Part 6, Page 99

Decree of the Reich Commissioner for the Occupied Dutch Territories referring to Jewish students

In accordance with section 5 of the Fuehrer's decree referring to the exercise of governmental authority within the Netherlands, dated 18 May 1940 (RGBl. I, S. 778), I decree that:

Section 1

This decree refers to:
1. Persons who are entirely or partly of Jewish blood, and have to register according to Decree Nr. 6/1941 on compulsory registration; exempt are those who have only one grandparential ancestor of pure Jewish race in the sense of this decree.
2. Persons who adhere to the Jewish religious faith.

Section 2

The enrollment at Dutch universities and colleges of persons classified under section 1 is restricted by regulations which are issued by the Secretary General of the Ministry of Education, Science- and Cultural administration.

Section 3

A person, classified under section 1, who did not matriculate in a Dutch university or college can only be admitted for examination in these institutions after permission has been granted by the Secretary General of the Ministry of Education-Science- and Cultural administration.

Section 4

This decree takes effect on the day of its proclamation.
The Hague, the 11 February 1941.

The Reich Commissioner for the
Dutch Occupied Territories
signed Seyss-Inquart.

Translation of Document 3326-PS. *Decree of the Reich Commissioner for the Occupied Dutch Territories in blocking the property of Jews who emigrated to the Netherlands, 18 September 1941.*

* * * * * * *

OFFICIAL GAZETTE FOR THE OCCUPIED DUTCH TERRITORIES, YEAR 1941
[Verordnungsblatt fuer die besetzten Niederlaendischen Gebiete] Part 39, Page 785.

Decree of the Reich Commissioner for the occupied Netherlands Territories, whereby an order is put into effect, issued by the Reich Minister of Economics regarding the blocking of property within the country belonging to Jews, who emigrated to the Netherlands.

Pursuant to section 5 of the Fuehrer's decree concerning the exercise of governmental authority in the Netherlands of 18 May 1940, I hereby order as follows:

Section 1

The order printed in the appendix—issued by the Reich Minister of Economics, concerning the blocking of property within the country belonging to Jews who emigrated to the Netherlands, herewith takes effect.

Section 2

Proper Foreign Exchange Control Offices in the sense of this order are those which are considered proper Foreign Exchange Control Offices in the German Reich in accordance with the prevailing regulations.

Section 3

Failure to comply with this order will be punished, pursuant to the rules of point VI of the law of Dec. 12, 1938 (RGBl. I pg. 1733) dealing with the control of foreign exchange. It will be considered a punishable act in the sense of Section 2, paragraph 2, of the decree No. 52/1940, which concerns German jurisdiction over crimes in the sense of the decree No. 123/1941.
The Hague, September 18, 1941.

The Reich Commissioner for the
occupied Netherlands territories
SEYSS-INQUART

Appendix
Order concerning the blocking of property within the country belonging to Jews who emigrated to the Netherlands.
Pursuant to section 60 of the Foreign Exchange Decree, I hereby order the following, to take effect as of Sept. 1st, 1941:

Jews, residing in occupied Netherlands territories, who emigrated from the German Reich after August 3rd, 1931, and who at that time were German citizens—can dispose their property—still remaining in parts of the German Reich—only with the consent of the proper Foreign Exchange Control office. Berlin, August 30, 1941.

For the Reich Minister of Economics
(s) Dr. Landfried

Translation of Document 3328-PS. *Excerpts from Decree of the Reich Commissioner for the Occupied Dutch Territories regulating all professional, industrial or other pursuits aimed at profits of Jews, 22 October 1941.*

* * *

OFFICIAL GAZETTE FOR THE OCCUPIED DUTCH TERRITORIES, YEAR 1941
[Verordnungsblatt fuer die besetzten Niederlaendischen Gebiete] Part 44, Page 841.

198

Decree of the Reich Commissioner for the Occupied Dutch Territories concerning the regulation of the professional activities of Jews.

By virtue of Article 5 of the decree of the Fuehrer concerning the exercise of governmental authority in the Netherlands of May 18, 1940 (Reichsgesetzblatt I S.778) I hereby order:

Article 1

The exercise by Jews of professional, industrial or other pursuits aimed at profits, may be made subject to permission or to conditions or may be prohibited by administrative orders. Arrangements for the termination and liquidation of work contracts, to which a person affected by this administrative order is a party, can be made at the same time.

Article 2

1. The administrative orders will be issued by the Reich Commissioner for the occupied Netherlands territories (Commissioner General for Finance and Economics) or by the department, authorized by him. They may apply to groups of persons or to individuals.

2. Administrative orders, applying to groups of persons will be announced in the legal gazette [Verordnungsblatt] of the occupied Netherlands territories, unless in a special case a different way of announcement is ordered.

* * * * * * *

Article 8

A Jew—in accordance with this decree—is a person, who, by virtue of the instructions of Section 4 of the decree No. 189/1940 concerning the registration of employers—is a Jew or is considered a Jew.

Article 9

1. The Reich Commissioner for the occupied territories of the Netherlands (General Commissioner for Finance and Economy) will take the necessary measures for the execution of this decree. He may delegate his authority to others.

2. The Reich Commissioner (Commissioner General of Finance and Economy) in case of doubts resulting from the application of the instructions of this decree may make generally binding legal decisions.

Article 10

This decree becomes effective on the day of its publication.
Den Haag, October 22, 1941.

The Reich Commissioner for the occupied
Dutch territories
SEYSS-INQUART

Translation of Document 3329-PS. Excerpts from Decree of the Reich Commissioner for the Occupied Dutch Territories prohibiting Jews from working in the fields of architecture, handicraft, music, literature, theatre, films and journalism, 22 November 1941.

* * *

OFFICIAL GAZETTE FOR THE OCCUPIED DUTCH TERRITORIES, YEAR 1941
[Verordnungsblatt fuer die besetzten Niederlaendischen Gebiete] Part 47, Page 901.

211

Decree of the Reichscommissioner for the Occupied Dutch Territories concerning the Netherlands Chamber of Culture [Kulturkammer].

Pursuant to Article 5 of the Decree of the Fuehrer concerning the exercise of governmental authority in the Netherlands of 18. Mai 1940 (RGBl I, p. 778) I order:

Chapter I
Task and aim of the Netherlands Chamber of Culture.

Article 1

1. Persons, who are active in the field of the plastic arts including architecture and handicraft, music, literature, theatre, films and journalism, will be united in guilds. These guilds will form the Netherlands Chamber of Culture.

2. It is the task of the Netherlands Chamber of Culture to promote the Netherland culture as it is represented by the people and country, by cooperation of its members, who are active in all of its spheres, to direct the technical, economic and social affairs of the cultural professions and to coordinate the different aims of the members of the various groups.

Article 2

The Netherlands Chamber of Culture is an incorporated public institution with rights and liabilities as defined in Article 152 of the constitution. Its domicile is in the Hague.

* * * * * * *

Article 10

1. Jews or persons with Jewish relatives by marriage can neither be members of the Netherlands Chamber of Culture, nor of an organization of persons, which in turn is a member of the Netherlands Chamber of Culture, or is supposed to be a member. It is further forbidden for these persons:
    1. To found or to participate in the founding of an organization of persons, which is a member of the Netherlands Chamber of Culture or is obliged to be a member.
    2. To credit or participate in the creation of a foundation and also to benefit directly or indirectly from the property of a foundation, if said foundation is a member of the Netherlands Chamber of Culture or is obliged to be a member.
    3. To work for an organization of persons as mentioned under I, or for a foundation as mentioned under 2, or to participate as a guest in the management of such organizations for persons or foundations.

(2) The Secretary-General of the Ministry for Popular Enlightenment and Arts may permit in special cases:
   1. That a Jew or a person with Jewish family ties become a member of the Netherlands Chamber of Culture.
   2. That organizations of persons or foundations, which must be a member of the Netherlands Chamber of Culture, be exempted from the obligation to become a member, if its members are exclusively Jewish, or if the foundation property is exclusively for the benefit of Jews.

Article 11

1. Jewish persons in the sense of this decree are—
    1. Persons who have more than one Jewish grandparent.
    2. Persons other than those mentioned under Nr. 1 who belonged to the Jewish religious community on May 9, 1940 or who have been accepted therein after this date.

2. Persons with Jewish relatives in the sense of this decree are such persons, who are married to a person as described under 3 or who live with such person in concubinary.

3. A grandparent is considered Jewish, if this grandparent has belonged to a Jewish religious community.

* * * * * * *

Article 36

This ordinance shall take effect as of the day of publication.
The Hague, November 22, 1941

The Reichscommissioner for the
Occupied Dutch Territories
SEYSS-INQUART

Translation of Document 3333-PS. *Excerpts from Decree of the Reich Commissioner for the Occupied Dutch Territories providing for the registration of all Jewish enterprises, 22 October 1940.*

* * *

OFFICIAL GAZETTE FOR THE OCCUPIED DUTCH TERRITORIES, YEAR 1940
[Verordnungsblatt fuer die besetzten Niederlaendischen Gebiete] Part 33, Page 546.

189

Decree of the Reich commissioner for the occupied Dutch territories concerning registration of business enterprises.

In accordance with article 5 of the decree of the Fuehrer on exercise of governmental authority dated 18 May 1940 [Reichsgesetzblatt I, p. 118] I decree the following:

Point 1
Enterprises Under Obligation To Register
Article 1
Definition of an Enterprise

Enterprises in the sense of this decree are:

1. Enterprises which, according to the law on Commercial registration of 1918 [Handelsregistergesetz - Handelsregister Wet 1918] must be registered in the General Commercial Register;

2. Enterprises of other associations of persons, furthermore enterprises of non-profit corporations, foundations and others formed for definite purposes insofar as they pursue economic objects;

3. Farm and forestry enterprises as well as horticultural and fishing enterprises, insofar as a commercial enterprise is connected with them;

4. Enterprises of craftsmen and peddlers are not included.

Article 2
Obligation to Register

Under obligation to register is every enterprise that on 9

May, 1940 corresponds or will correspond at a later date to the following definition

1. An enterprise which is operated by a person, if the owner is a Jew;
2. An enterprise which is operated by a company [Offene Handelsgesellschaft] or a corporation in which the liability is limited to one or more partners [Kommanditgesellschaft], if at least one personally liable partner [persoenlich haftender Gesellschafter] is a Jew.
3. An enterprise which is operated by a corporation or a stock corporation with limited liability.
   a. if at least one of the persons appointed to the legal representation or at least one of the members of the board of directors is a Jew.
   b. if Jews own essential interest in the capital or votes. It is considered to be an essential interest in the capital if more than a quarter of the capital belongs to Jews; it is considered to be an essential interest in votes, if the votes of the Jews reach the halfmark of the number of the total votes: if votes exist which contain preferential voting rights, it suffices if half of these votes belong to Jews;
4. an enterprise which is operated by an association of persons, a non-profit corporation formed for a definite purpose in the sense of article 1, section 2, if one of the definitions according to sections 2 or 3 of this article is applicable;
5. an enterprise, if it actually is under the controlling influence of Jews, the obligation to register will not be eliminated in case the property of the particular enterprise must be registered in accordance with Order No. 26/1940 concerning the treatment of enemy property. * * *

Article 4
Definition of a Jew

1. A Jew is one who is descended from at least three racially pure Jewish grandparents.
2. As a Jew is also considered one who is descended from two purely Jewish greatparents and
   1. either belonged to the Jewish religious community on 9 May, 1940 or will be admitted to it after the date, or
   2. was married to a Jew on 9 May, 1940 or marries a Jew after this date.
3. As pure-Jewish is automatically considered a greatparent if he belonged to the Jewish religious community.

* * * * * * *

This decree will become valid on the day of its promulgation.
The Hague
22 October, 1940

The Reich Commisioner for the
Occupied Dutch Territories
SEYSS-INQUART

Translation of Document 3334-PS. *Excerpts from Decree of the Reich Commissioner for the Occupied Dutch Territories prohibiting the employment of German nationals of German or related blood in Jewish households, 19 December 1940.*

* * * * * * *

OFFICIAL GAZETTE FOR THE OCCUPIED DUTCH TERRITORIES, YEAR 1940
[Verordnungsblatt fuer die besetzten Niederlaendischen Gebiete] Part 42, Page 761.

231

Decree of the Reich Commissioner for the occupied Dutch Territories concerning the employment of Germans in Jewish households.

By virtue of section 5 of the edict of the Fuehrer on the execution of governmental authority in the Netherlands of 18 May 1940 (RGBl. I. S. 118) I decree:

Section 1

(1) German Nationals of German or related blood cannot be employed in households of which a Jew is the head, nor in families of which a Jew is a permanent or temporary member for a non-interrupted period of more than four weeks.

(2) In the sense of paragraphs I are considered as Jews, those who according to the regulations of section 4 of decree Nr. 189/1940 concerning the registration of enterprises, are Jews or are considered as such. Employed in a household are those who, in order to work there, are entirely or partially, temporarily or continuously a member of the household or those who perform daily household work or other daily work directly or indirectly connected with the household without being a member thereof.

* * * * * * *

This decree becomes effective on the day of its publication.
The Hague, 19 December 1940

The Reichscommissioner for the
Occupied Dutch Territories
SEYSS-INQUART

Translation of Document 3336-PS. *Excerpts from Order of the Reich Commissioner for the Occupied Dutch Territories providing for the registration of all claims belonging to Jews, 21 May 1942.*

* * *

OFFICIAL GAZETTE FOR THE OCCUPIED DUTCH TERRITORIES, YEAR 1942
[Verordnungsblatt fuer die besetzten Niederlaendischen Gebiete] Part 13, Page 289.

58

Order of the Reich Commissioner for the Occupied Dutch Territories, concerning the treatment of Jewish property values.

By virtue of article 5 of the Fuehrer's decree concerning the exercise of governmental authority in the Netherlands of May 18th 1940 (RGBl. 1, S. 778) I hereby order as follows:

Chapter I
Claims and other rights.

Article 1

Claims of any kind have to be registered in writing with the banking firm of Lippmann, Rosenthal & Co., Amsterdam, if as on the effective date of this order or later, they belong wholly or partially to a person legally or really, who, according to the directives of article 4 of the decree No. 189/1940—concerning the registration of enterprises—is a Jew or has to be considered as a Jew. This does not concern claims of an enterprise that had to be registered by virtue of the decree No. 189/1940.

* * * * * * *

Article 6

The rules of articles 1-5 will not be applied:

1. to claims and rights dealt with in the order No. 148/1941 concerning the treatment of Jewish property values.

2. to such ownership of real property and such equal real property rights, rights of usufruct, let on lease or other rights of utilization, which have been properly registered in pursuance of article 2 of the Dejewfication order of Agriculture (No. 102/1941)

3. to such property like rights and mortgages which by virtue of article 3 of order No. 154/1941, concerning Jewish real property, have been duly registered; this also applies to the claims secured by mortgages.

* * * * * * *

Chapter III
Collections, articles of virtue, articles made of precious metals and jewels.

Article 10

Collections of all kinds, articles of virtue, articles of gold, platinum or silver as well as cut or raw precious or semi-precious stones and pearls have to be delivered to the banking firm of Lippmann, Rosenthal & Co., if they, legally or really, belong wholly or partially to a person mentioned in article 1. This does not apply to the property of an enterprise which has to register in pursuance of order No. 189/1940.

Article 11

(1) If a person according to the rules of article 4 of order No. 189/1940 is a Jew or being considered a Jew, is married to a person who is neither a Jew nor can be considered a Jew in accordance with the above mentioned rules, then article 10 will not be applied in cases where such articles belong to:

1. the Jewish husband, if there are descendants of this marriage who are not considered as being Jews according to the above mentioned rules;
2. the Jewish wife in case of a childless marriage.

(2) The rules of paragraph 1, number 1 are also valid, if the marriage does not exist any more.

(3) The regulations of par. 1 and 2 are not applied to marriages, which took place after May 9, 1940.

Article 12

Article 10 does not apply:
1. to individual wedding bands and the wedding band of a deceased husband or wife;
2. to silver wrist and pocket-watches being in personal use;
3. to silver-ware in use, with the consideration that each person belonging to the household of the owner is entitled to keep 4 pieces, namely: Knife, fork, table-spoon and tea-spoon.
4. to artificial denture, made of precious metals, as far as it is needed for personal use.

Article 13

(1) The articles, mentioned in article 10, have to be delivered also if they belong to a third person. Such rights have to be registered in writing with the banking firm of Lippmann, Rosenthal & Co. within a month after the delivery. The con-

sideration of rights which are claimed after the expiration of this time, can be refused without giving any reason.

(2) The banking firm of Lippmann, Rosenthal & Co. is responsible for claims, which are secured by rights as mentioned in par. 1. The person who is entitled to it can ask for an appropriate compensation for rights, which do not serve as the security of claims. The responsibility of the banking firm is limited to the extent of the selling value of the delivered goods.

(3) Legal security and executable measures which were ordered before this order has taken effect, are considered as being effective against the banking firm of Lippmann, Rosenthal & Co. after the delivery has been made.

Article 14

(1) The obligation for delivery rests with the owner (article 10).

(2) Besides, the following persons are also obliged to deliver:
1. Whoever is authorized to represent the owner
2. whoever in the Occupied Netherlands Territories administers, possesses, keeps in custody or guards articles, which according to the rules of articles 10 to 12 have to be delivered.

Article 15

The delivery has to be made immediately, latest until June 30, 1942. If the articles have been acquired after this date, they have to be delivered immediately, latest within one week after the acquisition.

Article 16

Only the banking firm of Lippmann, Rosenthal & Co. has the right of disposal of the articles, which have to be delivered according to the rules of articles 10-12. The provisions of article 7, paragraph 1-3 are to be applied accordingly.

Chapter IV
Obligatory Information

Article 17

(1) Whoever is asked for information by the banking firm of Lippmann, Rosenthal & Co., which is charged to carry out the directives of this order or order No. 148/1941 has to answer the questions completely and truly.

(2) If requested, books, vouchers and other material of evidence have to be presented to the banking firm.

Chapter V
Horses, land and water vehicles

Article 18

(1) If horses, land or water vehicles belong legally or really to a person in article 1, they have to be registered with the Central Office for Jewish Emigration, Amsterdam, until June 30, 1942.

(2) Only the Commissioner General of the Security Service has the right of disposal of the articles described in par. 1. The rules of article 7, par. 1-3 are applied accordingly.

* * * * * * *

Article 26

This order shall take effect as of the date of publication.
The Hague, the 21st of May 1942.

The Reich Commissioner for the
Occupied Dutch Territories
Signed: SEYSS-INQUART

Translation of Document 3358-PS (GB-158). German Foreign Office Circular, 31 January 1939, on "The Jewish Question as a factor in German Foreign Policy in the Year 1938".

* * *

Ministry for Foreign Affairs, 83-26 19/1 Ang. II

Berlin, 31st January 1939

Enclosed please find for your attention a circular which has been sent to the German authorities abroad on the subject of "The Jewish Question as a factor in German Foreign Policy in the year 1938".

By Order

Signed: Hinrichs.

To All Senior Reich Authorities and NSDAP Bureau for Foreign Affairs.

to No. 611—39 secret, Foreign

Secret

Foreign 6.2.39.
No. 611 39 Secret. Foreign If.
Copy to:
 Abw. I (Counter Intelligence I)
 W.Stab.
 Chief Dept. 3
 Att. Gr. of the Army General Staff
 OKM. Dept. 3. SKL
 Ob.d.L. (Z A)

III - 524

Ob.d.L. Dept. 5. General Staff.
Ausl. III
[Pencil note]
Chief W Wi.
                attention is requested.
By Order
1 Enclosure

Ministry for Foreign Affairs.   Berlin, 25th January 1939.
83-26 19/1
Contents:
The Jewish Question as a factor in German Foreign Policy in the year 1938.
1. The German Jewish Policy as basis and consequence of the decisions for the foreign policy of the year 1938.
2. Aim of German Jewish Policy: Emigration.
3. Means, ways and aim of the Jewish Emigration.
4. The emigrated Jew as the best propaganda for the German Jewish Policy.

It is certainly no coincidence that the fateful year 1938 has brought nearer the solution of the Jewish question simultaneously with the realization of the "idea of Greater Germany," since the Jewish policy was both the basis and consequence of the events of the year 1938. The advance made by Jewish influence and the destructive Jewish spirit in politics, economy and culture paralyzed the power and will of the German people to rise again more perhaps even than the power-policy opposition of the former enemy allied powers of the World War. The healing of this sickness among the people was therefore certainly one of the most important requirements for exerting the force which in the year 1938 resulted in the joining together of Greater Germany, in defiance of the world.
To All diplomatic and qualified consular representatives abroad.

The necessity for a radical solution of the Jewish question arose however also as a consequence of the foreign political development, which resulted in a further 200,000 Jews in Austria in addition to the 500,000 of the Jewish Faith living in the Old Reich. The influence of Jewry on Austrian economy which had grown to enormous proportions under the Schuschnigg Regime, made immediate measures necessary, with the aim of excluding Jewry from German economy and utilizing Jewish property in the interests of the community. The action carried out as reprisal for the murder of Legation Councillor von Rath accelerated this process to such an extent that Jewish shops—till then with the exception of foreign business—disappeared from the streets completely. The liquidation of the Jewish wholesale trade, manufacturing trade, and of houses and real estate in the hands of Jews, will gradually reach a point where in a conceivable time there will no longer be any talk of Jewish property in Germany. Nevertheless it must be emphasized that this is no seizure of Jewish property without compensation, as for instance the confiscation of Church Property during the French revolution. On the contrary the dispossessed Jew receives Reich Bonds for his goods, and the interest is credited to him.

The final goal of German Jewish Policy is the emigration of all the Jews living in Reich territory. It is foreseen that already the thorough measures in the economic sphere, which have prevented the Jew from earning and made him live on his dividends, will further the desire to emigrate. Looking back on the last 5 years since the assumption of power, it is, however, obvious that neither the Law for the Reestablishing of the Professional Character of the Civil Service nor the Nurnberg Jewish laws with their executive regulations, which prevented any tendency of Jewry being assimilated, contributed to any extent to the emigration of German Jews. On the contrary every period of domestic political tranquility has resulted in such a stream of Jewish immigrants returning, that the Gestapo has been obliged to put Jewish immigrants with German passports into a training camp for political supervision.

The Jew was excluded from politics and culture. But until 1938 his powerful economic position in Germany was unbroken, and thereby his obstinate resolve to hold out until "better times" came. Indicative of the tactics of this "delaying" resistance is the programme of a Jewish Party recently formed in Poland, to fight against all Polish measures aimed at Jewish emigration. As long as the Jew can earn money in Germany, then in the opinion of World Jewry the Jewish bastion in Germany need not be given up.

But the Jew has underestimated the consequences and the strength of the National Socialist purpose. The powerful Jewish positions in Vienna and Prague collapsed in 1938 at the same time as the system of states in Central Europe created at Versailles to keep Germany down. Italy stood at Germany's side, with her racial Laws in the fight against Jewry. An expert on the Jewish question, Prof. Goga, took over the Government in Bukarest with a programme aimed against Jewry, without however being able to carry it out because of overwhelming international pressure from Paris and London. Jewry in Hungary and Poland was subjected to special laws. Everywhere the success of German foreign policy now begins to shake Jewish strongholds which have been established for hundreds of years from Munich and in far off States, like the tremors of an earthquake.

It is also understandable that World Jewry, "which has selected America as its Headquarters" regards as its own downfall the Munich Agreement, which in American opinion signifies the collapse of the democratic front in Europe. For the system of parliamentary democracy has always, as experience proves, helped the Jews to wealth and political power at the expense of the people in whose country they live. It is certainly the first time in history that Jewry must evacuate a secure position.

This resolution was first formed in 1938. It showed itself in the efforts of the western democracies, particularly those of the United States of America, to put the now finally determined Jewish withdrawal from Germany, in other words Jewish emigration, under international control and protection. The American President Roosevelt "who it is well known is surrounded by a whole row of exponents of Jewry among his closest confidants" called a State Conference as early as the middle of 1938 to discuss the refugee questions, which was held in Evian without any particular results. Both of the questions, the answering of which is the first essential for organized Jewish emigration remained unanswered: firstly the question of *how* this emigration should be organized and financed and secondly the question: emigrate *to where?*

In answer to the first question, International Jewry in particular did not appear willing to contribute. On the contrary the Conference—and later the Committee formed by it in London under the direction of Rublee, an American—regarded its main task as that of forcing Germany by international pressure to release Jewish property to the greatest possible extent. In other words Germany was to pay for the emigration of her 700,000 Jews with German national property. It is at the same time to be doubted whether International Jewry ever seriously desired the mass emigration of their fellow Jews from Germany and other states at all, unless there was an equivalent of a Jewish State. The tactics hitherto employed in Jewish proposals, were in every case aimed less at mass emigration of Jews than at the transfer of Jewish property.

It goes without saying that the transfer of even a fraction of Jewish property would be impossible from the point of view of foreign exchange. The financing of a mass emigration of German Jews is therefore still obscure. Questions could be answered casually thus, that Germany for her part reckoned that International Jewry—particularly relatives of Jews who have emigrated—would support this emigration as vigorously as it made it possible for its destitute fellow Jews to immigrate to Germany, at a time when Germany was so weak that she could not stop the stream of Jews from the East. It should be emphasized, however, that according to police and taxation records, the greater proportion of Jews immigrated to Germany without means and made money in a few years or decades, while the German people lost their possessions as a result of the reparations imposed by the Treaty of Versailles or joined the ranks of the unemployed. Consequently Germany for her part had no sympathy for the compassion with which an ostensibly humanitarian world accuses Germany of illegally appropriating property which was taken away from the German people by Jewish business methods.

The second question, to what country should an organized Jewish emigration be directed, could similarly not be answered by the Evian Conference, as each of the countries taking part, having announced that they were fundamentally concerned with the refugee problem, declared that they were not in a position to take large numbers of Jewish emigrants into their territory. After over 100,000 Jews even in 1933/34 had succeeded either legally or illegally in escaping abroad and establishing themselves in someone else's country either with the help of their Jewish relatives living abroad or circles sympathetically disposed from a humanitarian point of view, almost every State in the World has in the meantime hermetically sealed its borders against these parasitical Jewish intruders. The problem of Jewish emigration is therefore for all practical purposes at a standstill. Many States have already become so cautious, that they demand a permit made out by German authorities from Jews travelling in the ordinary way with German passports, saying that there is nothing against them returning.

The emigration movement of only about 100,000 Jews has already sufficed to awaken the interest if not the understanding of many countries in the Jewish danger. We can estimate that here the Jewish question will extend to a problem of international politics when large numbers of Jews from Germany,

Poland, Hungary and Rumania are put on the move as a result of increasing pressure from the people of the countries where they are living. Even for Germany the Jewish problem will not be solved when the last Jew has left German soil.

It is even today an important duty of German policy to control and when possible direct the flow of Jewish emigration to be sure there is no incentive to cooperate with other countries such as Poland, Hungary and Rumania, who themselves are striving for the emigration of the Jewish sections of their population, in an attempt to solve this problem. From experience with this procedure interests clash, although directed towards the same goal, and retard the realization of Germany's urgent claim for German Jews to be admitted into other particular countries.

It is true that the Rumanian Government sent an official appeal to the Reich Government in the name of human ethics and justice, to join with them in an international action to solve the Jewish question. On the other hand, Poland at the end of October last year issued a decree, the execution of which has made it practically impossible for 60,000 Jews of Polish Nationality residing in Germany to return to Poland. As is well known, the Reich Government had then to decide to deport to Poland 60,000 Jews of Polish Nationality who will be followed by their families, shortly before the Polish Decree came into force. The Hungarian Government, it is true, appreciates the German Jewish policy in so far as they themselves have in mind the "Aryanization" of Hungarian-Jewish businesses in Germany, that is, Jewish owners of firms will be replaced by Hungarians. In general, however, it is apparent that the States concerned are more egotistically interested in deporting their own Jewish elements than in any international solution. Germany will therefore take the initiative herself, in order next of all to find ways, means and destination for Jewish emigration from Germany.

Palestine—which has already become the slogan of world opinion, the land for the emigrants—cannot be considered as the target for Jewish emigration, because it is incapable of absorbing a mass influx of Jews. Under the pressure of Arab resistance, the British Mandatory Government has restricted Jewish immigration into Palestine to the minimum. For the time being Jewish emigration to Palestine was helped to a great extent, as far as Germany was concerned, by the signing of an agreement with the representatives of Jewry in Palestine, which made it possible to transfer Jewish property in the form of additional exports (Haavara-Agreement). Apart from the fact that emigration was made possible by this method for a small number of wealthy Jews only, but not for the mass of *Jews without means*, [Pencil note: Are there such people] there were fundamental considerations of foreign policy against this type of emigration: the transfer of Jewish property out of Germany contributed to no small extent to the building of a Jewish State in Palestine. Germany must regard the forming of a Jewish State as dangerous, which even in miniature would form just such an operational base as the Vatican for political Catholicism. The realization that World Jewry will always be the irreconcilable enemy of the Third Reich, forces the decision to prevent any strengthening of the Jewish position. A Jewish State, however, would bring an international increase in power to World Jewry. Alfred Rosenberg expressed this idea in his speech in Detmold on 15 January this year as follows:

"Jewry is striving today for a Jewish State in Palestine. Not to give Jews all over the world a homeland but for other reasons: World Jewry must have a miniature State, from which to send exterritorial ambassadors and representatives to all countries of the world and through these be able to further their lust for power. But more than anything else they want a Jewish centre, a Jewish State in which they can house the Jewish swindlers from all parts of the world, who are hunted by the Police of other countries, issue them new passports and then send them to other parts of the world. It is to be desired, that those people who are friendly disposed to Jews, above all the Western Democracies who have so much space in all parts of the world at their disposal, place an area outside Palestine for the Jews, *of course in order to establish a Jewish Reserve and not a Jewish State.*"

That is the programme expressing the foreign policy attitude of Germany towards the Jewish question. Germany is very interested in maintaining the dispersal of Jewry. The calculation, that as a consequence boycott groups and anti-German centres would be formed all over the world, disregards the following fact which is already apparent. The influx of Jews in all parts of the world invokes the opposition of the native population and thereby forms the best propaganda for the German Jewish policy.

In North America, in South America, in France, in Holland, Scandinavia and Greece, everywhere, wherever the flood of Jewish immigrants reaches, there is today already a visible increase in anti-semitism. A task of the German foreign policy must be to further this wave of anti-semitism. This will be achieved less by German propaganda abroad, than by the propaganda which the Jew is forced to circulate in his defense. In the end, its effects will recoil on themselves. The reports from German authorities abroad emphasize the correctness of this interpretation:

The press and official correspondents continually report anti-semitic demonstrations by the population of North America. It is perhaps indicative of the domestic political development in USA, that the listening-audience of the "Radio Priest" Coughlin, who is well known to be Anti-Jewish, has grown to over 20 millions. The Embassy in Montevideo reported on 12 December last year "that the Jewish influx continues for months, week by week. It goes without saying, that anti-semitism is growing"—Salonica reported on 30 November 1938: "that forces are at work to stir up the hate against the Jews" and that at the same time Greek Freemasonry is endeavoring to stem the anti-semitic movement. In France, the Paris Town Council (Stadtversammlung) was in April of this year to discuss a proposal, by which the naturalization of Jews was in future to be refused. The meeting on the Jewish question ended with the speaker being beaten up—Lyon reported on 20 December last year: "The immigration of Jewish refugees has lately led to undesirable occurrences. The antipathy towards the new intruders based on business and competitive grounds, which is general throughout France, is unmistakable." This aversion has grown to such an extent meantime that a Jewish defense has already been organized against the anti-semitism in France (Report Paris dated 19 November last year).—The Embassy at the Hague reported on 30 December last year: "Under the pressure of countless immigrants from Germany, who make themselves objectionable particularly in Amsterdam, anti-semitism is growing very much in Holland. And if this continues, it can easily come to pass that Dutchmen will not only appreciate Germany's action against the Jews but will also find themselves wishing to do the same as we."—The embassy at Oslo reported on 8th April last year: "While only a few years ago, the streets of Oslo were hardly marred by Jews at all, lately a great change has come about here. On the streets, in restaurants and above all in the coffee houses, Jews sit around in hideous cluster. The Norwegians are being crowded out, more and more. The Norwegian Press, which formerly did not understand the Jewish question at all, suddenly realized what it meant to have the Children of Israel invade the country like a swarm of locusts. It will be a very salutory lesson, which is being meted out to the Norwegians".

These examples from reports from authorities abroad, can, if desired, be amplified. They confirm the correctness of the expectation, that criticism of the measures for excluding Jews from German Lebensraum which were misunderstood in many countries for lack of evidence would only be temporary and would swing in the other direction the moment the population saw with its own eyes and thus learned, what the Jewish danger was to them. The poorer and therefore the more burdensome the immigrant Jew is to the country absorbing him, the stronger this country will react and the more desirable is this effect in the interests of German propaganda. The object of this German action is to be the future international solution of the Jewish question, dictated not by false compassion for the "United Religious Jewish minority" but by the full consciousness of all peoples of the danger which it represents to the racial composition of the nations.

By Order

Schaumburg

Translation of Document 3363-PS. *Special Delivery Letter, 21 September 1939, from Chief of the Security Police to Chiefs of all detail groups of the Security Police concerning the Jewish problem in occupied zone.*

* * *

Copy
Berlin, 21 September 1939

The Chief of the Security Police
PP (II)—288/39 secret
Special Delivery Letter
To *The Chiefs of all detail groups [Einsatzgruppen] of the Security Police*
Concerning: The Jewish problem in the occupied zone.

I refer to the conference held in Berlin today, and again point out that the *planned joint measures* (i.e. the ultimate goal) are to be kept *strictly secret*.
Distinction must be made between
    (1) the ultimate goal (which requires a prolonged period of time) and
    (2) the sectors leading to fulfillment of the ultimate goal, each of which will be carried out in a short term).

The planned measures require thorough preparation both in technique and in the economic aspect.

Obviously the tasks at hand cannot be laid down in detail from here. The following instructions and directives serve at the same time for the purpose of urging chiefs of the detail groups to practical consideration of problems.

I

The first prerequisite for the ultimate goal is first of all, the concentration of the Jews from the country to the larger cities.
This is to be carried out speedily. In doing so distinction must be made:
(1) between the zones of Danzig and West Prussia, Poznan, Eastern Upper Silesia; and
(2) the other occupied zone.

If possible, the zone mentioned under item 1 shall be cleared completely of Jews, or at least the aim should be to form as few concentration centers as possible.

In the zones mentioned under item 2, there shall be established as few concentration points as possible so that future measures may be accomplished more easily. One must keep in mind that only such cities are chosen as concentration points which are located either at railroad junctions or at least along a railroad.

On principle, all Jewish communities *under 500* heads are to be dissolved and to be transferred to the nearest concentration center.

This decree does not count for the zone of detail group I, which is located East of Cracow and bounded by Bolanico, Jaroskaw, the new demarcation line and the previous Polish-Slovakian border. Within this zone merely an improvised census of Jews should be carried out. Furthermore, Councils of Jewish Elders as discussed below are to be set up.

II

Councils of Jewish Elders

(1) In each Jewish community, a Council of Jewish Elders is to be set up which, as far as possible, is to be composed of the remaining influential personalities and rabbis. The Council is to be composed of 24 male Jews (depending on the size of the Jewish community).

It is to be made *fully responsible* (in the literal sense of the word) for the exact execution according to terms of all instructions released or yet to be released.

(2) In case of sabotage of such instructions, the Councils are to be warned of severest measures.

(3) The Jewish Councils are to take an improvised census of

the Jews of their area, possibly divided into generations (according to age)
- *a.* up to 16 years of age,
- *b.* from 16 to 20 years of age,
- *c.* and those above and also according to the principal vocations—

and they are to report the results in the shortest possible time.

(4) The Councils of Elders are to be made acquainted with the time and date of the evacuation, the evacuation possibilities and finally the evacuation routes. They are, then, to be made personally responsible for the evacuation of the Jews from the country.

The reason to be given for the concentration of the Jews to the cities is that Jews have most decisively participated in sniper attacks and plundering.

(5) The Councils of Elders of the concentration centers are to be made responsible for the proper housing of the Jews to be brought in from the country. The concentration of Jews in the cities for general reasons of security will probably bring about orders to forbid Jews to enter certain wards of that city altogether, and that in consideration of economic necessity they cannot, for instance, leave the ghetto, they cannot go out after a designated evening hour, etc.

(6) The Council of Elders is also to be made responsible for the adequate maintenance of the Jews on the transport to the cities.

No scruples are to be voiced, if the migrating Jews take with them all their movable possessions, as far as that is technically at all possible.

(7) Jews who do not comply with the order to move into cities are to be given a short additional period of grace when there is good reason. They are to be warned of strictest penalty if they should not comply by the appointed time.

III

All necessary measures, on principle, are always to be taken up in closest agreement and collaboration with the German civil administration and the competent local authorities.

In the execution of this plan, care must be taken that economic security suffer no harm in the occupied zones.

(1) The needs of the army should particularly be kept in mind e.g. it will not be possible to avoid leaving behind here and there some Jews engaged in trade who absolutely must be left behind for the maintenance of the troops, for lack of any

other way out. In such cases, the immediate Aryanization of these plants is to be planned for and the emigration of the Jews is to be completed later in agreement with the competent local German administrative authorities.

(2) For the preservation of German economic interests in the occupied territories it is self understood that Jewish war and ordinary industries and factories and those important to the 4-Year Plan must be kept going for the time being.

In these cases also, immediate Aryanization must be planned for and the emigration of the Jews must be completed later.

(3) Finally, the food situation in the occupied territories must be taken into consideration. For instance, as far as possible, real estate of Jewish settlers should be provisionally entrusted to the care of neighboring German or even Polish peasants to be worked by them in order to insure harvesting of the crops still in the fields, or cultivation.

In regard to this important question contact should be made with the agricultural experts of the (C.d.Z.).

(4) In all cases in which a conformity of interests of the Security Police [Sicherheitspolizei] on the one hand, and the German civil administration on the other hand, can be reached.

I am to be informed of the individual measures in question as quickly as possible before their execution and my decision is to be awaited.

IV

The Chiefs of the detail groups [Einsatzgruppen] are to report to me continuously on the following matters:

(1) Numerical survey on the Jews present in their territories (if possible according to the above mentioned classification).

The number of Jews who are evacuated from the country and those who are already in cities are to be listed separately.

(2) Names of cities which have been designated as concentration points.

(3) The time set for the Jews to be evacuated to the cities.

(4) Survey of all Jewish war and ordinary industries and factories or those important to the 4-Year Plan in their territory.

If possible the following should be specified:
    a. Kind of factory (also statement on possible reconversion of factory to really vital or war-important factories or those important to the 4-Year Plan);
    b. which factories should be most urgently Aryanized (in order to avoid loss); what kind of Aryanization is suggested? Germans or Poles, (the decision depends on the importance of the factory);

c. number of Jews working in these factories (include leading positions).

Will it be possible to keep the factory going after the Jews have been removed or will German or Polish workers respectively have to be assigned for that purpose? To what extent?

If Polish workers have to be used, care should be taken that they are mainly taken from the former German provinces in order to somewhat ease the problem there. These questions can only be solved by incorporation and participation of the labor offices [Arbeitsaemter] which have been set up.

V

For the fulfillment of the goal set, I expect the full cooperation of all forces of the Security Police [Sicherheitspolizei] and the Security Service [Sicherheitsdienst].

The Chiefs of the neighboring detail groups shall immediately establish contact with each other in order to be able to cover completely the territories in question.

VI

The High Command of the Army [OKH]; the commissioner for the 4-Year Plan (c/o State Secretary Neumann, Staatssekretaer); the Reich Minister of the Interior (c/o State Secretary Stuckart); the Reich Ministry for Food and Economy [fuer Ernaehrung und Wirtschaft] (c/o State Secretary Landfrie(d)); as well as the Chief of the civil administration of the occupied territories have received copies of this decree.

Signed: Heydrich
Certified:
signed: Schnidt
Office employe.

Responsible for
correct copy
signed: signature
Major on the General Staff (Major i. G.)

Excerpt from Document 3418-PS. *Prophecy of Destruction of Jewish Race in Europe in the event of another World War, from The Archive, January 1935, p. 1605.*

* * *

THE ARCHIVE [Das Archiv] Jan 1935, reference book for Politics Economy-Culture, edited by Alfred Ingemar Berndt, assisted by Ernest Jaenicke. Publisher: Otto Stollberg/Berlin W 9, Page 1605.

If international finance-Jewry inside and outside Europe should succeed in throwing the nations into another *World War*, the result will not be the Bolshevization of the earth, and thus the victory of Jewry, but the *destruction of the Jewish race in Europe!*

Translation of Document 3428-PS (USA 827). Letter from Kube, Commissioner General for White Ruthenia, 31 July 1942, on Combating of Partisans and Action Against Jews in the District General of White Ruthenia, describing liquidation of 55,000 Jews.

* * *

SECRET
Department II a No 2407/428
Seal   Eagle Swastika
Minsk, on July 31, 1942
The Commissioner General for White Ruthenia
 Dept. Regional leader /G 507/42 g
   To Reich Commissioner for the East Land
     Regional leader Hinrich Lohse
       Riga Fs 10/8/42 rec.
The Reich Commissioner for the Eastern Territory
 Journal No 1122/42
Secret
   Seal of Reich Commissioner Ostland Chief dept.
       7 August 1942.
       II pol. II adm.
Re: *Combating of Partisans and action against Jews in the District General of White Ruthenia.*

In all the clashes with partisans in White Ruthenia it has been proven the Jewry, in the former Polish section as well as in the former Soviet sections of the District General, together with the Polish movement of resistance in the East and the Red Guards from Moscow, is the main bearer of the partisan movement in the East. In consequence, the treatment of Jewry in White Ruthenia, in view of the endangering of the entire economics, is a matter of political prominence, which should in consequence not be solved only according to an economic, but also according to a political viewpoint. In exhaustive discussions with the SS Brigadier General Zenner and the exceedingly capable Leader of the SD, SS Lieutenant Colonel Dr. jur. Strauch, we have liquidated in the last ten weeks about 55,000 Jews in White Ruthenia. In the territory Minsk-Land [county]

III - 537

Jewry has been completely eliminated, without endangering the manpower commitment. In the predominantly Polish territory Lida 16,000 Jews, in Zlonin 8,000 Jews, and so forth, have been liquidated. Owing to an encroachment in the army rear zone, already reported thither, the preparations made by us for liquidation of the Jews in the area Glebokie have been disturbed. The army rear zone, without contacting me, has liquidated 10,000 Jews, whose systematical elimination had been provided for by us in any event. In Minsk-City approximately 10,000 Jews were liquidated on the 28 and 29 of July, 6500 of them Russian Jews, predominantly aged persons, women and children—the remainder consisted of Jews unfit for commitment of labor who, in their overwhelming majority, were deported to Minsk in November of last year from Vienna, Bruenn, Bremen and Berlin, by order of the Fuehrer.

The area of Luzk too has been relieved of several thousand Jews. The same applies to Novogrodek and Wilejka. Radical measures are imminent for Baranowitschi and Hanzewitschi. In Baranowitschi alone, approximately 10,000 Jews are still living in the city itself; of these, 9,000 Jews will be liquidated next month.

In Minsk City 2,600 Jews from Germany are left over. In addition to that all the 6,000 Russian Jews and Jewesses, who remained as employes with such units, which employed them during the action, are still alive. Even in the future, Minsk will still retain its character as the strongest center of the Jewish element, necessitated for the present by the concentration of the armament industries and the tasks of the railroad. In all the other areas, the number of Jews to be drafted for labor commitment will be limited by the SD and by me to 800 at the most, but if possible to 500, so that after completion of future actions as announced, we will retain a remainder of 8,600 Jews in Minsk and of about 7,000 in the other 10 areas, including the jewless areas of Minsk-Land [county]. The danger, that the partisans can rely essentially upon Jewry in the future, will then exist no longer. Naturally, after the termination of demands of the armed forces, the SD and I would like it best, to eliminate Jewry once and for all in the District General of White Ruthenia. For the time being, the necessary demands of the armed forces, which are the main employers of Jewry, are considered. Besides the fact of this unequivocal attitude toward the Jewry, the SD in White Ruthenia has in addition the grave task to transfer continually new contingents of Jews from the Reich to their destiny. This is an excessive strain on the physical strength of the men in the SD and keeps them away from their duties, which are awaiting them in the area of White Ruthenia proper.

Therefore, I would be grateful if the Reich Commissioner could possibly stop additional deportations of Jews to Minsk at least until the peril of the Partisan movement has been subdued conclusively. I need the SD in its total force (100% commitment) against the partisans and against the Polish Resistance movement, both of which are occupying the entire strength of the not overwhelmingly strong SD units.

After completion of the action against the Jews in Minsk, SS Lieutenant Colonel Dr. Strauch reported to me tonight with just indignation that suddenly, without directives of the Reichleader SS, and without notification to the Commissioner General, a transport of 1000 Jews from Warsaw has arrived for this air-force administrative-command. I beg the Reich Commissioner (already prepared by telegram) to prevent transports of such a kind, in his capacity as supreme Plenipotentiary for the Eastern Territory. The Polish Jew is, exactly like the Russian Jew, an enemy of Germanism. He represents a politically dangerous element, the political danger of which exceeds by far his value as a skilled worker. Under no circumstances may administrative offices of the armed forces or of the air forces import Jews to an area of civil administration without the approval of the Reich Commissioner or from the Government General or any other place, as they will endanger the entire political work and the safeguarding of the District General. I fully agree with the commander of the SD in White Ruthenia, that we shall liquidate every shipment of Jews, which is not ordered or announced by our superior offices, to prevent further disturbances in White Ruthenia.

The Commissioner General for White Ruthenia
sig. Kube

Translation of Document 3430-PS. *Excerpt from "Four Years in Holland", 1944, by Reichsminister Seyss-Inquart, expressing implacable hatred toward Jews.*

* * *

[Page 57]

The Jews are the enemy of national socialism and the national socialistic Reich. From the moment of their emancipation, their methods were directed to the annihilation of the common and moral worth of the German people and to replace national and responsible ideology with international Nihilism. The fatal meaning of Judaism became completely clear to the German people during the years of the world war. It was really they who stuck the knife in the back of the German army which broke the resistance of the Germans, and in the year 1918 it was they who wanted to dissolve and decompose all national tradition and also moral and religious beliefs of the German people. The Jews for us are not Dutchmen. *They are those enemies, with whom we can come neither to an armistice nor to peace.* This applies here, if you wish, for the duration of the occupation. Do not expect an order from me which stipulates this, except regulations concerning police matters. *We will beat the Jews wherever we meet them* and those who join them must bear the consequences. *The Fuehrer declared that the Jews have played their final act in Europe*, and therefore they played their final act.

Translation of Document 3450-PS (USA 888). *Excerpts from Law of 18 November 1938 concerning the confiscation of property of enemies of the people and the State of Austria.*

* * *

Law of 18 November 1938 concerning the confiscation of property of enemies of the people and the State in Austria.

On the basis of Article 3 of the Law concerning the re-union of Austria with the German Reich of 13 March 1938 (Reichsgesetzblatt I p. 237) the following is decreed:

(1) The Reichsstatthalter [Austrian Governor] in Vienna or the office empowered by him can confiscate for the benefit of Austria property of persons or societies which have promoted efforts inimical to the people of the State, as well as articles and rights which were used or destined to promote such efforts. The Reich Minister of the Interior or office empowered by him is to determine which efforts are to be considered as inimical to the people of the State. After conference with the Reich Commissar for the re-union of Austria with the German Reich and with the consent of the Reich Minister of the Interior, confiscation can also be made in favor of another person as defined by the law.

(2) The Reichsstatthalter [Austrian Governor] in Vienna in consent with the Reich Commissar for the re-union of Austria with the German Reich disposed of the property confiscated in favor of Austria.

* * * * * * *

(7) Confiscations which were ordered by the Secret State Police before this decree took effect are considered confiscations in the sense of this decree. Instead of Paragraph 6, the rules of Paragraphs 8 - 15 are valid for these confiscations.

* * * * * * *

Translation of Document 3460-PS (USA 437). *Excerpt from Speech of Hermann Goering urging inexorable elimination of Jews from economic life of Vienna.*

* * *

HERMANN GOERING, SPEECHES AND PAPERS,
[Reden und Aufsaetze] by E. Gritzbach, Munich, 1938,
Pages 348-349.

I must address myself with a serious word to the city of Vienna. The city of Vienna can no longer rightfully be called a German city. So many Jews lives in this city. Where there are 300,000 Jews, you cannot speak of a German city.

Vienna must once more become a German city, because it must perform important tasks for Germany in Germany's Ostmark. These tasks lie in the sphere of culture as well as in the sphere of economics. In neither of them can we, in the long run, put up with the Jew.

This, however, should not be attempted by inappropriate interference and stupid measures but must be done systematically and carefully. As Delegate for the Four-Year Plan I commission the Reichstatthalter in Austria jointly with the Plenipotentiary of the Reich, to consider and take any steps necessary for the redirection of Jewish commerce, i.e., for the Aryanization of business and economic life, and to execute this process in accordance with our laws, legally but inexorably.

Translation of Document 3468-PS (USA 705). *Excerpts from Decrees of General Government of Poland, October-November 1939, concerning forced labor for Jews, requiring Jews to wear Star of David, and requiring Jewish enterprises to be marked by Jewish Star.*

* * *

DOCUMENTS OF GERMAN POLITICS
[Dokumente der Deutschen Politik]
1939, Part 2, Berlin, 1940, Pages 674-682.

131b. Decree of Governor General Dr. Frank of 26 Oct 39 concerning the establishment of forced labor for the Jewish population of the General Government.

On the basis of Article 5 Paragraph 1 of the decree of the Fuehrer and Reich Chancellor of 12 Oct 39 concerning the administration of the occupied Polish territories, I decree:

Article 1

For the Jews domiciled in the General Government forced labor is established, to take effect immediately. For this purpose the Jews are to be concentrated into Forced Labor Troops.

Article 2

The regulations required for the execution of this decree are issued by the Senior SS and Police Leader. He can fix territories east of the Vistula where the execution of this decree is not carried out.

---

134. Decree of the Governor General Dr. Frank as of 23 November 1938, concerning the markings of Jews and Jewesses in the General Government.

On the basis of Art. 5, Par. 1, by the Fuehrer and Reichschancellor as of 12 October 1939, concerning the administration of the occupied Polish territory (Reichsgesetzblatt I, p. 2077), I order

Art. 1

All Jews and Jewesses who are residing in the General Government and who are over ten years of age are required from 1 December 1939 on to wear on the right sleeve of their clothing a white band at least ten centimeters in width marked with the Star of Zion.

Art. 2

These armbands are to be procured by the Jews and Jewesses themselves and marked with the corresponding sign.

Art. 3

(1) Violations are punished by imprisonment.
(2) The Special Courts are competent for the trial.

The necessary rules for its execution are released by the executive of the Department of Internal Administration in the office of the General Government.

---

135. Decree of the Governor General Dr. Frank of 23 Nov 39 concerning the specification of business within the General Government.

Based upon Article 5, Par. I of the Decree of the Fuehrer and Reichschancellor of 12 October 1939 concerning the administration of the occupied Polish areas (Reichsgesetzblatt I, pp. 2077), I decree:

Article 1
Businesses whose owners are Germans have to be identified as German businesses. They may also carry Polish firm names.

Article 2
Businesses whose owners are Poles have to carry Polish firm names. They may also be provided with a German firm name.

Article 3
Jewish businesses are to be identified with the Star of Zion in such a manner that it will be plainly visible from the street; they are not allowed German firm names.

Article 4
(1) Violations will be punished by imprisonment.
(2) The Special Courts are competent for the trial.

Copy of Document 3544-PS (USA 660). Excerpts from interrogation of Walter Funk, 22 October 1945, concerning anti-Jewish economic measures.

* * * * * * *

Pre-trial interrogation of Walter Funk, taken at Nurnberg, Germany, 22 October 1945, 1430-1645, by Lt. Col. Murray Gurfein, IGD, OUSCC. Also present: Capt. H. W. Frank, Interpreter and John Wm. Gunsser, Court Reporter.

Q. Returning for a moment to this question of the fine against the Jews that we discussed in 1938, Funk, you were a party to all the laws that were put into effect in November 1938 after the Cristar Week?

A. I was only participating so far as the legal rulings of the Jewish property was concerned. So far as the fine was concerned I had not participated in that. This was a matter for the minister of finance.

Q. All the decrees excluding the Jews from industry were yours, were they not?

A. Yes. We had to do this because otherwise Jewish property would have been free for everybody to loot, and we had to do something to protect it. And it was my proposal that the Jews should be allowed to retain any shareholdings, and that any property which they had to give over to other people would receive an interest from the recipient. And their retaining their shareholdings, their retention of their shareholdings, was refused by Goering during a meeting, and so far as the interests on their property was concerned that was later refused by the minister of finance. I must explain something to you in this connection. So far as my participation in this Jewish affair is concerned, that was my responsibility and I have regretted it later on that I ever did participate. The Party had always brought pressure to bear on me previously to make me agree to the confiscation of Jewish property, and I had refused repeatedly. But later on, when the anti-Jewish measures and the force used against the Jews came into force, something legal had to be done to prevent the looting and confiscation of all Jewish property.

Q. You know that the looting and all that was done at the instigation of the Party, don't you?

(Here witness weeps)

A. Yes, most certainly. That is when I should have left in 1938. Of that I am guilty. I am guilty. I admit that I am a guilty party here.

Q. Well, now, just to make the record clear, this law which prohibited Jews from operating retail stores and wholesale establishments and other things was a law that you drafted yourself, was it not?

A. Yes, because we had to make such legislation simply because if we hadn't done it the Jews would have been subjected to uncontrolled looting as had already been done. All that was a point as the result of which I should have resigned.

Q. As a matter of fact, you predicted as the result of these decrees and other things that the Reich would become the possessor of a half billion shares of capital stock?

A. Yes, that was my estimation of the Jewish property. But to start with—and this must be in the document—I demanded at the beginning of this affair that the shares should not be taken away from them.

Q. Tell me, Funk, these measures against the Jews, weren't they taken at that time in 1938 partly as a preparation for the war, because you didn't want any important parts of the German industry to be under the control of Jews when the war came?

A. I had never thought at that time that a war could happen. After all, that was in 1938.

Q. In any event, with respect to the fine of a billion marks, you were present at the meeting where that was discussed, weren't you?

A. Yes. It came from Goering or the minister of finance, and the minister of finance carried it out.

The Documentary Evidence   3545-PS

Translation of Document 3545-PS (USA 659). *Excerpt from Speech by Walter Funk, 15 November 1938, on elimination of Jews from the German economy.*

* * *

FRANKFURTER ZEITUNG, 17 November 1938

Speech by Funk in Berlin on 15 November 1938.

The state and the economy constitute a unity. They must be directed according to the same principles. The best proof thereof has been rendered by the most recent development of the Jewish problem in Germany. One cannot exclude the Jews from the political life, but let them live and work in the economic sphere. The fact that the last violent explosion of the disgust of the German people, because of a criminal Jewish attack against the German people, took place at a time when we were standing just before the termination of the economic measures for the elimination of the Jews from the German economy—this fact is a result of the other fact that in the last years we had not handled this problem sufficiently early and consistently. In any event, the basis of a complete elimination of the Jews also from the economy had already been laid by the decrees of the Commissioner for the Four Year Plan, Field Marshal Goering, who was the first to undertake the solution of this problem. In the meantime, by means of Aryanization performed under governmental supervision, the Jews had already been excluded completely from the stock exchanges and the banks and almost completely from the larger businesses and all important industrial enterprises. According to estimates, of the net property of approximately 7 billion marks, determined pursuant to the decree for the registration of Jewish property, 2 billion marks have already been transferred into German possession.

Translation of Document 3569-PS. *Political Testament of Adolf Hitler, 29 April 1945, urging upon German nation merciless opposition to Jews.*

* * *

The Secretary of the Fuehrer, Reichsleiter Martin Bormann
                                        Fuehrer Headquarters
                                                29.4.45
        Postal address Munich 33, Fuehrerbau.
Dear Admiral of the Fleet,
    As, owing to the non-arrival of all divisions, our position

appears hopeless, the Fuehrer last night dictated the enclosed political Testament.

Heil Hitler!
Your
[signature illegible, presumably Martin Bormann]

[Seal]
ADOLF HITLER
My Private Will and Testament

As I did not consider that I could take responsibility, during the years of struggle, of contracting a marriage, I have now decided, before the closing of my earthly career, to take as my wife that girl who, after many years of faithful friendship, entered, of her own free will, the practically besieged town in order to share her destiny with me. At her own desire she goes as my wife with me into death. It will compensate us for what we both lost through my work in the service of my people.

What I possess belongs—in so far as it has any value—to the Party. Should this no longer exist, to the State, should the State also be destroyed, no further decision of mine is necessary.

My pictures, in the collections which I have bought in the course of years, have never been collected for private purposes, but only for the extension of a gallery in my home town of Linz a.d. Donau.

It is my most sincere wish that this bequest may be duly executed.

I nominate as my Executor my most faithful Party comrade, Martin Bormann.

He is given full legal authority to make all decisions. He is permitted to take out everything that has a sentimental value or is necessary for the maintenance of a modest simple life, for my brothers and sisters, also above all for the mother of my wife and my faithful coworkers who are well known to him, principally my old Secretaries Frau Winter etc., who have for many years aided me by their work.

I myself and my wife—in order to escape the disgrace of deposition or capitulation—choose death. It is our wish to be burnt immediately on the spot where I have carried out the greatest part of my daily work in the course of a twelve years' service to my people.

Given in Berlin, 29th April 1945, 4:00 o'clock.

(Sd.)   A. Hitler.

As Witnesses:
(Sd.) Martin Bormann

(Sd.) Dr. Fuhr.   As Witness:
    (Sd.) Nicolaus von Below.

[Seal]
ADOLF HITLER

My political Testament

More than thirty years have now passed since I in 1914 made my modest contribution as a volunteer in the first world war that was forced upon the Reich.

In these three decades I have been actuated solely by love and loyalty to my people in all my thoughts, acts, and life. They gave me the strength to make the most difficult decisions which ever have confronted mortal man. I have spent my time, my working strength, and my health in these three decades.

It is untrue that I or anyone else in Germany wanted the war in 1939. It was desired and instigated exclusively by those international statesmen who were either of Jewish descent or worked for Jewish interests. I have made too many offers for the control and limitation of armaments, which posterity will not for all time be able to disregard, for the responsibility for the outbreak of this war to be laid on me. I have further never wished that after the first fatal world war a second against England, or even against America, should break out. Centuries will pass away, but out of the ruins of our towns and monuments the hatred against those finally responsible, whom we have to thank for everything, International Jewry and its helpers, will grow.

Three days before the outbreak of the German-Polish war I again proposed to the British ambassador in Berlin a solution to the German-Polish problem—similar to that in the case of the Saar district, under international control. This offer also cannot be denied. It was only rejected because the leading circles in English politics wanted the war, partly on account of the business hoped for and partly under influence of propaganda organized by international Jewry.

I also made it quite plain that, if the nations of Europe are again to be regarded as mere shares to be bought and sold by these international conspirators in money and finance, then that race, Jewry, which is the real criminal of this murderous struggle, will be saddled with the responsibility. I further left no one in doubt that this time not only would millions of children of Europe's Aryan peoples die of hunger, not only would millions of grown men suffer death, and not only hundreds of thousands of women and children be burnt and bombed to death in the towns, without the real criminal having to atone for this guilt, even if by more humane means.

After six years of war, which in spite of all set-backs will go down one day in history as the most glorious and valiant demonstration of a nation's life purpose, I cannot forsake the city which is the capital of this Reich. As the forces are too small to make any further stand against the enemy attack at this place and our resistance is gradually being weakened by men who are as deluded as they are lacking in initiative, I should like, by remaining in this town, to share my fate with those, the millions of others, who have also taken upon themselves to do so. Moreover I do not wish to fall into the hands of an enemy who requires a new spectacle organized by the Jews for the amusement of their hysterical masses.

I have decided therefore to remain in Berlin and there of my own free will to choose death at the moment when I believe the position of the Fuehrer and Chancellor itself can no longer be held.

I die with a happy heart, aware of the immeasurable deeds and achievements of our soldiers at the front, our women at home, the achievements of our farmers and workers and the work, unique in history, of our youth who bear my name.

That from the bottom of my heart I express my thanks to you all, is just as self-evident as my wish that you should, because of that, on no account give up the struggle, but rather continue it against the enemies of the Fatherland, no matter where, true to the creed of a great Clausewitz. From the sacrifice of our soldiers and from my own unity with them unto death will in any case spring up in the history of Germany the seed of a radiant renaissance of the National-Socialist movement, and thus of the realization of a true community of nations.

Many of the most courageous men and women have decided to unite their lives with mine until the very last. I have begged and finally ordered them not to do this, but to take part in the further battle of the Nation. I beg the heads of the Armies, the Navy and the Air Force to strengthen by all possible means the spirit of resistance of our soldiers in the National-Socialist sense, with special reference to the fact that also I myself, as founder and creator of this movement, have preferred death to cowardly abdication or even capitulation.

May it, at some future time, become part of the code of honour of the German officer—as is already the case in our Navy—that the surrender of a district or of a town is impossible, and that above all the leaders here must march ahead as shining examples, faithfully fulfilling their duty unto death.

* * *

Second Part of the Political Testament

Before my death I expel the former Reichsmarschall Hermann Goering from the party and deprive him of all rights which he may enjoy by virtue of the decree of June 29th, 1941, and also by virtue of my statement in the Reichstag on September 1st, 1939, I appoint in his place Grossadmiral Doenitz, President of the Reich and Supreme Commander of the Armed Forces.

Before my death I expel the former Reichsfuehrer-SS and Minister of the Interior, Heinrich Himmler, from the party and from all offices of State. In his stead I appoint Gauleiter Karl Hanke as Reichsfuehrer-SS and Chief of the German Police, and Gauleiter Paul Giesler as Reich Minister of the Interior.

Goering and Himmler, quite apart from their disloyalty to my person, have done immeasurable harm to the country and the whole nation by secret negotiations with the enemy, which they conducted without my knowledge and against my wishes, and by illegally attempting to seize power in the State for themselves.

In order to give the German people a government composed of honourable men—a government which will fulfill its pledge to continue the war by every means—I appoint the following members of the new Cabinet as leaders of the nation:

President of the Reich: Doenitz.
Chancellor of the Reich: Dr. Goebbels.
Party Minister: Bormann.
Foreign Minister: Seyss-Inquart.
Minister of the Interior: Gauleiter Giesler.
Minister for War: Doenitz.
C-in-C of the Army: Schoerner.
C-in-C of the Navy: Doenitz.
C-in-C of the Air Force: Greim.
Reichsfuehrer-SS and Chief of the German Police: Gauleiter Hanke.
Economics: Funk.
Agriculture: Backe.
Justice: Thierack.
Education and Public Worship: Dr. Scheel.
Propaganda: Dr. Naumann.
Finance: Schwerin-Grossigk.
Labour: Dr. Hupfauer.

Munitions: Saur.
Leader of the German Labour Front and Member of the Reich Cabinet: Reich Minister Dr. Ley.

Although a number of these men, such as Martin Bormann, Dr. Goebbels etc., together with their wives, have joined me of their own free will and did not wish to leave the capital of the Reich under any circumstances, but were willing to perish with me here, I must nevertheless ask them to obey my request, and in this case set the interests of the nation above their own feelings. By their work and loyalty as comrades they will be just as close to me after death, as I hope that my spirit will linger among them and always go with them. Let them be hard, but never unjust, above all let them never allow fear to influence their actions, and set the honour of the nation above everything in the world. Finally, let them be conscious of the fact that our task, that of continuing the building of a National Socialist State, represents the work of the coming centuries, which places every single person under an obligation always to serve the common interest and to subordinate his own advantage to this end. I demand of all Germans, all National Socialists, men, women and all the men of the Armed Forces, that they be faithful and obedient unto death to the new government and its President.

Above all I charge the leaders of the nation and those under them to scrupulous observance of the laws of race and to merciless opposition to the universal poisoner of all peoples, international Jewry.

Given in Berlin, this 29th day of April 1945.   4:00 a.m.

Adolf Hitler.

Witnessed by
Dr. Josef Fuhr.   Wilhelm Buergdorf.
Martin Bormann.   Hans Krebs.

Translation of Document 3575-PS (USA 781). *Excerpt from Top Secret Memorandum concerning the meeting of the Reich Defense Council, 18 November 1938, in which it was reported that fine imposed on Jewry and Aryanization of Jewish enterprises relieved very critical situation of the Reich Exchequer.*

* * *

[Rubber Stamp] Submitted to the Minister
[Hand-written note] Dispatched 20 November
Berlin, 19 November 1938

The Documentary Evidence   3575-PS

TOP SECRET

Memorandum concerning the meeting of the Reich Defense Council [Reichsverteidigungsrat] on 18 November 1938
Chairman: Field Marshal Goering

All Reich Ministers and State Secretaries, with a few exceptions, were present, as were the Commander-in-Chief of the Army, the Commander-in-Chief of the Navy, the Chiefs of the General Staff of the three branches of the Armed Forces, Reichsleiter Bormann for the Deputy of the Fuehrer, General Daluege, SS Major General [SS Gruppenfuehrer] Heydrich, the Reich Labor Leader [Reicharbeitsfuehrer], the Price Control Commissar, the President of the Reich Labor Office, and others.

The meeting consisted solely of a three-hour lecture by the Field Marshal. No discussion took place.

---

3. *Finances*

Very critical situation of the Reich Exchequer. Relief initially through the billion [milliarde] imposed on Jewry, and through profits accruing to the Reich in the aryanization of Jewish enterprises.

Prospect of a "National Thanksgiving Sacrifice" (without commitment to this term) in the form of a single surrender of property, which will represent many times the value of the Armament Contribution [Wehrbeitrag] of the pre-war era. No details about date and particulars. Its task is to secure armament production, on a large scale.

Strict economy measures at all points.

Additional task of the Reich Defense Council: new formulation of all war-time legislation.

Concerning foreign policy the Field Marshal mentioned that it would have to be conducted in such a way that the planned armament program could be carried out.

(Signed)   Woermann

Translation of Document 3577-PS. *Letter from Josef Buerkel, Deputy of the Fuehrer for the Plebiscite in Austria, to Goering, 26 March 1938, concerning Aryanization of Jewish-held business in Austria and disposition of resulting funds.*

* * *

Gauleiter Josef Buerkel, the Deputy of the Fuehrer for the Plebiscite in Austria

Vienna, 26 March 1938
I., Parliament Building
Telephone: R-50-5-60

To the Minister President General Field Marshal Hermann Goering
present address: Vienna

Most honored General Field Marshal

I refer to this morning's talk and would like to approach you with the following request:

1. A fund of about 2-3 million Reichsmarks will be made available for the removal of economic difficulties that arise during the time of the change-over.

2. A fund of about 20-30 million Reichsmarks will be made available for the dispossession of the Jews from business and trade.

By means of press and radio I have just given the order that only those Aryan stores which are in Aryan possession and under Aryan management may have the inscription "Aryan store" [Arisches Geschaeft]. The carrying of all other inscriptions is forbidden. In this way, the inscriptions which have been in common use up to now, such as "This store is under Aryan management", "this store is administered by the NSBO", et cetera, will be caused to disappear at once.

It is pointed out emphatically in press and radio that a clear difference, visible even from the outside, has now been made between Aryan and Jewish stores. I was in a position to give that order after I had been informed that the Reich Minister of Interior and the Reich Labor Minister will, with your approval, publish this very day the regulations suggested by me concerning social-political questions. According to these regulations, very far-reaching protection is granted against the giving of notices, and the dismissal of Aryan employees and workers is made very difficult. It is to be anticipated that a renewed, very strong boycott movement will start against the Jewish stores, due to my order. In view of the uncertainty of the situation and in view of the declaration which you, my dear General Field Marshal, intend to issue today concerning the Jewish question, and which underlines the statements I made the day before yesterday, it can be anticipated that the Jews will be ready to sell their stores and companies at the cheapest prices. I think it will be possible, in this way, to bring a large part of Jewish property into Aryan hands under the most favorable economic terms. The only task of the fund would be to simplify the financing of the change-over in business. No losses would be incurred by the Reich Treasury. It also seems to me that such a measure is necessary to protect the interests of the employees.

I should like to request that the emergency fund mentioned under point 1 be left to my administration and that there be appointed for the fund mentioned under point 2 a trustee who would work in the closest possible cooperation with me.

Heil Hitler!
Yours faithfully,
[illegible signature]

Copy of Document 3589-PS (USA 720). Supplement No. 6 to Official Czechoslovak Report "German Crimes Against Czechoslovakia", 7 January 1946, reporting that many thousands of Czechoslovak Jews were killed in gas chambers at Auschwitz.

* * *

Nurnberg, 7 January 1946.
Supplement No. 6 to the Official Czechoslovak Report called "German Crimes Against Czechoslovakia" Presented by order of the Czechoslovak Government by General Dr. B. Ecer, Plenipotentiary, Czechoslovak Representative to the Commission of the United Nations for the Investigation of War Crimes in London, at present Chairman of the Czechoslovak Delegation to the Nurnberg Proceedings

By order of my Government I submit No. 6 of the Czechoslovak Report in accordance with art. 21 of the Charter the following statement:

During the tenure of office of defendant Wilhelm Frick as Reich Protector of Bohemia and Moravia from August 1943 until the liberation of Czechoslovakia in 1945, many thousands of Czechoslovak Jews were transported from the Terezin Ghetto in Czechoslovakia to the concentration camp at Oswieczien (Auschwitz) in Poland and were there killed in the gas chambers.

Affidavits of eyewitnesses in the official files of the Czechoslovak Government constitute the basis for this report.

for General Dr. B. ECER
Capt. Dr. A. Hochwald

Translation of Document 3611-PS. *Excerpt from Decree, 31 May 1941, authorizing Military Commander in Belgium and Northern France to order Jews to shut down their businesses or sell their assets.*

* * *

OFFICIAL GAZETTE OF THE MILITARY COMMANDER IN BELGIUM AND NORTHERN FRANCE
[VOBL—Verordnungsblatt des Militaerbefehlshabers in Belgien und Nordfrankreich] 1940-41, Page 620.
Decree on economic measures against Jews (3rd decree against Jews) dated 31 May 1941.
Sec. 17
Special Regulations

The Military Commander can forbid the continuation of business to Jews and firms obligated to register. He can furthermore order Jews and firms obligated to register to shut down or sell their business as well as to sell shares or other assets. If these orders are not complied with within a period to be determined, the Military Commander can appoint a commissionary administrator for the execution of the decreed measures.

Translation of Document 3663-PS (USA 825). *Letter from Leibbrandt (in charge of Main Division 2 of the Ministry for the Occupied Eastern Territories concerned with political affairs), 5 November 1941, to Reich Commissioner for the Ostland (Baltic Countries and White Russia), on subject of execution of Jews, and reply, 15 November 1941.*

* * *

The Reich Minister
For the Occupied Eastern Territories
Berlin W 35, 31 October 19
Rauchstrasse 17/18
Telephone: 21 95 15 and 39 50 46
Cable address: Reichsministerost

No. I / 2591 /41
It is requested to refer to this number and the subject matter in future correspondence

[Stamp:]
Reich Commissioner East
5 November 1941
Main Division IIa

To the Reich Commissioner for the East (Ostland)
in Riga
Hermann Goering Street 26
III - 554

The Reich and Security Main Office has complained that the Reich Commissioner for the East has forbidden executions of Jews in Liepaja (Libau). I request a report in regard to this matter by return mail.

By order
Signed: Dr. Leibbrandt
certified
[illegible signature]
Regierungsinspektor

[Stamp:]
Reich Ministry for the
Occupied Eastern
Territories

SECRET

The Reich Commissioner for the East
IIa 4 M 219/41 secret •

Riga 15 November 1941

1) To the Reich Minister for the Occupied Eastern Territories
Berlin
Rauchstr. 17/18
Re: Executions of Jews
District of Erlau 31 October 1941 I/2591/41
Reporter: Reg.Rat[Trampedach?]

I have forbidden the wild executions of Jews in Liepaja because they were not justifiable in the manner in which they were carried out.

I should like to be informed whether your inquiry of 31 October is to be regarded as a directive to liquidate all Jews in the East? Shall this take place without regard to age and sex and economic interests (of the Wehrmacht, for instance in specialists in the armament industry)?

[note in different handwriting:] Of course the cleansing of the East of Jews is a necessary task; its solution, however, must be harmonized with the necessities of war production.

So far I have not been able to find such a directive either in the regulations regarding the Jewish question in the "Brown Portfolio" [Brau Mappe] or in other decrees.

Tr. 8.11.

2) Resubmit 1.12.41   Submitted 1.12.
[initialed]

Translation of Document 3666-PS. (USA 826). *Letter from Braeutigam (first assistant to Leibbrandt who was in charge of Main Division 2 of the Ministry for the Occupied Eastern Territories concerned with political affairs), 18 December 1941, on clarification of the Jewish question in the East.*

* * *

[pencilled note] 28
The Reich Minister of the occupied Eastern Territories
Berlin, W 35, 18 Dec. 1941
Rauchstrasse 17/18
Telephone: 219515 and 395046
Cable Address: Reichsministerost
[illegible initials] 12/I
Received 22/12 [illegible initial]
TOP SECRET

No. I/1/157/41 Top Secret
Please use this business sign and subject in further correspondence.
Journal No. 394/41
[stamp] TOP SECRET
[pencilled note] A
6 J 1

1.) To the Reich Commissioner for the East [Ostland]
Riga / Leitort Tilsit
Adolf Hitler Street

Subject: Jewish Question re correspondence of 15 Nov. 1941

Clarification of the Jewish question has most likely been achieved by now through verbal discussions. Economic considerations should fundamentally remain unconsidered in the settlement of the problem. Moreover, it is requested that questions arising be settled directly with the Senior SS and Police Leaders.

By order
[signed] Braeutigam

2.) Filed II. a 4 Ma 26./1.

Translation of Document 3688-PS. *Notice from the German Foreign Office, 24 September 1942, concerning evacuation of Jews from occupied territories (Slovakia, Croatia, Rumania, Bulgaria, Hungary and Denmark) and regulation of the Jewish question in Italy.*

* * *

U.St.S.–D.–Nr. 6862

I have instructions [in longhand and unidentified]
Berlin, 24 September 1942

NOTICE

The RAM (Reich Foreign Minister) has instructed me today by telephone to hasten as much as possible the evacuation of Jews from different countries in Europe since it is certain that Jews incite against us everywhere and must be made responsible for acts of sabotage and attacks. After a short lecture on the evacuations now in process in Slovakia, Croatia, Rumania and the occupied territories, the RAM has ordered that we are to approach the Bulgarian, Hungarian and Danish Governments with the goal of getting the evacuation started in these countries.

In respect to the regulation of the Jewish question in Italy, the RAM has reserved further steps to himself. This question is to be discussed personally either at a conference between the Fuehrer and the Duce or between the RAM and Count Ciano.
Herewith

    Mr. State Secretary v. Weizaecker
    presented to you with request to acknowledge it.
    Any steps to be taken by us will be presented
    to you in advance for authorization.

Copies: Signed: Luther.
    Herrn U.St.S.PW.
    Herrn U.St.S.R.
    Herrn Dir.HaPol
    D II
    D III

Translation of Document 3710-PS (USA 557). Affidavit of Walter Schellenberg, 26 November 1945, on activities of Combat Groups (Einsatzgruppen) of the SIPO and SD (Security Police and Security Service) in executing Jewish prisoners of war on Eastern front and in carrying out mass executions of Jews in the East (Documents L-180, 078-PS, 502-PS, and R-102).

* * *

SWORN STATEMENT

In the middle of May 1943, as far as I remember, the Chief of Amt 4 of the RSHA (SS-Brigadefuehrer Mueller), in the name of the Chief of the RSHA (SS-Gruppenfuehrer Heydrich), held discussions with the Generalquartiermeister of the

Army (General Wagner) about questions connected with the operations of the SIPO and SD within the bounds of the Field Army during the imminent campaign against Russia. Wagner could come to no agreement with Mueller and therefore asked Heydrich to send another representative. I was at that time Chief of Section E in Amt 4 of the RSHA under Chief of Amt Mueller and was selected by Wagner because of my experience in matters protocol to be sent to Heydrich for the purpose of drawing up the final agreement. According to the instructions given to me, I was supposed to make sure that this agreement would provide that the responsible headquarters in the Army would be firmly obligated to give complete support to all activities of the Combat Groups and Combat Commandos of the SIPO and SD. I discussed the problem of this mutual relationship in great detail with Wagner. In accordance with this discussion I then presented him with the completed draft of an agreement, which met with his full approval. This draft of an agreement was the basis for a final discussion between Wagner and Heydrich towards the end of May 1941.

The contents of this agreement, as far as I remember, were substantially as follows. Its basis was the Fuehrer's command, mentioned at the very beginning of the agreement, that the SIPO and SD should operate within the combat elements of the Field Army, with the mission of utterly smashing all resistance in conquered front-line areas as well as in conquered rear-supply zones by every means and as quickly as possible. The various areas were then set down in which the SIPO and SD were to be active and operating. The individual Combat Groups were then assigned to the army groups whch were to take part in the campaign and the individual Combat Commandos to the respective armies which were to take part in the campaign.

The Combat Groups and Combat Commandos were to operate in detail:

(1) In front-line areas: In complete subordination to the Field Army, tactically, functionally, and administratively;

(2) In rear operational areas: In merely administrative subordination to the Field Army, but under the command and functional control of the RSHA;

(3) In rear Army areas: Arrangement as in (2);

(4) In areas of the civil administration in the East: Same as in the Reich.

The tactical and functional authority and responsibility of front-line headquarters of the Field Army over the Combat Commandos found no limitation in the agreement and therefore needed no further clarification.

The agreement made it clear that the administrative subordination embraced not only disciplinary subordination but also the obligation for rear headquarters of the Field Army to support the Combat Groups and Combat Commandos in matters of supply (gasoline, rations, etc.) as well as in the use of the communications network.

This agreement was signed by Heydrich and Wagner in my presence. Wagner signed it either "acting for" or "by order of" the OKH.

After Wagner and Heydrich had affixed their signatures, both of them asked me to leave the room for half an hour. Just while leaving I heard how they both wanted to discuss in complete privacy the Fuehrer's command, which was apparently known in advance by each of them personally, and its far-reaching implications. After the half hour was over I was called in once more just to say goodbye.

Today I read the "Operational and Situational Report No. 6 of the Combat Groups of the SIPO and SD in the USSR (covering the period from 1 to 31 October 1941)," as well as the "Comprehensive Report of Combat Group A up to 15 October 1941." The whole substance of these reports shows that the prime mission of the Combat Groups and Combat Commandos of the SIPO and SD was to undertake and carry out mass executions of Jews, Communists, and other elements of resistance. It is also clear from the above-cited "Comprehensive Report," which embraces no more than the first four months of these operations, that the cooperation of the respective Oberbefehlshabers with Combat Group A was "in general good and in individual instances, for instance that of Panzergruppe 4 under Colonel General Hoeppner, very close, in fact almost cordial" (page 1). From an enclosure to this same report, bearing the title "Summary of the Number of Executed Persons," particularly from the figures arranged according to the successively conquered areas, it is evident that the SIPO and SD operated in front-line areas so as to fully carry out their prime function of conducting mass executions of all elements of resistance even from the very beginning of the advance against Russia. I acknowledge the reliability and authenticity of both of the above-cited reports. Therefore I must today express my firm conviction that during the secret oral discussion between Wagner and Heydrich the extensive future activity of the Combat Groups and Combat Commandos within the combat elements of the Field Army was obviously discussed and delineated so as to include even planned mass executions. The close cooperation between the Field Army and the Combat Groups cited above as taking place even in the first weeks of the Russian campaign makes me today give expression to my firm conviction that the Oberbefehslhabers of the army groups and armies which were to take part in the Russian campaign were accurately informed through the normal OKH channels of communication about the extensive future mission of the Combat Groups and Combat Commandos of the SIPO and SD as including planned mass executions of Jews, Communists, and all other elements of resistance.

In the beginning of June 1941 all of the Ic counterintelligence officers, and, as far as I remember, all of the Ic officers of all army groups, armies, army corps, and some of the divisions which were to take part in the coming Russian campaign were called in by Wagner, together with Heydrich and the Chief of the Amt for Counterintelligence Abroad in the OKW (Admiral Canaris) for a general conference in the OKW Building at Berlin. The responsible leaders of the Combat Groups and Combat Commandos of the SIPO and SD were for the most part likewise present. I was also there. The essential substance and purpose of this meeting was to outline the military strategy against Russia and to announce the above-mentioned details of the written agreement reached by Wagner and Heydrich.

This group of Ic counterintelligence officers and Ic officers remained at Berlin a few days longer and was carefully instructed in several additional conferences, at which I was not present, about further details of the coming Russian campaign. I assume that these discussions were concerned with the exact delineation of the Fuehrer's command "to smash utterly all resistance in occupied areas by every means and as quickly as possible," including even planned mass executions of all elements of resistance. Otherwise the cooperation between the Field Army and the Combat Groups, which in the above-cited documents is clearly revealed as existing but a few weeks thereafter, could not in my opinion have been forthcoming. In any event there is hardly any reason to doubt that these Ic counterintelligence officers, immediately upon their return from Berlin, accurately informed their own superiors, including all Oberbefehlshabers of the army groups and armies which were to march against Russia, about the full extent of the agreements.

[signed] WALTER SCHELLENBERG
26. XI. 45

CITY OF NURNBERG: SS

Before me, Paul A. Neuland, Major, QMC, ASN O–385720, an officer duly qualified to take oaths, appeared Walter Schellenberg, to me known, who in my presence signed the foregoing statement consisting of five pages in the German language, and who swore that the same was true on the 26th day of November 1945.

I further certify that the two reports cited on pages 2 and 3 of the foregoing statement are documents contained in the official files of the Documentation Section of the Office of the U. S. Chief of Counsel at Nurnberg, Germany. I further certify that the document whose title is "Taetigkeitsund Lageberricht Nr. 6 der Einsatzgruppen der Sicherheitspolizei und des SD in der UdSSR (Berichtszeit vom 1.–31.10.1941)" is document No. R–102, and that the document bearing the title "Gesamtbericht der Einsatzgruppe A bis zum 15. Oktober 1941" is document No. L–180.

[signed]   Paul A. Neuland
PAUL A. NEULAND
Major, QMC
O–385720

Copy of Document 3720-PS (USA 220). *Excerpt from interrogation of Albert Speer, 18 October 1945, on subject of forced labor of Hungarian Jews.*

* * *

Pre-trial interrogation of Albert Speer, taken at Nurnberg, Germany, 18 October 1945, 1430-1700, by Lt. Col. M. I. Gurfein, AUS, OUSCC, Also present: Pfc. Sonnenfeld, Interpreter, and Miss Evelyn Low, Reporter.

Q. Were there any other special categories of foreign workers that were separately treated as, for example, Jews?
A. In 1942 for instance we used Jews in German factories.
Q. Foreign Jews or German Jews?
A. I believe German Jews.
Q. Put your mind on foreign Jews. Did you use those for forced labour in Germany?

A. As far as foreign Jews are concerned, Hungarian Jews were used in the building program.

Q. And when was that—in 1944?

A. Yes that was in 1944.

Q. Who made the decision to use the Hungarian Jews for this building work?

A. There is a history to that. Do you want me to tell you about it?

Q. Yes please, briefly?

A. Hitler had the intention to build great underground aeroplane factories in the fall of 1943. He gave an order to that effect. However, I did not concur in that and therefore I did not execute the order in all its strictness. In March of 1944 the director of the Central Organization Todt office submitted plans for those to Hitler. This was during the period of my illness. In this connection he stated that the building should be finished within six months. Hitler gave Dosch a direct order to build these six factories outside the normal competence of my Ministry. There were several big differences in this question between Goering and myself and also between Hitler and myself. As a result of these differences I received a written order from Hitler that Dosch was to build the six factories. The order should still be there. As far as I know the Hungarian Jews were made available for the building of these six factories by direct negotations that Dosch carried out.

Q. Carried out with whom?

A. I don't know exactly and I cannot say this because all this took place during the period of my illness but I believe there is a note about that with the official papers that are in your possession.

Q. When did you recover from your illness?

A. In the middle of May 1944.

Q. Did you transact any business during April 1944 before you were completely recovered?

A. Of course I always had to do a few things in spite of my illness.

Q. Where were you actually while you were ill?

A. At first I was in Hohenlychen, that was because I had an infection of the knee, from there I went to Klessheim, near Saltzburg and from there to Merano.

Q. And where were you in April 1944?

A. In Merano.

Q. Did you transact business from Merano?

A. Yes, I did this in a restricted measure. I was there to recover but every three or four days something came up.

Q. And did your people bring you papers to sign also?

A. Yes, I believe, yes.

Q. I want to ask you again, did you not personally order the arrangements to be made for the deportation of 100,000 Hungarian Jews for the project you have described?

A. No, I did not order that personally.

Q. I want to show you a letter of 17 April 1944, a photostat, and ask you to read it through and tell me whether you wrote that letter or dictated it?

A. As is apparent from the two letters TAE and the No. 474-44 it is evident that this originated in the Technical Department. The minutes of the discussions with the Fuehrer were always published under my name in order to give them the greatest possible authority. This is the result of such a discussion which took place during my illness. I did not write this. Sauer was the author of this document.

Q. And before this document was written you already knew and participated in the discussions as you have previously told us, about the obtaining of 100,000 Hungarian Jews for this Dosch project?

A. I believe that this is the same but it is out of the question that I participated in it because I was sick at the time.

Q. But you did tell us the history of the thing a little while ago concerning the requirements for the Dosch project and as I understood it you said that you knew that the Hungarian Jews were to be brought into Germany for purposes of this project. Is this correct?

A. I only didn't know the date any more. I didn't know whether this was before or after. At any rate it was not before the discussion that took place with Hitler at that time.

Q. What was not before, the letter or the knowledge?

A. What I mean to say is that I didn't know about the coming of those 100,000 Hungarian Jews to Germany before this letter was written or before the discussion took place with Hitler.

Q. But when you recovered and before the Hungarian Jews actually came you knew about it, is that what you mean?

A. When I recovered, of course I knew that those Hungarian Jews were coming to Germany. I didn't know at this time they actually were in Germany and had been obtained for this program.

Q. Did you object in any way to the use or to the transport of these Hungarian Jews by force?

A. No.

III - 563

Translation of Document 3762-PS (USA 798). *Affidavit of Kurt Becher, formerly a Colonel in the SS, 8 March 1946, to effect that Himmler ordered end of further liquidation of Jews between the middle of September and October 1944.*

* * *

I, Kurt Becher, formerly a colonel in the SS, born 12 September 1909, at Hamburg, declare the following under oath:

Between the middle of September and October 1944 I caused the Reichsfuehrer SS Himmler to issue the following order, which I received in two originals, one each for SS Generals [Obergruppenfuehrer] Kaltenbrunner and Pohl, and a carbon copy for myself:

"Effective immediately I forbid any liquidation of Jews and order that, on the contrary, hospital care [pflege] should be given to weak and sick persons. I hold you (and here Kaltenbrunner and Pohl were meant) personally responsible even if this order should not be strictly adhered to by lower echelons."

I personally took Pohl's copy to him at his office in Berlin and left the copy for Kaltenbrunner at his office in Berlin.

In my opinion Kaltenbrunner and Pohl bear the full responsibility after this date for any further killings of Jewish prisoners.

When visiting the the Concentration Camp Mauthausen on 27 April 1945 at 9:00 a.m. I was told under the seal of strictest secrecy by the Commandant in the Camp, SS Colonel Ziereis, that "Kaltenbrunner gave me the order that at least a thousand persons have still to die at Mauthausen each day."

The facts mentioned above are true. This declaration is made by me voluntarily and without coercion. I read through them, signed them, and confirmed the statement with my oath.

Oberursel, the 8th of March 1946.

[signed] Kurt Becher
Kurt Becher, SS Colonel in Reserve

Subscribed to and sworn before us at Oberursel, Germany this 8th day of March 1946.

[signed] Richard A. Gutman
Richard A. Gutman, 1st Lt. AUS
[signed] Kurt L. Ponger
T/e Kurt L. Ponger 32968282

The Documentary Evidence   3803-PS

Translation of Document 3803-PS (USA 802). Covering letter enclosing a letter from Kaltenbrunner, 30 June 1944, concerning forced labor of Jews in Vienna.

* * *

HEADQUARTERS
UNITED STATES FORCES IN AUSTRIA
Office of the Judge Advocate
APO 777, U. S. Army
15 March 1946

SUBJECT: Letter of Transmittal

TO: Office of United States Chief of Counsel, Nurnberg APO 163, U. S. Army.

1. Transmitted herewith original letter of Kaltenbrunner, and letter of transmittal from Mayor of Vienna.
2. For your information, Bleschke is presently confined at Camp Marcus W. Orr, Salzburg, Austria.

FOR THE JUDGE ADVOCATE:
ARTHUR T. RATCLIFFE
Major   JAGD
Asst Judge Advocate

Telephone VIENNA A-20472
Copy to Judge Advocate General, War Crimes Branch, Wiesbaden

Vienna, on the 11 March 1946

Mayor of the City of Vienna:
To the Legal Division USFA:
Vienna IX, Otto Wagnerplatz

I permit myself to refer to you a letter of the former Chef of the Sicherheitspolice and of the SD, Dr. Kaltenbrunner, to Blaschke, the former mayor of the city of Vienna, with the request to transmit same to the court at Nurnberg. This letter was found in the files of the Viennese City Hall and is in my opinion an important document of proof for the war criminal case at Nurnberg. I transmit this letter to you since Nurnberg lies in the American occupied zone.

A copy of this letter goes at the same time to the minister of Justice, Dr. Geroe.

The mayor of the city of Vienna:
s/ KOERNER

III - 565

Chief of the Security Police and of the SD
IV A 4b—3433/42g (1446)
(In reply refer to above and date)
                      Berlin SW 68, 30 June 1944
                      Prinz-Albrecht Strasse 8
                      Telephone: 12 00 40
                      SECRET
                      [Stamp]
                  Immediate action

TO: Buergermeister of the City of Vienna, SS Brigadefuehrer Blaschke, Vienna.

SUBJECT: Assignment of Labor Force to essential war work in the city of Vienna.

RE: Your letter of 7 June 1944

Dear Blaschke!

    For the special reasons cited by you I have in the meantime given orders to ship several evacuation transports to Vienna-Strasshof, SS Brigadier Dr. Dellbruegge had, as a matter of fact, already written to me concerning the same matter.

    At the present 4 shipments with approx. 12,000 Jews are pending. They should reach Vienna within the next few days.

    According to previous experience it is estimated that 30% of the transport will consist of Jews able to work (approx. 3,600 in this case) who can be utilized for the work in question, whereby it shall be understood that they are subject *to be removed at any time*. It is obvious that only a well guarded, enclosed place of work and a secured camplike billeting arrangement can be utilized and this is an absolute prerequisite for making these Jews available. Women unable to work and children of these Jews who are all kept in readiness for special action [Sonderaktion], and therefore one day will be removed again, have to stay in the guarded camp also during the day.

    Please discuss further details with the State Police Headquarters in Vienna, SS Obersturmbannfuehrer Dr. Ebner and SS Obersturmbannfuehrer Krumey from the Special Action Command Hungary [Sondereinsatzkommando Ungarn] who at the present happens to be in Vienna.

    I hope that these transports will be of help to you in carrying out these urgent work details of yours.

                                    Heil Hitler!

                    (signed)   Your Kaltenbrunner

The Documentary Evidence   3840-PS

Copy of Document 3840-PS (USA 803). *Affidavit of Karl Kaleske, adjutant to SS and Police Leader Stroop, 24 February 1946, concerning action against the Warsaw ghetto, April 1943.*

* * *

Before me, Major Luke P. Rogers, being authorized to administer oaths, personally appeared Karl Kaleske, who, being duly sworn, through the interpreter, made and subscribed the following statement:

My name is Karl Kaleske. I was Adjutant to Doctor von Sammern-Frankenegg from November 1942 until April 1943, while he was SS and Polizeifuehrer of Warsaw. I then was Adjutant to SS and Polizeifuehrer Stroop until August 1943. The action against the Warsaw ghetto was planned while von Sammern-Frankenegg was SS and Polizeifuehrer. General Stroop took over the command on the day of the commencement of the action. The function of the Security Police during the action against the Warsaw ghetto was to accompany the SS troops. A certain number of SS troops were assigned the task to clear a certain street. With every SS group there were from four to six Security policemen, because they knew the ghetto very well. These Security policemen were under Doctor Hahn, Commander of the Security Police for Warsaw. Hahn received his orders not from the SS and Polizeifuehrer of Warsaw, but directly from Kaltenbrunner in Berlin. This pertains not only to the ghetto action but to all matters. Frequently Doctor Hahn came to our office and told the SS and Polizeifuehrer that he had received such and such an order from Kaltenbrunner about the contents of which he wanted to inform the SS and Polizeifuehrer. He would not do this with every order, but only with certain ones.

I remember the case of three hundred foreign Jews who had been collected in the Polski Hotel by the Security Police. At the end of the ghetto action, Kaltenbrunner ordered the Security Police to transport these people away.

During my time in Warsaw the Security Police had been in charge of matters concerning the underground. The Security Police handled these matters independently of the SS and Polizeifuehrer, and received its orders from Kaltenbrunner in Berlin. When the leader of the underground in Warsaw was captured in June or July 1943, he was flown directly to Kaltenbrunner in Berlin.

I have read the statement over and I have understood it completely. I have made the statement freely and without compulsion. I swear before God that this statement is in accordance with the full truth.

[Signed] Karl Kaleske

Subscribed and sworn to before me at Wiesbaden, Germany, on this 24th day of February 1946.
[Signed] Luke P. Rogers
        Major   CMP
        Investigating officer

Copy of Document 3841-PS (USA 804). Affidavit of Juergen Stroop, SS and Police Leader of Warsaw District, 24 February 1946, to effect that he conducted action against the Warsaw ghetto in April 1943 pursuant to order of Himmler.

*   *   *

Before me, Major Luke P. Rogers, being authorized to administer oaths, personally appeared Juergen Stroop who, being duly sworn, through the interpreter, made and subscribed the following statement:

My name is Juergen Stroop. I was SS and Polizeifuehrer of the District of Warsaw from the 17th or 18th of April 1943, until the end of August 1943. The action against the Warsaw ghetto was planned by my predecessor, SS Oberfuehrer Doctor von Sammern-Frankenegg. On the day of the commencement of this action I took over the command and von Sammern-Frankenegg explained to me what was to be done. He had the order from Himmler before him, and in addition I received a teletype from Himmler which ordered me to clear the Warsaw ghetto and raze it to the ground. To carry this out, I had two battalions of Waffen-SS, one hundred army men, units of Order Police, and seventy-five to a hundred Security Police people. The Security Police had been active in the Warsaw ghetto for some time, and during this program it was their function to accompany SS units in groups of six or eight, as guides and experts in ghetto matters. Obersturmbannfuehrer Doctor Hahn was commander of the Security Police of Warsaw at this time. Hahn gave the Security Police its orders concerning their tasks in this action. These orders were not given to Hahn by me, but came from Kaltenbrunner in Berlin. As SS and Polizeifuehrer of Warsaw I gave no orders to the Security Police. All orders came to Hahn from Kaltenbrunner in Berlin. For example, in June or July of the same year, I was together with Hahn in Kaltenbrunner's office and Kaltenbrunner told me that while Hahn and I must work together, all basic orders to the Security Police must come from him in Berlin.

After the people had been taken out of the Ghetto, numbering from fifty to sixty thousand, they were brought to the railroad station. The Security Police had absolute supervision of these people, and was in charge of the transport of these people to Lublin.

Immediately after the ghetto action had been completed, about three hundred foreign Jews had been collected at the Polski Hotel. These people had partly been here before the action, and partly brought here during the action. Kaltenbrunner ordered Hahn to transport these people away. Hahn himself told me that he had received this order from Kaltenbrunner.

All executions [literally, carrying out death sentences] were ordered by the Reich Main Security Office, Kaltenbrunner.

I have read this statement over and I have understood it completely. I have made the statement freely and without compulsion. I swear before God that this is the full truth.

[signed] Juergen Stroop

Copy of Document 3868-PS (USA 819). *Affidavit, dated 5 April 1946, of Rudolf Franz Ferdinand Hoess, Commandant of Auschwitz Extermination Camp from 1 May 1940 to 1 December 1943, concerning execution of 2,500,000 persons and death from starvation and disease of another 500,000, most of whom were Jews.*

* * *

AFFIDAVIT

I, Rudolf Franz Ferdinand Hoess, being first duly sworn, depose and say as follows:

1. I am forty-six years old, and have been a member of the NSDAP since 1922; a member of the SS since 1934; a member of the Waffen-SS since 1939. I was a member from 1 December 1934 of the SS Guard Unit, the so-called Deathshead Formation [Totenkopf Verband].

2. I have been constantly associated with the administration of concentration camps since 1934, serving at Dachau until 1938; then as Adjutant in Sachsenhausen from 1938 to May 1, 1940, when I was appointed Commandant of Auschwitz. I commanded Auschwitz until 1 December 1943, and estimate that at least 2,500,000 victims were executed and exterminated there

by gassing and burning, and at least another half million succumbed to starvation and disease making a total dead of about 3,000,000. This figure represents about 70% or 80% of all persons sent to Auschwitz as prisoners, the remainder having been selected and used for slave labor in the concentration camp industries. Included among the executed and burnt were approximately 20,000 Russian prisoners of war (previously screened out of Prisoner of War cages by the Gestapo) who were delivered at Auschwitz in Wehrmacht transports operated by regular Wehrmacht officers and men. The remainder of the total number of victims included about 100,000 German Jews, and great numbers of citizens, mostly Jewish from Holland, France, Belgium, Poland, Hungary, Czechoslovakia, Greece, or other countries. We executed about 400,000 Hungarian Jews alone at Auschwitz in the summer of 1944.

3. WVHA (SS Main Economic and Administration Office), headed by Obergruppenfuehrer Oswald Pohl, was responsible for all administrative matters such as billeting, feeding and medical care, in the concentration camps. Prior to establishment of the RSHA, Secret State Police Office (Gestapo) and the Reich Office of Criminal Police were responsible for arrests, commitments to concentration camps, punishments and executions therein. After organization of the RSHA, all of these functions were carried on as before, but, pursuant to orders signed by Heydrich as Chief of the RSHA. While Kaltenbrunner was Chief of RSHA, orders for protective custody, commitments, punishment, and individual executions were signed by Kaltenbrunner or by Mueller, Chief of the Gestapo, as Kaltenbrunner's deputy.

4. Mass executions by gassing commenced during the summer 1941 and continued until fall 1944. I personally supervised executions at Auschwitz until the first of December 1943 and know by reason of my continued duties in the Inspection of Concentration Camps WVHA that these mass executions continued as stated above. All mass executions by gassing took place under the direct orders, supervision, and responsibility of RSHA. I received all orders for carrying out these mass executions directly from RSHA.

5. On 1 December 1943 I became Chief of AMT I in AMT Group D of the WVHA and in that office was responsible for coordinating all matters arising between RSHA and concentration camps under the administration of WVHA. I held this position until the end of the war. Pohl, as Chief of WVHA, and Kaltenbrunner, as Chief of RSHA, often conferred personally

and frequently communicated orally and in writing concerning concentration camps. On 5 October 1944 I brought a lengthy report regarding Mauthausen Concentration Camp to Kaltenbrunner at his office at RSHA, Berlin. Kaltenbrunner asked me to give him a short oral digest of this report and said he would reserve any decision until he had had an opportunity to study it in complete detail. This report dealt with the assignment to labor of several hundred prisoners who had been condemned to death—so-called "nameless prisoners."

6. The "final solution" of the Jewish question meant the complete extermination of all Jews in Europe. I was ordered to establish extermination facilities at Auschwitz in June 1941. At that time, there were already in the general government three other extermination camps; Belzek, Treblinka, and Wolzek. These camps were under the Einsatzkommando of the Security Police and SD. I visited Treblinka to find out how they carried out their extermination. The Camp Commandant at Treblinka told me that he had liquidated 80,00 in the course of one half-year. He was principally concerned with liquidating all the Jews from the Warsaw ghetto. He used monoxide gas and I did not think that his methods were very efficient. So when I set up the extermination building at Auschwitz, I used Cyclon B, which was a crystallized prussic acid which we dropped into the death chamber from a small opening. It took from 3 to 15 minutes to kill the people in the death chamber depending upon climatic conditions. We knew when the people were dead because their screaming stopped. We usually waited about one-half hour before we opened the doors and removed the bodies. After the bodies were removed our special commandos took off the rings and extracted the gold from the teeth of the corpses.

7. Another improvement we made over Treblinka was that we built our gas chambers to accommodate 2,000 people at one time, whereas at Treblinka their 10 gas chambers only accommodated 200 people each. The way we selected our victims was as follows: we had two SS doctors on duty at Auschwitz to examine the incoming transports of prisoners. The prisoners would be marched by one of the doctors who would make spot decisions as they walked by. Those who were fit for work were sent into the Camp. Others were sent immediately to the extermination plants. Children of tender years were invariably exterminated since by reason of their youth they were unable to work. Still another improvement we made over Treblinka was that at Treblinka the victims almost always knew that they were to be exterminated and at Auschwitz we endeavored to

fool the victims into thinking that they were to go through a delousing process. Of course, frequently they realized our true intentions and we sometimes had riots and difficulties due to that fact. Very frequently women would hide their children under the clothes but of course when we found them we would send the children in to be exterminated. We were required to carry out these exterminations in secrecy but of course the foul and nauseating stench from the continuous burning of bodies permeated the entire area and all of the people living in the surrounding communities knew that exterminations were going on at Auschwitz.

8. We received from time to time special prisoners from the local Gestapo office. The SS doctors killed such prisoners by injections of benzine. Doctors had orders to write ordinary death certificates and could put down any reason at all for the cause of death.

9. From time to time we conducted medical experiments on women inmates, including sterilization and experiments relating to cancer. Most of the people who died under these experiments had been already condemned to death by the Gestapo.

10. Rudolf Mildner was the chief of the Gestapo at Kattowitz and as such was head of the Political Department at Auschwitz which conducted third degree methods of interrogation, from approximately March 1941 until September 1943. As such, he frequently sent prisoners to Auschwitz for incarceration or execution. He visited Auschwitz on several occasions. The Gestapo Court, the SS Standgericht, which tried persons accused of various crimes, such as escaping Prisoners of War, etc., frequently met within Auschwitz, and Mildner often attended the trial of such persons, who usually were executed in Auschwitz following their sentence. I showed Mildner throughout the extermination plant at Auschwitz and he was directly interested in it since he had to send the Jews from his territory for execution at Auschwitz.

I understand English as it is written above. The above statements are true; this declaration is made by me voluntarily and without compulsion; after reading over the statement, I have signed and executed the same at Nurnberg, Germany, on the fifth day of April 1946.

[signed]   Rudolf Hoess
RUDOLF FRANZ FERDINAND HOESS

Subscribed and sworn to before me this
  5th day of April 1946, at Nurnberg, Germany.
[signed] Smith W. Brookhart Jr.
SMITH W. BROOKHART, JR.,
LT. COLONEL, IGD.

Translation of Document R-96 (GB-268). Correspondence from files of Minister of Justice, April-August, 1941, in preparation of discriminatory decree of 4 December 1941 (2746-PS) regarding criminal justice against Poles and Jews in annexed Eastern territories.

* * *

Copy

The Reich Minister of Justice
9170 Ostgeb/2—Ha 2-1826.41

Berlin W.8, 30th June 1941
Express Letter

To the Reich Fuehrer SS and Chief of the German Police in the Reich Ministry of the Interior.

Subject: Administration of Criminal Justice in the annexed Eastern territories.

Reference: Letter to the Reich Minister and Chief of Reich Chancellery, dated 16th May 1941—II A 2 (new) No. 127/41 173/1 and the letter addressed to me by the Main Office of Reich Security, dated 29th May 1941 — 11 a 2 (new) No. 205|41—176-7.

2 enclosures.

In the enclosure I transmit the following documents on which I would ask you to give your opinion at an early date:

1. draft of an ordinance concerning the administration of criminal justice against Poles and Jews in the annexed Eastern territories and the area of the former Free City of Danzig;

2. copy of my letter to the Reich Minister and Chief of the Reich Chancellery, dated 17th April 1941—9171 Ostgeb. 2 IIa 2 996/41—giving the reasons for this draft.

The draft has now been supplemented by Article XIII concerning the procedure of courts-martial. This supplementary article is based on a decision of the Fuehrer, of which I was informed through a letter from the Reich Minister and Chief of the Reich Chancellery dated 27 May 1941—Rk 7760 B; according to this decision the Reich Governor in the Reich Gau Wartheland is to be empowered to introduce courts-martial against Poles in his district.

In order to obtain a quick settlement of this urgent matter which is of importance for the war, I should be grateful if a personal discussion could be arranged. I ask for telephone call to fix the time for a conference.

Charged with the conduct of affairs

Reich Main Security Office
II A 2—No. 342/41—170—

Berlin SW 11, 11th July 1941
8 Prinz-Albrecht Street
Copy

Subject matter: Administration of Criminal Justice in annexed Eastern Territories.

1. *Note:*

The ordinance draft, which was sent to us for consideration by the Reich Minister for Justice with a covering letter of 30th June 1941 (pages 161 ff. of the file), was discussed at an informative meeting of the competent officials of the Reich Main Security Office and of the Reich Civil Police Main Office, Reich Fuehrer SS—Reich Commissioner for the Consolidation of the German Race—took part in the discussions, because the invitation, dated 7th July 1941, arrived late.

The discussion had the following results:

I. The general lines of the provisions of chapter 1 (criminal law) and chapter 2 (criminal procedure) are to be approved. They correspond to the principles followed by the police in dealing with Poles.

It should however, be suggested to the Ministry of Justice to insert in Chapter 2, Paragraph XII, a minimum of legal guarantees for the legal procedure; this might be done by adding to the present version the following sentences:

"In any case, however, the defendant should be granted a hearing, if need be with the help of an interpreter.

The names of the judges and of the defendant, the evidence on which the sentence is based, and the offence, the sentence with a brief opinion, and the date of the sentence should be taken down in writing in each case."

II. Chapter 3 (procedure under martial law) requires several modifications or clarifications:

1. The Reich Governors (Statthalter) are to be bound not only by the consent of the Reich Minister for Justice, but also by the consent of the Reich Minister of the Interior. This amendment is needed to safeguard the influence the police must have on introduction and procedure of martial law. Under the

present provision, which requires only the consent of the Minister of Justice, there is the risk that the intended martial law becomes a martial law under the supervision of the administration of justice and not a martial law for the purpose of the police.

2. The Reich Governors must have authority to declare martial law uniformly for the whole area [Gaue] under their administration. The present wording [districts] — Bezirke does not make it quite clear whether they have such authority.

3. The persons who are subject to the procedure under martial law should be the same as those to whom the other provisions of the ordinance refer. Therefore in Par. XIII Jews as well as Poles must be mentioned.

4. The jurisdiction of the courts-martial as stated in the bill is too narrow. They must given authority:

> *a.* to pass judgment under martial law on all excesses, not only on more serious ones against Germans,
> *b.* to pass judgment under martial law, even on minor offences which seriously endanger the German reconstruction work because of their frequency.

The words "more serious" before "excesses" and before "punishable offenses" must therefore be deleted from the draft.

5. Confinement to a concentration camp is, by definition, not a punishment but a measure of precaution. The provision whereby the court acting under martial law may sentence an offender to confinement in a concentration camp must therefore be amended.

The courts acting under martial law need, however, the authority to punish by imprisonment—though in this case it is for the Secret State Police and not for the law administration to carry out the sentence. The present wording of Paragraph XIII, sec. 2 must therefore be changed to read as follows:

"The penalties to be inflicted by the courts acting under martial law are the death penalty or imprisonment (penal camp). The execution of the penalty of imprisonment is the duty of the Secret State Police."

6. It must be made clear whether the Reich Governors are authorized to implement independently the provisions regarding the nomination of judges for the procedure of courts-martial, or whether the Reich Minister for Justice intends to reserve the right to withhold his consent for a declaration of martial law unless the Reich Governors refer to him any steps they take in these matters.

III. The present wording of chapter 4 (extension of jurisdiction and authorization) does not take into consideration that the police is authorized at present to inflict penalties for minor offences of Polish civilian workers within the territory of the Reich. This power is based upon an authorization granted to the Reich Fuehrer SS by the Reich-Marshal. The provision as drafted would therefore mean a deterioration of the legal position of the police in favor of the judiciary.

Provision must therefore be made for one of two alternatives:
- *a.* either the competence of the police as defined hitherto must be maintained expressly,
- *b.* or martial law must be made applicable to Poles within the whole territory of the Reich.

The latter proposal is preferable because it should be the ultimate goal to make Poles subject to the jurisdiction of the police.

IV. The items mentioned under No. I—III are to be discussed by department II A 2 with the Reich Ministry of Justice. It should be ascertained to what extent the Ministry of Justice is prepared to meet the wishes of the police. Thereafter the draft embodying the final position of the police toward the Reich Minister of Justice is to be submitted to the Reich Fuehrer SS. The draft is to be signed by all police departments who participate in the discussion.

Copies to
- *a.* Main Office Civil Police, c/o Ministerial Counselor Dr. Daemper,
- *b.* Reich Fuehrer SS, Reich Commissioner for the Consolidation of the German Race,
- *c.* Office III—III A 3
- *d.* Office IV—IV D 2 } of the Reich Main Security Office
- *e.* Office V—V A 1

following my letter of the 7th July 1941—II A 2 No. 205 VIII/41—176-7, for information.

      by order: signed: Neifeind.

[stamp]
The Reich Fuehrer SS, Reich Commissioner
for the Consolidation of the German Race
Received: 14th July 1941 4 W
File No.: COI/28R/5th Aug. 1940.

1. Dr. Bilfinger Office II V informs me on enquiry that the draft has been amended by agreement with the Reich Minister of Justice and has been submitted to SS-Group Fuehrer Wolff

for signature. The draft will be forwarded to the Reich-Minister of Justice and will be described as the final opinion of the Police.

We shall receive copy.

2. To be submitted again 19th August.

initialled: 30th July.

Copy

The Reich Fuehrer SS and
Chief of the German Police in the Reich Ministry of the Interior
S II A 2 No. 342/41—176.

Berlin SW 11, 1st August 1941
8 Prinz-Albrecht Street

I have no objections against the proposals.

Signed: Dr. Kr 27th Aug.

c—3/1-3

To the Reich Minister for Justice
Berlin, W.8.
Wilhelmstr. 65

Subject Matter: Administration of Criminal Justice in the Annexed Eastern Territories.

Reference: Express letter dated 30th June 1941—9170 Ostgeb/2-II a 2 1826.41

With reference to the discussion held by our respective officials on 14 July 1941, I wish to make the following comments on the draft you have submitted:

Generally I agree to the draft and welcome the special conditions to which Poles and Jews are to be subject both with regard to criminal law and criminal procedure. The reintroduction of martial law in the annexed Eastern Territories conforms with the wishes I have expressed several times.

I request you, however, to take into consideration the following specific points:

1. According to Paragraph XII the procedure is to be arranged by the court and the public prosecutor as they think fit in consideration of their duty. On principle I agree with this. However, in the earlier draft for a court-martial procedure which was worked out with your collaboration, a minimum of legal guarantees was provided for. This I would like to see preserved in future also. The present wording of Paragraph XII would result in an unusual situation whereby the rules for ordinary procedure would be less stringent than those for the procedure under martial law. Therefore, please amend the wording of

Paragraph XII accordingly.

2. In Paragraph XIII (procedure under martial law) please provide for the consent of the Reich Minister of the Interior in addition to consent of the Reich Minister of Justice.

3. During the discussion of the bill by the officials concerned, it became clear that the Reich Governors [Reichsstatthalter] should be authorized to declare martial law for any parts of their area as well as for the whole of their area. The present wording is open to doubt, I propose therefore the following wording:

" * * * for the area of his administration or specified parts thereof".

4. Although it may safely be assumed that in the future there will be no more Jews in the annexed Eastern territories, I am of the opinion that under present circumstances it is very urgent to provide martial law not only for Poles but for Jews as well. Therefore please insert in Paragraph XIII after the word "Poles" the words "and Jews".

5. Concerning the clause "and for other more serious offences which gravely endanger the German reconstruction work", please delete the words "more serious" so that martial law may be applied also to those cases which in themselves are not particularly serious but which might become a serious danger to the German reconstruction work because of their frequency (e. g. smuggling), and which urgently require immediate and draconic action for purposes of intimidation.

6. So far, the Secret State Police alone imposes protective custody. Furthermore, protective custody is by definition not a punishment but a measure of precaution and education. Therefore please amend section 2 of Paragraph XIII to read perhaps as follows:

"The penalty to be inflicted by the courts under martial law is the death penalty. The courts proceeding under martial law may, however, dispense with punishment and order transfer to the Secret State Police instead."

In this way due consideration would be given to the wishes of the Fuehrer and the aforementioned difficulties of terminology would be avoided.

7. I agree also to the extension of jurisdiction as provided in Paragraph XIV. But as you know, Reich Marshal Goering, in his ordinance of 8 March 1940, has delegated to me the responsibility for the proper conduct of the Poles. He has authorized me to issue the legal and executive provisions necessary for this purpose. I have made use of this authorization by issuing

The Documentary Evidence   R-96

the ordinances dated 8 March 1940—S IV D 2 No. 382/40—
and 3 September 1940—S IV D 2 No. 3382/40. These ordinances are also known to you. The present wording of Paragraph XIV does not make it quite clear whether this arrangement will remain unaffected. I note that the draft is not intended to bring about any change in this arrangement; I consider it necessary, nevertheless, to make it quite clear by means
of a brief remark in Paragraph XIV, that the aforementioned
authorization granted to me by Reich Marshal Goering and
the ordinances issued by me remain unaffected.

    By order:

                                Signed: Heydrich.

Reich Main Security Office
II A 2 No. 342/41—176—   Berlin, the 11th August 1941

Copy
    to Reichs Fuehrer SS—Reich Commissioner for the
    Consolidation of the German Race c/o attorney
    Dr. Kraeuter—or his deputy—in Berlin
        By order:

                                Signed: Neifeind.
Certified (signed) Heybutzki, secretary.

Stamp of:
    The Reich Fuehrer SS and Chief of the German Police in the
    Reich Ministry of the Interior.
    The Chief of the Security Police and the SD (Security-
    Service).

Stamp of:
    The Reich Fuehrer SS, Reich Commissioner for the Consoli-
    dation of the German Race. B
    Received: 14th August 1941.
    File No: C—3/1/—3/1st Aug. 1941.

Submitted to Dr. Kraeuter for action 15 Aug.   [initials].

Translation of Document R-102 (USA 470). *Excerpts from Activity and Situation Report No. 6 of the Task Forces (Einsatzgruppen) of the Security Police and the Security Service in the USSR, 1-31 October 1941, listing measures taken against Jews and the executions of hundreds and thousands of Jews in various locations in the East.*

                      *   *   *

(Rubber Stamp)
TOP SECRET
(GEHEIME REICHSACHE)
100 copies
Copy No. 42

ACTIVITY AND SITUATION REPORT NO. 6 OF THE TASK FORCES (EINSATZGRUPPEN) OF THE SECURITY POLICE AND THE SD IN THE U.S.S.R.
(Time covered by report: 1-31 October 1941)

Table of Contents

	Page
I. Stations.	1
II. Activities.	
A. *Eastern Territory* (Ostland)	
a.) Partisan activity and counteraction	1
b.) Situation in Leningrad	2
c.) Jews	7
B. *White Ruthenia.*	
a.) Partisan activity and counteraction	8
b.) Arrests and executions of communists, officials and criminals	11
c.) Jews	12
d.) Enemy propaganda activity	14
e.) Material seized	15
C. *Ukraine*	
a.) Partisan activity and counteraction	16
b.) Arrests and executions of communists, officials and criminals	17
c.) Jews	18
d.) Enemy propaganda activity	19
e.) Material seized	20
III. *Economy, Commerce and Culture.*	
A. *White Ruthenia*	
a.) Economy and commerce	20
b.) Supplies and provisions	21
c.) Agriculture	21
d.) Culture—Church	22
B. *Ukraine*	
a.) Economy and commerce	23
b.) Supplies and provisions	24
c.) Agriculture	25
d.) Culture	

         1. Schools   25
         2. Church   26
IV. Attitude of foreign groups.
     A. White Ruthenians
         Attitude towards Germanism   27
     B. Ukrainians
         a.) Attitude towards Germanism   28
         b.) Tendencies to autonomy   29
         c.) Attitude towards Bolshevism   29
V.   The German Racial Group in the area around
     Landau.
                    (Page 1 to Page 2—line 5)
I. STATIONS.
During the period covered by this report the stations of the Task Forces of the Security Police and the SD have changed only in the Northern Sector.
The present stations are:
    Task Force A: since 7 October 1941 Krasnowardeisk.
    Task Force B: continues in Smolensk.
    Task Force C: since 27 September 1941 in Kiew.
    Task Force D: since 27 September 1941 in Nikolajew.
The Action and Special Commandos (Einsatz und Sonder Commandos) which are attached to the Task Force continue on the march with the advancing troops into the sectors which have been assigned to them.
II. ACTIVITIES.
     A. Eastern Territory (i.e. Baltic area)
         a) Partisan activity and counteraction.
The activity of the Bolshevist partisans in area of task force A has *quieted down somewhat*. Nevertheless, Intelligence work has been further extended through the dispatching civilian agents, and the enlistment of the village elders and of the population. The results of the preliminary intelligence work served as a basis for several actions in the active combatting of the partisans. From a captured activity report of a partisan group it can be ascertained that the partisans anticipate in view of the approaching winter season that they will not be able to hold out longer than the middle of November.

         *   *   *   *   *   *   *

                (Page 7 line 7 to Page 14 line 14)
    c) *Jews*. In 1940 there were in Estonia approximately 4,500 Jews almost exclusively in Reval, Dorpat, Narwa and Pernau. There were only a few Jews in the country districts. After the occupation of the Eastern territory by German troops there

were still approximately 2000 Jews. The larger part had left the country in an easterly direction together with the Soviet authorities and the Red Army.

Spontaneous demonstrations against Jewry followed by pogroms on the part of the population against the remaining Jews have not been *recorded*, on account of the lack of adequate indoctrination.

However, the Estonian Protective Corps (Selbtschutz), formed at the time of the entry of the Wehrmacht, immediately started a *comprehensive arrest action of all Jews*. This action was under the direction of the task force of the Security Police and the SD.

The measures taken were:
1. Arrest of all male Jews over sixteen.
2. Arrest of all Jewesses from 16-20 years, who lived in Reval and environs and were fit for work; these were employed in peat cutting.
3. Comprehensive detention in the synagogue of all Jewesses living in Dorpot and its environs.
4. Arrest of the Jews and Jewesses fit for work in Pernau and environs.
5. Registration of all Jews according to age, sex, and capacity for work for the purpose of their detention in a camp is being prepared.

The male Jews over 16 were executed with the exception of doctors and the elders. At the present time this action is still in progress. After completion of this action there will remain only 500 Jewesses and children in the Eastern territory.

As an *immediate action* the following has been ordered by the task force of the Security Police and the SD:
1. Identification of all Jews.
2. The prohibition to carry on a public trade.
3. Prohibition of use of sidewalks and public transportation as well as of visits to theaters, cinemas and restaurants.
4. Prohibition of attendance at schools.
5. Seizure of all Jewish property.

B. *WHITE RUTHENIA*
   a) Partisan activity and Counteraction.

Contrary to the situation in the North sector the activity of the partisans in the area of task force B has increased slightly. In Welikij Luki alone 19 reports of attacks by partisans were received. However, the main weight of partisan activity lately has been shifting over to the *perpetration of acts of sabotage*. It has been noted that the strongest groups divide themselves into smaller ones. This results in a better camouflage and mobility. How far this camouflage goes is shown by three cases where partisans married into three villages in order to appear unsuspected. Furthermore Red Army men were unmasked as partisans; they had obtained certificates surreptitiously from units of the Wehrmacht showing them to be unsuspected as political prisoners who were to be left at large. When interrogated by the Action Commandos of the Security Police and the SD, they admitted after long denials that *they had received the order to pass themselves off as political prisoners or as forced laborers* and to take up the fight again as partisans behind the front.

Again and again it can be observed that the *population refuses to support the partisans* and in several instances they have even acted actively against the partisans if by this action the destruction of their property could be prevented.

In several actions against smaller partisan groups, a number of partisans would be shot.

At Choslawitschi 4 partisans who had shot at a German soldier were apprehended and liquidated.

Southeast of Demidow, five partisans were captured after a search of the forests; they admitted to have killed 14 German soldiers. They were liquidated.

In several actions northwest of Welish 27 partisans were apprehended and shot.

In the village Michalowo, after careful reconnaissance through civilian agents, 8 partisans were surprised in a house by the same Commando of the Security Police and the SD. They were arrested and hanged the next day in this particularly partisan-infested village.

The president of the District Region Soviets in Tarenitsch and his secretary were shot because of their connections with partisans.

During an action approximately 70 kilometers south of Mogilew, *25 Armenians, Kirghizs and Mongols* were apprehended with false identification papers with which they tried to conceal the fact that they belonged to a partisan group. They were liquidated.

In the same district two partisan leaders were captured and shot.

An Action Commando of the Security Police and the SD shot 3 partisans at Iwniki who shortly before capture had thrown their weapons into a brook.

In Wultschina 8 juveniles were arrested as partisans and

shot. They were *inmates of a children's home*. They had collected weapons which they hid in the woods. Upon search the following were found: 3 heavy machine guns, 15 rifles, several thousand rounds of ammunition, several hand grenades, and several packages of poison gas Ebrit.

    b) *Arrests and Executions of Communists, Officials and Criminals.*

A further large part of the activity of the Security Police was devoted to the combatting of communists and criminals. A special Commando in the period covered by this report executed 63 officials, NKVD agents and agitators.

In the vicinity of the Tytschinino railway station 4 girls were shot because they attempted to derail a train by loosening the fish-plates.

Three communist officials and one Politruk were liquidated at Gorodnia.

18 persons were executed at Mogilew; they had acted as political officials and Politruks. Weapons were found in their possession.

An Action Commando convicted a *member of the Supreme Council of the White Russian Soviet Republic* of arson in Witsbsk. He was shot.

Blood-Cellar in Tschernigow   In the NKVD building in Tschernigow a *blood cellar* was discovered. It was soundproof and lightproof. One room served as the place for executions. The wall was covered with boards serving as butts with sawdust strewn in front of it which was completely soaked with blood.

Lunatics   The Red Troops had opened the insane asylum at their departure and had armed some of the inmates. 21 insane persons were apprehended in the meantime and liquidated. In Minsk 632 and in Mogilew 836 persons were shot.

In Mogilew in addition 33 looters were executed.

The liquidations for the period covered by this report have reached a total of 37,180 persons.

    c) *Jews.*

Now as ever it is to be noted that the population on their own part refrains from any action against Jews. It is true that the population reports collectively of the terror of the Jews to which they were exposed during the time of the Soviet regime, or they complain about new encroachments of the Jews, but nevertheless, they are not prepared to take part in any pogroms.

All the more vigorous are the actions of the task forces of the Security Police and the SD against the Jews who make it necessary that steps be taken against them in different spheres.

In Gorodnia 165 Jewish terrorists and in Tschenrigow 19 Jewish communists were liquidated. 8 more Jewish communists were shot at Beresna.

It was experienced repeatedly that the *Jewish women showed an especially obstinate behaviour*. For this reason 28 Jewesses had to be shot in Krugoje and 337 at Mogilew.

In Borissow 321 Jewish saboteurs and 118 Jewish looters were executed.

In Bobruisk 380 Jews were shot who had engaged to the last in *incitement and horror* propaganda (Hetz-und Greuelpropaganda) against the German army of occupation.

In Tatarsk the Jews had left the Ghetto of their own accord and returned to their old home quarters, attempting to expel the Russians who had been quartered there in the meantime. All male Jews as well as 3 Jewesses were shot.

In Sadrudubs the Jews *offered some resistance* against the establishment of a Ghetto so that 272 Jews and Jewesses had to be shot. Among them was a political Commissar.

Mogilew   In Mogilew, too, the Jews attempted to sabotage their removal to the Ghetto. 113 Jews liquidated.

Wit   Moreover four Jews were shot on account of *refusal to work* and 2 Jews were shot because they had illtreated wounded German soldiers and because they did not wear the prescribed markings.

In Talka 222 Jews were shot for anti-German propaganda and in Marina Gorka 996 Jews were shot because they had sabotaged orders issued by the German occupation authorities.

At Schklow 627 more Jews were shot, because they had participated in acts of sabotage.

Witebsk   On account of the extreme danger of an epidemic, a beginning was made to liquidate the Jews in the ghetto at Witebsk. This involved approximately 3000 Jews.

* * * * * * *

(Page 16 line 7 to page 19 line 10)

C. *UKRAINE.*

a) *Partisan activity and counteraction.*

Although partisan activity in the south sector is very strong too, there is nevertheless the impression that spreading and effective partisan activity are strongly affected by the flight of higher partisan leaders and by the lack of initiative of the subordinate leaders who have remained behind. Only in one case a commando of the Security Police and the SD succeeded in a fight with partisans *in shooting the Secretary of the Communist Party for the administration district of Nikolajew-Cherson, who was at the time Commissar of a partisan group for the district Nikolajew-Cherson-Krim.*

The leader of a partisan group of five was captured after an exchange of shots near Odessa. He had the task of spotting artillery positions and of reporting them to a Soviet command post.

An action against partisans near Kostromka resulted in the arrest of 16 persons, among them a Politruk, a Unit leader of an annihilation brigade as well as 3 communist revolutionaries.

The Jew Herschko Salomon, who had belonged to a parachute Defense-Assault battalion, was located at the city hospital in Nikolajew. The screening of PWs resulted in the discovery of 3 Jews who were members of a partisan company.

In Belabanowka the former president of the village soviet, who had attempted to form a partisan group of his own, was arrested.

Furthermore a *member of the Polit Bureau and president of a workers union*, at present organiser of partisan groups, was arrested and liquidated.

14 partisans were shot at Kiev.

In the course of an action at Cherson 2 persons were apprehended who attempted to carry information behind the Bolshevik lines. At the same time the leader of a band of partisans was shot after a lengthy fight.

b) *Arrests and Executions of Communists and Officials.*

The search for leading communists resulted in the arrest of Kaminski, former GPU chief of Cherson. In the years 1919/21 he had carried out the liquidation of the Czarist officers. The head of the prison work shops of the NKVD was also caught.

In Kiev a number of NKVD officials and political commissars were rendered innocuous.

c) *Jews.*

The embitterment of the Ukrainian population against the Jews is extremely great because they are thought responsible for the explosions in Kiev. They are also regarded as informers and agents of the NKVD, who started the terror against the Ukrainian people. As a measure of retaliation for the arson at Kiev, all Jews were arrested and altogether 33,771 Jews were executed on the 29th and the 30th September. Money, valuables and clothing were secured and put at the disposal of the National-Socialist League for Public Welfare (NSV) for the equipment of the National Germans (Volksdeutschen) and partly put at the disposal of the provisional city administration for distribution to the needy population.

Shitomir   In Shitomir 3145 Jews had to be shot, because from experience they have to be regarded as bearers of Bolshevik propaganda and saboteurs.

Cherson   In Cherson 410 Jews were executed as a measure of retaliation for acts of sabotage. Especially in the area east of the Dnieper the solution of the Jewish question has been taken up energetically by the task forces of the Security Police and the SD. The areas newly occupied by the Commandos were purged of Jews. In the course of this action 4891 Jews were liquidated. At other places the Jews were marked and registered. This rendered it possible to put at the disposal of the Wehrmacht for urgent labor Jewish worker groups up to 1000 persons.

Translation of Document R-124 (USA 179). Minutes of Discussions between Speer and Hitler, 6 and 7 April 1944, concerning the importation of 100,000 Jews from Hungary for forced labor.

* * *

p. 132
Minutes of Discussions with
the Fuehrer
on 6th and 7th April 1944
State Secret

The Director of the   Berlin, 9th April 1944.
Technical Office
TA Ch S/Kr.
17)

"Suggested to the Fuehrer that, due to lack of builders and equipment, the second big building project should not be set up in German territory, but in close vicinity to the border on suitable soil (preferably on gravel base and with transport facilities) on French, Belgian or Dutch territory. The Fuehrer agrees to this suggestion if the works could be set up behind a fortified zone. For the suggestion of setting this plant up in French territory speaks mainly the fact that it would be much easier to procure the necessary workers. Nevertheless, the Fuehrer asks an attempt be made to set up the second works in a safer area, namely in the Protectorate. If it should prove impossible there, too, to get hold of the necessary workers, the Fuehrer himself will contact the Reichsfuehrer 'SS' and will give an order that the required 100,000 men are to be made available by bringing in Jews from Hungary. Stressing the fact that the building organization of the Industriegemeinschaft Schlesien Silesia was a failure, the Fuehrer demands that these works must be built by the O.T. exclusively and that the workers should be made available by the Reichsfuehrer 'SS'. He wants to hold a meeting shortly in order to discuss details with all the men concerned."

signed Speer.

Translation of Document R-135 (USA 289). Correspondence May and June 1943 from the General Commissar in White Ruthenia and the Reich Commissar in the Ostland (Baltic Countries and White Russia) to the Reich Minister for the Occupied Eastern Territories concerning the executions of Jews and the action of one prison warden of breaking out the gold bridgework, crowns and fillings of Jews one or two hours prior to execution.

* * *

Copy

The Reich Commissar　　　stamp: Personal Staff-
　for the Ostland　　　　　　Reichsfuehrer SS
Diary No. 3628/43 secret　　Documents-Administration
(Der Reichs Kommissar fuer　File No. Secret/227
　das Ostland)

Riga, 18 June 1943
SECRET

To the
　Reich Minister for the Occupied Eastern Territories
　Berlin

The attached secret reports received from General Commissar KUBE deserve special consideration.

The fact that Jews receive special treatment requires no further discussion. However it appears hardly believable that this is done in the way described in the report of the General Commissar of 1 June 1943. What is Katyn against that? Imagine only that these occurrences would become known to the other side and exploited by them! Most likely such propaganda would have no effect only because people who hear and read about it simply would not be ready to believe it.

The fight against bands also is taking on forms which are highly questionable if pacification and exploitation of the several territories are the aims of our policy. Thus, the dead,

III - 588

who were suspected of belonging to bands and whose number was indicated in the report of 5 June 1943 about the "Cottbus" project to have amounted to 5,000, in my opinion, with few exceptions would have been suitable for forced labor in the Reich.

It should not be ignored in this connection that in view of the difficulties of making oneself understood, as generally in such clean-up operations, it is very hard to distinguish friend from foe. Nevertheless, it should be possible to avoid atrocities and to bury those who have been liquidated. To lock men, women and children into barns and to set fire to these, does not appear to be a suitable method of combatting bands, even if it is desired to exterminate the population. This method is not worthy of the German cause and hurts our reputation severely.

I am asking that you take the necessary action.

(signed:) signature
stamp: Personal Staff Reichsfuehrer SS

The General Commissar Document Administration
for White Ruthenia File No. Secret/227
Gauleiter/BA Minsk, 5 June 1943
Diary No. 428/43 secret Secret
To the
 Reich Minister for the Occupied Eastern Territories
 Berlin
 through the Reich Commissioner for the Ostland
 Riga
Subject: Results of police operation "Cottbus" as reported so far for the period of 22 June to 3 July 1943.

SS Brigadefuehrer, Major General of Police von GOTTBERG reports that the operation "Cottbus" had the following result during the period mentioned:

Enemy dead	4 500
Dead suspected of belonging to bands	5 000
German dead	59
German wounded	267
Dead of foreign racial stock	22
Wounded of foreign racial stock	120
Captured members of bands	250
Destroyed enemy camps	57
Destroyed enemy positions	261
Apprehended male labor	2 062

Apprehended female labor	450
Sunk larger boats	4
Sunk floats	22

Booty consisted of:

1 airplane, 12 tow-gliders, 10 15 cm guns, 2 anti-tank guns, 9 grenade throwers, 23 heavy machine guns, 28 light machine guns, 28 machine pistols, 492 rifles, 1,028 grenades and bombs, 1,000 mines, 31,300 rounds rifle ammunition, 7,300 rounds pistol ammunition, 1,200 kg explosives, 2 complete radio installations with transmitter, 1 picture establishment, 30 parachutes, 67 wagons, 530 horses, 1 field kitchen, 430 sleighs, great amounts of medical drugs and propaganda material.

The operation affects the territory of the General District White Ruthenia in the area of Borissow. It concerns in particular the two counties Begomie and Pleschtschamizy. At present the police troops together with the army have advanced to Lake Palik and have reached the whole front of the Beresina. The continuance of the battles takes place in the rear zone of the army.

The figures mentioned above indicate that again a heavy destruction of the population must be expected. If only 492 rifles are taken from 4,500 enemy dead, this discrepancy shows that among these enemy dead were numerous peasants from the country. The battalion Dirlewanger especially has a reputation for destroying many human lives. Among the 5,000 people suspected of belonging to bands, there were numerous women and children.

By order of the Chief of Band-Combatting, SS Obergruppenfuehrer von dem BACH, units of the Wehrmannschaften have also participated in the operation. SA Standartenfuehrer KUNZE was in command of the Wehrmannschaften, among whom there were also 90 members from my office and from the District-Commissariat Minsk City. Our men returned from the operation yesterday without losses. I decline the use of officials and Reich employees of the General Commissariat in the rear zone of the army. The men who work for me were not deferred from army service in order to actively participate in combat against bands in the place of the armed forces and of the police.

Of the Wehrmannschaften, 1 railroader has been wounded (shot in lungs). The political effect of this large-scale operation upon the peaceful population is simply dreadful in view of the many shootings of women and children. In December, the town of Begomie was evacuated by the armed forces and the police. At that time, the population of Begomie was preponderantly on our side. In the course of the fighting, Begomie, which was built up as a strong point by the partisans, has been destroyed by German air attacks.

The General Commissar in Minsk
(signed:) signature

Court Prison

stamp: Personal Staff Reichsfuehrer SS
Document Administration
File No. Secret/227
Minsk, 31 May 1943

To the General Commissar
for White Ruthenia
Minsk

Subject: Actions against Jews.
Reference: Oral report on 31 May 1943.

On 13 April 1943 the former German dentist Ernst Israel TICHAUER and his wife, Elisa Sara TICHAUER, nee ROSENTHAL, were committed to the court prison by the Security Service (SD) (Hauptscharfuehrer RUEBE). Since that time all German and Russian Jews who were turned over to us, had their golden bridgework, crowns and fillings pulled or broken out. This happens always 1 to 2 hours before the respective action.

Since 13 April 1943, 516 German and Russian Jews have been finished off. On the basis of a definite investigation, gold was taken only in two actions, on 14 April 1943 from 172, and on 27 April 1943 from 164 Jews. About 50% of the Jews had gold teeth, bridgework or fillings. Hauptscharfuehrer RUEBE of the Security Service (SD) was always personally present and he took the gold along too.

Before 13 April 1943 this was not done.

(signed) GUENTHER
Prison Warden

R-135

stamp: Personal Staff Reichsfuehrer SS
Document Administration
File No. Secret/227

The General Commissar
for White Ruthenia

Minsk, 1 June 1943

Gauleiter/Wu.
Diary No. 414/43 secret.

Secret

To the
  Reich Minister for the
  Occupied Eastern Territories
  Berlin

  through the Reich Commissioner
    for the Ostland
    Riga

Subject: *Actions against Jews in the Prison of Minsk.*

The enclosed official report from the warden of the prison in Minsk is submitted to the Reich Minister and the Reich Commissar for information.

The General Commissar in Minsk
(signed:) signature.

Enclosure
Ed. I/1168/43 secret.

BIOGRAPHICAL DATA

1. PRINCIPAL OFFICIALS OF THE REICH GOVERNMENT

LEADER AND REICH CHANCELLOR (*Fuehrer und Reichskanzler*) .... ADOLF HITLER
Designated Successors .... HERMANN GOERING, RUDOLF HESS (until 1941)
Successor named to form a Government after the collapse in May 1945.. KARL DOENITZ
Head of Presidential Chancery (*Praesidialkanzlei*) and State Minister (*Staatsminister*) .... OTTO MEISSNER

REICH CABINET (*Reichsregierung*):
Chancellor (*Reichskanzler*) .... ADOLF HITLER
Vice-Chancellor .... FRANZ von PAPEN (until 1934)
Reich Ministers:
  Reich Chancery .... HANS LAMMERS
  Air .... HERMANN GOERING
  Armaments and War Production.... ALBERT SPEER (predecessor, Todt, Minister for Armaments and Munitions—until 1942)
  Church Affairs .... HERMAN MUHS, Acting (predecessor, Hans Kerrl)
  Economics .... WALTER FUNK (predecessors, Schacht, Schmitt, Hugenberg)
  Education .... BERNARD RUST
  Finance .... LUTZ GRAF SCHWERIN von KROSIGK
  Food and Agriculture .... HERBERT BACKE, Acting (predecessor, Walter Darre)
  Foreign Affairs .... JOACHIM von RIBBENTROP (predecessor, Constantin von Neurath)
  Interior .... HEINRICH HIMMLER (predecessor, Wilhelm Frick)
  Justice .... OTTO THIERACK (predecessor, Schlegelberger—acting, Guertner)
  Labor .... FRANZ SELDTE
  Labor Service .... KONSTANTIN HIERL
  Occupied Eastern Territories .... ALFRED ROSENBERG
  Posts .... WILHELM OHNESORGE (predecessor, Eltz von Ruebenach)
  Propaganda .... PAUL JOSEF GOEBBELS
  Transport .... JULIUS DORPMUELLER (predecessor, Eltz von Ruebenach)
  War .... WERNER von BLOMBERG (until 1938)

Ministers without Portfolio but with
Rank of Reich Minister .... WILHELM KEITEL (von Brauchitsch until December 1941)
KARL DOENITZ (Raeder)
MARTIN BORMANN (Hess)
HANS FRANK
ARTHUR SEYSS-INQUART (Roehm, until 1934)
Ministers after loss of portfolio....... WILHELM FRICK
CONSTANTIN von NEURATH
HJALMAR SCHACHT
State Ministers acting as Reich Ministers:
Head of the Presidential Chancery.. OTTO LEBRECHT MEISSNER
State Minister for Bohemia-Moravia. KARL HERMANN FRANK
Other Participants in Cabinet Meetings:
Chief of Foreign Organization of Party .... ERNST WILHELM BOHLE
Prussian Minister of State and Finance .... DR. JOHANNES POPITZ
Government Press Chief .... OTTO DIETRICH (predecessor, Walter Funk)
Reich Youth Leader............... ARTHUR AXMANN (predecessor, Baldur von Schirach)

SECRET CABINET COUNCIL (*Geheimer Kabinettsrat*)
President .... CONSTANTIN von NEURATH
Secretary .... HANS LAMMERS
Members .... JOACHIM von RIBBENTROP, HERMANN GOERING, PAUL JOSEF GOEBBELS, ERICH RAEDER, WILHELM KEITEL, RUDOLF HESS (until 1941), MARTIN BORMANN, WALTER von BRAUCHITSCH

REICH DEFENSE COUNCIL (*Reichsverteidigungsrat*) (Status in 1938)
Chairman .... ADOLF HITLER
Reich Minister of Air and Supreme Commander of Air Force (*Reichsminister der Luftfahrt und Oberbefehlshaber der Luftwaffe*) .... HERMANN GOERING
Supreme Commander of the Army (*Oberbefehlshaber des Heeres*) .... WALTER von BRAUCHITSCH
Supreme Commander of the Navy (*Oberbefehlshaber der Kriegsmarine*) ERICH RAEDER
Chief of the OKW (*Chef des Oberkommandos der Wehrmacht*) .... WILHELM KEITEL
Deputy of the Leader (*Stellvertreter des Fuehrers*) .... RUDOLF HESS
Chief of Reich Chancery (*Chef der Reichskanzlei*) .... HANS LAMMERS
President of Secret Cabinet Council (*Praesident des Geheimen Kabinettsrats*) .... CONSTANTIN von NEURATH
Plenipotentiary for Reich Administration (*Generalbevollmaechtigter fuer die Reichsverwaltung*) .... WILHELM FRICK

Biographical Data

Plenipotentiary for Economics (*Generalbevollmaechtigter fuer die Wirtschaft*) and Reich Finance Minister (*Reichsminister der Finanzen*) ..... WALTER FUNK

Reich Minister of Foreign Affairs (*Reichsminister des Auswaertigen*).. JOACHIM von RIBBENTROP

Reich Minister of Interior (*Reichsminister des Innern*) .... WILHELM FRICK

Reich Minister for Propaganda (*Reichsminister fuer Volksaufklaerung und Propaganda*) .... PAUL JOSEF GOEBBELS

President of Reich Bank Directory (*Praesident des Reichsbankdirektoriums*) .... HJALMAR SCHACHT

REICH DEFENSE COMMITTEE
(*Reichsverteidigungsausschuss*) ...... KEITEL, GOERING, SCHACHT, FUNK, FRICK and Defense Officials (RD Referenten)

MINISTERIAL COUNCIL FOR DEFENSE OF THE REICH
(*Ministerrat fuer die Reichsverteidigung*)
Chairman .... HERMANN GOERING
Secretary .... HANS LAMMERS
Plenipotentiary for Reich Administration .... HEINRICH HIMMLER (predecessor, Wilhelm Frick)
Plenipotentiary for Economics ...... WALTER FUNK
Chief of OKW .... WILHELM KEITEL
Deputy of the Fuehrer .... RUDOLF HESS (followed by Head of the Party Chancery, Martin Bormann)

THREE-MAN COLLEGE (*Dreier-Kollegium*)
Plenipotentiary for (War) Economy.. WALTER FUNK (predecessor, Schacht)
Plenipotentiary for Administration... HEINRICH HIMMLER (predecessor, Frick)

Chief of the OKW .... WILHELM KEITEL (predecessor, Minister of War—Blomberg)

OFFICE OF THE DELEGATE FOR THE FOUR YEAR PLAN
(*Beauftragter fuer den Vierjahresplan*)
Delegate (*Beauftragter*) .... HERMANN GOERING
State Secretary and Permanent Deputy PAUL KOERNER
Plenipotentiaries-General (*Generalbevollmaechtigte*):
  Control of Building .... ALBERT SPEER
  Special Chemical Production ...... CARL KRAUCH
  Economics in Serbia .... FRANZ NEUHAUSEN
  Metal Mining in the Southeast.... FRANZ NEUHAUSEN
  Armaments .... ALBERT SPEER
  Manpower .... FRITZ SAUCKEL

III - 595

OCCUPIED TERRITORIES (Administrators directly responsible to Hitler)
Reich Commissioners:
    Netherlands (*Reichskommissar fuer die besetzten niederlaendischen Gebiete*) Reich Commissioner ... ARTHUR SEYSS-INQUART
    Norway (*Reichskommissar fuer die besetzten norwegischen Gebiete*) Reich Commissioner .... JOSEF TERBOVEN
    Ostland (*Reichskommissar fuer das Ostland*) .... HINRICH LOHSE
    Ukraine (*Reichskommissar fuer die Ukraine*) .... ERICH KOCH
    Protectorate of Bohemia and Moravia (*Reichsprotektorat Boehmen und Maehren*) (Czechoslovakia)
        Reich Protector .... WILHELM FRICK (predecessor, Constantin von Neurath)
        State Minister .... KARL HERMANN FRANK
    General Government (*General gouvernement*) (Poland)
        Governor-General .... HANS FRANK
Chiefs of Civil Administration:
    Alsace—Chief of Civil Administration (*Chef der Zivilverwaltung im Elsass*) .... ROBERT WAGNER
    Bialystok—Chief of Civil Administration (*Chef der Zivilverwaltung in Bezirk Bialystok*) .... ERICH KOCH
    Carinthia and Carniola—Chief of Civil Administration (*Chef der Zivilverwaltung in den besetzten Gebieten Kaerntens und Krains*) .... FRIEDRICH RAINER
    Lorraine—Chief of Civil Administration (*Chef der Zivilverwaltung in Lothringen*) .... WILHELM STOEHR (predecessor, Josef Buerckel)
    Lower Styria—Chief of Civil Administration (*Chef der Zivilverwaltung in der Untersteiermark*) .... SIEGFRIED UIBERREITHER
    Luxembourg—Chief of Civil Administration (*Chef der Zivilverwaltung in Luxemberg*) .... GUSTAV SIMON
Military Administration:
    Denmark:
        Military Commander .... GEORG LINDEMANN (predecessor, Hermann von Hanneken)
        Plenipotentiary .... WERNER BEST
    France:
        Military Commander .... STUELPNAGEL
        Chief of Administration .... SCHMIDT
        Diplomatic Representative .... OTTO ABETZ

THE REICHSTAG:
    President .... HERMANN GOERING
    Vice-President .... HERMANN ESSER
    Head of Administration (*Ministerialdirigent*) .... KIENAST

Biographical Data

POLICE:

Reich Leader of SS and Chief of German Police (*Reichsfuehrer SS und Chef der Deutschen Polizei*) .... HEINRICH HIMMLER

Chief of the Order Police (*Chef der Ordnungspolizei*) .... WUENNENBERG (predecessor, Kurt Daluege)

Chief of Security Police and SD (*Chef der Sicherheitspolizei und SD*) .... ERNST KALTENBRUNNER (predecessor, Reinhardt Heydrich)

Reich Main Security Office (*Reichssicherheitshauptamt*):
Chief .... ERNST KALTENBRUNNER (predecessor, Reinhardt Heydrich)
Chief of Personnel (Dept. I) ...... ERWIN SCHULZ
Chief of Organization, Administration, and Law (Dept. II) .... HAENEL (predecessor, Siegert)
Chief of Security Service (SD) (Dept. III) .... OTTO OHLENDORF
Chief of Secret State Police (Gestapo) (Dept. IV) .... HEINRICH MUELLER
Chief of Criminal Police (Kripo) (Dept. V) .... PANZINGER (predecessor, Nebe)
Chief of Security Service (SD) Occupied Territories (Dept. VI) ... WALTER SCHELLENBERG
Chief of Ideological Research (Dept. VII) .... DITTEL (predecessor, Six)
Military Office .... WALTER SCHELLENBERG

2. PRINCIPAL OFFICIALS OF THE NAZI PARTY

Leader of the Party (*Fuehrer*) .... ADOLF HITLER
Deputy of the Fuehrer (*Stellvertreter des Fuehrers*) .... RUDOLF HESS (until 1941)
Chief of the Party Chancery and Secretary of the Fuehrer (*Leiter der Partei Kanzlei und Sekretaer des Fuehrers*) . MARTIN BORMANN
Chancery of the Fuehrer (*Kanzlei des Fuehrers*):
Head .... PHILIPP BOUHLER
Chancery of the Party (*Kanzlei der Partei*)
Head .... MARTIN BORMANN
Deputy Head .... HELMUT FRIEDRICHS
Heads of Divisions:
Internal Party Affairs .... HELMUT FRIEDRICHS
Constitutional Law .... GERHARD KLOEPFER
Finance .... KARL WINKLER
Personnel .... WALKENHORST
Reich Party Directorate (*Reichsleitung*):
Chancery of Fuehrer and Party Censorship .... PHILIPP BOUHLER
Chancery of the Party .... MARTIN BORMANN
Colonial Policy .... FRANZ RITTER von EPP
Ideology and Foreign Policy .... ALFRED ROSENBERG
Legal Office .... HANS FRANK (until 1942)
Municipal Policy .... KARL FIEHLER
Nazi Reichstag Delegation .... WILHELM FRICK
Organization and Labor Front....... ROBERT LEY
Party Tribunal .... WALTER BUCH
Peasantry .... WALTER DARRE (on leave, Herbert Backe, acting)

Press Control (political)............ OTTO DIETRICH
Press Control (economic) .... MAX AMANN
Propaganda .... PAUL JOSEF GOEBBELS
Reich Labor Service .... KONSTANTIN HIERL
SS and Germanization .... HEINRICH HIMMLER
Treasury .... FRANZ XAVER SCHWARZ
Youth Education .... BALDUR von SCHIRACH
Heads of Party Formations
  Elite Guard (SS) .... HEINRICH HIMMLER
  Storm Troops (SA)................ WILHELM SCHEPMANN (predecessors, Victor Lutze, Ernst Roehm)

  NS Motor Corps (NSKK) .... ERWIN KRAUS

  Hitler Youth (HJ) ....ARTHUR AXMANN (predecessor, Baldur von Schirach)

  NS Flying Corps (NSFK) (with status similar to that of a formation)..... ALFRED KELLER

  NS German Student League (NSDSB) GUSTAV-ADOLF SCHEEL
  NS University Teachers League (NSDoB) .... GUSTAV-ADOLF SCHEEL
  NS Women's League (NSF) .... GERTRUD SCHOLTZ-KLINK

3. HEADS OF THE ARMED FORCES

Supreme Commander (*Oberster Befehlshaber der Wehrmacht*) .... ADOLF HITLER

Highest ranking officer (Rangaeltester Offizier) .... HERMANN WILHELM GOERING (Reichsmarschall)

C. in C. Army (*Oberbefehlshaber des Heeres*) .... ADOLF HITLER (precedessors, Walter von Brauchitsch, Werner von Fritsch)

C. in C. Navy (*Oberbefehlshaber der Kriegsmarine*) .... KARL DOENITZ (predecessor, Erich Raeder)

C. in C. Air Force (*Oberbefehlshaber der Luftwaffe*) .... HERMANN WILHELM GOERING (succeeded in 1945 by Robert von Greim)

  A. HIGH COMMAND OF THE ARMED FORCES (*Oberkommando der Wehrmacht*: OKW)
Chief of High Command (*Chef des Oberkommandos der Wehrmacht*) .... WILHELM KEITEL

Chief of Operation Staff (*Chef des Wehrmachtfuehrungsstabes*) .... ALFRED JODL

Deputy Chief .... WALTER WARLIMONT

  B. ARMY HIGH COMMAND (*Oberkommando des Heeres*, OKH)
C. in C. Army
  (*Oberbefehlshaber des Heeres*) ...... ADOLF HITLER (predecessors, Walter von Brauchitsch, Werner von Fritsch)

Biographical Data

Chief of Staff, Army (*Chef des Generalstabes des Heeres*) .... HANS KREBS (predecessors, Heinz Guderian, Kurt Zeitzler, Franz Halder and Ludwig Beck)
C. NAVY HIGH COMMAND (*Oberkommando der Kriegsmarine*: *OKM*)
C. in C. Navy (*Oberbefehlshaber der Kriegsmarine*) .... KARL DOENITZ (predecessor, Erich Raeder)
Admiralinspekteur .... ERICH RAEDER (after 1943)

4. INDEX OF INDIVIDUALS

ABETZ, OTTO
German Ambassador to the Petain Government.

AMANN, MAX
Reich Leader for the Press (Reichsleiter fuer die Presse); President of the Reich Press Chamber (Praesident der Reichspressekammer); Head of Central Publishing House of the Party (Zentral Verlag, Franz Eher Nachf).

ARNIM, JURGEN von
Generaloberst 1941-2; leading Panzer units in Russia, Jan. 1943; Commander in Tunis; surrendered May 1943.

AXMANN, ARTHUR
Reich Youth Leader (Reichsjugendfuehrer) since 1940.

BACH-ZELEWSKI, ERICH, von dem
General of Police and of Waffen-SS; Chief of Anti-Partisan Units on the entire Eastern front, 1943-44; in charge of the defense of Warsaw until it was liberated; commander of a Waffen-SS Corps on the Western front.

BACKE, HERBERT
Acting Reichsminister for Food; in charge of Ministry of Food and Agriculture; Head of Reichsnaehrstand.

BERGER, GOTTLIEB
Chief of Central Office of SS; SS-Obergruppenfuehrer; General d. Waffen-SS; Inspector-General of Prisoners of War; Head of Policy Division of Reich Ministry for Eastern Territories.

BEST, DR. WERNER KARL
German Plenipotentiary in Denmark, formerly chief of the legal office of the Gestapo.

BLASKOWITZ, JOHANNES
Generaloberst.

BLOMBERG, WERNER EDWARD FRITZ von
Generalfeldmarschall; Minister of War until Feb. 4, 1938.

BOCK, FEDOR von
Generalfeldmarschall.

BODENSCHATZ, KARL HEINRICH
General in Air Corps; Chief of Staff to Goering.

BOHLE, ERNST WILHELM
Staatssekretaer in Foreign Office; Gauleiter, Head of Foreign Organization (AO) of NSDAP.

BORMANN, MARTIN
Secretary of the Fuehrer; Head of the Party Chancery; Member of Cabinet vested with power of Reich Minister; Ministerial Council for Defense of the Reich; Reichsleiter; Executive Head of the Volkssturm; member of the Reichstag; SS Gruppenfuehrer.

BOUHLER, PHILIPP
Chief of the Chancery of the Fuehrer; Reichsleiter; Chief of the Party Censorship Committee for the Protection of NS Literature; Chief of the Study Group for the German History Book and Educational Material.

BRAEUTIGAM
First assistant to Leibbrandt, who was in charge of Main Division 2 of the Ministry for the Occupied Eastern Territories concerned with political affairs.

III - 599

BRANDT, DR. KARL
Reich Commissioner for Health and Medical Services; SS Standartenfuehrer.
BRAUCHITSCH, WALTER HEINRICH HERMANN ALFRED von
Generalfeldmarschall, retired December 1941; formerly C. in C. Army (OKH).
BRUEGMANN, DR. ARNOLD
Chief of the Archives of the Party; Divisional Head in the Reichsstudentenfuehrung.
BUCH, WALTER
Reichsleiter; Supreme Party Judge; Advisor on Population and Racial Policy; SS Obergruppenfuehrer.
BUMKE, DR. ERWIN
President of the Supreme Court, Leipzig.
BURGDORFF, WILHELM
General d. Infanterie; Head of Personnel Division, OKH; Chief Military ADC. to Hitler.
BUSCH, ERNST
Generalfeldmarschall.
CANARIS, WILHELM
Admiral; Head of Intelligence in OKW (Abwehr); removed from post and executed.
CONTI, DR. LEONARDO
Staatssekretaer and Chief of Health Divisions (Abteilungen III & IV), Reich Ministry of the Interior; Head of Public Health Department of Party Reichsleitung.
DALUEGE, KURT
Chef der Ordnungspolizei; (Deputy) Reich Protector of Bohemia-Moravia; Generaloberst d. Polizei; SS-Oberstgruppenfuehrer.
DARRE, WALTER RICHARD OSKAR
Reichsleiter; Reichsbauernfuehrer; Reich Minister for Food and Agriculture; Head of Reichsnaehrstand; on leave since April 1942.
DIETRICH, DR. OTTO
Staatssekretaer; Chief of Press Divisions in Reich Ministry of Propaganda; Press Chief of Reichsregierung; Reichsleiter; Reich Press Chief of NSDAP.
DITTMAR, KURT
Generalleutnant; in Propaganda Division of the OKH; broadcaster of weekly military commentaries.
DOENITZ, KARL
Grossadmiral and C. in C. of OKM after 1943; previously C. in C. of Submarine Arm of German Navy; Head of Government formed in May 1945.
DORPMUELLER, DR. JULIUS*
Reich and Prussian Minister of Transport; Director-General of German State Railways.
DORSCH, XAVER FRANZ
Ministerialdirektor in Reich Ministry for Armaments and War Production; Head of Field Command in Organization Todt.
EICHMANN, ADOLF
Head of Dept. IV A4 of RSHA, and Chief of Sub-section "b" thereof charged with "The Solution of the Jewish Question".
EPP, FRANZ RITTER von
Reichsleiter; Reichsstatthalter Bayern; SA-Obergruppenfuehrer; Head of Colonial Policy Office of Party; General der Infanterie.
ESSER, HERMANN
Staatssekretaer and Head of Tourists Division in Reich Propaganda Ministry; Praesident of "Reich Group Tourist Traffic" (Fremdenverkehr); Vice-President of the Reichstag; State Minister (retd).

Biographical Data

FALKENHAUSEN, ALEXANDER von
Generaloberst—Commander of Belgium and Northern France.

FALKENHORST, NIKOLAUS von
Generaloberst—Commander in Norway.

FIEHLER, KARL
Reichsleiter; Chief of the Party Department for Municipal Policy; SS-Obergruppenfuehrer; Chairman of the Congress of German Municipalities; Oberbuergermeister Muenchen; Member of the Academy for German Law.

FISCHER, ERICH
Head of Home Press Division in the Reich Propaganda Ministry; Head of office for "German Press" in the Press Department of the Government; Head of Political Press section with Reichspressechef (RL).

FISCHER, HUGO
Head of Culture and Exhibitions sections in Reich Propaganda Department of RL.

FOSTER, ALBERT
Gauleiter, Reichsstatthalter and Reichsverteidigungskommissar Danzig-Westpreussen.

FRANK, DR. HANS
Governor-General of Poland; Reichsleiter until 1942; Reich Minister without portfolio; SS-Obergruppenfuehrer; President of the International Chamber of Law (1941-42) and of Academy of German Law; Member of the Reichstag; Leader of National Socialist Lawyers Bund (1933-1942).

FRANK, KARL-HERMANN
German Minister of State with rank of Reich Minister; Hoeherer SS und Polizeifuehrer "Protectorate" and Sudetenland.

FREISLER, DR. ROLAND
President of the People's Court; Prussian State Councillor; Member of the Academy of German Law.

FRICK, WILHELM
Minister of Interior (1933-1943); Reichsprotector of Bohemia and Moravia; Reichsdirektor of Elections (1933-1943); SS-Obergruppenfuehrer; Reichsleiter; Head of Nazi Reichstag Delegation; Member of Reich Defense Council; General Plenipotentiary for the Administration of the Reich (1935-1943); Reichsminister without Portfolio (1943-1945).

FRIEDRICHS, DR. HELMUT
Head of Section for Internal Party affairs in and deputy head of Chancellery of the Party.

FRITZSCHE, HANS
Ministerialdirektor, Reich Ministry of Propaganda; Plenipotentiary for the Political Supervision of Broadcasting in Greater Germany; Head of Broadcasting Division in Propaganda Ministry.

FUNK, DR. WALTER
Reich Minister of Economics; Member of the Ministerial Council for Defense of the Reich; Plenipotentiary for Economics; President of the Reichsbank; Vice-President of the Reich Chamber of Culture; formerly Chief of Press of the Reich Government (1933-1937); member of Reichstag (1932-1933); and State Secretary in the Ministry for Public Enlightenment and Propaganda (1933-1937).

GLAISE-HORSTENAU, DR. h. c. EDMUND von
General der Infanterie; SA-Gruppenfuehrer; Minister in Seyss-Inquart Cabinet; German General Plenipotentiary in Austria in 1944.

GLUECKS, RICHARD
Chief of "Amtsgruppe D" in the Economic and Administrative Main Office (Wirtschafts- and Verwaltungshauptamt) of SS; Commander of Concentration Camps; SS-Gruppenfuerer; General-leutnant d. Waffen-SS.

GOEBBELS, DR. PAUL JOSEF
Reich Minister of Public Enlightenment and Propaganda; Member of the Secret Cabinet Council; Chairman of the Interministerial Committee on Air-Raid Damage; Reichspropagandaleiter of the NSDAP; Reichsleiter; President of the Reich Chamber of Culture; Stadtpraesident, Gauleiter, Reichsverteidigungskommissar of Berlin; Reich Plenipotentiary for Total War Effort.

GOERING, HERMANN WILHELM
Successor designate No. 1 to Hitler; Reich Minister for Air; President of the Ministerial Council for the Defense of the Reich; member of the Secret Cabinet Council; Reich Forest Master; Commander-in-Chief of the Air Force; Prime Minister of Prussia; President of the Prussian State Council; President of the Reichstag; Plenipotentiary for the Four Year Plan; Head of the "Reichswerke Hermann Goering"; Reichsmarschall; SS-Obergruppenfuehrer; SA-Obergruppenfuehrer.

GREIM, ROBERT RITTER v.
Generaloberst, C.-in-C. of the Air Force (OKL) 1945.

GROSS, DR. WALTER
Head of Racial Policy Department of the Party; high official in the Chancery of the Party; Hauptdienstleiter; Head of the Science Division in Ideology Department (Amt Rosenberg).

GUDERIAN, HEINZ
Generaloberst, Chief of Staff of the Army (OKH).

GUENTHER, DR. HANS K. F.
Professor of Racial Science at Jena.

HAENEL
Head of Amt II, Reich Main Security Office; SS-Obersturmbannfuehrer.

HALDER, FRANZ
Colonel-General; Chief of Staff of OKH (until summer 1942).

HANNEKEN, HERMANN von
General der Infanterie; Military Commander in Denmark until 1945.

HAUSHOEFER, DR. KARL
Professor; Generalmajor (retd); President of Society for Geopolitics; Publisher of periodical "Die Geopolitik."

HENLEIN, KONRAD
Gauleiter and Reichsstatthalter Sudetenland; SS-Obergruppenfuehrer; member of the Reichstag.

HESS, RUDOLF
Successor Designate No. 2 of the Fuehrer; Deputy of the Fuehrer for all Party affairs; Reich Minister; member of the Reichstag until 1941.

HEYDRICH, REINHARDT
Formerly SS-Obergruppenfuehrer and Chief of the RSHA.

HIERL, KONSTANTIN
Reichsleiter; Reichsarbeitsfuehrer; Reichsminister; member of the Reichstag; Generalmajor.

HIMMLER, HEINRICH
Reichsfuehrer SS und Chef der Deutschen Polizei; Reich Commissar for the Strengthening of German Folkdom; Reich Minister of the Interior; Reichsleiter; Chief of the Replacement Army; Military Chief of the Volkssturm.

HITLER, ADOLF
Fuehrer u. Reichskanzler; Fuehrer of NS Party and Movement; Commander-in-Chief of the Wehrmacht; Commander-in-Chief of Army; Chief of Cabinet; Chief of Reich Defense Council; Chief of SA.

HOSSBACH, FRIEDRICH
General der Infanterie.

Biographical Data

JODL, ALFRED
Colonel-General (1944); Chief of Operation Staff of High Command of OKW (1939-1945).

JUETTNER, HANS
Head of SS Operational Main Office and Command of the Combat SS; Permanent Deputy to Himmler as Commander of the Replacement Army; SS-Obergruppenfuehrer; General d. Waffen-SS.

JUETTNER, MAX
Chief of SA Command and Permanent Deputy of the Chief of Staff; Chief of Mounted SA; SA-Obergruppenfuehrer; Member of the Reichstag.

KALTENBRUNNER, DR. ERNST
Chief of Security Police and Security Service; Chef des Reichssicherheitshauptamtes (Reich Security Main Office); Member of the Reichstag; SS-Obergruppenfuehrer; General der Polizei.

KEITEL, WILHELM
Generalfeldmarschall; Chief of the High Command of the Armed Forces (OKW); Member of Cabinet with rank of Reichsminister; Member of Secret Cabinet Council; Member of Ministerial Council for Defense of the Reich; Member of Reich Defense Council.

KESSELRING, ALBERT
Generalfeldmarschall; C.-in-C. South West and Army Group C.

KITZINGER, KARL
General der Flieger.

KLAGGES, DIETRICH
Ministerpraesident, Minister of the Interior, of Finance and of Education, in Braunschweig; SS-Obergruppenfuehrer.

KLEIST, EWALD von
Generalfeldmarschall.

KLOPPER, DR. GERHARD
Ministerialdirektor; Staatssekretaer and Expert for Government Affairs in Party Chancery; Oberdienstleiter; SS-Gruppenfuehrer.

KOCH, ERICH
Oberpraesident and Gauleiter of Ostpreussen; Reich Defense Commissioner for Wehrkreis I; SS-Gruppenfuehrer; Reich Commissioner of Ukraine, Bialystak.

KOERNER, PAUL
Staatssekretaer to the Plenipotentiary for the Four Year Plan (Goering); Prussian State Councillor; Chairman, Board of Directors, Hermann Goering Werke Saltzgitter; SS-Obergruppenfuehrer.

KRAUCH, DR. KARL
Plenipotentiary of the Board of the Four Year Plan for questions of chemical production; acting head of the Department for Expansion of Economic Life (Wirtschaftsaufbau); Chairman, board of directors, I. G. Farben; Wehrwirtschaftsfuehrer.

KRAUS, ERWIN
Commander-in-Chief of the NSKK; Inspector for Motor Training in the Volkssturm; Member of the Reichstag; Plenipotentiary for Motor Transport in War Industry (under the Four Year Plan).

KREBS, HANS
General der Infanterie; Chief of Staff of OKH.

KRUPP von BOHLEN und HALBACH, ALFRED
President of Friedrich Krupp Company, took over sole ownership in 1943; Deputy Chairman of the Board of Directors of the Reichsvereinigung Eisen; joined NSDAP in 1936.

KRUPP von BOHLEN und HALBACH, GUSTAV
Chairman of Board of the Friedrich Krupp A.G.; Pioneer of Labor; awarded Party's Golden Honor Badge and the Eagle Shield of the Reich.

III - 603

LAHOUSEN, ERWIN
Generalmajor; Assistant to Admiral Canaris, Head of Intelligence Section OKW (Abwehr); became Chief of Abwehr Section II in 1939.

LAMMERS, DR. HANS HEINRICH
Reichsminister; Chief of the Reich Chancery; SS-Obergruppenfuehrer; Member of and Secretary to the Secret Cabinet and the Ministerrat fuer die Reichsverteidigung; Preussischer Staatsrat; member of the Academy of German Law.

LANGE, DR. KURT
Commissioner for Currency, Banking, Insurance in Reich Ministry of Economics; Vice-President of Reichsbank; Deputy President of Deutsche Gold Discount Bank; NSFK-Brigadefuehrer.

LEY, ROBERT
Reichsleiter; Chief, Party Organization; Leader of the German Labor Front; Reich Housing Commissioner; SA-Gruppenfuehrer.

LIEBBRANDT
In charge of Main Division 2 of the Ministry for the Occupied Eastern Territories concerned with political affairs.

LINDEMANN, GEORG
Generaloberst; C.-in-C. Denmark beginning of 1945.

LINDEMANN, KARL
President of the Reich Chamber of Commerce; Stattsrat; Chairman Board of Directors, Atlas Werke AG. and Norddeutscher Lloyd.

LOEHR, ALEXANDER
Generaloberst der Luftwaffe; C.-in-C. of an Army Group in the South East.

LOHSE, HINRICH
Fauleiter, Oberpraesident, and Reich Defense Commissioner Schleswig-Holstein; Reich Commissioner "Ostland"; SA-Obergruppenfuehrer; Praesident of the Nordic Society.

LUETZOW, FRIEDRICH von
Vice-admiral; Radio Commentator on Naval matters.

MACKENSEN, EBERHARD von
Generaloberst.

MANSTEIN, FRITZ, ERICH von LEWINSKY
Generalfeldmarschall, Army Group South (early 43-April 44).

MEISSNER, DR. OTTO LEBRECHT
Staatsminister; Chef der Praesidialkanzlei, curator of Political Academy (Berlin); president of Italo-German Society; member of the Academy of German Law.

MEYSSNER, AUGUST
Hoeherer SS and Polizeifuehrer Serbia; SS-Obergruppenfuehrer; Generalleutnant der Polizei; member of People's Tribunal.

MILCH, ERHARD
Generalfeldmarschall; Staatssekretaer and permanent deputy to the Reich Minister of Air; Inspector General of the Air Force; member of the Armaments' Council.

MODEL, WALTER
Generalfeldmarschall; G. in C. of an Army Group in the West.

MUELLER, HEINRICH
Head of Amt IV (Gestapo), Reichssicherheitshauptamt (RSHA); SS-Gruppenfuehrer; Generalleutnant der Polizei.

MUSSERT, ANTON
Founder of Dutch Nazi Party in 1931; in December 1942 received the title of "Leader of the Dutch people" from Hitler.

Biographical Data

NEUHAUSEN, DR. FRANZ
General Plenipotentiary for Economics in Serbia (under the Four Year Plan); Consul-General; Chairman of the Board of the Yugoslav Bank; Head of Military Administration in the South East.

NEURATH, CONSTANTIN H. K. FRIEHERR von
Reichsminister without Portfolio (formerly Reichsminister of Foreign Affairs 1932, 1933, 1938); President of the Secret Cabinet Council; Member of Reich Defense Council; Reich Protector for Bohemia and Moravia, 1939-1943.

OHLENDORF, OTTO
Head of Amt III, SD (Security Service) of Reich Main Security Office; permanent deputy to the Staatssekretaer Reich Ministry of Economics; SS-Gruppenfuehrer; Generalleutnant d. Polizei.

OHNESORGE, DR. WILHELM
Reich Post Minister.

PAPEN, FRANZ von
Vice-chancellor and member of Cabinet (Feb. 1933-July 1934); Commissar for Saar District Plebiscite; Minister to Austria; Ambassador with special mission 1936-1938; Ambassador at large; Ambassador to Turkey after 1939.

PAULUS, FRIEDRICH
Generalfeldmarschall, captured at Stalingrad.

PEUCKERT, RUDI
Head of Labor Division, Reich Ministry of Occupied Eastern Territories; in charge of Agricultural Manpower under the Plenipotentiary for Manpower.

PFEIFFER, HANS
Personal Adjutant to the Fuehrer; SS-Hauptsturmfuehrer.

POHL, OSWALD
Chief of Administration and Economic Main Office of SS; Ministerialdirektor Reich Ministry of the Interior; SS-Obergruppenfuehrer; General der Waffen SS.

RAEDER, ERICH, DR. h. c.
Grossadmiral and Chief of OKM until 1943; thereafter Admiralinspecteur of German Navy; wearer of Golden Party Badge of Honor; Member of Cabinet with rank of Reichsminister; Member of Secret Cabinet Council.

RASCHER, DR. SIGMUND
Hauptsturmfuehrer in the Air Forces, later transferred to the SS; in charge of experiments on human beings at Dachau Concentration Camp.

RAINER, DR. FRIEDRICH
Reichsstatthalter, Gauleiter and Reichsverteidigungskommissar of Kaernten; Head of Zivilverwaltung, North-West Yugoslavia; Supreme Commissioner "Adriatisches Kuestengebiet"; SS-Obergruppenfuehrer.

REINECKE, HERMANN
General der Infanterie; Chief of the General Department of OKW (Allgemeines Wehrmachtamt); Chief of the NS Political Guidance Staff OKW; honorary member of the Special Senate of the People's Tribunal.

REINHARDT, FRITZ
Staatssekretaer and Head of Abteilung V, Reich Ministry of Finance, Berlin; expert on Labor Problems, Finance and Taxation in the Party Chancery; SA-Obergruppenfuehrer; Member of Reichstag; Hauptdienst-leiter of Party.

REINHARDT, GEORG HANS
Generaloberst.

RIBBENTROP, JOACHIM von
Minister for Foreign Affairs (1938-1945); Ambassador to Great Britain (1936-1938); Ambassador at Large (1935-1938); Special Delegate for Disarmament Questions (1934-1937); Member of the Secret Cabinet Council; Member of the Fuehrer's Political Staff at General Headquarters (1942-1945); Member of Reichstag; SS-Obergruppenfuehrer.

III - 605

RICHTHOFEN, WOLFRAM, Frhr. von
   Generalfeldmarschall.
RIECKE, HANS-JOACHIM
   Head of Food and Agriculture Division, Reich Ministry of Occupied Eastern Territories; Staatssekretaer in Reich Ministry of Food and Agriculture; SA-Gruppenfuehrer.
RINTELEN, EMIL von
   Minister (Gesandter) (for special duties); deputy head of the political division, Foreign Office.
ROEHM, ERNST
   Reichsminister, Staatskommissar, Staatssekretaer, Staatsrat, Stabs chef der SA; Shot June 30, 1934 for alleged conspiracy.
ROSENBERG, ALFRED
   Reich Minister for the Occupied Eastern Territories; Reichsleiter; head of RL Departments for Foreign Policy and for Ideology; chief of Einsatzstab Rosenberg, Special Staff for seizing Jewish property, libraries, and art treasures; SS-Obergruppenfuehrer; SA-Obergruppenfuehrer.
RUNDSTEDT, KARL RUDOLF GERD von
   Generalfeldmarschall.
RUST, DR. BERNHARD
   Reich Prussian Minister of Science and Education; SA-Obergruppenfuehrer.
SAUCKEL, FRITZ
   Reichsstatthalter, Reich Defense Commissioner and Gauleiter of Thuringia; Plenipotentiary-general for Manpower (Four Year Plan); SS-Obergruppenfuehrer; SA-Obergruppenfuehrer; member of Reichstag.
SCHACHT, HJALMAR
   Reich Minister without portfolio until 1943; formerly Minister of Economics, President of the Reichsbank, and General Plenipotentiary for the War Economy.
SCHELLENBERG, WALTER
   Chief of Security Service, Occupied Territories (Amt VI) in Reich Main Security Office; Chief of Military Office RSHA; SS-Brigadefuehrer.
SCHIRACH, BALDUR von
   Reichsleiter for Youth Education; Reichsleiter; Reich Defence Commissioner; Reichstatthalter; Mayor and Gauleiter of Vienna; Member of Reichstag; SA-Obergruppenfuehrer; Leader of Hitler Jugend, and Leader of Youth in the German Reich.
SCHMIDT, DR. PAUL (II)
   Chief of the Bureau of the Reich Foreign Minister with the rank of Gesandter; Ministerialdirigent; attached to Foreign Office, acted as Hitler's personal interpreter in all diplomatic negotiations.
SCHMUNDT
   Chief of Army Personnel Dept., Generalleutnant, later Hitler's adjutant.
SCHULZ, ERWIN
   Head of Amt I (Personnel) of Reich Main Security Office (Reichssicherheitshauptamt); SS-Brigadefuehrer.
SCHWARZ, XAVER FRANZ
   Reich Treasurer of the Party; Reichsleiter; SS-Obergruppenfuehrer; SA-Obergruppenfuehrer.
SCHWERIN von KROSIGK, LUTZ GRAF
   Reich Minister of Finance; Reich Minister for Foreign Affairs (since May 1945).
SELDTE, FRANZ
   Reich Labour Minister; Labour Minister for Prussia; SA-Obergruppenfuehrer.
SEYSS-INQUART, DR. ARTUR
   Reich Commissioner for the Occupied Netherlands; Reich Minister without portfolio; SS-Obergruppenfuehrer; member of the Reichstag; Minister in Austrian Cabinet.

Biographical Data

SIMON, GUSTAV
  Chief of Civil Administration, Luxembourg; Reichsstatthalter, Reichsverteidigungskommissar and Gauleiter of Moselland.

SPEER, ALBERT
  Reichleiter; Reichsminister for Armaments and War Production; Head of the Organisation Todt; General Plenipotentiary for Armaments in the Four Year Plan; head of Armaments Office of German High Command; member of Reichstag; member of Central Planning Board; wearer of Golden Badge of Honor of Party.

SPERRLE, HUGO
  Generalfeldmarschall, Third Air Fleet.

STOEHR, WILHELM
  Reichsstatthalter and Gauleiter, Westmark.

STRASSER, GREGOR
  Leader of Storm Troops (SA) in Lower Bavaria; Reich Organization Leader until 1932; executed on June 30, 1934.

STREICHER, JULIUS
  Gauleiter of Franconia; Editor and Publisher of *Der Stuermer;* SA-General; member of Reichstag.

STUCKART, DR. WILHELM
  Leading Staatssekretaer in Reich Ministry of Interior Territories; Head of the Abteilung II in this ministry.

STUDENT, KURT
  Generaloberst; G. in C. of Army Group "H" on Western Front.

STUMPFF, HANS-JUERGEN
  Generaloberst; C.-in-C. of Air Fleet "Reich"; member of the People's Tribunal.

TERBOVEN, JOSEF
  Gauleiter Essen; Reich Commissioner for Occupied Norway; SS-Gruppenfuehrer.

THIERACK, DR. OTTO GEORG
  Reich Minister of Justice; SS-Brigadefuehrer; SA-Gruppenfuehrer; President of the Academy for German Law; Head of NS Lawyer's League.

THOMA, WILHELM RITTER von
  General der Panzertruppen.

THOMAS, GEORG
  General der Infanterie; Head of Economy and Armaments Division, OKW (until Oct. 1944); member of the Armaments Council.

TODT, FRITZ
  Reichsleiter; 1940 Reich Minister for Armaments and Munitions; killed in 1942 in crash.

UIBERREITHER, DR. SIEGFRIED
  Reichsstatthalter, Reichsverteidigungskommissar and Gauleiter of Steiermark; Head of Civil Administration in Untersteiermark.

UTIKAL
  Staff Official in Rosenberg's Ministry for Occupied Eastern Territories, Chief of Staff of "Einsatzstab Rosenberg".

VIETINGHOFF-SCHEEL, OTTO-HEINRICH von
  Generaloberst; C.-in-C. "South".

WAGNER, ROBERT
  Reichsstatthalter, Reichsverteidigungskommissar and Gauleiter of Baden; Chief of Civil Administration in Alsace.

WARLIMONT, WALTER
  General; Deputy Chief of Operations Staff of OKW.

WEICHS, MAXIMILIAN, Frhr. von
  Generalfeldmarschall, Commander in Chief, Southeast and Army Group F.

WIEDEMANN, FRITZ
German Consul General in Tientsin and San Francisco; formerly Adjutant to Hitler.

WEIZSAECKER, ERNST FREIHERR von
German Ambassador to the Holy See.

WINKLER, KARL
Manager of the Party Chancery.

WISLICENY, DIETER
Hauptsturmfuehrer in Slovakia; Specialist on Jewish matters in Slovakia with Amt IV A4, Reichssicherheitshauptamt (Reich Main Security Office) 1940-1944.

WOLFF, KARL
Supreme SS and Police commander in Italy; Commander of the Italian SS Legion; General of the Waffen-SS at the Fuehrer's Headquarters; chief of the personal staff of the Reichsfuehrung SS; SS-Obergruppenfuehrer.

ZEITZLER, KURT
Generaloberst.

GLOSSARY OF COMMON GERMAN AND NAZI TITLES, DESIGNATIONS AND TERMS, WITH THEIR OFFICIAL ABBREVIATIONS

Abbreviation	German	English
	A	
	Abschnitt	Regional unit of SS and SD (about divisional strength)
Abt.	*Abteilung*	Division
	Abteilung Deutsche Presse	German or Home Press Department
	Abwehr	Intelligence and counter-intelligence department of OKH
ADtsch R.	*Akademie fuer Deutsches Recht*	Academy for German Law
	Amt	Office
AG	*Aktien-Gesellschaft*	Joint Stock Company
	Amtsgericht	Local Court
	Angriffskrieg	War of Aggression
	Anklagebehoerde	Office of Public Prosecutor
	Ausland	The world outside the borders of the Reich
AO	*Auslands-Organisation*	Foreign Organization of the NSDAP
	Auslandsdeutsche	German citizens residing outside Germany
APA	*Aussenpolitisches Amt*	NSDAP Bureau for Foreign Affairs
aD	*ausser Dienst*	Retired
AA	*Auswaertiges Amt*	Ministry for Foreign Affairs

Glossary

Abbreviation	German	English

B

	Beauftragter	Commissioner, delegate
BdF	*Beauftragter des Fuehrers fuer die Ueberwachung der gesamten geistigen und weltanschaulichen Schulung und Erziehung der NSDAP*	Delegate of the Fuehrer for the Total Supervision of Intellectual and Ideological Training and Education of the Party (Rosenberg)
	Beauftragter fuer den Vierjahresplan	Delegate for the Four Year Plan (Goering)
BdO	*Befehlshaber der Ordnungspolizei*	Commander of the Order Police
BdS	*Befehlshaber der Sicherheitspolizei*	Commander of the Security Police
	Befehlsleiter	Rank in Party Administration
	Bereichsleiter	Rank in Party Administration
Bev	*Bevollmaechtigter*	Plenipotentiary
	Bewegung	The movement, i.e., the Nazi Party, including Party formations, affiliated and supervised organizations
	Block	Smallest unit of the Nazi Party, including several houses
	Blockleiter	NSDAP leader of a block
	Botschafter	Ambassador
BDM	*Bund Deutscher Maedel*	German Girls' League (female Hitler Youth)
BGB	*Buergerliches Gesetzbuch*	German Civil Code

C

Ch	*Chef*	Chief, head, commander, superior
	Chef der Zivilverwaltung	Head of civil administration (e..g of an annexed area)
	Chefsache	Classified document for general officer only

D

DAF	*Deutsche Arbeitsfront*	German Labor Front
DFW	*Deutsches Frauenwerk*	German Woman's Organization (sub-organization of the NSF)
DGT	*Deutscher Gemeindetag*	German Municipal Congress
DHD	*Deutscher Handelsdienst*	German Commercial Service (News Agency)

III - 609

Abbreviation	German	English

DNB......... *Deutsches Nachrichten-*
              buero .... Official German News Agency
              Dienstleiter .... Rank in Party administration
              Drang nach Osten...... Drive to the East
              Dreierkollegium .... The College of Three (the two Plenipotentiaries for War Economy and Administration, and the Chief of the OKW)
DPK......... *Deutsche diplomatisch-politische Korrespondenz* .... German Diplomatic and Political Correspondence (News Letter of the Foreign Office)
DRK.........*Deutsches Rotes Kreuz*.. German Red Cross

E

eh............. *ehrenhalber* .... Honorary
              Einsatzgruppe .... Special (Gestapo and SD) formation used for special purposes, e.g., executing Nazi race policy, policing and raiding occupied areas
              Einsatzstab .... Special Purpose Staff
              Einsatzstab Rosenberg .. Rosenberg's staff for seizing Jewish property, libraries, and art treasures
EK...........*Eisernes Kreuz* .... Iron Cross

F

              Freikorps .... Illegal terrorist military formations of former officers and ex-servicemen in Germany after World War I
              Fuehrerbefehl .... Fuehrer Order
              Fuehrererlass .... Fuehrer Edict
              Fuehrerkorps .... Corps of political leaders of the NSDAP
              Fuehrerprinzip .... Leadership principle of the NSDAP
Fuest..........*Fuehrungsstab* .... Operational Staff
FdR..........*Fuer die Richtigkeit*.... True or accurate copy

G

              Gau .... Largest NSDAP unit; 42 in the Reich and one for all Party groups outside the Reich
              Gauamtsleiter .... Administrative head of the Party *Gauleitung*
              Gauleiter .... NSDAP leader of a *Gau*
              Gauleitung .... Center of Party administration in a *Gau*
              Gaurichter .... Judge in a *Gau* Party Court
              Gauschatzmeister ...... Treasurer of the Party *Gauleitung*
              Geheimer Kabinettsrat .. Secret Cabinet Council

Glossary

Abbreviation	German	English

GKos.......... Geheime Komman-
　　　　　　　dosache .... Top Secret (military classification)
　　　　　　　Geheime Reichssache ... Top Secret (civil classification)

Gestapo....... Geheime Staatspolizei .. Secret State Police. The political police system established in Prussia and extended throughout the Reich and the occupied territories
　　　　　　　Generalbeauftragter .... Commissioner-General
　　　　　　　Generalbevollmaechtigter Plenipotentiary-General

GBA.......... Generalbevoll-
　　　　　　　maechtigter fuer den
　　　　　　　Arbeitseinsatz .... Plenipotentiary-General for Labor Allocation (Sauckel)

　　　　　　　Generalbevollmaechtigter
　　　　　　　fuer die Kriegswirt-
　　　　　　　schaft .... Plenipotentiary-General for War Economy (Schacht)

　　　　　　　Generalbevollmaechtigter
　　　　　　　fuer die Reichsver-
　　　　　　　waltung .... Plenipotentiary-General for Administration (Frick-Himmler)

GG........... Generalgouvernement .. Government-General (Poland)
　　　　　　　Generalkommissar ..... Commissar-General

Genst......... Generalstab .... General Staff
　　　　　　　Gesandter .... Minister (diplomatic rank)

GmbH........ Gesellschaft mit
　　　　　　　beschraenkter Haftung Limited liability company
　　　　　　　Gleichschaltung .... The process of compulsory coordination of German organizations of all types to conform to the Nazi racial pattern and accept Party control

　　　　　　　Gliederungen der
　　　　　　　NSDAP .... Party Formations

H

　　　　　　　Hauptstelle .... Main Bureau
H. Gr......... Heeresgruppe .... Army Group
　　　　　　　Herausgeber .... Published of a Newspaper or Publishing Firm
　　　　　　　Herrenvolk .... Master race

HJ........... Hitlerjugend .... Hitler Youth
　　　　　　　Hohe Schule .... Center for Nazi ideological research
　　　　　　　Hoheitstraeger .... NSDAP bearer of sovereignty within a specific area of Party jurisdiction, i.e., a leader of a Gau, Kreis, Ortsgruppe, Zelle or Block

HSSPf........ Hoeherer SS-und
　　　　　　　Polizeifuehrer .... Higher SS—and Police Leader

III - 611

Abbreviation	German	English

I

IA		Operations officer or section; cf. G-3
IB		Supply officer or section; cf. G-1
IC		Intelligence officer or section; cf. G-2
iA	*im Auftrag*	By order of (above a signature)
iG	*im Generalstab*	Attached to the General Staff
iV	*in Vertretung*	Per (signature); acting for

K

KZ	*Konzentrationslager*	Concentration Camp
KdF	*Kraft durch Freude*	Strength through Joy (German Labor Front subsidiary)
	Kreis	Largest NSDAP subdivision of a *Gau*
	Kreisleiter	NSDAP leader of a *Kreis*
	Kriegsmarine	German Navy
Kripo	*Kriminalpolizei*	Criminal Police
	Kripo-Leitstelle	Regional Criminal Police office, directly under Reich Criminal Police authority
	Kripo-Stelle	Smaller than *Kripo-Leitstelle*, but also directly under Reich Criminal Police authority

L

	Land	One of the federal states of Germany (e.g., Prussia, Bavaria, Saxony, etc.)
	Landesgruppe	The Nazi Party organization in any country outside Germany
	Lebensraum	Living space
	Leiter der Parteikanzlei	Chief of the Party Chancellery (Bormann)
Lw	*Luftwaffe*	German Air Corps

M

Mil. Bef	*Militaerbefehlshaber*	Military Commander (commanding non-operational troops in occupied territories)
	Ministerrat fuer die Reichsverteidigung	Ministerial Council for the Defense of the Reich
	Ministerialdirektor	High Civil Servant (chief of a main section of a Ministry)
	Ministerialdirigent	High civil servant, ranking below *Ministerialdirektor*
	Ministerialrat	High civil servant, ranking below *Ministerialdirigent*
	Mit deutschem Gruss	With German salute (equivalent to *Heil Hitler*)
MdR	*Mitglied des Reichstags*	Member of the Reichstag

Glossary

Abbreviation	German	English

N

NS	Nationalsozialismus	National Socialism
NSBO	Nationalsozialistische Betriebszellen Organisation	National Socialist Factory Cells Organization
NSDAP	Nationalsozialistische Deutsche Arbeiterpartei	National Socialist German Workers' Party; Nazi Party
	Nationalsozialistischer Deutscher Studentbund	NS German Students' Bund
	Nationalsozialistischer Dozentenbund	NS University Teachers' Bund
NSFK	Nationalsozialistisches Fliegerkorps	NS Flying Corps
NSF	Nationalsozialistische Frauenschaft	NS Women's League
NSK	Nationalsozialistische Korrespondenz	NS Official News Letter
NSKK	Nationalsozialistischer Kraftfahrkorps	NS Motor Corps
	Nuernberger Gesetze	Nurnberg anti-Semitic laws

O

OB	Oberfehlshaber	Commander in Chief
ObKom	Oberkommando	High Command
OKL	Oberkommando der Luftwaffe	Air Force High Command
OKM	Oberkommando der Marine	Navy High Command
OKW	Oberkommando der Wehrmacht	Armed Forces High Command
OKH	Oberkommando des Heeres	Army High Command
OSAF	Oberste SA-Fuehrung	Supreme Command of the SA
ORPO	Ordnungspolizei	Order Police
OT	Organisation Todt	Labor Corps organized by Todt
	Ortsgruppe	Largest NSDAP subdivision of a *Kreis*
	Ortsgruppenleiter	NSDAP leader of an *Ortsgruppe*
	Ostland	Baltic countries and White Russia
	Ostmark	Austria

III - 613

Abbreviation	German	English

P

PPK	*Parteiamtliche Pruefungskommission zum Schutze des NS-Schriftums*	Official Party Examining Commission for the Protection of National Socialist Publications
Pg	*Parteigenosse*	Party Member (male)
Pgn	*Parteigenossin*	Party Member (female)
	Preussische Gesetzsammlung	Prussian Legal Gazette

R

	Ratsherr	Town Councillor
	Reichsamtsleiter	Head of a department in the Party Reichsleitung
RAD	*Reichsarbeitsdienst*	Reich Labor Service
RAM	*Reichsaussenminister*	Reich Foreign Minister
RDB	*Reichsbund der Deutschen Beamten*	German Civil Servants' League
	Reichsdeutsche	German citizens residing in Germany
RFSS	*Reichsfuehrer SS*	Reich Leader of the SS (Himmler)
RGBl	*Reichsgesetzblatt*	Reich Legal Gazette
	Reichshauptamtsleiter	Head of the central departments of the Party
	Reichsinnenminister	Minister of Interior (Frick, succeeded by Himmler)
RJF	*Reichsjugendfuehrung*	Reich Youth Leadership
	Reichskriegsminister	Reich War Minister
RKK	*Reichskulturkammer*	Reich Chamber of Culture
	Reichsleiter	Member of the Supreme Party Directorate, in general the top level leader of an NSDAP function
	Reichsleiter fuer die Jugenderziehung	Reich Leader of Youth Education (von Schirach)
	Reichsleiter des Reichsrechtsamtes	Head of the Legal Office of the Party (Hans Frank)
RL	*Reichsleitung*	Supreme Party Directorate
RM	*Reichsmark*	The mark; pre-war value about $.40
RMfdbO	*Reichsminister fuer die besetzten Ostgebiete*	Reich Minister for Occupied Eastern Territories (Rosenberg)

Glossary

Abbreviation	German	English
	Reichsministerium fuer Volksaufklaerung und Propaganda	Reich Ministry for Popular Enlightenment and Propaganda (Goebbels)
	Reichsnaehrstand	Reich Food Estate (compulsory association of all persons engaged in agriculture) (Backe)
	Reichsparteitag	Reich Party Rally (annual Nazi Congress at Nurnberg)
RPL	*Reichspropagandaleitung*	Party Propaganda Department
	Reichsregierung	Reich Cabinet
RRG	*Reichs-Rundfunkgessellschaft*	Reich Broadcasting Corporation
RSHA	*Reichssichterheitshauptamt*	Reich Main Security Office (Kaltenbrunner)
RT	*Reichstag*	Reich Parliament
	Reichstatthalter	Reich Governor (of a *Land* or *Reichsgau*)
RVR	*Reichsverteidigungsrat*	Reich Defense Council
	Reichswehr	The Germany Army of the Weimar Republic

S

	Schulungslager	A Party training camp for political indoctrination
SS	*Schutzstaffel*	Elite Guard of NSDAP (black shirts); personal bodyguard of the Fuehrer, used for military and policing purposes
SD	*Sicherheitsdienst*	Security Service; Intelligence and counter-intelligence Agency of SS
SIPO	*Sicherheitspolizei*	Security police. This was the name given to the Gestapo and Kripo considered jointly
	Staatssekretaer	Under Secretary of a Ministry
Stalag	*Stammlager*	Prisoner of War Camp (for enlisted men)
	Standardtenfuehrer	Rank in a Party formation, roughly equivalent to Colonel
	Stapo	*Gestapo*, Secret Police on the regional level
	Stapo-Leitstelle	Regional *Gestapo* office, directly under central command of *Gestapo*

III - 615

Abbreviation	German	English
SA	*Sturmabteilung*	Storm Troops of NSDAP (brown shirts)
	Systemzeit	System Era (Nazi designation of the Era of Weimar Republic, 1918-1933)

T

TV	*Totenkopfverbaende*	Death-Head units of the SS (Concentration Camp Guards)
TO	*Transozean*	Transocean (Official News Agency)
TP	*Transkontinent Press*	Transcontinent Press (News Agency)
	Treuhaender der Arbeit	Trustee of Labor

U

	Unterstaatssekretaer	Civil Servant, of a grade lower than *Staatssekretaer*

V

VT	*Verfuegunstruppen*	SS Units for Special Tasks
	Verlag	Publishing House
VOBl	*Verordnungsblatt*	Ordnance Gazette
	Vierjahrsplan	Four Year Plan
	Volk	Folk, people, race: all persons of German blood
VDA	*Volksbund fuer das Deutschtum im Ausland*	League for Germanism Abroad
	Volksdeutscher	A person of German blood but of non-German citizenship residing abroad, and considered a member of the German people
	Volksgericht	People's Court, highest court for political crimes
	Volksgemeinschaft	People's or racial community; the world-wide community composing all people of German blood
	Volksgenosse	Racial comrade; a person of German blood regardless of citizenship

W

WSS	*Waffen-SS*	Armed SS
	Wehrkreis	Military District
	Wehrkreiskommando	Military authority in charge of a *Wehrkreis*
	Wehrmacht	Armed Forces (Army, Navy, and Air Force)
WFSt	*Wehrmacht-Fuehrungsstab*	Operational Staff of Armed Forces
	Wehrwirtschaftsfuehrer	Title awarded to prominent industrialists for merit in armaments drive

III - 616

Glossary

Abbreviation	German	English
Wi-Rue	*Wehrwirtschaftsund Ruestungsamt*	War Economy and Armament Office (in OKW)
	Weltanschauung	World-view or philosophy
WHW	*Winterhilfswerk*	Winter Relief Organization
WVHA	*Wirtschaft-und-Verwaltungs Hauptamt*	Economic and Administration Main Office (of SS) in charge of Concentration Camps

Z

	Zeitung	Newspaper
	Zelle	NSDAP subdivision of an *Ortsgruppe*
	Zellenleiter	NSDAP leader of a Party cell
zbV	*zur besonderen Verwendung*	For special missions or duties
zV	*zur Verfuegung*	At disposal

III - 617

TABLE OF COMMISSIONED RANKS IN THE GERMAN ARMY, NAVY, AND SS WITH THEIR EQUIVALENTS IN THE AMERICAN MILITARY FORCES

Germany				United States	
Army	Navy	SS		Army	Navy
Leutnant	Leutnant zur See	Untersturmfuehrer		2d Lieutenant	Ensign
Oberleutnant	Oberleutnant zur See	Obersturmfuehrer		1st Lieutenant	Lieutenant (j.g.)
Hauptmann	Kapitaenleutnant	Hauptsturmfuehrer		Captain	Lieutenant
Major	Korvettenkapitaen	Sturmbannfuehrer		Major	Lieut. Commander
Oberstleutnant	Fregattenkapitaen	Obersturmbann-fuehrer		Lieut. Colonel	Commander
Oberst	Kapitaen zur See	Standartenfuehrer		Colonel	Captain
		Oberfuehrer			
Generalmajor	Konteradmiral	Brigadefuehrer		Brig. General	Commodore
Generalleutnant	Vizeadmiral	Gruppenfuehrer		Major General	Rear Admiral
General der Infanterie, Artillerie, etc.	Admiral	Obergruppen-fuehrer		Lieut. General	Vice Admiral
Generaloberst	Generaladmiral	Oberstgruppen-fuehrer		General	Admiral
Generalfeldmar-schall	Grossadmiral	Reichsfuehrer		General of the Army	Admiral of the Fleet

736
Am

Nazi Germany's war against the Jews.

DATE DUE			
Jan.25/93			

BETH HILLEL LIBRARY
WILMETTE, ILLINOIS

WITHDRAWN